Lecture Notes in Computer Science 10949

Commenced Publication in 1973
Founding and Former Series Editors:
Gerhard Goos, Juris Hartmanis, and Jan van Leeu

AF738426

More information about this series at http://www.springer.com/series/7407

Simon K. S. Cheung · Lam-for Kwok
Kenichi Kubota · Lap-Kei Lee
Jumpei Tokito (Eds.)

Blended Learning

Enhancing Learning Success

11th International Conference, ICBL 2018
Osaka, Japan, July 31 – August 2, 2018
Proceedings

Springer

Editors
Simon K. S. Cheung
The Open University of Hong Kong
Hong Kong
China

Lap-Kei Lee
The Open University of Hong Kong
Hong Kong
Hong Kong

Lam-for Kwok
City University of Hong Kong
Hong Kong
China

Jumpei Tokito
Kwansei Gakuin University
Osaka
Japan

Kenichi Kubota
Kansai University
Osaka
Japan

ISSN 0302-9743 ISSN 1611-3349 (electronic)
Lecture Notes in Computer Science
ISBN 978-3-319-94504-0 ISBN 978-3-319-94505-7 (eBook)
https://doi.org/10.1007/978-3-319-94505-7

Library of Congress Control Number: 2018947351

LNCS Sublibrary: SL1 – Theoretical Computer Science and General Issues

Printed on acid-free paper

This Springer imprint is published by the registered company Springer International Publishing AG part of Springer Nature
The registered company address is: Gewerbestrasse 11, 6330 Cham, Switzerland

Preface

Welcome to the proceedings of the 11th International Conference on Blended Learning (ICBL 2018). This year, ICBL 2018 was held at the Kansai University, Osaka, Japan, from 31 July to 2 August 2018.

Blended learning is one of the promising approaches to teaching and learning. It aims to integrate traditional learning with innovative means, such as e-learning, analytics, game-based learning, and open educational resources, in order to create a new learning environment to enhance learning effectiveness and enrich learning experience. Like the previous conferences in the series, ICBL 2018 provided a platform for knowledge exchange and experience sharing among researchers and practitioners in this field.

The theme of ICBL 2018 was "Blended Learning: Enhancing Learning Success." To cope with the recent technological advances, our focus is placed on how blended learning can enhance learning effectiveness and enrich learning experience that ultimately help engage students and enhance learning success. ICBL 2018 attracted a total of 94 paper submissions. After a rigorous review process, 35 papers were selected for inclusion in this volume. The selected papers cover various areas in blended learning, including the experience of blended learning, content development and assessment for blended learning, computer-supported collaborative learning, improved flexibility of learning processes, open educational resources, and pedagogical and psychological issues.

We would like to take this opportunity to thank the following parties who made the conference a success: (a) the conference Organizing Committee; (b) the international Program Committee; (c) the conference organizers and co-organizers; (d) the conference sponsors, and (e) all the conference participants.

We trust you will enjoy reading the papers.

July 2018

Simon K. S. Cheung
Lam-for Kwok
Kenichi Kubota
Lap-kei Lee
Jumpei Tokito

Conference Organization

International Program Committee

Chairs

Simon K. S. Cheung	The Open University of Hong Kong, Hong Kong, SAR China
Keith Lee	The Open University of Hong Kong, Hong Kong, SAR China
Junpei Tokito	Kwansei Gakuin University, Japan

Members

Oliver Au	The Open University of Hong Kong, Hong Kong, SAR China
Jinnong Cao	Hong Kong Polytechnic University, Hong Kong
C. S. Chai	The Chinese University of Hong Kong, Hong Kong, SAR China
Keith Chan	The Hong Kong Polytechnic University, Hong Kong, SAR China
Peter Chan	Brigham Young University, USA
Chih-Tsan Chang	National Chung Cheng University, Taiwan
Wei Chen	Chinese Academy of Agricultural Sciences, China
Guo-Li Chiou	National Taiwan Normal University, Taiwan
Thomas Chiu	University of Hong Kong, Hong Kong, SAR China
Mike Chui	Education University of Hong Kong, Hong Kong, SAR China
Giuliana Dettori	Istituto di Tecnologie Didattiche del CNR, Italy
Yoshiko Goda	Kumamoto University, Japan
Owen Hall Jr.	Pepperdine University, USA
Tianyong Hao	Guangdong University of Foreign Studies, China
Andreas Henrich	University of Bamberg, Germany
Yoko Hirata	Hokkai-Gakuen University, Japan
Yoshihiro Hirata	Hokkai-Gakuen University, Japan
Wai Shing Ho	Caritas Institute of Higher Education, Hong Kong, SAR China
Norio Hosaki	Waseda University, Japan
Jenq-Muh Hsu	National Chiayi University, Taiwan
Ronghuia Huang	Beijing Normal University, China
John Hui	City University of Hong Kong, Hong Kong, SAR China
Ryohei Ikejiri	University of Tokyo, Japan
Jane Jie	China Jiliang University, China
Morris Jong	The Chinese University of Hong Kong, Hong Kong, SAR China
Insung Jung	International Christian University, Japan
Yukari Kato	Kyoto University of Foreign Studies, Japan
Jacky Keung	City University of Hong Kong, Hong Kong, SAR China
Takayuki Konno	Meisei University, Japan

Kenichi Kubota	Kansai University, Japan
Mayumi Kubota	Kansai University, Japan
Haruo Kurokami	Kansai University, Japan
Reggie Kwan	The Open University of Hong Kong, Hong Kong, SAR China
L. F. Kwok	City University of Hong Kong, Hong Kong, SAR China
Chiu Lin Lai	National Taiwan University of Science and Technology, Taiwan
Ivan Lai	Caritas Institute of Higher Education, Hong Kong, SAR China
Jeanne Lam	HKU SPACE, Hong Kong, SAR China
Jun Le	Guangdong Radio and TV University, China
Min Hsien Lee	National Taiwan Normal University, Taiwan
Victor Lee	City University of Hong Kong, Hong Kong
K. C. Li	The Open University of Hong Kong, Hong Kong, SAR China
Yan Li	Zhejiang University, China
Yi Li	Nanjing University, China
Heng Luo	Central China Normal University, China
Will Ma	Technological and Higher Education Institute of Hong Kong, Hong Kong, SAR China
Jason MacLeod	Central China Normal University, China
Kousuke Mouri	Kyushu University, Japan
Masayuki Murakami	Kyoto University of Foreign studies, Japan
Junko Nemoto	Ehime University, Japan
Steven Ng	University of Sunderland, Hong Kong, SAR China
Hiroaki Ogata	Kyushu University, Japan
Makiko Oyama	Osaka University, Japan
Wakio Oyanagi	Nara University of Education, Japan
Diana Perez-Marin	Universidad Rey Juan Carlos, Spain
C. K Poon	Caritas Institute of Higher Education, Hong Kong, SAR China
Petra Poulova	University of Hradec Králové, Czech Republic
Jacky Pow	Hong Kong Baptist University, Hong Kong, SAR China
Yanghui Rao	Sun Yat-sen University, China
Junjie Shang	Peking University, China
Yinghui Shi	Central China Normal University, China
Ju Ling Shih	National University of Tainan, Taiwan
Raymond So	The Open University of Hong Kong, Hong Kong, SAR China
Yanjie Song	Education University of Hong Kong, Hong Kong, SAR China
Niwat Srisawasdi	Khon Kaen University, Thailand
Liana Stanescu	University of Craiova, Romania
Cai Su	Beijing Normal University, China
Vincent Tam	University of Hong Kong, Hong Kong, SAR China

Jeff Tang	Caritas Institute of Higher Education, Hong Kong, SAR China
Jay Tashiro	University of Ontario Institute of Technology, Canada
Kosuke Terashima	Osaka Kyoiku University, Japan
Stefanie Trausan-Matu	University Politehnica of Bucharest, Romania
Shikui Tu	Shanghai Jiao Tong University, China
Aihua Wang	Peking University, China
Cong Wang	City University of Hong Kong, Hong Kong, SAR China
Fu Lee Wang	Caritas Institute of Higher Education, Hong Kong, SAR China
Shu Ming Wang	Chinese Culture University, Taiwan
Shudong Wang	Shimane University, Japan
Billy Wong	The Open University of Hong Kong, Hong Kong, SAR China
Crusher Wong	City University of Hong Kong, Hong Kong
Gary Wong	University of Hong Kong, Hong Kong, SAR China
Raymond Wong	City University of Hong Kong, Hong Kong, SAR China
T. L. Wong	Douglas College, Canada
Di Wu	Central China Normal University, China
Haoran Xie	Education University of Hong Kong, Hong Kong, SAR China
You Ru Xie	South China Normal University, China
Toshiyuki Yamamoto	Kansai University, Japan
Harrison Yang	State University of New York at Oswego, USA
W. L. Yeung	Lingnan University, Hong Kong
Y. T. Yu	City University of Hong Kong, Hong Kong, SAR China
Liming Zhang	University of Macau, Macau, SAR China
Guodong Zhao	Peking University, China
Jianhua Zhao	South China Normal University, China
Yunxiang Zheng	South China Normal University, China
Ying Zhou	Beijing Normal University, China
Sha Zhu	Central China Normal University, China

Keynote Speakers and Panel Chairs

Keynote Speakers

Li Chen	Beijing Normal University, Beijing, China
Siu Cheung Kong	Education University of Hong Kong, Hong Kong, SAR China
Noyuri Mima	Future University Hakodate, Japan
Jayshiro Tashiro	University of Ontario Institute of Technology, Canada

Panel Chairs

Horace H. S. Ip	City University of Hong Kong, Hong Kong, SAR China
Harrison Yang	Central China Normal University, China, and State University of New York at Oswego, USA

Organizers

Kansai University

City University of Hong Kong

Co-organizers

Japan Association for Educational Media Study

Japan Society for Educational Technology

Hong Kong Society for Multimedia and Image Computing

Sponsors

Hong Kong Pei Hua Education Foundation

Springer Science+Business Media

BEE NET

Contents

Pedagogical and Psychological Issues

Keynotes

The Challenge for Higher Education Reform in Japan by Seven Samurai

Noyuri Mima(✉)

Future University Hakodate, Hokkaido 0418655, Japan
noyuri@fun.ac.jp

Abstract. This is an autobiographical account of a unique university that has been designed and implemented from scratch and is still in operation. The focus of this paper is not only to look back at past developments, but also to extract essences and principles for designing sustainable learning environments. To fulfill this purpose, the paper begins with the educational philosophy written at the time of the university's opening in 2000. After that, eighteen years of the university's educational practices and policies are summarized. Ultimately, the design of the learning environment as a whole will be discussed. It is argued that the challenge of effective design should be expanded from the conventional blend of real and digital classroom environments to a new perspective that coordinates space, activity and community. It is reasoned that this holistic perspective will contribute to future blended learning models for innovation in schools, organizations and society as a whole.

Keywords: Space · Activity · Community · Project-Based learning
Fabrication · Peer tutoring · Collaborative meta-cognition · Social motivation

1 Background and Aim

1.1 Background

In June 1996, seven researchers in their mid-thirties, all computer related scientists, were gathered and entrusted to make a new university from scratch. As a result, the learning environment to be introduced in this paper was developed, and the school building was awarded the Architectural Institute of Japan Prize. The philosophy behind the university's spirit became "Open space, Open mind."

There was a lot of turbulence in the process of creating a new university: the path to creating a university was very steep, and required us to overcome many obstacles. At long last, our university evolved through the kind of innovation and foresight that comes not from a plan prepared by a think tank specializing in the creation of a university, but by participatory design. I believe we became the "Seven Samurai" of Higher Education reform in Japan.

Even before the first syllabus was written, the first thing we did when we started designing the university was to ask ourselves a seemingly simple question: What is learning? "Learning" is different in kind from "teaching." No matter how much we

S. K. S. Cheung et al. (Eds.): ICBL 2018, LNCS 10949, pp. 3–16, 2018.
https://doi.org/10.1007/978-3-319-94505-7_1

teach, people may not necessarily learn. We started our university by rethinking learning.

1.2 Aim

The paper is an autobiographical paper of a unique university that has been designed and implemented from scratch and is still in operation. The focus of this paper is not only to look back at past developments, but also to extract essences and principles for designing sustainable learning environments. To fulfill this purpose, the paper begins with the educational philosophy written at the time of the university's opening in 2000. After that, eighteen years of the university's educational practices and policies are summarized. Ultimately, the design of the learning environment as a whole will be discussed. It is argued that the challenge of effective design should be expanded from the conventional blend of real and digital classroom environments to a new perspective that coordinates space, activity and community.

The following section was written as a collaboration between Noyuri Mima and Hillel Weintraub, written six months before the university's opening in September 1999 and reviewed by Weintraub [1]. It could be said that this is our educational philosophy.

2 Future UNiversity (FUN) - Hakodate as a Learning Organization

2.1 Traditional Universities and the Knowledge Acquisition Model

The traditional components of a university have been faculty, students, and general supporting staff. For generations, classroom instructors have stood in front of the blackboard, using standard style textbooks, and lecturing to their students. In this environment, intellectual work is thought to be an act of knowledge transfer. The human mind is seen as a container and learning is seen as the pouring of knowledge into it and saving it. (This is similar to the well-known "Banking Metaphor" of Paulo Freire, so it certainly isn't limited to Japan!)

With this view of knowledge acquisition, studying is considered as individual work. On the whole, teachers give importance only to the process of acquiring and saving information, and doing this effectively was the goal of education. Over the years, this has developed into the traditional style of university education in Japan.

It is not only the conservative nature of humans in general that makes traditions hard to change, but the accompanying institutions and other cultural support that grow up around such traditions. For example, the tests that students need to take to enter universities in Japan support this view of learning as "gathering up information." All teachers in pre-college institutions from elementary school to high school feel pressure to prepare their students for this kind of exam. Furthermore, after university, in the usual exams given to enter graduate school or companies, or even the National Bar Exam or the hundreds of other exams given to grant licenses for certificates (various teachers' licenses, for example) students' ability to perform successfully is evaluated by the information and memories stored inside their heads.

But of course, we know that in our real lives, whether as students, workers, parents, friends, we don't only depend on the remembered information we carry with us. In our daily lives, we solve problems not only with our personal pre-attained knowledge but more often with knowledge constructed through interacting with new situations and people. When we meet a new problem, we try to solve it by collecting information in various ways, such as consulting with others, doing research in some printed material or on the internet, or using tools or toys of some kind. Also, we need to recognize that solving problems is not just a means to gain knowledge. Human study is not "knowledge acquisition" so much as it is an interpersonal activity which takes place in conversation and in communication that is inseparable from situations or the context. Learning should be defined as the process of interaction which occurs in social relationships within a community containing a multitude of things beyond any single individual.

2.2 Designing Our New University

First Design Principle. No Space Barriers: Learning Without Walls in Open Spaces

There are a lot of boundaries in traditional university education. In Future University-Hakodate, we have designed a new learning environment which values learning without walls and attempts to remove various partitions - between classrooms, subjects, and learners. Faculty have traditionally stood on a raised surface, "delivering" lectures to students, who were expected to listen passively. Taking away these platforms and having completely open teaching areas or ones with glass used to limit noise but not the exchange of ideas, is our way of creating open style environments which will make interaction among students and between teachers and students very natural.

With these open spaces, students or teachers walking by an interesting class or workshop might think, "Hey! What's going on in there?" Or "Wow! That looks interesting. I'll just walk in and join them." Such an open atmosphere would be unthinkable in most universities in Japan where both psychological and physical doors are kept tightly shut.

At FUN, we also intend to have a lot of teamwork. Or perhaps the concept of "teamplay" may fit our spirit better. In any case, team teaching and team learning will be rife! Our students will be actively involved with designing learning environments which will be playfully serious, intellectually challenging and mysteriously engaging. Our open physical and emotional spaces will promote stimulating human activity which will we lead to deep, meaningful learning.

Second Design Principle. No Course Barriers: Introduction of Project Based Learning

In university lectures, it is usually thought best to teach systematically, starting with what is usually called "the basics." While this style of teaching has a long history and is comfortable for some teachers and learners, it also makes many students disengaged because it is difficult to relate their learning with their lives. Furthermore, in this systematic style, students have difficulties connecting their school activities with their future work and lives. Social value or intrinsic pleasure from the act of learning itself is lacking. Earning credits or the grade itself becomes the main goal.

Project Based Learning (PBL) is very different from this systematic style which is exemplified in ordinary lectures which present knowledge set in every field. The Project Based Learning Approach takes away the barriers among subjects. Most human activities, in society or at work are not limited to one subject or another, but cross into many disciplines. In the same way, the project based approach is a way of gaining a comprehensive experience in meaningful human activity. Educational research indicates that people learn more through significant social and personal activities. Furthermore, learners can apply how they learn to new situations which arise in their life, since PBL encourages design skills, research skills, experimentation, simulation and modeling practice and creative problem solving - what they learn Students collect information, carry on experimenting, making a model, doing a simulation, creating ideas to solve assignments given to projects they participate in. Students are not limited to one discipline, but can learn in a more realistic, interdisciplinary style. The focus on grades is replaced by a focus on meaningful learning.

Third Design Principle. No Personal Barriers: Cooperative Learning and Team Teaching

In creating our new university, we have focused on the concept of Cooperative Learning as one of our key design concepts. CL is a total shift of learning philosophy and style. People we are learning with become part of our community, there to support us, challenge us to move to new depths of understanding, thus affecting both how we learn and what we learn. It is generally accepted that cooperative social and work environments are healthier and more productive, but this concept has not become a part of most university designs. Future University (FUN) Hakodate will be a learning community in which all aspects of the university, from physical structure through the open relationships among learners, including teachers, will promote learning cooperatively.

If we look at learning outside of most formal classroom situations, it is apparent that it is both cooperative and social, as well as being supportive of individual expression and growth. Learning stagnates if there is no feedback loop; we need the opportunity to hear our own thoughts and see them reflected from others, particularly in a critically constructive environment. Moving away from the metaphor of pouring established information into the minds of students to a more constructionist and collaborative model, FUN Hakodate is designing itself as learning community where problems can be solved together through a commonly developed set of shared meanings. These understanding will never be seen as dogma, but through the open exchange with others both locally and universally, and will constantly be challenged, re-examined and refined or re-built.

In order to create this kind of atmosphere, we need to remove the kinds of situations which encourage learners to focus on individual performance on tests and rather design spaces which encourage cooperative interaction - research, rethinking, presentation through various media. This does not mean that students will lose their identity in group work, but instead will find and develop their own strengths and unique talents, still thinking how they can work together with others, rather than working against others as in most competitive situations. Furthermore, by encouraging teachers with different perspectives and fields of research to take part in projects together, the idea that diversity is valued and that students should constantly be stretching themselves to think both widely and deeply. Through team teaching, the content of project becomes enriched, and students' work can be evaluated from many different aspects.

Fourth Design Principle. No Language or Communication Barriers: Acquisition of Communication Skills

Communication ability - the ability to listen to others and express ourselves - is very important for self-development and self-realization. At FUN Hakodate, our theories of communication will grow out of our own lively, engaging, and authentic practice. So-called expert theories will not be handed meaninglessly to students to memorize, but rather our theories will develop through reflection of learners' own work, as well as an understanding of the theories of others. In keeping with our concept of barrier-free learning spaces, communication, including the use of English and all sorts of media, is not something only taught in special classes held at particular times a week; it is an integral part of university life, with every subject stressing both the "science and practice of communication" along with the "communication and practice of science."

Both research and presentation are part of the heart of learning. One of the important aims of FUN Hakodate is to help learners see the value of research and presentation in their personal and professional lives, and to begin to develop their confidence as communicators in a wide range of situations, utilizing a wide range of media. Working in schools, homes for the aged or handicapped, on newspapers/radio/TV, and even street performances are ways we will enter into dialogue about the arts, science and technology with the local community. Furthermore, this dialog will be expanded beyond our local community of learners to the universe of learners through the internet and AV conferencing, bi-lingual journals and TV shows as well as summer or year-long exchange programs. With this design, foreign language skills will not be imposed but developed from the felt needs of the students.

The contents of Project Based Activities will include presentation and exhibition design, technique of media use, theories of human cognition and communication, cooperative problem solving, and project design itself. A wide range of final outcomes will be honored - such as a traveling performance with acts demonstrating particular scientific principles that might be given to children, an interactive scientific exhibition in our university museum, a journal or TV show aimed at audiences around the world. In this way, students' ability to communicate scientific ideas in real world situations will be developed; a very different situation from the traditional university structure where knowledge is presented in rather limited ways only to a teacher.

Fifth Design Principle. No Age or Learning Style Barriers: Diversity of Learners

One of the barriers in traditional universities is that only teacher and students in one location are taking part in the learning activities. We are planning to remove this partition in project work culminating in authentic communication activities. In this way, learners of all ages and cultures will interact. Some examples of such projects would be designing facilities for lifelong education like a library or an aquarium in a town, or creating toys for disabled children's use, or planning ways that a local bookstore could develop to meet the needs of our university.

If our students themselves are valued as knowers-in-progress, they will also begin to value others in the same way. Interacting with learners of all ages to understand their intuitive and developed theories of science will be most rewarding - from children in kindergarten through high school, to retired people and other adult learners, perhaps experts in a particular field, perhaps changing jobs. Bringing such people into our university life will change the way all members of community begin to see themselves as taking part in the life-long process of learning.

Furthermore, we are greatly aware of the lack of women in the sciences and have taken it on ourselves to change this situation. Although the number of women students in science majors in Japan is increasing, it is still very low, so FUN Hakodate will search for ways to encourage young women scientists to join us at every possible turn, and our goal is to accept half men and half women as students.

By taking part in a respectful dialog with a diversity of learners, we will begin to see a wide range of styles and intelligences. Different study styles, learning styles, presentation styles; different kinds of intelligences - for problem solving, for thinking creatively, for social interaction, for artistic or dramatic expression - each person will feel his/her own power both individually and as a part of the learning community of FUN Hakodate. We have even created a special museum space in our university where learners of all ages, from all sectors of society, with all styles of learning, can interact and share their visions.

2.3 Students as the Center of Learning

In traditional school education, transferring knowledge using set textbooks and then evaluating that knowledge solely based on memorization is the standard approach. This style has created the mistaken view that meaningful study activities are closed, and simply necessitate individual work inside a university. Yet this is different from what experts do in real society. Scientists' activities include searching for meaningful issues, generating hypotheses, and finding ways to verify them. In contrast with this, education today focuses on memorizing propositions and formulas, or on proving an issue already known. Classes tend toward a drill and practice mentality so that so-called "basic knowledge" will be deeply instilled.

2.4 Students as Apprentice Researchers

Objectifying knowledge in this way removes all the mystery, surprise and relevancy of learning. It encourages passive learning and, ultimately, disengaged learners. In order to change the situation, at FUN Hakodate we regard our students as "apprentice researchers." This means that they will take an active and vital role in research and will be seen and learn to see themselves as "theory-makers", rather than as simply "theory-takers." They will learn from their own mistakes and develop new attitudes about the value of mistakes.

Faculty staff as a "senior researchers" have to show what they do consciously, thinking out loud as they work, and provide opportunities for students to join them in authentic activities. In this way, students can begin to see learning as exciting, challenging and meaningful. They see themselves as active learners. This development of their own strong identity, in a world where young people's individuality is often submerged by the deluge of images from new media and high-tech, we hope they can find new and joyful meaning in living. By giving students a chance to do real art, real science, real communication, we want them to become engaged in the joyful aspects of meaning-making, and finding a place for themselves in today's and tomorrow's world.

2.5 Portfolio as Achievement

In university education at present, students can have their ability evaluated mostly through their performance on tests. But we believe that meaningful education is beyond simplistic evaluation which focuses on a single moment of a learner's life. Future University Hakodate will encourage our students to develop awareness of how their behavior affects our environment and society. We value their process of social and intellectual growth because we see learning as a process, rather than something that can be evaluated at a particular moment. Evaluation within a total context of the students' learning is as important as learning in the total context of their lives. What a student doesn't know but is in the process of learning, is much more important to us than what the student can demonstrate s/he already knows.

This attitude totally changes the way learning is seen. Students immediately recognize the hypocrisy of saying "Learn in the context of your lives!" but are then evaluated based on a single event performance such as an exam. We want to avoid such hypocritical actions: trust and respect among learners is vital to everyone's growth!

Thus, our evaluation system will not aim to grade "objectively" or "relatively", but will focus on "development through feedback." Students will create their own portfolio of learning experiences over four years. Their portfolio will demonstrate a process of learning, what kind of technical knowledge or cultural theories they are developing, or what kind of projects they have been engaged in. This portfolio is accumulated from the time of entering our university, and will be used as a record of their growth as learners. Their Graduation thesis will represent a culmination of their work with us and become part of their portfolio, which can then be used to show their progress in learning, rather than a simple curriculum vitae when they are looking for work or planning to attend a Graduate school.

2.6 Prospect for the Future - University as Learning Community

Providing the learning surroundings described above, Future University Hakodate intends to redefine "community" to include our students, our faculty and administrative staff, people in Hakodate and neighboring towns, people in the region of Hokkaido, and expanding throughout Japan and the world, offering learning opportunities to everyone within physical or digital reach. We want to redefine humans as lifelong learners through our sharing of meaningful learning and living experiences.

3 The Result of Learning Environment Design

Informed and guided by the educational philosophy described in the previous section, the university building was designed in collaboration with a professional architect. Researchers with a background in Cognitive Science had the opportunity to establish the new university and designed its learning environment from the outset. Research in Cognitive Science related to learning such as memory, understanding, problem solving, and meta-cognition were applied to design its educational philosophy, the curriculum, the university building, the information environment, and faculty development. These have been improving over the past eighteen years. We are also continuously developing our curriculum, informed by practicing our philosophy for the past eighteen years. The following is a synopsis of selected outcomes presented as Cases.

3.1 Background of the Cases

The subject of this study is the university as a whole. Future University Hakodate and its history may be summarized as:

- Public university in Hakodate City, population 266,000
- 1100 total including Doctoral students
  - 240 students per grade,
- 70 faculty members and 60 staff
- Key dates:
  - 1996 Start planning committee for opening university
  - 2000 Open the university with the new building and start team teaching in several compulsory classes
  - 2002 Start a year-long course entitled 'Project-Based Learning' as a compulsory 3rd year class
  - 2008 Start a course entitled 'Learning through Fabrication' as a compulsory class in 2nd semester of the first year
  - 2012 Open a learning support center termed 'Meta-Learning Lab' and adopted peer tutoring

3.2 Cases

The research presented in this paper is informed by the design of the university building and the observations derived from five Cases summarized below. The analysis is a descriptive account exemplifying the five aforementioned Design Principles.

Case 1: Open-Transparent Building
To support our first design principle (No space barriers: Learning without walls in open spaces), the university school building was the result of discussions between the architect and we Seven Samurai. A large internal space, called Open Studio, with an unenclosed ceiling to the fifth level gives people a feeling of a free and shared space, and a sense of membership of the learning community (see Fig. 1(a)). All facilities such as classrooms, the library, gym, faculty laboratories, administration offices and all

other rooms are walled by transparent glass (see Fig. 1(b)). These are located in a single large building.

Fig. 1. (a) Open Studio; (b) Transparent glass wall

In this way, everyone can view what is happening on campus with each other and it motivates people to learn [2]. A variety of activities, including group work, discussions, programming, design, fabrication, communication and presentations are carried out based on curricula and extra-curricular programs developed in conjunction with this arrangement of space.

Case 2: Project-Based Learning
Our second design principle (No course barriers) has been implemented by Project-based learning, which is compulsory for all third-year students. It is not learning individually, but learning collaboratively, dealing with current and anticipated problems in society. Project-based learning provides students different learning opportunities from regular classes. It is a complement of regular lectures, and attempts to deliver and utilize organized knowledge of each discipline. Project-based learning provides an opportunity to solve real-world problems associated with multiple subjects while engaging in team collaboration (see Fig. 2). The students in a Project-based learning 'labs' each address one theme per year. Faculty play advisory roles on each team and are responsible for its development.

The third design principle (No personal barriers: Cooperative learning & team teaching) is also enacted since the theme is chosen not only from the contents directly related to classes but also from the real-world problems, students also work collaboratively with others outside the university. Through its implementation students actually experience the process from problem finding to problem solving. By utilizing the prior knowledge acquired in various classes, students themselves acquire know-how and skills necessary for undertaking projects through authentic experiences. As a result, the outcome of the project-based learning is realized inside and outside the campus and fed back to cooperating companies and the local community. Several studies have confirmed that students who had low motivation in regular lectures and exercises actively work, acquire knowledge and skills, and grow in Project-based Learning. [3, 4]. In an interview survey for graduate students, most students recall Project-based

Fig. 2. Project-Based Learning in action

Learning as a valuable experience that remains memorable after the four years of undergraduate study.

Case 3: Creativity Spreads from Hakodate to the World
Our fourth design principle (No language or communication barriers) can be best exemplified by two fourth-year students who in 2017 demonstrated their 3D education game entitled 'Japanese History Explorer' at The European Conference on Game-based Learning in Graz, the second largest city in Austria (see Fig. 3(a)). Competitors included undergraduate and post-graduate students from around the world, as well as start-up companies developing games for education. Of sixty-eight (68) worldwide participants, the FUN students were awarded third prize. This success exemplifies the interdisciplinary philosophy of FUN's education. For instance, to achieve this triumph the students had to utilize their design and programming skills, further their Project-Based Learning ideas through a research-focused implementation, then promote their game by effectively communicating to an international audience (see Fig. 3(b)). Their communication skill, curiosity, investigative spirit and motivation to make an effort to attain the goal exemplify the fundamental attributes nurtured at Future University Hakodate [5]. If students have the motivation to 'try' and the 'will' to challenge, the environment, the opportunities and the support are all available at FUN. It may therefore be said that world-class creativity is fostered in Hakodate.

Case 4: Meta-Learning Lab
The fifth design principle (No age or learning style barriers: Diversity of learners) is exemplified by our Meta-learning lab. Introductory education, literacy education and supplementary education in Higher Education in Japan have become issues of concern in recent years. In order to solve the problems, a learning support system adopted throughout the university and an integrated learning support system including staff development have been developed.

A Meta-Learning Lab provides peer-tutoring or one-to-one individualized study guidance between tutor and tutee (see Fig. 4(a)). The purpose of peer-tutoring is to encourage tutees to become autonomous learners by improving their self-study habits so that they can choose appropriate learning styles.

Fig. 3. (a) Scene from Japanese History Explorer; (b) Sharing through presenting

From this practice, the keys to making students autonomous learners have become clear: (1) develop meta-learning ability; (2) acquire and utilize learning strategies tailored to the situation; (3) progress from tutee to tutor.

In addition, the timing and contents of effective stepwise support for university students were examined. Based on the research results, the support system and teaching materials to promote stepwise growth of university students and the model of support were developed (see Fig. 4(b)) [6].

The Stepwise Growth Model
LEVEL 0: University Entrance Level: learning experience until high school
LEVEL 1: Tutee Level: consciousness of meta-learning
LEVEL 2: Tutor Level: learning support aware of meta-learning is possible
LEVEL 3: Master Tutor Level: advanced learning support is possible
LEVEL 4: Autonomous Learner Level: self-tutoring is possible

Case 5: Learning through Fabrication
This class was developed in collaboration with the Faculty of Design and Computer Science and exemplifies the inter-disciplinary nature of FUN's education (i.e. students at

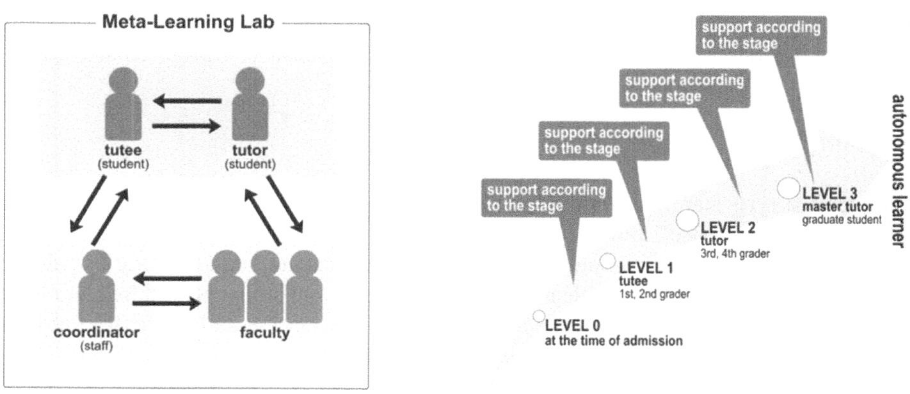

Fig. 4. (a) Meta-Learning Lab; (b) The Stepwise Growth Model

the center of learning). The purpose of this class, which is held in the second semester of the first year, is to develop skills for planning and implementing information expression, skills for documentation, and skills for presentation (see Fig. 5(a) (b)).

Fig. 5. (a) Learning through Fabrication Class; (b) Student's work

The design is termed augmented reality equipment; a Rube Goldberg machine seamlessly connecting the real world with the digital world using the programming skills learned in the first semester. Students learn the concept of control of devices by using sensors and actuators as the basic technology of expression. At the same time, they develop new, expressive creation skills and cultivate comprehensive expressive ability that integrates the engineering technologies of physical equipment as one system.

In the process of fabrication of artifacts in the classroom, it is important to consider the presence of others and a social meaning of the artifacts. The presence of others provides an opportunity to discover differences and write about it. Fabricating meaningful artifacts in society in the classroom facilitates students' collaborative metacognition and promotes their social motivation [7].

Engineering design is also promoted in this course [8]. It is a framework of thinking that extracts principles from the experiences of problem-solving given certain imposed constraints. In a modern society in which complex and unfamiliar amorphous tasks are emerging, acquiring engineering design skills is thus expected to be widely useful not only in engineering but also useful in an intuitive and sensitive design context [9].

4 Conclusion

The blended type learning environment of "real" and "digital" at Future University is characterized as "space" and "activity."

One of our aims was to change traditional style of teaching and learning in order to create an interactive channel of learning among faculty and students, and help students to learn from one another. With the approach used today, time and space are used for learning while students are on campus.

The result of our learning environment design and educational practices can be represented by the concept of "visibility." The visibility in the real environment is provided by the university's huge open space, and various learning and educational spaces with transparent glass walls. Students and faculty members can select them according to purpose and preference. Visibility in a digital environment is provided by an e-portfolio system, a bulletin board system, a class feedback system, and a voting system for theme selection of projects.

Regular and extracurricular activities in our open and transparent building cultivate our learning community. Close relationships among faculty and students who are members of the community characterize our intellectual environment, which naturally supports open-minded thinking, autonomous problem solving, spontaneous learning, and collaboration.

It is argued that our challenge has shown that effective design foci should be expanded from the conventional blend of real and digital situated in a classroom environment to the new perspectives that blend space, activity and community. Given our eighteen years of practice and continuous learning, it is reasoned that our design foci will continually contribute to blended learning models for innovation in schools, organizations and society as a whole.

Our philosophy lies behind the university's spirit of "Open space, Open mind." I believe we became "Seven Samurai" in Higher Education reform in Japan and hopefully in the world.

Acknowledgements. Gratitude to all current and previous Future University Hakodate staff and students for their creativity and inspiration. Special thanks to colleague Dr. Michael Vallance for evocative interactions and suggestions. This work was supported by JSPS KAKENHI Grant Number 15H02932.

References

1. Weintraub, H.: The Playful Scientist as Language Learner: redefining the relationships between learners, knowledge, spaces and media: an experiment at FUN - Future University - Hakodate (2002). https://www.childresearch.net/papers/playing/2002_01.html. Accessed 10 Apr 2018
2. Mima, N., Yamauchi, Y.: Design for Learning Environments: Space, Activity and Community. University of Tokyo Press, Tokyo (2005). (in Japanese)
3. Mima, N.: Designing a project-based learning in a university with new theory of learning. Jpn. Soc. Eng. Educ. **57**(1), 45–50 (2009). (in Japanese)
4. Mima, N.: Co-creation of social value in project learning with three-way satisfaction. Serviceology **4**(2), 10–15 (2017). (in Japanese)
5. Sasaki, T., Vallance, M., Magaki, T., Naito, N., Sumi, K., Bagenda Kasujja, D., Tsubakimoto, M.: Japanese History Explorer with Nozomi-chan for elementary school children. In: Proceedings of the 11th European Conference on Game-Based Learning ECGBL 2017, The FH JOANNEUM University of Applied Science, Graz, Austria, 4–6 October 2017, pp. 562–570 (2017)
6. Mima, N.: Design research for higher education in Japan based on collaborativity and sociality of learning. In:16th Annual Hawaii International Conference on Education (2018)
7. Mima, N.: Design research for learning environments based on collaborativity and sociality of learning. Ph.D. thesis, University of Electro-Communications, Tokyo (2010). (in Japanese)

8. Mima, N.: Possibilities of learning environments developing "Engineering Design" in higher education. In: Proceedings of the 32nd Annual Conference of Japan Society for Educational Technology, pp. 745–746 (2016). (in Japanese)
9. Martinez, S.L., Gary, S.: Invent to Learn: Making, Tinkering, and Engineering in the Classroom. Constructing Modern Knowledge Press, California (2013)

Can an Evidence-Based Blended Learning Model Serve Healthcare Patients and Adult Education Students?

Jayshiro Tashiro(✉), Patrick C. K. Hung, and Miguel Vargas Martin

Faculty of Business and Information Technology, University of Ontario Institute of Technology, Oshawa, ON, Canada
jay.tashiro@uoit.ca

Abstract. We explore the possibilities for evidence-based blended learning models that benefits both adult healthcare patients with chronic illness and also adults completing basic education programs designed to help them achieve high school equivalency with improved readiness for college and career. Ten chronic disease areas consume disproportionate percentages of healthcare resources. Adult education programs have become essential components of strategies to reduce education gaps and prepare unemployed or under-employed adults for college and career readiness. Consequently, in many countries these two populations of learners are critical to economic stability and sustained growth in technology-oriented careers. Ongoing research provided a model that combines emerging educational technologies and courseware in ways that allow customization of instructional strategies yet accommodate training in diverse content and skills. In this paper, we present the model and suggest a set of recommendations to improve educational support of adults with chronic diseases as well as to improve educational frameworks for adults preparing for college and career readiness.

Keywords: Patient education · Adult education · Blended learning
Evidence-based instruction · Educational technology · Courseware
Adaptive learning engines

1 Introduction

1.1 The Promise and Reality of Blended Learning

Previous impact analyses of healthcare technologies on care planning and delivery revealed important analogues between the transformation of healthcare and the transformation of evidence-based practices in patient education [1]. These types of analyses identified a variety of problems within patient education. During recent studies, we found very interesting commonalities between adult patient education and education of adults in college and career readiness programs.

However, a broad literature review revealed 10 gaps in knowledge about how educational environments "really work" to change an individual's learning outcomes and willingness as well as ability to sustain behaviors related to learning [2–5]. In brief,

S. K. S. Cheung et al. (Eds.): ICBL 2018, LNCS 10949, pp. 17–42, 2018.
https://doi.org/10.1007/978-3-319-94505-7_2

we argue that there is scant empirical evidence on the structure and function of educational environments that could personalize education in ways to optimize individual learning outcomes.

Earlier studies by the United States National Research Council [6–8], described several knowledge gaps, as did reports by the American Association for the Advancement of Science [9] and Federation of American Scientists [10]. Tashiro *et al.* studied the critical issues outlined in these five reports and expanded the research literature review to discover a broader set of knowledge gaps [2, 11–14]. Below, we present 10 gaps in our knowledge about how educational materials "really work" to change an individual's learning outcomes and willingness as well as ability to sustain behaviors related to learning:

1. How does an educational environment impact disposition to engage in a learning process?
2. What are the relationships of learning outcomes to the level of realism and relevance in an educational environment?
3. How do we measure the thresholds of experience within an educational environment that leads to measurable learning outcomes?
4. What are the knowledge domains being instantiated during learning?
5. In what knowledge domains are learning instantiations being retained and how stable is the retention?
6. What is the disposition to act on knowledge gained?
7. How accurately can instantiated knowledge be transferred?
8. What learning outcomes are developed during the learning process (e.g., conceptual and performance competencies)?
9. How are misconceptions developed during and sustained after working within an educational environment?
10. How is learning impacted by teacher-student and student-student social networks or e-communities?

Since these 10 gaps have not been bridged, truly inclusive and adaptive educational environments have been hard to build and evaluate. To complicate matters, and despite a rapid increase in the use of blended and totally online courses, there are few sensible and empirically supported theoretical frameworks for design and implementation of blended and totally online courses. From a humanist but also from an economic perspective, we began a detailed analysis of commonalities in problems related to adult patient education and adult education for college and career readiness.

1.2 Critical Issues in Patient Education

In many other countries, healthcare systems have begun to deal with increased incidence of chronic diseases. For the United States, the Centers for Disease Control and Prevention (CDC) provide data on American economic costs of different diseases (see the CDC site: https://www.cdc.gov/chronicdisease/overview/index.htm#ref17).

Chronic diseases and conditions are made worse by continued engagement of adults engaging in health risk behaviors. Estimates in the United States during recent years reveal that chronic health issues account for over 80% of the American $2.7

trillion annual health care expenditures. Many have argued these costs can be lowered substantially if educational outreach reduced health risk behaviors.

If you examine annual cardiovascular disease costs, the United States averaged $316.1 billion a year from 2012–2013. Costs for cancer in 2010 dollars amounted to $157 billion, while estimated cost of diagnosed diabetes in 2012 was $245 billion. Costs associated with arthritis and related conditions amounted to roughly $128 billion in 2003. Obesity resulted in enormous costs to healthcare systems. In the United States, medical costs related to obesity during 2008 were estimated at $147 billion. An interesting note: the average yearly medical costs for obese individuals averaged $1,429 higher than people with weights within normal limits. The costs associated with smoking have been increasing world-wide. In the United States during the period 2009–2012, the total economic impact from costs related to smoking was estimated to be $300 billion or greater each year. The above costs include direct medical care, but also can be disaggregated to reveal costs for lost productivity and premature death.

In 2012, the CDC concluded that about half of all American adults—117 million people—suffered from one or more chronic health problems. Indeed, 25% of adults had two or more chronic health conditions. Yet, the CDC also noted that unhealthy behaviors can be changed, including four health risk behaviors that cause a high percentage of illness, suffering, and early death from chronic disease—lack of exercise or physical activity, poor nutrition, tobacco use, and drinking too much alcohol.

Tan et al. argued that models of blended learning coupled to patient monitoring could be a critical pathway for helping individuals manage chronic disease or reduce the potential for developing chronic conditions [1]. Insight into the 10 knowledge gaps, online access, and healthcare providers' face-to-face as well as remote support can be gleaned from a review of studies on the patient portals now becoming popular in the United States and other countries. In brief, patient portals are digital communication platforms designed to provide patients with health information and support health communication between patients and their healthcare providers. Many include access to patient records. Many also provide educational links that allow a patient to explore information related to their health issue. We examined the literature from 2007 to present. Four studies provided systematic reviews of patient portal effectiveness in enhancing health communications and improving health outcomes [15–18].

The projected positive impacts of patient portals and other types of healthcare-related sites have not been fully realized. We feel five of the best sites are: WebMD—https://www.webmd.com/; Mayo Clinic—https://www.mayoclinic.org/patient-care-and-health-information; the United States National Institutes of Health—https://www.nih.gov/health-information; the American Diabetes Association—http://www.diabetes.org/; Cleveland Clinic—https://my.clevelandclinic.org/health; and MedlinePlus—https://medlineplus.gov/. Each of these sites provides substantive and interesting information, all have user-friendly designs (if a patient has at least a 6–8 grade reading level and a low-to-medium level of computer literacy), and each could be very useful to patients if a healthcare provider engaged with the patient sufficiently to help them find key pathways to information relevant to the respective patient's condition. These sites also provide evidence-based information, have multiple language options, and are free to use.

We concluded that the literature on patient portals and health information sites we have reviewed do not adequately address the barriers presented by the 10 knowledge gaps. That being said, we do believe that the sites listed above could become part of a blended learning environment that has potential for engaging patients and helping them understand and commit to changes in health behaviors that improve their outcomes or at least reduce health risks. In summary, the majority of patient portals in the United States were not designed to be part of a sensible blended learning teaching-learning-assessment environment [1, 11, 15–18].

Framed from the perspective of blended learning environments, we also identified some other barriers. Let us suppose that healthcare providers could introduce patients to online resources that had an evidence base for changing patients' behaviors toward life styles with reduced health risks or helped a patient manage chronic disease. Depending on the particular chronic illness, a teaching-learning-assessment environment could be designed to engage a patient in learning activities appropriate to their respective needs. We might be able to decrease health risks or improve management of chronic disease if a healthcare provider introduced a patient to online resources that had an evidence base for helping the patient understand their health problems and encouraged them to change health risk behaviors,

The teaching-learning-assessment environment would have to engage a patient in learning activities appropriate to their respective needs. But three barriers are obvious. First, a patient would need access to devices (computers, cell phones) and internet connections that allow affordable, easy, and on-demand access to the online elements of an educational program. Second, the majority of patients would require face-to-face time with a skilled healthcare educator who could coach each patient to find and use the online support as well as provide ongoing support, including help with content and context of educational materials and activities, but also referral to a technical support group. The blended environment must evolve as a sensible articulation of face-to-face activities with more independent online learning. Third, the patient education environments need adaptive capacities that create educational environments specific to each individual patient. This would mean online environments must bridge the 10 knowledge gaps mentioned in Sect. 1.1. The effectiveness of such an environment could be measured as significant improvement in patient outcomes or shifts toward healthy behaviors.

1.3 Critical Issues in Adult Education for Career and College Readiness

The United States Department of Education's National Center for Education Statistics reported data that suggest adults in the United States have an average literacy and numeracy significantly lower or not significantly different from international averages in literacy and numeracy. The Program for International Assessment of Adult Competencies (PIACC) collects extensive data on literacy-numeracy levels [19–21]. Among the 22 members of PIACC, literacy scores ranged from 250 in Italy to 296 in Japan, with an international average of 270 and the United States average at 273. Twelve countries had higher literacy scores than the United States. Measures of numeracy ranged from 246 in Spain to 288 in Japan. The United States numeracy average was 253, compared to the PIACC international average of 269, which placed the United

States below 18 other PIACC participating countries, higher than 2 countries, and not significantly different from 2 countries [19–21]. A point relevant to efforts in adult education is the score gaps in literacy and numeracy between those American adults without a high school degree and those attaining at least an associate degree.

In 2014, the passage of the Workforce Innovation and Opportunity Act in the United States [22], brought attention to the need to reframe strategies for adult education with a focus on ways and means to close education gaps and reduce social stratification as well as economic disenfranchisement of significant numbers of American citizens. For example, Education and Career News reported that 88 million adults—about half of the American workforce ages 18–64—have an educational level of high school equivalency or less [23]. However, projections for 2018 suggest that over 60% of jobs available to the U.S. workforce require education and/or training beyond a high school level. Furthermore, some groups of American adults are impacted more than others. Data on high school graduation rates reveal approximately 87% of Caucasian students graduate from high school on time, while for African-Americans the rate is 73% and for Hispanic students 76% [23]. Consequently, not only is there disenfranchisement due to achieved knowledge and skills but also differential disenfranchisement of minority groups.

As is the case for adults with chronic illness, education could be a critical pathway for adults working toward achieving educational levels of high school equivalency as well as higher levels of education and training that opened pathways to fulfilling and economically viable careers. The 10 knowledge gaps listed above are also key barriers to effective teaching-learning-assessment environments that could improve mastery of content and skills domains crucial to literacy, numeracy, and problem-solving (particularly problem-solving in technology-oriented careers). We compared educational needs and barriers for chronically ill adult with those of adults on educational pathways to take them beyond high school, including readiness for college and careers. Our research team studied teaching-learning-assessment systems that might be able to improve educational outcomes and behavioral changes consistent with improved health outcomes for adults with chronic illness, but also improved retention and learning outcomes for adults working toward higher levels of education and training that opened stable employment opportunities.

Tashiro *et al.* reviewed a large and diverse literature base to better understand "What really works in blended learning, for whom, why, how, and with what outcomes" [24]. Learning management systems, courseware systems, adaptive learning environments, and associated instructional materials offered by private software developers and academic publishers still have many weaknesses. Tashiro [25] examined the ethical failures of publishers and faculty when they do not use evidence-based materials and methods to create the teaching-learning-assessment environments for their courses and curricula frameworks. Why, for example, have educators not demanded the analogs of clinical trial research for instructional methods and materials? Indeed, a very interesting absence in research is cross-theory testing of models of cognition and learning.

As was the case for the patient education systems we reviewed, blended learning systems for K-12, undergraduate, graduate, professional development, and adult education do not adequately bridge the 10 knowledge gaps. That being said, we do believe there are a few blended learning models with potential for engaging diverse adult learners and helping them understand and commit to changes in patterns of learning that improve their conceptual and procedural knowledge to enhance options for college and career readiness. However, we have analyzed barriers to implementing blended learning within adult education programs. Adult education instructors often have been mandated to introduce blended learning environments into their adult education courses. Yet, the selected teaching-learning-assessment environments may not engage adult learners in activities appropriate to improving knowledge and skills, especially those essential for college and career readiness. The same barriers impeding the introduction of blended learning into patient education also plague adult education.

First, an adult learner would need access to devices (computers, cell phones) and affordable internet connections with easy and on-demand access to the online elements of an educational program. Second, learners would have to spend time with an educator (even if through asynchronous or synchronous online interactions) so they received help with content and context of educational materials and activities, but also could easily access a technical support group. The blended environment must have a well-developed balance and articulation of face-to-face activities (or online meetings) integrated with independent online learning activities. Finally, such teaching-learning-assessment environments must have adaptive capacities that monitor learners' progress and incorporate sensible and engaging remediation opportunities.

2 Case Studies of Blended Learning for Patient Education and Adult Education

2.1 Levels of Complexity

As we studied patient education and adult education for college and career readiness, we had to analyze the similarities—like those mentioned above—but also the differences. One of the differences is breadth and depth of the learning process. Patients with chronic illnesses require a focus on their particular chronic illness and causes, treatments, health behaviors, and routine as well as emergent care related to that illness. Their educational plan may have depth related to the disease, but usually not breadth related to other diseases and broader coverage of anatomy, physiology, pharmacology, and unrelated healthcare treatments. Adult learners in programs designed to improve college and career readiness encounter both breadth and depth in their studies. For example, many programs have two curricular strands—reading-writing and mathematics. Yet, almost all adult education programs also interlace within the two curricular strands content related to science, social studies, civics, and there is increasing focus on inclusion of modules related to healthcare, technology, and business. Often adult education programs also have parallel education programs for English Language Acquisition or English as a Second Language. In brief, adult learners usually have a broader content and skills repertoire to master.

Based on previous studies of healthcare and adult education, we sorted educational problems into one of three levels of complexity—micro, meso, and macro levels [3].

- Micro level problems occur at the individual or small-group level—the individual learner, the learner and instructor, and small groups of learners working together or with an instructor. From our perspective, the critical micro level problems are how to bridge the 10 gaps in our knowledge related to educational environments and their effectiveness [4, 5, 24]. In academic situations, these include interactions among students and students with instructors of a course. In healthcare settings, micro problems evolve between a patient and one or more healthcare educators and clinical staff.
- Meso level problems occur at the level of administrator and instructor interactions that shape the content, learning activities, program planning, implementation, and management of an educational program. In academic settings, such meso problems occur within the interactions (or lack thereof) among college vice presidents and deans, program directors, heads of departments or units, and instructors. All or some collaborate (or not) in selection of educational materials courseware and learning management systems or other educational technologies brought into teaching-learning-assessment environments. Analogous types of meso problems are evident in healthcare within the interactions of administrative staff, clinical staff, and healthcare educators when they choose or build patient-portals or other types of online educational offerings (sometimes in blended frameworks, sometimes not).
- Macro problems evolve at the level of institutional organizations, interactions between institutions and state organizations, and state-federal government interactions. Examples in academia include: department structures within a college; collaboration of colleges within a university; the impact of government mandates typically found within both state-funded universities and also community colleges in the United States supported by a county, city, or indigenous nation (for example, Native American tribal colleges); and state and federal guidelines or mandates imposed on educational institutions, such as accreditation, licensing requirements for professional education, state mandates, federal mandates, and federal as well as state funding. For healthcare, macro problems manifest in similar kinds of interactions: among administrators in hospital units and/or among administrators within a hospital cluster; collaboration of departments or units within a hospital or hospital cluster; the impact of government and insurance mandates that control reimbursements by diagnostic categories; federal and state accreditation; licensing requirements for healthcare professionals; evidence-based standards for patient education; and patterns as well as predictability of state mandates, federal mandates, but also stability of federal, state, and private funding.

Certainly, we do not make the claim that micro, meso, and macro problems are independent of each other. Indeed, their interdependence often adds to the complexity. However, proposed changes for education should have some kind of empirical support for improving educational outcomes and we need to understand the complexity within educational institutions and programs [2, 4]. Sadly, such empirical foundations are the exception rather than the rule.

2.2 A Patient Education Case Study

Tan et al. developed a model for patient education and behavioral change—***Ehealthlifestyle*** [1]. Tan's research team designed this educational and monitoring platform to provide e-Health outreach through remote monitoring of patients in their homes or long-term care settings so that trends towards exacerbations and other facets of chronic conditions could be better managed. This platform could facilitate both reduced healthcare costs and improved quality of life.

Ehealthlifestyle evolved from specific solutions in management of patients by remote systems to: (1) bridge patients' knowledge gaps; (2) enhance chronically ill individuals' technology adoption and sustained usage; (3) provide ongoing sampling of patient data; and (4) offer customized e-Health technologies to improve disposition to adhere to treatment regimens and encourage shifts toward health promotion behaviors. As a use case for ***Ehealthlifestyle***, the authors' examined management of COPD to explore how and why such a system collects data and predicts trends towards exacerbations by low-cost, high-frequency remote sampling of a patient's disease process. However, this system also provides ongoing blended learning types of environments in which case managers and other healthcare personnel could work with patients to improve health as well as reduce health risk behaviors. Tan et al. concluded effective patient education should be re-conceptualized as a type of blended learning. Based on a taxonomy for blended learning [13], patient education would usually include a low face-to-face component and a high online component. However, ongoing monitoring of the patient could be built into an adaptive teaching-learning-assessment environment that sent a clinical flag to the patient's care manager if the patient deviated from a care plan or suffered an exacerbation of a chronic illness. In such a case, the patient would be contacted by a healthcare provider who could provide support through face-to-face synchronous online chats, with or without video to help the patient find care for an exacerbation or re-engage with the care plan.

2.3 An Adult Education Case Study

Since research on blended learning in adult education has been underdeveloped relative to patient education, our case study will provide more detail about micro, meso, and macro levels of complexity in adult education. As a starting point, we note that research has not bridged the 10 gaps we listed in Sect. 1.1. We found little significant research related to adult education that provides a sound evidence-base in the areas of building and evaluating truly inclusive and adaptive educational environments likely to improve learning outcomes. To complicate matters, and despite a rapid increase in development of blended and totally online courses, design and implementation of such courses usually have not been driven from grounded theory in cognition and learning or from ground theory in behavioral change [2, 12]. Tashiro et al. discussed the lack of theory-driven and evidence-based approaches to building and evaluating educational technologies, learning management systems, and courseware systems, but also developed a taxonomy that reveals the diversity of blended learning models and the reasons instructors are not aware of this diversity [13]. The critical point is evidence-based studies of adult education are relatively rare and generally have small sample sizes [26, 27].

One of the authors (Tashiro) had the opportunity to study an American adult education program during January–December 2017 and will continue this research as a multi-year longitudinal study through May 2019. In this paper, we provide a summary of Phase 1 of the study, which we completed in December 2017. Phase I evolved as an ethnographic analysis of change management during the implementation of blended learning into the curricular threads of an adult basic education program focused on improving college and career readiness. Since the research is ongoing, we de-identify the research site and simply call it the "ABE" program.

We simplify here, but in the United States adult education programs are supported by federal and state funds that have very specific guidelines, with funding written into law at both the federal and state levels. The United States Department of Education provides funds to states who administer this support based on formula funding falling under a category of discretionary funds. Adult education programs receive a budget allocation appropriated and approved annually by the respective state legislature (interested readers can find more information about American adult education in: *Federal Adult Education—A Legislative Survey 1963–2013*).

Recently many states have initiated efforts to introduce more online learning into adult education programs. Our research site—ABE—is nested within a community college in a state that selected a courseware system and learning management system (LMS) that the state Department of Education hopes can be integrated to improve adult education and help adult education programs become more cost-effective. An expert panel composed of adult education administrators and instructors used a rubric to evaluate different courseware systems. The panel recommended the courseware *Odysseyware* (OW). The college in which ABE is nested uses an LMS called *Desire to Learn—D_2L*. ABE will use the D_2L *Brightspace Version*.

ABE and other adult education programs in the state proposed how they would use OW in blended learning teaching-learning-assessment environments and also delineated plans for integrating the courseware with a LMS. Since our research is ongoing, and regarding OW and D_2L, we disclose that we are not advocating for or against use of either. Our study will develop an evidence-based framework for improving learning outcomes within ABE and promoting transitions for adult students into meaningful opportunities for attending college and/or entering a career. Since we have not completed the planned longitudinal studies, we do not have enough evidence to provide favorable or unfavorable reviews of OW or D_2L.

Study Site. ABE is a unit within a community college in the western region of the United States. The college is a county-funded, two-year associates degree institution and houses ABE within campuses and learning centers. This college has partnerships with industry, but also well-developed articulation programs that facilitate transfers from the college into four-year baccalaureate and university systems within the state in which it is located. The ABE educational offerings are built around two curricular threads: (1) Reading and Writing; and (2) Mathematics. However, each thread is interlaced with educational units focused on science and social studies (including civics and history), with additional integrative and career readiness themes related to healthcare, technology, and business. The program also offers specialized classes: (1) Math Bridge (intensives for preparing students to take the GED testing but also preparing for college readiness); (2) Integrated Basic Education and Skills Training—I-BEST [26, 27]; and (3) classes in English Language Acquisition for Adults. The program had 110 instructors and staff in 2017, with 1,618 enrolled students during 2017 (demographics: 550 males, 1068 females, 1,403 minority students, and a student age range of 18–70 years old).

Odysseyware and D_2L. OW is not significantly different from many courseware systems. This courseware comes preloaded with courses. At the start of ABE's license, most of these courses covered content commonly taught in the United States from grades 3–12. Courses are most usually comprised of units, with each unit comprised of lessons, projects, quizzes, and tests. The lessons in most of the courses have short quizzes inside the lesson, which allows an assessment of a student's knowledge of the lesson. Unit quizzes and unit-clusters or course tests are linked to units and/or lesson clusters that appear before the placement of the quiz or test in the lesson sequence. OW has a "Flex" system that links quiz and test to subject matter in lessons. If a lesson is deleted during customization of a course, the Flex functionality adjusts the quizzes and tests for a unit so they do not contain assessment items from any deleted lessons. For a more complete perspective, visit the OW website at https://www.odysseyware.com/ to learn more about course management tools, strategies for building courses, assessment engines, instructor-student communication capacities, the gradebook structure, and how to generate student activity reports.

The learning management system D_2L (*Desire to Learn*) has been used in K-12 and higher educational systems. A preview of the *Brightspace Version* used at ABE can be found at: https://www.d2l.com/products/learning-environment/. Like many LMSs designed for academic institutions, there are tools designed for faculty that allow relatively easy course builds. D_2L has been designed to facilitate compliance with accessibility standards and can support a variety of online teaching-learning-environments. Course management tools offer the capacity for building courses with personalized learning pathways for students. Important features for instructors include: step-by-step instructions for building courses (including an HTML editor), an Instructional Design Wizard for aligning course content with learning objects and curricular standards, drag and drop functions for creating and organizing course content, relatively easy cloning or imaging capacities to create new courses from extant courses (through the timing and efficiency of such cloning often depends on the IT services of the educational institution or program), capacities for creating a variety of assessments or using extant assessments (with an interesting video feedback system called *VideoNote*), capacities for creating rubrics, options for integrating *TurnItIn*, and a variety of ways to create new course content through integration of multimedia and video links. The *Brightspace Version* of D_2L also offers a variety of analytics coupled to performance dashboards and progress reports for classes and individual students. As in many LMSs, *Brightspace* has capacities for automated notifications to instructors that provide information about students' progress and outcomes within a course.

Research Model. The overarching foci for our research have been the nested questions: "What works in a classroom rotation model of blended learning for adult education students, why, how, and with what transferable learning outcomes." Our approach used the 10 knowledge gaps presented in Sect. 1.1 as a framework to develop our research design. We created a mixed qualitative-quantitative research model. Integrated into this model are quantitative measures of students' and instructors' attributes related to each of the 10 knowledge gaps, such as perceptions of courseware and LMS usability, dispositions to learn, learning outcomes, and planning to act on knowledge gained [28–32]. However, our analysis of complexity within micro, meso, and macro levels of the impact on implementation of a blended learning environment for students also led us to design qualitative studies of ABE students, instructors, and administrators, as well as state Department of Education personnel. The qualitative probes use a methodology that explores perceptions of processes of change as instructors and students adopt and use a new courseware, a new learning management system, and ancillary educational technologies. The qualitative research model has been derived from connective ethnography studies used to better understand online/offline literacy networks [33, 34].

The recently completed Phase 1 was called "Grounding," because it provided a descriptive qualitative analysis of instructors' initial experiences planning for and implementing a blended learning environment into their courses. Phases 2–4 are mixed quantitative-qualitative studies of the micro, meso, and macro interactions that unfold within ABE as first OW and then OW integrated with D_2L are implemented. Phase 2 focuses on student experiences during blended learning, especially the micro levels of student-instructor and student-student interactions. Phase 3 overlaps with Phase 2 but focuses on instructor roles within meso levels of complexity during course and curricular planning, factors shaping course implementation and scheduling, and interactions with program administrators. Phase 3 overlaps with both Phases 2 and 3, layering over these phases a detailed study of macro levels of complexity, with specific probes of ABE program administrators, college administrators, as well as state Department of Education staff.

With this model of phased research, the Phase 1 Grounding provided a critical foundation because we were able to start the research at a very important moment—shortly after the state's Department of Education passed down the decision to adult education programs that OW should be integrated into each program's instructional practices. Thus, our research began in July 2017, at the very beginning of the change management process of implementing OW. However, the instructors (except for only a few individuals) knew very little about OW and none had access to it until after completing a mandatory training by OW staff (August–September 2017).

Phase 1 Grounding provided us with an important type of baseline for instructor knowledge of how and why OW could be integrated into their instructional strategies. Furthermore, administrators at ABE had decided to use the blended model of classroom rotation, which meant that instructors had to work through how to use OW to create blended teaching-learning-assessment environments, but also how such environments imposed shifts on their current instructional strategies for a classroom rotation model. To understand the micro interactions of instructor-student and the meso-level interactions of instructor-instructor as well as administrator-instructor, we needed a baseline of information on instructors' knowledge of, interest in, willingness to use, and sense of workload issues as OW was brought online for ABE's students. Instructors also had to plan for integration of OW and D_2L. Phase 1 Grounding offered an unusual opportunity to study a complete change management process from perspectives of different levels of complexity in the implementation of a blended learning environment as well as the evolution of OW use by ABE instructors and students. As mentioned, Phase 1 now has been completed. Phase 2 is underway. In this paper, we report the results of Phase 1 and its implications for subsequent research phases.

The Methodology of Research Phase 1. Grounding studies began in August 2017. Instructors were introduced to the plan for incorporating use of OW into the instructional strategies for delivering ABE's curricula and their embedded courses. ABE instructors participated in Professional Learning sessions. Following these sessions, instructors were invited (but not required) to comment on concerns and interests in the use of OW and eventual integration of this courseware with D_2L. A shared Google document allowed instructors to comment (anonymously) on the implementation of OW and the shift toward a blended learning classroom rotation model of instruction. This document had a table format with three columns, using the K-W-L rubric: Column 1—What Do You Know, Column 2—What Do You Want to Know, and Column 3—What Have You Learned [28]. We adapted the K-W-L model as a kind of discussion board to follow instructors' thoughts on and feelings about the initial stages of OW implementation. Instructors added commentary relevant to each column's heading. The research team reviewed and collated comments. Additionally, one of the authors (Tashiro) served during Phase I as both a course instructor in mathematics and as an Education Technology Coach. Separate from the K-W-L commentaries, he recorded ethnographic research notes on his class experiences as well as his interactions with instructors as they began to implement OW.

During October through December, instructors' comments were analyzed for thematic threads. By "thematic" we mean clusters of related commentary entered by instructors in the three K-W-L columns. The research team delineated themes. Four themes emerged. In this same time period, Tashiro's parsed his ethnographic notes into categories of meso, micro, and macro issues that evolved during discussions with his students and with instructors seeking his assistance to implement OW. We organized comments related to micro, meso, macro issues into a cross-tabulation of levels of complexity with the themes emerging from instructors' K-W-L commentaries after Professional Learning sessions.

Results of Phase 1 Research. While the K-W-L model has many values, analysis of themes can be confounded across what a person knows, what that person wants to know, and what the same person has learned. The four themes emerging from instructors' comments are presented below as organizing questions, below which we present interpretive analysis. We also describe the micro, meso, and macro levels of interactions relevant to each theme (as summarized from Tashiro's ethnographic notes and analysis).

Theme 1.—What are the ABE goals for blended learning and how are program goals articulated with student goals?

On the positive side, instructors had many ideas about how blended learning with OW might help them achieve the learning goals and student learning outcomes delineated by the state and interpreted into course designs by ABE. Instructors imagined how using OW could improve students' technology literacy and familiarity with computer systems as well as content and skills that would improve their opportunities for achieving college and career readiness goals. Instructors noted opportunities for blended learning models providing ongoing educational scaffolding outside of face-to-face (F2F) class time. Such opportunities could offer added benefits of increasing outreach to students who, in addition to taking classes, had family obligations as well as heavy employment workloads.

On the negative side, over 50% of the instructors did not really know how to design and implement a classroom rotation model of blended learning, and this issue was made more complicated by the variety of classroom rotation models that can be found in diverse educational settings. A particularly interesting set of discussions evolved around what a student would gain outside of F2F classroom activities, which suggested these instructors had not thought through how to build a classroom rotation model that sustained complementary but integrated elements of F2F and independent, outside-of-class work in OW.

Micro Level Issues.—When these early Professional Learning sessions were held, only a small percentage of the ABE instructors had used OW in a class, so they had little first-hand knowledge of student reactions to OW as well as to the classroom rotation models for blended learning. This meant that the majority of instructors did not know what the student-student and instructor-student interactions might be like or how to create a teaching-learning-assessment environment that facilitated meaningful learning experiences among students as well as between a student and their instructor.

Meso Level Issues.—At the meso level, instructors worked with each other to envision patterns of classroom rotation blended learning and effective use of OW that would not dramatically increase their workload—especially the part-time instructors who were paid for eight hours each week for teaching a class (six hours in the classroom and two hours for class preparation, office hours, and preparing as well as managing a course in OW).

Macro Level Issues.—A key macro issue evolved from discussions about who chose OW and what were the criteria for the choice. Only a tiny percentage of the instructors were involved in any way during the deliberations on selecting a courseware system and planning for its implementation. In terms of a change management process, this finding suggests a breakdown in communication between state Department of Education staff, ABE administrators, and ABE instructors. The end result could impede a smooth integration of a classroom model of blended learning with the OW courseware, if for no other reasons (and this was born out in October–December 2017), use of OW within a classroom rotation model did increase workloads and these increases were differentially harder on part-time instructors.

Theme 2.—What types of teaching-learning-assessment activities should instructors implement face-to-face (F2F) and which should be implemented within the online environment of the courseware? The instructors at ABE are a remarkably creative and dedicated group who are committed to serving adult students in this adult education program. In the Professional Learning sessions, instructors listed many interesting examples of student learning activities and parsed these between those that would more likely work F2F and those suitable for online and/or homework activities that did not require F2F instructor modeling, facilitation, or scaffolding. Instructors described ideas they had previously used with success in F2F classroom activities. With some coaching from instructors familiar with courseware (and some of the instructors had used My

Foundation Lab as well as Plato), the session discussions and subsequent comments in the K-W-L commentaries demonstrated a rich array of learning activities, assignments, assessments, and projects that could be sensibly allocated either to the F2F teaching-learning-assessment environment or to the out-of-classroom work that would predominantly be within OW.

By the end of November, most instructors had created a course in OW and were beginning to use the courseware in their classes. On the negative side, many instructors still did not have a clear sense of how to design and implement a classroom model of blended learning. However, many instructors quickly adapted what they had done prior to the transition to the new instructional model, integrating tried and true learning activities into F2F time and mapping content from class discussions and activities to course materials in OW.

Micro Level Issues.—Based on Tashiro's notes as an Education Technology Coach, a majority of instructors reported positive student-student and instructor-student interactions. About 40% had initial problems with OW, but these were generally solved quickly and satisfactorily by the instructors themselves or working with one of the Education Technology Coaches provided by ABE or with one of the full-time teachers in ABE. Over 75% of instructors wanted a faux student to be enrolled in their classes so the instructor could observe OW from the students' perspective and better understand the courseware functionality available to the students. Education Technology Coaches found a way to create faux students for instructors.

Meso Level Issues.—Discussions among instructors suggested that the fall term in which OW was implemented felt busier than usual. There were few complaints and conflicts reported in the K-W-L commentaries or observed between instructors and administrators of ABE.

Macro Level Issues.—A few issues arose among ABE administrators, the state Department of Education, and the developers of OW. These mostly focused on the number of seats available in the site license from OW. There also were discussions among these three groups about the need for more courses built to meet the needs of adult education.

Theme 3.—What are strategies for F2F and online work that addresses different levels of technology skills among ABE students? Instructors frequently commented on ABE's lack of hard data about how many students had computers at home as well as internet services with download/upload speed that allowed easy use of OW (and beginning in 2018, integrated use of OW an D2L). Instructors and administrators also expressed concerns about ABE students' general level of technology literacy. Many creative ideas were expressed about ways to help students achieve higher levels of technology skills: (1) integrate computer basics into courses (including use of smart phones during a class session); (2) peer mentoring by engaging pairs of students in online activities to improve computer and educational technology skills; (3) modeling and scaffolding for sensible steps toward computer literacy; (4) increased use of the Tech Corner—F2F tutoring and consultation by members of the community college's IT services; and (5) thinking about course articulation within each curricular thread so that students developed technological skills in lower-level classes and then could expand their skills in upper-level classes. For students without computers or smart phones as well as for those without adequate home internet service, instructors provided information to students about access to computers at county libraries and within computer laboratories available to ABE. Even so, instructors recognized a high percentage of ABE students have family and work obligations that reduce the time for working on computers to complete schoolwork at home. We estimated roughly 25% of ABE students did not have a computer at home and/or did not have easy access to good internet services.

Micro Level Issues.—From the perspective of Tashiro's work as an Education Technology Coach, there is considerable diversity in students' technical skills as well as diversity among instructors in knowledge about and effective use of educational technologies. Thus, creating and sustaining student-student and student-instructor interactions likely to lead to improved learning outcomes might be a good focus for future Professional Learning sessions. Another type of session for instructors could be training about how to teach technology skills as well as how to introduce students to use of OW accessed through a portal in D_2L.

Meso Level Issues.—Observations and notes about instructor-instructor and instructor-administrator interactions suggest needs assessments of students' technology skills and interests in online learning options should have been conducted prior to selection of the best blended learning model, a courseware system, and a model for courseware-LMS coupling.

Macro Level Issues.—At the state and federal levels there appear to be strong interests in improving the technological literacy of the American public, including efforts to improve college and career readiness among individuals who may be disenfranchised by lower levels of education that inhibit or outright prevent their participation in the American workforce. While there are interactions among staff in the state Department of Education and the ABE administrators and instructors, a smooth transition toward effective use of blended learning that drives improved learning outcomes will require better articulation among these stakeholders.

Theme 4.—During classroom rotation activities, what strategies can instructors use to facilitate the transition of students from F2F into online activities? When the first training sessions for OW were implemented at ABE, instructors raised a number of concerns. Most of these focused on how a classroom rotation model of blended learning could be operationalized, both in general terms, but also by individual instructors who already had developed instructional strategies that seemed to work for their students, often integrated online resources, but did not yet have a model for integrating OW as a source of course content, learning activities, and assessment. As partially described above, two other student-related issues also shaped questions about transitions from predominantly F2F teaching strategies to integration of a courseware in a blended learning strategy: (1) students would be required to study within the OW environment but outside of the classroom—how would that impact and in some cases disenfranchise students with limited access to computers and/or internet services; and (2) how could instructors, especially given workload constraints, have time to learn more about blended learning models, but also redesign existing courses to fit sensibly into a classroom rotation model of blended learning.

Interestingly, during the period from training how to use OW (July–August 2017) through introduction of OW in most courses (August–December 2017), instructors' perceptions began to shift. These shifts were not reflected as much in the Professional Learning sessions as in the notes of the Educational Technology Coach.

Micro Level Issues.—Despite assigned reading for Professional Learning sessions, the majority of ABECC instructors had not been exposed to or trained in the variety of courseware types, learning management systems, or the many types of blended learning courses. Individually and as a group, they were dedicated teachers and have worked hard to train themselves in these areas. Yet, workloads for individual instructors were problematic. Again, if a part-time instructor is paid for only 8 h per class, with 6 h F2F in classes per week (which usually included facilitating students' engagement in OW and other online resources), the 2 remaining hours left little time for self-education or group professional development in these areas. Even so, all teachers made efforts to copy or create an OW course and began to integrate courses into their instructional strategy.

Meso Level Issues.—Micro level issues spill over into meso level issues, because administrator-instructor interactions become confounded when workloads are barriers to systematic implementation of a blended learning model for instruction ABE did offer Professional Learning sessions to help instructors learn more about blended learning, courseware systems, and learning management systems. Yet, notes from the Education Technology Coach reveal more training would have helped instructors guide students through the transition toward effective blended learning teaching-learning-assessment environments.

Macro Level Issues.—Macro level issues emerged in the areas of funding and workload issues related to the change management during implementation of blended learning at ABE and also are reflected in the micro and meso issues alluded to above: (1) training for OW, (2) training for an upcoming integration of OW into the *Brightspace* version of D_2L, (3) availability of computers for every classroom, (4) full-time instructor workloads, (5) part-time instructor workloads, and (6) communication of a coherent vision of blended learning that could be implemented and rigorously evaluated for cost-efficiency and student outcomes.

3 *Gedanken* Experiments Based on Results of Phase 1 Research

3.1 Implications of Phase 1 Grounding

The Phase 1 research at ABE allowed us to compare the potential for blended learning to improve patient education and adult education. As we had hoped, Phase 1 provided a baseline for a rigorous study of "What works in a classroom rotation model of blended learning for adult education students, why, how, and with what transferable learning outcomes." We recognize that our ongoing study is not necessarily generalizable to all adult education programs in the United States as well as in other countries. What we hope to show is a systematic approach to studying the process of implementing courseware, LMSs, and models of blended learning within environments focused on adult learners, with our principle focus on patient education and adult education programs designed to improve adult learners' progress toward college and career readiness.

We returned to the 10 knowledge gaps presented in the Introduction of this paper. Certainly, the gaps we describe are not independent of each other. Furthermore, the gaps are shaped by the complex interactions of micro, meso, and macro interactions. We mapped the knowledge gaps into each of these levels of interactions. As a starting point in this discussion, we restate the knowledge gaps in terms of key the issues of each gap.

1. Disposition to engage in a learning.
2. Impacts of realism and relevance on learning outcomes.
3. Threshold of experience to learn.
4. Knowledge domains instantiated.
5. Learning retention and stability of retention.
6. Disposition to act on the knowledge gained.
7. Accuracy of instantiated knowledge and skills.
8. Measurable learning outcomes.
9. Misconception development.
10. Impacts of social networks or e-communities.

Our current work comparing blended learning model for adult patients and adult basic education students led a series of *Gedanken* experiments to study models for improving adaptive learning capacities for systems that might serve both patients as well as learners in adult education programs. These *Gedanken* experiments followed the model used during a study of a blended, competency-based CIT curriculum at Northern Arizona University [2]. As a brief summary, our team had studied healthcare systems and the transformation of clinical systems for collecting, storing and analyzing electronic patient data in electronic health records (EHR). We realized an analogue to an EHR would be an Electronic Learning Record (ELR) [1, 23]. Research funded by the Social Sciences and Humanities Research Council of Canada allowed us to integrate middleware into online environments to stream data into an ELR similar to data streaming into EHRs. We concluded adult patients and adult education students could be served by an ELR, but only if there were connections to the following: (1) for adult patients, the ELR should be connected through a two-way portal allowing data from a patient to be reviewed by a care manager of clinician; and (2) for students in adult education programs, the ELR should be connected through a two-way portal allowing data from an adult student to be reviewed by an instructor or tutor.

While some patient portals and some courseware systems and LMSs have communications portals, there are very few that have truly adaptive capacities for assessing a patient's progress in managing a chronic illness or in deviating from a care plan. The same is true for adult education—that is, there are few courseware or courseware-LMS combinations that are adaptive in ways that assess a learner's progress within an adult education program and provide feedback to student and instructor about deviations from a program of study. We analyzed how to enhance adaptive learning capacities of a system that could be coupled to a two-way ELR portal, with a focus on middleware layered into the data collection and analysis of student outcome data. In addition, we studied how to add a powerful knowledge system that connected databases of learning objects in ways a student could receive detailed feedback on their progress, as well as recommendations and remediation activities for improving their learning. During the period July 2014–January 2017, we conducted a *Gedanken* experiment to study ways and means to add adaptive capacity to a type of teaching-learning-assessment system that could serve adult patient education as well as learners in adult education programs. We note here that the same type of system could be used for pediatric patient education as well a K-12 student education in the United States if we built the system to accommodate differences in cognitive development and learning of children and adults.

3.2 Gedanken Experiments

During the period 2002–2016, the authors built and studied the research platform called **SIGNAL**—Serial Integration of Guiding Nodes for Adaptive Learning [2]. This platform allowed creation of a Space-Time mapping of each individual's conceptual and performance competencies to their decisions during engagement in educational and knowledge transfer activities [35–38]. An assessment system [2, 4] identified misconceptions of each individual as they explored learning activities within an online or computer-based system. Each misconception identified could then be mapped to Learning Activities in which a student or patient engaged.

Our *Gedanken* experiments created abstractions for our **SIGNAL** environment. By "abstraction" we mean a competency map of learning: for each Competency Domain we delineated the Objectives; for each Objective its Lessons; for each Lesson its Topics; for each Topic its Learning Activities; and for each Learning Activity its Learning Objects. We modelled each element of the concept map as dynamic compartments, that is, as linked software engines and/or databases able to send and receive signals that created database linkages. **SIGNAL** allowed linkages to assemble components of a teaching-learning-assessment environment related to a particular Learning Activity nested in a particular Topic of a Lesson associated with an Objective. For this *Gedanken* experiment, we then delineated two versions of **SIGNAL**: (1) one for patient education [1]; and (2) a second version of **SIGNAL** for an adult education courses at ABE [1, 2].

Our *Gedanken* experiments used **SIGNAL** to model adult patients learning how to manage COPD. A parallel *Gedanken* experiment with **SIGNAL** modelled student progress through two adult basic education courses—Reading-Writing and Mathematics, both taught by Tashiro during the period January–December 2017. As in earlier studies, we noted the critical nature of signals received and sent by any compartment of the teaching-learning-assessment environment. We realized that the dynamic nature of any given compartment is critically important to building truly adaptive educational environments that adapt to individual patients or students as they worked within a compartment. We use "compartment" herein to represent a Learning Object for a Learning Activity associated with a specific Topic of a specific Lesson within a particular Competency Domain. For example: (1) a patient learning activity related to behaviors that minimize exacerbations of COPD; or (2) for adult learners, how authors use pattern and variation in sentence length and word choice to convey emotional tonality in a piece of literary fiction.

Each *Gedanken* experiment led to a refinement of **SIGNAL**. The principal refinements evolved as we projected hypotheses for the nature of the dynamic features of monitoring middleware necessary to parse the dynamics and analyses of signals as well as the distribution of key data across compartments that could record each student's navigational and engagement decisions as well as time spent in various activities. Consequently, we derived model frameworks for monitoring data coupled to learning assessment outcomes within online simulations to map a learner's instantiation of knowledge and skills by comparing learning and competency outcomes against expectations delineated by expert panels [39–42]. These hypotheses can now be tested in rigorous research, such as we have planned for Phases 2–4 of our longitudinal studies at ABE.

Figure 1 shows a diagrammatic representation of **SIGNAL** as refined from Gedanken experiments. The result is a set of interconnected software engines that monitor educational activities of either a patient or an adult learner in an adult education program. In Fig. 1, the image shows a clinician who has received a clinical flag from a COPD patient and has begun to examine the patient's misconceptions about the management of their disease as well as the potential for serious exacerbations. Note, however, that an analogous image could show an instructor at an adult basic education program monitoring a learner's progress, especially misconceptions about the content area they are studying and the potential for these misconceptions to impede progress toward passing the American high school equivalency examinations.

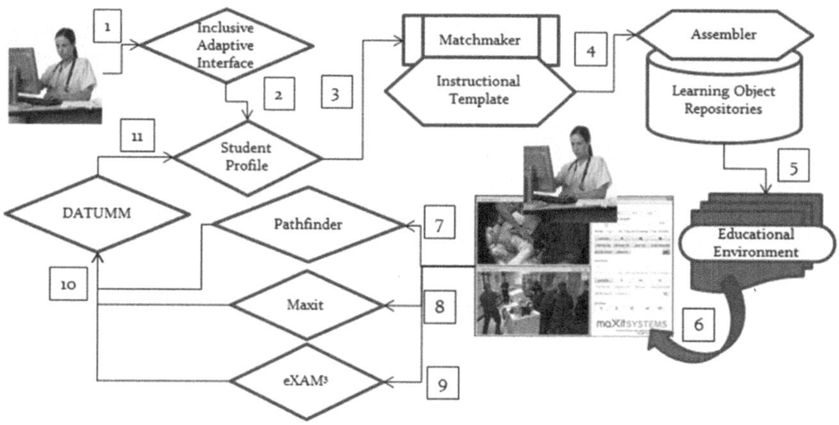

Fig. 1. Diagrammatic representation of the SIGNAL environment for patient education or education of adults in an adult basic education program [from 24].

Below, we describe the components of SIGNAL evolving from the *Gedanken* Experiments. We have included the knowledge gaps that each component can bridge.

(1) A clinician monitoring a patient or an instructor monitoring a student examines how well the patient or adult student is progressing within a Competency Domain's Lessons, Topics, and their respective Learning Activities and associated Learning Objects. The clinician or instructor has access to the two-way portal, so they can evaluate the progress of the patient or adult student (hereafter,

the "learner") and provide feedback. On the other side of the portal a learner has access to a Web-based interface, designed as a personalized Inclusive-Adaptive System that assesses a learner's accessibility needs and preferences for a personalized educational environment. The two-way portal combined with the Inclusive-Adaptive system helps bridge Gap 1—Disposition to engage in learning, but also re-engage in learning if the learner has been having difficulties with the Competency Domain's Lessons, Topics, and their respective Learning Activities and associated Learning Objects.

(2) The Inclusive-Adaptive Interface (IAI) collects data on the learner's needs and preferences, creating a Leaner Profile (LP) database that becomes part of an Electronic Learning Record (ELR). The IAI, LP, and ELR create learning opportunities to improve a learner's disposition to engage (Gap 1) as well as providing a record of student activities relating to Gaps 2–10.

(3) The LP data stream to a MatchMaker (MM) system that selects an Instructional Design Template (IDT) based on a theory of cognition and behavioral change selected by an instructor and consistent with the course content but informed by a learner's needs and preferences. MM and IDT work together in ways that can improve disposition to engage in learning as well as disposition to act on knowledge gained (Gap 6). However, these systems also work together in ways that bridge Gap 2—the learner's preferences for realism and relevance in the learning environment, and also Gap 3—the threshold of experience to learn (because the IDT-MM couple receives feedback from learner outcome systems described in more detail below).

(4) The MatchMaker engine then reads the metadata from the template.

(5) The Assembler Engine (AE) reads the IDT and metadata brought to it by MM, searches Learning Object Repositories (LOR) to find and collate learning activities, resources, educational scaffolding, learning assessments, and feedback personalized for the learner, and then organizes the assemblage to create a Web-based personalized teaching-learning-assessment-diagnostic Educational Environment (EE). AE, IDT, MM, LOR, and EE work in concert to create teaching-learning-assessment environments that are responses to data about the individual learner's interactions and learning outcomes within the environment created. Thus, there is an adaptive capacity for EE creation, monitoring of learner outcomes within EE, and automated adjustments to meet a learner's preferences as well as progress toward achieving learning outcomes (bridging Gaps 4–9, and also Gap 10 if the learner is integrated into social networks and/or e-communities).

(6) Learners engage within the EE (and, for some types of blended classes, learners also engage in face-to-face settings—such as clinician or instructor mentoring, live skills labs, low-fidelity or high-fidelity educational simulations related to a content domain area).

(7) Within the Web-based Educational Environments, each learner is constantly monitored by middleware called PathFinder (PF) that follows choices made within the Educational Environments and also times a student's engagement in learning activities, resources, assessments, and use of diagnostic feedback. PF contributes information to critical SIGNAL systems that together add individual learner data to the ELR (data important to bridging Gaps 1–10).

(8) Within the F2F moments—a clinician meeting with a patient or an instructor working with a student—a learner can be monitored as they demonstrate learning outcomes or skills. Our system for this component is a video-capture and analysis system called MAXIT. MAXIT efficiently collects assessment data on learners' performance competencies and bridges Gaps 4–5 as well as Gaps 7–9 [11, 36–38].

(9) Prior to, simultaneously with, or after learning-demonstration activities, learners enter an assessment engine called $eXAM^3$ [11], which assesses their learning outcomes within a cognitive taxonomy selected by the faculty member (e.g., Bloom's Revised Taxonomy or a skills-based rubric or a clinical expert panel rubric for a Competency Domain). $eXAM^3$ evolved as an assessment engine with diagnostic feedback capacities and provides data that help bridge Gaps 7–9.

(10) PathFinder, MAXIT, and $eXAM^3$ stream a learner's data to a data analysis and knowledge system called DATUMM.

(11) DATUMM, in turn, analyzes the data, creates new information about the learner, and sends information back to the Learner Profile. These new information sets integrate into the Learner Profile, with revised data and information facilitating adaptive changes to the flow beginning with the MatchMaker and ending in new configurations of the Educational Environment. Importantly, data from the Learner Profile also streams into a subcomponent—the Electronic Learning Record, through time creating a longitudinal record of a learner's progress [39–42]. DATUMM is most similar to the analytics engines now used widely in a number of applications.

The **SIGNAL** platform collects learners' data to create a very detailed Electronic Learning Record. The ELR also can be constructed to receive data and information from multiple courses, and so create a much more detailed and informative multidimensional learner transcript. Preliminary studies of this platform provide evidence that it will complement faculty efforts without increasing workload, while providing new tools and types of data for more authentic assessment of students' conceptual and performance competencies. SIGNAL also will allow detailed analysis of cognitive processes and behavioral choices to trace development of misconceptions [1, 2].

3.3 Ongoing Research

We now plan to use the **SIGNAL** framework to determine if **SIGNAL's** components could be duplicated through creative use of a typical courseware like OW and a typical LMS like D_2L. As an example of this type of experiment, we studied **SIGNAL** components and hypothesized how the capacities of these components could be achieved in a course using OW integrated within D_2L. We then created OW-D2L usage scenarios to see if we could reject specific hypotheses. One particularly challenging research design focused on the following hypothesis:

H_0: OW can be integrated within the LMS D_2L in ways that create an Inclusive-Adaptive Interface and Learner Profile for students that will automatically customize a teaching-learning-assessment environment for each student.

We began by looking at nine SIGNAL components—Inclusive-Adaptive Interface, Learner Profile, Electronic Learner Record, MatchMaker, Instructional Design Template, Assembler, Learning Object Repositories, the Educational Environment, and the PathFinder. Our logical sequence focused on what components in OW or {OW+D_2L} could duplicate the outcomes of the eight **SIGNAL** components. We tried various combinations of course management tools and content repositories within OW and D_2L that could be coupled within an educational strategy to provide outcomes close to our identical to the nine **SIGNAL** components. Our plan is to study student outcomes and faculty workload in two conditions: (1) an OW-D_2L integrated system; and (2) one of our **SIGNAL** models. This work is ongoing; however, preliminary time and outcome models suggest that an {OW-D_2L} coupling cannot duplicate a **SIGNAL** model without drastically increasing faculty workload. We continue to work on this project, because we feel such evidence-based comparisons are critical to advances in blended learning models using courseware and LMSs that "really work," especially in the contexts of improving learner outcomes without increasing instructor workload.

4 Conclusions and Recommendations

During the period 1998 to 2014, we studied how cognitive and learning sciences could inform instructional design, especially in development and evaluation of complex learning objects within online course components. This work led us to examine several theories of cognition and learning as well as theories of behavioral change. Sophisticated courseware-LMS combination could be constructed and could be used to test theoretical frameworks that have been proposed for cognition—for example cognitive load theory, cognitive flexibility theory, adaptive character of thought theory, and situated learning theory [35]. Some of these theories cluster into more individualistic structured learning—such as the adaptive character of thought and cognitive load theories. Others fit within what many educators call constructivist learning theories—such as cognitive flexibility theory and situated learning theory [35]. However, most developers of educational products have not driven development from grounded theory and have not conducted large-scale research on students' learning outcomes in different instances of their teaching-learning-assessment environments using different theoretical frameworks or a synthesis of frameworks to inform the design and various engines of the simulations. We found no rigorous large-scale studies (i.e. analogous to clinical trials) of courseware design that would give us an empirical foundation for "what really works" to improve student learning outcomes or bridge the knowledge gaps described earlier in this paper.

As use of blended and totally online courses increased, we recommended careful choices of educational systems that mapped sensibly to the developmental stage and prior knowledge of the end users—learners. As an example, when we designed clinical simulations for a virtual hospital and a virtual medical office, we immersed ourselves in the culture and practice of healthcare education. Common educational priorities and praxis led us to build virtual hospital and virtual medical office simulations grounded in the situated learning theory of cognition. This constructivist theory posits that learning develops within the activity, context, and culture in which it is situated. From an instructional design perspective, a simulation based on situated learning would involve learners in what some call a cognitive apprenticeship that provides a variety of engagements to support learning in knowledge-skills suites by enabling learners to develop and use their cognitive tools within authentic activities of the knowledge-skills domain (see, http://otec.uoregon.edu/learning_theory.htm#SituatedLearning). We believed that our simulations for healthcare students and practitioners could be built around situated learning theory because that theory fits with the processes common in planning and delivering healthcare.

Now, we have turned to patient and adult education and plan ongoing research to develop teaching-learning-assessment environments that best fit adult education programs. From Phase 1 studies at ABE, we feel a single theory of learning and cognition probably will not work for all adult education educational settings. For example, bridge programs from adult education into healthcare provider certificate and degree programs might use a situated learning theory as a framework within which to build suitable teaching-learning-assessment environments. However, other types of adult education programs might be better served by other theoretical foundations. Research Phases 2–4 at ABE will allow foundational work focused on how to use OW and D_2L is ways that best approximate our SIGNAL model. We anticipate our research at the ABE site will help create new types of courseware and simulation environments with an administrative dashboard built to allow any educational program to select a grounded theory in what we call the courseware's Assembler engine, which automatically configures learning activities, learning objects, and authentic assessments consistent with the selected theory.

What would we need? We would need flexible but powerful systems similar to prototypes with the capacities we built into **SIGNAL** [1, 2, 11–14, 36–42]. Capacities allowing researchers to choose a theory of cognition and learning must be coupled to engines that create the teaching-learning-assessment environment consistent with the theory selected. Learning activities with their embedded learning objects, respective learning assessments, and associated diagnostic feedback and educational scaffolding would all be dictated by the grounded theory selected. The courseware functionality would be driven by the selected theory. Thus, loading and configuring learning activities, learning objects, assessments, diagnostics feedback and scaffolding would have to be consistent with the selected theory. Teaching-learning-assessment environments with such characteristics and other truly adaptive learning environments must increase flexibility in types of theory-specific repositories of learning-assessment objects that could be assembled into the dynamic formations yielding a teaching-learning-assessment environment consonant with a particular theoretical framework. In the decade of "big data" analytics, we are poised to step towards educational research and praxis that is evidence-based and as predictive as the best clinical care in the world.

References

1. Tan, J., Hung, P., Dohan, M., Trojer, T., Farwick, M., Tashiro, J.: Gateway to quality living for the elderly: charting an innovative approach to evidence-based e-health technologies for serving the chronically ill. In: Proceedings of the 13th IEEE International Conference on Computational Science and Engineering (CSE-2010), 11–13 December 2010, Hong Kong (2010)
2. Tashiro, J., Hung, P., Martin, M.V., Hurst, F., Brown, A.: Personalized-adaptive learning—an operational framework for developing competency-based curricula in computer information technology. Int. J. Innov. Learn. **19**(4), 412–430 (2016)
3. Johnson, K., Tashiro, J.: Interprofessional care and health care complexity: factors shaping human resources effectiveness in health information management. In: Kabene, S.M. (ed.) Human Resources in Healthcare, Health Informatics and Healthcare Systems, pp. 250–280. IGI Global, Hershey (2010)
4. Tashiro, J., Hurst, F., Brown, A., Hung, P.C.K., Martin, M.V.: Personalized-adaptive learning – a model for CIT curricula. In: Cheung, S.K.S., Fong, J., Zhang, J., Kwan, R., Kwok, L.F. (eds.) ICHL 2014. LNCS, vol. 8595, pp. 266–277. Springer, Cham (2014). https://doi.org/10.1007/978-3-319-08961-4_25
5. Garcia-Ruiz, M.A., Tashiro, J., Kapralos, B., Martin, M.V.: Crouching tangents, hidden danger: assessing development of dangerous misconceptions within serious games for health care education. In: Hai-Jew, S. (ed.) Virtual Immersive and 3D Learning Spaces: Emerging Technologies and Trends, pp. 269–306. IGI Global, Hershey (2011)
6. National Research Council: How People Learn: Brain, Mind, Experience, and School. National Academy Press, Washington, DC (2000)
7. National Research Council: Knowing What Students Know: The Science and Design of Educational Assessment. National Academy Press, Washington, DC (2001)
8. National Research Council: How Students Learn: History, Mathematics, and Science in the Classroom. National Academies Press, Washington, DC (2005)
9. American Association for the Advancement of Science: Invention and Impact: Building Excellence in Undergraduate Science, Technology, Engineering and Mathematics (STEM) Education. American Association for the Advancement of Science, Washington, DC (2004)
10. Federation of American Scientists: Summit on Educational Games – Harnessing the Power of Video Games for Learning. Federation of American Scientists, Washington, DC (2006)
11. Tashiro, J., Choate, D.: Method to Assess a Person's Knowledge of a Subject Area. US Patent Application, No. 60/521,329. U.S. Patent and Trademark Office, Washington, DC (2004)
12. Tashiro, J., Martin, M.V., Hung, P.C.K.: MISSED – studying students' development of misconceptions in hybrid courses. In: Cheung, S.K.S., Fong, J., Fong, W., Wang, F.L., Kwok, L.F. (eds.) ICHL 2013. LNCS, vol. 8038, pp. 364–376. Springer, Heidelberg (2013). https://doi.org/10.1007/978-3-642-39750-9_34
13. Tashiro, J., Hung, P.C.K., Martin, M.V.: Evidence-based educational practices and a theoretical framework for hybrid learning. In: Kwan, R., Fong, J., Kwok, L., Lam, J. (eds.) ICHL 2011. LNCS, vol. 6837, pp. 51–72. Springer, Heidelberg (2011). https://doi.org/10.1007/978-3-642-22763-9_6
14. Tashiro, J., Hung, P.C.K., Martin, M.V.: ROAD-MAP for educational simulations and serious games. In: Tsang, P., Cheung, S.K.S., Lee, V.S.K., Huang, R. (eds.) ICHL 2010. LNCS, vol. 6248, pp. 186–204. Springer, Heidelberg (2010). https://doi.org/10.1007/978-3-642-14657-2_18

15. Alpert, J., Krist, A., Aycock, R., Kreps, G.: Applying multiple methods to comprehensively evaluate a patient portal's effectiveness to convey information to patients. J. Med. Internet Res. **18**(5), e112 (2016)
16. Irizarry, T., DeVito Dabbs, A., Curran, C.: Patient portals and patient engagement: a state of the science review. J. Med. Internet Res. **17**(6), e148 (2015)
17. Ammonwerth, E., Schnell-Inderst, P., Hoerbst, A.: The impact of electronic patient portals on patient care: a systematic review of controlled trials. J. Med. Internet Res. **14**(6), e162 (2012). https://doi.org/10.2196/jmir.2238
18. Wald, H., Dube, C., Anthony, D.: Untangling the web—the impact of internet use on health care and physician-patient relationship. Patient Educ. Couns. **68**, 218–224 (2007)
19. National Center for Education Statistics. https://nces.ed.gov/naal/. 20 Dec 2018
20. National Center for Education Statistics. https://nces.ed.gov/surveys/piaac/. 20 Dec 2017
21. Mamedova, S., Sparks, D., Hoyer, A.: Adult Education Attainment and Assessment Scores. Institute of Education Statistics—National Center for Education Statistics. U.S. Department of Education, NCES 2018-007 (2017)
22. Workforce Innovation and Opportunity Act, Public law No. 105-206, 29 U.S.C. Sec. 2801 (et seq) (2014)
23. Media Planet—Education and Career News: Leading the Charge to Raise Awareness About the Many Faces of Adult Education. http://www.educationandcareernews.com/online-learning/educate-amp-elevate-leading-the-charge-to-raise-awareness-about-the-many-faces-amp-relevancy-of-adult-education. Accessed 20 Dec 2017
24. Tashiro, J., Hung, P.C.K., Martin, M.V., Tashiro, R.R.: What really works in hybrid learning: a cognitive perspective. In: Cheung, S.K.S., Kwok, L., Yang, H., Fong, J., Kwan, R. (eds.) ICHL 2015. LNCS, vol. 9167, pp. 15–35. Springer, Cham (2015). https://doi.org/10.1007/978-3-319-20621-9_2
25. Tashiro, J.: Ethical analysis of publisher and faculty roles in building and using electronic educational products. J. Electron. Commer. Organ. **7**(1), 1–17 (2009)
26. Pappalardo, M., Schaffer, W.: Using research to design integrated education and training programs. J. Res. Pract. Adult Lit. Second. Basic Educ. **5**(3), 35–39 (2016)
27. Emory, D., Raymond, L., Lee, K., Twohy, S.: The academic I-BEST: a model for precollege student success in college transfer programs. J. Res. Pract. Adult Lit. Second. Basic Educ. **5** (3), 43–49 (2016). https://ccrc.tc.columbia.edu/publications/how-i-best-works.html
28. National Education Association—Know, Want to Know, Learned. http://www.nea.org/tools/k-w-l-know-want-to-know-learned.html. 20 Dec 2017
29. Cacioppo, J.T., Petty, R.E., Feinstein, J.A., Jarvis, W.B.G.: Dispositional differences in cognitive motivation: the life and times of individuals varying in need for cognition. Psychol. Bull. **19**(2), 197–253 (1996)
30. Sadowski, C.J., Gülöz, S.: Elaborative processing mediates the relationship between need for cognition and academic performance. J. Psychol. **130**(3), 303–307 (1996)
31. Sullins, E., Hernandez, D., Fuller, C., Tashiro, J.: Predicting who will major in a science discipline: expectancy-value theory as part of an ecological model for studying academic communities. J. Res. Sci. Teach. **32**(1), 99–119 (1995)
32. Aronson, E., Brewer, M., Carlsmith, J.M.: Experimentation in social psychology. In: Lindzy, G., Aronson, E. (eds.) Handbook of Social Psychology, 3rd edn, pp. 441–486. Random House, New York (1985)
33. Kendall, L.: The conduct of qualitative interviews – research questions, methodological issues, and researching online. In: Coiro, J., Knobel, M., Lankshear, C., Leu, D.J. (eds.) Handbook of Research on New Literacies, pp. 133–149. Lawrence Erlbaum Associates, New York (2008)

34. Leander, K.A.: Toward a connective ethnography of online/offline literacy networks. In: Coiro, J., Knobel, M., Lankshear, C., Leu, D.J. (eds.) Handbook of Research on New Literacies, pp. 33–65. Lawrence Erlbaum Associates, New York (2008)
35. Patel, V.L., Yoskowitz, N.A., Arocha, J.F., Shirtliffe, E.H.: Cognitive and learning sciences in biomedical and health instructional design—a review of biomedical informatics education. J. Biomed. Inform. **42**, 176–197 (2009)
36. Tashiro, J., Tashiro, R., Alvarado-Yule, J.: Adaptive Intervention and Management for Health Care Systems. U.S. Patent Application, No. 60/938,682. U.S. Patent and Trademark Office, Washington, DC (2008)
37. Martin, M.V., Hung, P.C.K., Tashiro, J.: Method for Competency Assessment of Healthcare Students and Practitioners. US Patent Application No. 61/162,587. US Patent and Trademark Office, Washington, DC (2009)
38. Tashiro, J., Hung, P.C.K.: Method for Assessing an Individual's Physical and Psychosocial Abilities. U.S. Patent Application, No. 61/549,5789. U.S. Patent and Trademark Office, Washington, DC (2011)
39. Fernandez, A., Regts, M., Tashiro, J., Martin, M.V.: A neural network prediction model for a digital media learning environment. In: International Conference on Information and Knowledge Engineering, Las Vegas, 16–19 July 2012
40. Fernandez, A.: Cluster techniques and prediction models for a digital media learning environment. Thesis, Master of Computer Science. University of Ontario Institute of Technology, August 2012
41. Regts, M., Fernandez, A., Martin, M.V., Tashiro, J.: Methodology for studying health science students' development of misconceptions. In: International Conference on Advances in Databases, Knowledge, and Data Applications, pp. 112–119, Reunion Island, 1–5 March 2012
42. Regts, M.: A look at simulated online learning environments and undergraduate health science students' development of misconceptions. Thesis, Master of Health Informatics. University of Ontario Institute of Technology, December 2012

Experiences in Blended Learning

An Expert System Approach to Support Blended Learning in Context-Aware Environment

Cixiao Wang(✉) and Feng Wu

Graduate School of Education, Peking University, Beijing 100871, China
wangcixiao@yeah.net, wufeng@pku.edu.cn

Abstract. With the development of mobile internet and devices, the flexibility and portability of digital learning have improved continuously. Students can interact with mobile devices to support blended learning in context-aware environment. In this study, an expert system named Plant-expert which can provide decision-making questions for students to acquire knowledge about plant classification was developed. To explore the learning effectiveness of Plant-expert, another app named Plant-general that only contains information pages of target plants was designed. An experiment has been conducted on a secondary school biology course to evaluate the effectiveness of the proposed method. The experimental group with 46 students using Plant-expert in campus with target plants and the control group with 47 students using Plant-general in the same campus. We conducted pre-test, post-test and delayed test to evaluate learning achievement of students and used the Paas (1992) cognitive load rating scale to measure the mental effort of students invested into blended learning activities. The experimental results show that the proposed approach can improve the learning achievements of the students, and not increases mental effort.

Keywords: Blended learning · Mobile learning · Expert system
Plant learning · Mental load

1 Introduction

In the increasing pervasiveness of today's digital society, mobile devices are changing the face of education. Based on mobile devices, Mobile learning has been seen as a digital learning method [1, 2] and enable learners to learn whenever they are curious. In blended learning, the importance of students' self-motivation and self-management increases because there is less in-class time and more emphasis on self-regulated learning [3]. In context-aware environment, such as campus, museums and aquarium, students can learn by interacting with nature, space and artifact. Meanwhile, to conduct blended learning in context-aware environment, students need to have more support to take required learning tasks. Thus, it is the learning process and learning materials deserve to explore, so as to provide a more effective learning activity during blended learning in context-aware environment. As a cognitive tool, mobile application can be a solution to help learners absorb knowledge from complex situation [4]. Learning plants

S. K. S. Cheung et al. (Eds.): ICBL 2018, LNCS 10949, pp. 45–56, 2018.
https://doi.org/10.1007/978-3-319-94505-7_3

with the support of mobile devices in authentic environment has proved to be able to bring better learning performance for learners [5, 6].

In this study, we proposed a mobile application based on expert system to support blended learning in campus, as campus is a sort of context-aware environment. The classification and recognition of plants in a biology course of middle school is one of the key points in the curriculum standards in China. The mobile system developed in this study is focus on plant classification and can provide prompts for students to experience blended learning outside their classroom. However, when using mobile devices in context-aware environment, students may have more cognitive load as they need to interact with both the learning materials and environment [e.g. 7]. Moreover, cognitive load is associated with learning performance in cognitive load theory [8]. From this context, to evaluate the effectiveness of the proposed approach, the following research questions are investigated:

(1) Do the students who learn with the expert-based mobile app show better learning achievements than those who learn with the conventional one without expert system mechanism?
(2) Does the expert-based mobile app increase the students' cognitive load in comparison with the conventional one?
(3) Do the students who learn with the expert-based mobile app show higher acceptance degree in terms of perceived ease of use and perceived usefulness than those who learn with the conventional one?

2 Relevant Studies

Learning in authentic context or environment has been considered as context-aware ubiquitous learning [9]. Some studies show that mobile applications that provide guidance and clues for learners to observe the learning objects can help learners get better results in context-aware environment. Chen et al. [10] designed a mobile learning system called Bird-Watching Learning (BWL) for students to acquire outdoor bird knowledge by searching information through the system, and the study shows that the experimental group using BWL performed better than the control group using a learning sheet with a guide book. Hwang and Chang [11] developed a mobile system called Formative Assessment-based Mobile Learning (FAML) for students to gain historical and cultural knowledge by leading students to observe the learning object via asking some questions; the study shows the experimental group performs better than control group with conventional tour-based learning approach. By contrast, Chu [7] developed a mobile system based on formative assessment approach and found that there were negative effects on students' learning achievement and cognitive load mainly because of overloading of working memory; that is students have to interact with both the digital materials and environment.

Cognitive load is the total amount of mental activity that applied to individual cognitive system within a given time, and there are three types of cognitive load [8, 12]: intrinsic, extraneous, and germane load, and the sum of the three is the total cognitive load. Besides, Paas and Van Merrienboer [13] divided cognitive load into assessment factors and causal factors, and the assessment factors include mental load, mental effort and behavior performance. It is revealed that mental effort is usually used to reflect real cognitive load [14]. Some studies show that mental effort in experimental group was lower than that in control group [e.g. 15]; some draw an opposite conclusion [e.g. 7]; while others show there was no significant difference between two groups [16]. Hence, in order to evaluate the effectiveness of use, when a new approach of mobile learning is proposed, the mental effort that students put into learning activities need to be measure.

Previous studies have reported that mobile systems can support students to learn plants knowledge in context-aware environment [e.g. 6]. Huang et al. [17] developed a mobile plant learning system (MPLS) provides relevant questions for students to interact with and information by observing features of leaves. Chu et al. [18] proposed a two-tier test approach to help students answer a question about the characteristics of the plant and gain a better understanding by answering reasons for the last question. Chen et al. [19] designed a mobile application for campus plant learning, and learners can scan a QR-code to get prompts to observe plant characteristics and answer related questions; the study proposed a progressive prompting approach, that is, prompts of wrong answers are gradually increasing in different stages. Most of learning processes of mobile learning in previous studies include multiple-choice questions with feedback or prompts.

Learning plants by expert system in authentic environment has proved to be able to bring better learning experience for students [20]. Compared to novices, experts pay more attention to the characteristics of situations or problems, that is, there is a great difference between experts and novices in their attention, which suggests that one may not simply learn from other people's experience, but also need to learn to experience it [21]. Expert system means a system that has a domain expert knowledge experience, and rule-based expert system, also called the generative rules system, is to use a series of rules to express expert knowledge [22]. Therefore, an expert system approach was proposed to support blended learning in context-aware environment.

3 An Expert System Approach to Support Blended Learning

3.1 Mobile Learning Mechanism Based on Expert System

In this study, a rule-based expert system is proposed to support plants learning in context-aware environment for secondary school students, and it can help students to take botany course in accordance with authentic teaching plan. This study sought to combine the plant related knowledge in secondary school curricula with the characteristics of mobile learning, as well as design a plant factual information database. Facts stored in the database include objects, attributes and values; objects are selected plants, and value of a certain attribute that used to describe characteristics of plants is assigned as "yes" or "no". The rule in the database is a series of IF-THEN statements, which means attributes are associated with each other.

Students can use the rule-based expert system in mobile learning to observe characteristics of target plants and make decisions by answering "yes or no" questions, which will improve learners' participation in mobile learning and frequency of observation of plant characteristics. The rule based expert system provides questions for students to gain information and practice relevant knowledge, which is similar to the systems developed in previous studies [11, 23]. It is important to note that the innovation of the plant learning system this study lies in the database is not constituted with questions in tests but a decision tree made up with "yes or no" attributes. The "yes or no" questions which are related with each other can help students understand how the classification of plants actually does, also provide them an opportunity to know how botanist work with plants classification.

3.2 Mobile Applications for Plants Classification

As seed plants are the most common plants on campus, this learning contents were focus on the classification of seed plants according to biological curriculum standards for compulsory education in China. Plant database in this study was composed of ten plants: Cedar, Ginkgo Biloba, Palm, Phyllostachys propinqua, Pittosporum tobira, Crape myrtle, Camphor tree, Chinese holly, Koelreuteria paniculata and Dandelion.

The reasoning mechanism of rule-based expert system enable learners to infer plant information through characteristics of plant, and it can improve availability and accuracy of knowledge. The factual information databases in this study is in the form of a Binary Tree (see Fig. 1). First, students find a target plant on campus and stand in front of it. Next, students visit the root node and answer the first question by interacting with the mobile application; if students choose "yes", then visit left subtree, otherwise, visit right subtree; each node has one "yes" or "no" question for students to answer by observing characteristics of the plant. Until there is no child node, the mobile system will present an information page of the related plant.

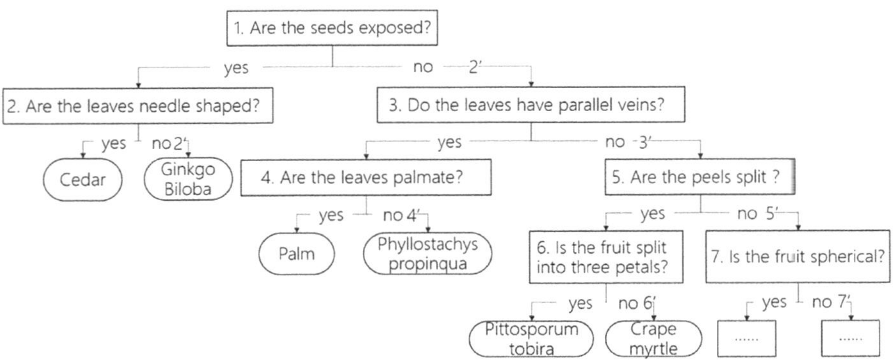

Fig. 1. Data structure diagram of plant binary tree

In this study, we developed two types of mobile learning system. Plant-expert with questions is based on expert system, and Plant-general with no questions was used to make a contrast. After students read their learning objectives presented on start interface, Plant-expert provides questions about plants' characteristics, while Plant-general shows a list of target plants (see Fig. 2).

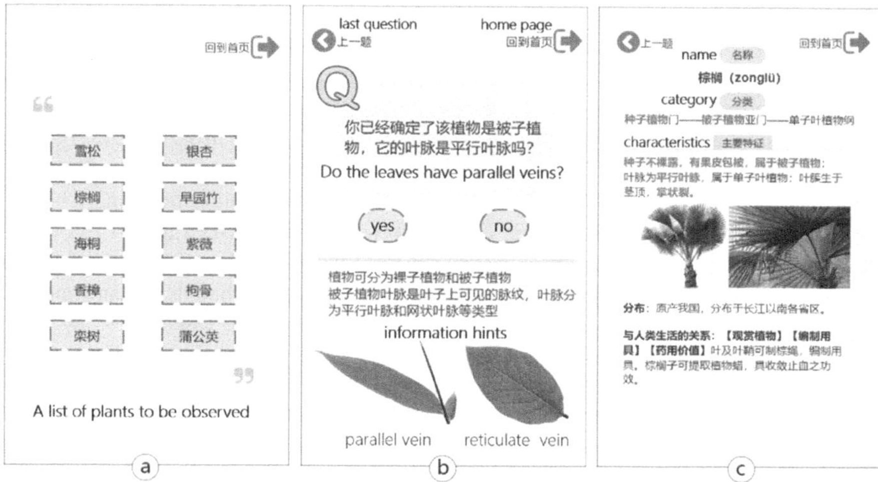

Fig. 2. Software interface of mobile applications: a. Plants list interface in Plant-general; b. Question page in Plant-expert, including the question about observed characteristics of target plant and information hints; c. Information page in Plant-general and Plant-expert, including name, category and characteristics of target plant.

In Plant-general, students can switch from any plants by clicking the buttons in plants list page, and they can get the same information pages as in the Plant-expert. Thus, students in control group can find a target plant in the campus, and then observe features of the plant according to the corresponding information page.

4 Experiment Design

4.1 Participants

The subjects of this study included two classes of seventh graders of a secondary school in southern China. The two classes were randomly assigned to an experimental group and a control group. The students are aged between 12–14 years and they all have previous experience with mobile phones and computers. The experimental group, including 46 students (25 boys, 21 girls), learned with Plant-expert with the expert-based mechanism in campus with target plants, while the control group students with 47 students (24 boys, 23 girls) learned with Plant-general in the same campus. All of the students were taught by the same instructor who had more than three years' experience of teaching biology courses.

4.2 Research Tools

The Research tools in this study included a pre-test, a post-test, a delayed test, and a questionnaire to measure the students' cognitive load and perception of proposed learning method and systems.

The pre-test contains nice one-choice questions and one short-answer question about the basic knowledge of plants with total scores of 90 and 10, respectively. The post-test includes memory test and the transfer test and each part accounted for 50 scores, and it consists of eight one-choice questions, one fill-in-the-blanks question with several blanks, and one short-answer question with total scores of 80, 10 and 10. The post-test aimed to assess students' knowledge of plant classification, while the delayed test with the same proportion of question types as post-test aimed to evaluate students' retention of relevant knowledge. All tests were developed by the instructor, and one teacher who had taught the plant course for more than ten years and one biologist from a famous university were consulted to check the tests.

The questionnaire used after learning activities contains a cognitive load scale, a perception scale and two open questions. We used the Cognitive Load rating scale [24] which only contains an item to measure students mental load invested into learning activities. The perception scale was developed by Hwang et al. [25] based on Technology Acceptance Model [26], including 5 items for "perceived usefulness" and 5 items for "perceived ease of use". Items in the questionnaire are all in nine-point Likert rating. The Cronbach's alpha values of perceived usefulness, and perceived ease of use are 0.832 and 0.884, respectively, which implies that the scales used in the study have high reliability. Moreover, we used two open questions about students' views on the pros and cons of proposed mobile applications and learning methods.

4.3 Experiment Procedure

The experiment procedure is shown in Fig. 3.

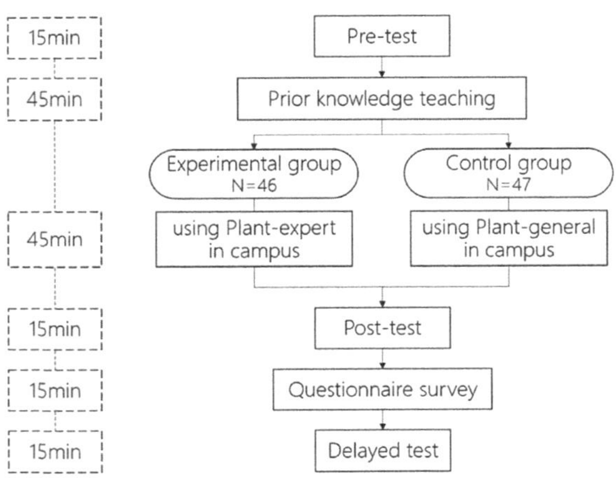

Fig. 3. Diagram of experiment procedure

At the beginning of the quasi-experiment, the students took the pre-test. Before the blended learning activity, the teacher conducted prior knowledge teaching about plants. During the learning activity, students in experimental group learned via answering related questions provided by Plant-expert in campus where the target plants in learning content were planted; those in control group learned with Plant-general in the same context-aware environment. After completing the learning tasks, students were asked to take post-test and questionnaire survey. Finally, one week later, students took a delayed test.

5 Experimental Results

5.1 Analysis of Learning Achievement

The mean values and standard deviations of the pre-test scores were 49.65 and 17.88 for the experimental group, and 47.36 and 17.30 for the control group. The t-test result ($t = 0.63$, $p > 0.05$) shows that there was no significant difference between the two groups, confirming that the two groups of students had equivalent prior knowledge before the learning activity.

After the learning activity, the post-test was conducted to evaluate the students' knowledge about plants classification. A t-test was performed on the post-test results including memory and transfer scores of the two groups, as shown in Table 1. It was found that there was no significant difference between the experimental group and the control group on students' post-test results ($p = 0.467 > 0.05$), neither the memory score ($p = 0.118 > 0.05$) and the transfer score ($p = 0.804 > 0.05$).

Table 1. t-test result of the post-test scores of the two groups.

Group	Post-test			Memory score			Transfer score		
	Mean	SD	t	Mean	SD	t	Mean	SD	t
Experimental group	62.65	16.12	0.628	30.91	8.97	1.58	31.74	11.80	−0.25
Control group	60.00	18.76		27.66	10.78		32.34	11.46	

The delayed test aimed to evaluate students' retention of plants classification knowledge. The mean values and standard deviations of the delayed test scores were 69.63 and 16.42 for the experimental group, and 59.26 and 19.94 for the control group. According to the t-test result ($t = 2.71$, $p = 0.007 < 0.05$), there was a significant difference between the two groups with $d = 0.568$, showing a medium effect size [27]. This implies that the mobile learning approach with the expert system strategy benefited the students more than the conventional approach on the retention of relevant plants knowledge.

Moreover, as shown in Fig. 4, there was a slight decline from post-test to delayed test on result of the control group, while delayed test result of experimental group was significant higher than its post-test result. These results of tests also imply that the difference of learning achievement was more remarkable in delayed test which was conducted a week later after the experiment than the difference in post-test. It means that students in the experimental group experienced a more complex interaction during the learning activity as they learned by Plant-expert, and they need to have further processing of knowledge after the learning activity to gain better performance (Table 2).

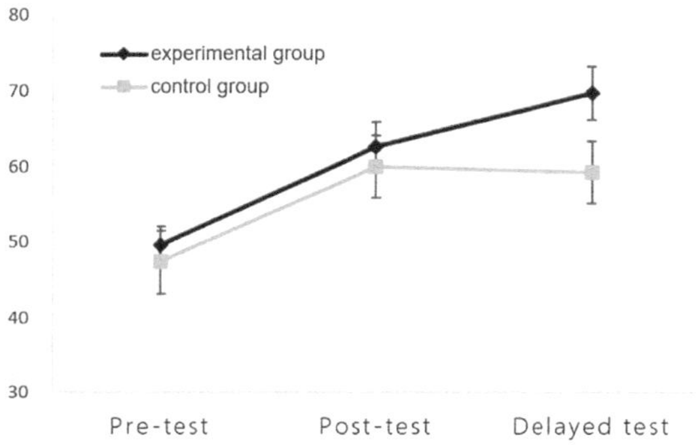

Fig. 4. Result changes in the two groups

5.2 Analysis of Mental Effort

To investigate the cognitive load of the students during blended learning activities, the Paas cognitive load rating scale was used in the questionnaire survey. As shown in Table 3, the mental effort in the control group (Mean = 5.43, SD = 1.85) was lower than that in the experimental group (Mean = 5.63, SD = 1.82), while the difference of mental effort between the two groups was not significant ($t = 0.54$, $p = 0.591 > 0.05$).

Mental effort refers to cognitive capacity required to complete the learning task, and can be imposed by improper instructional design; that is, it reflects cognitive load related to the way of structuring and presenting the learning content or the strategy used to guide students [13]. Therefore, the result means that the expert system approach won't increase more mental effort invested into the learning task compared with that using conventional mobile learning approach. Meanwhile, this indicates the format and the manner in which information is presented in the expert system approach is appropriate.

5.3 Analysis of Perceived Ease of Use and Usefulness

To better understand the students' perceptions of the use of Plant-expert, this study collected the students' feedback regarding "perceived usefulness" and "perceived ease of use" as shown in Table 4. It is found that most students gave positive feedback concerning the two dimensions of the expert system approach. The average ratings for "perceived usefulness" were 7.06 and 6.97 for the experimental group and the control group, respectively; moreover, their average ratings for "perceived ease of use" were 6.32 and 6.53. In comparison with the ratings given by the control group, the ratings for

Table 2. t-test result of the delayed test scores of the two groups.

Group	N	Mean	SD	t
Experimental group	46	69.63	16.42	2.74**
Control group	47	59.26	19.94	

**p < .01

Table 3. t-test result of the mental load of the two groups.

Group	N	Mean	SD	t
Experimental group	46	5.63	1.82	0.54
Control group	47	5.43	1.85	

"perceived usefulness" ($t = 0.33$, $p = 0.75 > 0.05$) and "perceived ease of use" ($t = 0.60$, $p = 0.55 > 0.05$) in the experimental group were similar, implying that the perceptions and attitudes of students using the two mobile applications were not significant different.

Table 4. t-test result of students' perceived ease of use and usefulness

	Group	N	Mean	SD	t
Perceived usefulness	Experimental group	46	7.06	1.46	0.33
	Control group	47	6.97	1.36	
Perceived ease of use	Experimental group	46	6.32	1.71	0.60
	Control group	47	6.53	1.67	

Moreover, students' views on the pros and cons of proposed learning methods were collected at the end of the questionnaire. It is discovered that there was no obvious difference between the two groups on the pros and cons, which coincided with the perceptions of students. In terms of its advantages, students pointed out the novel and interesting activities, convenience of knowledge acquisition, improvement of interest in learning, and more focused, and more relaxed, and so on. Since Plant-expert were used in the experimental group, some students reported the advantages of "providing information through topics", "having clearer learning objectives and knowledge points" according to the learning interaction of Plant-expert. In terms of shortcomings, students generally pointed out the disadvantages of "mobile devices can damage vision", "students who are not self-sufficient can easily become distracted"; some students also noted that the learning methods reduces communication between teachers and students, and students' cooperation. In addition, due to the complexity difference in the interactive learning processes, there are individual differences in time and information perception, such as students in the experimental group considered learning time was tense, while students in the control group thought that the information is not enough.

6 Discussion and Conclusions

In this paper, an expert system approach for blended learning in context-aware environment is presented, along with the experimental results of the "plant classification" learning content of a secondary school biology course. From the experimental results, it is found that the rule-based expert system mobile application cannot only improve the students' learning achievement after the learning activity, but also help students perform better than those learning by traditional mobile materials on retention of relevant knowledge retention. In this context, we can draw a conclusion that the students who learn with the expert-based mobile app show better learning achievements than those who learn with the conventional one without expert system mechanism.

Meanwhile, the mental effort of students was investigated by the Paas cognitive load rating scale [24] that only contains one item, and the results show that there was no significant difference between the two groups, implying that the expert system approach won't cause more mental effort during the learning activity than conventional approach. Thus, the rule-based mobile learning expert system proves to be a potential method for students to learn in context-aware environment. The findings seem to conform to the mental efforts in mobile learning between the two groups addressed by several researchers, such as Chang et al. [16]. However, the measurement of cognitive load includes many different techniques [14], and as mentioned earlier, the influence of mobile application and its learning process on learner's cognitive load has not been consistently reached [7, 10, 11]. Hence, the effect of the interaction of learning process in mobile applications on students' cognitive load and learning achievement could be a meaningful research topic.

The questionnaire results show that most students gave positive feedback concerning "perceived usefulness" and "perceived ease of use" to the expert system approach. Nevertheless, the perceptions and attitudes of students towards the two mobile applications were not significant different. In terms of students views on the pros and cons of proposed learning methods and systems, some students in the experimental group thought that they may experience stressful learning feelings. Such negative experiences show that an expert system is not always effective or can even cause negative impacts if researchers or instructors do not carefully consider when and how it can be applied to a learning process in outdoor blended learning.

In summary, this finding provides a good reference for those who intend to develop mobile application for plants classification. Future work may introduce more research tools to explore the cognitive process in blended learning in context-aware environment supported by the expert system approach. Also, the learning process and the interaction of the mobile application could be improved by investigating students' attitudes and learning effectiveness.

Acknowledgement. This research was conducted in Xinhuang Academy of the First high school of Changsha. The authors thank also all the teachers and students who have participated in the experiment.

References

1. Tabuenca, B., Kalz, M., Drachsler, H., Specht, M.: Time will tell: the role of mobile learning analytics in self-regulated learning. Comput. Educ. **89**, 53 (2015)
2. Wang, Y.S., Lin, H.H., Luarn, P.: Predicting consumer intention to use mobile service. Inf. Syst. J. **16**, 157 (2006)
3. So, H., Brush, T.A.: Student perceptions of collaborative learning, social presence and satisfaction in a blended learning environment: relationships and critical factors. Comput. Educ. **51**, 318 (2008)
4. Shadiev, R., Hwang, W.Y., Huang, Y.M., Liu, T.Y.: The impact of supported and annotated mobile learning on achievement and cognitive load. Educ. Technol. Soc. **18**, 53 (2015)
5. Jeno, L.M., Grytnes, J.A., Vandvik, V.: The effect of a mobile-application tool on biology students' motivation and achievement in species identification: a self-determination theory perspective. Comput. Educ. **107**, 1 (2017)
6. Zacharia, Z.C., Lazaridou, C., Avraamidou, L.: The use of mobile devices as means of data collection in supporting elementary school students' conceptual understanding about plants. Int. J. Sci. Educ. **38**, 596 (2016)
7. Chu, H.C.: Potential negative effects of mobile learning on students' learning achievement and cognitive load—a format assessment perspective. J. Educ. Technol. Soc. **17**, 332 (2014)
8. Van Merrienboer, J.J., Sweller, J.: Cognitive load theory and complex learning: recent developments and future directions. Educ. Psychol. Rev. **17**, 147 (2005)
9. Looi, C.K., Zhang, B., Chen, W., Seow, P., Chia, G., Norris, C., Soloway, E.: 1:1 mobile inquiry learning experience for primary science students: a study of learning effectiveness. J. Comput. Assist. Learn. **27**, 269 (2011)
10. Chen, Y.S., Kao, T.C., Sheu, J.P.: A mobile learning system for scaffolding bird watching learning. J. Comput. Assist. Learn. **19**, 347 (2003)
11. Hwang, G.J., Chang, H.F.: A formative assessment-based mobile learning approach to improving the learning attitudes and achievements of students. Comput. Educ. **56**, 1023 (2011)
12. Sweller, J., Merrienboer, J., Paas, F.: Cognitive architecture and instructional design. Educ. Psychol. Rev. **10**, 251 (1998)
13. Paas, F., Van Merrienboer, J.: Instructional control of cognitive load in the training of complex cognitive tasks. Educ. Psychol. Rev. **6**, 351 (1994)
14. Paas, F., Tuovinen, J.E., Tabbers, H., Van Gerven, P.W.M.: Cognitive load measurement as a means to advance cognitive load theory. Educ. Psychol. **38**, 63 (2003)
15. Lin, Y.T., Lin, Y.C.: Effects of mental process integrated nursing training using mobile device on students' cognitive load, learning attitudes, acceptance, and achievements. Comput. Hum. Behav. **55**, 1213 (2016)
16. Chang, C., Shih, J.L., Chang, C.K.: A mobile instructional pervasive game method for language learning. Univ. Access Inf. Soc. **16**, 1 (2017)
17. Huang, Y., Lin, Y., Cheng, S.: Effectiveness of a mobile plant learning system in a science curriculum in Taiwanese elementary education. Comput. Educ. **54**, 47 (2010)
18. Chu, H.C., Hwang, G.J., Tsai, C.C., Tseng, J.C.R.: A two-tier test approach to developing location-aware mobile learning systems for natural science courses. Comput. Educ. **55**, 1618 (2010)
19. Chen, C.H., Hwang, G.J., Tsai, C.H.: A progressive prompting approach to conducting context-aware learning activities for natural science courses. Interact. Comput. **26**, 348 (2014)

20. Wang, C.X.: The research on the application of plant identification and mobile learning APP based on expert system. In: 9th International Conference on Computer Supported Education, vol. 332, Porto (2017)
21. Sawyer, R.: The Cambridge Handbook of the Learning Sciences. Cambridge University Press, Cambridge (2006)
22. Clancey, W.J.: The epistemology of a rule-based expert system —a framework for explanation. Artif. Intell. **20**, 215 (1983)
23. Hwang, G.J.: Development of a mobile learning system based on a collaborative problem-posing strategy. Interact. Learn. Environ. **24**, 1 (2016)
24. Paas, F.G.: Training strategies for attaining transfer of problem-solving skill in statistics: a cognitive-load approach. J. Educ. Psychol. **84**, 429 (1992)
25. Hwang, G.J., Yang, L.H., Wang, S.Y.: A concept map-embedded educational computer game for improving students' learning performance in natural science courses. Comput. Educ. **69**, 121 (2013)
26. Davis, F.D.: A technology acceptance model for empirically testing new end-user information systems: theory and results. Massachusetts Institute of Technology (1985)
27. Cohen, J.: Statistical Power Analysis for the Behavioral Sciences, 2nd edn. L. Erlbaum Associates, Hillsdale (1988)

Learning English Through the Adaptive Model of e-Learning Reflecting Learner's Sensory Characteristics

Katerina Kostolanyova[1(✉)] and Ivana Simonova[2]

[1] University of Ostrava, Ostrava, Czech Republic
katerina.kostolanyova@osu.cz
[2] University of Jan Evangelista Purkyne, Usti nad Labem, Czech Republic
ivana.simonova@ujep.cz

Abstract. The main objective of the article is (1) to introduce the adaptive model of e-learning, which was designed by the University of Ostrava, Czech Republic, and (2) to present and discuss results of two researches conducted within the model and focusing on self-study activities reflecting learners' sensory preferences in learning English. In both researches, data were collected by standardized English grammar tests, by VARK questionnaire and non-standardized pre-tests and post-tests. Four hypotheses were tested; two of them focusing on the role of learner's sensory preferences, other two ones examining the support of visual and aural study materials in listening comprehension and reading comprehension. Results were not statistically significant; however, slight impact of visual materials in reading comprehension and aural materials in reading comprehension was detected.

Keywords: Adaptive learning · English · Sensory preferences
VARK · Listening comprehension · Reading comprehension

1 Introduction

Currently, the individualization of learning has been a frequently discussed topic, particularly in relation to the fast development of latest information and communication technologies (ICT). Generally, there exist numerous methods, strategies and approaches how learning content can be mediated to the learners in foreign language instruction, e.g. [1–3]. In face-to-face school instruction, a wide scale of didactic means is usually exploited. However, in the after-school learning activities, i.e. in home preparation for lessons, individual learning preferences can be easily satisfied and the process of learning can be tailored to learner's needs [4]. Therefore, materials for practising and fixing learner's knowledge are required to reflect individual preferences. Within this research, the main focus is paid on sensory characteristics. We agree with a widely accepted opinion expecting the learner to reach better results in learning if the process reflects his/her individual characteristics [5–8].

The main objective of this article is to introduce and apply an adaptive model of e-learning reflecting learner's sensory preferences in foreign language learning and

S. K. S. Cheung et al. (Eds.): ICBL 2018, LNCS 10949, pp. 57–68, 2018.
https://doi.org/10.1007/978-3-319-94505-7_4

present results of research monitoring whether learners reach better knowledge when exploiting it for after-school preparation.

2 Theoretical Background

Generally, any type of programmed learning can be considered a method which directs the process of acquiring new knowledge, skills, attitudes through appropriate learning content and feedback, and reflects learner's individual needs and preferences, even if the process is not directly managed by the teacher. In other words, it is an educational technique characterized by self-paced, self-administered instruction presented in logical sequence and with much repetition of concepts [9]. Learner's activities arise from precisely defined learning objectives, learner's diagnostics, appropriate learning conditions, proper knowledge of the learning process, learning content and learner's answers; all these components are implemented in the programme directing learner's process of learning.

The process of adjusting the e-learning process to learner's sensory preferences starts from programmed learning by Skinner [10] working with operant conditioning, learner's feedback and responsibility for the learning carried. Sequencing of the learning content ensures that learning objectives are reached step-by-step. The behavioral theory of programmed learning exploiting the trial-error approach was designed by Pressey; and Crowder, a contemporary of Skinner, proposed intrinsic (branching) programming, when the selection of the correct answer from multiple-choice alternatives lead the learner to fixing new knowledge. This approach was considered the starting phase of adaptive strategy in learning [11] as it enabled a certain extent of optimization when reflecting learner's characteristics and preferences before the beginning of the learning process.

The theory of adaptive e-learning reflecting sensory characteristics relates to three fields – educational science, psychology and informatics [12]. The personalized approach is based on adjusting the learning process to learner's sensory preferences, needs, i.e. on the adaptation of the learning content [7]. In other words, the process of instruction is expected to reflect results of learner's characteristics before the learning process starts, then the detected characteristics are reflected in appropriate learning materials for practising, fixing new knowledge and defining adaptive algorithms. Of course, this approach is not new; it originates from the principles of programmed learning, which started from adaptation in navigation and presentation, consequently focusing on learning content and user's interest, and currently exploiting mobile devices [13]. However, what is new in the adaptive model described below, is the way of considering sensory characteristics by automatic adaptive algorithms.

In the field of foreign language teaching and learning, the process of personalization is different compared to general and technical subjects – it focuses on different type of knowledge and skills, particularly the active production of language. Until now, the individualized e-learning has been solved within e.g. CALL (Computer Assisted Language Learning), ICALI (Intelligent Computer Assisted Language Instruction), MALL (Mobile Assisted Language Learning) etc., in testing knowledge the CALT (Computer Assisted Language Testing or CBLA (Computer Based Language

Assessment) approaches were exploited, and also the term of adaptive testing appears. However, the individualization is based on the level of knowledge, and sensory or any other type of learner's characteristics and preferences have not been reflected [14]. In the adaptive model of e-learning, study materials were based on the SLA approach (Second Language Acquisition) arising from Krashen's theory [15] which defines input characteristics of the second language and the way how the learning content should be acquired by the learner so as to provide positive impact on the development of linguistic skills.

To detect learning characteristics of an individual, learning objectives should be categorized in a way which corresponds to single language skills, consequently relating to sensory characteristics and preferences. The language skills considered within this research are reading comprehension and listening comprehension. The e-learning environment provides numerous tools for their development, compared to writing and speaking skills where different strategies are required. Sensory characteristics do not work independently; they mutually penetrate and work on different intensity levels, as Shimojo and Shams discovered within neurobiology research [16: 505–508]. On the other side, Coffield et al. [17] examining correlation between student's sensory preferences and methodology items implemented into study materials did not find out any evidence, so they concluded every learning content requires specific didactic means to be acquired regardless sensory preferences. Similarly, Marzano [18] found out that graphical presentation of learning contents had positive effect on forming knowledge, even if sensory characteristics were not considered. Compared to these results, other authors (e.g. Oxford and Ehrman [19] discovered that students with visual preference reached better results in reading comprehension compared to aural ones. Additionally, Felder and Henriques [20: 23–26] proved that students with visual preference learned better if they could see the text first, and then listen to it. Identically, the preference of aural students is to listen first, and then to read the text, Oxford stated, and she also verified good ability to perceive information from the written text with visual students [21: 3]. Providing visual students with instruction orally only is confusing for them; they do not prefer oral communication compared to verbal students, Felder states [20]. On the other side, aural students do not need visual means so as to acquire the learning content but they do not avoid it. They prefer active learning strategies, sometimes they may have problems with acquiring the content in the written form only [21: 3–4]. In the field of cognitive learning styles, the magnetic resonance discovered that visual students transformed the content into visual-mental images when reading, while verbal students watching images changed them into aural form of language [22].

2.1 Adaptive Model of e-Learning

The first version of adaptive model applied in this research was designed at University of Ostrava, Czech Republic in 2009–2012 within the project "Adaptive individualized instruction in eLearning". Its main objective was to design a complex adaptive system. Compared to widely exploited Learning management systems, this one differs to e.g. Moodle by having automatic adaptive algorithms embedded. The model comprises of three main parts (Fig. 1): Author, Virtual Teacher and Student. Before the process of learning starts, student's characteristics are monitored in two fields relating to the

(1) starting knowledge in a subject and (2) learning (in this case sensory) preferences. Author works as a modifier of student's learning; data from both fields are considered by the system, and study materials are adjusted to the individual preferences. Then, Virtual Teacher reads information on the starting level of knowledge and sensory preference(s) and recommends an optimal way (process) of learning. Within this phase pedagogic rules and didactic principles are taken into consideration and the final process of learning is thus individualized, i.e. tailored to student's level of knowledge and sensory preferences [12: 47–48].

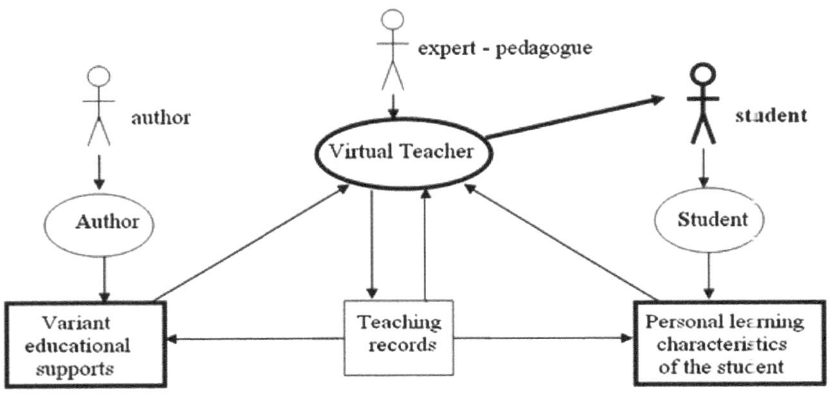

Fig. 1. Adaptive model of e-learning reflecting sensory characteristics [12: 48]

However, the adaptive model of e-learning was originally intended for teaching general and technically-oriented subjects (mathematics, physics, science, geography etc.). The question is whether it can be also exploited in (an)other subject(s), e.g. foreign languages, and particularly English which applies different approaches to acquiring the learning content(s), and whether students reach better knowledge when using this adaptive model of e-learning compared to those who do not exploit it.

Reflecting the above mentioned, the learning content in the adaptive model of e-learning for English language was structured into frameworks (topic), layers (motivation to learning and relaxation between single activities, explanation, summary, fixation and testing new knowledge) and components (new vocabulary, grammar explanation and exercises, listening comprehension, reading comprehension) within each topic. The concrete content was given by the (1) learning objective, (2) starting level of learner's knowledge in English and (3) individual sensory preferences. Totally 30 lessons were designed in two versions – for students with visual preferences (visual students) and students with aural preferences (aural students). Each version consisted of 210 components providing learners with the same learning content which could have been acquired through different didactic means and learners were directed by instructions in different forms reflecting their sensory preferences.

3 Methodology

The adaptive model of e-learning was applied in learning English as a foreign or second language (EFL, ESL). The model can be used in many ways, e.g. in face-to-face lessons; however, within this research it was exploited for learners' after-school preparation and practising new knowledge. Before the process of learning started, learner's level of knowledge and sensory preferences were tested. Then, students learned through the model. Finally, the increase/decrease in students' knowledge was tested, results were compared and discussed.

3.1 Research Objectives and Hypotheses

The research is structured in two parts: Research 1 and Research 2. The main objective was to explore the process of learning through adaptive model of e-learning in after-school preparation for English lessons and find out whether students learn more if the process of learning either (1) reflects their sensory preference (Research 1), or (2) is supported by different types of study materials irrespective of student's sensory preference (Research 2).

In Research 1, the research question was defined as follows: Does student's sensory preference (visual, or aural) have impact on the level of knowledge in selected language skills in English? Particularly, are students with visual preference better in reading comprehension, and are students with aural preference better in listening comprehension? To answer these questions, following hypotheses were tested:

H1: Students with visual preference score higher in reading comprehension compared to listening comprehension.
H2: Students with aural preference score higher in listening comprehension test compared to reading comprehension.

"To score higher" refers to the statistically significant difference (DIF) in the test score of reading comprehension (RC) test compared to listening comprehension (LC) within the group of students with visual preference (VISp) and within the group of students with aural preference (AURp), i.e. DIF RC VISp: DIF RC AURp; DIF LC VISp: DIF LC AURp. The differences were compared and the statistical significance was considered.

In Research 2, the type of study material another approach was applied. The research question was defined as follows: Does the type of study material (visual, or aural) have impact on the level of knowledge in selected language skills in English? Particularly, do students learn more if they study from materials reflecting visual preference (visual materials), or from materials reflecting aural preference (aural materials)? To answer these questions following hypotheses were tested:

H3: Students score higher in reading comprehension test compared to listening comprehension if they study from visual materials.
H4: Students score higher in listening comprehension test compared to reading comprehension if they study from aural materials.

In this case, "to score higher" refers to the statistically significant difference (DIF) in the test score of reading comprehension (RC) test compared to listening comprehension (LC) within the group of learners studying from visual materials (VISm) and within the group of learners studying from aural materials (AURm) irrespective of their sensory characteristics, i.e. DIF RC VISm: DIF RC AURm; DIF LC VISm: DIF LC AURm). The differences were compared and the statistical significance was considered.

3.2 Research Process

The method of pedagogical experiment was applied for the process of testing hypotheses. Before the pedagogical experiment started, entrance data from each respondent were collected by several tools.

In Phase 1, data defining respondent' level of English knowledge and sensory preferences were collected. For this purpose, (a) English grammar test, (b) English listening comprehension and reading comprehension test and (c) VARK questionnaire [23] were used.

Ad a) Respondents' general knowledge of English grammar was tested by standardized Quick Placement Test, version 2, edited by Oxford University Press and University of Cambridge Local Examinations Syndicate (UCLES). Reflecting the test score students were included in appropriate group according to CEFR (Common European Framework of Reference for Languages) [24]. The test consisted of 60 items and lasted 30 min. Results of grammar test were scaled from A2 to B1 of CEFR.

Ad b) Skills of listening comprehension and reading comprehension were tested by standardized KET (Key English Test for elementary level) and PET (Preliminary English Test for lower intermediate level) tests (by the same editors). Each test consisted of 50 items (25 on listening comprehension, 25 for reading comprehension; following the methodology, KET lasted 62 min, PET lasted 83 min, maximum score was 50 points each test.

Ad c) Sensory preferences were detected by standardized VARK (Visual, Aural, Read/Write, Kinesthetic) questionnaire [23], version 7.8, which consists of 16 items, maximum score is 16 points. Respondents' performance was scored according to standardized methodologies provided by the test authors and summarized in the form of table (Table 1). The data were inserted in the adaptive model of e-learning which then tailored (adapted) the learning process towards learners' sensory preferences and levels of knowledge.

Table 1. Test scores: sample student.

Student	Test score in Grammar	Level in CEFR	V	A	R	K	Test score in LC	Test score in RC
S1	18	A2	4	4	2	6	9	14

LC: Listening Comprehension; RC: Reading comprehension

In Phase 2, didactic pre-test (see detailed description under the phase 4) was administered before the process of adaptive e-learning started; it monitored knowledge in listening comprehension, reading comprehension and writing relating to the learning content to be acquired.

In Phase 3, the process of adaptive e-learning was conducted.

In Phase 4, didactic post-test was applied after the process of adaptive e-learning; it monitored knowledge acquired in listening comprehension and reading comprehension relating to the learning content acquired in the process of adaptive e-learning. Both the didactic pre-tests and post-tests of listening comprehension and reading comprehension were of identical structure (five questions with four multiple-choice answers, one answer was correct, maximum score was one point per correct answer) but they differed in content, i.e. the text the questions related to). All tests were designed in Google Forms and the link was inserted in the adaptive model of e-learning under the subject of English language. Finally, differences in test scores (didactic post-test minus didactic pre-test in listening comprehension and in reading comprehension) were calculated by appropriate statistic tests and exploited for testing the hypotheses.

Identical research design was applied both in Research 1 and Research 2.

3.3 Research Sample

The research sample consisted of 185 respondents; 92 of them participated in the Research 1 (61 students of A2 level according to CEFR; 31 students of B1 level) and 93 in the follow-up Research 2 (69 of A2 level; 24 of B1 level). They all were higher education students in the first or second year of study, specialized in natural science-related study programmes (physics, chemistry, biology, informatics, mathematics).

Reflecting the results of VARK questionnaire, they were divided in two groups according to the sensory preference: students having high scores in visual and read/write activities/tasks were included in the *group of visual students* (46 in Research 1; 47 in Research 2); those reaching high scores in aural and kinaesthetic activities/tasks formed the group of *aural students* (46 in Research 1; 46 in Research 2).

4 Research Results

Collected data were processed by SPSS statistic software. Research results are structured into two subchapters. First, results of Research 1 are presented, then results of Research 2 follow.

4.1 Results of Research 1

Pre-test scores of listening comprehension and reading comprehension tests were used for proving the normality of data distribution. One-sample Kolmogorov-Smirnov test was applied on .05 significance level. Normal distribution was detected neither in listening comprehension test, nor in reading comprehension test. Results are displayed in Table 2.

Table 2. Normality data distribution in Research 1.

	Listening comprehension test	Reading comprehension test
N	92	92
Kolmogorov-Smirnov Z	1.533	1.589
Asymp. Sig. (2-tailed)	.018	.013

In both tests the Asymp. Sig. value is lower than .05. Therefore, non-parametric two-sample Kolmogorov-Smirnov test was used for two independent samples to test whether or not the maximum absolute difference in the overall distribution of the two groups is significant. First, the difference (DIF) between post-test score and pre-test score was calculated, separately for reading comprehension (RC) test and for listening comprehension (LC) test, and for students with visual preferences (VISp) or aural preferences (AURp). Second, the differences were compared and their statistical significance was considered.

Hypothesis H1, stating that students with visual preference score higher in reading comprehension test compared to listening comprehension, was verified – the difference in test score was in favour of reading comprehension test (Z = –3.619c; Sig. = .000).

Hypothesis H2, stating that students with aural preference score higher in listening comprehension test compared to reading comprehension, was falsified – the difference in test score was in favour of reading comprehension test (Z = –3.229c; Sig. = .001).

To sum up, in both groups (i.e. with students with visual preferences and students with aural preferences), statistically significant differences in test scores of reading comprehension and listening comprehension tests were detected in favour of reading comprehension. Thus we can state that the way how these two language skills were acquired (i.e. learning through the adaptive model of e-learning) does not relate to prevailing sensory characteristic (preference) of the students in the Research 1 sample.

The question appears what the reasons of higher scores in reading comprehension tests in both groups might have been? Can the strategies students developed in previous foreign language learning students be applied? As Brown states, ESL (English as second language) and EFL (English as foreign language) taught in the culture different from the native one are more strongly oriented on language knowledge in reading than on listening comprehension [25: 77–79]. Thus we can suppose that aural students adapted to the situation they found themselves in. To take a deeper insight in the problem, Research 2 was conducted in which another approach was applied.

4.2 Results of Research 2

Before results of Research 2 are presented, it should be emphasized that another group of 93 students participated in Research 2 (47 students with visual preferences, 46 students with aural preferences). They were proportionally divided in two groups: (1) students (24 visuals and 23 aurals) studying in the adaptive model of e-learning using visual materials, (2) students (23 visuals and 23 aurals) studying in the adaptive model of e-learning using aural materials. Identical research design was applied as in Research 1 (see Sect. 3.2), i.e. the test of English grammar, listening comprehension and reading comprehension from KET and PET tests, VARK questionnaire, didactic pre-test and post-test were conducted.

Pre-test scores of listening comprehension and reading comprehension tests were used for proving the normality of data distribution. One-sample Kolmogorov-Smirnov test was applied on .05 significance level. Normal distribution was detected neither in listening comprehension test, nor in reading comprehension test. Therefore, non-parametric test was applied. Results are displayed in Table 3.

Table 3. Normality data distribution in Research 2.

	Listening comprehension test	Reading comprehension test
N	93	93
Kolmogorov-Smirnov Z	1.650	1.935
Asymp. Sig. (2-tailed)	.001	.009

In both tests the Asymp. Sig. value is lower than .05. Therefore, non-parametric two-sample Kolmogorov-Smirnov test was used for two independent samples to test whether or not the maximum absolute difference in the overall distribution of the two groups is significant. First, the difference (DIF) between post-test score and pre-test score was calculated, separately for reading comprehension (RC) test and for listening comprehension (LC) test, and for learners studying from visual materials (VISm) or aural materials (AURm). Second, the differences were compared and their statistical significance was considered.

Hypothesis H3, stating that students score higher in reading comprehension test if they study from visual materials, was verified – the difference in test score was in favour of reading comprehension test ($Z = -4.701$; Sig. = .000).

Hypothesis H4, stating that students score higher in listening comprehension test if they study from aural materials, was falsified – the difference in test score was in favour of reading comprehension test ($Z = -1.397$; Sig. = .162).

To sum up, in both groups, i.e. (1) students exploiting visual materials or (2) students exploiting aural materials, statistically significant differences in test scores between reading comprehension and listening comprehension tests were detected in favour of reading comprehension. Thus we can conclude that type of study material students learn from did not provide impact on the results in the Research 2 sample.

5 Discussions and Conclusions

Reflecting the results in Research 1 and Research 2, we can summarize that our expectations were not met – in learning English through the adaptive model of e-learning students reached higher scores (i.e. better knowledge) in reading comprehension irrespective the criterion of individual sensory preference, or type of study material they learned from. The question is what the causes might have been. We do not think that any of those listed below was the only or main reason; however, if considered as a whole, they may provide impact on the process of adaptive e-learning.

First, the presented results are limited by the *total amounts* of research samples (92 and 93 students) in both researches, so they cannot be generally applied.

Second, the exploitation of adaptive model of e-learning was monitored in the field of *after-school activities* towards preparation for English lessons only, and the school face-to-face instruction was not analyzed.

Third, learners' *motivation* both to studying English and working in the adaptive model of e-learning was not monitored within the research – most of the were positively motivated by the newness learning through the adaptive model of e-learning.

Fourth, despite the fact that learners generally have a high level of computer literacy, some *technical and/or methodological problems when working with the adaptive model* may have appeared if working from home, which may have provided impact on the results and could lower the motivation to learning.

Last but not least, as the positive contribution of the same adaptive model of e-learning was found out e.g. by Horký [26], Bradáč [27], Bradáč et al. [28], Juříčková [5] who analyzed the learning process from other views than sensory characteristics, another approach to evaluation of learning foreign languages within the model should be applied in the future. Starting from the learning preferences, a hybrid model was designed by Hasibuan and Nughoro [29] which combined traditional Felder-Silverman Learning Style Model with VARK; however, the results of model application into practice have not been published yet. VARK questionnaire was also applied in researches conducted by Stojanova et al. [30] who exploited not only reading/listening approach in teaching subject Data structures and algorithms but they also implemented visualizations through watching video-recordings and animations and didactic software. In ESP (English for Specific Purposes), learning preferences were analyzed from the gender and sensory view by Jaki and Md Yunus [31] and VARK results discovered that most male respondents (89%) were visual and kinaesthetic learners while female students were mostly of reading type. Unfortunately, in Researches 1 and 2 the student's gender was not monitored. Toktarova and Panturova proved [32] that when combining VARK with Gregorc's learning style model within the university electronic educational environment, the increase in knowledge was detected also in English language.

Currently, the adaptive model of e-learning is analyzed from the view of deeper identification of individual learning styles, particularly following aspects as learning theories in e-learning environment, predictors of online learning styles and their automatic classification and application, as also worked out by Truong [33]. Identically to our approach, he proposes three phases: (1) questionnaire survey before the instruction, (2) tracking student's process of acquiring the learning content and (3) analytic evaluation of the learning style. For the further development of the adaptive model of e-learning, gamification as a strong phenomenon in current education is considered to some extent, its principles should be also implemented in adaptive e-learning, focusing particularly on recognizing the learners, adapting the learning materials to their individual needs and preferences, eliciting learners' interaction through technologies and helping them define their own learning objectives [34].

References

1. Cohen, A.D.: Strategies in Learning and Using a Second Language. Longman, New York (1998)
2. Ehrman, M.E., Lou, E.B., Oxford, R.L.: A brief history of individual differences in second language learning. System **31**, 313–330 (2003)
3. Harmer, J.: How to Teach English, New edn. Pearson Education, Harlow (2007)
4. Garrison, R.D.: e-Learning in the 21st Century. Routledge, New York (2011)
5. Juříčková, R.: Optimalizace výuky cizích jazyků prostřednictvím eLearningu [Optimization of foreign language learning through eLearning]. Dissertation thesis. Ostravská univerzita, Ostrava (2015)
6. Šimonová, I., et al.: Styly učení v aplikacích eLearningu [Learning styles in eLearning applications]. Gaudeamus, Hradec Kralove (2010)
7. Šimonová, I., Poulová, P.: Learning Style Reflection Within Tertiary E-education. Gaudeamus, Hradec Kralove (2012)
8. Nedbalová, Š.: Uplatnění senzorických vlastností v adaptivní výuce cizích jazyků [Sensory characteristics applied in adaptive foreign language instruction]. Dissertation thesis. Ostravská univerzita, Ostrava (2015)
9. Malach, A.: Programované vyučování [Programmed learning]. Akademie, Praha (1977)
10. Skinner, B.F.: Teaching machines. IRE Trans. Educ. 14–22. http://ieeexplore.ieee.org/lpdocs/epic03/wrapper.htm?arnumber=4322064. Accessed 14 Jan 2018
11. Kulič, V.: Člověk – učení – automat [Man – learning – automat]. SPN, Praha (1989)
12. Kostolányova, K.: Teorie adaptivního e-learningu [Theory of adaptive e-Learning]. Ostravská universita, Ostrava (2012)
13. Brusilovsky, P.: Adaptive navigation support for open corpus hypermedia systems. In: Nejdl, W., Kay, J., Pu, P., Herder, E. (eds.) AH 2008. LNCS, vol. 5149, pp. 6–8. Springer, Heidelberg (2008). https://doi.org/10.1007/978-3-540-70987-9_2
14. Fulcher, G.: Practical Language Testing. Hodder Education, London (2010)
15. Krashen, S.D.: Principles and Practice in Second Language Acquisition. Pergamon, New York (1982)
16. Shimojo, S., Shams, L.: Sensory modalities are not separate modalities: plasticity and interactions. Current Opinion in Neurobiology **11**(4), 505–509 (2001). http://linkinghub.elsevier.com/retrieve/pii/S0959438800002415. Accessed 12 Jan 2018 (2001)
17. Coffield, F., et al.: Learning styles and pedagogy in post-16 learning. Learning and Skills Research Centre (2004). http://www.lsda.org.uk/files/PDF/1543.pdf. Accessed 28 Dec 2017
18. Marzano, R.J.: A theory-based meta-analysis of research on instruction. Mid-continent Regional Educational Laboratory, Aurora. http://www.peecworks.org/peec/peec_research/I01795EFA.2/Marzano%20Instruction%20Meta_An.pdf. Accessed 30 Nov 2017
19. Oxford, R.L., Ehrman, M.: Second language research on individual differences. Ann. Rev. Appl. Linguist. **13**, 188. http://www.journals.cambridge.org/abstract_S0267190500002464. Accessed 29 Dec 2017
20. Felder, R.M., Henriques, E.R.: Learning and teaching styles in foreign and second language education. Foreign Lang. Ann. **28**(1), 21–31 (1995)
21. Oxford, R.L.: Language Learning Styles and Strategies: An Overview. Learning Styles & Strategies, pp. 1–25. GALA, Oxford (2003)

22. Kraemer, J.M., Rosenberg, L.M., Thompson-Schill, S.L.: The neural correlates of visual and verbal cognitive styles. Journal of Neuroscience **29**(12), 3792–3798 (2009). http://www.jneurosci.org/content/29/12/3792.short?sid=5e847a46-9990-4e4b-bb8d-84775155b0b2. Accessed 21 Dec 2017
23. Fleming, N.D.: VARK, http://vark-learn.com/the-vark-questionnaire/. Accessed 13 Dec 2017
24. CEFR (Common European Framework of Reference for Languages). https://www.examenglish.com/CEFR/cefr.php. Accessed 23 Jan 2018
25. Brown, H.D.: Teaching by Principles. An Interactive Approach to Language Pedagogy, 3rd edn., pp. 77–79 Pearson, Longman, USA (2007)
26. Horký, E.: Autonomní učení cizích jazyků v eLearningu [Autonomous learning of foreign languages]. Dissertation thesis. Ostravská universita, Ostrava (2014)
27. Bradáč, V.: Adaptivní e-learningový system pro výuku jazyků [Adaptive e-Learning system for language learning]. Dissertation thesis. Ostravská universita, Ostrava (2015)
28. Bradáč, V., Smolka, P., Klimeš, C.: Personalization of foreign language education in the LMS Moodle environment. In: Vincenti, G., Bucciero, A., Vaz de Carvalho, C. (eds.) eLEOT 2015. LNICST, vol. 160, pp. 27–34. Springer, Cham (2016). https://doi.org/10.1007/978-3-319-28883-3_4
29. Hasibuan, M.S., Nugroho, L.: Detecting learning style using hybrid model. In: IEEE Conference on e-Learning, e-Management and e-Services (IC3e), pp. 107–111 (2016)
30. Stojanova, A., Stojkovikj, N., Kocaleva, M., Zlatanovska, B.: Application of VARK learning model on data structures and algorithm course. In: 8th IEEE Global Engineering Education Conference, EDUCON 2017, Athens, pp. 613–620 (2017)
31. Jaki, V.A., Md Yunus, M.: Language learning styles among TESL undergraduate students in Universiti Kebangsaan Malaysia from different gender group. Asian EFL J. **6**, 74–86 (2016)
32. Toktarova, V.I., Panturova, A.A.: Learning and teaching style models in pedagogical design of electronic educational environment of the university. Mediterr. J. Soc. Sci. **6**(3), 281–290 (2015)
33. Truong, H.M.: Integrating learning styles and adaptive e-Learning system: current developments, problems and opportunities. Comput. Hum. Behav. **55**, 1185–1193 (2016). https://doi.org/10.1016/j.chb.2015.02.014. Accessed 05 Feb 2018
34. Monterrat, B., Desmarais, M., Lavoué, É., George, S.: A player model for adaptive gamification in learning environments. In: Conati, C., Heffernan, N., Mitrovic, A., Verdejo, M.F. (eds.) AIED 2015. LNCS (LNAI), vol. 9112, pp. 297–306. Springer, Cham (2015). https://doi.org/10.1007/978-3-319-19773-9_30

Enhancing Learning Success Through Blended Approach to Learning and Practising English Grammar: Research Results

Ivana Simonova(✉)

University of Jan Evangelista Purkyne, Usti nad Labem, Czech Republic
ivana.simonova@ujep.cz

Abstract. Blended learning has become standard in foreign language instruction, particularly in acquiring English grammar. The main objective of the article was to find out whether blended approach enhances the process of acquiring new knowledge. The research was conducted at the Faculty of Informatics and Management, University of Hradec Kralove, Czech Republic, and the research sample consisted of 61 part-time bachelor students Data were collected in three phases: (1) face-to-face pre-testing to monitor entrance knowledge before the process of blended learning starts, (2) post-testing1 applied after the blended approach and (3) final face-to-face post-testing2 administered at the end of semester. Four hypotheses were tested to discover whether there exist statistically significant differences in test scores. The results entitle the described blended learning to be applied as appropriate approach to acquiring English grammar in ESP.

Keywords: Blended learning · Higher education · English grammar E-learning · ESP · English for Specific Purposes

1 Introduction

Blended learning, combining the best of online learning and face-to-face instruction for the purpose of enhancing the process of learning, is appreciated by most students as they prefer courses that have some online components [1]. Blended approach also provides more flexibility for students and instructors, some technologies allow for more learning to take place, they facilitate a specific kind of learning activity that might not be possible without the technology, students can use different ways to engage into learning and also to demonstrate what they learned; and last but not least, both teachers and students have the opportunity to develop their skills in using latest devices and applications [2].

As discovered in detail by Poon [3], the flexibility for student learning is particularly meant in terms of learning style and pace. Considering a wide range of delivery methods, blended learning increases and improves students' engagement and consequently their knowledge. The experience in blended learning proved that well-designed blended courses not only enhanced students' learning but also increased retention of their knowledge, even in large classes [4].

S. K. S. Cheung et al. (Eds.): ICBL 2018, LNCS 10949, pp. 69–80, 2018.
https://doi.org/10.1007/978-3-319-94505-7_5

Consequently, the main question appears whether, or not the blended approach should be applied so as learners acquired the learning contents with less effort, in shorter time-period, in a more natural way etc. In other words, first, it is necessary to think about what the teacher is going to teach, and what s/he wants students to learn, i.e. what the learning objective and outcomes are. Second, the proposal of methods (scenario) should be designed and learning outcomes measured. Finally, having all these criteria in mind, the decision comes whether/to what extent the blended learning will be applied to acquiring the learning content. Within the decision-making process, learners' effort, time spent on learning and the appropriateness of blended learning should be considered. Moreover, learners' ability to work independently, even if supported by electronic guidelines and teacher's immediate feedback, plays important role, as well as the competence in using technologies for educational purposes [2].

Reflecting the above mentioned, the main objective of this article is to introduce the concept of blended learning for acquiring English grammar within English for Specific Purposes and present results of research conducted in this field.

2 Blended Approach to Learning English Grammar in ESP at the Faculty of Informatics and Management

In the part-time bachelor study programmes of Applied Informatics and Information Management, English for Specific Purposes (ESP) is taught for four semesters (ESP1 – ESP4). In the Czech Republic the upper secondary school graduates are required to reach B1 level of CEFR (Common European Framework of Reference for Languages) [5]. Despite this fact, however, the real state differs. Some university applicants do not meet this pre-condition. So as to enable them to reach the required knowledge, special courses are held for the first-year university students; and consequently ESP courses start in the third of six semesters of bachelor studies. Moreover, students' knowledge is summarized in ESP1 course which focuses on English grammar. Then, other courses target at developing the skill of reading comprehension of professional texts (ESP2), written communication (ESP3) and oral communication and presentation (ESP4). Before bachelor graduation, students are required to reach the B2 level of CEFR.

In each semester (12 weeks long) the blended approach is applied combining 24 face-to-face hours taught in four six-hour blocks in the classroom and autonomous learning within appropriate ESP course in the learning management system (LMS) Blackboard. The courses can be accessed from personal computers, notebooks, tablets or other mobile and smart devices irrespective of the operational system. LMS Blackboard was originally designed as the learning environment, so it is able to meet all the requirements and features that enhance the process of teaching and learning. It means it provides tools for displaying study materials in various forms (fulltext, hypertext, presentations, animations, figures, table etc.), for conducting teacher/student and student/student communication, sharing materials and messages, practising and testing new knowledge with immediate correction, explanation and link to the appropriate part of study materials so as to focus on deeper learning, which is highly important particularly in autonomous (e-)learning.

3 Methodology

In spite of the fact the blended learning has been considered a standard approach, researches in this field are highly required. The basic question is whether learning results developed within this process entitle teachers and educational institutions to apply it so as learners reached required knowledge.

3.1 Research Objective

The main objective of this research is to explore how much students learn, if selected phenomena of English grammar in ESP are acquired within the process of blended learning which in this case combines face-to-face lessons with autonomous e-learning within LMS Blackboard.

3.2 Research Method, Tool, Process and Hypotheses

The research process was structured into three steps.

First, the pre-test was administered on the first face-to-face lesson of ESP1 course before the process of acquiring new learning content started. Students received a list of 44 grammar phenomena in electronic form (the terminology was both in English and Czech language). They were to write a simple sentence containing each phenomenon in appropriate context. For the purpose of the research the phenomena were divided in two groups which followed the CEFR requirements for A2 (Basic user – elementary level) and B1 (Independent user – intermediate level) groups:

In A2 group, following 20 phenomena were listed (G1-20): Irregular Noun in plural; Uncountable Noun; Comparative or Superlative form of Adverb; Present Simple tense; Present Continuous; Past Simple Past Continuous; Future action expressed by Will, Going to, Present Continuous; Present Perfect Simple; Present Perfect Continuous; Past Perfect; Past Perfect Continuous; Modal verbs; There is/There are; Would rather; Had better.

In B1 group, following 24 phenomena were included (G21-44): three types of Conditional sentences; Future Perfect Simple; Future Perfect Continuous; Wish clauses for the Present and Past; expressing the Purpose; Time clause for future actions; Relative clause; word order in Indirect speech; Sequence of tenses; Subject with Infinitive structure; Object with Infinitive structure; Modal verb with Past Infinitive; Gerund or Infinitive form; Have Something Done structure; Used to with Infinitive; Used to with -ing form; Make/Do sentences; Who/What question; Question tags; So am I/Neither am I.

The time period for completing the list was 70 min. After the lesson, the list was submitted to the LMS Blackboard. Each sentence was assessed by the teacher (one point per correct sentence; maximum test score was 20 points for G1-20 part, and 24 points for G21-44 part. These results are called the pre-test scores further on.

Second, as autonomous homework, students read texts relating to their field of study and work, i.e. professional books, articles in journals, manuals etc. They focused on the listed grammar phenomena, and when it was found, the whole sentence containing the appropriate grammar phenomenon was added to the list (including the reference to the source). So as to create as good as possible list of sentences, students were allowed (or even encouraged) to use both printed and e-sources for reading and to exploit various learning aids, e.g. presentation providing the summary with description of all required grammar phenomena and few samples, which was created by the teacher, any grammar book or student's book with exercises and the key, web pages relating to learning English, printed and e-dictionaries etc. Moreover, they could conduct discussions, both in the LMS or on social networks, to consider the appropriateness (in/correctness) of single sentences, to share sources and methods of searching for single phenomena.

Totally, 2,684 sentences should have been submitted. Despite students were informed that the task would not be considered completed if they did not fill in all 44 phenomena, eight sentences were missing. In total, 2,676 sentences were submitted; 2,194 sentences (82%) were collected from e-sources. The total time for completing the list was six weeks; then, it was submitted through the LMS and assessed by the teacher as post-test1. Identically to the pre-test, one point per each correct sentence was scored (maximum score was 20, resp. 24 points). Within the assessment the teacher provided feedback to each student – correct and incorrect sentences were distinguished and links to study materials with further explanations were provided to the student. As the amount of sentences was high, the feedback was sent within two weeks, one month before the end of semester as minimum. Advanced students completed the list of sentences in the time shorter than six weeks, so the "first come first served" principle in providing the feedback was applied by the teacher. Then, student's task was to study the results of assessment, and continue the process of acquiring the learning content of ESP1 course; and if needed, to contact the teacher for further support. Thus the blended earning approach was applied combining face-to-face lessons and autonomous work supported by latest devices and technologies.

Third, student's final knowledge was tested at the end of semester in the form of face-to-face credit test. The task was to write simple sentences using professional vocabulary and showing each grammar phenomenon in context. This task was rather difficult because not only the knowledge of grammar phenomena, their structure and spelling, but also the context and professional vocabulary were required. No didactic aids were allowed during the testing. Identically to the pre-test and post-test1, one point per each correct sample was scored (maximum score was 20, resp. 24 points). This result is called the post-test2 score.

So as to reach the main research objective, i.e. to discover how much students learn, if selected phenomena of English grammar in ESP are acquired within the process of blended learning, four hypotheses were set:

H1: There exists the statistically significant difference between pre-test and post-test1 scores in the group of grammar phenomena G1-20.
H2: There exists the statistically significant difference between post-test1 and post-test2 scores in the group of grammar phenomena G1-20.
H3: There exists the statistically significant difference between pre-test and post-test1 scores in the group of grammar phenomena G21-44.
H4: There exists the statistically significant difference between post-test1 and post-test2 scores in the group of grammar phenomena G21-44.

3.3 Research Sample

Totally 61 students of the Faculty of Informatics and Management, University of Hradec Kralove, Czech Republic, enrolled in the subject of ESP1 in Applied Informatics and Information Management part-time bachelor study programmes participated in the research. Their knowledge of general English was estimated according to the results of entrance exam test and students' self-evaluation: A1 of CEFR level – 14 students, A2 – 28 students, B1 – 17 students, B2 – 2 students. Other four students reached C1 level certificates, two students had C2 certificates. They all worked with English-speaking companies; therefore, their learning content in ESP1 was individualized (e.g. they co-operated in ESP project) so as to reflect and develop their higher-level of knowledge; they were not included in the research sample. Despite the gender and age were not considered within the research results, ten students were females (16.4%), the age of 48 respondents (78.7%) was in the interval of 24–36 years, the whole sample was spread in the interval of 19–44 years.

4 Results

Collected data were not compared to those from any type of non-blended process of learning. Within this research test scores produced in pre-test, post-test1 and post-test2 in G1-20 and G21-44 phenomena were processed by appropriate statistic methods and statistical significance of differences was considered. Results are structured into two parts: (1) descriptive statistics and (2) testing hypotheses.

4.1 Descriptive Statistics

Results of descriptive statistics are displayed in Table 1 for grammar phenomena G1-20 and in Table 2 for G21-44 grammar phenomena. They present the values of total amount of respondents (N), Mean, Standard Deviation (SD), Minimum and Maximum score, Score range, Median, Mode and results of two tests of normality data distribution (Shapiro-Wilk W test and Kolmogorov-Smirnov test).

As clearly seen mainly in Mean values, the pre-test score was 15 points for grammar phenomena G1-20 (Table 1). After six-week long study period in the ESP1 course, the post-test1 score increased to 18 points. However, in the final post-test2 the score decreased to 17 points (maximum score was 20 points in each test).

Table 2 displays test scores for grammar phenomena G21-44. The Mean values show that the pre-test score was 14 points. After six-week long study period in the ESP1 course, the post-test1 score increased to 17 points. However, in the final post-test2 the score decreased to 13 points (maximum score was 24 points in each test).

The normality of data distribution was rejected by both the statistic tests in pre-test, post-test1 and post-test2 in both groups G1-20 and G21-44. Reflecting this result, non-parametric test (Wilcoxon Signed-Rank test) was applied for verification of all hypotheses.

Table 1. Descriptive statistics: G1-20.

Heading level	Pre-test	Post-test1	Post-test2
N	61	61	61
Mean	15.52459	18.11475	17.21312
SD	3.495743	1.89823	2.921842
Min	4	13	6
Max	20	20	20
Range	16	7	14
Median	16	19	18
Mode	16	20	18
Normality: Shapiro-Wilk W	0.7762979 (R)	0.8616919 (R)	0.7808502 (R)
Normality: Kolmogorov-Smirnov	0.2753996 (R)	0.2205023 (R)	0.2291058 (R)

R: Reject normality

Table 2. Descriptive statistics: G21-44.

Heading level	Pre-test	Post-test1	Post-test2
N	61	61	61
Mean	13.81967	17.4918	12.93443
SD	6.18468	5.448617	6.500946
Min	0	1	1
Max	24	24	24
Range	24	23	23
Median	15	18	14
Mode	17	24	–
Normality: Shapiro-Wilk W	0.9556006 (R)	0.9231352 (R)	0.9571066 (R)
Normality: Kolmogorov-Smirnov	0.1181878 (R)	0.1199856 (R)	0.08558426 (R)

R: Reject normality

4.2 Testing Hypotheses

Hypotheses were tested in two steps: (1) results of hypotheses H1 and H2 dealing with grammar phenomena G1-20 are presented; (2) results of hypotheses H3 and H4 dealing with grammar phenomena G21-44 are displayed.

Grammar Phenomena G1-20

First, the paired difference for pre-test score and post-test1 score was calculated for grammar phenomena G1-20 by Wilcoxon Signed Rank test. Reaching the Z-value = 6.3755, the first hypothesis **H1 was verified** ($\alpha = 0.05$; probability level = 0.000000). This result means that statistically significant difference was discovered between the pre-test and post-test1 scores (Fig. 1, left histogram).

Second, the paired difference for post-test1 score and post-test2 score was calculated for grammar phenomena G1-20 by Wilcoxon Signed Rank test. Reaching the Z-value = 1.6783, the second hypothesis **H2 was falsified** ($\alpha = 0.05$; probability

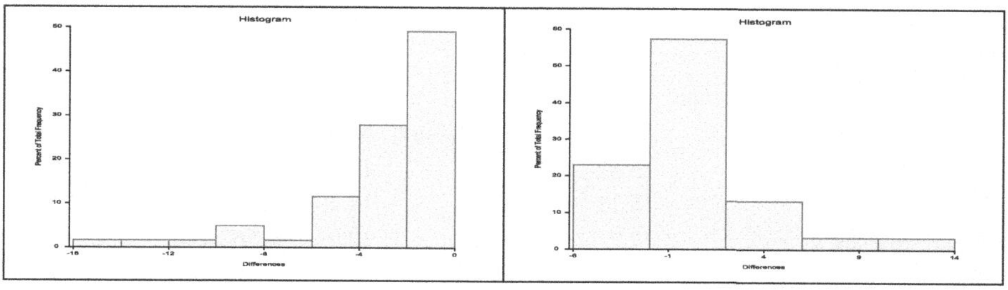

Fig. 1. G1-20: Differences in test scores in pre-test versus post-test1 (left), in post-test1 versus post-test2 (right).

level = 0.093288). This result means that statistically significant difference was not discovered between the post-test1 and post-test2 scores (Fig. 1, right histogram).

Grammar Phenomena G21-44

Third, the paired difference for pre-test score and post-test1 score was calculated for grammar phenomena G21-44 by Wilcoxon Signed Rank test. Reaching the Z-value = 6.1518, the third hypothesis **H3 was verified** ($\alpha = 0.05$; probability level = 0.000000). This result means that statistically significant difference was discovered between the pre-test and post-test1 scores (Fig. 2, left histogram).

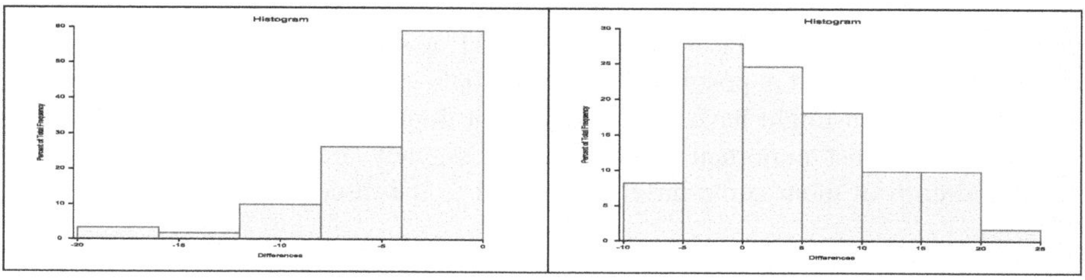

Fig. 2. G21-44: Differences in test scores in pre-test versus post-test1 (left) and post-test1versus post-test2 (right).

Fourth, the paired difference for post-test1 score and post-test2 score was calculated for grammar phenomena G21-44 by Wilcoxon Signed Rank test. Reaching the Z-value = 4.0515, the fourth hypothesis **H4 was verified** ($\alpha = 0.05$; probability level = 0.000051). This result means that statistically significant difference was discovered between the post-test1 and post-test2 scores (Fig. 2, right histogram).

To sum up, hypotheses H1, H3 and H4 were verified; hypothesis H2 was falsified. So as to have a more practical insight, Mean values in single tests are compared in Table 3.

In G1-20 group the results show the statistically significant increase in post-test1 score compared to pre-test (+2.59); however, the decrease was detected in post-test2 score compared to post-test1 (−0.9). In G21-44 group the statistically significant increase was even higher in post-test1 compared to pre-test (+3.68); however, the sharp

Table 3. Descriptive statistics: Summary of Mean values in Pre-test, post-test1 and Post-test2 in G1-20 and G21-44.

Grammar phenomenon	G1-20			G21-44		
Test score	Mean	Dif.	Stat. sign.	Mean	Dif.	Stat. sign.
Pre-test	15.52			13.81		
Post-test1	18.11	+2.59	Yes	17.49	+3.68	Yes
Post-test2	17.21	−0.9	No	12.93	−4.56	Yes
Total		+1.69			−0.88	

Stat. significance: result is statistically significant

and statistically significant decrease was discovered in post-test2 score compared to post-test1 (−4.56). When total differences between pre-test and post-test2 scores are compared, the increase of +1.69 was calculated in G1-20 group and the decrease of −0.88 in G21-44 group of English grammar phenomena.

5 Discussions and Conclusions

Reflecting the size and structure of the research sample, the research results cannot be generalized, they are valid for the sample groups only. As displayed in Table 3, blended learning approach enhanced students' success in learning in the group G1-20, where easier English grammar phenomena (relating to A2 level of CEFR) were included. In the group G21-44 (relating to B1 level of CEFR), the decrease in knowledge was detected in post-test2 compared to the pre-test. The question is what the causes of this result might have been. We do not think any of those listed below will perform as the most important one. Nevertheless, they are interconnected to some extend and each of them could have contributed to the discovered finding.

Starting level of English knowledge: Despite the level of student's knowledge was clearly defined before they enrolled in the ESP1 course, not all of them met the requirements (see 3.3 Research sample). As reflected by the course teacher, some of them worked hard – they attended private lessons, paid preparatory courses held by the faculty, contacted the ESP teachers for consultations before the course started and during the semester. Nevertheless, they had difficulties and/or were not able to acquire the whole learning content of the ESP1 course – either from the reason of low entrance level of knowledge, or lack of effort. This constraint was reflected in the result of G21-44 phenomena, which are of advanced level and students, false beginners, were not able to master them. Finally, it resulted in decrease of mean score in post-test2 compared to pre-test.

Appropriateness and/or effectivity of autonomous study in acquiring still unknown learning content: Reflecting the low level of English knowledge with some students described above, we agree it is very difficult to acquire completely new and difficult learning content, even if the blended learning comprises of face-to-face lessons are held (when students can ask for immediate additional explanation, examples, feedback) and autonomous homework supported by other explanations and tests in LMS course.

Student's effort and ability to learn autonomously: To be honest, it should be mentioned that not all students are able to learn and/or practise the learning content autonomously. As generally accepted, this ability refers to motivation, level of previous knowledge, general intelligence and many other personal characteristics [6]. Irrespective of how strongly the learner is enhanced (by the teacher, LMS, or other didactic means), the positive effects of learning may not appear. Moreover, as reflected by ESP teachers at the faculty, students do not have so strong problems in ESP2-4 courses which deal with reading comprehension of professional texts and oral and written communication in ESP. So the grammar itself might not be the core problem. Regardless the fact how helpful face-to-face lessons and autonomous work are [7], the blended approach cannot work efficiently in acquiring new and demanding learning content with not-hard-working students.

Student's high self-evaluation of own knowledge and performance: In accord with high self-confidence and self-assurance of an individual, which are required by current system of personality presentation, these features are also developed by educational institutions and companies. However, reflection to the real state is highly needed. Failing that, students and young undergraduates may overestimate their knowledge, strengths, and fail in their activities in the end [8].

Last but not least, being aware of the fact that the task required in post-test2 was difficult, as the *application of new knowledge always* is, the low test score is not so surprising. Students had been informed that their activities and efforts relating to grammar would be part of their final credit test but they did not know the concrete form of the task. As a result, they were not able to actively produce appropriate sentences without the support of various learning aids, as they were allowed in post-test1 (e.g. search engines, electronic grammar books etc.).

As summarized by Uskov et al. [9], student's personal characteristics, particularly motivation to learn but also learning style preferences, student's effort to learn, level of starting knowledge, appropriateness of didactic means used in the process of (blended) teaching/learning, are the main criteria which play substantial role, whatever type of learning we have in mind. The blended learning concept has been applied in higher education for years, and currently, it has been mainly conducted within smart environments and approached through smart devices. However, to compare the research results to identical/similar ones was not possible because not such a research design was described in publications listed in recognized databases. Learners' progress was considered by Elhoseny et al. [10] who focused on innovations, particularly making the learning environment adaptable to learner's individual needs (dealing with both sensory preferences and level of knowledge). Additionally, Klimova [11] analyzed the teacher's role under the new conditions and concluded it was still based on the same didactic principles as in the past. Unfortunately, her study revealed that despite living in the e-society, some teachers were not able to efficiently implement latest technologies in their teaching.

On the other side, blended learning is positively accepted by numerous students. Pinto-Llorente et al. [12] conducted a quantitative study of 358 students (aged 29–58 years) focusing on the process of improving grammatical competence. Students mainly highlighted the learning autonomy in learning ESL (English as Second Language) – pace, time, sentences for practising single phenomena in real context, and the possibility of online testing. Authors also proved that students' knowledge of English grammar, including theoretical rules, improved [13]. Another research of quantitative/qualitative methodology was conducted by Wright [14]. He also focused on the blended learning concept in learning grammar within EFL (English as foreign Language) having the sample of 112 students. They appreciated pace and place of online learning together with the role of teacher as their motivator. Students' results were not mentioned, but the importance of teacher's skill enhancing the success of the process was strongly emphasized.

The implementation of SAMR model reflecting the Bloom's taxonomy of educational objectives applied in blended learning and teaching of general English and ESP was proposed by Netolicka and Simonova [15]. The model applies two phases (the enhancement and augmentation) and four steps within the process of acquiring new knowledge – (1) substitution (i.e. technology acts as direct tool substitute without no technology change), (2) augmentation (i.e. technology acts as direct tool substitute with functional improvements), (3) modification (i.e. technology allows for significant task redesign) and (4) redefinition (i.e. technology allows creation of new task, previously inconceivable) [16]. Authors provided a detailed methodology how the model can be efficiently implemented and introduced results of pilot testing, including learners' and teachers' feedback. Follow-up results proved both significantly better knowledge and differences in learners' performance in the group working with iPads compared to students not using them [15].

Liu et al. [17] developed a new computer-assisted learning system called starC which enhances teachers and learners to operate the learning activity through the whole learning process. They proposed a new learning pattern based mainly on the collaborative learning in the flipped environment and applied it in English classes on the higher education level. They discovered that within this pattern, students in the experimental group produced better results particularly in speaking but also in grammar, reading and writing compared to the control group where this approach was not applied.

Last but not least, teaching/learning English grammar enhanced by LMS Moodle was researched by Shecher [18]. After analyzing the available tools, he proposed a model which paid strong attention to engaging students in learning activities, and discussed parameters which should be considered in designing a blended learning course, focusing mainly on acquiring the vocabulary, grammar, reading, and on testing new knowledge. The main objective of his work was to give teachers confidence and basic inspiration how to enhance the process of teaching English.

However, a few years after Shecher's research (in 2018), technologies provide numerous, much more interesting tools and strategies which are expected to attract learners' attention and work efficiently. Even though the didactic principles are identical for centuries [19], fast development of latest technologies offers both the teachers and learners new ways how to exploit them for educational purposes. Reflecting this state, teachers are facing new IT skills to be mastered and the teacher's role is changing. However, s/he will always work as an important factor in the process of acquiring the new knowledge, irrespective of the extent the technologies will take within the process of blended learning.

Acknowledgements. This paper was supported by IGA project 2018 "ICT in FL education", Faculty of Education, University of Jan Evangelista Purkyne, Usti nad Labem.

References

1. ECAR National study of undergraduate students and information technology, 2011 Report (2012). https://library.educause.edu/resources/2011/10/ecar-national-study-of-undergraduate-students-and-information-technology-2011-report. Accessed 22 Feb 2018
2. Blended learning. https://www.cte.cornell.edu/teaching-ideas/teaching-with-technology/blended-learning.html. Accessed 20 Feb 2018
3. Poon, J.: Use of blended learning to enhance the student learning experience and engagement in property education. Prop. Manag. **30**(2), 129–156 (2012)
4. Amaral, K., Shank, J.: Enhancing student learning and retention with blended learning class guides (2010). https://er.educause.edu/articles/2010/12/enhancing-student-learning-and-retention-with-blended-learning-class-guides. Accessed 18 Feb 2018
5. Common European Framework of Reference for Languages: learning, teaching and assessment. Provisional edition. Council of Europe (2017). https://www.coe.int/en/web/common-european-framework-reference-languages/?. Accessed 30 Dec 2017
6. Kim, C.: The role of affective and motivational factors in designing personalized learning environments. Educ. Tech. Res. Dev. **60**(4), 563–584 (2012)
7. Spector, J.M., Merrill, M.D. (eds.) Effective, efficient and engaging (E3) learning in the digital age. Distance Educ. Spec. Issue **29**(2), 187–198 (2008)
8. Rican, J.: Metakognice a metakognitivní strategie jako teoretické a výzkumné konstrukty a jejich uplatnění v moderní pedagogické praxi (Metacognition and metacognitive strategies as theoretical and research constructs and their application in moderm pedagogical practice). 1st edn. Hnevin, Most (2016)
9. Uskov, V.L., Bakken, J.P., Penumatsa, A., Heinemann, C., Rachakonda, R.: Smart pedagogy for smart universities. Smart Innov. Syst. Technol. **75**, 3–16 (2017)
10. Elhoseny, H., Elhoseny, M., Abdelrazek, S., Riad, A.M.: Evaluating learners' progress in smart learning environment. Adv. Intell. Syst. Comput. **639**, 734–744 (2018)
11. Klimova, B.: Smart teacher: innovations in smart universities. Smart Innov. Syst. Technol. **75**, 321–329 (2017)
12. Pinto-Llorente, A.M., Sanchez-Gomez, M.C., Garcia-Penalvo, F.J., Casillas-Martin, S.: Students' perceptions and attitudes towards asynchronous technological tools in blended-learning training to improve grammatical competence in English as a second language. Comput. Hum. Behav. **72**, 632–643 (2017)
13. Pinto-Llorente, A.M., Sanchez-Gomez, M.C., Garcia-Penalvo, F.J.: Student perception on the use of a blended-learning model to improve grammatical competence. In: Alvez, G.R., Felgueiras, M.C. (eds.) TEEM 2015, Third International Conference on Technological Ecosystems for Enhancing Multiculturality, pp. 91–98 (2015)
14. Wright, B.M.: Blended learnings student perception of face-to-face and online EFL lessons. Indones. J. Appl. Linguist. **7**(1), 64–71 (2017)
15. Netolicka, J., Simonova, I.: SAMR model and bloom's digital taxonomy applied in blended learning/teaching of general English and ESP. In: ISET 2017, Proceedings of International Symposium on Educational Technology, pp. 277–281 (2017)
16. Schrock, K.: SAMR and Bloom's. http://www.schrockguide.net/samr.html. Accessed 18 Feb 2018

17. Liu, T., Chen, Z., Lesgold, A.M., Feng, X., Wang, C.: Novelty blended learning pattern and its application in English language teaching. In: ICDTE 2017: International Conference on Digital Technology in Education, ACM International Conference Proceedings Series volume, Part F, vol. 131203, pp. 7–12 (2017)
18. Shechter, D.A.: Blended language learning using Moodle: analyzing the design of a university Turkish course as a model for other languages. In: Chova, L.G., Martinez, A.L., Torres, I.C. (eds.) INTED2015: International Technology, Education and Development Conference, pp. 1169–1169 (2015)
19. Comenius, J.A.: Didactica magna. Dědictví Komenského (Comenius Heritage), Praha (1930)

Cultivating Situational Interest in Blended Learning Environment

Yan Keung Hui(✉), Chen Li, Sheng Qian, and Lam-for Kwok

Department of Computer Science, City University of Hong Kong, 83 Tat Chee Avenue, Kowloon, Hong Kong
{john.ykhui, cslfkwok}@cityu.edu.hk,
{richard.li, sqian9-c}@mycityu.edu.hk

Abstract. According to the theories of interest and self-determination in education psychology, students' academic performance will be positively affected by situational interest and learning motivation. For improving the design of an engineering course at the City University of Hong Kong in a blended learning environment, we apply these two theories to form a new conceptual model and verify it through an experimental study in which a total number of 61 undergraduate students participated during a whole 13-week course. In this study, we aim at finding out how situational interest can be cultivated. The data analysis results show that the learning motivation can further cultivate the situational interest on top of the individual interest, and the perceived usefulness of instructional design can enhance students' learning satisfaction and learning motivation. Our findings make theoretical contributions by combining these two theories and demonstrate the importance of these theories on the instructional design.

Keywords: Situational interest · Theory of Interest
Self-determination Theory · Instructional design

1 Introduction

It is believed that students with learning motivation and feel interested in the learning environment can improve their cognitive and emotional outcomes and therefore achieve better academic performance [1]. Many researchers have focused on this topic and proposed various educational psychology theories in recent decades. Among the proposed theories, the most representative two are the theory of interest (ToI) and self-determination theory (SDT). Specifically, they explore antecedents in cultivating students' psychological states in order to enhance their academic performance. The ToI focuses on the person-object relationship, while the SDT focuses on content specifics [2]. Based by combining these two theories, various studies such as the study on integrating the two theories with the Big Five personalities [1] and the study on the two theories on the technological pedagogical content knowledge framework [3] have been conducted in previous research studies [1]. However, learning outcomes based on these theories are difficult to be empirically proven [4].

S. K. S. Cheung et al. (Eds.): ICBL 2018, LNCS 10949, pp. 81–92, 2018.
https://doi.org/10.1007/978-3-319-94505-7_6

In this study, we proposed a conceptual model consisting seven hypotheses based on the two theories and empirically verified the model using a dataset which we collected from a 13-week engineering course at the City University of Hong Kong. We aim to identify a predictive path of academic performance in the proposed model based on the ToI and SDT.

Specifically, we first verify the goodness of model fitting through measurement assessment and model assessment. Then we identify a predictive path with high predictive power. Specifically, this path consists of five sequentially organized nodes as follows: *perceived usefulness of instruction design, learning satisfaction, learning motivation, situational interest, and academic performance*.

The findings provide both theoretical and practical contributions. Theoretically, we identify a model to apply both theories with empirical support. Practically, we investigate how to cultivate students' situational interest through the development of learning satisfaction and learning motivation. In addition, we also discover the importance of perceived usefulness of instructional design in developing them.

The remaining of the paper is organized as follows. Firstly, we make a brief introduction to theoretical backgrounds and the proposed conceptual model in Sect. 2. Secondly, we explain the research methods in detail in Sect. 3. Then, we perform data analysis and show the analysis results in Sect. 4. Furthermore, we discuss both the theoretical implication and practical implication in Sect. 5. Finally, we make a conclusion of this paper in Sect. 6.

2 Theoretical Background and Research Model

2.1 Self-determination Theory

Self-determination theory (SDT) was developed by Deci and Ryan [5, 6] based on their prior research on the distinction between intrinsic and extrinsic motivation [7]. Intrinsically motivated behavior represents prototype of self-determined behavior. Some extrinsically motivated behaviors were found to be self-determined later [8].

Students being motivated normally have the characteristics of curiosity, exploration, and interest [1], which aligns with the ToI. In education domain, we propose that learning motivation (LM) can cultivate students' situational interest.

Satisfaction of basic psychological needs is the prerequisite of self-determined motivation, while basic psychological needs in the education domain refer to the learning environment including the instructional design [1]. Therefore, we propose that the perceived usefulness of instructional design will first improve learning satisfaction and then learning motivation.

2.2 Theory of Interest

Early in the 1970s, ToI was widely used to describe and explain the process and result in learning [1] and was mainly applied in research of teaching and learning [9]. Specifically, ToI discusses the relationship between a person and an object, and classifies the interests into situational interest (SI) and individual interest (II).

SI refers to the psychological state which a person feels interested in something at a particular time and environment [10]. In the education domain, it refers to the teaching and learning environment including the pedagogy of the course, the learning management system, textbook, notes, team members of a group project, and classroom equipment. It also includes the instructional design on how the course is to be delivered by combining all the environmental elements. We propose that proper instructional design can directly cultivate students' SI.

Students being motivated and having higher SI normally engage in the learning process better than others. They also have a long-term commitment and longer retention of what they have learned. They are also willing to apply the learned knowledge more actively and frequently than others. In the long-term, students with higher SI can achieve better academic performance [1, 11].

On the other hand, II is a relatively stable psychological state. In this study, it refers to the original stable psychological state of each student prior to a course. The theory also mentions that SI is supported by strong motivation and II [10]. We propose that both II and LM can cultivate students' SI.

2.3 Research Model

In order to find out the most important elements on how students' SI can be cultivated and whether SI can affect the academic performance (AP), we combined the above two theories and proposed a conceptual model as shown in Fig. 1 and evaluated the model empirically afterward. We proposed a basic hypothesis that SI, varying on time and situation, could be influenced by three factors: (1) II, (2) instructional design, and (3) LM. Among them, II means the prior interest before taking a course; and instructional design is measured in a reflective way and named as the perceived usefulness of instructional design (PUID). Moreover, LM heavily relies on the precondition of learning satisfaction (LS), which can be cultivated by instructional design. Finally, the AP can be influenced by SI.

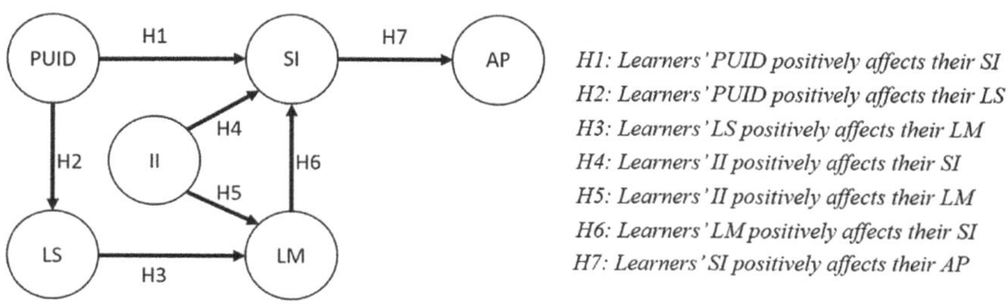

Fig. 1. The proposed conceptual model based on ToI and SDT

3 Methods

3.1 Research Context

The course Software Engineering Principles and Practice is offered as a core course to students in Creative Media Major, which aims to produce creative media professionals proficient in computing technology. Students are expected to gain a solid foundation in the creative processes, including video, sound, photography, storytelling, game design, animation, computer graphics, installation, and interactive digital media production. However, some of these students are more media oriented towards their studies resulting in not having much motivation in studying this course.

This software engineering course aims to provide practical knowledge and skills in software development using unified modeling language by going through the software engineering process from software requirement analysis, design, and implementation to testing. It also covers more theoretical topics such as software processes, design principles and project management. The course delivery takes the form of 2-h lecture and 1-h tutorial/laboratory every week for 13 weeks. Students are asked to work on a semester-long group project. Since they do not have much experience in software development and show less interest in the subject, some of these students find it extremely difficult in studying this course.

Traditionally, we asked students to work on some typical software development projects like library systems and facility management systems etc. Since students were not familiar with the knowledge domains of the chosen projects and thus, with less interest in the course, they found it hard to achieve the learning outcomes and there was a certain percentage of failure every year.

In the academic year 2015–2016, we modified the approach of teaching and learning of this course. We aimed to choose a knowledge domain that they might be interested in for the project work; to provide plenty of video learning resources to students as part of the flipped learning; to plan the project work with a series of phase submissions instead of submitting a large piece of work at the end; to provide templates and guidance at every phase; and to provide feedback immediately after the submission so that they were able to improve their work in the next phase.

We chose a game on the Unity3D platform as the basis for the semester project. Unity3D provides a large number of short videos on various topics. We asked students to watch some videos on the selected game before starting the project. We asked students to attempt a short quiz to test their understandings on Unity3D. We guessed that game development was an interesting topic that creative media students might have more interests in learning software engineering practice in this domain. We then asked students to model the chosen game using unified modeling language technique with the help of the software engineering tool Visual Paradigm. We also suggested students to watch video learning resources in Visual Paradigm and the programming language C Sharp. We delivered software engineering knowledge during the lectures and we showed practical skills in using Unity3D and Visual Paradigm during the tutorial/laboratory sessions. Since we guessed that students might have interests in game development on the Unity3D platform, we specifically included some tips in using Unity3D in most tutorial/laboratory sessions so as to cultivate their situational interests. Students are expected to understand the concepts and apply them to complete the project by using the software tools Visual Paradigm and Unity3D.

In order to monitor changes in students' perception on the knowledge domain using this approach, interests on the topics, and the efforts in studying, we asked students to fill a survey prior and during the course.

3.2 Survey Instrument Data Collection

Based on relevant researches on LM [12], LS and PUID [13], we defined several measurement items in this study. Specifically, II and SI are to be measured by a list of questions about students' interest on various topics covered by the course. AP is collected after the examination.

According to the above measurement items, we designed a questionnaire for the course in the academic year 2015/16. In this questionnaire, all questions are measured by a 5-point Likert-scale ranging from "strongly disagree (1)" to "strongly agree (5)".

The questionnaire was distributed to students for measuring the II at the beginning of the course, and for measuring the other constructs at a later stage. Among the whole 71 students in the course, 62 students submitted their questionnaires. One student has submitted twice and his questionnaire was dropped. As a result, 61 valid records were used in this study.

In order to eliminate questions with high collinearity, we conducted the collinearity check for all items of each construct. Table 1 shows the resulting items in each construct to be used in the subsequent data analysis.

Table 1. Number of items in each construct being used for analysis

Name of construct	Original number of items	Final number of items
II	10	7
LM	20	12
AP	N/A	N/A
LS	10	7
SI	10	5
PUID	10	6

3.3 Techniques for Data Analysis

Partial least square was used to test the research model, which is a second generation structural equation modeling technique. It can assess the construct validity by estimating the loadings of indicators on constructs, and the causal relationships among constructs in multi-stage models [14]. In addition, it has fewer statistical identification issues than covariance-based structural equation modeling and is suitable for constructs with relatively small samples [15]. Therefore, we conduct the data analysis using the SmartPLS tool (version 3.2.7) available at https://www.smartpls.com/.

4 Data Analysis and Results

To validate the proposed model, we performed a two steps evaluation: (1) Measurement model assessment, and (2) Structural model assessment. Measurement model assessment is to ensure the reliability and validity of the construct measures in order to support the suitability of including them in the path model. Structural model assessment is to check the strengths of path coefficients, impacts and explanatory powers of paths from independent variables to dependent variables [15].

4.1 Measurement Model Assessment

To assess the measurement model, we first examine the absolute importance of each item (observable variables) to its corresponding construct [16] by verifying the outer loadings of each observable variable for the corresponding construct. This can ensure each observable variable is measuring for the corresponding construct but not others. Secondly, we examine the internal consistency reliability of each construct by measuring the Cronbach's alpha [17], composite reliability value and average variance extracted. This is to ensure each construct has sufficient internal consistency reliability to warrant modeling analysis [18, 19]. Thirdly, we examine the convergent validity of each construct by evaluating the outer loadings and t-values of each observable variable [18]. Finally, we examine the discriminant validity by evaluating the cross-loadings of the observable variables [20], the square root of average variance extracted [18, 19] and Heterotrait-Monotrait Ratio [21].

Firstly, given that all constructs in the model are reflective constructs, the absolute importance of each item to its corresponding construct is measured by the outer loadings. From Table 2, all outer loadings are ranged from 0.763 to 0.891, higher than the threshold (0.708) [16]. These results indicate that all items are more important to its corresponding construct than any other constructs.

Table 2. Outer loading (OL) and t-value of each observable variable in each construct

		Observable variables											
		1	2	3	4	5	6	7	8	9	10	11	12
PUID	OL	.802	.813	.861	.786	.856	.849						
	t-value	13.506	11.052	18.055	10.224	15.371	16.575						
SI	OL	.855	.864	.882	.793	.884	.856						
	t-value	24.24	25.063	18.201	14.196	26.932	20.637						
II	OL	.889	.763	.865	.867	.891	.796	.815					
	t-value	7.95	5.049	7.333	7.842	7.586	4.565	5.803					
LM	OL	.858	.806	.887	.821	.816	.873	.814	.824	.813	.890	.808	.765
	t-value	18.523	15.577	24.123	10.358	13.67	19.282	12.504	18.278	13.186	28.071	13.907	11.045
LS	OL	.838	.841	.840	.786	.847	.857	.827					
	t-value	13.299	17.46	17.299	8.637	13.261							

Secondly, internal consistency reliability is evaluated by Cronbach's alpha, composite reliability, and average variance extracted of each construct with their respective observable variables [17]. From Table 3, Cronbach's alpha values and composite reliability values are greater than the threshold value (0.708), and all average variance extracted values are greater than the required threshold (0.50). These results indicate that all the constructs have sufficient internal consistency reliability to warrant modeling analysis [18, 19].

Table 3. Cronbach's alpha, composite reliability, and average variance extracted of each construct

Construct	Cronbach's alpha	Composite reliability	Average variance extracted
PUID	0.908	0.929	0.686
SI	0.927	0.943	0.733
II	0.938	0.945	0.709
LM	0.959	0.964	0.692
LS	0.927	0.941	0.695

Thirdly, convergent validity of all constructs is examined by loading levels and t-values. From Table 2, all observable variables have outer loadings substantially and significantly larger than the recommended loading level (0.50) [18]. Moreover, all of the t-values of all constructs are high, which means that low standard errors exist. Therefore, the convergent validity of all constructs is well justified.

Finally, the discriminant validity of each construct is examined using three methods: (1) Verify the cross-loadings of the observable variables to ensure that the loading of each observable variable in its corresponding construct is higher than its cross loading in other constructs [20]. It shows positive using this method. (2) Compare the square root of average variance extracted with its correlation coefficient associated with all other constructs. From Table 4, discriminant validity cannot be justified between LS and LM, as well as between PUID and LS. It is because the square root of the average variance extracted of the construct is smaller than the corresponding value of corresponding inter-construct correlation [18, 19]. (3) Verify the Heterotrait-Monotrait Ratio to see if there exists all these values are higher than the threshold (0.9) [21]. From Table 4, discriminant validity cannot be justified because it contains two values over the threshold.

Table 4. Construct correlation matrix and the square root of average variance extracted

	II			LM			LS			PUI			SI		
	A	B	C	A	B	C	A	B	C	A	B	C	A	B	C
II	**.842**					1.011									1.062
LM	.231	.212		**.832**											3.291
LS	.102	.152		*.897*	*.949*	1.011	**.834**								
PUID	.149	.160		.827	.884		*.878*	*.941*	1.000	**.828**					3.187

Note: The figures in **bold** are the square root of average variance extracted of the corresponding construct. The figures with italic font show discriminant validity issues. A: inter-construct correlation; B: Heterotrait-Monotrait Ratio; C: variance inflation factor.

Given that the discriminant validity problem existed, we further conducted the multi-collinearity assessment for all exogenous constructs. All inner variance inflation factor values are less than 5.00 as shown in Table 4. Therefore, it is not an issue that the multicollinearity among the exogenous constructs could further impact structural equation modeling investigation of causal relationships [18, 19].

4.2 Structural Model Assessment

Structural model assessment is performed by evaluating the path coefficient, the coefficient of determination (R^2 means the variance that can be explained by the model), effect size (f^2), relative predictive relevance (Q^2) and the goodness of model fitting [19]. In order to generate these values, bootstrapping and blindfolding procedures in SmartPLS are employed [22–24].

Firstly, we evaluate the path coefficients of each hypothesis, examine the significant level of each path coefficient, and evaluate the level of R^2. As shown in Fig. 2, we observe that all path coefficients are significant with $p < 0.05$ in H1, H4 and H5, while others are very significant with $p < 0.01$. The R^2 of SI, LM, and LS are strong with a value over 70%. However, the R^2 of the AP is weak with value about 10%.

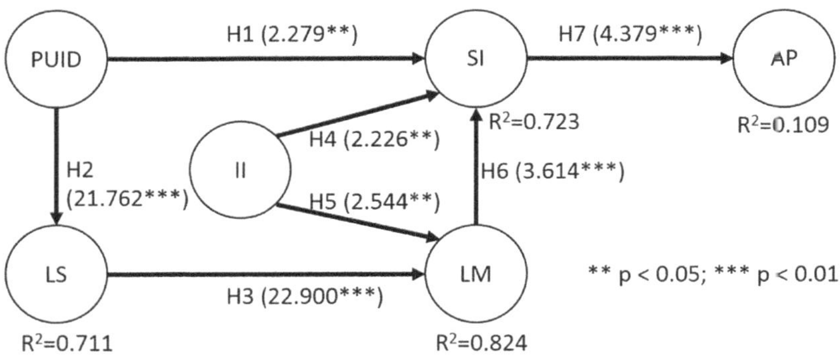

Fig. 2. Path coefficient and R2

Secondly, we examine the impact of a specific predictor construct on an endogenous construct by evaluating the f^2 value, which is defined as having small, medium and large effect if the f^2 value is larger than 0.02, 0.15 and 0.35 respectively [19]. The result shows that II ($f^2 = 0.110$) has a small effect while LS ($f^2 = 4.375$) has a large effect in producing the R^2 of LM. On the other hand, PUID ($f^2 = 0.134$) and II ($f^2 = 0.097$) have small effect while LM ($f^2 = 0.265$) has medium effect in producing the R^2 of the SI. SI ($f^2 = 0.142$) has a small effect in producing the R^2 of the AP. PUID ($f^2 = 3.361$) has a large effect in producing the R^2 of the LS.

Thirdly, the model's predictive relevance is examined by evaluating the Q^2 values, which is defined as having small, medium and large effect if the Q^2 value is larger than 0.02, 0.15 and 0.35 respectively [19]. The result shows that LM ($Q^2 = 0.507$), LS ($Q^2 = 0.477$) and SI ($Q^2 = 0.489$) are having large predictive relevance while AP ($Q^2 = 0.116$) has small predictive relevance.

Finally, model fit can be evaluated by evaluating the standard root mean square residual. The value is found to be 0.084, which is smaller than the threshold (0.10) [25]. Therefore, the model has a good model fit.

5 Discussion and Implication

5.1 Discussion

This study shows that the research model of combining the ToI and the SDT is valid with the good model fit and accepts all proposed hypotheses. Firstly, it was found that SI significantly predicts AP. Students feel interested in the 13-week course significantly perform better than those feel uninterested in the course. Since we chose an interesting knowledge domain for the course project in the academic year 2015–2016, this change in instructional design can enhance students' AP.

Secondly, LM has much higher predictive power than II and the direct effect of PUID. Since we split the whole project into multiple phases, the type of course instructional design allows students to achieve the goal by stages with encouragements and motivations through immediate feedbacks after each stage. Although the instructional design can cultivate students' SI directly, the indirect effect via enhancing LM is more important.

Thirdly, the PUID is critical to enhance the LM through the LS. LS was achieved in this course by providing plenty of video learning resources as part of the flipped learning. In addition, templates and guidance to help students achieve the specific goal of each stage.

Finally, we can identify the main path based on the effect size of each path coefficient in the model. The main path tells that a proper instructional design can induce students' learning satisfaction, which in turn can improve their learning motivation. Then, the learning motivation can cultivate their situational interest and eventually improve their academic performances.

However, although all hypotheses are positively accepted, the R^2 of academic performance is relatively small. It is clear that psychological state may not have a clear direct impact on the actual performance. It may have a long-term effect and may not be observed in a 13 weeks period in the course [1, 11]. Further research should be conducted to identify the missing path between psychological state and the actual performance.

5.2 Theoretical Implication

Theoretically, we proposed a model based on the above two theories and verified it empirically. Practically, we identified the main path in our model on how to cultivate students' situational interest through the development of learning satisfaction and learning motivation. In addition, we also identified the importance of perceived usefulness of instructional design in developing them.

5.3 Practical Implication

Practically, our findings point out the importance for lecturers to enhance students' psychological state including learning satisfaction, learning motivation and situational interest, towards learning. The ultimate goal is to cultivate students' SI through enhancing their LM. LM is enhanced by increasing students' LS through proper instructional design.

For example, lecturers can choose interesting topics to attract students SI directly, or design the course in such a way that students can feel being satisfied and being encouraged, and eventually be motivated to learn.

In a blended learning environment, technology only provides tools and platforms to assist teaching and learning. A well-planned instructional design with the proper use of technology is the key to improve the teaching and learning processes. This aligns with our recent research on the importance of instructional design adopting the flipped classroom in a blended learning environment [26].

5.4 Limitation

Further study is needed to address a few limitations in our study. First, this study focuses only on the psychological factors such as satisfaction, motivation, and interest, without taking into account other factors such as demographic information of students, prior academic performance, and other types of abilities of students.

Second, this study focuses only on students' behaviors in one academic year of one course in one institution using subjective survey, which limits the generalizability of the proposed model. In the future, we need to perform a further study on either expanding horizontally by including students from more courses and/or more institutions or even multiple geographic locations, or vertically by including multiple years of students.

Finally, although the sample size of 61 students is considered as sufficient according to the 10 times rule [19] and has more than two times of the required samples size already, it can have a higher statistical explanation power if the data could be collected from a larger number of samples.

6 Conclusion

In terms of competency and academic performance, achieving the intended learning outcomes is the ultimate goal of the process of teaching and learning. Developing students' psychological states such as motivation and interest are frequently discussed and thus two major educational psychological theories, ToI and SDT, were established. By using data collected from a software engineering course, we built a model and verified the model empirically.

Measurement assessment and model assessment, by using Partial least square, were used to assess the goodness of model fit. We identified that learning motivation has a high predictive power for the situational interest, which predicted the academic performance significantly. Moreover, experimental results also show that the instructional design is critical in enhancing students' learning satisfaction and then the learning motivation.

Theoretical implications on building a research model with empirical support and practical implications for identifying the criticalness of instructional design in a blended learning environment for cultivating students' SI was discussed. Limitations were reviewed and further studies were proposed.

References

1. Muller, F., Louw, J.: Learning environment, motivation and interest: perspectives on self-determination theory. S. Afr. J. Psychol. **34**(2), 169–190 (2004)
2. Krapp, A.: An educational psychological theory of interest and its relation to SDT. In: Deci, E.L., Ryan, R.M. (eds.) Handbook on Self-determination Research, pp. 405–427. University of Rochester Press, Rochester (2002)
3. Urban-Woldron, H., Hopf, M.: TPACK - A Prerequisite for Successful Technology Integration into The Classroom? (2011)
4. Rheinberg, F., Vollmeyer, R., Burns, B.D.: Motivation and self-regulated learning. Pattern Recogn. **131**(1), 81–108 (2000)
5. Deci, E.L., Ryan, R.M.: Intrinsic Motivation and Self-determination in Human Behavior. Plenum Press, New York (1985)
6. Deci, E.L., Ryan, R.M.: Overview of self-determination theory: an organismic dialectical perspective. In: Deci, E.L., Ryan, R.M. (eds.) Handbook of self-determination research, pp. 3–33. University of Rochester Press, Rochester (2002)
7. Deci, E.L.: Intrinsic Motivation. Plenum Press, New York (1975)
8. Deci, E.L., Ryan, R.M.: Promoting self-determined education. Scand. J. Educ. Res. **38**(1), 3–14 (1994)
9. Hoffmann, L., Krapp, A., Renninger, K.A., Baumert, J.: Interest and learning. In: Proceedings of the Seeon Conference on Interest and Learning. IPN, Kiel (1998)
10. Dewey, J.: Interest and Effort in Education. Southern Illinois University Press, Carbondale (2009)
11. Rotgans, J.I., Schmidt, H.G.: Situational interest and academic achievement in active-learning classroom. Learn. Instr. **21**(1), 58–67 (2011)
12. Pintrich, P.R.: A Manual for the Use of the Motivated Strategies for Learning Questionnaire (MSLQ) (1991)
13. Klein, H.J., Noe, R.A., Wang, C.W.: Motivation to learn and course outcomes: the impact of delivery mode, learning goal, orientation, and perceived barriers and enablers. Pers. Psychol. **59**(3), 665–702 (2006)
14. Fornell, C., Bookstein, F.L.: Two structural equation models: LIS-REL and PLS applied to consumer exit-voice theory. J. Mark. Res. **19**(4), 440–452 (1982)
15. Hair, J.F., Ringle, C.M., Sarstedt, M.: PLS-SEM: indeed a silver bullet. J. Mark. Theory Pract. **19**(2), 139–152 (2011)
16. Cenfetelli, R.T., Bassellier, G.: Interpretation of formative measurement in information systems research. MIS Q. **33**(4), 689–707 (2009)
17. Churchill, G.A.: A paradigm for developing better measures of marketing constructs. J. Mark. Res. **16**(1), 64–73 (1979)
18. Fornell, C., Larcker, D.F.: Evaluating structural equation models with unobservable variables and measurement error. J. Mark. Res. **18**(1), 39–50 (1981)
19. Hair, J.F., Hult, G.T.M., Ringle, C.M., Sarstedt, M.A.: Primer on Partial Least Squares: Structural Equation Modeling (PLS-SEM). Sage Publications, Los Angeles (2014)

20. Chin, W.W.: Issues and opinion on structural equation modeling. MIS Q. **22**(1), VII–XVI (1998)
21. Henseler, J., Ringle, C.M., Sarstedt, M.: A new criterion for assessing discriminant validity in variance-based structural equation modeling. J. Acad. Mark. Sci. **43**(1), 115–135 (2015)
22. Cohen, J.: Statistical Power Analysis for the Behavioral Sciences. Lawrence, Erlbaum Associates, Hillsdale (1988)
23. Gefen, D., Rigdon, E.E., Straub, D.W.: An update and extension to SEM guidelines for administrative and social science research. MIS Q. **35**(2), iii–xiv (2011)
24. Hair, J.F., Sarstedt, M., Ringle, C.M., Mena, J.A.: An assessment of the use of partial least squares structural equation modeling in marketing research. J. Acad. Mark. Sci. **40**(3), 414–433 (2012)
25. Henseler, J., Dijkstra, T.K., Sarstedt, M., Ringle, C.M., Diamantopoulos, A., Straub, D.W., Ketchen, D.J., Hair, J.F., Hult, G.T.M., Calantone, R.J.: Common beliefs and reality about partial least squares: comments on ronkko & evermann (2013). Organ. Res. Methods **17**(2), 182–209 (2014)
26. Hui, Y.K., Mai, B., Qian, S., Kwok, L.F.: Cultivating better learning attitudes: a preliminary longitudinal study. Open Learn. J. Open Distance e-Learn. **33**(2), 155–170 (2018)

Application of Gamification to Blended Learning in Elementary Math Instructional Design

Ruonan Hu and Junjie Shang(✉)

Graduate School of Education, Peking University, Beijing 100871, China
rnhu@gse.pku.edu.cn, jjshang@pku.edu.cn

Abstract. Gamification in education can be supported with digital technologies, which offers the instructor the benefits of both face-to-face traditional instruction and online learning. But gamification is not a universal panacea. Applying gamification in education is not as easy as in other fields; regular practice of combining gamification elements with learning content might make students be distracted by game elements. In this study, gamified math lessons are designed and applied in an elementary school to tackle problems existed in gamification in education. Then the fun-based gamified instructional designing method and fun-based design principles have been put forward. Whether ARCS motivation strategies used in the class reflects teachers' role and design in the gamified activity. As a result, videos of the gamified math class have been analysed. From the results, it is found that differentiated teaching method by corresponding technology facilitates students' comprehension and connection between game rules and knowledge point.

Keywords: Gamification · Fun in education · Video analysis

1 Introduction

Mathematics is not only the foundation of natural science and technology science, but also plays a more and more important role in the humanities and social sciences. As an important part of human culture, math is the basic quality of modern citizens. The math achievement in elementary school greatly determines the future study of mathematics. The earlier the difficulties in mathematics learning are identified, the earlier the appropriate education intervention can be implemented. While teaching math, blended learning concept greatly helps facilitating comprehension of abstract concept in math.

'Gamification' is a much newer concept than game-based learning. It is about deploying elements, mechanics, dynamics, and frameworks derived from video-game design in a variety of contexts, rather than about using individual video games. It has great potential in education. While applying gamification in education, two critical questions emerged: What should we do when students are attracted by game related elements, and lose intrinsic motivation for knowledge? Whether cognitive or psychomotor capabilities or attitudes acquired during game play can be generalized to other nongame contexts, such as exam, life? Gamification in education equipped with

S. K. S. Cheung et al. (Eds.): ICBL 2018, LNCS 10949, pp. 93–104, 2018.
https://doi.org/10.1007/978-3-319-94505-7_7

technology, gamified design and knowledge can offer the instructor the benefits of both face-to-face traditional instruction and online learning, which means it is a type of blended learning. As a predictable trend of educational revolution, blended learning or teaching is not only combining face-to-face learning technique with online learning on the level of technology. Rather, it is the combination of elements in the treatment conditions, especially the inclusion of different kinds of learning activities, that has been proved to be effective across studies [1]. Just as Clark has cautioned against interpreting studies of instruction in different media as demonstrating an effect for a given medium, conditions may vary with different instructor and content variables. It means that in blended learning, activities instead of technology is the core of the instructional design. The above points on gamification and blended learning can be summed up as the research question: How to make gamification design and blended teaching design facilitate learning effectiveness? Tracing the origin of gamification, fun is the essence, because people play for fun. Tracing the origin of education, knowledge fun is the essence, because people learn to get fun in life and taste fun in knowledge. A well-designed gamification learning system can help learners take on meaningful roles that are fruitful for learning. To better balance between gamification and education, technologies and learning activities, this paper makes contributions to instructional design using the gamified method and pedagogic content, with cases illustrated in elementary math. Fun-based gamified instructional design principles are also summarized and combined with video analysis to guarantee keeping students' attention and motivation in learning activities.

2 Related Studies

2.1 Gamification in Education

Gamification in education has been proved to lead to greater student engagement and participation [2], higher task completion rate [3], more interest in learning [4] and better performance [5].

Gamification is normally realized in three ways: The first way is using game elements in educational design. Nah et al. [6] synthesized the literature on gamification of education and identified several game design elements that are used in education, including points, levels, badges, peer interaction and collaboration, freedom to choose difficulty level, storytelling, feedback and so on. Given these game elements, it seems that such method may fail to make students engage in for a longer time. On the contrary, video games and virtual worlds excel at engagement [7]. The second way is mixing game mechanics into education, which aims to deliver concrete challenges that are perfectly tailored to the learner's skill level. Games provide complex systems of rules for players to explore through active experimentation and discovery. One critical game design technique is to deliver concrete challenges that are perfectly tailored to the player's skill level, increasing the difficulty as the player's skill expands [8]. The third way is the use of video game in learning or instruction, which is normally referred to as digital game-based learning. There's always a wrong idea thinking that game is the way to teach, that's why the three techniques are all about using games for education. Human all are eager to play and own fun instinctively and spontaneously, which means as soon as game is used wrongly or only as a means, it will result in fatigue and frustration. It's desperately in need to create game activity rather than to use game activity, and it's in need to make game activity for fun rather than only for profitable target.

2.2 Fun

Gamers voluntarily invest countless hours in developing their problem-solving skills within the context of games mainly for the fun in game [9]. Fun is the key of game and gamification. For many years, dopamine was suggested to be the brain's "pleasure chemical". Brain mechanisms involved in fundamental pleasures (food and sexual pleasures) overlap with those for higher-order pleasures (for example, monetary, artistic, musical, altruistic, and transcendent pleasures) [10]. Pleasure is a complex psychological concept with many different sub-components which include 'liking', 'wanting', and 'learning' components [11]. Games provide many positive emotional experiences, such as optimism and pride [12]. This research uses "fun" to cover players' positive experience and emotion, including pleasure and happiness.

Based on different understanding and research, what fun is and how to get it are analyzed. Psychologists generally use the happiness index to reflect the happiness of a person: the happiness index = the realization value/expectation value. It's also a double factor function $H = F(n, m)$, where n is the self-perceptions index, and m is the evaluation index from the outside world. That means happiness of individual depends on self-expectation, actual realization state, self-perception, and evaluation from the outside world.

Existing theories about fun can be classified into pattern matching theory, natural funativity theory, fun system theory. Koster [13] argued that people are amazing pattern matching machines and fun is a process of discovering patterns. As long as we see a pattern, we usually delight in tracing it and try to grasp it until we become bored with it. When we play a game, we are analyzing patterns. Natural Funativity theory [14] divides fun into three categories: (1) Physical fun, which mainly refers to enjoyment connected with our evolutionary past, like sport, hunting, gathering, exploring, dancing. (2) Social fun, which originates from our tribe life, and is about trade, competition, cooperation and communication. (3) Mental fun, which comes from human ability to perceive and use patterns, such as puzzle game. There is another idea from XEO Design company. Based on independent contextual interviews of 60 players playing their favorite games, 4 keys to fun were put forward, includes hard fun and easy fun. Hard fun is the emotion, with people might feel relaxed, sad, proud, when players overcome obstacles, take meaningful challenges, solve puzzles. Easy fun is the sheer experiencing enjoyment, such as curiosity, surprise, fantasy, creativity. People fun is the same as social fun in Natural Funativity. Serious fun is the enjoyment from players' internal experiences, in which they enjoy changes in their internal state during and after play.

What are the elements of fun? Caillois [15] thought that competition, chance, role play, sensory change are the four main elements in game. Garneau [16] analyzed fourteen forms of fun. These fourteen forms of fun are, in no particular order: Beauty, immersion, intellectual problem solving, competition, social interaction, comedy, thrill of danger, physical activity, love, creation, power, discovery, advancement and completion, and application of an ability.

In addition, playfulness requires freedom – the freedom to experiment to fail, to explore multiple identities, to control one's own investment and experience [17]. So does fun. Enough freedom to quest and experience is funny.

3 Research Questions

The following questions were mainly researched in this study:

1. What should we do when students are attracted by game elements, lose intrinsic motivation for knowledge itself?
2. Whether cognitive or psychomotor capabilities or attitudes acquired during game play can be generalized to other nongame contexts?

4 Gamified Math Instructional Design

As for the problem of transfer, comparable cognitive processes and maximizing the overlap between the gamified activity and external tasks are desired [18]. To tackle the above questions in practice, this study was conducted in an elementary school in Beijing, China. The mathematics class of grade 3 in the elementary school was selected, and the gamified instructional design in mathematics was conducted in 4 experimental classes. People involved in the design include: research staff, teachers, mathematics teachers group, researchers on gamification of education, and students. Research staff and mathematics teacher group are involved in the design and evaluation mainly from the perspective of subject content and methods. Teachers participated in the design of the task, from the students' requirements. And gamification researchers mainly work on the gaming learning tasks and the overall pace of gaming on the control to participate in the design. The students' participation is mainly designed through the feedback of the trial. The design process generally follows the idea in Table 1, which is implemented more than twice in each class, and the class video is recorded.

The following is a list of representative design, corresponding activities and technology used.

Table 1. Gamified math activities

Learning objectives	Traditional teaching activities	Gamified teaching activities
A preliminary understanding of the fraction	Understanding the meaning of the average distribution; Understanding the meaning of fraction in real life	Spite foods from different animals and human Find fraction in the house Learning fraction on the number line: board role-playing game,3D video game

(*continued*)

Table 1. (*continued*)

Learning objectives	Traditional teaching activities	Gamified teaching activities
Making manual division with one-digit divisor and 0 in the middle of dividend	Explain the rules of vertical operation and practice then apply them	Money division game Three people go to dinner and go Dutch, it is in need to calculate how much each person spends. Who can divide the money in your hands into three group? Invented game for exercise
Know features of an angle Compare the size of different angles Draw different angles with rulers	The composition and size of the angle are explained by the adjustable ruler	Touch and guess, look whose description is right Turing a circular sticky note into angle monster Angle hand puppet play
Understand the meaning of rectangles and squares, and calculate the perimeter of rectangles and squares correctly	Feel the rectangles and squares in life and explain the concepts	Calculate perimeter of different leaves Invented game of the perimeter calculation on a hundred sheets of paper to occupy the territory
The need for a preliminary feeling of 24-h and can select timing method appropriately Know that 24 h is a day and can represent time by 24-h time reckoning	Use the clock to demonstrate calculation and conversion of 24-h and 12- h and discovery rule	The card matching game, finding the 12-h card and 24-h card according to the clock card Learning clock game in app store
Experience the process of matching and cultivate students' ability of orderly thinking	Clothes matching, diet matching, and route choose activity	Game of who can match faster for Susan Code-breaking for a music box Dress up game in app store

According to the design process mentioned above, the design process is illustrated with the example of "A preliminary understanding of the fraction" and "The 24-h time reckoning".

In the class of "A preliminary understanding of the fraction", the whole learning flow is "review the average distribution and division—cognitive conflict in representing half thing—learn about the history of fraction—learn about all parts in a fraction—dividing cookies with different shapes to compare fraction in different cookies. (see Fig. 1)—find fraction in the house (see Fig. 2)—strengthen fraction on the number line with fraction board game and video game (see Figs. 3, 4)". At the beginning of the fraction class the teacher asked students about 'how to divide the bamboo to two pandas', 'is it ok if the division is not fair?', 'how to represent half bamboo in math? How to represent half peach?'.

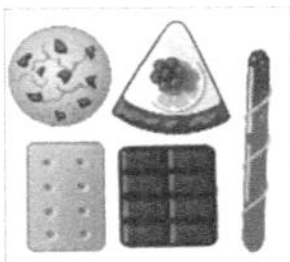

Fig. 1. Cookies with different shapes

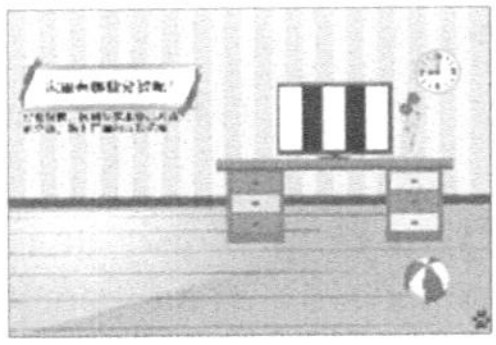

Fig. 2. Find fraction in house

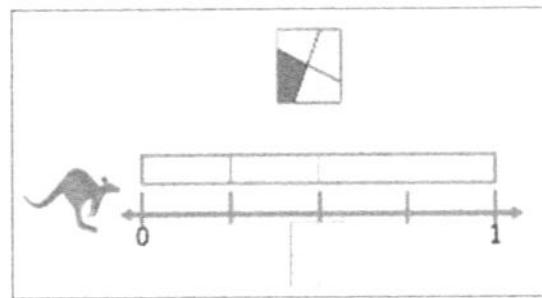

Fig. 3. Kangaroo jump board game

Fig. 4. Interface of Run fraction game

The Kangaroo jump board game is designed to help students learn fraction on the number line. It not only can build the connection between integer and fraction but also helps facilitate whether the fraction is big or small. The Run fraction game is developed to gather user data while choosing the position of the target number on the number line. On the whole, the preliminary understanding the fraction adopts both traditional learning tools and video game to strengthen the understanding of fraction.

In the class of "The 24-h time reckoning", the main point in learning includes knowing that 24 h is a day and can represent time by 24-h time reckoning, for which the gamified activities include card matching game (see Fig. 5) and the video game 'Learning to tell time' from app store. In addition, in the second lesson of "The 24-h time reckoning", how to convert between 12-h and 24-h in real-life situations is practiced using question-answer online system. The questions are divided into different levels according to the difficulty, covering business hour calculation, runtime of train calculation, etc. (Fig. 6). All the data from students, including the accuracy of every question and the rate of every option, can be gathered and seen with the teachers' account (Fig. 7). Such immediate feedback greatly helps teachers explain the difficulties.

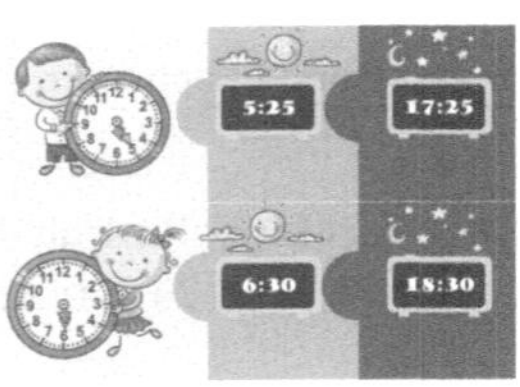

Fig. 5. Card matching game

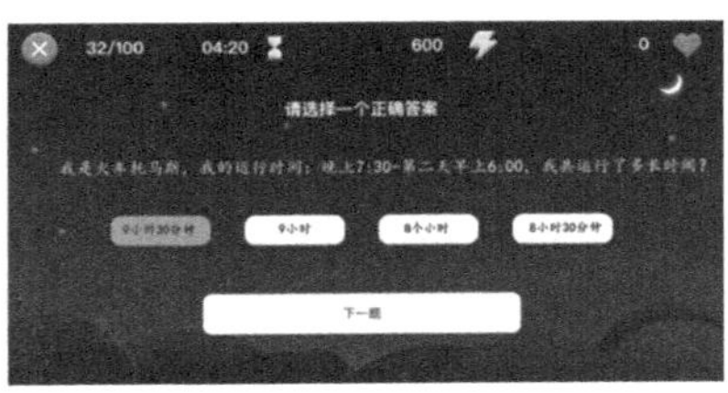

Fig. 6. Question-answer online system

Fig. 7. Students' data

5 Design Process

The design process of gamifying math lessons is summarized according to the theories and practice. As Gagne [19] stated, the system view of instructional design includes many steps, starting with the evaluation of needs and purposes, and the decision of each teaching step should be based on empirical evidence. Each step leads to a new decision, which becomes the next step. Hence with subject and student centered, the gamified instructional design process is built upon instructional design principle and idea from the spiral structure in software engineering. As Fig. 8 shown below, whether the subject content targets are satisfied and whether learning requirements are met are considered at each stage in the iteration.

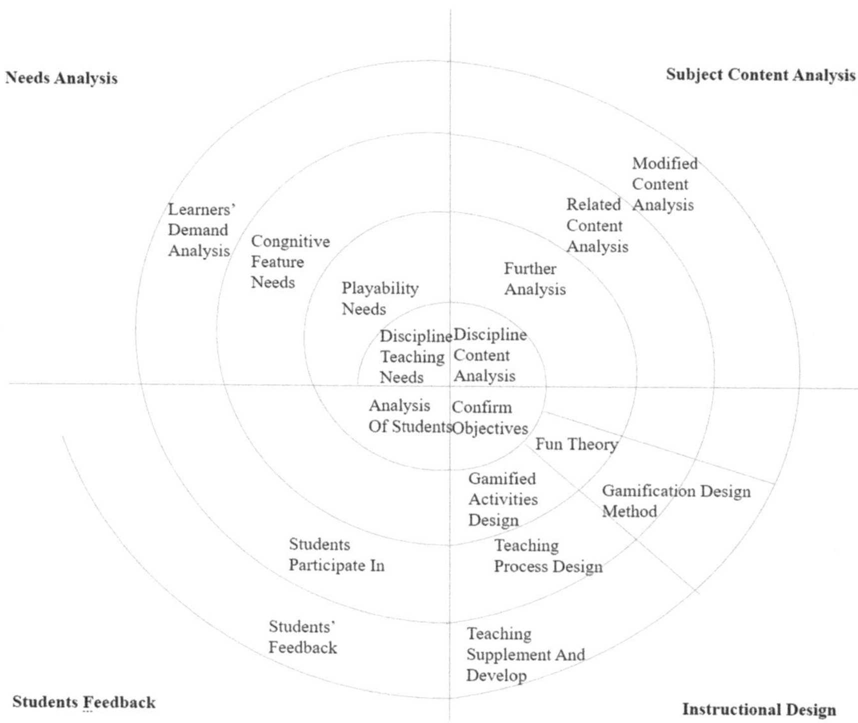

Fig. 8. Gamified math instructional design process

5.1 Needs Analysis

In the gamified instructional design process, the needs from subject-based pedagogy, cognitive development, different learning individuals, and playability are all involved. All our design must be based on exploring how people learn, and how competence is acquired. The concrete method in need analysis includes making survey among students about their likings or disliking, making surveys on all the existing games or cartoons mainly for knowing what students are in need from knowledge to play, from cognitive figure to personal demands. For example, the generalization ability of middle grade of elementary school students is at the stage of image abstraction, transition from concrete thinking to abstract thinking, then in teaching activity, the principle or knowledge should be concrete firstly and be abstracted secondly.

5.2 Subject Content Analysis

Gamified instructional design is content dominated to ensure subject-oriented approach and content can be integrated into game activities. Multilevel analysis of subject content should be made to realize the real scientific nature of game-based learning. As for math, all principles and concept ought to be understood by students. If the math concept and computing methods are taught without enough understanding to the content, without understanding how it is summarized, the knowledge students learnt is like swallow food ignoring the absorption of its nutrition. Teachers should figure out clearly what, why, and how by themselves.

5.3 Instructional Design

As an instructional designer, the first question to ask is not "What the students want to learn?" but "What will they do after they have finished learning?" As a result, learning goal determination is the precondition of designing learning tasks and the whole teaching process. Different from traditional instructional design, adapted from the ideas of blended learning, gamified instructional activity combined with effective online resource or video games are one aspect of the design process.

Gamified and funny learning activities are for students to have enough time and freedom to experience and grasp patterns in class, which is the core in all design, for it matters whether students like the class or not. Further, teaching process matters whether students learn from game. Nobody and nothing can take place of teacher. In the gamified activity, personal guidance is possible and connection between knowledge and activities is strengthened.

5.4 Students' Feedback

The learners are the co-designer in the teaching. Observation of students' participation in the gamified activity directly reflects whether they enjoy the activity, which decides whether they love learning. Their performance can show which level they are in. Then teaching can be adjusted according to feedback.

6 Design Principle

In looking at how to make fun for people, according to the reviews above, the following elements are summarized (Table 2).

Games with the above elements provide clues to design activity. When students or players experience the above actions, fun in activities could be tasted more.

Table 2. Different fun and examples

Dimension	Actions	Example
Easy fun	Exploration	Exploring new worlds
	Fantasy	Excitement and adventure
	Creativity	Wanting to figure it out Seeing what happens in the story Feeling like me and my character are one Liking the sound of cards shuffling Growing pets
Hard fun	Goals	Playing to see how good I really am
	Obstacles	Playing to beat the game
	Strategy	Having multiple objectives Requiring strategy rather than luck
People fun	Compete	Compete with others
	Cooperate	Cooperate with teammates
	Communicate	Communicate with teammates and competitors
Nature fun	Physical fun	Dance Doing Whole body participate in
	Immersion	Forget time Fully engaged
	Freedom	Free to choose Free to think Free to quest

7 Video Analysis to Evaluate the Gamified Math Class

All the gamified math lessons were applied in the elementary school, and the students gain Video (and previous film images) have been used in research for a long time, mainly in anthropology, sociology, psychology and education. Based on the classroom video observation and analysis, combining with the questionnaire survey data, the "effective teaching" program, initiated by Bill Gates and Melinda Gates Foundation, aims to research the effective teaching behavior for students' academic achievements [20]. For example, working from a cognitive perspective, Roschelle [21] pioneered the use of video to study science learning. A historically significant project was the Third International Mathematics and Science Study [22], which was the first to videotape a comparative sample of classrooms for making international comparisons of mathematics teaching. This study set a standard for international sampling.

The purpose of this study using video analysis is analysis and research on the problems in gamified math class from the perspective of the game design to improve teaching. This study uses 4 keys to fun theory as coding scheme for video analysis. At the same time, the three-level ARCS motivation structure model with 4 first-level strategies, 22 secondary strategies and 60 three-level strategies were used as the coding scheme for video analysis [23].

The video analysis was carried out using 4 classes video picked randomly. Refer to the common practice of video analysis in class, the researcher selected 30 s as time slice to make observation record. Firstly, the course video was observed and recorded, namely, the teaching process was recorded objectively as observing the video repeatedly. After completing the recording, the video is coded according to the three-level strategy of ARCS, which is completed in two steps. The first step, according to the classroom observation record, encodes the current strategy in the time period. Because a strategy can take up more than one time, the second step of the code is to combine and mark (Table 3).

Video analysis was conducted using Nvivo11, on 4 class videos of 232 min.

Table 3. Result of video analysis

Motivation strategy	Percentage	Motivation strategy	Percentage	Motivation strategy	Percentage
Contradict the learner's past experience	10.03%	R1.1 State how instruction relates to future activities	4.05%	C5.1 Independent in learning and practicing a skill	12.21%
A1.3 Introduce two equal facts, only one of which can be true	7.11%	A5.1 Create analogies and associations	5.07%	C4.2 Verbalize successes and failures	5.11%
A6.1 Participate	6.13%	A5.2 Problem solving	12.27%	S3.4 Motivating feedback	5.13%
A3.4 Break up print materials	6.05%	A3.3 Vary the medium of instruction	4.10%	S2.1 Unexpected rewards	3.03%
A3.2 Vary the format of instruction	5.07%	A4.1 Use play on words	4.07%	S3.2 Personal attention	13.33%
S1.3 Students help each other	17.41%	S3.3 Informative, helpful feedback	8.12%	S1.1 Use a newly acquired skill	7.11%
S1.2 Intrinsic pride in accomplishing difficult task	6.11%	S3.1 Verbal praise	6.10%		

From the perspective of the ARCS motivation model, teachers in gamified math lessons use a large number of motivational strategies, among which satisfaction strategy, "Allow a student who masters a task to help others who have not yet done so" is the mostly used, which is inseparable from the cooperative activity strategy used in the design. Secondly, one of most used strategies is personalized attention, which belongs to satisfaction strategies. In the process of students' independent gamified activities, teachers can have more time to focus on students' individual character, effective differentiation of counseling, which in this way, makes up for the students who only play very happily but learnt nothing. In addition, it helps to make inferior students participating in the game. Attention strategy is the most frequent strategy, teachers use the conflict strategy—introducing a fact that seems to contradict the learner's past experience. The largest proportion of all may be concluded into two reasons: the first is related with mathematical disciplines; more students need to build connection between prior knowledge and new knowledge, and realize the internalization. The second is that in the process of creating cognitive contradictions frequently between teachers and students, students' attention is attracted to achieve deep interaction with teachers on cognitive level. Our gamification classroom is not a surface activity and prosperity but should pay more attention to cognitive level students' cognitive participation.

8 Conclusion

In the process of object's self-development, through two times negation, it will show cycles with spiral periodicals. Fun-based instructional design is only one technique to combine subject tightly with gamified activity, which is to be verified and modified through more practice. But ensuring learner motivation has always been a critical aspect of good instructional design [24]. What is in need for all of us is to design gamified learning so as to help students master what they need to learn instead of participating in game. Fun in game can be applied in learning activities through different ways. In this research, the design process and design principles of gamified math instructional design has been conducted and summarized. But the research also needs to be further conducted to test and verify the design method and principles.

Acknowledgements. This study is based on the project "Studying Game-based Learning from the Perspective of Learning Sciences", which belongs to the 2017 General Projects of Educational Research for the 13th Five-year Plan and was financed by China National Social Science Foundation NO. BCA170072.

References

1. Means, B., et al.: The effectiveness of online and blended learning: a meta-analysis of the empirical literature. Teach. Coll. Rec. **115**, 134–162 (2013)
2. Barata, G., Gama, S., Jorge, J., Goncalves, D.: Engaging engineering students with gamification. In: International Conference on Games and Virtual Worlds for Serious Applications, pp. 1–8 (2013)
3. Brewer, R., et al.: Using gamification to motivate children to complete empirical studies in lab environments, pp. 388–391 (2013)
4. Kumar, B.: Gamification in education - learn computer programming with fun. Int. J. Comput. Distrib. Syst. **2**(1), 69–78 (2012)
5. O'Donovan, S., Gain, J., Marais, P.: A case study in the gamification of a university-level games development course. In: Proceedings Saicsit, pp. 242–251 (2013)

6. Nah, F.F.-H., Zeng, Q., Telaprolu, V.R., Ayyappa, A.P., Eschenbrenner, B.: Gamification of education: a review of literature. In: Nah, F.F.-H. (ed.) HCIB 2014. LNCS, vol. 8527, pp. 401–409. Springer, Cham (2014). https://doi.org/10.1007/978-3-319-07293-7_39
7. McGonigal, J.: Reality is Broken: Why Games Make Us Better and How They Can Change the World. Penguin Press, New York (2011)
8. Lee, J.J., Hammer, J.: Gamification in education: what, how, why bother? Acad. Exch. Q. **15**, 1–5 (2011)
9. Koray, O., et al.: Enhancing problem-solving skills of pre-service elementary school teachers through problem-based learning. Asia-Pacific Forum Sci. Learn. Teach. **9**, 1–18 (2008)
10. Kringelbach, M.L.: The hedonic brain: a functional neuroanatomy of human pleasure. In: Kringelbach, M.L., Berridge, K.C. (eds.) Pleasures of the Brain, pp. 202–221. Oxford University Press, New York (2010)
11. Berridge, K., Kringelbach, M.: Pleasure systems in the brain. Neuron **86**, 646 (2015)
12. Mcgonigal, J.: Reality Is Broken: Why Games Make Us Better and How They Can Change the World. Penguin (Non-Classics) (2011)
13. Koster, R.: A Theory of Fun for Game Design. Paraglyph Press, Scottsdale (2004)
14. AWHF Yet: 2.1 Understanding Fun-The Theory of Natural Funativi-ty.cw.metu.edu.tr
15. Caillois, R., Barash, M.: Man, Play and Games. Thames and Hudson, London (2001)
16. Fourteen forms of fun. http://www.gamasutra.com/view/feature/227531/fourteen_forms_of_fun.php
17. Klopfer, E., Osterweil, S., Salen, K.: Moving learning games forward. HAL-SHS (2009)
18. Tobias, S., Fletcher, J.D., Wind, A.P.: Game-based learning. In: Spector, J., Merrill, M., Elen, J., Bishop, M. (eds.) Handbook of Research on Educational Communications and Technology, pp. 485–503. Springer, New York (2014). https://doi.org/10.1007/978-1-4614-3185-5_38
19. Gagné, R.M., Briggs, L.J., Wager, W.W.: Principles of Instructional Design. Harcourt Brace Jovanovich College Publishers, Fort Worth (1992)
20. Foundation, B., Gates, M.: Working with Teachers to Develop Fair and Reliable Measures of Effective Teaching. MET Project. Bill & Melinda Gates Foundation, p. 16 (2010)
21. Roschelle, J.: Learning by collaborating: Convergent conceptual change. J. Learn. Sci. **2**(3), 235–276 (1992)
22. Stigler, J.W., et al.: The TIMSS videotape classroom study: methods and findings from an exploratory research project on eighth-grade mathematics instruction in Germany, Japan, and the United States. A Research and Development Report. Education Statistics Quarterly, p. 180 (1999)
23. Keller, J.M.: Development and use of the ARCS model of instructional design. J. Instr. Dev. **10**, 2–10 (1987)
24. Martin, B.L., Reigeluth, C.M.: Affective education and the affective do-main: implications for instructional-design theories and models. Open Educ. Res. **11**, 86 (2004)

Developing Digital Campus by Application-Driven: Experience and Challenges in Mainland China

Yu Jiang[1(✉)], Lizhen Jiao[2], and Lingyu Xu[3]

[1] National Center for Educational Technology, Beijing 10031, China
jiangy@moe.edu.cn
[2] Tsinghua University, Beijing 10084, China
[3] Beijing University of Posts and Telecommunications, Beijing 100876, China

Abstract. "Digital campus" is an inevitable school pattern of its development in the information age. Under the guidance of the state and localities, some experiences have been gained in the promotion of school informatization with application-driven as the basic principle or working principle. In the present study, digital campus in the first batch of information pilot units of the Ministry of Education was taken as representatives, and their practice was analyzed to understand the nature of application-driven. Meanwhile, this paper further introduced the typical experience of digital campus construction and application driven by three forces—problem-driven, demand-driven and idea-driven. These experiences can provide references for schools in different development stages and different levels of development. Furthermore, the article analyzed issues of the aforementioned different types of power-driven, and proposed suggestions such as highlight the development of "human" ability, give full play to the advantages of "cloud computing", as well as emphasize network security and localization management and services.

Keywords: Digital campus · Application-driven · Education informatization

"Digital campus" is an inevitable product of school informationization in information age. Since the emergence of the digital campus in 2000, it is still the main theme of the promotion of information environment in primary education school in China. With the implementation of the "three connections and two platforms" project, school informatization condition has greatly raised, whereas 94% primary and secondary schools have had access to the Internet. The concept of "application-driven" is an important policy of the national informatization, which also reflected in the development and change of "digital campus". Since the 12th Five-Year Plan, the state and localities have carried out relevant pilot projects of digital campus construction. Under the guidance of the application-driven policy, schools has begun a series of successful explorations according to its specific conditions. The process has yielded a fruitful experience in terms of school information construction and its application, however, their still remains a certain gap with the requirements of "deepening the application".

S. K. S. Cheung et al. (Eds.): ICBL 2018, LNCS 10949, pp. 105–114, 2018.
https://doi.org/10.1007/978-3-319-94505-7_8

1 Concept of Digital Campus

It is generally believed that the concept of "digital Campus" originated from the "e-campus" project proposed by the MIT in the 1970s. If considering the concept of "digital earth", the digital campus should be regarded as a virtual system closely related to network, virtual reality technology. Academic published articles usually add the word "construction" beside digital campus, which means the construction of the digital campus, or a part of a virtual system of building digital campus. Around 2000, a number of universities set up independent campus network. while with the increasing information and application of the school internet, IT-supported departments urgently requires a unified management and unified user authentication mechanism to secure the network covering the whole school [1]. On the basis of this, the hierarchical and overall view was adopted in planning and implementing school's information construction, and finally realize an overall digitalization in terms of the environment, resource and activity [2]. It has become one of the important trends of education reform in the world to use various computer technologies to create an internet-based virtual campus parallel to the real campus, and rely on various technical tools and means to promote the all-round reform of universities. while in the field of basic education, it is generally believed that the purpose of the construction of digital campuses in primary and secondary schools is to use information to expand the function of education, teaching and education management. Meanwhile, expand the real digital campus space to improve the quality of education and teaching efficiency. Compared with the concept of digital campus in colleges and universities, the concept of digital campus in primary and secondary schools emphasizes more on the learning space. In fact, although the concept of space is practical, but more complex, it is more complicated and not a strict academic definition. There are obvious differences in the construction of digital campus among primary and secondary schools and colleges and universities, such as different network infrastructure, information level of the service object, scale of service objects, insufficient support for teaching and learning. However, it still lacks of systematic and in-depth research. Therefore, the digital campus construction in the basic education stage has always been a problem that puzzles the development of primary and secondary schools.

On the construction of digital campus of primary and secondary schools, Huang, R.H. et al. put forward the fourth-generation concept of digital campus construction in primary and secondary schools from the perspective of learning environmental change. The first generation of digital campus has basic information service, but the system cannot interconnect; the second generation digital campus has more resources and business system, which has certain support to education, teaching, research, management and service. The third generation of digital campus has rich digital resources, in which application system can be integrated, as well as related services. Support software facilities are open and extensible, and can effectively support teaching and learning [3]; The fourth generation of digital campus refers to the wisdom campus, it can effectively support the teaching and learning, enrich the school campus culture, expand dimensions of space and time and take service oriented as the basic concept to build a business process, resource sharing, intelligent flexible education teaching environment. This is based on the dimensions of the school's information-based environment construction, integration on different levels of interconnection and interoperability, and the division of the effects of education and teaching service support services. The division of Huang is easy to operate, which has a wide influence on the digital campus construction of elementary and secondary schools in China, the primary and secondary schools can understand their four stages according to the characteristics of the school information environment. The higher the stage, the better the information environment. Based on the requirement of school organizational change in the information age, Gao, T.G., etc. thought the core purpose of digital campus construction is to establish an education form that is compatible with the information society. The main body of change in the digital campus construction is the school-cell education system. The transformation of school organization is the core of the digital campus construction [4]. Whether it is the environment of digital campus construction or the organizational change view of digital campus construction, they all emphasize that the construction of digital campus is the process of continuous development of technology. The implementation of digital campus construction is school, and the target audiences are school teachers and students.

In conclusion, the construction of digital campus originates from the elements of the real campus (such as environment, resources, activities, etc.) digitalization, in order to meet the needs of further school informatization. It has experienced the construction of the technology platform to support school education, the development of complementary virtual reality learning space, and the overall improvement of the school's information environment. The goal and connotation of its construction are also Growing. National Education Medium and Long-term education Reform and Development Plan Outline (2011–2020) pointed out that "promoting the construction of digital campus" is the first time that our country has put forward the concept of digital campus in official documents. Subsequently, the "network school pass" project has greatly promoted the construction of the digital campus of primary and second schools across the country. "Digital campus" has become the key content of school information construction and application.

2 "Application-Driven" is the Basic Principle for Digital Campus Construction in Primary and Secondary Schools in China

At the national education informatization conference in 2017, education deputy minister DU ZY pointed out that, China's education informatization has achieved satisfying results during the 12th five-year plan period. As one of the two basic principles, "application-driven" is considered as useful experience in the promotion of informatization with Chinese characteristics. "Digital campus is not just a technology system, it's… in the innovation service application, we can better integrate people, technology, practice and value in education activities." [5]. Therefore, "application" itself is also an important content of digital campus, and its construction is for better application of services. Application-driven requirements are based on the objectives of education teaching and the needs of learners. To implement education informatization with the goal of promoting the application of information technology in education and teaching, and changing teaching methods and learning methods. Finally, to change the awkward situation of heavy construction and light application, and guide schools to promote construction with application.

What exactly is "application-driven"? The literal meaning of "drive" is "to drive action" or "to exert an external force to make it move forward". The meaning of "application-driven" is to drive the input of informatization with the school education and the practical application in the reform and development. Application is the external force driving the action, and the main body is education workers and students. The author believes the term includes at least three levels of meaning. First, the problems encountered in the reform and development of education in the school of informatization, and the application in the main battlefield of teaching and learning. This reflects society awareness of information technology in education has improved. Informatization is not a decoration, not a face project. On the contrary, it can play a role in the main battlefield of teaching and learning. It will only be persuasive to seize the application of solving real-life teaching and learning problems, in other words, applications must face the core issues and key aspects of teaching. Second, informatization should meet the requirements of promoting school education quality and the talent training. Meanwhile, to play a role in the daily teaching activity of teachers and students, as well as improve the existing teaching mode and method. Third, pay attention to innovation. Informatization environment is the prerequisite of the application, but application innovation should not solely depends on the advanced basic environment. The continuous development of technology can provide new momentum for the application, the development of education will also put forward new requirements for application. Therefore, modern education idea must be implemented to facilitate more personalized learning, and allow students to achieve comprehensive and personalized development. In this way, we can make alive some education concept which can not be realized in traditional environment.

Under the influence of the "application-driven" policy, and several major projects implemented by national organizations and the improvement of school informatization capabilities, there have been unprecedented calls for "application". For example in the first batch of education informationization pilot projects of the ministry of education, the pilot work is required to follow the principle of "demand oriented, application focused", and oriented by practical needs… Through the innovative application of information technology in education teaching, education management and service, we should give full play to the education informationization in solving various levels of actual problems, especially the hot difficult problems that people concerned about [6]. In the central electronic education project "the scheme of the digital campus construction", requirement of the "application innovation" is also put forward, which emphasizes applications that can improve students' information literacy, principal leadership and teachers' professional development. To promote the normal application and application innovation, so as to provide more experience for application in teaching and learning under the network environment. In these leading projects, there is no emphasis on environment construction of informatization, but highlight the informatization application in daily teaching, key link and large-scale, with appropriate innovation to promote the informationization achievements in assisting of education reform.

3 Typical Case Analysis of Application-Driven Digital Campus

In 2012, the ministry of education implemented the education information pilot project, and established 351 pilot units in primary and secondary schools. Through the analysis of the establishment of the pilot work, this article found that 47 schools chose digital campus or digital campus as the main content, including 19 primary schools, 28 secondary schools accounting for 13.3% of the total, and is the highest proportion in the pilot content classification. "digital green campus", "explore mechanism" are the keywords.

Recently, the ministry of education organized the acceptance work for the first batch of pilot units. At the same time, it also carried out the "Information Technology and Depth Fusion Demonstration Training" program. A number of application-driven digital campuses are typically highlighted in the two projects. Through the analysis of the typical school of digital campus construction or application, application-driven in primary and middle schools is mainly manifested in the following aspects:

Problem-Driven. In the process of school education development, some urgently needed solving practical problems are accumulated due to the geographical position, students foundation, surrounding social factors and school history. Therefore, digital campus construction was adopted in some schools in order to solve these problems. These problems is mainly divided into several categories: (1) Multi-campus management brings work pressure and burden to managers. It is difficult for managers to use traditional means to coordinate and manage collaboration in different school districts. Therefore, a management platform is built to assist managers in remote collaborative work, and resources of the main campus school are used to use information technology platforms. Sharing to the branch campus, the video conference system is the core technical support condition. (2) the averagely old teachers age, professional misappropriation, high teacher mobility, and the overall low level are all factors in the difficult guarantee of the teaching quality. In some rural areas, students are mainly outsourced. Schools take advantage of informatization to improve teaching quality and consider it as the only breakthrough when other factors are difficult to change in a short term. (3) the pressure of teachers' teaching management caused by large class sizes and the complexity of students, which requires the use of information technology to help teachers conduct student management, home-school communication, and reduce teacher workload.

Demand-Driven. The application of this type to drive digital campus is not to deal with the current problems to be solved, but to combine the improvement of the school environment and various tasks of school education, teaching and management. The benefits of digital campus work rely on the education and management of information technology, in which the application value is reflected. The requirements of this type of drive and the specific technical support usually included the following categories:

(1) improve management efficiency and optimize management style. (2) explore certain teaching modes to analyze the needs of technical and personnel capabilities.

Idea-Driven. In recent years, learning space change became the hot spot in the transformation of development in the information age. In particular, with the rising concept of the "future school", the demand for upgrading learning space such as traditional classroom, has become increasingly high. In the informatization environment construction, some schools do not have obvious problem-solving or application demand orientations. Instead, they are based on the trend judgement of the principal and other management teams under the reform and development of education in the information age. Therefore, this can be called concept-driven. It mainly displays in the following aspects: (1) the integration development of the existing school-running concept with the digital campus development. (2) the initial exploration of the concept of modern educational space, the transformation and upgrading of the existing classroom environment. (3) creation of a future learning space with driven-learning approaches. Classroom layout is designed according to different needs of the course study to better service students' inquiry learning and collaborative learning.

The three "application-driven" reflect three important driving force of digital campus construction. "Problem-driven" digital campus aims to solve the problem of current education teaching and shows a clear response orientation. The principal has clear expectations for digital campus, hoping to obtain visible and satisfactory achievements from the application of information technology. This embodies the "practical" value of digital campus. Schools that are at a comparative disadvantage in traditional education systems tend to be problem-driven. Seeing from the effect point of view, as long appropriate technical solutions are adopted, the problems can hopefully resolved gradually. "Demand-driven" focus on the heart. The digital campus update is based on school management and personnel training requirements. It is the development path chosen by the principal after comprehensive evaluation the effectiveness of information technology. The path is a kind of development drive that holds a leading role in the information age, which can be alternative by other paths. Schools with comparative advantage in traditional education systems tend to be demand-driven. "Idea driven" type focuses on the future. The principal acknowledges the revolutionary impact of technology on education, and believes that there have been major changes in education, talent, and social needs in the information age. They think about the relationship between space, curriculum, teaching and environment from the perspective of "change" and "innovation". Their digital campus project may not be effective in the short term, however, it is an important attempt and exploration of future schools. This type of driving mainly occurs in some new schools. These three driving forces initially reflected the characteristics of education informatization from 1.0 to 2.0. Vice Minister Du Zhanyuan proposed education informatization 2.0. Education informationization 1.0 is the introduction of external variables, while 2.0 is to transform these exogenous variables into endogenous variables, starting slowly from exogenous to internal which involves problems solving, self-requirements and future orientation.

Although these three drivers have relatively applicable school type with different starting point, they all have the following common points. First, it starts from the school standard and reflects school's main body position in the digital campus.

Gao et al. [4]. pointed out that school should be clarified as the real main body in the construction of digital campus, while other organizations and personnel are the leaders, participants, and service providers of this changes. Digital campus should not chase after technology, but follows the heart. It is a judgment made by the principal and his team based on the reality and future trend. Second, they fully embody the "technology is for my own use" point of view, and the concept that technology should serve the development of education. Technology development is very fast. In the field of education, not advanced technology can get very good application. The advancement of technology should not regarded as a criteria in judging a school's informationization work. Therefore, these schools are not selected because of their more advanced technology, but that benefits of "application". Third, the collective wisdom of principals and the leading groups guided by the school-running concept play an important role. The three application-oriented drive types do not cost huge amounts of money to purchase large numbers of hardware devices in the short term. Sustained, large-scale applications require more strategies and methods, in which the leadership and conduct of principal play a critical role.

Significant achievements have been made in the application-driven digital campus upgrade project. As *The development into the fast lane: elementary education teaching report in 2016* pointed out, the nation-wide active application of information technology in primary and secondary schools have greatly deepened the application of information technology. The scope has gradually evolved from the individualized pilot projects in a few schools, to the generalized application among primary and secondary schools. Meanwhile, the nationwide state of "informal use, regular use, and universal use" informatization-based teaching has taken shape [7]. Behind the emergence of this new normality is the continuous improvement of the school network condition, the provision of diversified education resources, the widespread use of multiple teaching terminals, and the improvement of various teaching systems. Through planning and the issuance of relevant documents, the state adheres to the "application-driven" basic house exhibitions. This has been widely accepted by schools, and also become the consensus of education workers to promote the development of teaching reform through the application of education informatization. And it will continue to play a vital role in the next phase of the informatization.

4 Current Issues Existing in the Construction of Application-Driven Digital Campus

Deepen the application is one of the four working principles of the "13th Five-year Plan" education informatization. It requires to promote environment construction and support the core business through application, around the target to carry out the training and performance evaluation, carry out training and performance evaluations around the application goals, and rely on education information to speed up the construction of learner-centered teaching and learning methods. The developed countries are increasingly emphasizing the application as the driving force to effectively promote the construction level of education informatization. However, at present the school informatization work still has certain gap with this requirement, and the revolutionary impacts of education reform and information technology has not yet been completely released. In terms of digital campus, its main problems lie in:

First, the common phenomenon that school business systems cannot communicate with each other. In order to meet the requirements of subject teaching, school's introduction of software platform lacks a unified plan. Meanwhile, the market does not yet have a multi-disciplinary application resource provision platform that integrates students' basic data. Consequently, the business systems within school are not connected to each other. The construction of teaching application system currently aims to build a teaching-centered information system, to help students' learning as well as promote the construction and application of students' independent, cooperative and inquiry learning information system. This still remains a weak link in primary and second schools [7].

Second, school resources cannot be shared and circulated. This can not well adapted to the needs for greater sharing of high-quality education resources, and for further innovation in school teaching and learning methods. As mentioned earlier, the main body of digital campus is school, however, with too much emphasis on the min body status of school will inevitably limit the construction vision. The resources can provide services for other schools, what's worse, some schools even deliberately use technology to increase barriers against other schools to avoid sharing of quality resources. The widespread of repeated resources and redundant storage generated a large amount of waste data. Therefore, there is an increased conflict between calls for higher resource sharing and the increasingly high data barriers.

Third, the increasingly high demand for multi-data processing capabilities and its contradiction with the ability of school's technical staff in supporting services. The increasingly wide application of information technology has shifted from the "information age" to "data age". And the ability for data collection, storage, analysis and processing has become increasingly demanding. Whatever the type of application, it needs to exert further value and the use of accumulated data is the key point. However, there is a lack of professionals in data management, and teachers' data reading ability is uneven, all these factors restrict the further improve the school information.

Four, the external motivation of teachers and students' application of information technology urgently needs to shift to internal motivation. The decisive influence of school principal is not institutionalized. The era of Education informationization 2.0 has transformed from exogenous forces to endogenous forces, which requires teachers to further change their ideas from "requested to use" to "want to use". In addition, there is a risk of over-reliance on the principal's personal digital campus work. It is necessary need to institutionalize, normalize, and legalize the informationization work, and school informatization work is not affected by personnel changes.

The future school is a research hotspot in the current education field. It advocates the re-design of schools, and explores the structural changes of schools under the background of "Internet plus" through the integration of space, curriculum and technology [8]. To achieve this kind of structural change, school must experience the two phases of environmental reconstruction and learning method reform. In the "application-driven" application of digital campus, the transformation of learning methods has begun to take shape, the basic environment has improved, and the real-world curriculum system for students has begun to show results. However, the revolution of learning space has not been changed, and the boundary of the classroom has not yet been broken, which in turn limit further changes of learning style. Students ubiquitous learning did not get effective technical support and learning resources support. Standardized, homogeneous class teaching is still the mainstream, teaching order still cling to tradition. These become limitations of modern learning in digital campus, whereas the hymns of factory-trained model of the industrial era are still sang in the "technology" pervasive environment.

5 Recommendations on Further Improvement of Digital Campus

Application-driven digital campus should further emphasize the developing "human" ability. The ultimate goal of school informatization is to promote the development of people and the construction of application-driven digital campus. Meanwhile, to promote the normalized application of information technology in education teaching as well as mainstream business. Support the optimization and reconstruction of school teaching, management and service process, and develop teacher and students' information literacy in the process of optimization and reconstruction. Specifically speaking, particular attention should be paid to students' information-based learning ability, teachers' information-based teaching capabilities, management personnel's information management abilities, and technical staff's information service capabilities. To improve the ability in the in-depth application of information technology, and the improved application subject can further push the application into various aspects.

Fully rely on the "cloud computing" supported services to make teachers and students more focused on core business. With the wide application of cloud computing, especially the continuous improvement of the national "three links and two platform" project, it can support more informationization primary and middle schools from a single campus construction to the cloud technology supported "end". Technological resources provided by national can be regarded as the "cloud", whereas schools serves as the "end". The main focus is to create the road between "cloud" and "end", so that the "end" can fully apply the resources, technology and service provided by the "cloud". Meanwhile, the "end" itself can better focus on its own core business, and focus on developing the information technology application ability of the entire school teachers and students. On the other hand, within the "cloud" supported digital campus, the high-quality education resources in the "end" can be widely shared by means of "cloud".

Pay more attention to the network security. Data will be the most important asset in the "Data Age", however, the network security in the educational field is a real a concern. with the popularization of school data, data management and learning system, the complexity of internet attacks including school-targeted blackmails also grows. Internet security has been a growing concern. The security of digital campus includes management security, application security and environmental security, and its core is data security. In addition, to help establish students' data security awareness and protect their data privacy, and apply students' data for conventions with schools, parents, and the third party software companies. For example, in the *American*

Education Technology Planning 2017, it put forward the data's "responsible use policy". The purpose is to reach an agreement between parents, students and schools, to stipulate rules that govern responsible use as well as the consequences of inappropriate use. At the same time, students are educated to become responsible citizens during the school period.

Pay more attention to network localization management. With the normalized development of school information technology application, the primary factors influencing the application among teachers and students is school network and learning terminals. Therefore, localization of network management and service becomes more important. Localized network management and the service content mainly includes: the operation and maintenance of the school's Internet access, teachers and students' use of terminal (including built-in terminal) network access support, understanding and management of student data, protection of teachers and students' data security, assistance in helping solve students' connection problems at home. In short, the content of the localization management and service has changed from auxiliary role on teachers' application of information technology resources to provide network support and security management for the increasing applications between teachers and students, thus creating a safe, stable and reliable network environment for applications in digital campus.

References

1. Peihua, S., Jiang, D.X.: Digital campus, Inf. Syst. Eng, 8, 10 (2002)
2. Zhao, G.D.: University digital campus and digital learning documentary research, pp. 19–22. Peking University press, Beijing (2012)
3. Huang, R.H.: The content and strategic focus in constructing of Digital campus of primary and secondary schools. J. Beijing Educ. **8**, 60–61 (2009). (General Education Edition)
4. Gao, T., Wang, R.: From the angle of change theory in construction of digital campus in basic education. China Educ. Technol. **12**, 24–27 (2012)
5. Yu, S.: Transformation and breakthrough of digital campus and its change trends. Prim. Second. School Manag. **5**, 4–9 (2015)
6. The notice of Implementing pilot of education informatization of the ministry of education 2012, No. 4 (taught), on 13 January 2012
7. Access to the development fast lane – 2016 The Report of educational information in elementary and secondary education. East China Normal University Press, Shanghai (2017)
8. Peijie, C.: The path of the future school – the position of "Internet + education" and sustainable development. Educ. Res. **10**, 46–51 (2016)

College Students' Acceptance and Willingness Towards Blended Learning Experience

Jinrui Dai(✉) and Yushun Li(✉)

Faculty of Education, School of Education Technology, Beijing Normal University, No. 19, XinJieKouWai St, 100875 HaiDian District, Beijing, People's Republic of China
jreene@163.com, lyshun@bnu.edu.cn

Abstract. Blended learning, which spreads the edges of online learning to off-line service, has combined the advantages of face-to-face learning and pure online learning and brought vigor to E-learning. The paper is based on the findings of an investigation on college students' willingness to provide and use off-line functions of an online learning platform. The difference in users are expected to be revealed for offering better category of resources and adaptive functions. To get a clear idea of the influence factors of blended learning and help the design of an individualized online learning platform, the paper will give some analysis about the possibilities and feasibility of blended functions of the platform.

Based on the results of descriptive analysis, Levene test, single factor ANOVA and the crosstab chi-square test, differences appearing in gender and grade need attaching importance to and taking care of. It is proved that learners in universities are willing and competent to take the instructional role to help each other in E-learning. As for how to achieve the blended process in E-learning in higher education, suggestions are offered as to build a location based system(LBS) and an inner-campus communication society on the learning platform. Knowing and accepting the difference, the design of the platform is also optimized to assist learners as well as to improve blended learning experience in the process.

Keywords: Blended learning · Online learning platform · Willingness
Higher education

1 Introduction

1.1 Background of the Study

According to the 40th Statistics Report for China Internet Development revealed on August the 4th from China Internet Network Information Center(CNNIC), up to June 2017, there are 751 million Internet users in China, occupying nearly 54.3% of Chinese population [1]. With the rapid development of E-commerce as well as E-learning, the way of learning has been changed a lot in China.

Beginning with Massachusetts Institute of Technology's storm in Open Educational Resources (OER), sharing of open, free and high-quality academic resources have been spread out across the country. Online courses form the three main course providers,

S. K. S. Cheung et al. (Eds.): ICBL 2018, LNCS 10949, pp. 115–125, 2018.
https://doi.org/10.1007/978-3-319-94505-7_9

namely Coursera, Udacity, and edX, have provided learners with easy access to resources in technology, language, culture and intellectual property.

As all these platforms provide a variety of resources online, students using them can handle their learning in their own pace so that individualized learning is realized. However, problems also come as misconception and difficulties that cannot be solved by learners themselves bother a lot. Lack of supervision in the process of learning results in low lesson-complete rate. Being faced with the situation, instructors in the online courses are playing a significant role in guiding students to learn. Thus, blended learning has taken the place of pure online courses in most cases naturally.

1.2 Aims of the Study

Facing the transition from being forced to learn to self-learning, college students always feel confused and uncomfortable. In common cases, the discomfort cannot be erased by themselves in a short time easily. Added up with the challenge of brand new way of learning, individualized learning can be just an idea in the air. As a result, enhancing students' willingness and self- consciousness to learn become an important issue when running a learning platform.

When it comes to individualized learning, what the difference is between learners is the key problem that should be figured out. In elementary education, the set of curriculum is carefully designed by experts in each discipline. At the same time, concepts like interdisciplinary knowledge and hierarchical teaching are the things to reform in elementary education while these challenges are what should be taken into account in courses for learners in universities.

Based on the design of an online learning platform, the research is aiming to make it clear how to provide an effective and efficient way to help learners. Empirical research will be used with questionnaires handed out to college students through the Internet to collect relevant data. From the result of the analysis, it is expected to get some ideas for learning platform design and how blended learning should function in higher education.

2 Literature Review

Blended learning is an education program that combines online digital media with traditional classroom methods [2]. With some element of student control over time, place, path, or pace, it requires the physical presence of both teacher and student [3]. Although a lack of consensus on a definition of blended learning has led to difficulties in research on its effectiveness in the classroom [4], the introduction of blended learning does help students to learn [5]. It is also confirmed that Blended learning methods can also result in high levels of student achievement compared with face-to-face learning and pure online learning [6].

At present, it is found that blended learning would affect students' motivation and interest for learning. Proponents of blended learning argue that incorporating the asynchronous Internet communication technology into higher education courses serves to facilitate a simultaneous independent and collaborative learning experience [7].

This incorporation is a major contributor to student satisfaction and success in such courses. The presence of online communication society has been found to improve student attitudes towards learning [8].

With the effect of blended learning confirmed, efforts have been put on how to attract learners and improve their learning experience. Seeing from the aspects of learners' experience, student satisfaction in blended learning are analyzed to figure out how to improve current courses [9, 10]. The influence of individual factors like learning styles and student perceptions of the use of interactive online tutorials have been checked systematically [11, 12].

The acceptance of a newly designed thing is usually measured under the framework like technology acceptance model (TAM) and its revised versions [13]. Taken marketing factors into consideration, Innovation Diffusion Theory (IDT) has focus the popularization of the creative new function [14]. In our cases, blended learning experience has brought the off-line function on spot. Thus, the willingness of college students to the new items need to be checked.

Back to the situation when designing an online learning platform, the willingness of learners towards specific functions like blended learning experience should be investigated. As acceptance of online learning is researched and taken care of [15], the personalized functions of the platform that transform students' way of learning into blended learning should be taken into consideration as well. In most cases, college students pick their lessons just follow their heart as it is assumed that they have the ability to handle most courses. Therefore, the Instructional Factors may be ignored. Take individual differences and lack of instructions into consideration, our platform is designed to provide opportunities for learners to help each other. The willingness of users to the function need to be checked.

When it comes to individualized learning, the resources in the courses nowadays are packed in fixed set. Without careful categorized resources, it is impossible to achieve personalized learning. So the differences between gender and grade of college students is what the research aim to find out.

3 Methodology

3.1 Research Design

Based on the findings in the literature review, the current study adopted the empirical methodology to address the research questions. As to data collection, a questionnaire on learners' willingness and acceptance towards using learning platforms is designed to check what is the individual difference like and how the learning system functions.

As participants in online learning programs are used to the way of learning without face-to-face interactions, the effects of adding blended learning activities to their study need to be confirmed. Specifically, the research aims to make it clear whether the off-line service designed in our platform is accepted by the target users. As a result, options on college students' acceptance and willingness towards blended learning experience are designed in the questionnaire to analyze the effects and feasibility of blended learning.

The questionnaire is handed out to college students through the Internet and collected by sojump. On the basis of reliability analysis, the result will be given from two aspects after further descriptive analysis, single factor ANOVA and the crosstab chi-square test. One is the whether the differences exist will affect customer behavior and the outcome of our learning. Another is the suggestions on the platform design for blending learning.

The research questions can be listed in following research hypotheses:

H1. College students' grade will positively affect willingness of providing off-line service.
H2. There is a significant difference between male and female in their attitudes towards college students' credit.
H3. There is a significant difference between male and female in their attitudes towards online learning platforms' using their credit reports.

3.2 Data Collection

The total number of participants of this questionnaire is 430. With 430 people covered, the response rate for the questionnaire was 100%. The effective return-ratio was higher than 98.83% as 425 of the questionnaires are valid. All the 425 respondents are college students, in which 152 are boys and 273 are girls, accounting for 35.76% and 64.24% respectively. The grade distribution of the respondents is shown in the Table 1.

Table 1. The grade distribution of the respondents

Options	Sum	Percentage
Freshman	68	16%
Sophomore	99	23.29%
Junior	191	44.94%
Senior	54	12.71%
Postgraduate	13	3.06%
Valid questionnaires	425	

According to the statistics, the questionnaire is mainly issued to junior students. And we are trying to know about their willingness to experience blended learning. To improve the customer experience of online learning platforms, the result of the survey is used to explore how individuals differ from each other. By knowing and attracting college students, we get to know about the obstacles that may exist in changing the traditional way of learning at the same time.

On the one hand, for designers, the following statistics can help understand the demand of learners. On the other hand, for college students, the research will help you know about the blended functions of the platform as well as why and how it is designed to be so.

3.3 Data Analysis

As what has been mentioned in research design, options on college students' acceptance and willingness towards blended learning experience in the questionnaire are focus on participants' willingness and acceptance towards the added blended learning activities. As a campus learning community online, the blended function of our platform means students can make appointment with their tutors online and learn from them both online and offline. The existing of off-line service makes our learning platform distinct from traditional MOOC courses. At the same time, the acceptance of the service should be checked from both the providers and the users.

In result, subjective questions are listed in the questionnaire to seek the willingness of college students towards the off-line service. As the off-line service is not provided for free, the payment function is in need to guarantee students' convenience while learning. However, college students' willingness to use payment function need to be activated according to the market research carried out earlier. According to the current situation, attempts have been made in the research to set a location based learning system so that students in the same school can help each other in study and enjoy the safer experience from their peers. Furthermore, a credit report is also offered for users of off-line service for better learning experience.

Before the checking of college students' acceptance and willingness towards the service mentioned, subjective questions in the questionnaire are selected to test its reliability in order to confirm the accuracy of the data before further statistical analysis. The result of the corresponding questions is shown in Table 2.

Table 2. The result of the subjective questions

Options	Very unwilling	Unwilling	Uncertain	Willing	Very willing
Willingness of using off-line service	20(4.71%)	29(6.82%)	134(31.53%)	117(27.53%)	125(29.41%)
Willingness of providing off-line service	16(3.76%)	28(6.59%)	127(29.88%)	137(32.24%)	117(27.53%)
Willingness of using credit report	14(3.29%)	20(4.71%)	102(24.00%)	148(34.82%)	141(33.18%)
Willingness of authorizing credit report	29(8.82%)	40(9.41%)	117(27.53%)	135(31.76%)	104(24.47%)

For the reason that only the data of the subjective questions can be tested by Cronbach α reliability coefficient for reliability analysis, we can calculate alpha for the subjective questions mentioned above first (Table 3).

Table 3. Reliability statistics

Cronbach's Alpha	Cronbach's Alpha based on standardized items	N of items
.846	.848	4

As the result has shown, $\alpha = 0.846$, meaning that the questionnaire is *very credible*. Based on the reliability test, we can continue to do some further analysis.

4 Findings and Discussions

In order to get a clear conclusion, the results of the questionnaire will be checked in this part to help offer more realistic countermeasures.

4.1 Relationship Between Grade and Willingness of Providing Off-Line Service

Taking the effect of grade difference into consideration, students' willingness of providing off-line service are checked through one-way ANOVA test. As the null hypothesis is that there is no significant difference in the total variance of the observed variables at all levels. With the total variance confirmed no significant difference, homogeneity of variance is picked as the method of the part of analysis (Table 4).

Table 4. The result of willingness of providing off-line service among grades

		N	Mean	Std. Deviation	Std. Error Mean	95% Confidence interval of the difference	
						Lower	Lower
Willingness of providing off-line service	Freshman	68	3.81	.981	.119	3.57	4.05
	Sophomore	99	3.72	1.040	.105	3.51	3.92
	Junior	191	3.67	1.021	.074	3.52	3.82
	Senior	54	3.80	1.219	.166	3.46	4.13
	Postgraduate	13	4.08	1.256	.348	3.32	4.84
	sum	425	3.73	1.052	.051	3.63	3.83

As shown in Table 5, there exists a significant difference among different grades on the willingness to provide off-line service. It is identified that students in higher grade are aware of their needs and adapt themselves to all kinds of learning modes better. As senior students are also those who have more experience in courses as well as other aspects of knowledge, their willingness to take the role of tutors makes sense. It becomes a key opportunity and challenge for online learning platform to attract them to use the platform.

Table 5. The result of ANOVA test on willingness of providing off-line service

			Sum of squares	df	Mean	F	Sig.
Between groups	combination		2.923	4	.731	.658	.622
	Linear term	Unweighted	.958	1	.958	.863	.354
		Weighted	.028	1	.028	.025	.874
		Deviation	2.896	3	.965	.869	.457
In the group			466.498	420	1.111		
sum			469.421	424			

4.2 Relationship Between Gender and Sense of Security

The results of the question on participants' sense of security when it comes to the use of O2O Apps are explored from the aspect of attitudes towards college students' credit. In result, the option in the questionnaire is exhibited as *how would you access college students' credit* so that college students' sense of security when using blended service is investigated. The results of group statistics show the standard error of the sample size, mean value, standard deviation and mean value of the male and female (Table 6).

Table 6. Group statistics

Options	Gender	N	Mean	Std. Deviation	Std. Error Mean
How would you access college students' credit?	Male	152	3.64	.896	.073
	Female	273	3.67	.753	.046

Spss 20.0 is used for the Levene test and the T test to check whether two gender groups are different from each other. Null hypothesis, which is also named H0, is set as there is a significant difference between male and female in their attitudes towards college students' credit.

The Levene test on homogeneity of variance and the results of T test on the equality of the mean are given in Table 7. The F statistic sig values $0.059 > 0.05$, which can be recognized as the equal variance assumption. Referring to the T-test results, bilateral sig value $0.694 > 0.05$, meaning that we should reject H0 and there is no significant difference in attitudes between men and women towards college students' credits. When we are trying to attract customers for online learning platform, the sense of security of different genders is almost the same.

Table 7. The results of independent samples test

		F	Sig.	t	df	Sig. (2-tailed)	Std. Error Difference
How would you access college students' credit?	Equal variances assumed	3.598	0.059	-0.394	423	0.694	0.082
	Equal variances not assumed			-0.375	270.12	0.708	0.086

4.3 Relationship Between Gender and Willingness of Credit Reports

Specifically speaking, things like acceptance and willingness towards the use of their credit report need to be confirmed before off-line instructions from students offered by the platform. The result of questions like Would you authorize the platform to use your credit report if you are one of the online learners? (1–> 5 says very unwilling –> very willing) is shown in Tables 8 and 9.

Table 8. The result of willingness of using credit reports

X\Y	Very unwilling	Unwilling	Uncertain	Willing	Very willing
Male	6(3.95%)	9(5.92%)	44(28.95%)	56(36.84%)	37(24.34%)
Female	23(8.42%)	31(11.36%)	73(26.74%)	79(28.94%)	67(24.54%)

Table 9. The result of group statistics

	Gender	N	Mean	Std. Deviation	Std. Error Mean
Would you authorize the platform to use your credit report if you are one of the online learners?	Male	152	3.72	1.026	.083
	Female	273	3.50	1.216	.074

The Levene test and the T test is used to check whether two gender groups are different from each other. Null hypothesis, which is also named H0, is set as there is a significant difference between male and female in their attitudes towards online learning platforms' using their credit reports.

The Levene test on homogeneity of variance and the results of T test on the equality of the mean are given in the Table 10. The F statistic sig values $0.002 < 0.05$, which can be recognized as the variances of the two groups are different. Referring to the T-test results, bilateral sig value $0.049 < 0.05$, meaning that we should accept H0 and there is a significant difference in attitudes between men and women towards college students' credits. We need to eradicate different individual characteristics adaptable design in this case.

Table 10. The result of independent samples test

		F	Sig.	t	df	Sig. (2-tailed)	Std. Error Difference
Would you authorize the platform to use your credit report if you are one of the online learners?	Equal variances assumed	9.345	0.002	1.878	423	0.061	0.117
	Equal variances not assumed			1.971	358.11	0.049	0.111

5 Conclusions

5.1 Major Findings of the Study

Although the network environment is relatively free and the market capacity seems huge, in fact it is influenced by a variety of factors. When it comes to turning learning platform into an O2O one, difference in people's acceptance towards the off-line function exist in specific ways.

With the result of the research, the online learning platform are designed location-based and off-line functions added. As for how to achieve the blended process in E-learning in higher education, suggestions are offered as to build an inner-campus communication society in the LBS. Social relationships are important while high-tech environments may compromise the balance of trust, care and respect between teacher and student. Therefore, college students are encouraged to take the instructional role themselves on and off the platform in the design of the system. Guaranteed by the belongingness of students to their own school, the location-based society makes them feel safe to communicate with each other. And from what have been proved in the study, the rule goes for both genders.

As for the detailed design of the learning content, adaptive instructional materials can be provided through tailor questions to each student's ability and calculate their scores. In the process of blended learning, students are encouraged to work both individually and socially or collaboratively as opportunities are offered to learn in different circumstances.

As a tool, or to say a new way to learn, technologies elaborate its function in altering our conception of learning. Knowing and accepting the difference, the design of the platform is also optimized to assist learners as well as to improve blended learning experience in the process.

5.2 Limitations and Suggestions for Future Research

The paper has concentrated on the differences of students and the interactions between our platform users. However, we haven't provided an efficient way to solve the potential problems. Although the sample for the research is more than 400, errors and deviations may exist when we use the features of the sample to speculate the overall situation. Thus the practicalities of the situation need to be substantiated in the implementation of the platform.

New technologies are frequently accompanied by unrealistic hype and promise regarding their transformative power to change education for the better or in allowing better educational opportunities to reach the masses. With the Internet and social media, using educational apps makes the students highly susceptible to distraction and sidetracking. Even though proper use has shown to increase student performances, being distracted would be detrimental. The introduction of blended learning cannot solve the problem thoroughly.

By far the greatest latitude of choice exists the very first time a particular instrument, system, or technique is introduced. In that sense technological innovations are similar to legislative acts or political findings that establish a framework for public order that will endure over many generations. And that's why we should think twice before taking action.

Acknowledgments. This work is supported by *Research on the Comparison and Promotion Strategy of Educational Informatization between China and Developed Countries* (NO. ACA160012) from National Social Science Fund for *13th Five-Year plan* key project in Education in 2016. The 13th Five-Year plan key project from the Chinese Society of Education named Research on key issues of promoting the development and application of cloud service in education under Internet plus background (No. 1601060835A) also supported this paper.

References

1. China Internet Network Information Center (CNNIC). Accessed 04 Aug 2017. http://cnnic.cn/gywm/xwzx/rdxw/201708/t20170804_69449.htm
2. Kirwin, S., Swan, J., Breakwell, N.: Comparing online learning with blended learning in a teacher training program. J. Res. Center Educ. Technol. **5**(2), 67–74 (2009)
3. Huang R.M., Lanqin, Z., Haisen, Z.: The theory of curriculum design based on blended learning. E-education Research, pp. 9–14 (2009)
4. Oliver, M., Trigwell, K.: Can "blended learning" be redeemed? E-Learning **2**(1), 17–26 (2005)
5. Riffell, S., Sibley, D.: Using web-based instruction to improve large undergraduate biology courses: an evaluation of a hybrid course format. Comput. Educ. **44**(3), 217–235 (2005)
6. Sarıtepeci, M., Çakır, H.: The effect of blended learning environments on student motivation and student engagement: a study on social studies course. Educ. Sci., 40(177) (2015)
7. Garrison, D.R., Kanuka, H.: Blended learning: uncovering its transformative potential in higher education. Internet High. Educ. **7**(2), 95–105 (2004)
8. Alexander, S.: Flexible learning in higher education. International Encyclopedia of Education, pp. 441–447 (2010)
9. Diep, A.N., Zhu, C., Struyven, K., Blieck, Y.: Who or what contributes to student satisfaction in different blended learning modalities? Br. J. Edu. Technol. **48**(2), 473–489 (2016)
10. Sun, P.C., Tsai, R.J., Finger, G., Chen, Y.Y., Yeh, D.: What drives a successful e-learning? An empirical investigation of the critical factors influencing learner satisfaction. Comput. Educ. **50**(4), 1183–1202 (2008)

11. Bolliger, D.U., Supanakorn, S.: Learning styles and student perceptions of the use of interactive online tutorials. Br. J. Edu. Technol. **42**(3), 470–481 (2011)
12. Lim, D.H., Morris, M.L.: Learner and instructional factors influencing learning outcomes within a blended learning environment. J. Educ. Technol. Soc. **12**(4), 282–293 (2009)
13. Wu, J.H., Wang, S.C.: What drives mobile commerce?: an empirical evaluation of the revised technology acceptance model. Inf. Manag. **42**(5), 719–729 (2005)
14. Lee, Y.H., Hsieh, Y.C., Hsu, C.N.: Adding innovation diffusion theory to the technology acceptance model: supporting employees' intentions to use e-learning systems. Educ. Technol. Soc. **14**(4), 124–137 (2011)
15. Lee, J.W.: Online support service quality, online learning acceptance, and student satisfaction. Internet High. Educ. **13**(4), 277–283 (2010)

The Influence of Culture on the Use of Information Technology in Learning in Hong Kong's Higher Education

Kwan-Keung Ng[1(✉)], Ching-Hong Luk[2], and Wai-Ming Lam[2]

[1] University of Sunderland, Hong Kong, Hong Kong, China
steven.ng@sunderland.edu.hk

[2] School of Business and Hospitality Management, Caritas Institute of Higher Education, Tseung Kwan O, New Territories, Hong Kong, China
{eluk,plam}@cihe.edu.hk

Abstract. Nowadays, information technology (IT) is widely used in learning in various ways, such as searching information from the internet, open-source learning methods like Moodle, Blackboard, and instant message applications like WhatsApp and WeChat, distance learning etc. The advances in information technology have significantly changed ways of teaching and learning in higher education. A number of researches investigate the acceptance of using technology based on various kinds of models, such as Unified Theory of Acceptance and Use of Technology (UTAUT) or Technology Acceptance Model (TAM) models [1–3]. However, there is a lack of literature talking about the direct antecedents of Hofstede's cultural dimensions on the behavioural intention and using behaviour of information technology in a learning context. This research is going to investigate the direct influence of culture on the use of information technology in learning in Hong Kong's Higher Education based on cross-cultural research literature, in which [4] widely cited dimensions of national culture, namely masculinity/femininity, individualism/collectivism, uncertainty avoidance, power distance. Five specific hypotheses are then formed to investigate how these dimensions influence the behavioural intention and the actual behaviour of information technology in learning. The results show that there is no relationship between masculinity/femininity and behaviour intention in using information technology in Hong Kong's Higher Education. However, individualism/collectivism, power distance and uncertainty avoidance will affect behavioural intention in using information, while behavioural intention will have an effect on actual behaviour in using information technology in Hong Kong/s Higher Education.

Keywords: Culture · Information technology · Behavioural intention
Actual behaviour · Higher education first section

1 Introduction

Information technology (IT) in education is still a hot topic and a concern. IT is being incorporated into teaching and learning process, not only through the availability of online courses, but also to support and assist student learning [5, 6]. The rapid development of

S. K. S. Cheung et al. (Eds.): ICBL 2018, LNCS 10949, pp. 126–135, 2018.
https://doi.org/10.1007/978-3-319-94505-7_10

e-learning appears since most of the higher education institutions are using web-based instruction system for teaching their online courses. The advancement in technology have facilitated new forms of information processing and formed new structures. This will not only complement universities but also transform them. Therefore, virtual classrooms become very common when new technologies are included in the University context. This is currently bringing together the possibilities of teaching-learning based upon a communication system using computers [7].

Instead of replacing traditional classroom teaching, information technology complements it and thousands of online courses are being offered by universities and colleges worldwide in this way. E-Learning, also known as Web-based learning is defined as an Internet-enabled learning process [8]. It is a crucial way to make learning methods more portable and flexible [9]. Particularly, these characteristics are even more important in modern higher education. E-learning adoption by university students' is growing at a world-wide level. However, courses completely online (without traditional classroom teaching) are less than 5%, and the number of students enrolled in at least a course with relevant online contents is ranged between 30% and 50% [10].

However, the diverse cultural origins and different background of tertiary students may derive from different perceptions and so as to evaluations of similar e-learning processes. However, given a common purpose and using technology that may minimise cultural differences, there is a question if it is possible for universities to overcome some of the cultural barriers to learning by using information technology. Moreover, what the influence of culture on how university students learn by using information technology is. This paper tries to address these questions. In addition, the presence of students from different nationalities enrolled in the same courses is a fact in this increasingly globalised world. Furthermore, the growing competence of colleges and universities trying to attract new students will negatively affect the reputation of those educational institutions who do not address these multi-cultural issues properly. Another important matter is related to the impact to the learning effectiveness of multicultural students using information technology.

2 Literature Review

2.1 Information Technology in Learning

Information Technology is becoming an increasingly important part of higher education in many different areas of knowledge. E-learning involves all forms of electronically supported learning and teaching, which are procedural in character and aim to have impact on the construction of knowledge with reference to individual experience, practice and knowledge of the learner. Information and communication systems, serve as specific media to implement the learning process, whether networked or not. There are many forms and ways of IT used in learning, such as Canvas, Blackboard, Moodle, as wells as various types of mobile applications, such as WeChat, Whatsapp, etc.

One of the main reasons for the widespread use of online learning in many institutions is that most students now have access to the Internet. As one of the examples, The University of British Columbia, in Vancouver, Canada, offered its first credit courses delivered entirely over the Internet to distance education students in 1996. The same year Murray Goldberg developed a software package called WebCT designed to enable Web-based courses to be offered over the Internet [11].

2.2 Hofstede's Cultural Dimensions

Culture is a set of routines that is practiced by a group of people on a regular o r even daily basis [12]. In last decades, cross-cultural studies have been developing. Importantly, these articles deal with studying differences in individual behaviour because of national culture. The core of these studies is culture. However, defining culture is difficult. Based on various definitions of culture, four main characteristics have emerged [13]. Firstly, it is a guide that people of the same group follow in order to be able to understand each other's behaviors, actions and events and a shared system of meaning. Secondly, there is no culture absolute, that is, culture is a relative notion. In other words, the way one national culture views the world is relative to how another culture views the world. Thirdly, culture is learned, instead of inherited. It is derived from an individual's social environment. Lastly, culture is a collective phenomenon rather than an individual one. There can be large variations in individual values and behaviours within one culture.

[14] article has developed this research line. In this work, Hofstede presented the results of his extensive study of national cultures. Based on data from 117,000 IBM employees from 40 different countries, he extracted four dimensions of culture, individualism vs collectivism, masculinity vs femininity, power distance, and uncertainty avoidance.

In addition to the measurement scales proposed by Hofstede, the use of values of each dimension obtained by a large number of nations has become the most common method of comparing national cultures used in academic research. These dimensions were published in [15] work. Based on this conceptual framework, cross-cultural analysis has been applied in marketing and management for a long time [16]. Recently, some of it has been applied to learning [17, 18] and technological scopes [19].

For some time, many articles have been showing that cross-cultural variables affect students' learning. [20] made a good review of this type of work. [21] found that some adult learners showed a strong preference for collaborative over competitive activities. Computer conferencing would be appropriate since it supports group activities such as discussion on a topic, problem-solving, role-playing, etc. [22] found that working together in collaborative teams with students from another study background and country offers high educational value and is highly appreciated. However, Hong Kong students experienced a global team feeling and trust towards their classmates.

Individualism reflects the way members emphasise their own needs over the group's needs. Individualism can be defined as a concern for one's self rather than a concern for the group to which one belongs. People with individualistic cultures tend to think of themselves as "I", they prefer to stand on their own two feet and classify themselves by their individual characteristics. Oppositely, in collectivistic cultures, the needs of the group or clan are more important than a single individual's needs. In collectivistic cultures, the group is seen as the major factor of loyalty and identity [23].

Power distance is the extent that large differentials of power and therefore inequality are accepted in a given culture. Power distance will affect the extent to which employees accept that their boss has more power than they have. For instance, high power distance can mean that employees will accept that their boss's decisions and opinions are correct because the person is the boss not because his or her opinions are qualitatively or quantitatively good. Employees in low power distance cultures accept that their boss has more power and is right only when the boss knows the best way to do something and knows the correct answers. Countries with high power distance emphasise hierarchical symbols while countries with low power distance are more egalitarian [23].

Uncertainty avoidance is the level of risk accepted by a culture, which can be gleaned by the emphasis on ritual behaviour, rule obedience, and labour mobility. This dimension examines the extent to which people feel threatened by ambiguous situations. Cultures with low levels of uncertainty avoidance have a bigger tolerance for ambiguity and less need for formal rules. Cultures with high levels of uncertainty will hold true for high uncertainty avoidance cultures [23].

Finally, masculinity/femininity refers to culture differentiation on the basis of gender and activity. For example, in masculine cultures, gender differentiation is quite pronounced, whereas in feminine cultures both sexes are more likely to engage in all types of professions or activities. Masculine cultures tend to emphasise work goals such as earnings, advancement, and assertiveness. On the other hand, feminine cultures tend to emphasise personal goals such as friendly atmosphere, getting along with the boss and others, and a comfortable work environment [23].

3 Methodology

This study used Hofstede's cultural dimensions to investigate the relationships between the constructs of masculinity/femininity, individualism/collectivism, uncertainty avoidance, power distance, behavioural intention and actual behaviour in using information technology in learning in the higher education context. This study investigates if the cultural dimensions affect the students' behavioural to their actual behaviour in using information technology in Hong Kong higher education context.

There are FIVE research hypotheses which are listed as follows (as shown in Fig. 1):

H1: Masculinity/Femininity will have an effect on Behavioral Intention in using information technology in Hong Kong's Higher Education.
H2: Individualism/Collectivism will have an effect on Behavioral Intention in using information technology in Hong Kong's Higher Education.
H3: Power Distance will have an effect on Behavioral Intention in using information technology in Hong Kong's Higher Education.
H4: Uncertainty Avoidance will have an effect on Behavioral Intention in using information technology in Hong Kong's Higher Education.
H5: Behavioral Intention will have an effect on Actual Behavior in using information technology in Hong Kong's Higher Education.

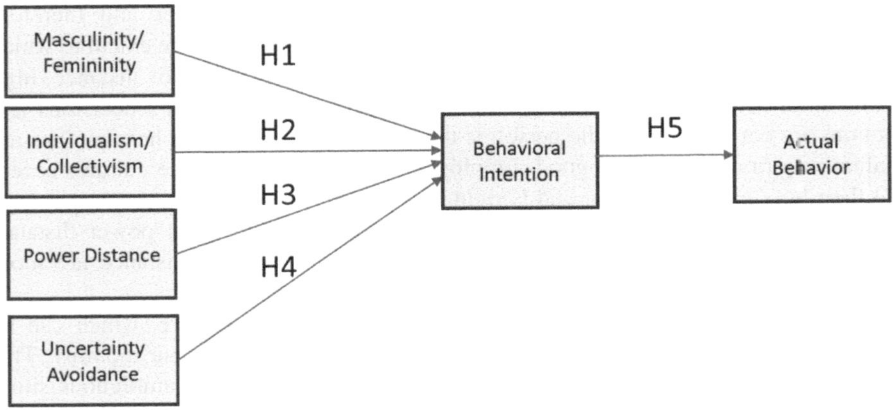

Fig. 1. Research model

There are 24 questions in the questionnaires including two questions for demographic inquiries. Questionnaires used a 5-point Likert-type scale, and total 148 questionnaires were received from students; 5 questionnaires were deleted because of the incompletion of responses. Finally, 143 questionnaires were input via Partial Least Squares regression (PLS) software for analysis.

4 Research Findings

For the descriptive analysis, the gender percentage between male students and female students is 47% vs 53% respectively. The local student's percentage vs non-local students percentage is 58% and 42% respectively. Besides, the mean scores of Masculinity/Femininity, Individualism/Collectivism, Power Distance, Uncertainty Avoidance, Behavioral Intention and Actual Behavior are ranged from 2.584 to 3.811 as shown in Table 1. There is one question (A4) which received the mean score lower than 2.5, the question is "Information Technology is more important for men than women" which reflects students believe no significant difference in male and female on the influence of culture on the using of information technology in learning in Hong Kong' higher education.

For the R Square analysis, as shown in Fig. 2, the R Square score of Behavioural Intention and Actual Behaviour are above 0.25 which reflects the equations apply to these five hypotheses are acceptable.

In addition, the researchers have performed a bootstrapping analysis via SmartPLS programme from 143 responses to 5000 samples so as to assess the significance of the path coefficients among these six constructs, which is listed in Table 2. PLS-SEM serves as the basis for the measurement operationalization using effect, causal, or composite indicators on the operational layer [24] (Fig. 3).

Table 1. Summary of students' responses to the influence of culture on the use of information technology in learning in Hong Kong's higher education

	A1	A2	A3	A4	MAS/FEM	B1	B2	B3	B4	B5	B6	IND/COL
MEAN	2.783	2.552	2.580	2.420	**2.584**	2.678	3.301	3.294	3.294	3.217	3.182	**3.161**
STDEV	1.273	1.197	1.269	1.213	**1.242**	1.098	1.035	0.879	0.956	0.920	0.932	**0.995**

	C1	C2	C3	PWR DIS	D1	D2	D7	UNC AVD
MEAN	2.650	2.657	2.524	**2.611**	3.392	2.783	3.161	**3.112**
STDEV	1.030	1.169	1.174	**1.125**	0.779	0.980	0.924	**0.931**

	E1	E2	E3	BEV IND	F1	F2	F3	ACT BEV
MEAN	3.937	3.895	3.902	**3.911**	4.112	3.622	3.699	**3.811**
STDEV	0.898	0.955	0.891	**0.913**	2.523	0.948	0.904	**1.652**

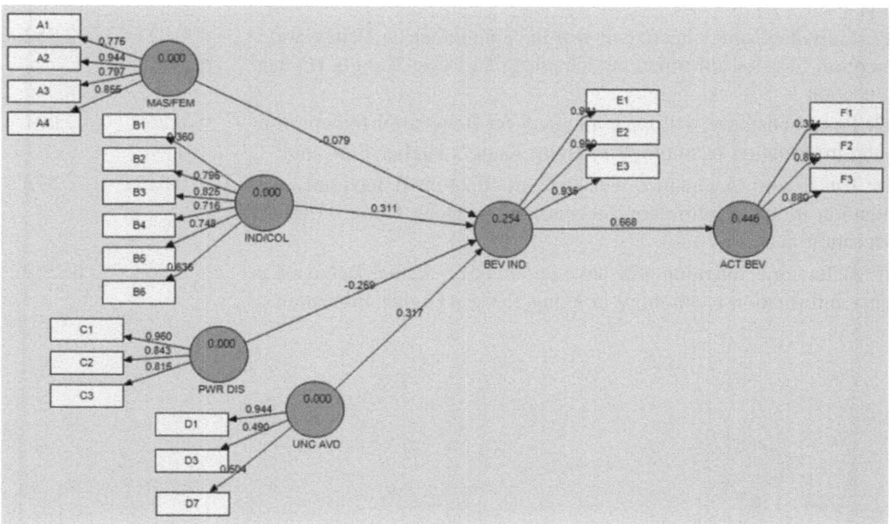

Fig. 2. R Square analysis of the influence of culture on the use of information technology in learning in Hong Kong's higher education

For the H1 hypothesis, the Beta Value and T-Statistics scores are −0.079 and 0.595, which reflect the research findings do not support this hypothesis. As aforementioned, students believe there is no significant difference in male and female on the influence of culture on the using of information technology in learning in Hong Kong' higher education. Our research results show that there is no significant relationship between masculinity/femininity with the behavioural intention and actual behaviour. Similar research results are shown in another research study [25]. In their study, the researchers found that Masculinity/femininity did not have any significant moderating effects, and the direction of the moderating effects was opposite to those of gender. Similarly, the direct effect of masculinity/femininity was opposite to that of gender. These findings suggest that masculinity/femininity, although based on gender roles, exerts different influences on users' technology adoption decisions. The relationship between gender and masculinity/femininity deserves further research. Therefore, the researchers suggested that further study of gender and masculinity/femininity is needed as these distinct individual differences may have a complex, interrelated influence on technology adoption.

Table 2. Research Test Results of the influence of culture on the use of information technology in learning in Hong Kong's higher education

FACTOR → BI (Behavioral Intention)	Beta Value	T-Statistics
H1: Masculinity/Femininity will have an effect on Behavioral Intention in using information technology in Hong Kong's Higher Education	−0.079	0.595
H2: Individualism/Collectivism will have an effect on Behavioral Intention in using information technology in Hong Kong's Higher Education	0.311	2.952
H3: Power Distance will have an effect on Behavioral Intention in using information technology in Hong Kong's Higher Education	−0.259	2.001
H4: Uncertainty Avoidance will have an effect on Behavioral Intention in using information technology in Hong Kong's Higher Education	0.317	3.573
H5: Behavioral Intention will have an effect on Actual Behavior in using information technology in Hong Kong's Higher Education	0.668	10.369

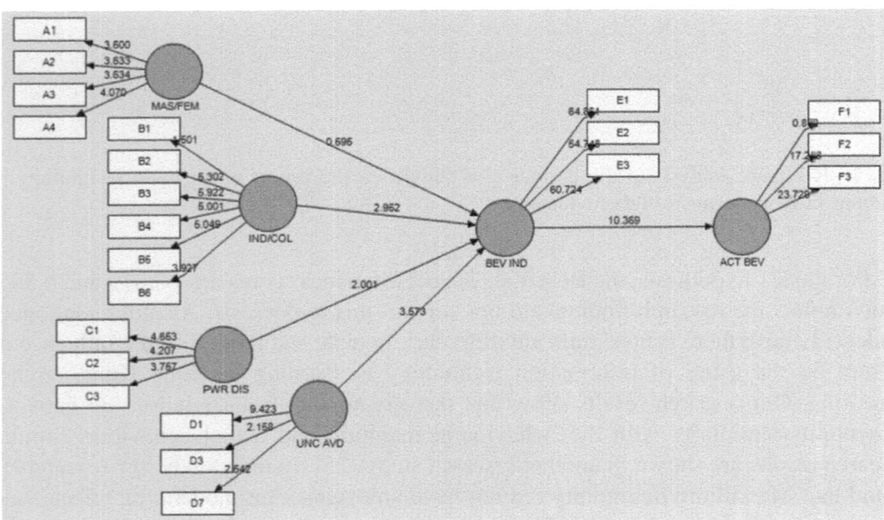

Fig. 3. PLS-SEM Path analysis of the influence of culture on the use of information technology in learning in Hong Kong's higher education

For the H2 hypothesis, the Beta Value and T-Statistics scores are 0.311 and 2.952, which reflect the research findings support this hypothesis, and show that Individualism/Collectivism has a positive effect on Behavioral Intention in using information technology in Hong Kong's Higher Education.

For the H3 hypothesis, the Beta Value and T-Statistics scores are −0.259 and 2.001, which reflect the research findings support this hypothesis, and show that Power Distance has a negative effect on Behavioral Intention in using information technology in Hong Kong's Higher Education. It is because nowadays students do not believe there is a power distance between them, especially in using information technology context. In the meantime, higher power distance will discourage them to use information technology. Students nowadays prefer to have self-decision rather than being instructed to use/do something.

For the H4 hypothesis, the Beta Value and T-Statistics scores are 0.317 and 3.573, which reflect the research findings support this hypothesis, and show that Uncertainly Avoidance has a positive effect on Behavioral Intention in using information technology in Hong Kong's Higher Education.

For the H5 hypothesis, the Beta Value and T-Statistics scores are 0.668 and 10.369, which reflect the research findings support this hypothesis, and shown that Behavioral Intention has a positive effect on Actual Behavior in using information technology in Hong Kong's Higher Education.

5 Limitations and Further Research

This is a preliminary research investigating the impact of cultural factors on the behavioural intention and actual behaviour in using information technology in Hong Kong's Higher Education. The sample size is limited. In addition, the variety of cultural background is limited. In future study, more samples and more different cultural background from different countries can be compared so that the impact of cultural factors on the use of information technology in learning can be compared for different students from different countries.

6 Conclusion

This study's results show that there is no relationship between masculinity/femininity and behaviour intention in using information technology in Hong Kong Higher Education. However, individualism/collectivism, power distance and uncertainty avoidance will have an effect on behavioural intention in using information technology, while behavioural intention will have an effect on actual behaviour in using information technology in Hong Kong Higher Education particularly. In future, more samples would be collected from different countries with different cultural background so that the impact of cultural factors on the use of information technology in learning can be extensively investigated.

References

1. Escobar-Rodriguez, T., Monge-Lozano, P.: The acceptance of Moodle technology by business administration students. Comput. Educ. **58**(2012), 1085–1093 (2012)
2. Cornell, R.M., Eining, M.M., Hu, P.J.: The effects of process accountability on individuals' use of a familiar technology. J. Inf. Syst. **25**(1), 109–128 (2011)
3. Dasgupta, S., Granger, M., McGarry, N.: User acceptance of r-collaboration technology: an extension of the technology acceptance model. Group Decis. Negot. **11**, 87–100 (2002)
4. Hofstede, G.: Cultures Consequences. SAGE Publications, Newbury Park (1984)
5. Martin, T., Serrano, A.: The role of new technologies in the learning process: Moodle as a teaching tool in physics. Comput. Educ. **52**, 35–44 (2009)
6. Romero, C., Ventura, S., García, E.: Data mining in course management systems: Moodle case study and tutorial. Comput. Educ. **51**, 368–384 (2008)
7. Ciudad, A.: Teaching innovation and use of the ICT in the teaching-learning process within the new framework of the EHEA, by jeans of Moodle platform. Am. J. Bus. Educ. **3**(13), 13–19 (2010)
8. Gunasekaran, A., Mcneil, R.D., Shaul, D.: E-learning: research and applications. Ind. Commer. Train. **34**(2), 44–53 (2002)
9. Zhang, D., Nunamaker, J.F.: Powering e-learning in the new millennium: an overview of e-learning and enabling technology. Inf. Syst. Front. **5**(2), 207–218 (2003)
10. OECD: E-learning in Tertiary Education: Where do We Stand?. OECD, Paris (2005)
11. Bates, A.W.: Technology, E-learning and Distance Education, 2nd edn. Routledge, Abingdon (2005)
12. Rahman, N.A., Voon, B.H., Firdaus, A.P.: Soc. Behav. Sci. **224**, 84–92 (2016)
13. Hoecklin, L.: Managing Cultural Differences: Strategies for Competitive Advantage. Addison-Wesley Publishing Company, Cambridge (1995)
14. Hofstede, G.: Culture's Consequences: International Differences in Work-Related Values. Sage, Thousand Oaks (1980)
15. Hofstede, G., Bond, M.H.: The Confucius connection: from cultural roots to economic growth. Organ. Dyn. **16**(4), 4–21 (1988)
16. Magnusson, P., Wilson, R.T., Zdravkovic, S., Zhou, J.X., Westjohn, S.A.: Breaking through the cultural clutter; a comparative assessment of multiple cultural and institutional frameworks. Int. Mark. Rev. **25**(2), 183–201 (2006)
17. Elenurm, T.: Applying cross-cultural student teams for supporting international networking of Estonian enterprises. Baltic J. Manag. **3**(2), 145–158 (2008)
18. Shipper, F., Hoffman, R.C., Rotondo, D.M.: Does the 360 feedback process create actionable knowledge equally across cultures? Acad. Manag. Learn. Educ. **6**(1), 33–50 (2007)
19. Lippert, S.A., Volkmar, J.A.: Cultural effects on technology performance and utilization: a comparison of U.S. and Canadian users. J. Glob. Inf. Manag. **15**(2), 56–90 (2007)
20. Economides, A.A.: Culture-aware collaborative learning. Multicult. Educ. Technol J. **2**(4), 243–267 (2008)
21. Sanchez, I., Gunawardena, C.N.: Understanding and supporting the culturally diverse distance learner. In: Gibson, C.C. (ed.) Distance Learners in Higher Education, pp 47–64. Atwood Publishing, Madison (1998)
22. Vogel, D., Van Genuchten, M., Lou, D., Verveen, S., Van Eekhout, M., Adams, T.: Distributed experiential learning: the Hong Kong-Netherlands project. In: Proceedings of the 33rd Hawaii International Conference on System Sciences, vol. 1, p. 1052. IEEE (2000)

23. Hoeklin, L.: Managing Cultural Difference: Strategies for Competitive Advantage. Addison-Wesley, Wokingham (1994)
24. Richter, N.F., Cepeda, G., Roldán, J.L., Ringle, C.M.: Eur. Manag. J. **34**(6), 589–597 (2016)
25. Li, X., Hess, T.J., McNab, A.L., Yu, Y.: Culture and acceptance of global web sites: a cross-country study of the effects of national cultural values on acceptance of a personal web portal. Database Adv. Inf. Syst. **40**(4), 62–87 (2009)

A Digital Storytelling Group Assignment for Fostering Sense of Belonging of First-Year Students

Andrew Kwok Fai Lui(✉), Maria Hiu Man Poon, and Sin Chun Ng

School of Science and Technology, The Open University of Hong Kong, 30 Good Shepherd Street, Ho Man Tin, Kowloon, Hong Kong SAR, China
{alui,mpoon,scng}@ouhk.edu.hk

Abstract. First-year students are vulnerable to dropout as they make the challenging transition into university life. Students with a strong sense of belonging to their peers are more likely to persist. Various types of interventions aiming at improving the social-emotional well-being of students have been proposed in the literature. Getting students to work together in a non-trivial task, in particular, can conjure interpersonal interaction opportunities. This paper aims to postulate that digital storytelling group assignment is an effective intervention for fostering sense of belonging among first-year students. The key features of the group assignment, the design of the evaluation methodology, and the findings of the study are de-scribed in the paper. The sense of belonging of first-year students was found to increase significantly during the period of the group assignment. In addition, the group assignment was found to be most effective if it was administered in the first few weeks of study. The flexible nature of digital storytelling makes blending into any course straightforward.

Keywords: Digital storytelling · Student retention · Sense of belonging First-year students · Computing · CS1

1 Background

First-year students are at their most vulnerable moment as they make the transition from high schools to universities. The curriculum, the teaching style, the campus, the schedule, and the peers are some of the novelties that they find both exciting to experience and challenging to overcome. The less academic or socially capable students often feel overwhelmed [12, 17]. According to various statistics, the majority of dropouts from universities happen during the first year of study, and this first-year dropout rate has been around 25% to 30% among the baccalaureate institutions in the United States [3, 12]. Some disciplines like computer science and engineering can experience even higher dropout rates [7, 11]. Student retention has been a top agenda item of many tertiary institutions around the world for the past couple of decades, under the backdrop of dwindling public funding and greater accountability of tertiary institutions [16]. Implementation of effective best practices to help students persist actually

S. K. S. Cheung et al. (Eds.): ICBL 2018, LNCS 10949, pp. 136–147, 2018.
https://doi.org/10.1007/978-3-319-94505-7_11

makes a lot of sense. Institutions will enjoy greater financial stability. Graduation is also a significant benefit to the individuals, the immediate families, and also to the related profession and the society.

Cultivating the sense of belonging of first-year students is a proven strategy for student retention. In the context of tertiary education, the sense of belonging describes the strength of connection between students and their institutions, faculty members and their peers [5, 15]. For adolescences, engagement with their peers is especially fundamental to meeting their basic needs as well as practical benefits in emotional and academic support [6]. They are more likely to enjoy positive learning experience and success as a result [10]. In the first few weeks of their university life, new students face uncertainties on their social life and they appreciate social opportunities to make friends [18]. In particular, quality friendship can ease the assimilation into university life, improve student engagement, and increase motivation to persist [2].

In developing measures to enhance sense of belonging, the literature agrees that getting first-year students to work together has a multitude of benefits. Group work creates ample of opportunities of personal interactions. Completing a task together makes one feel included and accepted as an important member of the group [10]. There is however a number of considerations of the type of tasks designed for maximizing the benefits. First, the task should be educationally meaningful that facilitates students engaging with their study [4]. Second, the collaborative element of the task should involve out-of-class activities so that building ties beyond the classrooms is encouraged [8]. Third, the background abilities of individuals should not hinder them making contributions. The disparity in the level of contributions can cause conflicts and it should be avoided. Conflict resolution and teamwork development should wait until a later time in the curriculum.

1.1 Digital Storytelling and Enhancing Sense of Belonging

Digital storytelling is a creative activity of telling stories with video, audio, images and other multimedia types. Recently, applying digital storytelling in educational context, especially that involving student group work, has begun to attract attention. Digital stories may be designed to inform or instruct on a topic or to share personal experience [13]. One example educational use of digital storytelling is to task students in an operating system course to produce videos that illustrate algorithms with daily life analogies [9]. Barrett [1] found that digital storytelling facilitates good teaching practices such as student engagement, deep learning, and project-based learning.

A digital storytelling assignment can offer genuine roles similar to a real-life video production team. Students should find it easy to take up a role in the team and make contributions, and therefore feel engaged. The work appears non-trivial and involves a number of tasks including theme setting, research, storyboard development, acting, recording, editing, and production [14]. Digital video and audio capture and editing is already part of daily social life of adolescences. Anyone with a smartphone is capable of producing video of reasonable quality. There are always acting roles that can serve as the last resort for ensuring participation.

This paper reports on a study of designing a digital storytelling group assignment for enhancing the sense of belonging of first-year computing students. The key features of the assignment are listed in the following:

- Timing and Group Formation. The group assignment should be introduced and initiated during the first lecture. The group membership should be randomly drawn and announced at the same time. Due to imbalanced gender ratio, students of the two genders are separately drawn.
- Theme of the Story. The theme of the assignment should be broadly specified and relevant to the programme of study. For the computing students in this study, the theme was set to be "Computer Programming in Daily Life".
- Objective of the Digital Story. The digital story should be educational allowing viewers to know more about computer programming.
- Variations in Presentation. To increase students' interest and variations between stories, each team should also be given a randomly drawn requirement that is related to presentation.
- Everyone involved in Acting. To ensure participation, a requirement should be imposed that every team member must visually appear in the video.

1.2 Research Questions

Concerning the effectiveness of digital storytelling group assignments for improving the sense of belonging of first-year computing students, this paper investigates the following research questions:

- Do students experience an increase in sense of belonging through the digital storytelling group assignment regardless of their year of study and gender?
- Does prior experience in video production or lack of it affect engagement in the assignment?

2 Methods

The research questions were investigated in a descriptive, prospective, one-group pre-test post-test study. The sense of belonging of test subjects was measured before the commencement of the digital storytelling group assignments and after the completion of the assignment.

2.1 Participants

The test subjects were students studying the course titled Introduction to Computer Programming in the Autumn 2017 term. There were totally three cohorts of students enrolled in the course: the first two cohorts were first-year students entering into Year 1 (n = 36) and Year 2 (n = 18) levels respectively of a computing degree programme, and the third cohort (n = 22), which was considered as a quasi-control group, consisted of students into their second year of study in an engineering degree programme. About 22% were female students (n = 17, male = 59).

Participation in the study was voluntary and student consent was obtained. The first part of the survey was carried out in the first day of the term. It was also their first face-to-face contact session in the university and the survey was completed in the class. The second part of the survey was submitted with their assignment work. Both surveys were paper-form.

2.2 Measures

The measures used in the study were adapted mainly from the College Mattering Scale [19]. The sense of belonging measure was operationalized through the two sub-scales: the General College Mattering (GCM) subscale and the Mattering versus Marginality (MVM) subscale. The GCM subscale reflects the degree how other individuals at the colleges are interested in a student's well-being and success. The MVM subscale reflects the degree of feeling belongingness or rejection. These two subscales were chosen because they were conceptualized on mattering, which is associated with sense of belonging both emotionally and cognitively [19, 20]. These two subscales were included in both the pre-assignment survey and the post-assignment survey. The scores were on a Likert Scale of 1 to 5 (i.e. 5 being strongly agree). The scores for MVM were transformed into the positive orientation, that is, higher scores represent more mattering.

The pre-assignment survey included, in addition to the above, other exploratory measures such as the number of friends they have made in the same cohort and the expectation of teamwork.

The post-assignment survey also included measures such as the number of friends, the roles assumed in the teamwork, and the perception of the teamwork and the outcome.

2.3 Justifications

The method described above should adequately address the two research questions. The first research question examined if there was a significant improvement in sense of belonging, and then examined if other factors such as year of study and gender had an influence. The second research question examined if digital storytelling group assignment would be particularly suitable for first-year students, considering the background knowledge of students would not affect participation. First-year students come from diverse background. Other types of group projects, such as pair programming, have been shown to cause conflicts due to disparity in abilities.

The absence of a real control group in the study design, due to ethical and practical reasons, can be regarded as a dent on the legitimacy of any conclusion. There could be other factors causing any change in the sense of belonging. However, during the period of the study, the digital storytelling group assignment was the only group project that involved all the test subjects. The second year engineering students, which were not new to one another, was used as a quasi-control group.

3 Results

3.1 Improvement in Sense of Belonging

To evaluate possible improvement in the sense of belonging among students, a paired t-test was performed between the pre-assignment and post-assignment GCM and MVM with a significant level of 0.05 as a cut-off. Table 1 lists the descriptive statistics and results of the pair-t tests on all cohorts (both first-year and second-year students). There were significant difference and improvement in the scores for pre-GCM (M = 3.25, SD = 0.72) and post-GCM (M = 3.40, SD = 0.67), for pre-MVM (M = 3.54, SD = 0.71) and post-MVM (M = 3.68, SD = 0.72), and also for the overall scores pre-assignment (M = 3.40, SD = 0.59) and post-assignment (M = 3.54, SD = 0.62).

Table 1. Pre-assignment and post-assignment scores of the subscales of the college mattering scale and the overall scores

	Paired differences					t	df	Sig. (2-tailed)
	Mean	S.D.	S.E. mean	95% confidence interval of the diff.				
				Lower	Upper			
P1: GCM (Pre) – GCM (Post)	−.15	.47	.05	−.26	−.04	−2.83	75	.006
P2: MVM (Pre) – MVM (Post)	−.14	.63	.07	−.29	.00	−1.99	75	.050
P3: Overall (Pre) – Overall (Post)	−.15	.41	.05	−.24	−.05	−3.18	75	.002

Table 2 displays a comparison between the first-year student cohorts and the second-year student cohort (i.e. the quasi-control group). Significant difference in the mean scores was observed between pre-GCM (M = 3.18, SD = 0.77) and post-GCM (M = 3.43, SD = 0.71), and between overall mattering scores pre-assignment (M = 3.40, SD = 0.65) and post-assignment (M = 3.58, SD = 0.67). No significant improvement in sense of belonging was found among the second-year cohort.

Table 2. Pre-assignment and post-assignment scores group by student cohorts

	Paired differences					t	df	Sig. (2-tailed)
	Mean	S.D.	S.E. mean	95% confidence interval of the diff.				
				Lower	Upper			
First-year students								
P1: GCM (Pre) – GCM (Post)	−.25	.40	.05	−.36	−.14	−4.59	53	.000
P2: MVM (Pre) – MVM (Post)	−.11	.65	.09	−.29	.06	−1.30	53	.198
P3: Overall (Pre) – Overall (Post)	−.18	.40	.05	−.29	−0.7	−3.34	53	.002
Second-year students								
P1: GCM (Pre) – GCM (Post)	.09	.53	−.11	−.14	.33	.80	21	.432
P2: MVM (Pre) – MVM (Post)	−.22	.61	.13	−.49	.05	−1.68	21	.109
P3: Overall (Pre) – Overall (Post)	−.06	.42	.09	−.25	.12	−.72	21	.480

Table 3 shows a comparison of the overall college mattering scale mean scores between the first-year cohorts and the second-year cohort. Note that the pre-assignment mean score of the second-year cohort is almost the same as that of the first-year cohorts.

Table 3. Comparison of pre-assignment and post-assignment mean overall scores between new first-year students and second-year students (bracketed figures are standard deviations)

	Overall (Pre)	Overall (Post)
First-year students	3.40 (0.65)	3.58 (0.67)
Second-year students	3.39 (0.41)	3.45 (0.51)

The internal consistency of the scores of the pre-assignment GCM (alpha = 0.90), pre-assignment MVM (alpha = 0.86), post-assignment GCM (alpha = 0.86), post-assignment MVM (alpha = 0.89) was examined and their descriptive statistics are listed in Table 4.

Table 4. Internal Consistency of the GCM and MVM items

Sub-scales	# of Items	Cronbach's alpha	Ranges of item-total correlation	Mean	SD
Pre-assignment GCM	4	0.90	0.75–0.84	3.25	0.72
Pre-assignment MVM	5	0.86	0.55–0.83	3.40	0.67
Post-assignment GCM	4	0.86	0.64–0.80	3.54	0.71
Post-assignment MVM	5	0.89	0.66–0.87	3.68	0.72

3.2 Gender

Tables 5 and 6 show the changes in GCM and MVM group by gender. The male group was found to have a significant improvement in GCM and overall college mattering. In addition, the female group appeared to have a higher mean in pre-assignment GCM but it was found to be not statistically significant according to Student's t-tests.

Table 5. Mean GCM and MVM group by gender

	Mean GCM (Pre)	Mean GCM (Post)	Mean MVM (Pre)	Mean MVM (Post)
Male	3.19 (0.70)	3.37 (0.67)	3.53 (0.69)	3.69 (0.67)
Female	3.46 (0.74)	3.51 (0.69)	3.55 (0.81)	3.65 (0.87)

Table 6. Pre-assignment and post-assignment scores of the male group

	Paired differences					t	df	Sig. (2-tailed)
	Mean	S.D.	S.E. mean	95% confidence interval of the diff.				
				Lower	Upper			
Male								
P1: GCM (Pre) – GCM (Post)	−.18	.46	.06	−.30	−.06	−2.97	58	.004
P2: MVM (Pre) – MVM (Post)	−.16	.66	.09	−.33	−.01	−1.86	58	.068
P3: Overall (Pre) – Overall (Post)	−.17	.42	.06	−.28	−.06	−3.06	58	.003

3.3 Perception of Teamwork in the Group Assignment

Table 7 lists the mean scores of other measures concerning the perception of teamwork in the group assignment. Student's t-tests were used and no significant difference was found between first-year students and second-year students, except for the item on the reluctant to work in the same group again, in which the first-year students tend to disagree more. No significant difference was found between the genders.

Table 7. Descriptive statistics of scores of teamwork perception in the group assignment

	Mean	Mean (first-year)	Mean (second-year)	Diff. between groups
It was easy to find a role in the group project	3.74 (0.66)	3.78 (0.63)	3.64 (0.72)	
The group worked well in the project	3.79 (0.77)	3.78 (0.82)	3.82 (0.66)	
I think other members appreciated my effort	3.55 (0.74)	3.57 (0.77)	3.50 (0.67)	
I do not want to work in the same group again	2.52 (1.02)	2.34 (1.04)	2.95 (0.84)	Sig. at $p < 0.05$
I feel frustrated after working in this group	2.32 (0.82)	2.22 (0.84)	2.55 (0.74)	
I rate highly the outcome of the project	3.72 (0.76)	3.76 (0.78)	3.64 (0.73)	
I have made friends with my group mates	3.55 (0.89)	3.50 (0.99)	3.68 (0.57)	

3.4 Prior Experience in Video Production

The subjects were asked to indicate the roles they actually took up in the project, and the roles which they had prior experience.

Table 8 lists the statistics for all cohorts, and also group by first-year and second-year cohorts. Two things to note are that all students were involved in acting, and no student from the second-year group had video editing experience.

Table 9 below shows that students who had prior experience in a task were likely to assume the related role, something that was expected and it matches with chi-square test. Then Student's t-test was applied to discover if involving in a certain task would affect the measures on perception of teamwork. Those who assumed a Research role had scored significantly higher in feeling appreciated by others (mean diff = 0.37,

Table 8. Descriptive statistics of prior experience

	All (n = 76)		First-year (n = 54)		Second-year (n = 22)	
	Prior experience	Actually involved	Prior experience	Actually involved	Prior experience	Actually involved
Research	34	35	28	28	11	7
Story development	32	51	21	35	24	16
Video recording	32	46	23	32	8	14
Acting	44	76	33	54	36	22
Video editing	35	23	25	16	0	7

sig = 0.031). Interestingly, those who were doing video recording felt more reluctant to work in the same group again others (mean diff = 0.19, sig = 0.04).

Table 9. Chi-square test of prior experience and actual involvement

Actually involved in	Has prior experience	New to the task	χ^2	Student's t-test with measures
Research	69%	31%	15.1 **	I think other members appreciated my effort. (mean diff = 0.37, sig = 0.031)
Story development	51%	49%	5.01 **	–
Video recording	52%	48%	4.85 **	I do not want to work in the same group again (mean diff = −0.19, sig = 0.04)
Acting	58%	42%	–	–
Video editing	73%	26%	10.3 **	–

** Sig (2-tailed) < 0.05 level

Over 90% of students took up more than one role, and in some cases all five roles. Figure 1 shows the frequency distribution of the number of roles taken up by each student. On average each student assumed three roles. The number of roles taken up implies the degree of involvement and also the amount of effort. It was found the number of roles is weakly correlated with reducing GCM measure, that is, the more roles to assume, the less is one feeling appreciated by others (correl = −0.23, sig = 0.045).

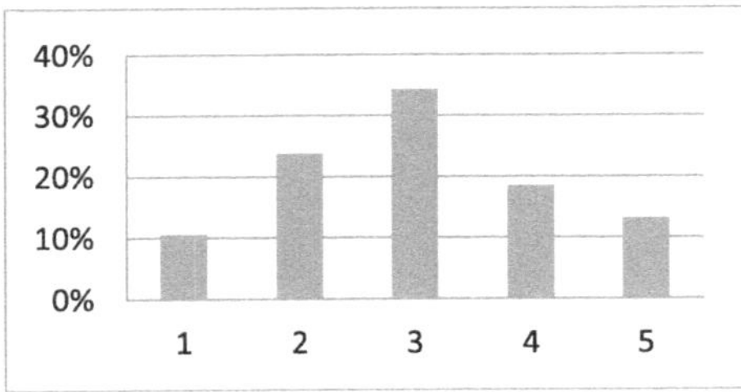

Fig. 1. Frequency of the number of roles taken up by a student

4 Discussion

For enhancing sense of belonging among first-year students, every type of intervention has benefits and limitations. Group assignments, due to its nature in coercing students to interact within an academic significant context, have been widely considered [22]. Certain dimension of group assignments can however influence the form of interaction, for example, the difficulty level, relevance to the programme, prior knowledge required among others. Table 10 lists some types of group assignments that have been used in the computing programmes at the author's institutions, and observations of their limitations for the purpose.

Table 10. Limitations of types of group assignments for enhancing sense of belonging

Group assignment types	Nature	Limitations
Final year project	Problem solving and system integration	Technically demanding
Blogging	Research and writing on a topic	Not easy to find a role because there are few unique roles
Pair programming	Complete programming tasks together	A technically weaker partner hard to get involved

This paper explored the effect of digital story-telling for this purpose. Digital storytelling offers a viable alternative due to the following reasons:

- The theme is flexible for instructors to set one that every student can contribute regardless of academic background.
- There are many genuine roles that are unique and easy to acquire the related skills.
- Producing a multimedia is generally satisfying [21].
- The collaboration and interaction can extend beyond the classroom or even the campus.

4.1 Sense of Belonging and the Group Assignment

Our findings showed that the sense of belonging, operationalized through the College Mattering Scale, was found to increase significantly for first-year students during the period of the digital story-telling group assignment. Obvious ethical and practical reasons prevented the design of an experiment to isolate the core variables. In fact, it would be naïve to consider the group assignment as the sole factor for any improvement in the sense of belonging. Instead, the group assignment was seen acting as a catalyst or icebreaker in the first few weeks of university life. It would give students a platform to know the first few acquaintances.

There was also a gender difference found from the analysis. Only the male group experienced a significant increase in the sense of belonging but the increase in the female group was not significant. The female group's pre-assignment overall mean score appears higher than the male group, but the difference was not significant. Male computing students have been suffered from a stereotype of being nerdy and asocial, and the initial low score could have come from this self-perception. The group assignment seems able to remove this wrong perception. The post-assignment scores were virtually at the same level across the male and the female groups.

No significant increase in the sense of belonging was observed among the second-year students, who had already spent one year with each other. Interestingly the pre-assignment overall score of second-year students was virtually the same as the first-year students (3.39 versus 3.40) but it did not increase. This group also scored significantly higher in the measure "I do not want to work in the same group again" (mean diff = 0.61, sig < 0.05). One interpretation is that they did not like some of the teammates assigned to them randomly, based on their experience in their first-year of study. The window of opportunity to build relation seems to have passed for these students, implying that intervention for enhancing sense of belonging should happen as early as possible.

4.2 Roles and Teamwork

Our findings showed that students could find a role easily (mean = 3.74) and enjoyed the teamwork (mean = 3.79). In fact, most students took up more than one role and made contributions. Students generally had confidence to pick up a new role. Around 30% to 40% of students were inexperienced in the role that they took up, with the exception of video editing, which is quite rightly a specialized role.

Another observation is that the beneficial effect of the group assignment appears to be independent of the number of roles or the certain roles assumed by a student. However, it was found that the gain in sense of belonging was reduced in a small way if a student was overburdened with tasks.

5 Conclusion

The study contains a few validity issues that may have affected the strength of conclusion. It was not feasible to set up a control experiment to attribute any effect directly to the digital storytelling group assignment, and also to compare digital storytelling with other group assignment types. The group assignment took several weeks, presenting insurmountable obstacles to eliminate other variables into the study. In addition, the subjects were computing students that could have biased the initial sense of belonging measure.

Nevertheless, the findings provided clues that digital storytelling group assignment is an effective intervention for enhancing sense of belonging among first-year students. The flexible nature of digital storytelling makes blending this group assignment into any course straightforward. Meeting the following two conditions should increase the likelihood of getting any benefit from this blended learning method:

- To better enhance sense of belonging, the group assignment should start right at the beginning when the class meet for the first time.
- The number of roles taken up by a student in the group assignment should be restricted.

Designing suitable interventions for better retention of first-year students has become an important job duty of faculty members. Computing students, both male and female, can be particularly inhibited by their own nerdy and asocial stereotype. Early intervention with suitable group assignment can break this stereotype, allowing the students to see the social side of their peers. Making the first few friends is the hard part, but the group work can facilitate its happening. The next stage of this study will examine this *catalytic* functionality of digital storytelling group assignment, and delve deeper into the patterns of making friends.

References

1. Barrett, H.: Researching and evaluating digital storytelling as a deep learning tool. In: Society for Information Technology and Teacher Education International Conference, vol. 2006, no. 1, pp. 647–654 (2006)
2. Bowman, N.A.: The development of psychological well-being among first-year college students. J. Coll. Stud. Dev. **51**(2), 180–200 (2010)
3. Credé, M., Niehorster, S.: Adjustment to college as measured by the student adaptation to college questionnaire: a quantitative review of its structure and relationships with correlates and consequences. Educ. Psychol. Rev. **24**(1), 133–165 (2012)
4. Gellin, A.: The effect of undergraduate student involvement on critical thinking: a meta-analysis of the literature 1991–2000. J. Coll. Stud. Dev. **44**(6), 746–762 (2003)
5. Kahu, E.R., Nelson, K.: Student engagement in the educational interface: understanding the mechanisms of student success. High. Educ. Res. Dev. **37**(1), 58–71 (2018)
6. Kiefer, S.M., Alley, K.M., Ellerbrock, C.R.: Teacher and peer support for young adolescents' motivation, engagement, and school belonging. Res. Middle Level Educ. **38** (8), 1–18 (2015)
7. Kinnunen, P., Malmi, L.: Why students drop out CS1 course? In: Proceedings of the Second International Workshop on Computing Education Research, pp. 97–108. ACM (2006)
8. Krause, K.L., Coates, H.: Students' engagement in first-year university. Assess. Eval. High. Educ. **33**(5), 493–505 (2008)

9. Lui, A.K.F., Poon, M.H.M., Ng, S.C.: The blending of student generated videos in an operating systems course. In: Proceedings of the International Conference on Open and Flexible Education. OUHK (2015)
10. Masika, R., Jones, J.: Building student belonging and engagement: insights into higher education students' experiences of participating and learning together. Teach. High. Educ. **21**(2), 138–150 (2016)
11. Moses, L., Hall, C., Wuensch, K., De Urquidi, K., Kauffmann, P., Swart, W., Dixon, G.: Are math readiness and personality predictive of first-year retention in engineering? J. Psychol. **145**(3), 229–245 (2011)
12. Reason, R.D., Terenzini, P.T., Domingo, R.J.: First things first: developing academic competence in the first year of college. Res. High. Educ. **47**(2), 149–175 (2006)
13. Robin, B.R.: The educational uses of digital storytelling. In: Society for Information Technology and Teacher Education International Conference, pp. 709–716. Association for the Advancement of Computing in Education (2006)
14. Robin, B.R.: Digital storytelling: a powerful technology tool for the 21st century classroom. Theory Pract. **47**(3), 220–228 (2008)
15. Thomas, L.: Student retention in higher education: the role of institutional habitus. J. Educ. Policy **17**(4), 423–442 (2002)
16. Tinto, V.: Research and practice of student retention: what next? J. Coll. Stud. Retent.: Res. Theory Pract. **8**(1), 1–19 (2006)
17. Van der Zanden, P.J., Denessen, E., Cillessen, A.H., Meijer, P.C.: Domains and predictors of first-year student success: a systematic literature review. Educ. Res. Rev. **23**, 57–77 (2018)
18. Wilcox, P., Winn, S., Fyvie-Gauld, M.: It was nothing to do with the university, it was just the people': the role of social support in the first-year experience of higher education. Stud. High. Educ. **30**(6), 707–722 (2005)
19. Tovar, E., Simon, M.A., Lee, H.B.: Development and validation of the college mattering inventory with diverse urban college students. Meas. Eval. Couns. Dev. **42**(3), 154–178 (2009)
20. Baumeister, R.F., Leary, M.R.: The need to belong: desire for interpersonal attachments as a fundamental human motivation. Psychol. Bull. **117**(3), 497 (1995)
21. Kearney, M., Schuck, S.: Spotlight on authentic learning: Student developed digital video projects. Australas. J. Educ. Technol. **22**(2) (2006)
22. Reed, A.: Exploring the perceptions of current computer science students and student affairs professionals on the factors influencing student retention and attrition (Doctoral dissertation), pp. 189–208 (2016)

Content Development for Blended Learning

Study on Visual Learning Based on Network Environment

Kedong Li(✉) and Ying Li

South China Normal University, Guangzhou 510631, China
likedong@gmail.com

Abstract. The paper describes a study of visual learning in a network environment, which includes a new instructional model, the STILE (situation, tools, interaction, lucubration, evaluation) model which is based on Problem Based Learning (PBL). We describe the process of blended learning through a teaching experiment which offers a good reference to teachers. We then describe how this model can be carried out in a network environment efficiently. The experimental results show that visual learning in a network environment can improve the learning effect, which promotes students' learning from passive to active and leads to a better communication and reflection. This study also shows the effects on improving teachers' professional development. One aim of this study is to develop students' 4C (Critical Thinking and Problem Solving, Collaboration, Communication and Creativity) abilities through a series of activities both offline and online. The other aim is to enrich the theory of visual learning based on network environment and to implement the application of visual technology and the concept of personalized learning into practical teaching.

Keywords: Visual learning · Network environment · STILE model

1 Introduction

It is essential for individuals be able to use visual content and materials in order to engage capably in a visually-oriented society [1, 2]. Visual learning usually refers to a type of learning styles in which teachers and learners utilize graphs, charts, maps and diagrams for learning [3]. In recent years, we have carried out visual learning action research in several schools in Guangdong province of China and have achieved great effects. We found that visual learning can change the traditional instructional pattern of which students just receive knowledge from teachers. To further our study based on the previous results, we attempted to explore how visual learning would work in a network environment. In this section, we will introduce visual learning and describe the technical supports in the network environment.

1.1 Visual Learning

In our study, visual learning includes three elements: knowledge visualization resources, thinking visualization tools and data visualization methods. Teachers can use knowledge visualization resources (such as videos, animation) to create a problem-based learning

S. K. S. Cheung et al. (Eds.): ICBL 2018, LNCS 10949, pp. 151–161, 2018.
https://doi.org/10.1007/978-3-319-94505-7_12

environment; students can use thinking visualization tools (such as Venn diagram, Fishbone diagram) to think and analyze the knowledge; and teachers and researchers can evaluate and assess students through data visualization methods (such as Radar map).

Knowledge Visualization Resources. Knowledge visualization resources refer to the construction, communication and presentation of complex knowledge by using graphic image techniques of two- or three-dimensional activities. These resources can effectively convey facts to students, and help students correctly remember, apply and reconstruct knowledge and generate new knowledge. The main representative forms of these resources include image, animation, picture and video. The most important aspect of knowledge visualization is the ability to create a real problem in a visual form so that students can explore and obtain knowledge.

Thinking Visualization Tools. In the teaching process, the way of thinking visually can help develop students' intuitive thinking, divergent thinking, imaginal thinking and innovative thinking, as well as in improving their cognitive structure [3].

Using thinking visualization tools refers to the visual process of using a series of graphical techniques to present the previously unseen thinking methods and thinking paths. Therefore, using the method and the process of "thinking" makes teachers more conveniently present visually; makes students understand and internalize the knowledge easily, and improves the efficiency of information processing and information transmission. There are various thinking visualization tools but the main tools include three categories: Mind Map, Graphical thinking tools, and Table thinking tools (PMIQ table).

Mind Map, as shown in Fig. 1, can help learners organize and represent divergent thinking. Graphical thinking tools as shown in Figs. 2, 3, 4 and 5, such as Venn diagram, X/Y/W diagram, Pyramid diagram and Fishbone diagram, can help develop students' diverse logical thinking. Table thinking tools such as PMIQ table as shown in Fig. 6, can promote students' ability to reflect and ask questions. There are four aspects of PMIQ: plus, minus, interesting and question. Plus means the knowledge students have acquired. Minus means the knowledge students have still not yet acquired. Interesting means the knowledge students are interested in. Question means the knowledge students still have questions.

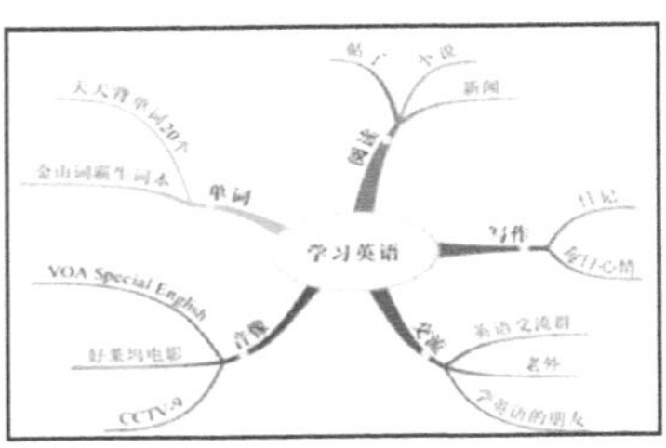

Fig. 1. Mind Map

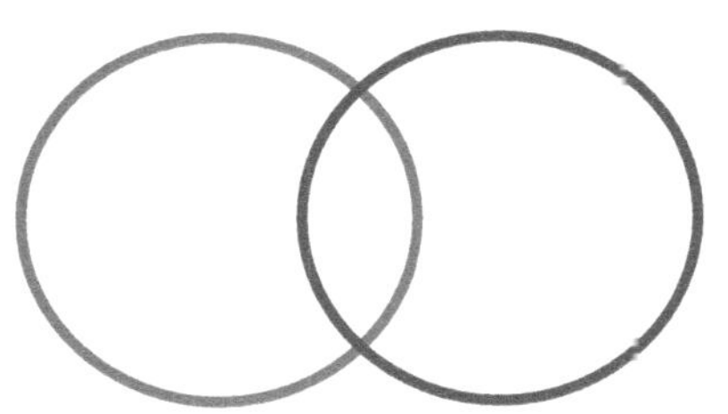

Fig. 2. Venn diagram

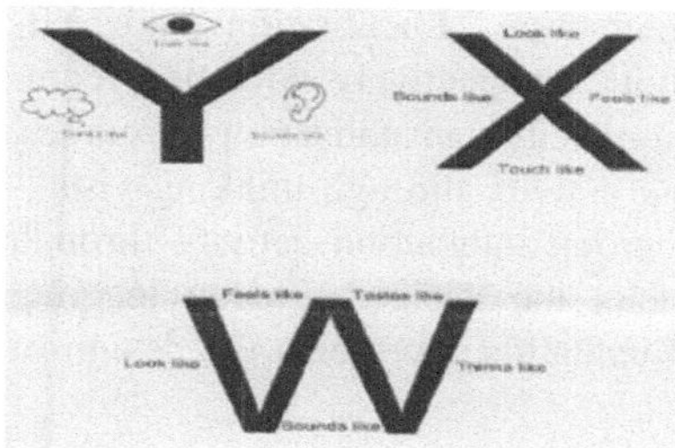

Fig. 3. X/Y/W diagram

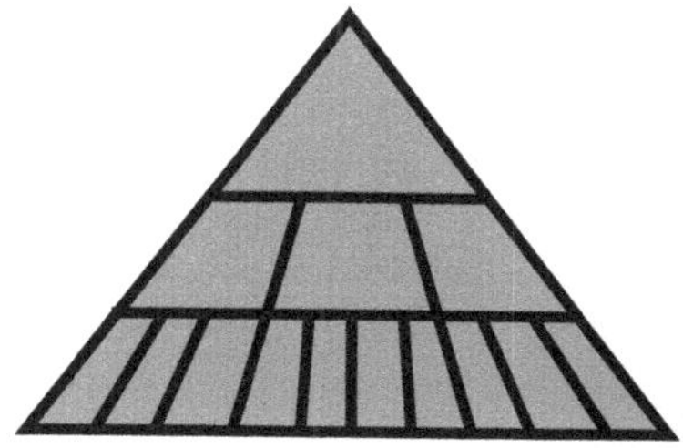

Fig. 4. Pyramid diagram

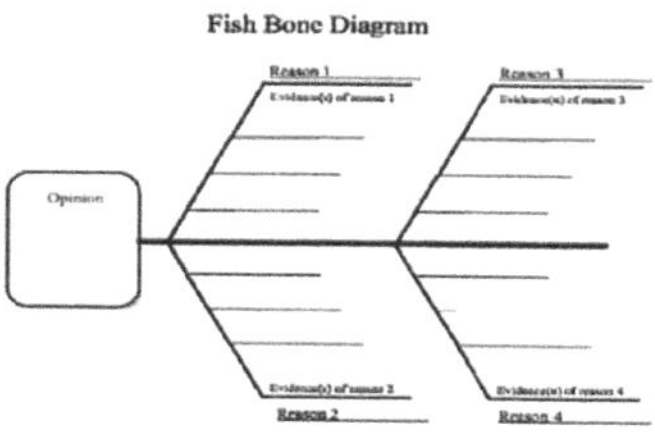

Fig. 5. Fishbone diagram

P (Plus)	M (Minus)	I (Interesting)	Q (Question)
①______( )	①______( )		
②______( )	②______( )		
③______( )	③______( )		
④______( )	④______( )		

Fig. 6. PMIQ table

Data Visualization Methods. Data visualization methods refer to the theoretical method and the use of computer graphics and image processing technologies which transform data into graphics or images visually seen on a screen and allow interactive processing. The main methods are radar map (Fig. 7) and scatterplot (Fig. 8) which can reflect the correlation or trend of data, and help teachers to observe and analyze data intuitively, and find the implicit rules in data.

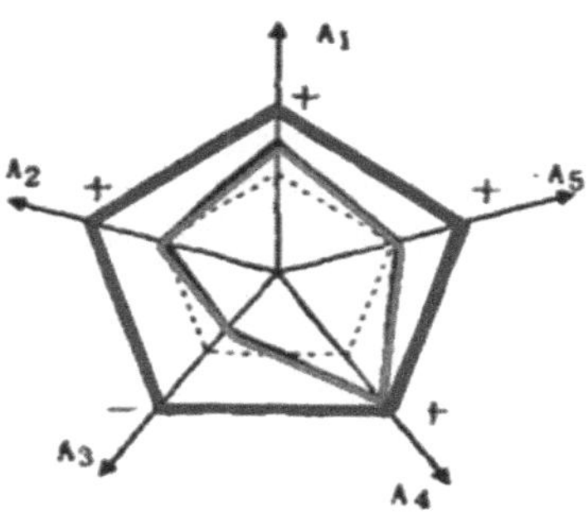

Fig. 7. Radar map

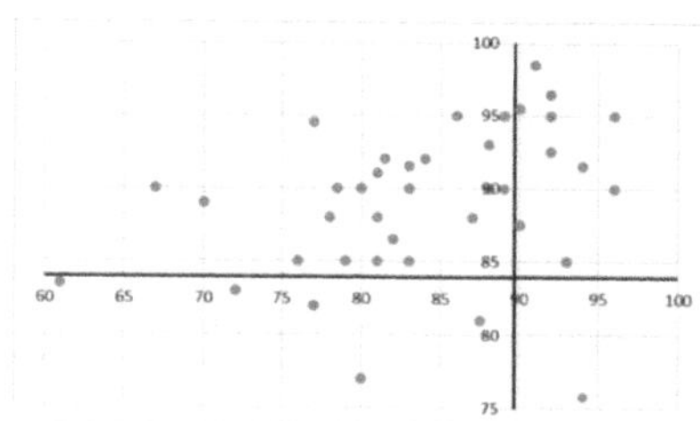

Fig. 8. Scatterplot

1.2 The STILE Model Based on PBL

To promote students' learning from passive to active, we adopted an instructional model named STILE (Fig. 9) through the action research [4]. The STILE model has five elements including Situation, Thinking, Interaction, Lucubration and self-Evaluation. These five elements represent five activities respectively. Situation represents the design of problem situation through knowledge visualization resources. Thinking represents the design of students' thinking activity through thinking visualization tools. Interaction represents the design of group interaction activity through thinking visualization works. Lucubration represents the design of deep learning activity under the guidance of an instructor. Self-Evaluation represents the design of students' reflection.

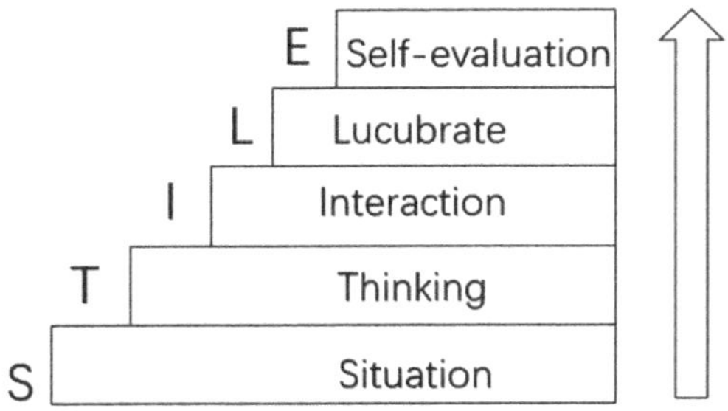

Fig. 9. The STILE model

1.3 The Network Environment

A network learning environment is required to meet the demands of students in self-study and in communicating with each other. There are several technical supports in providing services in a network learning environment. These supports include the infrastructure such as the WIFI system; the educational cloud platform comprising of the instructional resource repository, instructional service and students' space; learning devices including Pad or smart phone, display terminal and information analysis device. Teachers can design learning activities to promote students' active learning and take control on students' learning situation in a network learning environment.

In order to take the full advantages of a network learning environment, teachers need to master additional knowledge in technological pedagogical knowledge (TPK) and get themselves familiar with the concept and process of blended learning [5].

2 Purpose and Significance of the Study

In order to cope with the rapid advancement in technologies of the society and the corresponding demand on talents, New Media Consortium put forward the 21st century skills, which can be summarized as the 4Cs: Critical Thinking and Problem Solving, Collaboration, Communication and Creativity [6]. One aim of this study is to develop students' 4C abilities through a series of activities both offline and online. We adopted the Problem Based Learning (PBL) theory to guide our practice.

Terry Heick [7] described the nine characteristics of the 21st century study. These characteristics include (1) learner-centered, (2) media-driven, (3) personalized, (4) transfer-centered, (5) visibly relevant, (6) data-rich, (7) adaptable, (8) interdependent and, (9) diverse. The other aim is to enrich the theory of visual learning based on a network environment and to design and apply visual technology and the concept of personalized learning into real life teaching, so as to offer a good reference to the design of blended learning process.

3 Methods

3.1 Participants

Participants included students and teachers from 34 schools ranging 9 grades covering subjects in Chinese, Mathematics, Science and English. There were over 40 teachers and more than 200 students participating in this project. This paper described only one case of practice in Mathematics in a primary school in Foshan as an example. There were about 40 students and 1 teacher in this case. The topic of this case is "Line segment, Ray, Line".

3.2 The Process of Blended Learning

Learning activities were carried out in a specific learning environment under the guidance of the teacher. The learning community learned through exploration, cooperation and individual learning. Learning activities were designed to develop students' skills and attitudes [8]. Interactions between students and teachers were encouraged in the network learning environment to complete the specific learning tasks as assigned by the teachers. Blended learning combines the advantages of offline learning and online learning. These advantages include using blended learning activity in promoting deep learning, in integrating the teaching plan design with the subject matter, and learning elements supporting each other from goals to tasks and activities [9].

By reviewing the previous literature, we learned about the elements of blended learning and the design of the process. We summarized this blended learning process in Fig. 10. There are a total of ten activities including six offline learning activities and four online learning activities.

Offline learning activities include (1) students review old knowledge with the Pyramid diagram; (2) teachers play the video and create a problem situation with a question; (3) students collaborate with their group members using thinking visualization tools and answer the question which teachers put forward within the Venn diagram; (4) students lucubrate learning through games and perfect their diagrams; (5) students communicate with other groups; (6) teachers summarize the lesson and emphasize key point of the subject knowledge.

Online learning activities include (1) students watch the video repeatedly using the e-schoolbag system and think about the question; (2) students display the group's Venn diagram through the network; (3) students lucubrate learning through the repository of

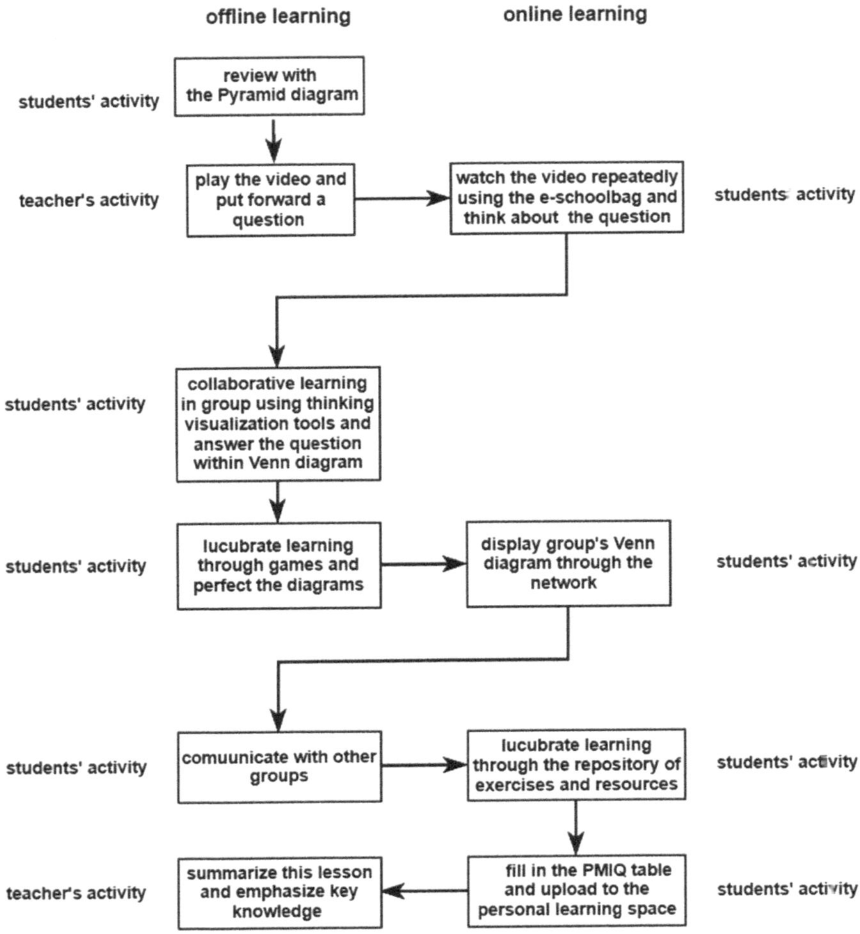

Fig. 10. The process of blended learning

exercises and resources; (4) students fill in the PMIQ table and upload it to the personal learning space.

As shown in Fig. 10, most of the activities are designed for students and there are just two activities for teachers in the whole blended learning process which reflects the adoption of the student-centered approach in designing the blended learning process.

The process was also designed with adoption to the STILE (situation, tools, interaction, lucubration, evaluation) model.

S (situation): In this case, the teacher asked the question that "What is the connection and difference among Line segment, Ray and Line?" to create the problem-situation through the video. This video was recorded by the teacher for the students in relation to daily life. At the end of the video, the teacher asked the question to inspire students to think. In addition, the teacher could also select appropriate resources in whatever forms from the Internet. Generally, the teacher needed to reorganize the resources properly and asked a question relating to the key knowledge points at the end.

T (tools): In this case, students chose to use the Venn diagram to facilitate the discussing and thinking about the question actively. They used the tool to learn by themselves through watching the videos repeatedly. Students could choose different thinking visualization tools to learn and answer the question according to different types of question and knowledge.

I (interaction): There are two kinds of interaction: students' communication in their own group and students' communication among groups with the following steps, discussing, communicating in own group, communicating among groups, displaying and explaining the work in a collaborative manner. There is an effective method for promoting collaborative learning in a group. The teacher set up different roles according to the different tasks respectively in advance, which might facilitate real cooperation rather than just becoming the captain's task. There are two ways of communication among groups. One is cross-group publication. The method we adopted is that each group arranged one member to stay in the own group displaying their work and answering questions, the remaining members then went to other groups and asked questions. Three to five minutes later, they came back and reported on what they had learned. The other is cross-group intersect. The implemented method is that group members went to other groups to compare others works with themselves and then improved their works. Both ways required effective guidance from teachers.

L (lucubration): In this case, it includes two kinds of lucubration, playing games offline and doing exercises online. Through this part, students could strengthen the understanding of the problem and complete their diagrams. Game playing was under the instruction and guidance of the teacher. Later, they did the exercises online according to their learning situation, a kind of personalized learning to realize layered teaching and self-paced learning.

E (evaluation): In this case, the main evaluation method is using the PMIQ table. Students filled in the table and asked some innovative questions. This would help students in extending their study. The most important aim of PMIQ is to develop the habit of asking questions and thinking critically.

In this process, students can use the network repository to study and deepen the learning. Students can use the network to share their ideas and reflect themselves. For teachers, they are required to learn asking questions rather than telling answers to students and they must have the ability to choose the appropriate resources and organize them effectively. Teachers can also use the instructional system to grasp students' learning situations and evaluate students' performance easily.

Table 1. Teacher's evaluation scale for visual learning

School name				
Name	Gender	Subject		Teaching experience
	Totally agree	Agree	Not agree	Totally disagree
1. You can select the visual resources and design questions through the network				
2. You can guide students to select and adopt visual tools to answer questions				
3. You can organize students to carry out group cooperative learning activities through the network				
4. You have a more profound understanding of the student-centered teaching idea through teaching practice				
5. You have a better understanding of problem - oriented teaching method through practice				
6. You can strengthen and deepen the students' learning with various teaching methods both online and offline				
7. You think visual learning activities can help students develop their thinking ability				
8. You think network environment can promote the visual learning				

Table 2. Students' evaluation scale for visual learning

School name				
Name	Gender	Subject		Class
Question	Totally agree	Agree	Not agree	Totally disagree
1. You are very interested in this class				
2. You can understand the issues raised in the micro video				
3. You can use the online instructional repository to self-study				
4. You can complete the task base on thinking tools by yourself				
5. You can take an active part in group learning activities				
6. You can use the online learning space to express your idea				
7. You can understand the content of this lesson				
8. You can use the PMIQ table to reflect and measure yourself				

4 Trial Effect

In order to evaluate the effect of visual learning in a network environment, we designed two scales [10]: Teacher's Evaluation scale as shown in Table 1 for Visual learning, and Students' Evaluation scale for Visual learning as shown in Table 2. We also conducted a deep interview with the teacher.

The questionnaire of teachers' evaluation scale had been distributed to 21 teachers, and 20 effective questionnaires were received. Among them, 14 teachers were skillful teachers who have worked for 2 years, the other 6 were new teachers who just joined this project for only half a year. The answers to the questions in the scales were represented by 2, 1, −1, −2 from "totally agree" to "totally disagree" respectively. The total score was calculated according to the two-way rating scale calculation formula $Fi = \sum ajnij/2N$. The calculated results are shown in Table 3. From the analysis results

Table 3. Data statistics for teachers' evaluation scale

No.	New teacher					Skilled teacher				
	Totally agree	Agree	Not agree	Strongly disagree	Fi	Totally agree	Agree	Not agree	Strongly disagree	Fi
1	3	3	0	0	0.75	12	2	0	0	0.93
2	3	3	0	0	0.75	13	1	0	0	0.96
3	3	3	0	0	0.75	12	2	0	0	0.93
4	2	4	0	0	0.67	13	1	0	0	0.96
5	1	5	0	0	0.58	13	1	0	0	0.96
6	2	4	0	0	0.67	12	2	0	0	0.93
7	1	5	0	0	0.58	13	1	0	0	0.96
8	3	3	0	0	0.75	12	2	0	0	0.93

shown in Table 3, we can see that the scoring rate Fi of all items for skillful teachers and new teachers are more than 0.5, which shows that both new teachers and skillful teachers have achieved obvious results in teaching ability after the practice of visual learning trail. In addition, the scoring rate Fi of skillful teachers is higher than that of new teachers, which shows that the long-term visual learning trail can improve the professional development of teachers and the thinking ability of students.

In order to investigate the effect of this research on students' ability development, 555 pieces of visual learning student's self-evaluation scales were distributed and 555 questionnaires with valid data were collected. Through calculating the scoring rate, each Fi is more than 0.5, the specific data analysis is shown as Table 4, which shows that students are interested in teaching activities with visual learning methods, and most students can understand the question asked in visual resources and can find solutions by use thinking visual tools. In addition, students can devote themselves to group learning interaction actively, and master the relevant knowledge after visual learning trail in a network learning environment.

Table 4. Data statistics for students' self-evaluation scale

No.	Totally agree	Agree	Not agree	Strongly disagree	Fi
1	428	120	3	4	0.87
2	362	181	11	1	0.80
3	394	151	9	1	0.84
4	409	135	9	2	0.85
5	406	145	4	0	0.86
6	405	145	5	0	0.86
7	420	125	8	2	0.87
8	425	125	5	0	0.88

During the interview, teachers said that there was a great improvement in their capability in searching for relevant learning resources and integrating data from various sources. Both students and teachers considered that visual learning in a network learning environment could improve the teaching and learning effect and could help develop students' capability of critical thinking and problem solving.

5 Conclusion

In our study, we summarize the process of visual learning in a network learning environment and have achieved encouraging results. With the rapid development of learning analysis tools, blended learning may play a more effective role in visual learning, which can help teacher know the learning of students.

However, there are also some challenges for teachers. On the one hand, teachers should improve their ability in designing blended learning activities in four aspects, associating the learning contents closely to the characteristics of learners, designing a blended learning activity carrier for deep learning; correlating the various integrative learning elements, and applying blended learning in an innovative manner.

On the other hand, teachers need to improve their ability in conducting class with blended learning design in four aspects too, viewing multiple learning theories, ensuring guidance with creativity, making prompt reaction to questions and situations in class, and applying up-to-date technology.

Of course, it is worth noting that teachers would not have a good grasp of designing and conducting the blended learning class, especially deep learning overnight, before they have a deep rational understanding of teaching. Rich teaching practice and constant reflection are required to deal with a complex and dynamic class. Meanwhile, teachers need to adapt to various teaching situations and form deep insight and acute responsiveness of visual learning in a network learning environment.

However, the application of blended learning theory to visual learning practice is still only a minority, so we have to devote ourselves to this research area in the future and to maximize its effectiveness. We now plan to promote it to more schools in Dongguan and Shenzhen.

References

1. Hattwig, D., Burgess, J., Bussert, K., Medaille, A.: Visual Literacy Competency Standards for Higher Education. Association of College and Research Libraries (2011)
2. Yang, H.H.: An integrated approach to developing visual literacy. In: Cheung, S.K.S., Fong, J., Fong, W., Wang, F.L., Kwok, L.F. (eds.) ICHL 2013. LNCS, vol. 8038, pp. 219–231. Springer, Heidelberg (2013). https://doi.org/10.1007/978-3-642-39750-9_21
3. Zhao, H.C., Wang, Y.: Retrospect and prospect of the research on visual of thinking in China: an analysis based on the 2003–2013 papers of China knowledge network. China Educ. Technol. **4**, 10–17 (2014)
4. Li, K.D.: Visual learning action research. Educ. Inf. Technol. **7**, 9–17 (2016)
5. Ao, Q., Liu, H., Jia, S.D.: Study on the "case - task" driven teaching mode in hybrid learning. Modern Educ. Technol. **03**, 122–126 (2013)
6. Trilling, B., Fadel, C.: 21st Century Skills: Learning for Life in Our Times. Wiley, Hoboken (2012)
7. Heick, T.: 9 Characteristics Of 21st Century Learning. Teach Thought (2012)
8. Li, H.M., Xu, W., Zhang, J.P.: Learning in an environment of virtual fusion, movement and design. China Educ. Technol. **1**, 23–29 (2013)
9. Peng, F.X., Yang, W.: How to deepen learning and how to support learning analysis with educational big data? Modern Distance Educ. **2**, 31–39 (2017)
10. Li, K.D., Sun, N.W.: Evaluation research of visual learning trial effect. In: International Conference of Media Education (2017)

Design and Implementation of an Immersive Virtual Reality Biological Courseware—Miraculous Eyeball

Qingtang Liu[1], Shufan Yu[1](✉), Luyu Lin[2], Suxiao Xu[1], and Linjin Wu[1]

[1] School of Educational Information Technology, Central China Normal University, Wuhan 430079, Hubei, China
yushufan1993@gmail.com
[2] National Engineering Research Center for E-learning, Central China Normal University, Wuhan 430079, Hubei, China

Abstract. In recent years, immersive interactive technologies are becoming more and more mature. A large number of schools actively carry out virtual experimental teaching and establish virtual laboratories. As a kind of immersive interactive technology, virtual reality technology is attracting increasing attention in education. This paper describes the characteristics of immersive VR, hardware and software types, summarizes the different forms of VR used in teaching and discusses the principles of biological virtual experiment construction in other research. Taking the teaching content of 'structure of eyeball' in middle school biology textbook as a case, this research designs and develops a virtual experiment courseware - Miraculous eyeball. The research suggests that to construct outstanding teaching experiments of VR not only needs mature equipment and technologies but also requires a combination of decent teaching theories and tactics.

Keywords: Interactive learning · Virtual reality · Immersive courseware Biological experiment

1 Introduction

Virtual reality is a digital environment integrated with vision, hearing and touching generated by computer technology. It combines with relevant science and technology and can be highly similar to the real environment within a certain range [1]. VR technology originated in the United States. As early as 1965, Ivan Sutherland proposed the basic idea that the VR system includes the interactive graphics display, force feedback device and voice prompt [2]. Then in 1966, Lincoln Studio in Massachusetts Institute of Technology officially started the research of HMD (head-mounted display). And in 1980, the first full-featured HMD was officially launched. After entering the 21st century, by applying robust 3D computing capabilities, rendering and data transmission, VR technology entered a completely new era. In 2013, Oculus released its HMD Oculus Rift, then HTC released its own HMD vive in 2015. With the participation of different giants, VR industry becomes much more matured. The media

S. K. S. Cheung et al. (Eds.): ICBL 2018, LNCS 10949, pp. 162–174, 2018.
https://doi.org/10.1007/978-3-319-94505-7_13

even regarded the year 2016 as "VR Year" [3]. "Virtual/Augmented Reality White Paper (2017)" released by the Chinese Academy of Information and Communication pointed out that in China, governments at all levels are actively promoting the development of virtual reality. VR has been listed in the "13th Five-Year" information planning, Internet plus and other major national documents. Till the end of 2016, nearly 20 provinces and cities began to develop the virtual reality industry.

Experiment is an important method of human cognizing and transforming the world. Laboratory experimentation plays an essential role in engineer and science education [4]. With the development of Educational Informatization and the innovation of new multimedia technologies, the employment of VR technology in teaching experiments has become popular. Various primary and secondary schools are actively setting up VR labs and carrying out VR teaching. It is generally believed that virtual experiments can provide learners with a flexible, open and independent learning environment and learning resources, thereby enhancing the teaching of science and engineering.

Numerous researches show that experimental teaching in the VR environment has the following advantages compared to the traditional classroom: 1. Can present the spatial relationship and the internal structure of the object perfectly 2. Can simulate a specific scene and perform dangerous experiments 3. Can save a considerable cost [5]. Thus, the immersive experience of teaching courseware and teaching environment has a high requirement. Existing virtual reality courseware designed for K-12 students is of varying quality, and most of them fail to achieve the desired effect. Many educators and manufacturers are actively exploring the best design method of VR courseware, considering how to integrate teaching in a better way.

Biological experiments are diverse in different environments. In a traditional classroom, when students engage in biological experiments, if some dangerous drugs need to be exposed, teachers should devote great efforts to arranging experiments in advance in order to prevent students from being in danger. Besides, sometimes microbiological structures cannot have the authentic feeling. But using VR technology can avoid many kinds of danger and enhance the sense of immersion and interaction [6]. This paper explores the application of VR in biology teaching under the premise of analyzing the application form of different virtual reality equipment in education. Taking the structure of the eyeball in the textbook of middle school as an example, this research designs and implements a VR-based biology courseware- Miraculous eyeball in order to make a probable attempt at immersive biological teaching.

The rest of this paper will be organized in the following order: The second part summarizes the different types of VR devices and explores their application in teaching. The third part introduces the design process of the biological teaching courseware. The last part is the summary and prospect of this article.

2 Immersive Virtual Reality Equipment and Analysis of Its Educational Application

VR has three major characteristics: Imagination, Immersion, Interaction. And according to different standards, VR systems have different categories, which usually be divided into the following three categories: 1. desktop virtual reality system (Desktop VR), this system is mainly using graphics workstations and monitors, a virtual scene is created and participants use peripherals such as a mouse and keyboard to interact. 2. Distributed VR, it is based on a networked virtual environment in which multiple users or virtual environments at different physical environments are connected each other, another circumstance is that multiple users are participating in the same VR environment, people interact and share information with other users through the computer. 3. Immersive VR, which is based on head-mounted devices and projection devices. It can provide users with the same scene in two different viewing angles so as to achieve an immersive 3D experience.

The diversity of VR technologies offers a variety of options for different types of instructional content. Currently, immersive VR teaching based on HMD is the mainstream solution in teaching. For biology class, immersive HMD can provide realistic interact and vivid demonstration. To a certain extent, it can also save manpower and material costs. Therefore, immersive VR is the main topic of this article, and immersive VR headset is selected to design the courseware in this research.

2.1 The Feature and Types of Immersive VR

Immersive VR provides a fully immersive experience for the participant, gives users a feeling of being in the real world. It encloses the visual, audible, and other senses of participants in a pre-designed virtual reality space which mixes sound, location tracker, data glove, and other hand-held input devices to give participants an immersive, focused experience. Autonomy, presence and interactivity have constituted its three core characteristics [7]. At present, HMD (head-mounted display) and projection VR system are the most common Immersive VR device.

2.1.1 HMD (Head-Mounted Display) VR System

- *Mobile VR headset*

In 2014, Google's I/O Developer Conference released a seemingly "chilly" cardboard box, but it had become the biggest surprise in this session. Google promotes VR into the ordinary mobile phone through this cheap approach, and mobile VR concept began to emerge. Mobile VR, as its' name implies, is a VR box with a pair of convex lenses attaching a mobile device based on the principle of binocular parallax. In order to bring immersive experience, the corresponding pictures of two eyeballs display on the two sides of mobile phone. Mobile VR has portable, cheap and other advantages. it brings many people who have no conditions to experience VR a viable way to feel it. By the end of 2017, the cardboard application download volume in the Google Play

Store has exceeded 10 million. After that, many manufacturers also released their own "cardboard", such as Storm Mirror, Xiaomi VR box, Samsung gearvr and so on.

However, due to mobile device limitations such as phone's inherent low-resolution and CPU/GPU weakness, the feeling of dizziness may be occurring when experience VR, and only through the gyroscope 360-degree operation walk and interact in space is impossible. In education, the applications of cardboard mainly focus on users' experience. For example, Nival continuous release several cardboard-based educational games such as Inmind and Incell. It is worth mentioning that Incell provides a scientific strategy for players to experience the microscopic world of human cells and to learn how to prevent the invasion of viruses in advance.

- *All-in-one VR headset*

All-in-one device is a VR headset with an independent processor. It possesses separate operation, input and output functions. Though the configuration is not as strong as the PC VR headset, All-in-one VR has no connection constraints. And it has a better experience compared to mobile VR since the higher degree of freedom. With the maturity of inside-out, slam and other technologies, all-in-one VR device also ushered in its spring. In the second half of 2017, oculus go, released by Facebook, supports three-dimensional head tracking (3DOF) with the "best optical system" and "wide field of vision". Fast switching technology, high visual clarity, making its experience closer to the pc VR. Its presence brings all-in-one VR machine an unlimited future.

In China, Pico and IdeaLens are two major companies providing equipment for STEM education in primary and secondary schools and they have established a large number of high-quality teaching resources through cooperation with various VR education companies. At present, teaching applications of all-in-one headset are also mainly for display, such as VR museums.

- *PC VR Headset*

For the perspective of demand, human-computer interaction becomes the core feature of VR compared to other inherent attributes of mobile phones and all-in-one devices. On the other hand, the VR terminal may degenerate into just a head-mounted TV/mobile phone without interaction. The use of outside-in technology in pc VR is a good solution to the problem of interaction. PC VR refers to VR display device with the high-performance computer. With sensing capabilities and interactive features, its data operations, image transmission, etc. completed by PC, has high quality [8]. PS VR, vive and oculus rift are the three most popular PC VR products at present.

In educational field, PC VR covers a wide range, including virtual tour, presentation, skill training and so on [9]. For instance, a group of Irish students rebuilt historic sites in OpenSim (a 3D environment) and ramble freely in it through the Oculus Rift headset. With the help of MissionV, this VR project provided Irish students with portable tools to build VR scenes.

2.1.2 Projection Virtual Reality System

In 1995, students at the University of Illinois established a three-sided projection room, in the middle of the it, users wear stereoscopic liquid crystal shutter glasses to watch VR movies. Based on this, they developed the CAVE (Cave Automatic Virtual

Environment) which we can see in the Fig. 1. CAVE is a projection-based immersive VR device that features high resolution, immersive and interactive characters. For Immersive experience and rich scientific research achievements, CAVE played a significant role in promoting modern virtual reality technology to the public [10]. In China, The VR-PLATFORM CAVE system developed by Vistandard has made a lot of innovations in military simulation, biomedicine, virtual disassembly, geology and topography education. Compared to HMD, the cave system is very expensive but more suitable for large class.

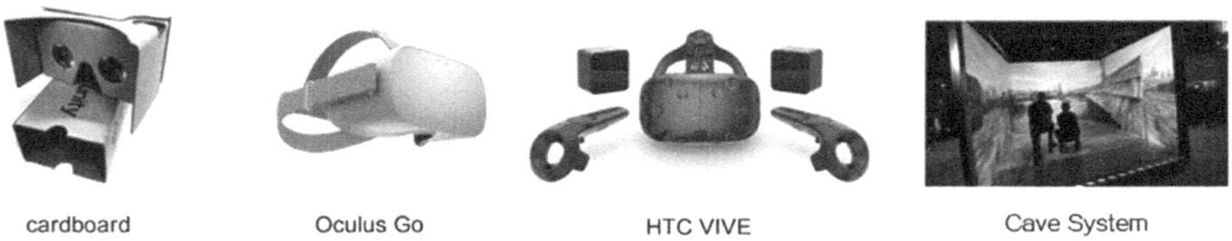

Fig. 1. Mobile VR, All-in-on VR, PC VR and CAVE system

For the four distinct categories of VR, we conducted a comparative evaluation of them in terms of immersion, interactivity, imagination, price and applicable class size and got the following results (Table 1).

2.2 Review of Educational Experiments of Immersive VR and Discussion of Its Construction Principle

As early as 1993, China University of Science and Technology was engaged in the research and development of campus virtual teaching experiment software. Two years later, the "WUJI Computer Simulation Experiment" system became the first VR learning software in the world, and many schools used this software for teaching [11]. Currently, there are also some web-based virtual engineering experiments developing by some companies such as Nobook. These Desktop-VR to some extent allow students to DIY and stimulate students' imagination. But the downside is low immersion and less interaction. Many researchers have been exploring the immersive VR teaching methods and theories based on HMD. Rong Cui has proposed five-point design principles of CAI Courseware based on VR. He believes that the difference between the construction of VR teaching resources and traditional teaching resources is the integration of student-centred concept and the idea of cultivating self-exploration capabilities [12]. Gao has corresponding research on the construction of VR virtual venues. He proposed the principles and strategies of constructing VR learning resources, including the advance of hardware selection, the elaboration of contents, the logical layout of structures, and the specialization of venue layout [8]. In the field of educational game, Wang et al. of Peking University Argue that VR/AR educational games and applications mainly have the following theoretical basis: situated learning theory, embodied cognition theory, flow theory and cooperative learning theory [13].

Table 1. Comparison of different VR

Comparison of different VR	Imagination	Immersion	Interaction	Price	Portability	Class size
Mobile VR headset	Low	Low	Simple interaction	Low	Portable	Medium size class (To some extent, it is not suitable for classroom teaching for the diversity of different mobiles)
All-in-one VR headset	Medium	Medium	Simple interaction	Medium	Portable	Large class
PC VR headset	High	Ultra	Rich interaction	High	Cumbersome	Small class (each student owns device), large class (3–5 students per device)
Cave automatic VR	Extreme	Medium	Lack of interaction	Ultra	Cannot carry	Small class (cave system), large class(9D movie)

Currently, experiment courseware based on immersive VR is mainly focused on engineering subjects. In biology, there are also some practices.

- Biological Experiment

Biological experiments include basic biology, biochemistry, biotechnology engineering, physiological anatomy, cell biology, molecular biology and microbiology and other experimental courses [14]. From another perspective, the preparation of biological experiments and the experimental process are time-consuming. In some more experiments, If the operation fails, students can not repeat the experiment again. Therefore, the use of VR can effectively save time and costs.

Jie Xu of Qingdao Experimental High School produced VR courseware "gene expression" which clearly expresses gene transcription and translation from curriculum introduction to classroom reflection through "Brain Tour", "Cell Structure", "Transcription" and "Translation" four scenes. Experiments show that VR can mainly reduce the cognitive load of students, convert abstract knowledge to figurative forms. And by interacting with the VR environment, students' idea can be inspired [15].

Chen of Central China Normal University designed and developed the "Bacillus subtilis isolation and culture" experiment based on HTC VIVE (pc headset). Except for the characteristics of bacillus morphological, students can understand the basic process and precautions of separating the target microorganism from the complicated environment. His combination of narrative theory in VR broadens courseware's perspective, attracts more attention and increases immersion in VR experiments [16].

As for the combination of VR and Biopsychology, Song et al. trained 116 pilots by self-designed VR levitation and relaxation feedback system. The experiment proves that the new biofeedback technology with VR technology as a carrier has an obvious effect on learners compared to traditional psychology technology and levitation technology [17].

More research shows that the principles below need to be followed in the production of VR courseware in biology:

1. Need to be different from the traditional multimedia courseware, the models should have an appropriate volume for a better demonstration and research
2. Need to construct reasonable scene in line with the corresponding learners' age and psychological characteristics
3. Need to combine the appropriate teaching theory, such as the embodied learning, spiral learning theory and so on
4. Need to control the learning time, it should be noted that VR courseware cannot completely replace the classroom, so the instructional design should be closely integrated into it

3 VR Courseware-Miraculous Eyeball

The structure of human eyeball is derived from the first section of chapter 4 in PEP (People's Education Press) Junior High School Biology Textbook Volume 7, and title of this section is "Body's perception of the external environment". This section consists of three parts: the basic function and structure of the human eye, the process of visual formation, the causes of myopia and its prevention.

The textbook introduces the basic structure and function of human eyeball through the principle of camera imaging. Then by illustrating a vivid example that cat's pupil can self-regulate in the environment of different brightness, it shows that the human eyeball can also be self-adjusted according to different environments. Finally, causes of myopia and principles to adjust will be introduced. The knowledge is well-structured by this book.

However, as for the textbook, it only shows a simple two-dimensional structure of eyes. Students can only construct the specific structure and details of the eyeball by imagining. Therefore, it is hard to explore the structure of the eyeball and the visual principle through traditional textbooks. If we employ VR technology, a lifelike eyeball can be created, and learners can freely scale, move, rotate it. By this way, not only can immersive sense be brought but also students' learning motivation can be stimulated.

Therefore, in order to create a better VR experience, this article uses the HMD device HTC vive to produce the immersive VR courseware. Guoxiang Zhang, teacher in the Cross-border Software Company in Suzhou which is committed to VR education, said that VR educational effect is able to be better if learning time is controlled under 15 min a day, and 7 min each time. For primary and junior high school students, the deterioration of eyesight caused by VR experience is not allowed. Therefore, it should be noted that VR courseware can only serve as an auxiliary role in the classroom. It can't replace a teacher's position.

3.1 Teaching Objectives of the Courseware

Following the standard of junior high school biology teaching book, we set the teaching target:

1. To make users know the structure of the eyeball, the visual principle of the eye, the cause of myopia and hyperopia
2. To stimulate learning motivation in biology
3. To achieve the sublimation of knowledge through self-exploration in a virtual environment

In VR class, teacher explains the knowledge and encourages students to carry out discussion after the simple exploration of the structure of eyes. Students take the Helix ascending learning through the courseware.

Based on this, this study suggests that the VR eyeball courseware can be set to four parts, including the structure of the eyeball, the principle of how eyeballs build images, the causes and correction methods of myopia and the expanded knowledge about hyperopia.

3.2 Interactive Design and Technical Detail

The interaction mainly contains the model design, scene design and human-computer interaction design.

Eyeball is the main resource for this system. To model it, we make a detailed design for each part of it. At the same time, we have modeled the experiment classroom and provided learners with the best experience in a highly simulated environment. (Figure 2) And there are two main scenes: scene one is the laboratory corresponding to the actual scenario and scene two is the virtual scene corresponding to the virtual environment. Learners have different interactive perspective in different situations.

As for the developing environment, we chose Unity3D which is the most popular game engine on the market. And two plugins were used: Steam VR and VR_TK. The design process of the system is as follows (Fig. 3).

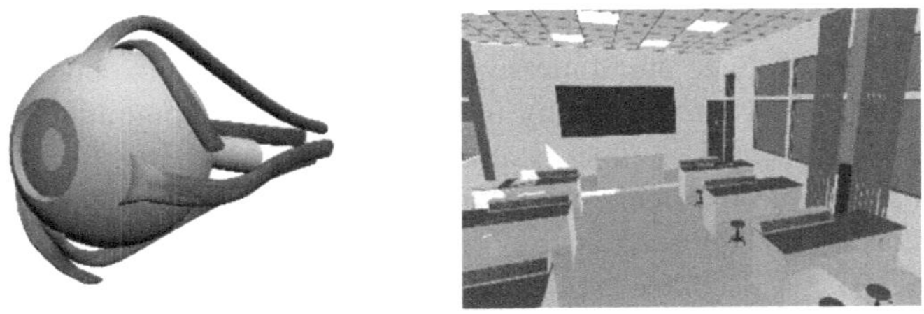

Fig. 2. Models of this courseware

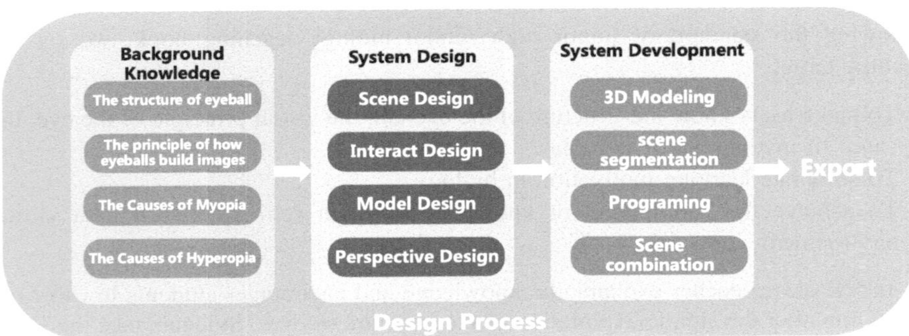

Fig. 3. Design process

3.3 Content Design

3.3.1 The Structure of Eyeball

1. Scene one. On the blackboard writes a chalk textured text "structure of human eyeball" right in front of the eye model. Users can rotate, scale and move the model freely to see its detailed structure.
2. Switch to "scene two". The detailed structure of eyeball is presented with descriptive texts floating next to corresponding parts. Users can interact with each part. (Figure 4)

In this section, the structure of the eyeball is introduced to enhance the student's impression of the eyeball and stimulate their learning motivation through self-exploration.

3.3.2 The Principle of How Eyeballs Build Images

Learners will be given a question of how human eyes can detect light through audio. With this question in mind, the elementary theory of how eyeballs build images will be illustrated through an example of how human will build an image of apple in brains.

In this part, with curiosity and doubt, users learn the principle of eyeballs to see objects and achieve a fusion of knowledge by an embodied cognition.

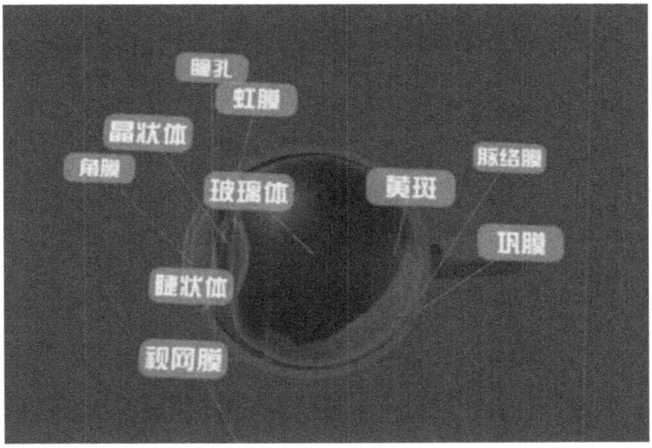

Fig. 4. The structure of eyeball in "scene two"

3.3.3 The Causes and Correction Methods of Myopia

1. Switch back to the "scene one" and play the record with the corresponding animation "myopia is one of the eye diseases modern adolescents suffer. When normal people see objects far away, the ciliary body relaxes and the lens becomes thinner, then the light passes through the lens and converges on the retina. Nonetheless, myopia is not like this".
2. One of the reasons for myopia - The lens is too thick.
   By pressing the vive joystick touchpad button to trigger the light, the image will be converged in front of the retina through thicker lens. Convergence point is highlighted and blinks twice. The corresponding explanations will be playing: There are two kinds of myopia: one is refractive myopia. The lens is too thick so that its refractive power becomes stronger, thus the light coming from a distant point will converge in front of the retina before reaching. It's not a point but a blurred bright spot when arriving at the final. After broadcasting all the animation, the "jump button" will appear which used to tell users another reason for myopia.
3. Another reason for myopia - Ocular axis is too long
   When the eyeball is too long in the anterior-posterior direction, light from a distance point will gather in front of the retina. The result is the same as the refractive myopia - when it arrives at the retina, it is not a point but a blurry bright spot. Similarly, the light triggered by Vive joystick touchpad-button passes through a long ocular axis, finally converges in front of the retina.
4. Embodied experience: From the perspective of the myopic eye in the virtual world, the scenery outside the window is blurred and the words on the book can only be seen in very close distance. (Figure 5 is the embodied experience)

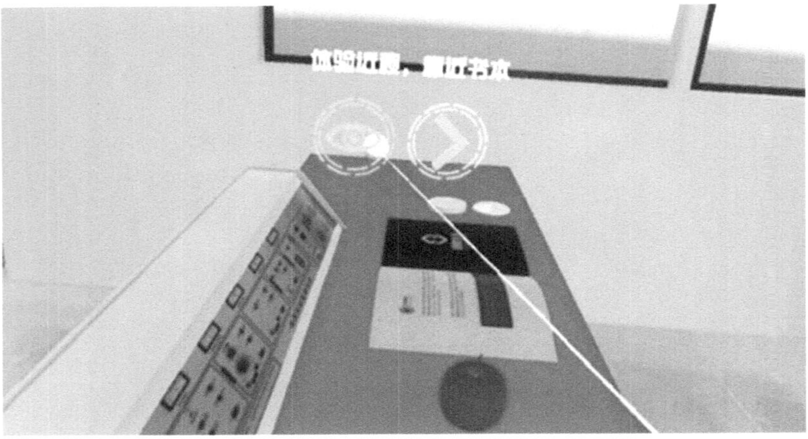

Fig. 5. Experience myopia in "scene one"

5. Myopia correction: In the virtual scene, put glasses on a myopic eye. The light will diverge through the concave lens and then converge on the retina through the lens and other parts. The convergence point will highlight and flash twice. Then the scene will be clear.

In normal classes, students already have a preliminary understanding of the textbook knowledge. Through this part of the experience, learners have a profound impression on the principle of eye myopia. And they can discuss the causes and correction of hyperopia. Finally, expanded knowledge will be introduced in the last part.

3.3.4 The Causes and Correction Methods of Hyperopia

Switch back to the "scene one" and play the record with the corresponding animation: Hyperopia is one of the eye diseases suffering modern adolescents. When normal people see objects far away, the ciliary body shrinks and the lens becomes thicker, then the light passes through the lens and converges on the retina.

The reason for hyperopia is Contrary to myopia, this section presents the two reasons for hyperopia (the lens is too thin/the ocular axis is too short) in the same method.

This part is to expand the student's horizon. The knowledge is also being improved and consolidated through Embodied experience.

4 Conclusion

The research reviews the virtual experiment based on various immersive HMD and its applications in teaching, designs and develops a set of HTC vive (PC VR headset) teaching courseware- Miraculous eyeball with the knowledge of high school biology. When designing the courseware, we considered and integrated instructional theory such as cooperative learning, embodied learning, inquiry learning and spiral ascension learning. The research aims to provide a VR experimental courseware model through the design and production of this product.

Through this study, we believe that the design and development of VR courseware resources not only need premium equipment and technology but also require to combine the correct teaching strategies and theories. A right teaching theory is the basis for guiding the classroom, is the strong support for teachers in class, is the fountain of student's motivation. The teaching will be colourful if the application of VR is controlled rightly in teaching time and manner.

At the same time, this study also has its own shortcomings. First of all, the content of system design is too much, which may cause cognitive load on some people. Secondly, we haven't conduct a wide range of teaching practice to prove the effect of courseware. Therefore, our future plan is to optimize the courseware on the basis of class teaching research.

The virtual reality technology is at the intersection of positively changing in 2018. As the multi-modal interaction technology becomes mature and AI become fiery. VR also seeks its own orientation in education. Although the new teaching model brought by VR technology is still only a prototype at present, and there is still a large space for us to imagine and improve. I firmly believe that, with the improvement of technology and the reduction of cost, VR will gradually become mature and will have more diversified applications in education and teaching in the future.

Acknowledgements. This research is supported by the Chinese National Natural Science Foundation Project "Research on Deep Aggregation and Personalized Service Mechanism of Web Learning Resources based on Semantic" (No.71704062), Hubei Province Technology Innovation special projects "Key technologies and demonstration applications of Internet + Precision Education" (No.2017ACA105) and Ministry of Education - China Mobile Research Fund 2017 Annual Project "Research and pilot of regional teaching and research mode supported by information technology"(No.MCM20170502).

References

1. Zhao, Q.P.: Review of virtual reality. Sci. China (Ser. F: Inf. Sci.) **39**(01), 2–46 (2009)
2. Sutherland, I.E.: The ultimate display. In: Multimedia: From Wagner to Virtual Reality (1965)
3. Didehbani, N., et al.: Virtual reality social cognition training for children with high functioning autism. Comput. Hum. Behav. **62**, 703–711 (2016)
4. Huang, R.H., Zheng, L.Q., Cheng, W.: The learners cognition and credibility of virtual experiments. Open Educ. Res. **18**(06), 9–15 (2012)
5. Ding, N., Wang, Y.M.: The application of virtual reality in education: advantages and challenges. Mod. Educ. Tech. **27**(2), 19–25 (2017)
6. Li, J.: Application of virtual reality technology in high school biology teaching. Prim. Second. Inf. Technol. Educ. **1**, 64–66 (2018)
7. Jonassen, D.H., et al.: Learning to Solve Problems with Technology. Pearson Education, London (2003)

8. Gao, Y.D., Yan, X.M., Li, X.: Design and implementation of immersive virtual reality venue: taking the development of red VR memorial in practical teaching of ideological and political courses as an example. eEduc. Res. **38**(12), 73–78+85 (2017)
9. Shi, T.J.: The application of virtual reality in education. Northeast Normal University (2008)
10. Zhou, Y.: Cardboard Interaction Design and Development of Virtual Reality Application. Hubei University of Technology (2017)
11. Yang, X.P.: Application Research of Virtual Reality Technology Based on Unity3D in Middle School Physics Teaching. Shanghai Normal University (2015)
12. Cui, R.: The Research of Realization and Effect of Independent Inquiry Learning Based on VR Technology–Take the Replication of DNA from Biology Course of High School for Example. Jiangxi Science and Technology Normal University (2015)
13. Wang, C.X., Li, H., Shang, J.J.: Application and development prospect of educational games based on virtual reality and augmented reality. China Educ. Tech. (8), 99–107 (2017)
14. Gu, H., Sun, Z.J., Li, Q.: Research of actual and virtual combined experimental teaching model in biology. Res. Explor. Lab. **35**(4), 108–110 (2016)
15. Xu, J., Sun, R., Deng, X.F.: Application of virtual reality (VR) technology in high school biology class. Biol. Teach. **42**(03), 46–47 (2017)
16. Chen, J.J.: Design and Application of Virtual Simulation Experiment Based on VR Narrative. Central China Normal University (2017)
17. Song, H.M.: The research design of handheld individual solider psychological adjustment instrument. In: Summary of the 19th National Conference on Psychological Science (2016)

Blended Learning Concept in Selected Tourism Management e-Courses with Focus on Content Development Including Recommender System

Miloslava Černá(✉) and Anna Borkovcová

Faculty of Informatics and Management, University of Hradec Kralove, Rokitanskeho 62, Hradec Kralove, Czech Republic
{miloslava.cerna,anna.borkovcova}@uhk.cz

Abstract. The paper covers two main areas that intertwine each other: content development of e-courses and recommender system with blended learning concept that spans over both themes. This paper approaches the educators' question on how to enhance learning, in this case from the perspective of improvement of students' learning performance by proper guiding in the virtual platform. There were two influencing stimuli for innovative changes in the e-courses on culture, geography and history of English speaking countries within the frame of Management of Tourism bachelor programme. Firstly, a recommender system was designed so that the great amount of study materials in the e-courses could be properly reorganized and clarified. The second stimuli was connected with the change of language subjects status from compulsory to voluntary subjects and inevitable drop of students' language competences and interest in language subjects because economic and managerial subject became preferential. Since the e-learning platform doesn't allow implementation of the advance recommendation system which enables, for example, algorithm for calculating the weight of documents, it was necessary to create a similar model using the available resources as the analyses of student attendance and number of downloads and evaluation. The result is an effective model that does not require a more advanced e-learning portal and, to a smaller amount, can be done by the instructor manually, and provides effective content filtering in the e-course. Students appreciated the fact that they do not have to decide which material is sufficient for their study. Appropriateness of the model was demonstrated by reduced failure rate.

Keywords: Content development · Recommender system
Tourism management · Rating · Learning environment

1 Introduction

Innovations in subjects History, Geography and Tourism of English-speaking countries and Culture of English-speaking countries with focus on literature, music, arts within the Management of Tourism Bachelor study programme are introduced in the paper. Students study these subjects in all six semesters, the content of these subjects is enormous; it covers history and culture of the United Kingdom and the USA, but also

S. K. S. Cheung et al. (Eds.): ICBL 2018, LNCS 10949, pp. 175–187, 2018.
https://doi.org/10.1007/978-3-319-94505-7_14

Australia, New Zealand, India and selected countries of Africa. There were two influencing stimuli for innovative changes in the discussed e-courses Firstly, *a recommender system was designed to give a kind of order to the great amount of study materials*, which had gathered during the years in the e-courses. The second stimuli was connected with the *change of language subjects status from compulsory to voluntary subjects* and inevitable drop of students' language competences and interest in language subjects because economic and managerial subject became preferential.

2 Methodology and Goals

2.1 Starting Point – Tourism Management - History and Current Situation

History, Geography and Tourism of English-speaking countries and Culture of English-speaking countries subjects have been taught for 25 years and have undergone crucial changes, which were caused by the changes in the policy of Faculty of Informatics and Management in the Tourism Management Bachelor study programme connected new re-accreditation criteria in 2004. With the incorporation of economic and managerial subjects, the amount of foreign language lessons substantially decreased. Many "language subjects" including History, Geography and Tourism Culture of English-speaking countries changed their status from compulsory to optional subjects. Originally, the strength and popularity of this bachelor programme was connected with its focus on languages but with the shift towards economic and managerial learning content the interest of applicants decreased 4 times, which means the number of applicants has been reduced to one-quarter of the original. Since 2005/2006 students even do not have to graduate from languages. Only students who want to sit for the state exam in languages have to attend and gain credits in the discussed subjects [1]. The consequences of implemented changes led not only to the mentioned drop in applicants but also to the significant *decrease in the entrance level of language knowledge of enrolled students*. Big effort has been devoted to the improvement of students' language competences; teachers have to be much more resourceful to raise students' interest in languages, history, geography and culture of English and German speaking countries. E-courses accompanying language subjects have been innovated and enriched with new motivating components [2, 3] and current topics like cultural studies and intercultural business communication [4]. The role of language in tourism is indisputable, Rahayu [5] considers language competence a necessary pre-condition for the work in the field of Tourism and Management and a tool towards reducing communication barriers but also cultural constraints. *The objective is to demonstrate another example of academics' endeavour to motivate and engage students into learning English language and lead students to final language state exam.*

2.2 The Aims and Methodological Frame

The paper deals with analysis of current and near future options for blended learning and content development in e-courses. *The main aim of the paper is finding possibilities for simpler e-learning portals that do not allow advanced features and designing own modified recommender system including working out of individual stages of its implementation.* The sub-goal is to demonstrate that students' results from an e-course where this model is implemented are significantly better that in an e-course where the method of recommender content was introduced.

Methodological frame consists of practical theory on the recommender system and its modification into a form usable on our educational server. Practical theory discusses: Document repository, Rating repository, Content-based filtering and Good learner's average rating. The other key section was adjusting the system to our learning management system Blackboard. It consists of Introduction of e-course and Rating of study materials. Two e-courses are described: one with the original design and the other one with implemented innovations. The core part represents Rating of study materials, which is divided into 4 phases: 1st phase – Students' rating, 2nd phase – Lecturer' rating, 3rd phase – Automatic system rating and the 4th phase – Filtered content.

The *analysis* was applied at the beginning of the research; individual elements of the chosen recommender system were divided into parts and examined in detail. This allowed us to find out how the parts work and what is essential to them. Thanks to this analysis, we were able to redraw individual elements to be applicable to our e-learning portal, yet they retained most of their features, effectiveness and efficiency. The analysis was also used in the phase when findings on students' success and satisfaction with the new content of recommended works were processed. Namely, it was *relational analysis*; we had to verify whether the changes in learners' results and their satisfaction do not depend on other aspects except for the implemented system. It was ensured by the questionnaire survey and by identifying possible circumstances such as a change in the study plan, change of subject status, etc. The *comparison method* was used when two courses with the similar content and structure were compared; one e-course was in the original design without implementation of the system and the other with the implemented system, regulated content based on filtering out the most suitable materials.

3 Literature Review

The paper covers two main areas that intertwine each other: content development of e-courses and recommender system with blended learning concept that spans over both themes. Literature review brings a set of selected relevant studies on these two areas.

Currently involvement of students into content development is widely discussed topic in the academic forum. Learning as a cognitive process is accompanied with affective determinants that have to be stimulated. Students are not only recipients but they are also creators; it depends on how students are motivated, how they are instructed and how their effort is evaluated [6]. Steyn et al. [7] believe that students can better grasp the content and increase their learning via utilization of virtual platform and working out own material there. Researchers consider as natural working in Blackboard, because their students are millennials generation growing up with the Internet.

Cheung [8] discusses open resources like open textbooks, open reference books, online dictionaries, and encyclopaedias from the perspective of perceived usefulness for study purposes. Students use them as alternative textbooks or reference books to acquire relevant knowledge and reinforce their understanding of studied concepts. Students voluntarily participated in the study; actively created and evaluated the content, e.g. diligently proof-read the e-books. Findings revealed that the accuracy, quality and comprehensiveness of contents are key concerns of using open educational resources for learning purposes. Here is a parallel with our paper which is the students' perception and evaluation of quality. We also strive to ensure quality of the study content, which was created by students themselves via recommending system.

Following selected study is based on students' development of mobile learning content where students were paid for their activity. Wang et al. 2015 [9] highlighted the importance of motivation. They stated that teachers dominated content development and the students as recipients of e-learning were seldom included. "In this study we hypothesized that if e-learning content were developed by students, it would be a source of learning motivation for the students and would provide material for a database of re-usable materials," p. 382 [9]. Researchers' idea was that it was possible and feasible to have students develop mobile learning content. It had to be done with teacher's guidance and supervision. Students were paid for their activity but they didn't consider it to be the main incentive. Surprisingly students in general lacked enthusiasm. At the beginning of the project, they were more active, but later their contributions diminished gradually. It is rather naive to believe that if students develop content, the teachers will save some time. The opposite is true. Teachers have to edit students' work and check also ethical issues which is time-consuming.

The other part of literature review focuses on approaches and applied concepts enabling filtering of study materials in the virtual environment. Soonthornphisaj et al. [10] describe web application with integrated recommender system within the e-learning concept. The authors highlight the *importance of the quality of the learning materials* that are predominantly provided by the instructor. According to them the other key factor influencing students' outcome are other *learners' recommendations*, that is why they developed a collaborative filtering mechanism which enables prediction of the suitable documents to the learners. Not only instructors but also students can upload new study materials into the virtual learning space and students can rate the currently available materials, as well. Authors define the recommender system as a software agent that gathers the rating information from all users in order to predict or recommend the most suitable materials to each user. Information on student's knowledge is gained via a quiz generator in the system.

Salehi et al. [11] designed a personalized recommender system. They claimed that existing systems lacked accuracy because preferences of learners and materials were not considered simultaneously. Sequential pattern mining and multidimensional attribute-based collaborative filtering was proposed in their recommender system framework. Learners were provided with the real-time up dated contextual information reflecting their preferences gained from Leaner Preference Tree and learners' rating.

4 Recommender System Based on Good Learners' Ratings and Content-Based Filtering

This is a scheme of a desired recommender system, see Fig. 1. This approach is just being tested on experimental data, but it seems to be an appropriate method. The document (in our e-courses 'a presentation'), which can be created by both the instructor and the student, is stored in the Document Repository. The Document Repository is a part of an e-learning platform to which neither a student nor an instructor has direct access. This part of the system is administrated by the ICT administrator of the faculty. A student can download each presentation from the Document Repository, review it and rate. The rating is stored in the Rating Repository (which is just as Document Repository 'detached'), the rating is further used in the filtering phase, which also includes automatically evaluated data from the Document Repository, which are in this context calculations of material similarity, term occurrence, etc. All these data are processed and evaluated and students get the right materials. This approach is based on [12, 13].

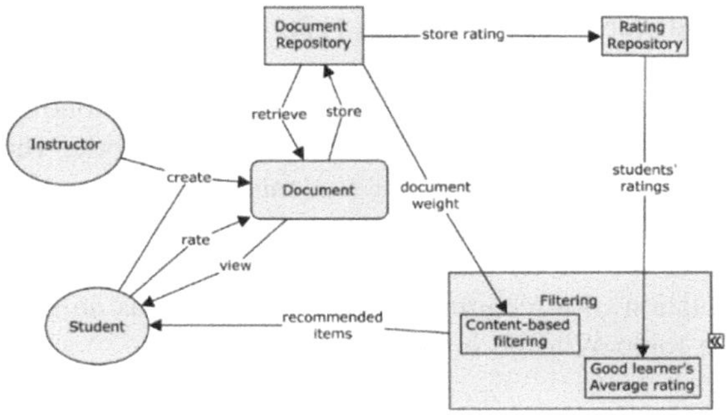

Fig. 1. Scheme of recommender system

The core terms are Content-based filtering and Good learners rating [14]. Similarity is calculated using the vector space model: it contains two main phases: weight calculation and cosine similarity calculation. The weight is calculated by the frequency of the term occurrence in the document and the total number of documents that may be recommended to the student. The calculation of cosine similarity is done by means of vectors, namely by the user profile vector and the document content vector. In this way, documents that have a good value in terms of the number of keywords, mentioned terms are filtered out. The average rating of the item by good learners is calculated by using the share evaluation of the item by good learner and a total number of good learners who rated the item. Any item, which has not yet been rated by a good learner, will get predicted rating by means of similarity with an already rated document. In this way, documents that are most popular with well-performing students will be brought to the recommended system.

5 Modified Solution

Our commercial educational server does not allow implementation of the system described in the Sect. 4, so the model had to be modified into a form that is easy to apply and produces the desirable results. Automatically evaluated data are replaced by the content recommendation, students' activity can be tracked in the Blackboard LMS but not the number of views and downloads of individual presentations.

Average item rating is conducted via implemented *star rating system*, which is available to students in the normal interface of the eLearning system.

5.1 Introduction of Compared Courses

A print screen in Fig. 2 from 'History, Geography and Tourism of New Zealand' e-course shows the course without the recommender system. It is compared with a 'Culture of Africa and India' course, where the system has been implemented. Structure of the e-courses on geography and culture are nearly the same, students feel familiar with the environment and due to appropriate navigation, they don't get lost in the amount of study materials. Design of the e-courses reflects the requirements of both didactics [15, 16] and web-design principles [17]. Each chapter consists of three parts: (1) Entry into the topic with motivating questions. In the entry part there are thoughtfully formulated objectives according to Bloom's taxonomy [18] and compulsory and voluntary tasks; (2) Main Content with full and brief version prepared by the teacher including the quiz that revises students' knowledge of studied topic and (3) Students' Gallery with many presentations. There is a problem because of accumulation of a great deal of study materials of various value and that calls for reorganization. Implementation of a recommender system seems as an appropriate solution. See structure of the topic Wildlife in New Zealand Fig. 2.

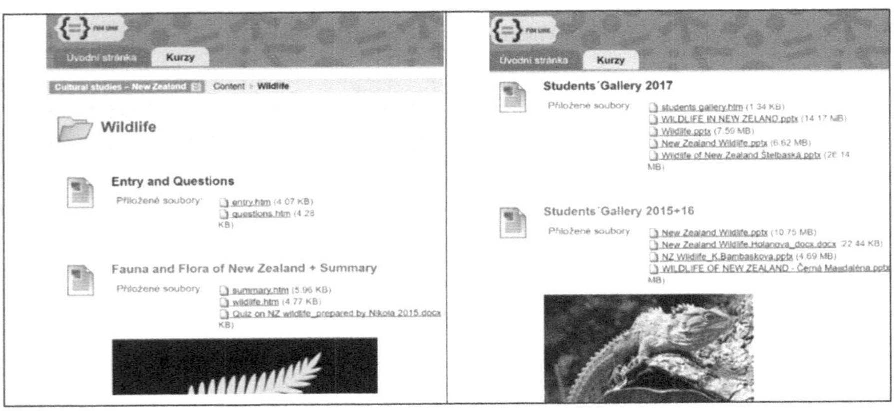

Fig. 2. Structure of the lesson in the e-course

We are looking for dependencies and differences between these two courses. The expected result is that students will attend the Culture of Africa and India course more frequently; they will be more satisfied with the course because they can find desired information in the large amount of study materials in an easier and convenient way. Consequently, their knowledge might improve, which is the goal because the effectiveness of the process of education is still assessed by gained knowledge and competences. The Recommender system is already applied in the Culture of Africa and India course. Students have access to the Students' gallery, where they can rate all presentations; they can also enter the Recommended Content, where one of the best presentations is filtered out for each topic.

5.2 Rating of Materials

Phase 1 – *Student's rating*

Figure 3 shows the user interface of the course as the student sees it. At the first stage, the instructor of the course places student presentations to the given topics in the e-course, checks whether the individual presentations meet formal and content requirements as discussed during present classes. All students can see the rating scale at each submitted presentation. The rating system displays five dots, which change after clicking into desired number of stars; the first star from the left equals 1 that is the worst evaluation, click on the last fifth dot displays 5 stars which equals 5 the best rating.

Fig. 3. Student's rating

At this stage of the changes in the rating system connected with the recommender system, students assess presentations in the e-course and during F2F classes, as well. Students present their presentations to the audience as an insight into the topic from the students' perspective. The audience is distributed *printed rating sheet*. Less active students ('lazy') can use the 1–5 scale rating where 1 is the worst and 5 is the best rating to rate individual parts of the presentation, e.g. clarity, content quality, contribution to the topic, formal presentation and overall impression. Students that are more active can add their comment to each of the rated areas. In the next phase of this research, the evaluation sheet will also be implemented directly in the e-course, so that the system could process and evaluate it automatically which will save teachers a lot of time. Worked out data from the electronic questionnaire will only be available to students attending the present classes and submitting their rating of the discussed presentation.

Phase 2 – *Lecturer's rating*
Figure 4 shows the user interface of the course as the lecturer sees it. The lecturer can see an *Overview of activities* where he/she learns which students are active, how often they rate presentations, whether they log on to the server on a continuous basis. Only the course instructor has access to this part of the system. Due to the Czech language localization of the system, the headings in the table are in the Czech language. 'Přehled aktivity' means Activity overview, Příjmení – Family name, Jméno – Name. Important columns follow: 'Poslední přístup ke kurzu' - Last Course Access which displays the date and time the user opened the course last time, 'Počet hodnocení' - Number of ratings which shows the number of all ratings the user has given and 'Příspěvků v diskusi' - Discussion Board which displays the number of posts for the user. In this e-course, the discussion is not being used very much. Most discussions and queries take place during weekly F2F classes and any individual issues are solved via private email conversation. Last column is 'Zobrazit hodnocení' - View Grades. When clicked on the icon, you will be redirected to the classification overview, see Fig. 5. System columns, which check the proper functionality of the entire course are hidden (grey) because they are not important for this paper. Only course instructor has access the *User Interface Classification*. The teacher can also enter grades (see below), he/she can see their overall rating and overall rating from the student assessment system.

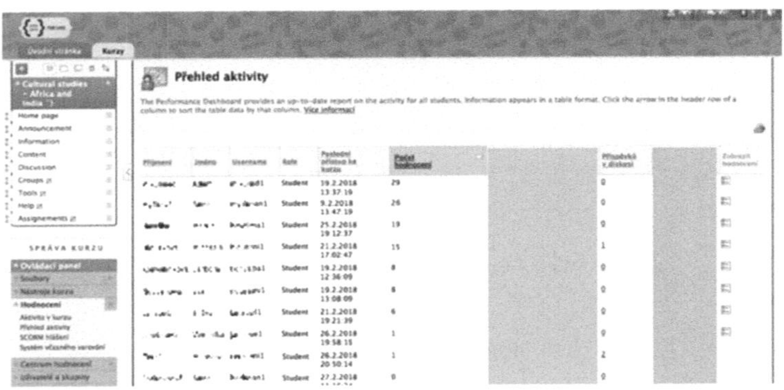

Fig. 4. Lecturer's rating – overview of students' activities

In addition to the issue of the recommender system, the teacher has an overview of the continual student's success rate. He/she can then focus on students with weaker performance and motivate them, give them additional tasks to improve the overall score, or simply show them poor results. In the Classification overview following columns are displayed: 'Hodnocení studentů' - *Student rating* which shows the average rating of all ratings for all the presentations that the student has received from all other

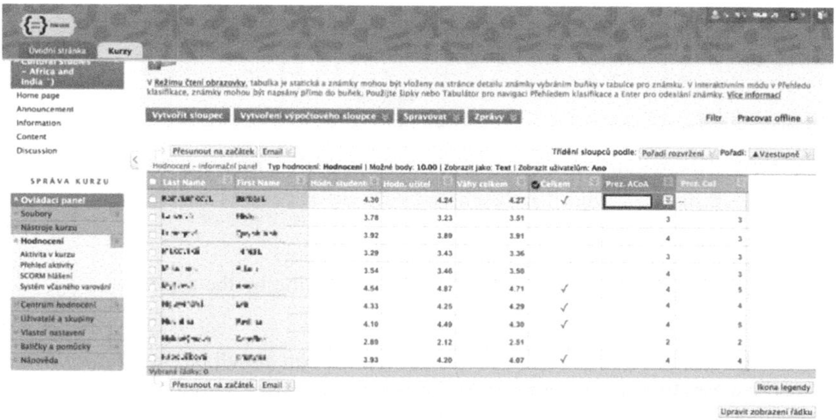

Fig. 5. Classification overview

students for all their presentations, 'Hodnocení učitele' - *'Teacher Rating'* shows the average rating of all students' presentations evaluated by the teacher. 'Váhy celkem' - Total Weights column shows the average student rating and teacher rating (average of all grades). The last column 'Celkem' – Total brings automatic system designation that is granted to all students who have a 'Total Weights' higher than 4. Students who reach rating 4 and higher are considered by the system 'good learners'. Students can be sorted according to the values in each column in an ascending order or descending order, by clicking on the column. Each column right from the column 'Celkem' – Total represents the rating of one lecture or one topic. These ratings are then averaged into 'Teacher rating'. In case of additional assignments, it is possible to create additional columns in which values/grades are inserted by the teacher manually. Teachers can use computational columns that calculate max/min, average, weight, and sum according to given values, which may be useful if teachers are interested in average scores from just a few lectures, or want to see an overview of the student's worst or best lectures.

Phase 3 – *Automatic System Rating*
Figure 6 shows a part from the 15 followed topics it represents an authentic sample of student's activity tracking, number of views and downloading of all presentations by one student can be seen. This is a way of automatically rated presentation, which is offered by the e-learning portal, and does not require further lecturer activity. Explanation of the main columns follow. 'Item Name and Type' displays the name of the visited page and its type. Here is a list of content folders (such as presentations), another type can be, for example, a discussion or announcement. 'Number of Downloads' shows how many times the content has been downloaded by the student. A higher number of downloads may mean that a student enters the e-course from multiple devices and it is easier to get a presentation that he/she is interested by retrieving it directly from the e-course than transferring it via the flash drive/email. 'Total Time Spent in Hours' shows the time spent on that page. Low values indicate that the content didn't impress the student, he/she may have found some inaccuracies. Last column 'Initial Access Date/Time' refers to the time

Student Activity by Item in the Course

Item Name And Type	Number of Downloads	Total Time Spent in Hours	Number of Times Accessed	Initial Access Date/Time
[illegible] Culture of India.doc Složka obsahu	1	0,01	2	27.2.2018 19:24
African Kingdoms [illegible].pptx Složka obsahu	1	0,02	2	18.2.2018 19:12
Ancient civilizations of Africa [illegible].pptx Složka obsahu	3	0,43	19	18.2.2018 19:14

Fig. 6. Automatic student's activity tracking by the system

and date of the student's first access to the content. It can also have *good tangible value* for the teacher, he/she can see whether the student prepares systematically or crams at the last moment before the exam/test.

Phase 4 – *Filtered content*

Last part of the described process on study materials rating deals with the *desired innovation which is the developed recommended content.* After the documents are filtered out, the best content as recommended item is displayed to students in the e-learning environment (Fig. 7).

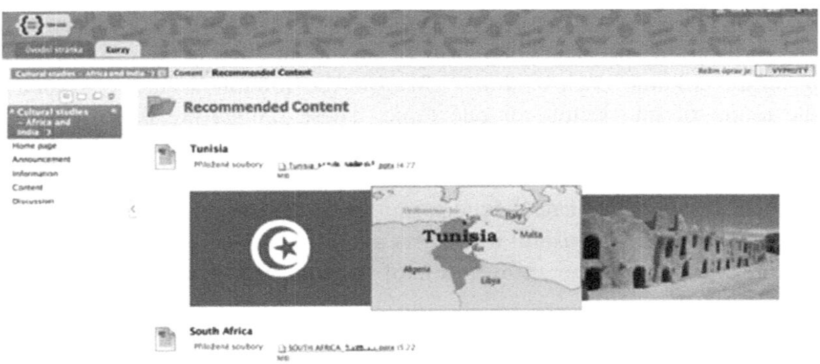

Fig. 7. Recommended content

Only one presentation per topic is chosen into the Content recommender; the selection is based on here presented recommender system. Other presentations from Student gallery stay in each lesson and serve as additional study material. The decision to select only one presentation is based on the Paradox of Choice, in other words on the decision paralysis theory which argues that if a person has more choices, they often do not even apply any of them because they do not want go through the decision phases and rather postpone the problem/obligation [19]. Students do not have to make decision, which study material to use, students are recommended one presentation in the recommended content was filtered as the best possible choice.

6 Conclusion and Discussion

This paper approaches the educators' question on how to enhance learning, in this case from the perspective of improvement of students' learning performance by proper guiding in the virtual platform. Shift to the virtual environment has brought teachers opportunity to supply students with unlimited amount of study materials, but what seemed a great advantage soon showed also its drawbacks. As discussed in the literature review, academics started to solve this problem more than decade ago. We have utilized blended learning concept in the Tourism Bachelor Study programme for fifteen years. With the every year influx of new students' presentations, we also started to face the problem of growing study material in the e-course Students' gallery section. It was necessary to reorganize study materials and to make order in a somewhat chaotic section that just accumulated students' presentations. Solution of the problem with a high quantity of materials we saw in the improvement of materials and implementation of recommender system based on the content filtering. In winter semester we implemented our solution into the first e-course. Currently we are introducing this proved innovation into three more e-courses on Culture and History.

On a commercial virtual platform that does not allow more advanced content filtering, we successfully introduced innovations utilizing rating of study materials. It can also be applied to very 'basic' e-learning systems; they only have to be able to count number of views and downloads, and provide some sort of rating. In case of less extensive courses, the instructor alone can also evaluate these data and filter the content. The majority of students said that filtered content facilitated their search for appropriate material in individual topics. The important was also the fact that filtered material, which was placed into the 'Recommended content' section, was agreed by the teacher so students knew that it was the appropriate or sufficient study material and appreciated this model. Visit rate in the e-course rose in the case of items that were recommended and dropped in the unorganized student gallery, where all the time was spent on the rating of presentations. The success rate of students in this course has also increased; the failure rate is reduced from about 30% to 10%. On the other hand, in the course that remained unchanged, no changes appeared, no increase in students' interest was recorded, the success rate changed only by a few units, which is statistically insignificant (Fig. 8).

Year	Total	Success	Failure	Failure in %
2013/14	23	17	6	26,09%
2014/15	31	17	14	45,16%
2015/16	24	16	8	33,33%
2016/17	19	12	7	36,84%
2017/18	11	10	1	9,09%

Fig. 8. An overview of the failure rate

In the next stage, implementation of the recommender system into other e-courses Management of Tourism programme will continue. The questionnaires on rating presentations that are presented by students during F2F classes will be transformed into the electronic form, so that manual evaluation and change of weight ratings of individual students could be done automatically in the system.

Acknowledgement. The paper is supported by the project SPEV 2018 at the Faculty of Informatics and Management of the University of Hradec Kralove, Czech Republic.

References

1. Simonova, I.: Blended learning as a mover in the tourism&management study programme? In: Cheung, S., Kwok, L., Lee, L.K., Ma, W., Yang, H. (eds.) Blended Learning. New Challenges and Innovative Practices. LNCS, vol. 10309, pp. 118–128. Springer, Cham (2017). https://doi.org/10.1007/978-3-319-59360-9_11
2. Klimova, B.: Teacher's role in a smart learning environment—a review study. In: Uskov, V. L., Howlett, R.J., Jain, L.C. (eds.) Smart Education and e-Learning 2016. SIST, vol. 59, pp. 51–59. Springer, Cham (2016). https://doi.org/10.1007/978-3-319-39690-3_5
3. Hubackova, S., Semerádová, I.: Comparison of on-line teaching and face-to-face teaching. Procedia Comput. Sci. **89**, 445–449 (2013). https://doi.org/10.1016/j.sbspro.2013.08.875
4. Pikhart, M.: Implementing new global business trends to intercultural business communication. Procedia Soc. Behav. Sci. **152**, 950–953 (2014). https://doi.org/10.1016/j.sbspro.2014.09.348
5. Rahayu, A.U.: The mastery of the english language in reducing cultural and communication barriers in tourism world. In: Morrison, A.M., Abdullah, A.G., Leo. S. (Eds.) Proceedings of the Asia Tourism Forum 2016 – The 12th Biennial Conference of Hospitality and Tourism Industry in Asia, vol. 19, pp. 574–578 (2016)
6. Černá, M.: Utilization of social applications as a way of student's engagement into a learning process. Adv. Sci. Lett. **23**(4), 2889–2893 (2017). SOSHUM 2016
7. Steyn, R., Millard, S., Jordaan, J.: The use of a learning management system to facilitate student-driven content design: an experiment. In: Huang, T.-C., Lau, R., Huang, Y.-M., Spaniol, M., Yuen, C.-H. (eds.) SETE 2017. LNCS, vol. 10676, pp. 75–94. Springer Cham (2017). https://doi.org/10.1007/978-3-319-71084-6_10
8. Cheung, Simon K.S.: Distance-learning students' perception on the usefulness of open educational resources. In: Cheung, S.K.S., Kwok, L.-F., Ma, Will W.K., Lee, L.-K., Yang, H. (eds.) ICBL 2017. LNCS, vol. 10309, pp. 389–399. Springer, Cham (2017). https://doi.org/10.1007/978-3-319-59360-9_34
9. Wang, S., Jarrell, D., Iwata, J.: Involving students in mobile learning content development: successes and challenges. In: Cheung, S.K.S., Kwok, L.-F., Yang, H., Fong, J., Kwan, R. (eds.) ICHL 2015. LNCS, vol. 9167, pp. 382–393. Springer, Cham (2015). https://doi.org/10.1007/978-3-319-20621-9_32
10. Soonthornphisaj, N., Rojsattarat, E., Yim-ngam, S.: Smart e-learning using recommender system. Computational Intelligence. LNCS (LNAI), vol. 4114, pp. 518–523. Springer, Heidelberg (2006). https://doi.org/10.1007/978-3-540-37275-2_63
11. Salehi, M., Nakhai Kamalabadi, I., Ghaznavi Ghoushchi, M.B.: Personalized recommendation of learning material using sequential pattern mining and attribute based collaborative filtering. Educ. Inf. Technol. **19**(4), 713–735 (2014). https://doi.org/10.1007/s10639-012-9245-5
12. Zheng, Y., Li, L.: A three-dimensional context-awareness model for peer recommendation in the e-learning context. Int. J. E-Learn. (IJEL) **7**(1), 153–168 (2008)

13. Khribi, M.K., Jemni, M., Nasraoui, O.: Automatic recommendations for e-learning personalization based on web usage mining techniques and information retrieval. Educ. Technol. Soc. **12**(4), 30–42 (2009)
14. Ghauth, K.I., Abdullah, N.A.: Learning materials recommendation using good learners' ratings and content-based filtering. Educ. Technol. Res. Dev. **58**(6), 711–727 (2010). https://doi.org/10.1007/s11423-010-9155-4
15. Comenius, J.A.: The Great Didactic of John Amos Comenius. Russell and Russell, New York (1967)
16. Černá, M., Poulová, P.: Reflection of comenius' didactic principles in ESP instruction. In: ICIBET 2013: International Conference on Information, Business and Education Technology. Atlantis Press, Paris (2013)
17. Krug, S.: Don't Make Me Think, Revisited: A Common Sense Approach to Web Usability. New Riders Publishing Thousand Oaks, CA, USA (2014)
18. Bloom, B.S.: Taxonomy of Educational Objectives: Cognitive Domain. David McKay Company, Inc., New York (1956)
19. Schwartz, B.: The Paradox of Choice. PhilosophersNotes website (2018). http://experiencelife.com/wp-content/uploads/2013/04/The-Paradox-of-Choice.pdf

Slide-Based Lecture Notes as a Student-Centered Alternative to Textbooks for Non-native English Speakers

Oliver Tat Sheung Au(✉), Raymond Man Hong Wong, and Lap-Kei Lee

School of Science and Technology, The Open University of Hong Kong, Ho Man Tin, Hong Kong
{oau, rmhwong, lklee}@ouhk.edu.hk

Abstract. Some non-native speakers struggle with lectures conducted in English. It may be hard for them to pick out key messages when reading books or lecture notes. Microsoft PowerPoint has an "add notes" feature. We propose to use it to attach lecture notes to individual slides instead of compiling all lecture notes in a conventional book form. Students learn key points from slides and detailed explanation from slide-based lecture notes. A suitable learning approach, deep or shallow, can be chosen according to personal learning goal on a slide-by-slide basis. Student-centered learning is empowered to a high level of granularity in a blended learning environment. Lecturers may update slide-based lecture notes more effectively and efficiently than separate sets of slides and lecture notes.

Keywords: Slide-based lecture notes · Student-centered learning
Blended learning · Non-native English-speaking students
Underprepared students

1 Introduction

In Hong Kong, English is the medium of instruction in universities though it is not the mother tongue of most students. A few students would write down on the course-end evaluation that they wish lectures were given in Chinese even they know that it is against university policies. Students have to struggle in lectures and with textbooks. Students prefer lecture notes written in direct and simple English than a long and winding textbook.

Microsoft PowerPoint is a popular slide creation tool. It has an "add notes" feature that allows users to associate notes to an individual slide. Presenters use it to prepare what to say during presentations. We use it to add detailed notes to explain the briefly stated key points on each slide. We propose to rearrange conventional lecture notes in a slide-based organization. The proximity of slides and explanation notes allows students to get to the details quickly and accurately as needed. Slide-based organization also reduces the lecturer's effort in keeping course contents up-to-date. Our preliminary survey proves that slide-based lecture notes are perceived by students to be very

S. K. S. Cheung et al. (Eds.): ICBL 2018, LNCS 10949, pp. 188–199, 2018.
https://doi.org/10.1007/978-3-319-94505-7_15

helpful. In this paper, we will share our experience of this novel lecture notes organization.

Superficially, blended learning is about using a mix of technologies with classroom teaching to enhance learning. Deep down, student autonomy is a desirable outcome of blended learning. Assorted learning activities allow students to choose the kinds that are most effective for them. The slide-based lecture notes approach that we propose broadens the choice available to students and is therefore highly relevant to the context of blended learning.

Section 2 has literature review which discusses aspects of student-centered learning and blended learning in which the proposed slide-based lecture notes approach will be good. Textbooks and reasons of their declining usage are explained. The section ends with a discussion of using PowerPoint slides in education, deep and surface learning approaches. Section 3 shows examples of slide-based lecture notes and the problems they try to solve. Section 4 discusses a student survey, observations and interpretation. Section 5 revisits the reasons that slide-based lecture notes are good for non-native English-speaking and underprepared students. It discusses potential criticism of our work and future work.

2 Literature Review

2.1 Student-Centered Blended Learning

In a traditional learning environment, teachers decide on the learning activities students should take part in. The role of students is passive. On the contrary, student-centered learning puts students first. It acknowledges that each student is unique and should have the autonomy to personalize his or her learning experience. Jones made suggestions on how to implement student-centered classrooms [1]. For example, students should work together without frequent intervention by lecturers. Equally important is that students should be convinced of the benefits for them to work together. Personalization makes learning experience rewarding to students. Students should be encouraged to find their own answers to the questions they asked for personalization of their learning. Learning activities can go back and forth between teacher-led and students-centered.

Blended learning combines the use of face-to-face and online learning activities. It enables learning activities to take place in various settings through different media. Students can choose to learn in the way that suit them best personally. Dickinson shows a strong link between autonomy and motivation of students in a literature review [2].

2.2 Textbooks

Declining Usage. In the same 30-year period, Consumer Price Index went up 250% but textbooks cost 800% more [3]. According to a 2006 report, 60% of university students did not buy textbooks due to their high costs [4]. In 2011, the number increased to 70% [5]. The trend of students not buying textbooks was evident though it may be stabilized by now. Students cannot benefit from books that they do not read.

Digital textbooks are cheaper, but many still prefer to read printed textbooks. Digital books cannot be resold after the course to recoup their costs.

Open Textbooks. Open educational resources (OER) are available free of charge. In a user survey, 80% of students find OER useful or very useful [6]. From 7 studies that report on the efficacy of OER, three studies show improved learning outcomes, three show no difference and one worsened [7]. Students' experience of OER was general favorable. But respectively only 10% and 20% of faculty were "very aware" and "aware" of OER [8]. Roughly one-half of the faculty thought that "there are not enough resources for my subject" and "it is too hard to find what I need". The adoption of open textbook was meagre at 9% in 2016-17 increased from 5% the year before. The supply of OER must be broadened and deepened for more adoption.

Custom Textbooks. Some publishers allow lecturers to select chapters from several books and be bound together in a single book customized for a course. Lecturers can contribute additional chapters to their custom textbooks. A customer textbook will be cheaper than the several textbooks from which its chapters were selected. It is still not cheap from students' perspective. Lecturers need to have a good idea of the class size to print the right number of copies. A publisher told us three years ago that the class size should be 200 or more for custom textbooks to be financially attractive.

Advantages of Using Textbooks. Collected from other sources, Gak summarized the advantages of using textbooks [9]. Textbooks help define course syllabus. They serve as a road map for students and provide visual elements that lecturers may not have time or knowhow to create.

Disadvantages of Using Textbooks. Authors naturally love to write books that appeal to a wide range of readers. A course taken from any degree program may have very specific needs to meet. The target students can have specific background and interests. It is not always easy for authors to write a textbook book meeting the very specific needs. Textbooks written for native English speakers will be challenging for non-native speakers.

Lecture Notes. Lecturers may write their own lecture notes in substitution of textbooks. For technology-related courses, lecturers will need to update lecture notes frequently. When we update PowerPoint slides, it is easy for us to forget to update corresponding parts in the lecture notes.

2.3 PowerPoint Slides

At the turn of the century, educators had a heated discussion about the use of PowerPoint slides for teaching. Students may be coaxed into not taking notes in class. On the one hand, passive listening is not conducive to deep learning [10]. Studies however show no difference in student performance when slides are used [11–13]. Just like many other technologies, it is up to the users to exploit or misuse PowerPoint slides. Instead of asking whether to use PowerPoint, we may ask how to use it for best results.

Textual Density on Slides. Brock and Joglekar surveyed 353 information management students in 17 classes taught by 12 lecturers [14]. They found that 3 bullet points and 20 words or less per slide are preferred. The low averages may be due to the fact that some slides hold mainly photos and drawings thus have reduced the amount of texts needed on slides. Berk surveyed 70 relevant studies to suggest 3 to 6 bullet points per slide as a good practice [15].

Slides vs Blackboard and Textbooks. Corbeil compares French as a second language courses for first year university students using (1) PowerPoint alone and (2) traditional blackboard with textbooks respectively. One hundred and five students participated in the 2-year study. While pre-tests and post-tests show no difference in learning outcomes of the two approaches, more students prefer the PowerPoint-only approach over the blackboard with textbook approach [16]. They like the slides for the clearly focused key points. They also found lengthy read of textbooks boring.

2.4 Learning Approaches

Marton and Säljö coined the terms "deep approach" and "surface approach" for learning that focus on understanding and reproducing respectively [17]. It is an influential paper that brought forth subsequent work by other researchers.

Deep Learning Approach. Students need to fulfill enabling conditions to employ the deep learning approach. They should have intrinsic motivation to learn. In other words, they have an interest in the subject matter. If they learn merely to avoid the consequence of failing a course, they are extrinsically motivated.

The choice between deep learning and surface learning also depends on the student's prior knowledge [18]. In fact, prior knowledge is more important than the amount of effort for students to perform well in a final year course [19]. The amount of materials in the curriculum also can affect the learning approach. An overwhelming amount of learning materials pushes students to adopt surface learning and thus compromise their understanding [20, Chap. 2].

Types of questions used in the assessment can affect the learning approach too [20, Chap 3]. If questions ask the relationship of various parts, deep learning approach will likely be adopted. If questions only demand reproduction of factual information, students are inclined to use surface learning approach.

If the teacher's intention is to transmit knowledge, students are more likely to adopt surface learning approach [21]. If teachers employ student-centered strategy that aims at changing students' conceptions and how they relate among themselves and with the outside world, students tend to adopt deep learning approach.

3 Slide-Based Lecture Notes

3.1 The Problem

Chinese is the language Hong Kong students use in their everyday lives. Universities and secondary schools have different policies in the language of instruction. University classes are taught in English while the majority of secondary school classes are taught in Chinese. The change of language used in class is a challenge for some students advanced to universities. For several years, we have been recording lectures to post online. Students can review the online lecture after attending the same lecture live to make up for their deficiency in English or prior background. The lecture recording posted online has been a popular feature of our course.

For some of our courses, we wrote 500-page lecture notes to supplement PowerPoint slides used in lectures. The lecture notes were printed in a textbook form. Since our courses are in computer science, slides and lecture notes must be updated annually. When we update the slides, we need to keep the lecture notes in sync. But lecture notes are provided to students at the beginning of the course which is earlier than the time we would use the slides. It is easy for slides and lecture notes to go out-of-sync. The need to update lecture notes and prepare for lecture on two separate time frames increased our workload.

The separate sets of slides and lecture notes are less than ideal for students. First, they may be out-of-sync to cause confusion. Second, the separate slides and lecture notes coax students to commit to one learning approach when they sit down to study. If they want to employ deep learning, they would study lecture notes. If they want to review before a test, reading the slides would be best. On encountering a slide that they feel the need to study more, they have to fumble through the pages of lecture notes to find the passage corresponding to the slide. Another way to use the conventional lecture notes is to skim through the pages. Doing so is quite easy for students to miss the key points.

3.2 Our Solution

Figure 1 was a slide that we used before adopting slide-based lecture notes. It was used in a course that we did not provide separate lecture notes to students. We tried to make the slide understandable when students used it for self-study. Lengthy wording made the slide less suitable for lecture presentation. But the slide still did not contain enough details to enable deep learning. The result was clearly a compromise.

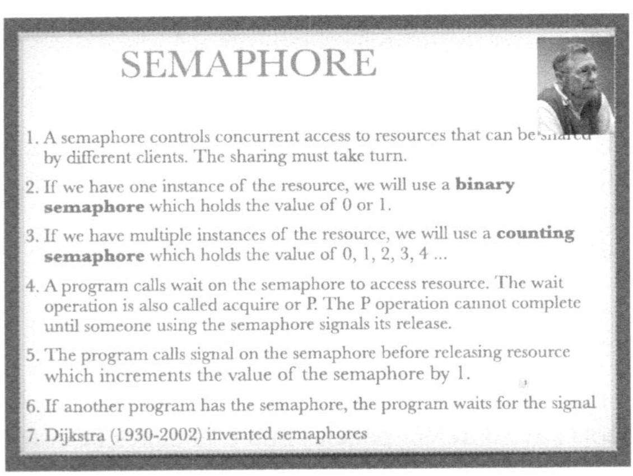

Fig. 1. A PowerPoint slide contains many words but not enough for deep learning

We use the Microsoft PowerPoint "add notes" feature to add detailed explanation to each slide. Figure 1 was transformed to Fig. 2. We can now afford to shorten the wording on the slide to facilitate lecture presentation and leave the detailed explanation to the slide-based lecture notes. In addition to explaining the key points, the notes may be enriched with stories to relate to other computer science courses or the outside world. The slide-based lecture notes enable deep learning. We generate two pdf files to give to students. One file holds slides paired with the lecture notes as in Fig. 2. The other file only holds the slides.

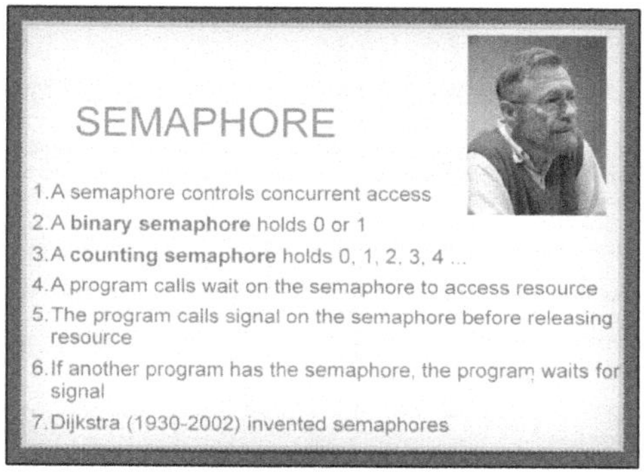

Point 1: Semaphores coordinate concurrent attempts to access the same resource. We assume that the resource can be shared by different programs but just not simultaneously. In other words, programs need to take turn to access the sharable resource.
Point 2: If there is only one instance of the resource, we could use binary semaphores.
Point 3: If there are multiple instances of a resource, we use counting semaphores.
Point 4: The wait operation is also called acquire or P. When a program calls P, it will tries to decrement the positive value in the semaphore by 1. If someone else is already using the semaphore, its current value would be zero. The P operation cannot complete until someone using the semaphore signals its release.
Point 5: A program using the semaphore will signal the release which increments the value of the semaphore by 1. Now that the semaphore is returned to positive value, a waiting program can complete its P operation to proceed to using the resource.
Point 7: Dijkstra is one of the best known computer scientists of all time. He made many contributions to computer science. In addition to the semaphores, he also invented a shortest path algorithm and the Reverse Polish Notation. The latter can be used to encode an arithmetic expression for easy evaluation by a computer than the equivalent expression in infix notation. For example,. "a b + c ×" is the reverse Polish notation that computers prefer over the equivalent infix notation "(a + b) × c".

Some students think that they cannot do certain tasks due to the limitations in their training. Dijkstra studied Physics as an undergraduate and proceeded to complete a computer science PhD. If you like a subject enough, your drive can make up the deficiency in your background. By the way, why are the wait and signal operations also called P and V? Dijkstra is Dutch. He named his invention using Dutch. Supposedly, P and V are the first letters of the operations in Dutch.

Fig. 2. A slide with slide-based lecture notes.

Figure 3 is an example in which the slide only has a diagram. The slide-based lecture notes are even more important. Without them, students will have a difficult time to understand the diagram during self-study.

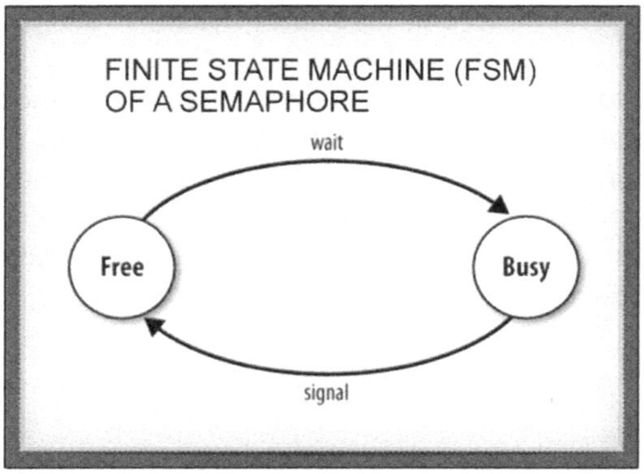

Recall that you have learned finite state machines (FSM) in your discrete structure course. It is more commonly called discrete mathematics course at other universities. Let's express the behavior of a semaphore with an FSM.

The two circles represent two possible states of a semaphore.

An arrow denotes a state transition. The label on the arrow names the event causing the transition.

Reading from left to right. When the current state of the semaphore is free, the wait event will change the state to busy.

Reading from right to left. When the current state of the semaphore is busy, the signal event will change the state to free.

Fig. 3. A slide with only a diagram well-explained by the slide-based lecture notes.

4 Results

4.1 The Survey

The entire class of 75 students in a final year distributed systems course in computer science were invited to participate; 46 students completed the survey. They were asked how often they took part in four learning activities: attending lectures, viewing lecture recordings, studying slides and studying slide-based lecture notes. Students answered on a 5-point Likert scale on two questions. The result is shown in Fig. 4.

Figure 5 shows the perceived usefulness of learning activities. The survey was conducted after the mid-term test, so students should have an idea how useful is an activity as far as assessment is concerned.

4.2 Observation and Discussion

We classify the four learning activities as two kinds: teacher-led and student-centered. Lecture attendance and viewing of lecture recording are teacher-led because their pace and progression are controlled by lecturers with relatively little input from students. Studying slides and studying lecture notes are student-centered; students can choose the learning pace and what to skip conveniently. Students can pause any time to do other things including digging deep on the topics that interest them.

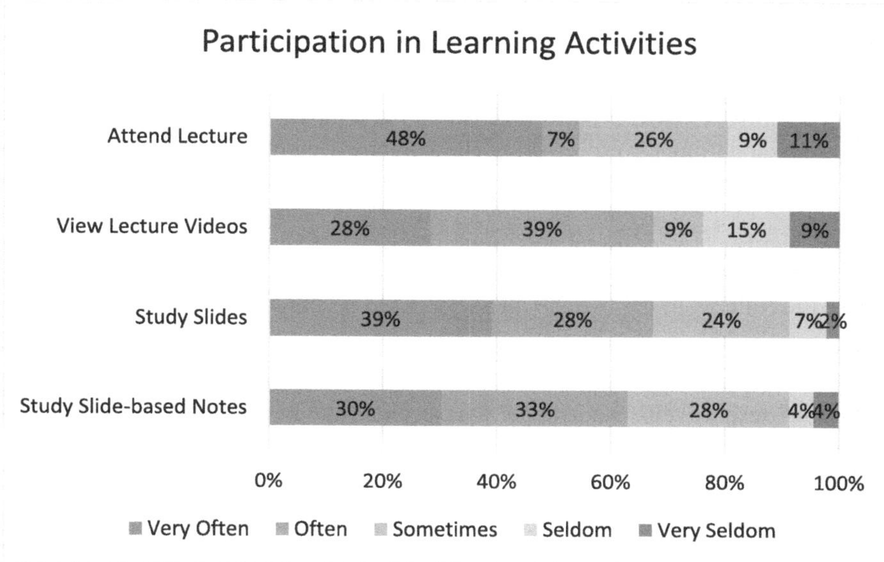

Fig. 4. Participation in learning activities.

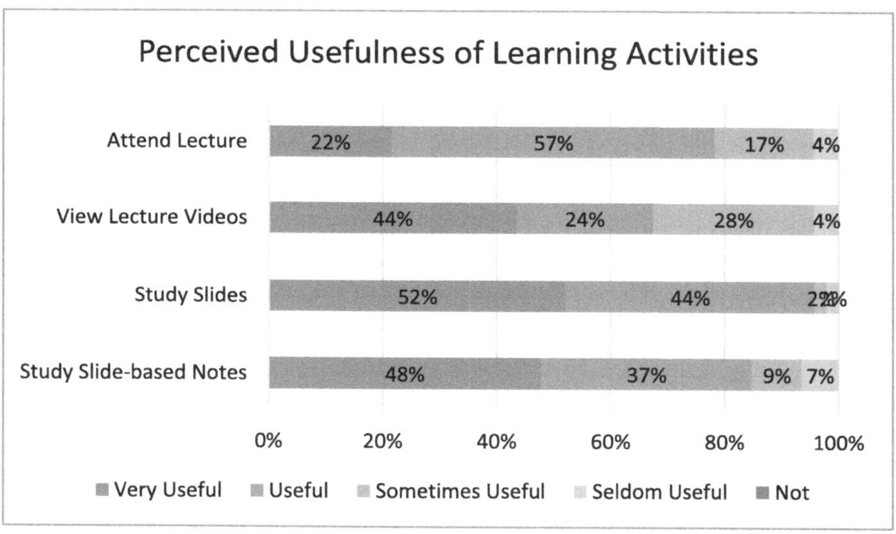

Fig. 5. Perceived usefulness of learning activities.

Lecture Attendance. Almost 50% of respondents attend lectures "very often". But only 6.5% respondents attend lectures "often". The huge gap in the two responses could be due to the effort required to commute to the campus. Though the university is served by two metro (underground railway) stations, the walking time to the university are 15 and 25 min respectively. The lecture attendance would be higher if lecture videos are not available. About 22% and 57% respondents find lecture attendance "very useful" and "useful" respectively.

Viewing Lecture Videos. Almost 30% and 40% of respondents view lecture videos "very often" and "often" respectively. The combined number is significantly higher than that of lecture attendance. Clearly our students embrace blended learning. About 44% and 24% respondents find viewing lecture videos "very useful" and "useful". The combined number of very useful and useful is lower than that of lecture attendance but the number of "very useful" is double that of "useful". It may be considered a tie in the perceived usefulness in the two alternative ways to access lectures: live and recorded.

Studying Slides. Around 39% and 28% of respondents study the slides "very often" and "often" respectively. Around 52% and 44% find studying the slides "very useful" and "useful" respectively. Students may have found the key points being highlighted on slides very useful.

Studying Slide-Based Lecture Notes. Around 30% and 33% of respondents study the slide-based lecture notes "very often" and "often" respectively. The number is slightly lower than that for studying the slides. Around 48% and 37% find studying the slide-based lecture notes "very useful" and "useful" respectively. The combined 85% assures the contribution of slide-based lecture notes to students' learning experience.

Since both slides and slide-based lecture notes are popular among students, we would no doubt continue to provide both to the students.

5 Conclusion

Blended learning facilitates independent and collaborative learning experience [21]. It holds the promise of student-centered deep learning [22]. The proposed slide-based lecture notes offer one more choice of learning activities to students who readily adopt and perceive as useful. Slide-based lecture notes contain explanation for a specific slide in as much detail as desired. The new organization of learning materials can contain the same amount of information as in lecture notes in the conventional book form. But it brings new benefits as follows.

Distinction of Key Points and Details. Underprepared students, who may have weak English and prior knowledge, often have trouble in the identification of key messages from textbooks and conventional lecture notes. They cannot learn deep even if they want to. The proposed slide-based lecture notes distinguish key message from details and can be used as bicycle training wheels for the gradual mastery of deep learning by underprepared students.

Student Autonomy for Deep Learning. A misunderstanding of deep learning is to think of it as an inborn personal trait of students. The learning approach to use, deep or shallow, depends on the student's interests and background in the topic. A student may want to use deep learning for one topic and shallow learning for another. Shallow learning is not all bad. Superficial knowledge of a topic paves the way for deep learning of the same topic in a later date. Slide-based lecture notes enable students to study deep or shallow at will on a slide-by-slide basis. Autonomy in learning improves motivation [2]. Affective benefit of slide-based lecture notes should enhance student performance.

Effective and Efficient Lecture Notes Updates. If separate sets of slides and lecture notes are used, lecturers need to do the updates at least twice: once at the beginning of the study term before printing the lecture notes and again before posting the slides. The multiple updates to learning materials consume time and are susceptible to causing slides and lecture notes to go out-of-sync. The new organization afforded by slide-based lecture notes streamlines the updating task of learning materials. When students have questions, they can accurately identify the difficult slide by its slide number. Lecturers may revise the detailed explanations in the slide-based lecture notes.

5.1 Potential Criticism of Our Work

Lacking a Control Group and Statistical Analysis. Neither a control group nor statistical analysis is employed in our study. We are not in a position to say whether the welcoming behavior by students can be reproduced with the next cohort. This class of students like the approach and perceive it as helpful. But we cannot say definitely that their learning outcomes will improve because of the slide-based lecture notes. A basic principle of blended learning is to provide students with a choice of learning activities. Students should be empowered to choose how they learn. At this moment, we do not care whether 75% or 90% of students like the approach. The exact figure depends on the characteristics of students which may vary from year to year. The proposed slide-based lecture notes should close the feedback loop by identifying the parts of learning materials that need improvements. Statistical analysis could be applied after we have gained more experience with slide-based lecture notes.

Predigestion of Learning Materials. The approach distinguishes for students what are key points and what are details. Are we predigesting the learning materials for students? What if one of the abilities we want students to acquire is the ability to identify the key message without help? This is a difficult question and its answer involves consideration of education philosophy. We do not have an easy answer here. After contemplation, we may end up with a position that the approach should be limited to, for example, years 1 and 2 of university students.

5.2 Future Work

We may set up future experiments with control groups to learn more about the impact of using the slide-based lecture notes. We may want to know exactly how it affects student performance. Eventually, we should try to answer the philosophical question of whether the slide-based lecture notes are predigested study materials for students and thus deprive them from becoming a complete independent student who can learn from any source and pick out the key points without assistance.

References

1. Jones, L.: The Student-Centered Classroom. Cambridge University Press, Cambridge (2007)
2. Dickinson, L.: Autonomy and motivation a literature review. System **23**(2), 165–174 (1995)
3. Weisbaum, H.: College textbook costs more outrageous than ever. CNBC (2014). https://www.cnbc.com/2014/01/28/college-textbook-costs-more-outrageous-than-ever.html. Accessed 6 Mar 2018
4. Kinzie, S.: Swelling textbook costs have college students saying 'pass'. Washington Post (2006). http://web.missouri.edu/~glaserr/current_news/Article_Textbook_Costs.pdf. Accessed 6 Mar 2018
5. Kirk, A.: Textbooks costs continue as barrier to higher education. Huffington Post (2006). https://www.huffingtonpost.com/dr-arthur-f-kirk-je/textbooks-costs-continue-_b_4612606.html. Accessed 6 Mar 2018
6. Cheung, S.K.S.: Distance-learning students' perception on the usefulness of open educational resources. In: Cheung, S.K.S., Kwok, L.-F., Ma, W.W.K., Lee, L.-K., Yang, H. (eds.) ICBL 2017. LNCS, vol. 10309, pp. 389–399. Springer, Cham (2017). https://doi.org/10.1007/978-3-319-59360-9_34
7. Hilton, J.: Open educational resources and college textbook choices: a review of research on efficacy and perceptions. Educ. Tech. Res. Dev. **64**(4), 573–590 (2016)
8. Seaman, J.E., Seaman, J.: Opening the textbook: educational resources in U.S. higher education. Babson Survey Research Group (2017). http://www.onlinelearningsurvey.com/reports/openingthetextbook2017.pdf. Accessed 7 Mar 2018
9. Wingfield, S., Black, G.: Active versus passive course designs: the impact on student outcomes. Tech Trends: Linking Res. Pract. Improve Learn. **48**(5), 36–38 (2004)
10. Gak, D.: Textbook – An important element in the teaching process. Diperoleh dari epub.ff.uns.ac.rs pada tanggal (2011)
11. Brown, K.: Technology: building interaction. J. Educ. Bus. **81**(2), 119–125 (2005)
12. Kozub, R.: Student attitude towards and use of powerpoint® slides as study guides in undergraduate introductory financial accounting. J. Coll. Teach. Learn. **7**(3), 39–45 (2010)
13. Kunkel, K.: A research note assessing the benefit of presentation software in two different lecture courses. Teach. Sociol. **3**(2), 188–196 (2004)
14. Brock, S., Joglekar, Y.: Empowering PowerPoint: Slides and Teaching Effectiveness. Interdisc. J. Inf. Knowl. Manag. **6**, 85–94 (2011)
15. Berk, A.: Research on PowerPoint®: from basic features to multimedia. Int. J. Technol. Teach. Learn. **7**(1), 24–35 (2011)
16. Corbeil, G.: Can PowerPoint presentations effectively replace textbooks and blackboards for teaching grammar? Do students find them an effective learning tool? CALICO J. **24**(3), 631–656 (2007)
17. Marton, F., Säljö, R.: On qualitative differences in learning: I - outcome and process. Br. J. Educ. Psychol. **46**(1), 4–11 (1976)
18. Student approach to Learning. Oxford Learning Institute. https://www.learning.ox.ac.uk/support/teaching/resources/#d.en.44131. Accessed 11 Mar 2018
19. Au, O., So, R., Lee, L.K.: Prior knowledge dwarfs hard work in achieving academic performance. In: Cheung, S.K.S., Kwok, L.-F., Ma, W.W.K., Lee, L.-K., Yang, H. (eds.) ICBL 2017. LNCS, vol. 10309, pp. 139–147. Springer, Cham (2017). https://doi.org/10.1007/978-3-319-59360-9_13

20. Marton, F., Hounsell, D., Entwistle, N. (eds.): The Experience of Learning, 2nd edn. Scottish Academic Press (1997)
21. Garrison, D., Kanuka, H.: Blended learning: uncovering its transformative potential in higher education. Internet High. Educ. **7**(2), 95–105 (2004)
22. Trigwell, K., Prosser, M., Waterhouse, F.: Relations between teachers' approaches to teaching and students' approaches to learning. High. Educ. **37**(1), 57–70 (1999)

Assessment for Blended Learning

Enhancing Teacher Assessment Literacy Using a Blended Deep Learning Approach

Wing Shui Ng[1(✉)], Haoran Xie[1], and Fu Lee Wang[2]

[1] The Education University of Hong Kong, Tai Po, NT, Hong Kong
ngws@eduhk.hk
[2] The Open University of Hong Kong, Ho Man Tin, Kowloon, Hong Kong

Abstract. Assessment literacy refers to educators' understanding of the principles and practices of sound assessment. It has been considered as a critical professional requirement in educational system since it to a great extent affects students' learning. However, research has shown that both pre-service and in-service teachers are weak in assessment literacy and lack confidence to implement effective assessment. The main reasons of unsatisfactory assessment literacy among teachers are the limited pre-service assessment education and a lack of research on the pedagogies on assessment education. To enrich effective practice of assessment literacy education, a blended deep learning approach for educating teacher assessment literacy was applied in this study. The strategy combined a face-to-face component for content-based teaching and an online learning component for process-based teaching. The online learning component with the focus on peer assessment engaged participants in a deep learning of assessment. Participants expressed that they had obtained an in-depth understanding on assessment literacy and particularly on peer assessment. They had developed better confidence and are willing to implement peer assessment in their future teaching. This study provides a case of using a blended learning approach on assessment education for reference.

Keywords: Assessment literacy · Blended learning · Peer assessment
Peer feedback · Assessment for learning · Deep learning

1 Introduction

In response to the development of society and educational needs, teachers have no longer solely served as knowledge providers. More importantly, a teacher is required to serve as a facilitator, a mentor or a coach to guide the process of students' learning [9]. A teacher should also help students learn effectively by designing authentic, meaningful and challenging learning activities that are related to students' experiences [2]. As stated by Dochy [9], the teacher in current educational practice is "a key to open the door to domains of knowledge and experience" (p. 11). The student, on the other hand, is responsible for his or her own learning. Learners are expected to engage in meaningful learning rather than rote or surface learning. Students should make sense of subject contents through a vigorous interaction with it. The goal is not only to produce high knowledgeable individuals. Students should also obtain trainings for developing

S. K. S. Cheung et al. (Eds.): ICBL 2018, LNCS 10949, pp. 203–214, 2018.
https://doi.org/10.1007/978-3-319-94505-7_16

various competencies, including cognitive, meta-cognitive, social and affective competencies, for the success of their future [2, 9]. Deep learning should be internally motivated and is associated with an intention to understand, rather than to simply pass an assessment task [16]. In this connection, assessment has been identified as a powerful aid to engage students into a more in-depth learning process and transform them into reflective practitioners [9, 11]. Teachers should therefore develop knowledge and skills on educational assessment. However, there is only a handful of research on the pedagogies of assessment education [7, 13, 24]. In this connection, this paper reports a study that applied a blended deep learning approach to enhance teacher assessment literacy.

2 Assessment Literacy as a Critical Teacher's Competence

Assessment is a core element in education. The term, assessment literacy, was coined by Stiggins [28]. It refers to educators' understanding of the principles of sound assessment, including the understanding of assessment terminology, the development and use of assessment methodologies and techniques, familiarity with standards of quality in assessment, and familiarity with alternative to traditional measurements of learning [22, 31]. It involves integrating assessment practices, theories, and philosophies to support teaching and learning in education [6].

As elaborated by Stiggins [29], assessment-literate educators should know what they assess, why they assess, how best they assess, how to generate sound samples of performance and how to prevent problems in assessment. They should also understand how to construct, administer, and score reliable assessments and communicate valid interpretations about student learning [6]. Teacher's assessment literacy has been considered as a critical professional requirement in educational system since it to a great extent affects students' learning [8, 23]. It is therefore critical that teachers should develop literacy on educational assessment.

However, research has shown that both pre-service and in-service teachers are weak in assessment literacy and lack confidence to implement effective assessment [1, 7]. It results in inaccurate assessment of students and consequently preventing them from achieving the desired performance [30]. Research has identified that the main reasons of unsatisfactory assessment literacy among teachers are the limited pre-service assessment education and a lack of research on the pedagogies of assessment education [7, 13, 24]. For the sake of enriching the research on pedagogies of assessment education, the researcher designed and applied a blended deep learning approach for educating teacher assessment literacy. The blended deep learning approach is elaborated in the following section. This study attempted to explore the following research question.

"What is the effectiveness of a blended deep learning approach on enhancing teacher assessment literacy?"

3 Method

This section reports the context of this study. It also elaborates the design and rationales of the blended deep learning approach.

3.1 Context of the Study

The study was conducted in a course entitled Problem-solving and Assessment in Design and Technology taught by the researcher and his colleagues in a Postgraduate Diploma of Education programme. The course aims to provide a deeper investigation of knowledge and issues associated with assessment methods. It develops theories and skills on assessment and addresses the use of instructional and assessment theories to enhance teaching and learning. Upon completion of the course, students should be able to construct appropriate assessment for secondary students. A total of nine pre-service teachers enrolled in the course with six males and three females. After explaining the purposes, all pre-service teachers were willing to sign a consent form to participate in this study. The blended deep learning approach for educating teacher assessment literacy was implemented in lesson 6 to 10 of the course. Their works in the learning activity were not counted in the final assessment grade of the course. The focus of other lessons was problem-solving skills and it was taught by other colleagues.

3.2 Blended Deep Learning Approach for Teacher Assessment Literacy Education

As suggested by McAllister and Irvine [17], teaching methods, such as assessment education pedagogy, can be divided into two components, namely content-based teaching and process-based teaching. The main purpose of content-based teaching is for transmission of knowledge and skills. It is usually conducted using a lecture-based didactic approach for learning educational policies, procedures and theories [14]. The content-based teaching approach has been commonly used in assessment education [14]. The process-based teaching methods, on the other hand, provide opportunities for students to carry out reflection and initiate meaningful dialogue. It aims to engage students in active learning. As stated by Shepard and her colleagues [27], teachers under training should experience how to design, score and interpret assessment. Particularly, formative assessment or assessment for learning, such as peer assessment strategy, should be emphasized since it engages teachers in a positive assessment experience and transforms them into reflective practitioners [21, 34].

In order to integrate content-based teaching and process-based teaching into a coherent pedagogy, a blended learning approach was adopted. Although different definitions have been suggested, blended learning is generally referred to the pedagogy that combines face-to-face classroom teaching with an online learning component [26]. The use of blended learning approach in designing courses, particularly in higher education, has been increasing [18]. With the inclusion of an online component, the time students spent on learning can be increased. Blend learning approach can make use of online technologies to implement asynchronous teaching and learning. Individual learning and learner autonomy can also be promoted by a blended learning approach [18, 26]. In the design of the pedagogy applied in this study, elements for engaging participants into deep learning were intentionally included and it constituted the blended deep learning approach. An overall structure of the blended deep learning approach is depicted in Fig. 1. In this design, both the face-to-face teaching and online learning components were implemented in the same period in parallel manner. The online learning component aimed to consolidate what they learnt in class to achieve a deep learning of assessment literacy.

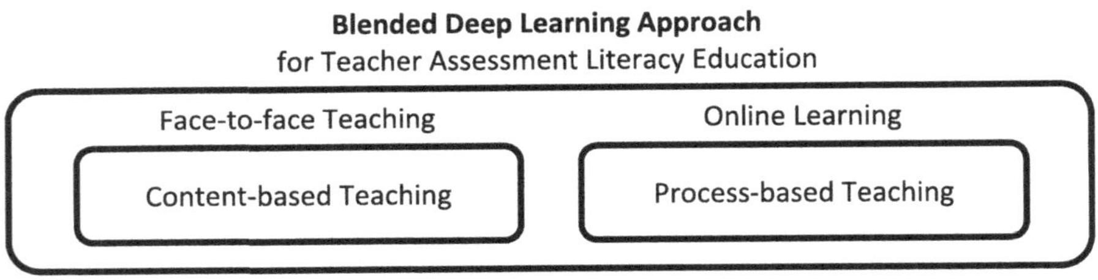

Fig. 1. Overall structure of blended deep learning approach

Face-to-face Teaching Component. The face-to-face teaching component aimed to enable the pre-service teachers to obtain in-depth theoretical knowledge of assessment. The following five topics were carefully selected.

- development of assessment culture
- peer assessment
- feedback for learning
- cases of assessment for learning
- teacher assessment literacy

The first topic addressed the development of assessment culture. In past few decades, the role of assessment in education has undergone significant changes [11]. The paradigm of assessment has shifted from the focus on measurement to the emphasis on improving learning [9, 11, 25]. The purpose of this topic was to enable pre-service teachers to have a holistic understanding on the development of educational assessment.

The second topic focused on the practice of peer assessment. The researcher elaborated various aspects of peer assessment, including its definition, benefits in learning, challenges, reliability and validity, and the procedures in implementation. Actually, the beneficial effects of peer assessment have been well documented in the literature [32]. It has been suggested that peer assessment activities are able to activate students to become learning resources for one another [3]. Research has confirmed that after being engaged in a peer assessment process, students become more reflective in their own working process and have a better understanding of task requirements, greater confidence to deal with assigned tasks and better performance in subsequent tasks [10, 33].

The third topic explored feedback strategy for effective learning. The researcher explained the functions of feedback in learning, principles of good feedback and how to provide effective feedback. As mentioned by Black and Wiliam [3], feedback is a critical component in assessment for learning to move learners forward. It provides information for learners to take actions to narrow the gap between their present stage and the desired goal. As the ultimate objective of assessment for learning is to improve learning on the basis of evidence obtained by peer assessment, high-quality feedback whose adoption is valuable for improving performance is crucial in the peer assessment process.

After strengthening knowledge of peer assessment and feedback, the researcher elaborated a few cases that applied peer assessment in learning process in the next lesson. For example in Ng's [19] study, peer assessment and feedback strategy was applied to enhance the effectiveness on learning computer programming. Students were required to work in pairs to complete learning tasks collaboratively on computer programming. The findings show that the students were satisfied with the peer assessment and feedback strategy in learning computer programming. Moreover, their actual performance was also better when compared with that achieved using traditional teaching method. In another study conducted by Ng [21], a series of assessment for learning strategies with self- and peer-assessment components were applied to transform a web developer into a reflective practitioner. Participants expressed that they became more active, serious, independent, critical and confident in the web design process. They also stated that they learned more and found the strategy beneficial.

The last topic in the face-to-face teaching component was teacher assessment literacy. The researcher explained the concepts and rationales of teacher assessment literacy to let the pre-service teachers understand the importance of educational assessment. Moreover, the classroom assessment standards suggested by the Joint Committee on Standards for Educational Evaluation [15] was also elaborated. With rich contents in the face-to-face teaching in different topics, pre-service teachers were expected to develop a good understanding on assessment literacy and particularly the implementation of peer assessment.

Online Learning Component. The purpose of online learning was to engage the pre-service teachers in active learning outside classroom. It aligned with the rationale that assessment education needs to engage teachers in complex and deep learning about assessment [34]. The online learning component was implemented in a wiki online platform (Fig. 2). The pre-service teachers could participate in online peer assessment anytime, anywhere. A wiki platform, which have the potential benefit of facilitating online collaborative learning, has been used as a learning environment for peer assessment activities [20, 21].

The online learning activity involved four stages (Fig. 3). At the beginning of the online activity, the pre-service teachers were clearly informed the following learning objectives. After the learning activity, they should be able to

- develop a structured peer assessment plan with supporting rationales;
- evaluate the quality of a peer assessment plan;
- provide appropriate and justified feedback on peers work;
- demonstrate an in-depth understanding of peer assessment; and
- identify necessary knowledge and skills of teacher assessment literacy.

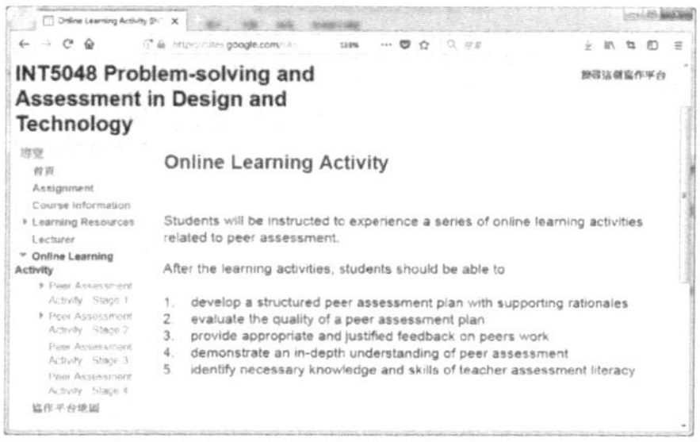

Fig. 2. Wiki platform for online learning

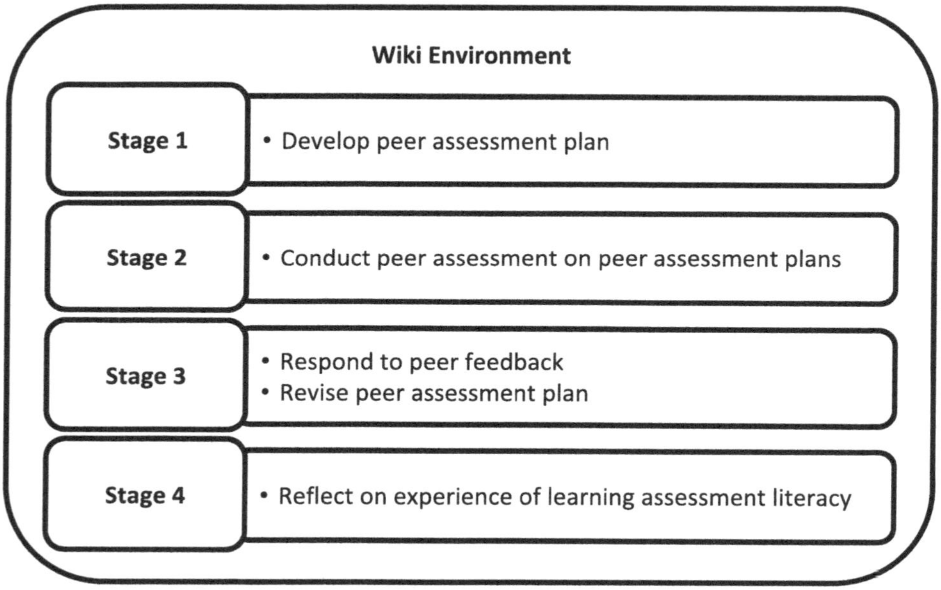

Fig. 3. Online learning component of the blended deep learning approach

In the first stage, the pre-service teachers were required to develop a peer assessment plan for students in junior secondary school level to learn knowledge of science, technology, engineering and mathematics. Since the pre-service teachers might have limited knowledge or experience to design peer assessment strategy, the researcher provided some samples of peer assessment plan that suggested by Carless and his colleagues [5] to serve as a scaffolding tool. This activity enabled the pre-service teachers to consolidate what they learnt in class. According to Bloom's [4] taxonomy of educational objectives, the development of peer assessment plan was an activity of synthesis. It involved the combination of parts of previous experience with new materials and to reconstruct it into a new and well-integrated whole. The development of peer assessment plan could be regarded as an activity of a very high level of learning.

In Stage 2 of the online learning activity, the pre-service teachers were instructed to assess the peer assessment plans of two classmates randomly assigned by the researcher. They were required to negotiate the criteria of assessment and the format of providing feedback. After discussion, they agreed that the peer assessment plan should be assessed based on innovation of practice, rationale of practice and feasibility of practice. They considered that qualitative comments were important and grade in the format of A to F should be provided. By engaging the pre-service teacher in peer assessment of peer assessment plans, they were brought to a meta-level of learning since the object of peer assessment was a peer assessment plan. This activity that involved evaluation was regarded as the highest level of learning in Bloom's [4] taxonomy of educational objectives. Together with the activity in Stage 1, the pre-service teachers were required to develop peer assessment plan, carry out peer assessment and review peer assessment plans. This design of strategy enabled them to engage in a deep level of learning on assessment.

In Stage 3, the pre-service teachers were instructed to respond to peer feedback. They were required to express whether they agreed with peer feedback. If they disagreed with peer feedback, they were required to provide justifications to defend. They were then required to revise their own peer assessment plan on the basis of received feedback. The activity in this stage enabled the pre-service teachers to initiate meaningful and critical dialogue on educational assessment. Moreover, they were required to engage in the necessary cognitive processes to thoroughly examine the received feedback, compare the performance with the received feedback, and decide whether to adopt the feedback to improve his or her work so as to close the feedback loop [12].

In the final stage, the pre-service teachers were required to review their experience in the whole teaching strategy. They were invited to express their opinions based on the questions given by the researcher. Details of the questions and the reflection from pre-service teachers are reported in the results section. The activity in this stage aimed to enable the pre-service teachers to reflect on what they learnt on educational assessment under the blended deep learning approach.

4 Results

This section reports the results obtained from Stage 4 of online learning component of the blended deep learning strategy. First of all, all the pre-service teachers expressed that they did not have any experience to implement peer assessment while about 67% of them experienced peer assessment previously as the role of learner.

4.1 Comments on Specific Designs of Pedagogy

When asking their opinions on the arrangement of assessing peer assessment plan, they expressed that they had a better understanding on the design of a peer assessment plan and this strategy promoted self-reflection. For example, some pre-service teachers mentioned that

"This design enables me to learn more about various Peer Assessment Plan design so that I can enhance my plan."

"This design enables me broaden my eyesight of others idea and the plan of lesson. It can let me reflect the good or bad of my plan."

Moreover, the researcher also requested the pre-service teachers to reflect on the arrangement of negotiating assessment criteria and feedback format. They expressed that it helped align the criteria of assessment and give a fair assessment.

"... it is important to align the focus of assessment before assessing. Otherwise, the assessing result may be very different. Some may have high grade but other may have low grade."

"... each student judging by the same standard criteria. It is a fair assessment."

The next question invited the pre-service teachers to comment on the feedback on peer feedback arrangement. They opined that it provided an opportunity for them to initiate academic dialogue.

"... This design enable me to improve communication and better understanding of expectations between each others."

"... that is a good chance for me to communicate and explain my plan with the fellows which would be benefit for both sides."

It also helped them to carefully review peer feedback and their own peer assessment plan to identify areas of improvement.

"This design enables me to improve my peer assessment plan by considering what is good and which point is needed to enhance from peers."

"... understand others comments and rethink what I can improve of modify for my plan."

4.2 Achievement of Learning Objectives

The researcher then consulted the pre-service teachers to what extent the learning objectives of the online learning activity were achieved. They were invited to respond using a 7-points Likert scale with 1 and 7 indicate Strongly Disagree and Strongly Agree respectively. They were also encouraged to express qualitative comments. As shown in Table 1, the mean scores range from 5.2 to 5.8. It suggests that the pre-service teachers considered all the learning objectives were reasonably achieved.

Table 1. Achievement of learning objectives from participants' perspective.

Learning objective	Mean score
Develop a structured peer assessment plan with supporting rationales	5.4
Evaluate the quality of a peer assessment plan	5.4
Provide appropriate and justified feedback on peers work	5.2
Demonstrate an in-depth understanding of peer assessment	5.8
Identify necessary knowledge and skills of teacher assessment literacy	5.7

They also expressed some positive comments as follows.

"it was an impressive activity to learn this topic."
"Lecturer provided rich knowledge of peer assessment."
"the lecture and the activity were well presented and the knowledge and information were adequate."
"Knowledge delivery is enough and I believed that the demonstration would be useful in my future teaching."

However, some participants expressed that they would like to have longer period to engage in the learning activity.

"If we have more lessons, that will be great! Because we can do more hands-on practice."
"...still need more practice on that area."
"... I just learnt in a few week and lack of experience, so it is hard to evaluate a peer assessment plan with suitable comment."

In addition, some participants expressed that they did not have sufficient confidence to provide high quality feedback. It suggests that to strengthen participants' content knowledge and provide assessment training are critical in the implementation of peer assessment.

"... I think I still don't have enough knowledge and experience to feedback."
"... the topic of the activity is a little bit difficult for a peer review discussion, since a good STEM activity is hard to defined."

4.3 Overall Reflection on Teaching Strategy

The researcher also invited the pre-service teachers to express their overall opinions on the teaching strategy. As shown in Table 2, they opined that they developed better confidence and will implement peer assessment in their future teaching. They were satisfied with the learning activity.

Table 2. Participants' overall opinions on the teaching strategy

Question	Mean score
Confident to implement peer assessment in the future ("1 - Not Confident", "7 - Very Confident")	5.6
Will implement peer assessment in future teaching ("1 - No, Not Likely", "7 - Yes, Definitely")	5.4
Satisfied with the peer assessment activity ("1 - Not Satisfied", "7 - Very Satisfied")	5.9

Finally, the pre-service teachers were invited to write qualitative comments on the learning activity. All of them expressed very positive comments. An example is as follow.

"I think this is an abundant activity for me to experience the whole process of peer assessment. Since I can design a lesson plan at the beginning. Then I can evaluate and comment to the peers' work to see how they planned their lessons. I also receive the feedbacks from my peers,

so this is an interactive activity for me to understand how to make a good peer assessment plan and provide some qualitative feedbacks to peers. Finally, I think peers and I can learn from each other by evaluate the other plans. Because different comments can be achieved, the planner can explore some new ideas and make further enhancement. This is a good activity for peer learning and making progress, so I will try to use peer assessment activity in future."

5 Discussion and Conclusion

As suggested by the results, the pre-service teachers have recognized that the rationale of conducting assessment is for offering effective feedback and for enhancing learning. By preparing peer assessment plan and engaging in peer assessment process, they have developed necessary competence and confidence to implement educational assessment. They have also been aware of the importance of negotiating assessment criteria and feedback format for ensuring the quality of assessment. All the participants appreciated the teaching strategy for developing their assessment literacy and they are willing to implement peer assessment in their future teaching. All these evidences suggest that the pre-service teachers have developed an in-depth understanding on assessment literacy after the experience of the blended deep learning approach of teaching.

However, due to limited class time, the strategy was implemented in only a few weeks. As stated by the pre-service teachers, the effectiveness of the teaching strategy on assessment education might be further enhanced if the participants could be engaged in a longer period. It aligns with the insight from Xu and Brown [34] that assessment education needs to be long enough to engage teachers in complex and deep learning about assessment. Moreover, training on conducting assessment is also an important factor in peer assessment. In addition, caution must be put on the small sample size of this study. Therefore, a future study with longer period, more training of peer assessment and larger sample size is therefore recommended. Notwithstanding the limitations, favorable results were obtained in this study and the strategy effectively enhanced assessment literacy of the pre-service teachers. The blended deep learning approach applied in this study enriched the pedagogy of assessment education in literature for future reference.

References

1. Beziat, T.L., Coleman, B.K.: Classroom assessment literacy: evaluating pre-service teachers. Res. **27**(1), 25–30 (2015)
2. Birenbaum, M.: Assessment 2000: towards a pluralistic approach to assessment. In: Birenbaum, M., Dochy, F. (eds.) Alternatives in Assessment of Achievements, Learning Processes and Prior Knowledge. Kluwer Academic Publishers, Boston (1996)
3. Black, P., Wiliam, D.: Developing the theory of formative assessment. Educ. Assess. Eval. Account. **21**(1), 5–31 (2009)
4. Bloom, B.S.: Taxonomy of Educational Objectives. Longman, London (1956)
5. Carless, D., Joughin, G., Liu, N.-F.: How Assessment Supports Learning: Learning-oriented Assessment in Action. Hong Kong University Press, Hong Kon (2006)

6. DeLuca, C., Bellara, A.: The current state of assessment education: aligning policy, standards, and teacher education curriculum. J. Teach. Educ. **64**(4), 356–372 (2013)
7. DeLuca, C., Klinger, D.A.: Assessment literacy development: identifying gaps in teacher candidates' learning. Assess. Educ. Princ. Policy Pract. **17**(4), 419–438 (2010)
8. DeLuca, C., LaPointe-McEwan, D., Luhanga, U.: Teacher assessment literacy: a review of international standards and measures. Educ. Assess. Eval. Account. **28**(3), 251–272 (2016)
9. Dochy, F.: A new assessment era: different needs, new challenges. Res. Dialogue Learn. Instr. **2**(1), 11–20 (2001)
10. Dochy, F., Segers, M., Sluijsmans, D.: The use of self-, peer and co-assessment in higher education: a review. Stud. High. Educ. **24**(3), 331–350 (1999)
11. Falchikov, N.: Improving Assessment Through Student Involvement: Practical Solutions for Aiding Learning in Higher and Further Education. RoutledgeFalmer, London (2005)
12. Gielen, S., Peeters, E., Dochy, F., Onghena, P., Struyven, K.: Improving the Effectiveness of Peer Feedback for Learning. Learn. Instr. **20**(4), 304–315 (2010)
13. Graham, P.: Classroom-based assessment: changing knowledge and practice through preservice teacher education. Teach. Teach. Educ. **21**(6), 607–612 (2005)
14. Grossman, P.L.: Research on pedagogical approaches in teacher education. In: Cochran-Smith, M., Zeichner, K.M. (eds.) Studying Teacher Education: The Report of the AERA Panel on Research and Teacher Education, pp. 425–476. American Educational Research Association, Washington, DC (2005)
15. JCSEE: The Classroom Assessment Standards. Joint Committee on Standards for Educational Evaluation (2015). http://www.jcsee.org/the-classroom-assessment-standards-new-standards. Accessed 3 Jan 2017
16. Marton, F., Saljo, R.: Approaches to learning. In: Marton, F., Hounsell, D., Entwistle, N. (eds.) The Experience of Learning, pp. 39–58. Scottish Academic Press, Edinburgh (1997)
17. McAllister, G., Irvine, J.J.: Cross cultural competency and multicultural teacher education. Rev. Educ. Res. **70**(1), 3–24 (2000)
18. Mozelius, P., Hettiarachchi, E.: Critical factors for implementing blending learning in higher education. ICTE J. **6**(2), 37–51 (2017)
19. Ng, W.S.: The impact of peer assessment and feedback strategy in learning computer programming in higher education. Issues Inf. Sci. Inf. Technol. **9**, 17–27 (2012)
20. Ng, W.S.: Students' perspectives on the process and effectiveness of a self- and peer-assessment strategy in learning web design within a Wiki environment. In: International Conference on Information, Communication Technologies in Education, ICICTE 2013 Proceedings, pp. 257–266. Southampton Solent University, Crete (2013)
21. Ng, W.S.: Enhancing the quality of educational website design through assessment for learning strategies. In: Sreedhar, G. (ed.) Design Solutions for Improving Website Quality and Effectiveness, pp. 24–51. Information Science Reference, USA (2016)
22. Popham, W.J.: Why assessment literacy is professional suicide. Educ. Leadersh. **62**(1), 82–83 (2004)
23. Popham, W.J.: Needed: a dose of assessment literacy. Educ. Leadersh. **63**(6), 84–85 (2006)
24. Popham, W.J.: Assessment literacy overlooked: a teacher educator's confession. Teach. Educ. **46**(4), 265–273 (2011)
25. Serafini, F.: Three paradigms of assessment: measurement, procedure, and inquiry. Read. Teach. **54**(4), 384–393 (2000)
26. Sharma, P.: Blended learning design and practice. In: Carrier, M., Damerow, R.M., Bailey, K.M. (eds.) Digital Language Learning and Teaching: Research, Theory, and Practice, pp. 167–178. Routledge, New York (2017)

27. Shepard, L., Hammerness, K., Darling-Hammond, L., Rust, F.: Assessment. In: Darling-Hammond, L., Bransford, J. (eds.) Preparing Teachers for a Changing World: What Teachers Should Learn and Be Able to Do, pp. 275–326. Jossey-Bass, San Francisco (2005)
28. Stiggins, R.J.: Assessment literacy. Phi Delta Kappan **72**(7), 534–539 (1991)
29. Stiggins, R.J.: Assessment literacy for the 21st century. Phi Delta Kappan **77**(3), 238–245 (1995)
30. Stiggins, R.J.: The unfulfilled promise of classroom assessment. Educ. Measur. Issues Pract. **20**(3), 5–15 (2001)
31. Stiggins, R.J.: Assessment crisis: the absence of assessment for learning. Phi Delta Kappan **83**(10), 758–765 (2002)
32. Topping, K.: Peer assessment between students in colleges and universities. Rev. Educ. Res. **68**(3), 249–276 (1998)
33. Topping, K.J., Smith, E.F., Swanson, I., Elliot, A.: Formative peer assessment of academic writing between postgraduate students. Assess. Eval. High. Educ. **25**(2), 146–169 (2000)
34. Xu, Y., Brown, G.T.L.: Teacher assessment literacy in practice: a reconceptualization. Teach. Teach. Educ. **58**, 149–162 (2016)

Evaluation of the Use of Mobile Devices for Clinical Practicum in Nursing Education

Kam Cheong Li, Linda Yin-King Lee, Suet-Lai Wong, Ivy Sui-Yu Yau, and Billy Tak-Ming Wong(✉)

The Open University of Hong Kong, Hong Kong, China
{kcli,yklee,slwong,isyyau,tamiwong}@ouhk.edu.hk

Abstract. This paper reports an evaluation of the use of mobile devices by nursing students in clinical practicum. In this learning environment, nursing students have to apply their nursing skills and follow specific clinical procedures in real-life situations. Following the Framework for the Rational Analysis of Mobile Education (FRAME), this study involved a total of 265 nursing students taking part in a questionnaire survey and 20 nursing students and relevant staff participating in interviews, showing their views, experiences and perceptions of the use of mobile devices for studying nursing materials and conducting clinical assessment in the practicum context. The results indicate their overall satisfaction of the mobile learning practice, in particular for the ubiquitous access of materials for situated learning in wards, and the effectiveness of supporting teachers to keep track of students' learning progress. Areas of improvements were also identified, which emphasise the network connectivity of devices, user training and technical support for the use and maintenance of the devices.

Keywords: Mobile learning · Nursing education · Learning motivation FRAME model · Clinical practicum

1 Introduction

Mobile learning has been identified as conducive to pedagogical flexibility and innovation on the strength of its "on the move" nature. Learning materials in textual, visual, or aural forms could be easily accessed by and delivered to learners [1, 2]. This facilitates particularly situated learning which occurs beyond the confines of classroom settings and conventional academic schedules.

Clinical practicum in nursing education presents a proper scenario for practising mobile learning. Nursing education involves not only the mastery of conceptual knowledge in classrooms and laboratories, but also the acquisition of practical and social skills in clinical wards. Through the use of mobile devices, nursing students can better access just-in-time information and participate in situated, experimental and contexualised learning activities [3]. Yet nursing education is context-dependent by nature [4], and therefore the extent to which mobile learning impacts on nursing students demands consideration of the nursing practicum environment.

This study aimed to evaluate how mobile learning impacts on nursing students' learning effectiveness in clinical practicum. It conceptualised mobile learning using the

S. K. S. Cheung et al. (Eds.): ICBL 2018, LNCS 10949, pp. 215–226, 2018.
https://doi.org/10.1007/978-3-319-94505-7_17

Framework for the Rational Analysis of Mobile Education (FRAME) model [2]. This model posits that mobile learning is a process driven by the interaction of mobile technologies, human learning capacities, and the social dimensions of learning.

This paper harnesses the FRAME model to highlight nursing students' perception of their mobile learning experience, showing the effectiveness of mobile learning in clinical practicum. It is based on the mobile learning practice for nursing education in a university in Hong Kong, summarising the views of nursing students, the course coordinator of clinical practicum and the instructional designer of mobile apps from different perspectives. The results also reveal possible ways to improve the effectiveness of mobile learning to address the diverse learning needs of nursing students.

2 Literature Review

2.1 Clinical Practicum in Nursing Education

Nursing education is a discipline which has widely incorporated mobile learning into pedagogical practice. Integrating mobile technology and digital literacy into nursing education has been deemed necessary by numerous councils and associations of nurses across the world [5]. Nursing educational programmes have also attempted curricula transformations with the aid of mobile devices [6].

As nursing education necessitates both the acquisition of conceptual knowledge and practical skills, it takes place in a variety of learning contexts, not only in schools but also in clinical wards. The situated, experiential and contextual nature of nursing education is therefore an ideal platform for mobile learning to take effect and realise its potential. For example, mobile devices can allow students to access the most up-to-date information and reliable resources on the internet in spite of physical locations and time constraints [3]. Advantages of using of mobile devices in nursing practice have been identified as an enhancement of information access, time-saving, patients' safety, quality of medical care, and confidence in performing professional tasks [7]. Other possibilities include the use of mobile devices to establish virtual communication among instructors, peers, and resources at the point of care [8]; and the use of mobile-based video clips to assist in clinical teaching, ultimately increased students' motivation, confidence, and satisfaction throughout the learning process [9].

In the nursing education in Hong Kong, nursing students have to gain most of their practicum experience outside classrooms and prepare themselves for professional adaptability in realistic contexts such as health care institutions and hospitals [10]. It has been suggested that nursing students in Hong Kong highly prioritise "support, respect, and recognition by all personnel in the clinical environment" as fundamental to their learning satisfaction; a supportive learning environment is thus vital [11]. Building up on previous studies' insights into nursing education in the Hong Kong's context, it is of utmost concern to investigate the role that mobile learning could play in facilitating students' learning in practicum [12].

2.2 FRAME Model

Koole's [2] Framework for the Rational Analysis of Mobile Education (FRAME) model suggests that mobile learning consists of an interaction among three factors: the mobile technologies (device), human learning capacities (learner), and the social aspects of learning (social). This model has been widely employed in evaluating, improving and further developing mobile learning in nursing education [13, 14], laying a theoretical foundation for advancing and assessing the development of learning materials and pedagogical strategies in this field.

The FRAME model contends that the effectiveness of mobile learning is highly correlated to whether the three aspects—device, learner and social—have fulfilled their potential during the process of their interaction. Previous studies [8] have similarly paid central attention to whether the three aspects have been fulfilled. According to Koole [2], in a most ideal case, learners through mobile learning can "assess and select relevant information, redefine their goals, and reconsider their understanding of concepts within a shifting and growing frame of reference" (p. 38).

3 Method

This study aimed to find out the effectiveness of the use of mobile devices for learning in clinical practicum. It covered the experiences and perceptions of nursing students, as well as the course coordinator of clinical practicum and the instructional designer for mobile apps.

3.1 Participants

A total of 265 Year-3 and Year-4 undergraduate nursing students studying in a university in Hong Kong were recruited to participate in the study. All the participating students had experiences in using mobile devices for learning in clinical practicum. For learning purposes, each student was supplied with an iPod Touch when they enrolled in the nursing programme. The device was used by the student throughout the study of the nursing programme and the student did not need to return back the device. Two mobile apps specially developed for the students' learning in clinical practicum were installed to the devices in advance. Training was provided to the students for the use of the devices and the apps. In addition, the course coordinator of clinical practicum and the instructional designer for the mobile apps also participated in the study. All participants were introduced the tasks involved in the study, and their consent to participate was obtained.

3.2 Experimental Procedure

The study focused on the students' mobile learning practice in clinical practicum. The students needed to use one of the apps to conduct clinical assessment with their mentors in the wards. Another app provided nursing videos on a broad range of clinical skills and procedures which the students had to master in order to pass the practicum.

Therefore the use of mobile devices in the practicum was compulsory for the students, meaning that the devices served as a tool which integrates with the students' learning, instead of being something "superimposed on" their practice [8].

The study involved interviews and a questionnaire survey. Two sessions of focus group interviews were conducted with a total of 20 participating students, and two individual interviews with the course coordinator and the instructional designer, respectively. The interviews focused on the participants' experiences of and views on the mobile learning practice. The interviews were structured based on the FRAME model. The participating students also took part in a questionnaire survey which studied their perception of the mobile learning experience.

3.3 Instruments

Mobile Learning Apps. Two mobile apps were developed and installed to the students' iPod Touch for their use in clinical practicum. One of the apps was used for clinical assessment. It contains a list of clinical assessment items, each of which has to be rated by the students and their mentors as 'achieved' or 'not achieved'. Another app provided nursing videos on a range of topics. The nursing videos were produced to help the students to do revision on relevant clinical skills and procedures.

Questionnaire. The questionnaire was developed to collect the students' feedback of their mobile learning experience. It follows the FRAME model to understand how the mobile learning process is perceived by the students. It contains altogether 66 items covering various aspects of the model. The questionnaire has undergone a review by an expert panel, followed by a pilot test conducted by 10 students (who were not involved in this questionnaire survey) to check their understanding of the items. A 7-point Likert scale is used for the questionnaire—ranging from '1 Completely dissatisfied' to '7 Completely satisfied', from '1 Not at all familiar' to '7 Extremely familiar', from '1 Not at all useful' to '7 Extremely useful', and from '1 Strongly disagree' to '7 Strongly agree'—depending on different types of the items. The survey was paper-based, and the students spent around 15 min on average to complete the questionnaire.

4 Results

4.1 Focus Group and Individual Interviews

The responses in the interviews of different parties in mobile learning practice, i.e., students, the course coordinator, and the instructional designer, reflect their perceived benefits from and obstacles of practising mobile learning. They also reveal the major concerns that need to be addressed in practising mobile learning in the clinical practicum setting. The interview data were analysed by categorising the participants' feedback into themes according to the FRAME model.

Interaction Learning Through Clinical Assessment with the Mobile App. Despite the design and function of the assessment app were overall satisfied by the participants, some students indicated issues related to use the mobile app for assessment, which hinder effective communication during the assessment. Student 'J' mentioned the difficulty of understanding some assessment items in the app:

> There was a time I have to consult my mentor about what an assessment item is asking about. It seemed that I had communication problems with my mentor because I misunderstood the items.

Some students raised the issue of flexibility in assessment using the app, claiming that the assessment app—which offers only binary options of 'achieved' and 'not achieved' for students' clinical procedures—was too simplistic and does not provide further comments or suggestions for students. Student 'Je' indicated:

> It may be better to rate our performance using a number point scale. The current assessment method giving only 'achieve or not achieve' cannot distinguish best performed students from the other less performed ones.

From the perspective of the course coordinator, the assessment app did benefit the teaching and learning process. It releases the teachers' burden to a large extent by enhancing the efficiency of the data entry process, and allowing teachers to access students' assessment record anytime. It also helps students to do revision and access what they learned through the mobile devices. The assessment process is simple for the students and mentors, that the students only need to upload their results through the app after the practicum.

It was also well aware of that some mentors, who practised the conventional paper-based assessment for years, take longer time to be familiar with and get used to the new way of assessment through the mobile devices. The course coordinator mentioned:

> It has been many years that our nursing training relied on hardcopy materials for assessment. Some mentors may not be familiar with and have not got used to the app.

In sum, the assessment app has improved the conventional clinical practicum in terms of allowing the assessment process be completed conveniently, so that teachers can release a considerable amount of workload, and students can benefit more from mentors' immediate feedback during the assessment. However, miscommunication existed occasionally in understanding the assessment criteria. Both the students' and teacher's responses showed that sufficient training and clear instruction on the use of mobile devices for assessment are significant for the success of the new practice of mobile assessment, especially for those who have long been practicing the conventional ways.

Learning Materials Delivered with a Mobile App. Another app, which is used to access the nursing videos, was positively received by the participants for doing revision of the nursing skills and procedures in clinical practicum. For example, student 'S' gave a positive view on the app that the nursing videos help students to visualise the clinical procedures and facilitate retention of the content:

> I often use the app for revision, because it contains a lot of videos that were helpful for us to practice nursing skills especially before assessment.

According to the course coordinator, the videos are comprehensive, updated, and appropriate for skill-wise practicum training. They serve as a means to standardise the basic nursing skills which were taught in different courses and by different instructors. The course coordinator said:

> The videos are common to all nursing practices and comprehensive enough. We produced a lot of videos ourselves that all students can access through the nursing video app.

To further improve the app, the course coordinator suggested extending it to support learning of both the classroom and practicum contexts, where students can access the materials for common topics in various courses and situated cognition can be facilitated. The course coordinator said:

> There is an app introducing electrocardiography used in some courses. It can also be used by the students when seeing such real examples in the practicum.

In addition to the nursing videos, the instructional designer introduced current work and future plans to provide interactive, multimedia contents on difficult topics:

> In the app, technology will be used to enhance the students' understanding how the cardiovascular system works, such as interactive illustration of the heart. There will be scenarios and case studies on heart diseases to help students learn how to identify where the problems lie within the cardiovascular system and the heart.

Teacher-Learner Interaction and Learner-Learner Interaction. The mobile app for assessment facilitated interaction between students and teachers/mentors. The interviewees pointed out areas for improving the communication, especially in terms of getting mutual agreement on key requirements for the assessment. For instance, some students raised the discrepancies between the students and mentors on understanding the materials and guidelines for assessment, which require further communication to resolve the issue. Student 'CH' said:

> The mentors might not be very clear about the assessment system. Some of them thought that giving a result of "not achieved" for a few assessment items was acceptable since they did not usually give full mark. However, it is mandatory for us to get all items "achieved" to pass the practicum.

The course coordinator explained that communication between students and mentors was mainly through the discussion during the assessment process:

> There are two parts in the assessment via the mobile app: the student first self-rates his/her performance and then the mentor gives another rating. It is expected that they will communicate during the process. The mentor is expected to explain and discuss with the student about the differences, if any, between the student's self-rating and the mentor's rating, which is a part of the student's learning during such interaction.

Device Usability. The participants pointed out the benefits of iPod Touch for its portability to be used in the ward environment. Some students emphasised that the size of a larger device was not preferred because it was heavy and inconvenient to carry. Student 'J' said:

> We have to carry our own stuff and walk around in the ward while working. It is not comfortable if I carry a large device and I worry about dropping the device down.

Other student views also existed. For instance, student 'Ch' preferred a device with a larger screen size for reading lecture notes:

> There would be a lot of notes since we study the nursing programme for a total of five years. If we have an iPad or a tablet we can check the notes anytime we want.

In general, the students were satisfied with the functions of the device in supporting learning, such as photo-taking and build-in dictionary. On the other hand, more user support is needed, such as warranty and repairs, to enhance the students' motivation to use the devices. As student 'Dor' suggested:

> It will be better if there are staff on campus responsible for technical support. It is important that there are clear instructions on who we can seek help from.

Social Technology. The limitation of the iPod Touch that it only has Wi-Fi connectivity has been highlighted and such limitation might constrain the use of it. The students had to connect the device to the internet through sharing their own mobile phone's 3G/4G network. As student "M" put it:

> I have to use my own smartphone to access the nursing videos when there is no Wi-Fi. I have to bring and use two devices at the same time, that is not convenient.

On the other hand, there was also a view that Wi-Fi connectivity is enough for accessing learning materials (i.e. knowledge function), and students can use other devices such as smartphones to fulfil the social function (e.g. instant messaging). It is not necessary to integrate the knowledge function and social function in one single device for learning.

Institutional Support. The importance of institutional support for the use of the devices has been emphasised in the interviews. In sum, the students wished to have more convenient channels for solving technical problems, and a longer warrant period for the devices covering the students' whole study period of the nursing programme. The staff interviewed highlighted that training was provided to university staff and hospital mentors, that would be reviewed and improved to enhance the students' motivation for using the devices for learning.

4.2 Questionnaire Survey

To evaluate the effectiveness of mobile learning in the clinical practicum following the FRAME model, the ratings on each of the variables of the FRAME model were summarised. Table 1 presents the descriptive statistics. The reliability of the ratings, as assessed by Cronbach's α, ranged from .78 to .96, indicating that the internal consistency of the composite items was at overall acceptable to excellent levels [15]. Using a seven-point Likert scale ('7' as the highest), the mean scores ranged from 3.48 to 5.21, showing a considerable variation across different variables in the FRAME model.

The device aspect received the highest mean rating ($M = 4.69$, $SD = 0.90$), reflecting a relatively high level of student satisfaction with the physical, technical and functional characteristics of the mobile devices. Among the variables of the device aspect, physical characteristics had the highest mean rating. File storage and retrieval

Table 1. Descriptive statistics for ratings on variables of the FRAME model (n = 231).

Variables of the FRAME model	Number of items	M	SD	SE	Cronbach's α
Device (D)	17	4.69	0.90	0.06	.93
Physical characteristics	3	5.21	1.12	0.07	.78
Speed	3	4.68	1.09	0.72	.90
Output capacities	3	4.67	1.15	0.08	.84
Error rates	3	4.57	1.11	0.73	.89
Input capacities	3	4.51	1.20	0.08	.81
File storage and retrieval	2	4.42	1.33	0.09	.91
Social (S)	6	3.77	1.21	0.08	.93
Social interaction	2	4.10	1.35	0.09	.93
Conversation and cooperation	4	3.61	1.24	0.82	.90
Learner (L)	13	3.93	0.95	0.06	.89
Context and transfer	1	4.13	1.26	0.08	–
Prior knowledge	7	3.97	1.06	0.07	.81
Memory	2	3.90	1.34	0.09	.86
Discovery learning	1	3.90	1.26	0.08	–
Emotions and motivations	2	3.71	1.34	0.09	.91
Social technology (DS)	5	4.24	1.16	0.08	.92
Device networking	3	4.37	1.23	0.08	.95
System connectivity	1	4.27	1.34	0.09	–
Collaboration tools	1	3.83	1.41	0.09	–
Device usability (DL)	11	4.10	1.10	0.07	.93
Satisfaction	3	4.52	1.17	0.08	.80
Portability	2	4.45	1.49	0.10	.96
Psychological comfort	4	3.82	1.34	0.09	.96
Information availability	2	3.69	1.42	0.09	.89
Interaction learning (LS)	7	3.97	1.24	0.08	.93
Interaction	4	4.04	1.30	0.09	.94
Learning communities	2	3.85	1.32	0.09	.80
Situated cognition	1	3.48	1.55	0.10	–
m-learning process (DLS)	7	3.83	1.19	0.08	.96
Knowledge navigation	2	4.01	1.27	0.08	.93
Information access	2	3.93	1.27	0.08	.94
Mediation	3	3.64	1.23	0.08	.91

received a relatively lower rating (M = 4.42, SD = 1.33), showing that the devices were perceived as less convenient in areas such as file storage capacity.

The social technology aspect was rated with lower mean scores. The networking functionality of the device, i.e. device networking, was the highest rated component (M = 4.37, SD = 1.23), followed by the device capability for connecting to other devices, i.e. system connectivity (M = 4.27, SD = 1.34). Collaboration tools received a relatively low mean rating of 3.83 (*SD* = 1.41), reflecting the nature of students' learning in clinical practicum which does not involve a lot of collaborative work among students.

The device usability received a relative large variance in the ratings of its variables. The students indicated a relatively high level of satisfaction with the satisfaction variable (*M* = 4.52, *SD* = 1.17), i.e. the physical appearance, functions and user-friendliness of the mobile devices and mobile apps. Comparatively, the rating on information availability (*M* = 3.69, *SD* = 1.42) was lower. The results were consistent with the interview findings that the Wi-Fi-only network connectivity of the mobile devices was raised by some students as inconvenient to use the devices anywhere.

Interaction learning received a mean score of 3.97 (*SD* = 1.24). It reflected mainly the students' experience in their interaction with mentors during clinical assessment with the app. The moderate ratings for the composite items in this aspect were consistent with the interview findings, that the students wished to have more effective learner-teacher and learner-learner communication, and a supportive environment for them to study and apply clinical skills in a real life situation.

The learner aspect received a mean score of 3.93 (*SD* = 0.95). Among its components, context and transfer was better rated (*M* = 4.13, *SD* = 0.26). The results showed that the students performed cognitive tasks using the mobile apps, especially in transferring the knowledge and skills learned in class to a real life context, at an acceptable level. Comparatively, the emotional and motivational aspect of mobile learning was rated at a lower level (*M* = 3.71, *SD* = 1.34). Together with the relevant interview findings, the result suggested that further institutional support was desirable to enhance the students' motivation to engage in mobile learning activities.

The social aspect was rated with the lowest mean rating (*M* = 3.77, *SD* = 1.21), which was mainly attributed to the mean score for conversation and cooperation (*M* = 3.61, *SD* = 1.24). Such result reflected that the communication and interaction with the aid of mobile devices, either among students and teachers/mentors, was not highly regarded by the students.

The mobile learning (m-learning) process, which integrates all variables in the FRAME model, represents the overall effectiveness of the mobile learning practice. It received only a moderate mean score (*M* = 3.83, *SD* = 1.19). Two of its variables—knowledge navigation and information access—were rated relatively high among the three, with the mean ratings of 4.01 (*SD* = 1.27) and 3.93 (*SD* = 1.27), respectively. They represent how effective the students learnt to locate accurate and suitable online information, and how effective they learnt to select, manage, and apply the information for their needs. Comparatively, the mediation variable was rated lower (*M* = 3.64, *SD* = 1.23). The students showed less confidence in stating that they were able to use the mobile devices to adjust their learning strategies, and to reshape their interaction with peers/mentors in clinical practicum using the devices.

5 Discussion

This study reveals the benefits of and issues about the use of mobile devices in clinical practicum. For nursing students, they can access learning materials in wards, which was deemed important for their revision and fostering their mastery of nursing skills and clinical procedures. The mobile app for clinical assessment facilitated their interaction with mentors, where useful feedback about their performance and ways for improvement can be obtained. For teachers/course coordinators, the clinical assessment conducted via mobile devices substantially reduced their efforts in keeping track of students' learning progress, and they can discover students' problems early and provide timely assistance if needed. Such findings supplement the benefits of mobile learning widely reported [16], providing specific advantages of the use of mobile devices for nursing students in the practicum context. The app for mobile access of nursing videos extend the findings reported in Ma and Yeh [17] for their use in supporting situated learning of nursing students.

From the students' experience, effective communication with mentors during the clinical assessment was seen as a challenge. This requires both parties to be familiar with the use of the mobile app and have the same understanding of assessment criteria. Extra user training, however, is not an ideal solution as it creates extra burden and workload for mentors [18]. Simplicity of the app design with built-in assistant features would be helpful for both the students and mentors in this regard.

Institutional support on warrant and repair of the devices was suggested, which can enhance the students' motivation to bring out and use the devices. The fear of losing the devices or getting them broken was reported as a demotivator for learners to actively use the devices [19]—a typical challenge following the conventional way of institution-provided devices. Initiatives such as bring-your-own-device and mobile personal learning environment were proposed [20]. Despite concerns about their suitability in the ward environment were raised [18], the feasibility of such initiatives should be explored, in relation to the growing acceptability of the use of mobile devices in every aspects of our lives.

The various ratings of the FRAME variables show that only certain aspects of the mobile learning practice in this study were better received by the students. This observation was also reported in other studies using the FRAME model to evaluate mobile learning effectiveness [19]. As a heuristic model in its originally proposed form [21], the hypothesised state of effective mobile learning practice—addressing all the three aspects (device, learner and social) of the model—could be revisited. Further work could be done to examine the potential variation of the model in disciplinary practices of mobile learning.

6 Conclusion

Focusing on the clinical practicum context, this paper has revealed the benefits of the use of mobile devices to facilitate nursing students' learning, and concerns which may hinder its effectiveness. The findings contribute to inform the design of mobile learning practices to cope with this specific learning environment in nursing education.

In addition to students, other parties in the mobile learning practice, such as teachers and mentors, should also be taken into consideration about their benefits in the practice.

The study also showed the application of the FRAME model to conduct both qualitative and quantitative evaluation of mobile learning practice. It suggests potential variations in the realisation of the model according to different device users, settings, and purposes. Future work could be done on capturing the influence of such variations, if any, on devising and evaluating mobile learning experiences, and investigating the roles of the model in this regard.

Acknowledgements. The work described in this paper was substantially supported by a grant from the Research Grants Council of the Hong Kong Special Administrative Region, China (UGC/FDS16/H10/14).

References

1. Evans, C.: The effectiveness of m-learning in the form of podcast revision lectures in higher education. Comput. Educ. **50**(2), 491–498 (2008)
2. Koole, M.L.: A model for framing mobile learning. Mob. Learn. Transform. Deliv. Educ. Train. **1**, 25–47 (2009)
3. Kukulska-Hulme, A., Traxler, J.: Mobile teaching and learning. In: Mobile Learning – A Handbook for Educators and Trainers, pp. 25–44 (2005)
4. McHugh, M.D., Lake, E.T.: Understanding clinical expertise: nurse education, experience, and the hospital context. Res. Nurs. Health **33**(4), 276–287 (2010)
5. Raman, J.: Mobile technology in nursing education: where do we go from here? a review of the literature. Nurse Educ. Today **35**(5), 663–672 (2015)
6. Clark, A., Glazer, G., Edwards, C., Pryse, Y.: Transforming nursing education with Apple technology. Nurse Educ. **42**(2), 91–94 (2017)
7. Johansson, P.E., Petersson, G.I., Nilsson, G.C.: Nursing students' experience of using a personal digital assistant (PDA) in clinical practice — an intervention study. Nurse Educ. Today **33**, 1246–1251 (2013)
8. Park, C., Van Neste-Kenny, J., Burton, P., Kenny, R.: A model of mobile faculty presence in nursing education practice. Can. J. Nurs. Inf. **5**(3), 21–42 (2010)
9. Lee, N., Chae, S., Kim, H., Lee, J., Min, J.H., Park, D.: Mobile-based video learning outcomes in clinical nursing skill education: a randomized controlled trial. Comput. Inf. Nurs. **34**(1), 8–16 (2016)
10. Ip, W.Y., Chan, D.S.K.: Hong Kong nursing students' perception of the clinical environment: a questionnaire survey. Int. J. Nurs. Stud. **42**(6), 665–672 (2005)
11. Chan, D.S.K., Ip, W.Y.: Perception of hospital learning environment: a survey of Hong Kong nursing students. Nurse Educ. Today **27**(7), 677–684 (2007)
12. Lee, L.Y.K., Lee, J.K.L., Wong, K.F., Tsang, A.Y.K., Li, M.K.: The establishment of an integrated skills training centre for undergraduate nursing education. Int. Nurs. Rev. **57**, 359–364 (2010)
13. Kenny, R.F., Park, C.L., Van Neste-Kenny, J.M.C., Burton, P.A.: Mobile self-efficacy in Canadian nursing education programs. In: Proceedings of the 9th World Conference on Mobile Learning, Valletta, Malta (2010)

14. Parscal, T., Sherman, K., Heitner, K., Lucas, G.: A new model to measure student engagement with a mobile learning tool integrating CoI and FRAME. In: Proceedings of Global TIME 2012, pp. 31–37. Association for the Advancement of Computing in Education (2012)
15. Tavakol, M., Dennick, R.: Making sense of Cronbach's alpha. Int. J. Med. Educ. **2**, 53–55 (2011)
16. Li, K.C., Wong, B.T.M.: A review of indicators of success in mobile learning. In: Proceedings of the Third International Conference on Open and Flexible Education, pp. 53–63, Hong Kong, China (2016)
17. Ma, F.T., Yeh, M.Y.: The development of the situated learning materials in the nursing and communication course. In: Proceedings of the 8th International Conference on Ubi-Media Computing, Colombo, pp. 298–302 (2015)
18. Colton, S., Hunt, L.: Developing a smartphone app to support the nursing community. Nurs. Manag. **22**(9), 24–28 (2016)
19. Kenny, R.F., Van Neste-Kenny, J.M.C., Park, C.L., Burton, P.A., Meiers, J.: Mobile learning in nursing practice education: applying Koole's FRAME model. J. Distance Educ. **23**(3), 75–96 (2009)
20. García-Peñalvo, F.J., Conde, M.Á.: The impact of a mobile personal learning environment in different educational contexts. Univ. Access Inf. Soc. **14**(3), 375–387 (2014)
21. Koole, M.L.: Mobile learning: is the FRAME model still current? (2011). http://kooleady.ca/thoughts/?p=619

A Meta-analysis of the Peer Evaluation Effects on Learning Achievements in Blended Learning Environment

Panpan Cui and Lanqin Zheng(✉)

School of Educational Technology, Faculty of Education, Beijing Normal University, Beijing 100875, China
cppbnu@mail.bnu.edu.cn, bnuzhenglq@bnu.edu.cn

Abstract. Blended learning has been widely used in the field of education. Previous studies revealed that peer evaluation was an effective way to implement blended learning. Therefore, the aim of this study was to explore the effects of peer evaluation on learning achievements in blended learning environment. The meta-analysis was conducted by integrating the quantitative findings of 23 empirical study from 2008 to 2017. The results indicated that the peer evaluation activity had a medium effect on students' learning achievements. Further, the present study analyzed the effect sizes of seven moderating variables. It was found that writing essays had the highest impacts on students' learning achievements. The anonymous evaluation was more effective than non-anonymous evaluation. Providing training for peer raters and teacher involvement produced the higher effect size. In addition, the effect size did not differ among different kinds of software and school levels. Social science learning domain yielded the better effect size than other learning domains. Finally, the results and future work were also discussed in detail.

Keywords: Learning effectiveness · Peer evaluation activity
Blended learning environment · Meta-analysis

1 Introduction

Blended learning, which is combined in the forms of online and face-to-face, has been received more and more attention in recent years [1]. Peer evaluation, which can be conducted in a collaborative way in the blended learning environment, is a valuable learning approach that can support students' learning processes and outcomes [2]. Despite their popularity and value, it remains unclear whether peer evaluation activities in blended learning environment are effective for students' learning achievements. This study aims to investigate the effectiveness of peer evaluation in blended learning context.

1.1 Literature Review

Peer evaluation activities involve students in an iterative process of evaluating peers' products, providing feedback, and revising products [3]. It is beneficial for both the assessor and assessee [4]. Several studies indicated that peer evaluation is an effective

S. K. S. Cheung et al. (Eds.): ICBL 2018, LNCS 10949, pp. 227–237, 2018.
https://doi.org/10.1007/978-3-319-94505-7_18

way to improve learners' achievements. For instance, Zheng et al. [5] conducted a peer evaluation experiment in a Chinese university and found that students' writing achievements was improved. Papadopoulos et al. [6] employed 54 sophomore students who participated in the peer evaluation work in the domain of Computer Networking. The results indicated that students all get better domain learning outcomes than the pre-test. Researchers also have conducted meta-analysis of peer evaluation. Marsh et al. [7] implemented a meta-analysis of the gender effect of peer evaluation and found that there were no gender difference. Li et al. [8] carried out a meta-analysis of comparing peer and teacher ratings of the peer evaluation in the digital age. It was found that the relationship between peer and teacher ratings was moderately strong.

Today's students tend to learn in an immediate and online way rather than by face-to-face lectures [9]. However, the learning approach of face-to-face has its own indispensable advantages. Hence, blended learning became more and more popular in education. It enabled students to learn and collaborate deeply and meaningfully [10]. For both instructors and students, blended learning is an effective way to rich teaching and learning experiences [11].

However, how to implement peer evaluation in blended learning environment is still a major concern. According to Nguyen [12], the implementation of blended learning usually can be done in four stages: making acquaintance, designing and testing, sharing and application, evaluation, and adjustment. Actually, evaluation is one of the critical stages during the implementation. Recent studies have found that formative evaluation and summative evaluation were two common forms of evaluation [13]. Additionally, peer evaluation is also an effective way. Only a few studies investigated the peer evaluation activity in blended learning environment. For example, Bi [14] conducted an evaluation of blended learning technologies in a systems engineering course. It was found that blended learning could promote feedback and interactions among students. Nguyen [15] presented a model using peer evaluation in blended learning courses. The results indicated that the peer evaluation activities lead to significant improvement in learning achievements. In addition, Çevik et al. [16] took the peer evaluation activity in the course of Teaching Methods II. The students took the theoretical and lab sessions in the form of face-to-face. The instructor created an online environment to supplement face-to-face sessions, allowing students to submit and evaluate the work of others. Hsia et al. [17] conducted a 7-week peer evaluation activity in the art class, a 45-min face-to-face class was took in the classrooms each week. Students were asked to develop and revise the script on paper based on a theme of Chinese story, then they would present it face-to-face. Moreover, the video of their presentation was uploaded to a learning system, which would be evaluated by peers. Babik [18] implemented the peer evaluation activity in a business course. The course was taught in two face-to-face sections, and the students also engaged in ten take-home assignments. Their assignment would be uploaded to the online learning system and peers would make comments and feedback on the submissions.

1.2 Research Questions

In the light of the literature reviewed, it was revealed that there were limited studies to conduct meta-analysis to explore the effectiveness of peer evaluation activity in blended learning environment. Therefore, the aim of this study was to conduct a meta-analysis of related papers of peer evaluation. According to the research purpose of the study, two research questions were addressed as follows: (1) What are the effects of peer evaluation activity on learning achievements in blended learning environment? (2) What id the effectiveness of moderating variables in peer evaluation activity withinblended learning context?

2 Method

2.1 Meta-analysis Research

Meta-analysis is a statistical technique to systematically combine data from several independent studies to reach a conclusion with greater statistical power [19]. Nowadays, meta-analytic research in education is becoming more and more popular. Meta-analysis can test the robustness of the over effect of the papers as well as identify the effect of moderating variables. By using effect sizes, the results of different studies can be converted into a scale, then the studies could be compared on similar constructs [20].

In this study, the software of CMA V2 was adopted to analyze the data of the studies collected from the database. Furthermore, the Q-value test (homogeneity) and effect size were taken into account to be calculated.

2.2 Literature Search

The papers was systematically searched from 2008 to 2017 through the electronic database of Web of Science. The keywords used for searching and locating the primary studies included "peer evaluation", "peer assessment", "peer review", "peer feedback". In addition, the articles were included and it should be reported in English. As a result, there were initially 1343 papers totally. The inclusion criteria used were: (1) the studies focusing on peer evaluation; (2) the studies included experiments implemented in blended learning environment; (3) the studies included the experimental group and the control group; (4) the studies reported the empirical results of peer evaluation activity and the necessary descriptive statistics such as the means, variances, and sample sizes related to effect sizes. After scanning the papers, 23 papers were selected to be further analyzed.

2.3 Study Feature Coding

Based on a careful review of the 23 selected papers, a coding scheme was revised to classify the feature of the 23 papers according to Li et al. [21]. The codes were categorized into seven themes: tasks being rated, evaluation modes, peer raters training, teachers involvement, software, school levels and learning domains. Tasks being rated included writing essays, project plans, artefacts or products. Evaluation modes included anonymous and non-anonymous. Training of peer raters included received training and without training. Teacher involvement included teacher involvement and without teachers. The software was classified according to the function, including software only for peer evaluation and software for general purpose. School levels included K-12 and higher education. Natural science, social science, engineering and technological science constituted the category of learning domains.

3 Results

3.1 Overall Effect Size

The studies on peer evaluation included in this meta-analysis (k = 23) involved 2184 students. When a study reported more than one dependent group of peer evaluation, the weighted means of them was calculated. However, a single study may include statistic data of multiple independent samples in some studies. Hence, the 23 studies provided data for 37 independent effect sizes.

As shown in Table 1, the effect sizes of the primary studies were heterogeneous ($Q = 545.667$, $df(Q) = 36$, $p < .001$). Therefore, the random effects model was suitable to be analyzed in this study [18]. The average effect size value in the random-effects model was 0.675 with a standard error of 0.156, indicating that there was a medium effect [22]. With a 95% confidence interval, the lower limit was 0.369 and the upper limit was 0.982. Therefore, the peer evaluation activity in the blended learning environment had significant impacts on students' learning achievements.

Table 1. Overall effect size.

Model	N	ES	SE	Variance	P-value	95% confidence interval	
						Lower	Upper
Fixed	37	0.155	0.037	0.001	0.000	0.081	0.228
Random	37	0.675	0.156	0.024	0.000	0.369	0.982

3.2 Moderator Analysis

The following sections describe the results of moderator variable. In order to analyze the effects of moderators, the information such as tasks being rated, evaluation modes, training of peer raters, teachers involvement, software, school levels, and learning domains were coded for all the selected papers. Next, the results of each moderator were explained in detail.

Tasks Being Rated

In Table 2, it was found that there was a significant difference among different tasks ($Q = 12.668$, $df(Q) = 2$, $p < .05$), indicating that different tasks in the peer evaluation activity in blended learning environment could produce different influence on students' achievements. The effect size of writing essays, project plans, artefacts or products were 1.468^{***}, 0.044, and 0.653^{***}, respectively. That is to say, writing essays had the highest impacts on students' learning achievements. Artefacts or products was taken the second place.

Table 2. Effect size of tasks being rated.

Task	N	ES	SE	Variance	95% confidence interval	
					Lower	Upper
Writing essays	9	1.468***	0.368	0.135	0.748	2.189
Project plans	9	0.044	0.197	0.039	−0.342	0.430
Artefacts or products	19	0.653*	0.234	0.055	0.195	1.111

Note: *, *** respectively indicate that the significance level is at 5% and 1‰.

Evaluation Modes

In terms of evaluation modes, the effect size of anonymous was 0.879*** and non-anonymous was 0.125 (see Table 3). The effect size of anonymous was larger than non-anonymous. Meanwhile, there was significant difference between the two evaluation modes (Q = 4.218, df(Q) = 1, $p < .05$). Therefore, anonymous evaluation was the most effective way to improve the achievements of students in the peer evaluation activity in the blended learning environment.

Table 3. Effect size of evaluation modes.

Evaluation mode	N	ES	SE	Variance	95% confidence interval	
					Lower	Upper
Anonymous	27	0.879***	0.190	0.036	0.507	1.252
Non-Anonymous	10	0.165	0.291	0.085	−0.405	0.736

Note: *, *** respectively indicate that the significance level is at 5% and 1‰.

Training of Peer Raters

As shown in Table 4, there was significant difference between training of peer raters (Q = 7.882, df(Q) = 1, $p < .05$), which indicated that training of peer raters in the peer evaluation activity in blended learning environment could produce different influence to students' achievements. The effect size of received training (0.991***) was larger than without training (0.213), showing that received training was more effective on peer evaluation activity in blended learning environment. That is to say, received training could significantly affect the achievements of students.

Teacher Involvement

As shown in Table 5, the effect size of teacher involvement was 1.190***. The effect size of teacher involvement was larger than without teachers. Meanwhile, there was significant difference between teachers involvement and without teacher

Table 4. Effect size of training of peer raters.

Peer raters training	N	ES	SE	Variance	95% confidence interval	
					Lower	Upper
Without training	15	0.213	0.191	0.036	−0.162	0.587
Received training	22	0.991***	0.201	0.040	0.597	1.385

Note: *, *** respectively indicate that the significance level is at 5% and 1‰.

Table 5. Effect size of teacher involvement.

Teacher involvement	N	ES	SE	Variance	95% confidence interval	
					Lower	Upper
Teacher involvement	18	1.190***	0.232	0.054	0.736	1.645
Without teacher	19	0.220	0.174	0.030	−0.121	0.561

Note: *, *** respectively indicate that the significance level is at 5% and 1‰.

($Q = 11.206$, $df(Q) = 1$, $p < .05$). Therefore, teacher involvement was a more effective way to improve the achievements of students in the peer evaluation activity in the blended learning environment.

Software

Comparing different effect sizes of the two kinds of software in Table 6, effect size of software for general purpose was 0.687***, which was larger than software only for peer evaluation (0.664***), but the difference was not statistically significant ($Q = 0.007$, $df(Q) = 1$, $p > .05$). It was indicated that there were no obvious variation between the two different kinds of software. The two kinds of software were both effective for students' learning achievements.

Table 6. Effect size of software.

Software	N	ES	SE	Variance	95% confidence interval	
					Lower	Upper
Software only for peer evaluation	15	0.664***	0.163	0.026	0.345	0.983
Software for general purpose	22	0.687*	0.226	0.551	0.245	1.129

Note: *, *** respectively indicate that the significance level is at 5% and 1‰.

School Levels

Table 7 presented the results of effect sizes of school levels. The effect size of K-12 was 0.636* and higher education was 0.717*. The effect size of higher education was larger than K-12. However, there was no significant difference between the two different school levels (Q = 0.076, df (Q) = 1, $p > .05$). That is to say, the two different school levels could improve the achievements of students in peer evaluation activity.

Table 7. Effect size of school levels.

School Levels	N	ES	SE	Variance	95% confidence interval		Test of heterogeneity in effect size
					Lower	Upper	Q
K-12	16	0.636*	0.186	0.035	0.271	1.001	0.076
Higher education	21	0.717*	0.230	0.053	0.267	1.168	

Note: *, *** respectively indicate that the significance level is at 5% and 1‰.

Learning Domains

As shown in Table 8, social science showed the largest effect among all learning domains (0.903***), which indicated that students performed best in social science learning. The effect size of engineering and technological science was 0.741* and the effect size of natural science was lowest. Furthermore, there was significant difference among learning domains (Q = 8.764, df(Q) = 2, $p < .05$), indicating that it would be most effective to carry out peer evaluation activity in social science domain in blended learning environment.

Table 8. Effect size of learning domains.

Learning domain	N	ES	SE	Variance	95% confidence interval	
					Lower	Upper
Natural science	6	−0.063	0.251	0.063	−0.554	0.428
Social science	19	0.903***	0.248	0.061	0.418	1.388
Engineering and technological science	12	0.741*	0.220	0.048	0.310	1.172

Note: *, *** respectively indicate that the significance level is at 5% and 1‰.

3.3 Publication Bias Analysis

To examine whether the publications were biased due to the effect sizes, a funnel plot was drawn (see Fig. 1), which indicated that the 37 effect sizes were distributed on both sides of the average. To explore the publication bias in the studies, the trim and fill method [23] was applied. If there is no publication bias, the distribution of effect sizes will be distributed symmetrically. In the present study, the funnel plot was a little asymmetric, showing a low value of the publication bias. Moreover, as shown in Table 9, the classic fail-safe N analysis [24] showed that it required 1128 studies in order to reduce the effect size value to zero. The number was larger than 195 (5 * 37 + 10). Therefore, the publication bias was demonstrated to be low in the present study.

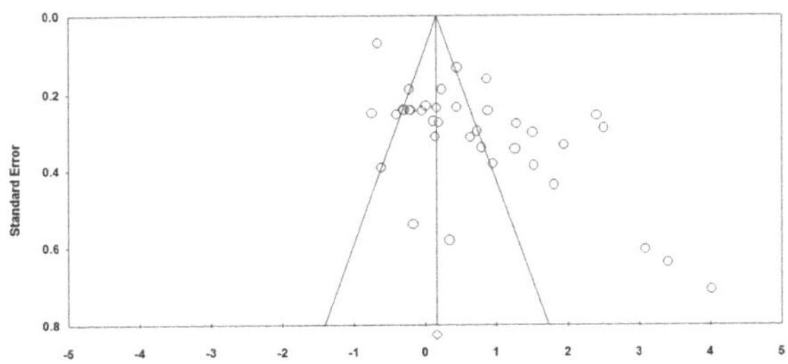

Fig. 1. Funnel Plot of Standard Error by Std diff in means

Table 9. Classic fail-safe N of observed studies.

Z-value for observed studies	10.99
P-value for observed studies	0.00
Alpha	0.05
Tails	2.00
Z for alpha	1.96
Number for observed studies	37
Number for missing studies that would bring p-value to > alpha	1128

4 Discussion

Twenty-three papers published between 2008 and 2017 were included in the present study. The average effect size value was 0.675 with a standard error of 0.156, showing that the peer evaluation activity in blended learning environment had the moderate impact on students' learning achievements.

Firstly, peer evaluation task in blended learning environment was a critical factor when evaluating the effectiveness of peer evaluation activity. In this study, writing essays and artefacts or products showed the larger effect size. That is to say, the English writing task would produce a great influence on students' achievements. It was in line with Yang [25], who reported that students had excellent achievements in a blended English writing class. Additionally, students would learn better when making artefacts or products in peer evaluation activity. For instance, Hsia et al. [17] investigated the story interpretation peer evaluation activity in blended learning environment and found that students' achievements had been significantly improved.

Secondly, evaluation modes, training of peer raters, teacher involvement, software were also important during the implementation of peer evaluation. In terms of evaluation modes, the present study found that anonymous evaluation produced the larger effect size, which indicated that anonymous evaluation would help students perform better in the peer evaluation activity. Anonymity was considered to guarantee fair evaluation [26]. Some studies have reported that students learned positively and efficiently when anonymity was assured [27]. When it comes to the training of peer raters, the meta-analysis found the effect size of received training was larger than without training. It enlightened us that the training was an effective way to enhance the effectiveness of peer evaluation. The implementation of training in peer evaluation was considered to be an important component in the peer evaluation activity [28]. The training process can assist the students to become familiar with the peer evaluation and rules of assessment, which was beneficial to their achievements. The results also indicated that teacher involvement had significant impacts on learning achievements with the effect size of 1.190. If a teacher participated in the peer evaluation process, students would concentrate more on their tasks and evaluation. In addition, a strong relationship between the score given by teachers and peers can be deemed as the proof of accuracy in the peer evaluation process [29]. Results from meta-analysis of software discovered that software for general purpose effect size was larger slightly than software only for peer evaluation, but there was no significant difference between them. The reason may be that both two kinds of different software could support peer evaluation process in the blended learning environment.

Lastly, the two different school levels had no significant difference. It was considered that peer evaluation activity was suitable for both higher education and K-12 education. For example, Azari [30] found that the undergraduate students gained higher achievements in the peer evaluation. Lee et al. [31] investigated that learning achievements of the participants in different peer evaluation groups in the 7th grade classes. It was found that the students' achievements were all significantly improved. In addition, there was significant difference in effect sizes of learning domains in the present study and social science showed the largest effect. It implied that peer evaluation activity would be more effective in the social science in blended learning environment. Lai [32] conducted a peer evaluation activity in an art course of an elementary school. It was found that the students' learning achievements was significantly improved.

5 Limitations and Future Work

To sum up, the present meta-analysis provided evidence of the effectiveness of peer evaluation activity in blended learning environment. It was found that peer evaluation activity had moderate impacts on students' learning achievements. In addition, the present study provided valuable references for teachers who conducted peer evaluation activities in blended learning environment. It is suggested that students can participate in peer evaluation activity in social science domain in an anonymous way. It would be better to provide training for the raters before peer evaluation. Teachers were also advised to participate in the peer evaluation activity.

Nevertheless, there were still several limitations in the present study. The first limitation was that the data source was limited to Web of Science, then some of the relevant research publications in other databases were not included. Secondly, the present study did not explore the moderating impacts of evaluation criterion and learning style in blended learning environment. Therefore, future study will examine the influences of learning style and evaluation criterion on the learning achievement in peer evaluation activities.

Acknowledgement. This study was funded by the project of English Course "Computer-Supported Collaborative Learning" in Beijing Normal University.

References

1. Bralić, A., Divjak, B.: Integrating MOOCs in traditionally taught courses: achieving learning outcomes with blended learning. Int. J. Educ. Technol. High. Educ. **15**(1), 1–16 (2018)
2. Shih, R.C.: Can Web 2.0 technology assist college students in learning English writing? Integrating Facebook and peer assessment with blended learning. Australas. J. Educ. Technol. **27**(5), 829–845 (2011)
3. Cheng, K.H., Hou, H.T.: Exploring students' behavioural patterns during online peer assessment from the affective, cognitive, and metacognitive perspectives: a progressive sequential analysis. Technol. Pedagog. Educ. **24**(2), 171–188 (2015)
4. Evans, C.: Making sense of assessment feedback in higher education. Rev. Educ. Res. **83**, 70–120 (2013)
5. Zheng, L., Cui, P., Li, X., Huang, R.: Synchronous discussion between assessors and assessees in web-based peer assessment: impact on writing performance, feedback quality, meta-cognitive awareness and self-efficacy. Assess. Eval. High. Educ. **43**(3), 500–514 (2018)
6. Papadopoulos, P.M., Lagkas, T.D., Demetriadis, S.N.: How to improve the peer review method: free-selection vs assigned-pair protocol evaluated in a computer networking course. Comput. Educ. **59**(2), 182–195 (2012)
7. Marsh, H.W., Bornmann, L., Mutz, R., Daniel, H.D., O'Mara, A.: Gender effects in the peer reviews of grant proposals: a comprehensive meta-analysis comparing traditional and multilevel approaches. Rev. Educ. Res. **79**(3), 1290–1326 (2009)
8. Li, H., Xiong, Y., Zang, X., Kornhaber, M.L., Lyu, Y., Chung, K.S., Suen, H.K.: Peer assessment in the digital age: a meta-analysis comparing peer and teacher ratings. Assess. Eval. High. Educ. **41**(2), 245–264 (2016)
9. Jukes, I., McCain, T., Crockett, L.: Understanding the Digital Generation: Teaching and Learning in the New Digital Landscape. Corwin Press, Thousand Oaks (2010)
10. Garrison, D.R., Kanuka, H.: Blended learning: uncovering its transformative potential in higher education. Internet High. Educ. **7**(2), 95–105 (2004)
11. Shih, R.C.: Blended learning using video-based blogs: public speaking for English as second language students. Australas. J. Educ. Technol. **26**(6), 883–897 (2010)
12. Nguyen, V.A.: A peer assessment approach to project based blended learning course in a Vietnamese higher education. Educ. Inf. Technol. **22**(5), 2141–2157 (2017)
13. Strijbos, J.W., Sluijsmans, D.: Unravelling peer assessment: methodological, functional, and conceptual developments. Learn. Instr. **20**(4), 265–269 (2010)

14. Bi, Y.: Evaluation of blended learning technologies in a large enrollment case-based systems engineering course. In: 121st ASEE Annual Conference & Exposition, pp. 1–20. Indianapolis (2014)
15. Nguyen, V.A.: Towards the implementation of an assessment-centred blended learning framework at the course level: a case study in a Vietnamese national university. Int. J. Inf. Learn. Technol. **34**(1), 20–30 (2017)
16. Çevik, Y.D., Haşlaman, T., Çelik, S.: The effect of peer assessment on problem solving skills of prospective teachers supported by online learning activities. Stud. Educ. Eval. **44**(44), 23–35 (2015)
17. Hsia, L.H., Huang, I., Hwang, G.J.: A web-based peer-assessment approach to improving junior high school students' performance, self-efficacy and motivation in performing arts courses. Br. J. Edu. Technol. **47**(4), 618–632 (2016)
18. Babik, D., Singh, R., Zhao, X., Ford, E.W.: What you think and what I think: studying intersubjectivity in knowledge artifacts evaluation. Inf. Syst. Front. **19**(1), 31–56 (2017)
19. Cohen, L., Manion, L., Morrison, K.: Research Methods in Education, 6th edn. Routledge, New York (2007)
20. Balta, N., Michinov, N., Balyimez, S., Ayaz, M.F.: A meta-analysis of the effect of Peer Instruction on learning gain: Identification of informational and cultural moderators. Int. J. Educ. Res. **86**, 66–77 (2017)
21. Rücker, G., Schwarzer, G., Carpenter, J.R., Schumacher, M.: Undue reliance on I2 in assessing heterogeneity may mislead. BMC Med. Res. Methodol. **8**(1), 1–9 (2008)
22. Cohen, J.: Statistical Power Analysis for the Behavioral Sciences, 2nd edn. Erlbaum, NJ (1988)
23. Duval, S.: The trim and fill method. In: Rothstein, H.R., Sutton, A.J., Bornstein, M. (eds.) Publication Bias in Meta-Analysis: Prevention, Assessment, and Adjustments, pp. 127–144. Wiley, Chichester (2005)
24. Rosenthal, R.: The file drawer problem and tolerance for null results. Psychol. Bull. **86**(3), 638–641 (1979)
25. Yang, Y.F.: Transforming and constructing academic knowledge through online peer feedback in summary writing. Comput. Assist. Lang. Learn. **29**(4), 683–702 (2016)
26. Joinson, A.N.: Social desirability, anonymity, and internet-based questionnaires. Behav. Res. Methods, Instrum. Comput. **31**(3), 433–438 (1999)
27. Vanderhoven, E., Raes, A., Montrieux, H., Rotsaert, T., Schellens, T.: What if pupils can assess their peers anonymously? a quasi-experimental study. Comput. Educ. **81**, 123–132 (2015)
28. Mulder, R.A., Pearce, J.M., Baik, C.: Peer review in higher education: student perceptions before and after participation. Act. Learn. High Educ. **15**(2), 157–171 (2014)
29. Güler, Ç.: Use of WhatsApp in higher education: what's up with assessing peers anonymously? J. Educ. Comput. Res. **55**(2), 272–289 (2017)
30. Azari, M.H.: Effect of weblog-based process approach on EFL learners' writing performance and autonomy. Comput. Assist. Lang. Learn. **30**(6), 529–551 (2017)
31. Lee, C.I., Yang, Y.F., Mai, S.Y.: The impact of a scaffolded assessment intervention on students' academic achievement in web-based peer assessment activities. Int. J. Distance Educ. Technol. (IJDET). **14**(4), 41–54 (2016)
32. Lai, C.L., Hwang, G.J.: An interactive peer-assessment criteria development approach to improving students' art design performance using handheld devices. Comput. Educ. **85**, 149–159 (2015)

Automatic Assessment via Intelligent Analysis of Students' Program Output Patterns

Chung Keung Poon[1], Tak-Lam Wong[2(✉)], Chung Man Tang[3], Jacky Kin Lun Li[1], Yuen Tak Yu[3], and Victor Chung Sing Lee[3]

[1] Caritas Institute of Higher Education, Tseung Kwan O New Town, Hong Kong SAR
[2] Douglas College, New Westminster, BC, Canada
tlwong@ieee.org
[3] City University of Hong Kong, Kowloon Tong, Hong Kong SAR

Abstract. Automatic assessment of computer programming exercises offers a number of benefits to both learners and educators, including timely and customised feedback, as well as saving of human effort in grading. However, due to the high variety of programs submitted by students, exact matching between the expected output and different output variants is undesirable and how to do the matching properly is a challenging and practical problem. Existing approaches to address this problem adopt various inexact matching strategies, but typically they are unscalable, incapable of expressing a diversity of program outputs, or require high level of expertise. In this paper, we propose Hierarchical Program Output Structure (HiPOS), which provides higher expressiveness and flexibility, to model the program output. Based on HiPOS, we design different levels of matching rules in the matching rule hierarchy to determine the admissible program output variants in a flexible and scalable manner. We conducted experiments and compare our approach of automatic assessment to human judgement. The results show that our proposed method achieved an accuracy of 0.8467 in determining the admissible program output variants.

Keywords: Automatic assessment · Programming education
Hierarchical Program Output Structure

1 Introduction

Many students find that learning computer programming is challenging. Studies have shown that they encounter many difficulties in problem formulation, algorithm design, logical thinking, and syntax when learning programming [8, 16]. To help students overcome these difficulties, instructors usually require students to do many programming exercises for practice and assessment. While designing tasks for students to assess their learning is no easy task, providing timely, useful, and informative feedback to students is even more challenging. Moreover, the class size of a typical introductory programming course in colleges is large. Manually verifying the source code of each student's submission and providing tailored feedback is time-consuming. The problem

S. K. S. Cheung et al. (Eds.): ICBL 2018, LNCS 10949, pp. 238–250, 2018.
https://doi.org/10.1007/978-3-319-94505-7_19

is magnified in massive open online courses (MOOCs), in which the volume of enrolled students can be huge. Many studies show that timely feedback can enhance students' learning effectiveness and experience, as well as their motivation and engagement in classes [7, 14, 16]. This raises the need of automatic or semi-automatic assessment systems that can provide instant and customized feedback to students based on their work. The feedback can advise students the possible cause of errors and refer students to study the relevant materials to tackle the problems.

Recently, universities have utilized automated program assessment systems (APASs) in their programming courses to assess students' work on programming exercises [1, 4, 5, 15, 20, 22]. In a typical programming course, instructors firstly design an assessment task, which is usually a programming exercise requiring students to write program code to solve a problem. For assessment tasks, instructors will prepare a number of test cases to verify the correctness of the students' program code. A test case consists of a test input to the program and the corresponding expected output produced by the program. These instructor-prepared test cases are then imported to an APAS. Students can submit their program source code to the APAS. The APAS automates the assessment by compiling the program code submitted by a student, executing the program with the instructor-prepared test cases, and comparing the output of students' program to the expected output in each test case. One use of the APAS by the instructor is to assess students' programming capability based on the number of correct outputs produced by the submitted program. Another use of the APAS is to prompt the students with informative feedback if there is any failed test case. Students can then revise the program until it is correct.

APASs have proliferated because they not only free up instructors' time for other creative educational tasks, but also offer tremendous benefits in many other aspects [11, 24] that can hardly be achieved otherwise, such as facilitating the design of effective pedagogy [2], provision of instant and personalized feedback to both instructors and students [9, 22, 28], and enhancing students' learning motivation [16].

The core function of an APAS is to automatically compare the output of students' program to the expected output in each test case. Most of the existing comparison approaches are too simplistic, rigid and incapable of adapting to different pedagogies such as providing suitable feedback and suggesting the possible cause of errors to students. More importantly, these existing APASs can accept only one output or a space-trimmed version of it as the correct expected output. A program output which the instructor may consider acceptable as correct (or *admissible*) can be inappropriately rejected by an APAS. This poses a difficulty in designing assessment tasks by the instructor, and often leads to undesirable learning effect to students. For example, students may feel frustrated and lose learning motivation when their submitted programs are repeatedly rejected by APASs due to some tiny difference between the outputs. There is a practical need to develop an automatic approach that can accept multiple *admissible output variants*, which may deviate from the expected program output but are still considered correct by the instructor. For example, consider the programming exercise **Ex.1** as shown in Fig. 1.

The expected output designed by the instructor is "`The average of 3 numbers is 74.33.`" when the input is "`56 81 86`". We denote this output by S^0. Such an output consists of a sentence-like structure with several components, and two of the

> **Ex.1**: *Write a program that asks the user to enter 3 numbers, obtains the 3 numbers from the user and prints a message showing the average of the 3 numbers.*

Fig. 1. An example programming exercise **Ex.1**

components contain values that vary among different test cases, namely, the number "`3`" and the average "`74.33`". The following actual outputs may also be considered admissible because a human can easily interpret that they have the same meaning as S^0.

S^1: "`74.33 is the average of 3 numbers.`"
S^2: "`Mean of 3 numbers: 74.3333`"
S^3: "`The average of 3 numbers is 74.`"

Previous approaches to deal with the issue of rigid APASs are either laborious to implement, inapplicable to a variety of programming exercises, or sensitive to small and insignificant output variations. In this paper, we propose a more robust framework for automatically modelling and analysing student program output variations based on a hierarchical structure called HiPOS. Our framework assesses student programs by means of a matching rule hierarchy, which not only produces a better verdict of correctness, but also provides more informative feedback to students for improving their learning. This paper substantially extends our previous work reported in [21]. We conducted an experiment on our framework by applying it to the assessment of real student programs and the results are indeed promising.

2 Related Work

Some formal approaches have been proposed to increase the flexibility of output matching in APASs. Some APASs require the instructor to write regular expressions [18], shell scripts [12] or parser scripts using *lex* and *yacc* [13] to recognize admissible variants by pattern matching. This strategy does relax the rigidity, but not all instructors would like to write scripts. Even if the instructor is competent, the scripts can be error-prone and tedious to write. Also, the limited expressiveness of simple scripting will restrict their matching capability. These drawbacks fundamentally hinder the wide-spread adoption of scripting strategies.

Recently, some approaches have been proposed that lead to a better solution to the problem. The framework of Fonte et al. [6] allows the flexibility of output comparison where the list of *admissible* or *partially admissible* output variants can be formally specified by the instructor in advance using their domain specific language *Output Semantic-Similarity Language* (OSSL), including the exact (partial) mark to be awarded. For example, Fig. 2 is a possible OSSL specification for the sample programming exercise "*Given a positive integer, compute the set of its divisors.*" extracted from [6].

Here, the OSSL specification defines two tests with the numbers `8` and `12` as inputs, respectively. The correct output for the first test is the *set* of divisors `<1,2,4,8>` and that for the second test is `<1,2,3,4,6,12>`. When

```
PROBLEM: SetDivisors   TESTS: 2   TOTAL: 3
INPUT:   8
OUTPUT:  SET <1,2,4,8>  (1)
         ALSO SET <2,4,8>   (0.5)
         ALSO SET <1,2,4>   (0.5)
INPUT:   12
OUTPUT:  SET <1,2,3,4,6,12>  (2)
         ALSO SET <2,3,4,6,12>   (0.5)
         ALSO SET <1,2,3,4,6>   (0.5)
```

Fig. 2. An example OSSL specification [6]

comparing the expected output with the actual ones produced by a student's program, the framework takes note of the semantics of the keyword `SET` and, hence, compares each value but ignores their order, ensuring that every combination of the specified numbers (such as `<3,12,6,2,4,1>` for the second test) is considered correct and awarded the full mark of `2` (indicated in the above OSSL specification within the bracket that follows the correct output) regardless of the ordering of the values. If the student's program output is `<1,2,3,4,6>` (or any permutation of it) for the second test, it will still be awarded a partial mark of 0.5 even though the extreme value `12` is missing. If the exercise is changed to compute the sequence (instead of set) of divisors in as*cending order*, then every instance of the keyword `SET` in the above OSSL specification can be replaced by the keyword `SEQ` to indicate that a *sequence* of numbers is expected, that is, the ordering of the numbers is significant and any deviation from the correct order will be considered inadmissible. However, an output missing an extreme value will still be awarded `0.5` mark as long as the ascending order is preserved.

In this framework, instructors can customize the OSSL grammar for each output variant to judge whether a program output is admissible or not. As a result, instructors are required to "predict" the anticipated admissible output variants and write the grammar in advance. Even if an experienced instructor may be able to know most of the admissible output variants, a large amount of human effort and a substantial degree of expertise is needed to write the grammar for each admissible output variant.

Another different framework that handles the output structure and its component items is proposed in [24, 25] in a more flexible manner. It adopts a *token pattern approach* (TPA) so that fine-grained (*pattern*) matching rules can be fed into an APAS for automatic processing without the need to write scripts. The TPA framework firstly automatically tokenizes a program output. After that, each token of the expected program output is tagged with its type, value and matching rules by the instructor. The matching rules, which are constructed by the instructor, are then applied to judge if an actual output is admissible when the token of the actual output is compared with that of the expected output. For a numeric token, the instructor may, say, choose a matching rule which specifies an output to be correct as long as it equals the expected value when rounded to a preset number of decimal places. Then extra trailing digits of 0, say, will not affect correctness. For a token representing an English word, the matching rule may specify that any synonym of the word, which is readily available from a digital dictionary, is also acceptable. If desired, the instructor may also specify the matching rule in such a way that a small typo (such as a misspelt letter) is also tolerated to a well-defined extent and treated as admissible (or partially admissible with partial marks awarded).

Table 1 illustrates the TPA framework applied to the example exercise **Ex.1**. The first three rows show the token pattern of the expected output S^0, which consists of a sequence of 8 tokens with their types, values and associated matching rules in each row, respectively. The last two rows show the values and types, respectively, of the corresponding tokens of the actual output S^2. In between these rows is the row that shows the matching results, that is, the results of comparing the corresponding tokens of the two outputs. Pairing of the corresponding tokens for matching can be done by using the *longest common subsequence* algorithm, whereas the comparison of individual pairs of tokens is done according to the instructor-specified (or default) matching rules. In this example, the stop words "`The`", "`of`" and "`is`" as well as the punctuation mark "`.`" (period) in S^0 are "*ignored*", that is, they are not mandatory to be present in the actual output. The remaining tokens are considered significant in meaning and so are mandatory in the actual output, but the two ordinary English words "`average`" and "`numbers`" are specified to allow "*approximate match*" so that the synonym "`Mean`" and the singular word "`number`", respectively, are still considered admissible, as indicated by the corresponding ticks (✓) in the row of matching result. Note also that for "approximate match", the character case (upper or lower) is ignored during comparison. On the other hand, the expected output integer "`3`" demands an *exact match* of integer value, while the expected output of average value "`74.33`", which is of type double precision floating point number, will be considered successfully matched with a corresponding actual output number if they are the same when rounded to "*at least two decimal places*", even though the two numbers are of different precision. Since all individual token pairs are matched successfully, the actual output S^2 is considered admissible by the APAS using the TPA framework.

On the other hand, the actual output S^3 is considered *not* admissible by the TPA framework because it fails the matching rule associated with the token of value `74.33`. Neither is S^1 because even though the words in it are the same as those in S^0, their token orders are different. The TPA framework currently cannot recognize similarity when the orders of tokens differ.

While TPA can assess more exercises automatically than existing methods, the range of such exercises is still inherently constrained. For example, an unordered set of numbers, say, should be handled as a group and not as individual units. Inspired by the TPA framework, this paper proposes a more robust framework based on natural language processing (NLP) to overcome the weaknesses of previous approaches.

3 Automatic Admissible Output Variant Assessment

3.1 Hierarchical Program Output Structure

As discussed in Sect. 2, the token pattern approach (TPA) has several shortcomings which we address in this paper. For example, the output variant S^1 will be considered inadmissible by using TPA because the orders of the output tokens are different. Second, TPA tokenizes the program output using simple delimiters and then identifies

Table 1. Applying the TPA Framework to Ex.1

Expected (S^0)	**Type***	SW	Word	SW	Int	Word	SW	Double	Pun
	Value	`The`	`average`	`of`	`3`	`numbers`	`is`	`74.33`	`.`
	Matching Rule	Ignored	Approximate match	Ignored	Exact match	Approximate match	Ignored	At least 2 decimal places	Ignored
Matching result			☞		☞	☞		☞	
Actual (S^2)	**Value**		`Mean`	`of`	`3`	`number`	`:`	`74.3333`	
	Type*		Word	SW	Int	Word	Pun	Double	

* For token types, the following abbreviations are used.
SW means a "stop word" which refers to common words that are usually filtered out before or after processing of natural language data, such as "`a`", "`an`", "`the`", "`is`", "`are`", "`of`", "`out`", etc.
Word means an ordinary English "word" other than stop words.
Int means a numeric "integer".
Double means a ("double" precision) floating point number.
Pun means a punctuation mark.

the token types (such as word and integer) using a set of simple predefined rules that are independent of the exercise, but the tokenization algorithm and the type of tokens are sometimes problem-specific and need disambiguation. For example, while the output string "`754-3010`" can be interpreted as a single token of a phone number, it can also be interpreted as being composed of three tokens representing the subtraction of two numbers. The criteria for accepting output variants should be decided by the instructor based on the problem context or other pedagogical reasons, which may vary from one exercise to another.

We have designed a structure called *Hierarchical Program Output Structure* (HiPOS) to enhance the expressiveness and robustness in determining the admissibility of program variants. After tokenizing a program variant, the HiPOS will be automatically constructed. A HiPOS is an ordered tree structure, where each leaf represents a token of the output variant. The subtree rooted at an internal node of HiPOS represents a block of tokens or a part of the program variant. Figure 3 depicts the HiPOS of the expected output S^0. **Ex.1** requires the learners to write a program to generate a message about the average of three numbers, which is expected to be in the form of free text or sentence. We adopted a natural language parser [19] to construct the HiPOS in this example. Each internal node is labeled by a tag in the tagset used for natural language parsing [19]. The parsed tree characterizes the syntactic structure of a sentence in natural language processing (NLP), where a sub-tree represents a contiguous phrase such as noun phrase, verb phrase, etc.

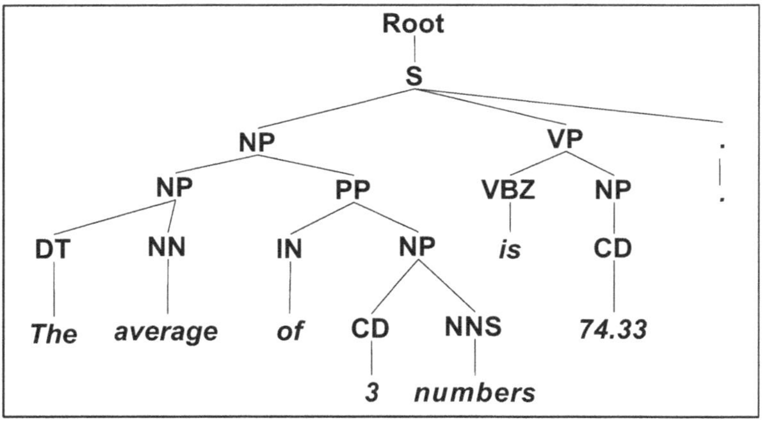

Fig. 3. The HiPOS* of the expected output (S^0) of **Ex.1,** * Each internal node of the HiPOS is labeled by a tag used for natural language parsing. (**S** = Simple declarative clause; **NP** = Noun phrase; **VP** = Verb phrase; **PP** = Prepositional phrase; **DT** = Determiner; **NN** = Noun, singular or mass; **IN** = Preposition or subordinating conjunction; **CD** = Cardinal number; **NNS** = Noun, plural; **VBZ** = Verb, 3rd person singular present)

3.2 Matching Rule Hierarchy

Based on the HiPOS of the expected output, instructors can decide the set of matching rules, *M*, to automatically determine the admissibility of a variety of output variants. In addition, automatic feedback can be provided to students if the output variant fails certain matching rules. To provide more useful and customized feedback to students, we have designed a hierarchy for the construction of matching rules.

Given a number of test cases prepared by the instructor, an individual HiPOS for a particular test case can be displayed graphically for easy browsing. The instructor can then create the matching rules according to his/her teaching needs. The hierarchy of matching rules *M* consists of four levels, namely, *problem-level*, *block-level*, *token-level*, and *test-case-level*. We continue to use **Ex.1** as the example to illustrate the idea and function of different levels of matching rules.

Problem-Level: Problem-level matching rules are designed for judging the basic criteria of correctly completing the exercise (*problem*). They are not specific to any test case, but are applicable to the entire HiPOS and all output variants of the exercise. For example, "The result needs to contain one or more numeric token." is a sample problem-level matching rule that applies to all test cases. Since the problem-level matching rule is a top-level criterion, the program will be treated as inadmissible once an output variant does not satisfy a problem-level matching rule. The instructor can then provide feedback to students about the program design for the exercise in general because students may have no or little idea in writing the program. A possible feedback is "The program needs to (1) obtain the three inputs of numbers, (2) calculate the results and store it in a variable, and (3) display the message."

Block-Level: Block-level matching rules are applicable to a *block*, that is, a subtree rooted at an internal node of a HiPOS of an output variant. For example, for an output variant to be admissible, a noun phrase (NP) of it must be sufficiently similar in semantics to the noun phrase "`The average of 3 numbers`" of the expected output. To do so, the instructor needs to specify the associated internal node (that is, the node **NP** at the second level of the HiPOS in Fig. 3). He/she can create a block-level matching rule "The subtree needs to be matched by semantic similarity with threshold 0.9." The semantic similarity between two phrases can be computed using the work described in [10]. With such a rule, the phrase "`Mean of 3 numbers`" in **Ex.1** will be considered admissible.

A block-level matching rule can also specify the order of subtrees to handle more variety of admissible output variants. Consider S^1: "`74.33 is the average of 3 numbers.`" Current APASs are likely to reject S^1 as inadmissible because the token orders differ. Our HiPOS can handle similar output variants in a more flexible manner. With respect to the HiPOS in Fig. 3, the instructor can create a block-level matching rule "Allow different orders for the first two subtrees." for the internal node labelled **S**, and another block-level matching rule "Allow different orders for all subtrees." for the internal node labelled **VP**. By imposing these two rules, the previous output variants are automatically judged to be admissible even though the subject and the object of the sentences are interchanged.

Token-Level: Token-level matching rules are applicable to a single *token*. They are associated with a leaf in HiPOS. For example, the matching rule "The token needs to be in 2 or more decimal places." can be added to the leaf `74.33` because the aim of the exercise is to develop students' concept of integer and floating point number handling in writing programs. Using the wrong types of variables will lead to the incorrect precision of the leaf `74.33`. Correspondingly, a finer feedback can be provided to the students. For example, "Float/double variable types should be used in the calculation." can be a feedback to remind students to become aware of the need and importance of choosing the correct variable types in program writing.

Test-Case-Level: Test-case-level matching rules are designed for a particular *test case*. For instance, "The token `0.002` needs to be in 3 or more decimal places." is a test-case-level matching rule for the test case with input "`0.001 0.002 0.003`". If the output variant only fails to match with some test-case-level matching rules, the program may be partially correct.

Figure 4 illustrates the matching mechanism in determining the admissibility by our framework. HiPOS provides a means to efficiently divide a program output into different meaningful and useful parts. The idea of the matching mechanism is that parts of an output variant will be matched with the relevant parts of the expected output to determine the admissibility, instead of comparing two HiPOSs, which is essentially a tree comparison problem. Figure 4(a) shows the HiPOS H^0 of S^0 tagged with different levels of matching rules decided by the instructor. Recall that H^0 is automatically generated by an NLP parser and no human effort is required. Since two block-level matching rules state that the subtrees rooted at the nodes S and VP can be unordered, some auxiliary HiPOSs will be automatically generated by enumerating different ordering of the subtrees. In addition, the "unordered" rule can also be specified as "unordered(i,j)"

where *i* and *j* refer to the *i*-th and *j*-th subtrees respectively. For example, in the output "`The roots are 3 and 5.`" (of an exercise for finding roots of a quadratic equation), an NLP parser can group "`3 and 5`" into a subtree and the rule "unordered(1,3)" will allow us to accept the output variant "`The roots are 5 and 3.`"

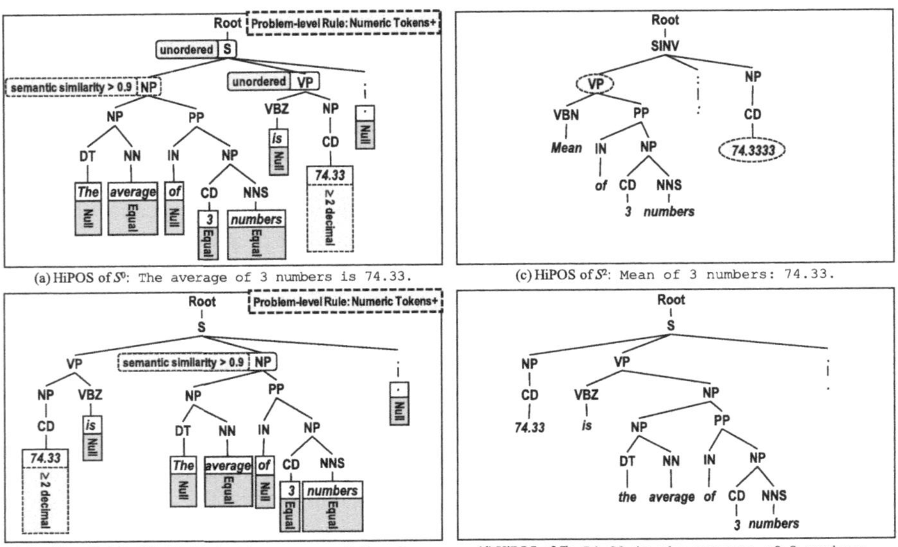

(a) HiPOS of S^0: `The average of 3 numbers is 74.33.`

(b) Auxiliary HiPOS of S^0: `74.33 is the average of 3 numbers.`

(c) HiPOS of S^2: `Mean of 3 numbers: 74.33.`

(d) HiPOS of S^1: `74.33 is the average of 3 numbers.`

Fig. 4. The matching mechanism of our framework, Note: Determination of the admissibility of a program output is based on HiPOS and different levels of matching rules. The shaded boxes with solid edges refer to the matching rules specified by the instructor. The yellow boxes with dotted edges refer to the matching rules triggered to determine the admissibility in our example. (Here **SINV** and **VBN** in (c) means "Declarative sentence with subject-aux inversion" and "verb, past participle" respectively.)

For example, Fig. 4(b) is one of the auxiliary HiPOSs generated from the HiPOS in Fig. 4(a). Since the number of nodes is limited and the use of the "unordered" matching rules is controlled by the instructor, the complexity of enumeration does not cause any runtime concern. After generating the needed auxiliary HiPOSs, matching is conducted in a top-down manner. Consider S^2: "Mean of 3 numbers: 74.3333", whose HiPOS H^2, which is generated by the same NLP parser, is depicted in Fig. 4(c). The problem-level matching rule "The result needs to contain one or more numeric token." will be firstly used to check if S^2 contains at least one numeric token. Our framework will traverse H^2 using depth-first-search and check if the part of the sentence represented by any subtree is similar in semantics to the part "`The average of 3 numbers`". It can be found that the part rooted at the node **VP** "`Mean of 3 numbers`" satisfies this matching rule as the semantic similarity is greater than 0.9 according to [10] (see also the online phrase similarity service provided by UMBC [26]). Next, the token-level matching rule "The token needs to be in 2 or more decimal places." will be applied to the leaf

"`74.33`". As H^2 satisfies all the matching rules, S^2 will be treated as admissible though it is not the same as S^0.

Consider S^1: "`74.33 is the average of 3 numbers.`", whose HiPOS H^1 is shown in Fig. 4(d). Note that the auxiliary HiPOS of H^0 is different from H^1 because the former is created by enumerating different ordering of the related internal nodes of H^0 while H^1 is created by parsing S^1 using an automatic NLP parser. Similarly, different levels of matching rules are used to determine the admissibility of S^1. However, the different ordering of the tokens leads to the incapability to match H^0. To handle this issue, our framework conducts matching to all the auxiliary HiPOSs of H^0 to see if S^1 can match with any of them. As H^1 satisfies the matching rules and ordering of the auxiliary HiPOS in Fig. 4(b), S^1 is considered admissible.

4 Experiment

We implemented HiPOS and the matching method as described above. We then conducted experiments to evaluate how well HiPOS can model the program output and the matching rule hierarchy can determine the correctness. In the experiment, 18 undergraduate students, who took an introductory course on C++ programming, were invited to participate. These students were asked to write a program for **Ex. 2** depicted in Fig. 5 in one of the tutorials. Students could submit their code to an APAS [28] any number of times until it is correct or the end of the class. Each submission was verified by running the program with 5 different test cases by the APAS. After the end of the class, we collected 274 program outputs by the students' submission. Each of these program outputs is separately judged by the instructor and by our automatic matching method to see how well our method agrees to human judgement.

Ex.2: *Write a program such that it first accepts an integer n* ($1 < n \le 20$) *which represents the number of students in a class. For each student, read the student's mark m* ($0 \le m \le 50$). *Store all marks into an array.*
After all marks are read, the program prints the average mark and the bar chart of the marks. You may assume that the input is valid (that is, data type is correct and the integers are within the valid range).
Example input:

```
3 30 20 50
```

Example output for the above input:

```
Average = 33.33
******************************
********************
**************************************************
```

Fig. 5. A second example programming exercise **Ex.2**

To apply our proposed method, the instructor was asked to design the matching rules based on his experience and prior knowledge on **Ex. 2**. Figure 6 shows the HiPOS of the example test case using a natural language parser. Although the output was not in the form of a sentence, the natural language parser could still successfully parse it to form a tree-like structure. The instructor could then create necessary matching rules to assess students' programs and provide customized feedback to enhance students' learning. In this tutorial, the instructor created the matching rules as shown in Fig. 6. Notice that the token-level matching rule for the token "`33.33`" is "The token needs to be in 0 or more decimal places." Recall that the learning objective of the tutorial was to practise the use of array and not related to the data types. Unlike the running example in Sect. 3, which focuses on the learning of data types, the instructor allowed the use of integers in this exercise. Therefore, the instructor can easily adjust the matching rules to facilitate different learning and teaching needs.

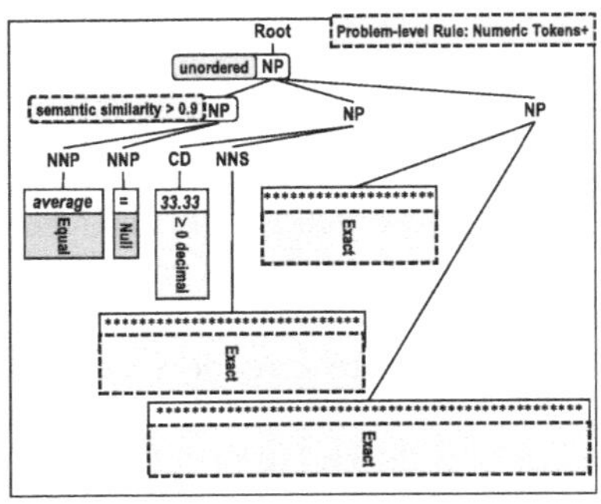

Fig. 6. The HiPOS of the expected output for **Ex. 2,** Note: The input/output are the same as the example input/output of **Ex. 2**. (**NNP** = Proper noun, singular)

We adopted the metric *accuracy* in our evaluation. Accuracy is defined as the total number of program outputs that are identically judged by both human instructor and our automatic method, divided by the total numbers of sample outputs. We achieved an accuracy of 0.8467 (232/274) in this set of experiment. We analyzed the output variants which lead to inconsistent judgment by the human instructor and our method. We found that inconsistency was mainly because the instructor set a looser standard in accepting the program output. For example, the following output variant was considered to be admissible by the instructor, but inadmissible by our framework due to the missing of the word "`average`" and low semantic similarity.

```
    33
    ******************************
    ******************** **************************************************
```

Besides, some output variants such as the following one were considered to be inadmissible by our framework since it cannot tokenize to separate the third token into "`33.3333`" and the series of asterisks.

```
    Average = 33.3333****************************** ********************
**************************************************
```

5 Conclusions

We have designed a structure called Hierarchical Program Output Structure (HiPOS) to model the program output. The automatically constructed tree-like structure can effectively capture the characteristics of a program output and provide higher expressiveness. A matching rule hierarchy is designed to determine to admissibility of program output variants in a flexible and robust manner. The matching rule hierarchy consists of different levels of matching rules to judge the correctness of a program output variant in different granularity. We conducted an experiment using real-world data from students of a introductory programming course to evaluate our approach. The results show that HiPOS and the matching rule hierarchy can consistently judge the admissible program variants.

Acknowledgement. The work described in this paper is fully supported by a grant from the Research Grants Council of the Hong Kong Special Administrative Region, China (Project No. UGC/FDS11/E02/15).

References

1. Academia Stack Exchange, Use of automated assessment of programming assignments. http://academia.stackexchange.com/questions/20578/use-of-automated-assessment-of-programming-assignments. Accessed 20 Dec 2015
2. Ala-Mutka, K.: A survey of automated assessment approaches for programming assignments. Comput. Sci. Educ. **15**(2), 83–102 (2005)
3. Chen, D., Manning, C.D.: A fast and accurate dependency parser using neural networks. In: Proceedings of the Conference on Empirical Methods in Natural Language Processing, pp. 740–750 (2014)
4. Curator: an Electronic Submission Management Environment, Computer Science @ Virginia Tech.. http://courses.cs.vt.edu/curator/. Accessed 20 Dec 2015
5. Douce, C., Livingstone, D., Orwell, J.: Automatic test-based assessment of programming: a review. ACM J. Educ. Resour. Comput. **5**(3) (2005). Article 4
6. Fonte, D., da Cruz, D., Gançarski, A.L., Henriques, P.R.: A flexible dynamic system for automatic grading of programming exercises. In: Proceedings of the Symposium on Languages, Applications and Technologies (SLATE 2013), pp. 129–144 (2013)
7. Gerdes, A., Heeren, B., Jeuring, J., van Binsbergen, L.T.: Ask-Elle: an adaptable programming tutor for Haskell giving automated feedback. Int. J. Artif. Intell. Educ. **27** (1), 65–100 (2017)
8. Gómez-Albarrán, M.: The teaching and learning of programming: a survey of supporting software tools. Comput. J. **48**(2), 130–144 (2005)
9. Gulwani, S., Radiček, I., Zuleger, F.: Feedback generation for performance problems in introductory programming assignments. In: Proceedings of the ACM SIGSOFT International Symposium on Foundations of Software Engineering (FSE 2014), pp. 41–51 (2014)
10. Han, L., Kashyap, A., Finin, T., Mayfield, J., Weese, J.: UMBC EBIQUITY-CORE: semantic textual similarity systems. In: Proceedings of the Joint Conference on Lexical and Computational Semantics, pp. 44–52 (2013)
11. Higgins, C., Gray, G., Symeonidis, P., Tsintsifas, A.: Automated assessment and experiences of teaching programming. ACM J. Educ. Resour. Comput. **5**(3) (2005). Article 5

12. Ihantola, P., Ahoniemi, T., Karavirta, V., Seppälä, O.: Review of recent systems for automatic assessment of programming assignments. In: Proceedings of the Koli Calling International Conference on Computing Education Research (Koli Calling 2010), pp. 86–93 (2010)
13. Jackson, D.: Using software tools to automate the assessment of student programs. Comput. Educ. **17**(2), 133–143 (1991)
14. Jacobs, C., Wilson, M., Barker, C.: Using the latest developments in mobile technology to improve students' engagement with assessment feedback. In: Proceedings of the 2015 IEEE Conference on Interactive Mobile Communication Technologies and Learning (IMCL), pp. 124–126 (2015)
15. Joy, M., Griffiths, N., Royatt, R.: The BOSS online submission and assessment system. ACM J. Educ. Resour. Comput. **5**(3) (2005). Article 2
16. Law, K.M.Y., Lee, V.C.S., Yu, Y.T.: Learning motivation in e-learning facilitated computer programming courses. Comput. Educ. **55**(1), 218–228 (2010)
17. Lewis, D.D., Jones, K.S.: Natural language processing for information retrieval. Commun. ACM **39**(1), 92–101 (1996)
18. Morris, D.S.: Automatic grading of student's programming assignments: an interactive process and suite of programs. In: Proceedings of the ASEE/IEEE Frontiers in Education Conference (FIE 2003), pp. S3F-1–6 (2003)
19. The Penn Treebank Project. https://www.cis.upenn.edu/~treebank/. Accessed 20 Dec 2015
20. Pieterse, V.: Automated assessment of programming assignments. In: Proceedings of the Computer Science Education Research Conference (CSERC 2013), pp. 45–56 (2013)
21. Poon, C.K., Wong, T.L., Yu, Y.T., Lee, V.C.S., Tang, C.M.: Toward more robust automatic analysis of student program outputs for assessment and learning. In: Proceedings of the 2016 IEEE 40th Annual Computer Software and Applications Conference (COMPSAC), pp. 780–785 (2016)
22. Tang, C.M., Yu, Y.T.: An exploratory study on instructors' agreement on the correctness of computer program outputs. In: Cheung, Simon K.S., Fong, J., Fong, W., Wang, F.L., Kwok, L.F. (eds.) ICHL 2013. LNCS, vol. 8038, pp. 69–80. Springer, Heidelberg (2013). https://doi.org/10.1007/978-3-642-39750-9_7
23. Tang, C.M., Yu, Y.T.: An exploratory study on instructors' agreement on the correctness of computer program outputs. In: Cheung, Simon K.S., Fong, J., Fong, W., Wang, F.L., Kwok, L.F. (eds.) ICHL 2013. LNCS, vol. 8038, pp. 69–80. Springer, Heidelberg (2013). https://doi.org/10.1007/978-3-642-39750-9_7
24. Tang, C.M., Yu, Y.T., Poon, C.K.: An approach towards automatic testing of student programs using token patterns. In: Proceedings of the International Conference on Computers in Education (ICCE 2009), pp. 188–190 (2009)
25. Tang, C.M., Yu, Y.T., Poon, C.K.: An experimental prototype for automatically testing student programs using token patterns. In: Proceedings of the International Conference on Computer Supported Education (CSEDU 2010), pp. 144–149 (2010)
26. UMBC Phrase Similarity Service. http://swoogle.umbc.edu/SimService/phrase_similarity.html. Accessed 20 Dec 2015
27. Wong, T.L., Lam, W., Chen, B.: Mining employment market via text block detection and adaptive cross-domain information extraction. In: Proceedings of the Annual International ACM SIGIR Conference on Research and Development in Information Retrieval (SIGIR 2009), pp. 283–290 (2009)
28. Yu, Y.T., Poon, C.K., Choy, M.: Experiences with PASS: developing and using a programming assignment assessment system. In: Proceedings of the International Conference on Quality Software (QSIC 2006), pp. 360–365 (2006)

Computer-Support Collaborative Learning

A Mobile Synchronous Peer-Tutoring System for Elementary Students' Learning in Chinese Language Arts

Mengping Tsuei[1(✉)] and Hsiu-Wen Huang[2]

[1] Graduate School of Curriculum and Instructional Communications Technology, National Taipei University of Education, Taipei, Taiwan
mptsuei@tea.ntue.edu.tw

[2] Department of Education, National Chia-Yi University, Chia-Yi, Taiwan

Abstract. Language skills are the most important academic skills for children. This study involved the development and implementation of a mobile synchronous peer-tutoring system for learning Chinese (iPTC) that provided various scaffolding tools facilitating children's Chinese language learning in a face-to-face context. Forty-eight fifth-grade students participated in the study. The results indicated that students benefitted from iPTC use, as demonstrated by improved achievement in Chinese characters. Students had positive attitudes toward online peer learning. Girls showed significantly stronger positive attitudes than did boys. The results also indicated that the peer-tutoring tools facilitated fifth graders' peer tutoring behavior.

Keywords: Mobile computer-supported collaborative learning
Peer tutoring · Elementary students

1 Introduction

Students who have stronger science, reading, and/or mathematics skills tend to be better at collaborative problem solving because managing and interpreting information and complex reasoning are always required to solve problems. The results of the 2012 Programme for International Student Achievement indicated that students in Taiwan performed in the top ninth of participating countries in reading. However, 11.6% of participating students in Taiwan read below level 2 [1]. A recent report indicated that an increasing number of students gains only superficial meaning when reading Chinese phrases and sentences, and cannot share that meaning with others in a comprehensive way [2]. Moreover, handwriting is a main learning objective in Chinese curricula, especially those for elementary students. Therefore, the enhancement of students' Chinese language arts skills is an increasingly important issue in Taiwan.

Peer learning is one of the most effective instructional strategies for language arts. A well-structured peer-assisted learning intervention involves the use of sequential learning activities and turn-taking mechanisms. The technique has been employed in classrooms and in computer-supported collaborative learning (CSCL) contexts [3–5]. The scaffolding tools that facilitate participation during online peer tutoring make a

S. K. S. Cheung et al. (Eds.): ICBL 2018, LNCS 10949, pp. 253–262, 2018.
https://doi.org/10.1007/978-3-319-94505-7_20

major contribution to successful CSCL [5, 6]. CSCL refers not only to connecting remote students, but also to the use of technology to shape face-to-face interactions [7], especially for elementary students. Therefore, face-to-face CSCL has emerged as an important approach to children's learning [5, 8–10].

As technology becomes ubiquitous, mobile computer-supported collaborative learning (mCSCL) has emerged in recent years to support the process and products of collaboration [11, 12]. Appropriate designs of peer-learning activities for students using mobile devices might include elements of scaffolding by the technology, by peers, or by the teacher that strengthen students' collaborative skills, such as instant messages, touch screen buttons [13]. However, much research on mCSCL implementation has focused on out-of-classroom and field-trip learning [14, 15]. As mobile devices become increasing prominent in the lives of children, many educators are becoming experienced with their use for educational purposes. This study argues that a mobile tablet environment can provide a better user interface than personal computer, in which students can naturally write Chinese characters on the screen. Building on prior mCSCL research, this study presented a mobile synchronous peer-tutoring system for Chinese language learning (iPTC) that provided children with various scaffolding tools facilitating Chinese learning in the face-to-face context.

2 Literature Review

The CSCL community has shown growing interest in determining the best way to adaptively support collaborating students [14, 16]. A previous study examined integrated face-to-face and networked collaborative learning technology and pedagogy in a secondary school history classroom [17]. Twenty-four students worked with CSCL software in small groups in the classroom using concurrently both the communication and the collaborative work software for 6 months. The results suggested that the degree of teacher control over the class was an important factor in the CSCL setting. The pedagogical design was another important factor facilitating peer learning in CSCL.

Few CSCL studies have involved the integration of peer tutoring design. Web-based peer-tutoring systems provide extra support for face-to-face peer tutoring and further enhance the effectiveness of teaching and learning. The study indicated that tutees liked the learning and teaching resources posted on the web by the tutors [18]. In one study [19], Cognitive Tutor Algebra, an intelligent tutoring system, was extended by integrating a reciprocal peer-tutoring activity, which increased students' conceptual learning. Peer tutors appear to engage naturally in reflective processes that lead to learning, but they may need more support for elaborative processes and the provision of appropriate help to their tutees.

Previous works have also documented the effectiveness of synchronous peer-tutoring systems in enhancing elementary students' mathematics learning [20]. Use of the G-Math system resulted in significantly greater increases in overall math scores, especially for arithmetic and application problems, and in self-concept and intrinsic goal orientation, than did a face-to-face control condition.

The use of wireless technology and mobile devices has also been incorporated in CSCL research. Wong et al. [21] developed the Chinese-PP character learning system, an in-class mobile synchronous collaborative learning game for constructing Chinese characters from components. The Chinese-PP system is based on 1:1 mCSCL activities by which children learn Chinese characters. Students must compose valid characters by correctly arranging components. Third-grade students using this system showed significantly improved individual ability to compose alternative characters from the components they were given.

3 The Mobile Synchronous Peer-Tutoring System for Chinese Language Learning (iPTC)

3.1 The iPTC System Framework

The iPTC was developed by using multiplayer architecture for synchronous screens (smartFox server). The system framework is displayed in Fig. 1. The iPTC is consisted of a learning activity management system (LAMS) for teachers and an application (app) for students. The LAMS helped teachers to initiate peer-tutoring activities by grouping students and assigning tutor and tutee roles. The teacher assigned peer-tutoring activities from the Chinese language arts item bank, which included questions from textbooks used in elementary schools in Taiwan. The activities had three themes: Chinese characters, word and vocabulary building, and sentence exercises.

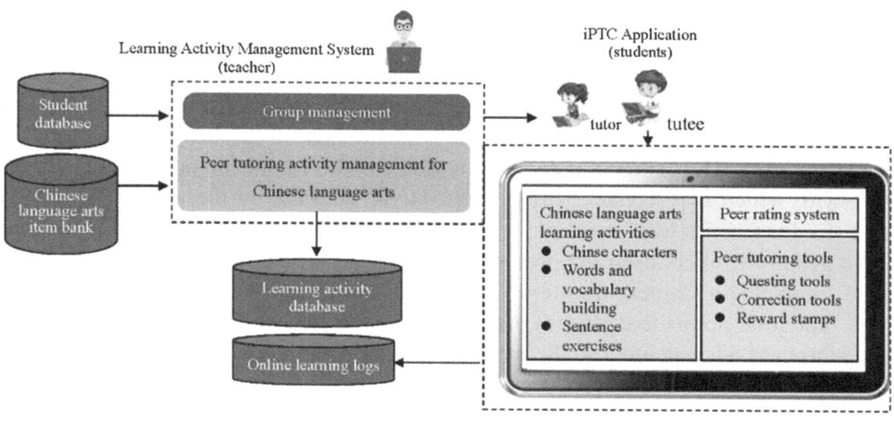

Fig. 1. The iPTC system framework.

After the teacher had assigned online peer-tutoring activities, students could log into the iPTC app on their tablets. Each student in the experiment group was provided with a tablet. In the app, a synchronous tutoring area is displayed in the middle of the screen (Fig. 2). Students could therefore learn on the three activity themes on synchronous screens. The questions had multiple-choice, fill-in-the-blank, fill-in-the-blank with Mandarin phonetic symbols, and drag-and-drop structures. For all except the multiple-choice questions, students had to write on the screen instead of typing text.

For this purpose, an enlarged rectangular of writing area popped up which represented the character in the answering area (Fig. 2). Thus, students could transfer their handwriting experience from tablet to paper.

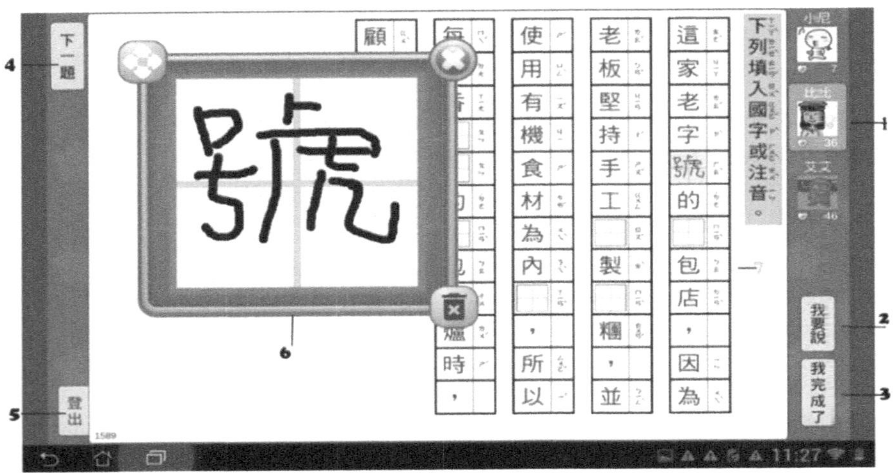

Fig. 2. Screenshot of the iPTC app: (1) avatar icon, (2) questioning tools, (3) complete notice, (4) next question, (5) log out, (6) writing area.

Peer-tutoring tools were provided to facilitate students' tutoring and interaction. The questioning tools for the tutor and tutee included various help prompts, feedback, and "asking for help" sentences. Students could choose these sentences during the online activities. The correction tools provided for the tutors including a pencil and eraser with which they could easily correct tutees' answers on the screen. As part of tutors' feedback on tutees' answers, reward stamps were provided for each question.

All group members used the peer-rating system to judge tutees' performance after he/she completed a Chinese question. The scores were then totaled for personal bonus points. The total points that student earned were converted to experience value, which counted toward advancement to the expert level. This module was designed to provide a "game-like" environment, to maintain students' motivation and facilitate their participation in the online process.

The system also provided correct answers, allowing students to reflect on their solutions after peer rating. This design thus encouraged metacognition.

3.2 Face-to-Face Online Peer-Tutoring Activities for Chinese Language Arts Learning

Before the experiment, students were paired heterogeneously by the teacher according to their Chinese achievement scores from the previous semester. In each dyad, one student took on the role of the tutor, providing content stimulus to the other student (the tutee). During this time, the tutor monitored and assessed the correctness of the tutee's responses. In the next section, the students switched roles. The teacher trained students in face-to-face peer tutoring to ensure that they followed the correct procedures.

In the online peer-tutoring process, the tutor started by pressing the "begin" button. The system automatically and randomly selected problems from the item bank assigned by the teacher in LAMS. The tutee had to answer the questions. During the peer-tutoring activities, students in the same group used various tools to guide the tutoring strategies. The question tools were located on the right side of the screen. Students could communicate with each other by choosing specific sentence buttons, such as prompting or questioning, offering help, asking for help, giving feedback, and providing praise. The selected sentences were shown to the right of the students' avatars. These features were included in the program to help with typing speed and to reduce errors at the elementary student level [3].

When a tutee asked for help, the tutor could use the correction tools on the left side of the screen. He or she could also use the reward stamps to give hints or feedback, such as "Some characters in the sentence are wrong", "Good Jobs!". (Fig. 3). Moreover, they could use the pencil tool to correct the answer.

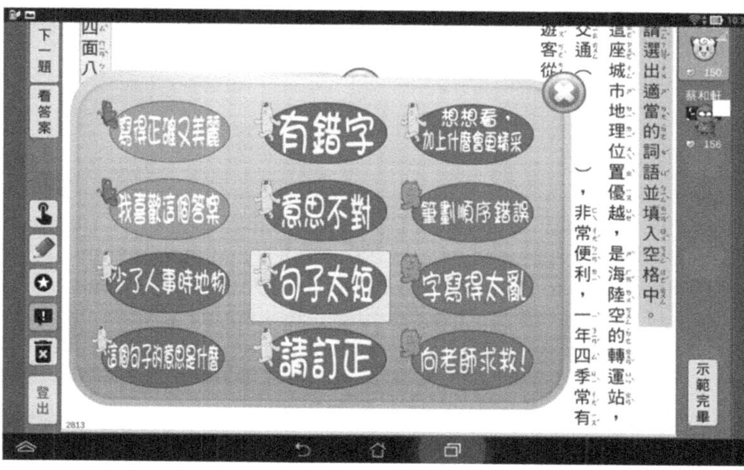

Fig. 3. Reward stamps of the iPTC app.

After the tutee completed the answers, all group members judged his/her performance using the peer-rating system. They determined whether each answer was correct or incorrect; the iPTC provided the correct answers during this process. For each incorrect answer, the tutee had to ask the tutor to teach him/her and redo the question. Students gained one point in experience value for each correctly solved problem. With five experience value points, the student advanced to the expert level. Images corresponding to experience levels (maximum 15 levels) were displayed beside students' avatars.

4 Study 1: Assessment of Attitudes Toward and Usability of the iPTC Among Elementary Students

This project was implemented for 2 years. Study 1 was implemented in the first year to assess attitudes toward and usability of the iPTC among elementary students.

4.1 Method

Participants. Twenty-seven fourth graders participated in this preliminary study for 3 weeks. Each student was provided with a mobile tablet for use of the iPTC app in the face-to-face classroom setting.

Questionnaire. The Attitudes toward Online Peer Tutoring in Chinese (APT-C) questionnaire was distributed to the students after the experiment. The 23-item APT-C assessed five constructs: self-efficacy and motivation in learning Chinese (six items), perceptions of peer learning (seven items), peer tutoring roles (three items), perceptions of scaffolding tool use (three items), and usability of the iPTC (four items). Responses were structured by a 5-point Likert scale ranging from 1 ("strongly disagree') to 5 ("strongly agree"). The Cronbach's alpha coefficient for the APT-C was 0.94, suggesting an adequate level of internal consistency.

4.2 Results

Overall, students showed strongly positive attitudes toward peer tutoring with the iPTC (mean [M] = 3.98, standard deviation [SD] = 0.62; Table 1). They were very satisfied with the usability of the system (M = 4.06, SD = 0.82) and indicated that synchronous peer tutoring helped them to learn (M = 4.07, SD = 0.76). Most students indicated that they liked to play the role of the tutor during peer tutoring (M = 4.08, SD = 0.96). Compared with boys, girls showed significantly more positive attitudes toward peer tutoring ($t = -2.47, p < 0.05$; $\overline{x}_{girls} = 4.23, \overline{x}_{boys} = 3.72$) and peer learning ($t = -2.20, p < 0.05$, $\overline{x}_{girls} = 4.40, \overline{x}_{boys} = 3.74$) with the iPTC.

Table 1. Means and standard deviations of responses to the attitudes toward online peer tutoring in Chinese questionnaire.

Factors	Mean	SD
Overall	3.98	0.62
SEM	3.91	0.74
PT	4.07	0.76
RO	3.93	0.79
ST	3.82	0.83
UB	4.06	0.82

5 Study 2: Effects of iPTC on Chinese Language Arts Learning Among Elementary Students

Study 2 was implemented in the second year to explore the effects of the iPTC on elementary students' learning and their online behaviors.

5.1 Method

Participants and Design. Forty-eight fifth-grade students (aged 11–12 years) from two classes in an elementary school in Taipei, Taiwan participated in this quasi-experimental study for 12 weeks. One class served as the experimental group and the other class served as the control group. Three Chinese language arts sessions (40 min each) were held per week. In the first two sessions in each week, students in both groups received whole-class instruction. In the third session, students in the control group worked face-to-face in dyads using the collaborative learning strategy, and students in the experimental group worked in dyads online using the iPTC in the classroom. Chinese achievement scores in the previous semester did not differ significantly between the experimental and control groups.

Instruments. Three Curriculum-based Assessment in Chinese language arts (CBA-C) tests, developed according to curriculum-based assessment principles, were administered to the students in both groups at 3-week intervals. All tests consisted of the same number of questions (32 questions) of the same types (Chinese characters, vocabulary, and sentence structure). The CBA-C tests were used to evaluate students' comprehension of three lessons in Chinese language arts. Three CBA-C were implemented in the study.

5.2 Results

Repeated-measures analysis of variance was used to assess the impact of iPTC use on students' CBA-C test scores. Overall, students' CBA-C scores did not differ significantly between groups ($F = 0.01$; Table 2). Students in the experimental group outperformed those in the control group on questions in the Chinese characters category ($F = 4.48$, $p < 0.05$).

Table 2. Means and standard deviations of CBA-C scores and results of repeated-measures analysis of variance.

CBA-C test category	Experimental group	Control group	F
	$\bar{x}$ (SD)	$\bar{x}$ (SD)	
Overall score	89.75 (1.49)	88.98 (1.43)	0.14
Chinese characters	93.59 (0.94)	90.86 (0.88)	4.48*
Vocabulary	94.81 (1.05)	94.48 (0.99)	0.05
Sentence structure	77.51 (3.39)	80.14 (3.10)	0.33

*$p < 0.05$.

5.3 Students' Online Behavior During iPTC Use

To explore students' behavior during online peer tutoring, students' learning logs were recorded in a database. Based on previous research [3, 20], students' online behavior was analyzed and coded according to a scheme comprised of 20 subcategories of participant behavior. The subcategories were derived from three patterns of peer interaction: tutor behavior, tutee behavior, and procedural behavior. Procedural behavior occurred most frequently during iPTC use; the "complete notice" function was recorded for 1239 questions (Table 3). Tutor behavior was logged more frequently than tutee behavior (n = 1641 [39.60%] vs. n = 548 [13.22%]). The most frequent tutor behavior was the use of the correction pen (28.21%). Tutors also gave tutees reward stamps very frequently (3.52%). The most frequent tutee behaviors were viewing answers (n = 186) and asking for demonstration of solutions (n = 121).

Table 3. Frequencies of online behaviors during iPTC use

Category	Code	Definition	Frequency	Percentage
Tutor behavior	GF	Giving feedback on tutee's answers	40	0.97
	IE	Indicating errors	50	1.21
	TW	Viewing answers	137	3.31
	RW1	Stamps for reward	146	3.52
	RW2	Stamps for guidance	32	0.77
	CA	Correction pen	1169	28.21
	TA	Trying again to correct the answer	28	0.68
	DS1	Demonstrating a solution	39	0.94
Tutee behavior	DS2	Demonstrating a solution	37	0.89
	AH	Asking for help from the teacher	6	0.14
	H1	Asking for help 1: please indicate the errors	39	0.94
	H2	Asking for help 2: giving hints	50	1.21
	H3	Asking for help 3: please demonstrate solutions	121	2.92
	PO	Posing a question about content	59	1.42
	EF	Giving feedback	22	0.53
	EW	Viewing answers	186	4.49
	TA	Trying again to correct the answer	28	0.68
Procedural behavior	PS1	Changing the operator (tutor or tutee)	644	15.54
	PS2	Complete notice	1239	29.90
	PS3	Clearing the canvas	72	1.74

6 Discussion and Conclusions

The present study revealed significant benefits of the use of a mobile synchronous peer-tutoring system, which improved children's Chinese character achievement scores. Students had very positive attitudes toward iPTC use in the classroom. They were also satisfied with the usability of the iPTC system. Girls had more positive attitudes than boys toward the peer learning environment. These results are in agreement with those of prior work in synchronous peer tutoring [20], and indicate that online peer-mediated learning can enhance student learning in Chinese language arts, as well as in mathematics.

In this study, tutor behavior was more frequent than tutee behavior during iPTC use. Tutees frequently requested that tutors demonstrate the answers to questions, in contrast to the tutee behavioral patterns observed during online peer tutoring in mathematics, where indicating errors occurred most frequently [20]. Most questions in Chinese language arts that were used in the present study required students to hand-write Chinese characters. When tutees did not remember how to write the characters, they asked tutors to demonstrate and then tried again. This process explains the more frequent occurrence of tutors' demonstration than in mathematics learning. Tutors also used reward stamps frequently. These tools prompted more instruction from tutors. Consequently, the present study adds to prior research [22, 23] documenting the efficacy of mobile peer tutoring with structured guidance in the CSCL environment.

References

1. PISA 2012 Results in Focus. http://www.oecd.org/pisa/keyfindings/pisa-2012-results-overview.pdf
2. Ministry of Education in Taiwan. https://www.edu.tw/
3. Smet, M.D., Keeper, H.V., Valcke, M.: Blending asynchronous discussion groups and peer tutoring in higher education: an exploratory study of online peer tutoring behavior. Comput. Educ. **50**, 207–223 (2008)
4. Webb, N.M., Mastergeorge, A.M.: The development of students' helping behavior and learning in peer-directed small group. Cognit. Instr. **21**, 361–428 (2003)
5. Tsuei, M.: Development of a peer-assisted learning strategy in computer-supported collaborative learning environments for elementary school students. Br. J. Educ. Technol. **42**, 214–232 (2011)
6. Janssen, J., Erkens, G., Kanselaar, G., Jaspers, J.: Visualization of participation: does it contribute to successful computer-supported collaborative learning? Comput. Educ. **49**, 1037–1065 (2007)
7. Dillenbourg, P., Järvelä, S., Fischer, F.: The evolution of research on computer-supported collaborative learning. In: Balacheff, N., Ludvigsen, S., de Jong, T., Lazonder, A., Barnes, S. (eds.) Technology-Enhanced Learning, pp. 3–19. Springer, Dordrecht (2009)
8. Roschelle, J., Rafanan, K., Estrella, G., Nussbaum, M., Claro, S.: From handheld collaborative tool to effective classroom module: embedding CSCL in a broader design framework. Comput. Educ. **55**, 1018–1026 (2010)
9. Zurita, G., Nussbaum, M.: Computer supported collaborative learning using wirelessly interconnected handheld computers. Comput. Educ. **42**, 289–314 (2004)

10. Stahl, G., Koschmann, T., Suthers, D.D.: Computer-supported collaborative learning. In: Sawyer, R.K. (ed.) The Cambridge Handbook of the Learning Science, pp. 409–425. Cambridge University Press, New York, NY (2006)
11. Ogata, H., Yano, Y.: Supporting Japanese mimicry & onomatopoeia learning with sensors'. In: Proceedings of IEEE International Workshop on Wireless, Mobile and Ubiquitous Technologies in Education (WMUTE 2006), pp. 111–115 (2006)
12. Sung, Y.-T., Yang, J.-M., Lee, H.-Y.: The effects of mobile-computer-supported collaborative learning: Meta-analysis and critical synthesis. Rev. Educ. Res. **87**, 768–805 (2017)
13. Boticki, I., Looi, C.-K., Wong, L.-H.: Supporting mobile collaborative activities through scaffolded flexible grouping. Educ. Technol. Soc. **14**, 190–202 (2011)
14. Chen, W., Tan, N., Looi, C.-K., Zhang, B.H., Seow, P.: Handheld computers as cognitive tools: technology-enhanced environmental learning. Res. Pract. Technol. Enhanced Learn. **3**, 231–252 (2008)
15. Cupic, M., Mihajlovic, Z.: Computer-based knowledge, self-assessment and training. Int. J. Eng. Educ. **26**, 111–125 (2010)
16. Rummel, N., Weinberger, A., Wecker, C., Fischer, F., Meier, A., Voyiatzaki, E., Koedinger, K. R.: New challenges in CSCL: Towards adaptive script support. In: Proceedings of the 8th International Conference for the Learning Sciences, vol. 3, pp. 338–345. International Society of the Learning Sciences (2008)
17. Baker, M., Bernard, F.X., Dumez-Féroc, I.: Integrating computer-supported collaborative learning into the classroom: The anatomy of a failure. J. Comput. Assist. Learn. **28**, 161–176 (2012)
18. Yip, W.: Web-based support for peer tutoring. In: Proceedings of the IEEE International Conference on Advanced Learning Technologies, pp. 619–623. IEEE Computer Society (2004)
19. Walker, E., Rummel, N., Koedinger, K.R.: Integrating collaboration and intelligent tutoring data in the evaluation of a reciprocal peer tutoring environment. Res. Pract. Technol. Enhanced Learn. **4**, 221–251 (2009)
20. Tsuei, M.: Using synchronous peer tutoring system to promote elementary students' learning in mathematics. Comput. Educ. **58**, 1171–1182 (2012)
21. Wong, L.-H., Looi, C.-K., Boticki, L.: Improving the design of a mCSCL Chinse character forming game with a distributed scaffolding design framework. Res. Pract. Technol. Enhanced Learn. **2017**, 12–27 (2017)
22. Tsuei, M.: Learning behaviours of low-achieving children's mathematics learning in using of helping tools in a synchronous peer-tutoring system. Interact. Learn. Environ. **25**, 147–161 (2017)
23. Thurston, A., Duran, D., Cunningham, E., Blanch, S., Topping, K.: International on-line reciprocal peer tutoring to promote modern language development in primary schools. Comput. Educ. **53**, 462–472 (2009)

The Effects of Smart Classroom-Based Instruction on College Students' Learning Engagement and Internet Self-efficacy

Yinghui Shi[1], Changling Peng[1], Shimeng Wang[1], and Harrison Hao Yang[1,2(✉)]

[1] Central China Normal University, Wuhan 430079, China
yhshi@mail.ccnu.edu.cn, {pengchangling, smwang}@mails.ccnu.edu.cn
[2] State University of New York at Oswego, Oswego 13126, USA
harrison.yang@oswego.edu

Abstract. The purpose of this study was to investigate the effects of smart classroom-based instruction on students' learning engagement and internet self-efficacy. A quasi-experiment study was conducted using a sample of 96 freshmen from a university in central China. While students in one class employed the smart classroom-based instructional approach, students in the other class employed the traditional one. Students in both classes studied the course of literature texts reading for three months. Students' pre- and post- surveys showed that the students with the smart classroom-based instructional approach had a significantly higher level of learning engagement and internet self-efficacy than did the students with the traditional one, which indicated that using smart classroom can increase students' learning engagement and internet self-efficacy when cooperated with an appropriate instructional approach.

Keywords: Smart classroom · College students · Learning engagement Internet self-efficacy

1 Introduction

As a new form of classroom learning environment and the product of the emerging information technologies (e.g., Internet of things, cloud computing and big data), the smart classroom, with deep interaction as its core feature, has been one of the research hotspots in the field of education (e.g., [1, 2]). It possesses a variety of features, such as the real-time interaction, environmental control, video monitoring and remote control [3]. Benefited from these functions and features, the smart classroom has the potential to enhance demonstration and presentation of instructional materials, to improve the quality of interactions among teacher, students and learning contents, and to promote classroom interaction and situational awareness [4]. Moreover, the smart classroom provides supports for various forms of teaching activities, which can help cultivate students' critical and creative thinking [5], and improve students' problem-solving abilities and application of information technology as well. Compared with traditional multimedia classroom, the smart classroom places more emphasis on using participatory teaching method to promote students' deep learning and knowledge internalization.

S. K. S. Cheung et al. (Eds.): ICBL 2018, LNCS 10949, pp. 263–274, 2018.
https://doi.org/10.1007/978-3-319-94505-7_21

In China, a growing body of teachers are taking several potential advantages of the smart classroom in classroom instruction, such as improving students' learning interest and motivation, enhancing the interaction and creation of classroom instruction. While a number of empirical researches have been done on the effects of the smart classroom on students' learning motivation, attitudes etc., relatively little attention has been paid on the effects of smart classroom-based instruction on college students' learning engagement and internet self-efficacy. Thus, this study takes freshmen of a university that is located in central China as the targeted participants, with the aim of investigating the effects of the smart classroom-based instruction on students' learning engagement and internet self-efficacy.

2 Literature Review

2.1 The Smart Classroom

Smart classroom is also known as intelligent classroom, classroom of future or classroom of tomorrow. Jawa et al. defined the smart classroom as a learning environment that could easily store information generated during teaching, generate timely teaching feedback on teaching activities, control equipment intelligently, and complete data and information search quickly [6]. He pointed out that the smart classroom which set cloud computing, sensor networks, wireless networks, artificial intelligence and other new generation of information technology functions in one was an important tool and means of the future classroom teaching, and it can support learning environment of teaching and learning style which required the creation of the real situation, inspiration of thinking, acquisition of information, sharing of resources, multiple interactions, independent inquiry, collaborative learning and so on [7]. Shi believed that the smart classroom was a new form of classroom, which can optimize the presentation of teaching content, make the sharing of learning resources convenient, promote classroom interaction development, and it also had the function of situational awareness and environmental management. What's more, smart classroom was a typical materialization of intelligent learning environment, and also was the high-end form of multimedia and online classroom [4].

In this study, the smart classroom can be regarded as a special type of digital learning environment. Smart classroom is defined as the environment of promoting interactive learning between teachers and students, cultivating students' self-learning, collaborative learning and problem solving abilities, and enhancing efficiency of classroom teaching.

2.2 Smart Classroom and Learning Engagement

Since the 1990s, learning engagement has drawn great attention from an increasing number of educators, and it has been defined from different perspectives. Skinner and Belmont argued that students' engagement referred to students who were engaged show sustained behavioral involvement in learning activities accompanied by positive emotional tone. They divided students' learning engagement into two parts: behavioral engagement and emotional engagement. Behavioral engagement refers to students' level of effort, attention, and persistence during the initiation and execution of learning activities, and emotional engagement refers to students' emotional reactions such as interest, happiness, anxiety and anger in academic-related activities [8]. Some scholars believe that learning engagement should also include the third aspect: cognitive engagement, that is, students' perceptions of themselves, their studies, their skills and their strategies for mastery learning (e.g., [9, 10]).

There is some evidence that the smart classroom-based instruction can increase student's learning engagement. For instance, Hwang et al. (2010) found that the learning in an authentic environment as well as in a virtual world had a positive impact on students' learning, especially in the field of emotion, including learning engagement, learning motivation and learning interaction [11]. In addition, Manny-Ikan et al. (2011) also found that that use of the smart classroom contributed to students' engagement in learning [12]. Zhang et al. found that, compared with the traditional lecture-based instruction, students in the smart classroom environment were more involved in emotion, and their behavioral engagement was more positive [13]. Based on the scale developed by Fredricks (2004), this study applied a quantitative scale to assess college students' learning engagement for understanding within the smart classroom-based instructional approach [9].

2.3 Smart Classroom and Internet Self-efficacy

According to Bandura (1977), self-efficacy was defined as "a person's own judgment in regarding to realize the capacity to successfully organize necessary events to achieve the objectives given" (p. 193) [14]. An individual's self-efficacy can affect their preferences and behaviors, both positively and negatively [15]. As a special type of self-efficacy, the internet self-efficacy refers to learners' confidence in their general skills or knowledge of operating Internet functions or applications in the Internet-based learning condition [16].

According to Xie et al. (2016), the application of e-learning space could gradually promote college students' e-learning internet self-efficacy and its cumulative application effect was very significant [17]. Finding from similar study conducted by Kim et al. (2013) indicated that a blogging centered course had impacts on the increases in students' internet self-efficacy, particularly for reactive/generative self-efficacy [18]. In addition, a considerable amount of studies pointed out that internet self-efficacy might play an important role in students' learning processes and learning outcomes (e.g., [19, 20]). In other words, students with a higher degree of internet self-efficacy tended to demonstrate better learning performance [21]. Some other studies, however, found that internet self-efficacy could not predict students' online learning outcomes [22]. Despite that internet self-efficacy plays a vital role in the process of students' learning, little attention has been paid on students' internet self-efficacy under the smart classroom environment.

2.4 The Research Questions

Previous studies have explored learning engagement and internet self-efficacy from theoretical and practical aspects in the development of e-learning and ICT in education.

However, there have been few studies that have addressed the effects of smart classroom-based instruction on students' learning engagement and internet self-efficacy. Therefore, the main purpose of this study will cover the following research questions:

1. Is there a significant difference in students' learning engagement between the smart classroom-based instruction and the traditional lecture-based instruction?
2. Is there a significant difference in students' internet self-efficacy between the smart classroom-based instruction and the traditional lecture-based instruction?

3 Method

3.1 Participants

The participants of this study were 96 freshmen majored in Chinese language and literature from two classes of a university that located in central China. Two classes were randomly divided into two groups: the experimental group (n = 47) and the control group (n = 49), with each group consisting of one class.

The same instructor was involved in this study, who taught both the experimental group and the control group. The instructor was trained to be proficient in using smart classroom technologies and had substantial teaching experiences and corresponding pedagogy to conduct instruction in the smart classroom. Illustration of the quasi-experiment is shown in Table 1.

Table 1. Illustration of the quasi-experiment

Group	Learning environment	Student number (N)	Instructional approach
Experimental group	Smart classroom	47	The smart classroom-based instructional approach
Control group	Traditional multimedia classroom	49	The traditional lecture-based instructional approach

3.2 Smart Classroom

The smart classroom referred in this study mainly includes one interactive whiteboards (IWB), six touch-control integrated devices (TIDs), wireless area network (WLAN) and cloud-based learning platform. IWB, instead of the chalkboard, was used in the smart classroom with the purpose of offering opportunities for teachers and students to interact with each other in a collaborative learning environment. The TIDs were used to display the learning contents and the contents of student discussions. Due to the full cover of WLAN in the smart classroom, students could connect with the teacher and peers through smart phones and tablet PCs. Not only could students search for relevant materials in the classroom, but also could they use the smart phone to scan the QR

(Quick Response) code that presented on the TIDs to complete related exercises. Moreover, the teacher could distribute learning tasks via the cloud-based learning platform and students could download them as well as additional instructional materials according to their needs.

Smart classrooms cannot just emphasize the richness of technology, but also requires a conceptually unique physical design. The physical design of smart classrooms should be comfortable and ergonomically appropriate to enable the required technology utilization, which is critical for shifting away from teacher-centered practices and toward participatory student-centered learning [23]. Additionally, adequate amounts of space should be provided to support the utilization of multiple learning resource formats, including physical textbooks, as well as students' group work interactions [24].

3.3 Instructional Approaches

A quasi-experimental study was conducted to examine the difference of the effects of smart classroom-based instruction and traditional lecture-based one on students' learning engagement and internet self-efficacy. Students in the experimental group employed the smart classroom-based instructional approach, while students in the control group employed the traditional lecture-based one.

The smart classroom-based instructional approach. The smart classroom-based instructional approach refers to the use of smart technologies (e.g., IWB, TIDs, cloud-based learning platform) and advanced instructional methods that are enabled by these smart technologies in the smart classroom, in order to display learning contents, to carry out learning activities, to realize instructional interaction between teachers and students, and to complete the whole process of classroom instruction in a smart way. Before class, the teachers assigned/uploaded related learning tasks and instructional materials on the cloud-based learning platform for students to read and explore more related knowledge. By reading relevant learning materials, students completed the task of teacher's arrangement. In class, the teacher and students could make use of smart technologies to conduct interactive demonstrations so as to realize the interaction among the teacher and students. After class, students could further digest the learning materials as well as continuing the discussion in the cloud-based learning platform.

In order to cultivate students' abilities to understand concepts and solve problems, the smart classroom-based instructional approach emphasized the student-centered learning environment to help students complete the self-construction of knowledge. In this model, cloud-based learning platform, IWB and TIDs were the main interactive tools in the smart classroom. They were not only used for displaying the learning contents, but also used for teacher's handwriting, notes and feedbacks, as well as students' answers. The framework of the smart classroom-based instructional approach is shown in Fig. 1.

In the smart classroom, the teacher could make use of the cloud-based learning platform, the IWB and the TIDs to carry out a variety of learning models, such as problem-driven learning. With the help of these smart technologies, teachers could provide students with a plenty of learning tools, course materials and learning services

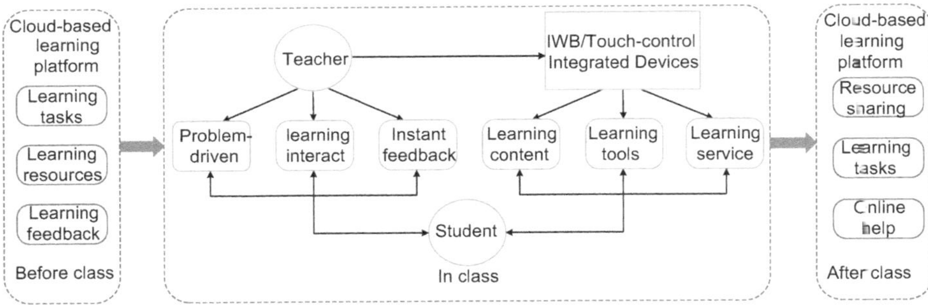

Fig. 1. Framework of the smart classroom-based instructional approach.

to satisfy the different needs of students, as well as implementing deep interaction with students. In addition, the interaction could also happen among students or between students and the IWB or the TIDs with the help of the built-in learning tools and learning services of the IWB or TID. Moreover, teachers could provide real-time feedback and evaluation for students via the IWB and cloud-based learning platform. What's more, the smart classroom-based instructional approach was aimed to develop students' autonomous, cooperative and inquiry learning ability, as well as their abilities to think independently and solve problems, with the purpose of helping students to complete self-construction of knowledge.

The traditional lecture-based instructional approach. The traditional lecture-based instructional approach refers to the traditional classroom teaching with the jointly use of projector, screen and chalkboard. Traditional lecture-based instruction is generally considered as teacher-centered and learning content-oriented, which is promoted by practices and drills with less classroom interaction between teachers and students. In the control group of this study, the traditional lecture-based instructional approach was used. The framework of the traditional lecture-based instructional approach is shown in Fig. 2.

In the traditional lecture-based instructional approach, teachers usually used the projector to display multimedia teaching resources for students, such as video and audio files, and various types of documents. Because teachers and students could not operate and write directly on the projector, and thus they had to write contents on the chalkboard, by which the interaction between teachers and students could be achieved. In the traditional lecture-based classroom, the chalkboard was mainly used for the teacher's handwriting and students' answers to exercise questions, while the projector was used only for the presentation of course material.

3.4 Learning Content

As a compulsory course of the major of Chinese language and literature, literature texts reading was taken as the experimental subject. The textbook for the literature texts reading course employed in this study was *Lectures on Literature* written by Vladimir Nabokov who was an American famous novelist and literary critic. The main purpose

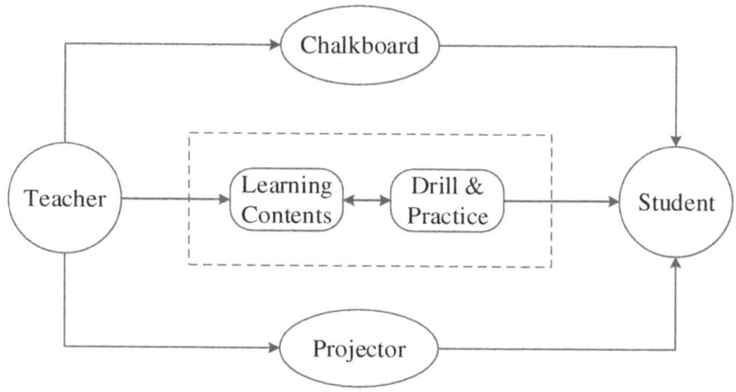

Fig. 2. Framework of the traditional lecture-based instructional approach.

of this course is to train students with a sense of understanding, appreciation, evaluation and critic capabilities to different types of literature.

3.5 Measures

To measure the effects of smart classroom-based instruction on students' learning engagement and internet self-efficacy, two scales were employed in this study. One is the Learning Engagement Scale (LES), and another one is the Internet Self-efficacy Scale (ISS). The LES was developed by Fredricks et al. (2004) to explore the relation between the learning environment and students' behavioral engagement (BE), emotional engagement (EE) and cognitive engagement (CE) [9]. ISS which is developed by Liang et al. (2011), includes two dimensions: Basic Self-efficacy (BSE) and Advanced Self-efficacy (ASE) [25].

The LES consists of fifteen items, which are expressed with a five-point Likert scale, ranging from 1 (strongly disagree) to 5 (strongly agree). A sample item of this scale in BE dimension is 'I will attend the class forum discussion'. The ISS consists of fifteen items, which are also expressed with a five-point Likert scale. A sample item of this scale in BSE dimension is 'I feel confident copying text on the Web into word'.

The LES and the ISS were translated into Chinese with the help of two educational experts. Results from the factor analysis indicated that all the items within the LES fell into three factors, while the ISS fell into two factors. The reliability alpha for LES in each dimension was 0.86, 0.78 and 0.90 respectively and the total reliability alpha is 0.94, while the reliability alpha for ISS in each dimension was 0.95 and 0.94 respectively and the total reliability alpha was 0.94, that indicates that the two scales are deemed to be sufficiently reliable for assess students' learning engagement and internet self-efficacy.

3.6 Procedure

All the participants were required to take LES and ISS surveys at the beginning and at the end of the course. One week before the start of the experiment, the pre-survey was conducted. After a three-month long teaching experiment, the post-survey was carried out simultaneously in the two groups. Data analysis was conducted using SPSS software.

4 Results

4.1 Students' Scores on the LES and ISS in the Pre-survey

To explore the effects of two different instructional approaches on students' learning engagement and internet self-efficacy, an independent sample t-test was conducted to examine the significance of the difference between the control group and the experimental group students who participated in the pre-survey. The independent sample t-test results are shown in Table 2.

Table 2. The results of t-test for students' LES and ISS scores in the pre-survey

Scale	Factor	Group				*t*	*p*
		Experimental group (N = 47)		Control group (N = 49)			
		Mean	SD	Mean	SD		
LES	BE	4.31	0.43	3.97	0.47	3.61	0.000***
	EE	4.28	0.50	4.10	0.47	1.87	0.065
	CE	4.07	0.54	3.97	0.53	0.96	0.342
ISS	BSE	4.35	0.56	4.33	0.39	0.24	0.813
	ASE	3.88	0.73	3.82	0.64	0.43	0.670

***$p < 0.001$.

As shown in Table 2, there was a significant difference between the experimental group and the control group with respect to the mean score of BE factor ($t = 3.61$, $p < 0.001$), this may be due to that students' behavior engagement, such as attention, can be improved in a short period of time, whereas the experimental group of students had been learning in the smart classroom for a week, and thus the experimental group had a significantly higher BE than that of the control group. However, no significant difference was found between the experimental group and the control group in ISS and the EE and CE factors in LES, which meant that the experimental group and the control group students had the same level of emotional engagement, cognitive engagement and internet self-efficacy.

4.2 Students' Scores on the LES and ISS in the Post-survey

After a three-months teaching experiment, the analysis of covariance (ANCOVA) was conducted to examine the difference between the control group and the experimental group with respect to students' learning engagement and internet self-efficacy in the post-survey, by using the pre-survey scores as covariate and the post-survey scores as dependent variables, in order to decrease the interference of the pre-survey scores on the experimental results. The adjusted mean and standard error (SE) for the two groups, as well as the F-value are revealed in Table 3.

Table 3. The results of ANCOVA for students' LES and ISS scores in the post-survey

Scale	Factor	Group				F	p
		Experimental group (N = 39)		Control group (N = 42)			
		Adjusted mean	S.E.	Adjusted mean	S.E.		
LES	BE	4.50	0.06	3.88	0.06	47.58	0.000***
	EE	4.52	0.07	3.83	0.07	53.90	0.000***
	CE	4.25	0.08	3.66	0.08	27.12	0.000***
ISS	BSE	4.56	0.07	4.30	0.06	7.61	0.007**
	ASE	4.09	0.08	3.73	0.07	11.79	0.001***

**$p < 0.01$; ***$p < 0.001$.

According to Table 3, there were significant differences between the experimental group and the control group of the mean scores of BE ($F = 47.58$, $p < 0.001$), EE ($F = 53.90$, $p < 0.001$) and CE ($F = 27.12$, $p < 0.001$). The results indicated that students in the experimental group had a significantly higher level of learning engagement than did the students in the control group.

In addition, there were significant differences between the experimental group and the control group of the mean scores of BSE ($F = 7.61$, $p < 0.01$) and ASE ($F = 11.79$, $p < 0.001$). The results indicated that the students in the experimental group had a significantly higher level of internet self-efficacy than did the students in the control group, which indicated that the use of smart classroom could increase students' internet self-efficacy when cooperated with an appropriate instructional approach.

5 Discussion and Conclusion

The purpose of this study was to investigate the effects of the smart classroom-based versus traditional lecture-based classroom instruction on students' learning engagement and internet self-efficacy. It was found that there were statistically significant differences on students' learning engagement and internet self-efficacy between the experimental group and the control group, with the experimental group had significantly higher scores toward the learning engagement and internet self-efficacy than did the control group. The result suggested that the smart classroom-based classroom instruction could improve students' learning engagement and internet self-efficacy.

The results showed that the smart classroom-based instruction could improve students' learning engagement. The results of this study were basically consistent with those of Zhang et al. (2016)'s research [13]. It might be because the experimental group students were taught in the smart classroom and they had a more appropriate learning environment which accompanied with a better learning experience. What's more, students in the experimental group had a better chance to interact with the instructor, peers and the learning contents. During the learning process, students' interests became more diversified, and the accumulation of experience would contribute to develop students' abilities and engagement, which led to the improvement of students' learning engagement [26].

The results also indicated that the rational use of smart classroom could effectively improve students' internet self-efficacy. By the nature of the instructional approaches, students in the smart classroom-based instructional approach had more opportunities to interact with their instructors comparing to the students in the traditional one. As students practiced and experienced more, their confidence of learning would be enhanced, which were thought to be positively related to students' self-efficacy [27]. This might explain why the experimental group students' internet self-efficacy was significantly higher than that of the control group students.

It should be noted that this study only examined the effects of smart classroom-based instruction on literature texts reading course for college students, and the findings of this study may not fully reflect the efficiency of the employment of smart classroom in other subject areas. To this end, future studies are suggested to apply the smart classroom-based instructional approach to more subjects, such as mathematics, geography, chemistry, physics and English. In addition, more attention should be paid to the design and implementation of appropriated instructional approaches for smart classroom-based instruction, in order to achieve an improvement in student's learning engagement and internet self-efficacy. Moreover, future studies are also suggested to explorer the full potential of smart classroom in supporting classroom interaction and students' self-construction of knowledge, in order to achieve an effective integration of information technology with classroom instruction.

Acknowledgement. The work was supported by the Fundamental Research Funds for the Central Universities of Central China Normal University (CCNU16A05037).

References

1. Huang, R.H., Hu, Y.B., Yang, J.F., Xiao, K.D.: The functions of smart classroom in smart learning age. Open Educ. Res. **18**(2), 22–27 (2012)
2. Chen, W.D., Ye, X.D., Xu, Y.F.: Future classroom: smart learning environment. J. Distance Educ. **30**(5), 42–49 (2012)
3. Yu, T., Ying, W.S., Sha, K.: Explore the medical curriculum teaching development in the smart classroom. Int. J. Inf. Educ. Technol. **7**(2), 130–134 (2017)
4. Shi, B.: Design and implementation of college smart classroom architecture in the age of the internet plus. J. Cent. China Norm. Univ. (Nat. Sci.) **S1**, 91–95 (2017)
5. Kwan, Y.W., Wong, A.F.L.: Effects of the constructivist learning environment on students' critical thinking ability: cognitive and motivational variables as mediators. Int. J. Educ. Res. **70**, 68–79 (2015)

6. Jawa, A., Datta, S., Nanda, S., Garg, V., Varma, V., Chande, S., Venkata, M.K.P.: SMEO: a platform for smart classrooms with enhanced information access and operations automation. In: Balandin, S., Dunaytsev, R., Koucheryavy, Y. (eds.) NEW2AN/ruSMART -2010. LNCS, vol. 6294, pp. 123–134. Springer, Heidelberg (2010). https://doi.org/10.1007/978-3-642-14891-0_12
7. He, K.K.: Wisdom classroom + classroom teaching structure reform – the fundamental methods of realizing educational informationization. Educ. Res. **36**(11), 76–81+90 (2015)
8. Skinner, E.A., Belmont, M.J.: Motivation in the classroom: reciprocal effects of teacher behavior and student engagement across the school year. J. Educ. Psychol. **85**(4), 571–581 (1993)
9. Fredricks, J.A., Blumenfeld, P.C., Paris, A.H.: School engagement: potential of the concept, state of the evidence. Rev. Educ. Res. **74**(1), 59–109 (2004)
10. Metallidou, P., Viachou, A.: Motivational beliefs, cognitive engagement, and achievement in language and mathematics in elementary school children. Int. J. Psychol. **42**(1), 2–15 (2007)
11. Hwang, G.J., Chu, H.C., Shih, J.L., Huang, S.H., Tsai, C.C.: A decision-tree-oriented guidance mechanism for conducting nature science observation activities in a context-aware ubiquitous learning environment. Educ. Technol. Soc. **13**(2), 53–64 (2010)
12. Manny-Ikan, E., Dagan, O., Tikochinski, T., Zorman, R.: Using the interactive white board in teaching and learning – an evaluation of the smart classroom pilot project. Interdiscip. J. E-Learn. Learn. Objects **7**, 249–273 (2011)
13. Zhang, Y., Zhu, Y., Bai, Q.Y., Zhu, Y.H., Li, X.Y.: Research of the teaching interaction behavior characteristics of primary mathematics in the smart classroom. China Educ. Technol. **37**(6), 43–48+64 (2016)
14. Bandura, A.: Self-efficacy: toward a unifying theory of behavioral change. Psychol. Rev. **84** (2), 191–215 (1977)
15. Shi, Y.H., Peng, C.L., Zhang, X., Yang, H.H.: Interactive whiteboard-based instruction versus lecture-based instruction: a study on college students' academic self-efficacy and Academic Press. In: Cheung, S.K.S., Kwok, L-f, Ma, W.W.K., Lee, L.-K., Yang, H. (eds.) ICBL 2017. LNCS, vol. 10309, pp. 319–328. Springer, Cham (2017). https://doi.org/10.1007/978-3-319-59360-9_28
16. Tsai, C.C., Chuang, S.C., Liang, J.C., Tsai, M.J.: Self-efficacy in internet-based learning environments: a literature review. Educ. Technol. Soc. **14**(4), 222–240 (2011)
17. Xie, Y.R., Sheng, C.X., Yang, X.T., Wu, W.Y.: The study on self-efficacy promotion effect with the application of e-learning space. China Educ. Technol. **1**, 34–40 (2016)
18. Kim, Y., Glassman, M., Bartholomew, M., Hur, E.H.: Creating an educational context for open source intelligence: the development of internet self-efficacy through a blog-centric course. Comput. Educ. **69**(4), 332–342 (2013)
19. Hoffman, B., Spatariu, A.: The influence of self-efficacy and metacognitive prompting on math problem-solving efficiency. Contemp. Educ. Psychol. **33**(4), 875–893 (2008)
20. Chang, C.S., Liu, E.Z.F., Sung, H.Y., Lin, C.H., Chen, N.S.: Effects of online college student's internet self-efficacy on learning motivation and performance. Innov. Educ. Teach. Int. **51**(4), 366–377 (2014)
21. Tsai, M.J., Tsai, C.C.: Information searching strategies in web-based science learning: the role of internet self-efficacy. Innov. Educ. Teach. Int. **40**(1), 43–50 (2003)
22. Bell, P.D.: Predictors of college student achievement in undergraduate asynchronous web-based courses. Education **127**, 523–533 (2007)
23. Looi, C.K., Seow, P.S.K., Zhang, B.H., So, H.J., Chen, W.L., Wong, L.H.: Leveraging mobile technology for sustainable seamless learning: a research agenda. Br. J. Educ. Technol. **41**(2), 154–169 (2010)

24. Macleod, J., Yang, H.H., Zhu, S., Li, Y.H.: Understanding students' preferences towards the smart classroom learning environment: development and validation of an instrument. Comput. Educ. **122**, 80–91 (2018)
25. Liang, J.C., Wu, S.H., Tsai, C.C.: Nurses' internet self-efficacy and attitudes toward web-based continuing learning. Nurse Educ. Today **31**(8), 768–773 (2011)
26. Lee, J.S.: The effects of the teacher – student relationship and academic press on student engagement and academic performance. Int. J. Educ. Res. **53**, 330–340 (2012)
27. Bandura, A.: Adolescent development from an agentic perspective. In: Pajares, F., Urdan, T. (eds.) Self-Efficacy Beliefs of Adolescents, pp. 1–43. Information Age Publishing, Greenwich (2006)

Learners' Experiences on Role-Playing Collaborative Learning Supported by ELS: A Case Study of Virtual Company Program

Ting Qiu(✉), Haiyuan Liu, and Enshan Yin

Guangdong University of Finance & Economics, Guangzhou 510320, China
Qssd205@163.com, {liuhaiyuanxn,yes}@gdufe.edu.cn

Abstract. For the purpose of improving the students' comprehensive practical ability in economic and management undergraduate education, we have designed a Virtual Company Program supported by E-learning space (ELS), using the strategy of role-playing collaborative learning. This study focuses on the students' collaborative learning experiences in this program, and investigates learners' perception of collaborative process, learning output, and supports of E-learning space. It found that most students gained a good learning experience in this activity, during which E-learning space played an important role in resource support, collaborative support and evaluation support. But they also met some troubles due to their different knowledge background, unconsciousness of seeking help and failure to use collaborative tools. Suggestions are put forward to promote the depth of interaction and generation of collaborative process.

Keywords: Learners' experiences · Role-playing collaborative learning
E-learning space · Virtual Company

1 Introduction

Nowadays, the demand for economic and management talents is increasing, and the demand for their ability is getting higher. However, it is common that in some teaching activities teachers often just repeat what the book says but never cultivate students' practical ability, which also becomes the bottleneck of economic and management education. It leads to the difficulties to meet the requirements of work department and a long period of adaption in their new jobs for graduates. We hope to solve the problems above by social practice, but it's ineffective at the end due to the limitations of the following conditions. Firstly, the company must keep the business secret, so interns are unable to penetrate into the operation of the enterprise in depth and integrity. Therefore, most of the time is spent on the peripheral and simple service jobs, but little is achieved on the application of professional knowledge and professional skills training. Secondly, due to the short practice time, students can only contact some links of professional practice activities, but cannot systematically and completely understand the whole process of professional practice activities. As a result, most practical activities become formalistic.

S. K. S. Cheung et al. (Eds.): ICBL 2018, LNCS 10949, pp. 275–286, 2018.
https://doi.org/10.1007/978-3-319-94505-7_22

For the purpose of improving the students' comprehensive practical ability in economic and management undergraduate education, we design a Virtual Company Program supported by E-learning space, breaking the discipline boundaries, integrating the instructional goals of knowledge and ability together, and setting up a multidisciplinary comprehensive virtual practice system for all the economics and management undergraduate students in our University. Students from different specialties are allocated to different jobs of virtual companies, virtual management institutions and virtual service organizations, in which they simulate enterprise operation in a complex and dynamic virtual market environment according to the actual business processes and rules.

The essence of the Virtual Company Program is a role-playing collaborative learning supported by E-learning space. In order to explore the collaborative learning activities to improve the program performance, this study will investigate the participants' learning experience and focus on the following research questions:

- What are the learners' perception of role-playing collaborative process and learning output?
- What are the learners' perceptions of supports of E-learning space for role-playing collaborative learning?
- How to improve the performance of the Virtual Company Program by optimizing the learners' learning experiences?

2 Literature Review

2.1 Virtual Company: A Role-Playing Collaborative Learning

Role-play teaching method is a psychosocial technology created by American psychiatrist Moreno (1960). It is to put people in the social position of others temporarily, and to act according to the way and attitude required by this position, so as to get a better understanding of their own social roles and others and to learn to perform their own roles more effectively [1]. At present, it has been widely used in the teaching of various levels and different contents, and is one of the main forms of collaborative learning activities.

Virtual Company is the most typical application of role-playing collaborative learning in the instruction of economic and management. As an instructional model, it refers to Teaching Co. established by students according to relevant business activities rules under the guidance of teachers, which originated from Germany. It is regarded as a kind of business practice teaching model with low cost, less consumption and higher efficiency [2]. Virtual Company in Germany, economic and management instruction in different countries is constantly being reformed and innovating, which makes Virtual Company have various teaching modes in many countries. In 1994, the new form of practical teaching was introduced to China, and since then some instructional laboratories have been set up. But in practical application, there are still some bottlenecks in the teaching method so it cannot be applied further and extensively.

Problems of Resources Support. Virtual Company is a kind of complexity learning activity with a large number of rules. In the process of participation into the activities, students need help and support from massive resources, such as professional knowledge resources, management rules and operating documents, which can be accessed anytime and anywhere in the process, or it may directly lead to the stagnation or error actions.

Problems of Collaboration Support. The basis of the operation of the Virtual Company group is whether the learners from different specialties can work together successfully or not. Troubles brought by different professional background, limited time of face to face and deep cooperation demand more support for collaboration.

Problems of Process Evaluation. As a role-playing collaborative learning activity, the real value of the Virtual Company is not the results of the operation of the business, but the improvement of students' practical skills. Therefore, process evaluation is an important way to evaluate the output of learning. However, the traditional teaching environment lacks this process evaluation.

2.2 E-learning Space

E-learning space (ELS) is a virtual space for formal learning and informal learning running on a learning support service platform. From the perspective of functional characteristics, E-learning space has the following key features: (1) E-learning space supports effective learning process and activity management, and provides learning resources and learning scaffolding to direct students' learning. (2) E-learning space provides a social network for collaborative learning. Learners can share individual learning content to peer and get comments and feedback which will stimulate learning motivation and reflective thinking. (3) E-learning space supports knowledge management and persistent, iterative learning records, which can be used in process assessment [3, 4].

This shows that as a role-playing collaborative learning activity, E-learning space provides effective resources, collaboration and evaluation support for Virtual Company.

2.3 Collaborative Experience and Technology Acceptance

Firstly, learning experience is a learning process, including learners' external learning experience and internal mental activities. Secondly, it is a learning result, including cognitive and emotional responses [5]. Emotion is the core of experience, and positive emotion as a driving force can effectively drive the learners to accept and absorb what they have learned, and then devote themselves to learning wholeheartedly. Karaman and Özen survey of students' experiences of collaborative virtual learning activities using a five-stage model [6]. Miao et al. explored the online collaborative experiences of MOOC learners, by investigating learners' perception of collaboration process, cooperative learning output and challenges in interaction process [7]. Zhu designed a collaborative learning scale according to the basic principle of collaboration, from the dimensions of "deep interaction", "information convergence", "collective thinking", "collaborative construction" and so on [8]. The model proposed by Wang and Zhu is used for the evaluation of collaborative process perception [9]. As what the research have discussed above, learners' collaborative learning experience will be evaluated from three aspects: learners' willingness, perception of collaborative learning process and perception of collaborative output.

The Technology Acceptance Model (TAM) proposed by American scholar Davis, was initially used to explore the influence factors of the universal use of computers [10]. It is now widely used to analyze the reason why users accept a certain kind of information technology product. In TAM, there are two key factors: perceived usefulness and perceived ease of use. The two together determine the user's attitude to the use of an information technology product. With perceived usefulness, user's attitude affects their willingness and behavior, and their willingness ultimately determines the use behavior of the product. TAM provides guidance for learners to evaluate their learning experience of using E-learning space in the Virtual Company Program What help (perceived usefulness) or challenge (perceived unease of use) have E-learning space brought for learners in the process of role-playing collaborative learning?

3 Context and Methodology

3.1 Program Design

We set up a multi-disciplinary Virtual Company Program, based on the role-playing collaborative learning strategy and E-learning space support. The program was provided in the first semester of the grade four undergraduate, with a total length of 6 weeks, finally about 240 h, of which 120 in class and 120 outside of class. It is a compulsory module of 13 undergraduate majors, including accounting, financial management, business management, marketing, human resources management, logistics management, finance, economics, statistics, international business, information management and information system, finance, financial engineering, etc.

The main body of Virtual Company Program is virtual manufacturing companies. In the process of operation of the virtual manufacturing companies, students need to carry out the following virtual experiments, including the establishment of companies, business analysis, environment and strategy for the development of the annual business plan, market development, adjustment plan and budget, fund raising, investment, human resources, production conditions, production plan, production preparation, operation, sales tax operation scheme business, and enterprise management information system design and development. Besides, another important part of the program is virtual circulation companies and virtual financial institutions, which constitute the external economic environment and market environment of company operation (Fig. 1).

In the program, we have designed three levels of role-playing collaborative organization.

Level 1. Students from different majors were mixed into groups. There were 13–16 students in a group, forming a relatively complete group of knowledge structure, providing multiple role resources for virtual operation.

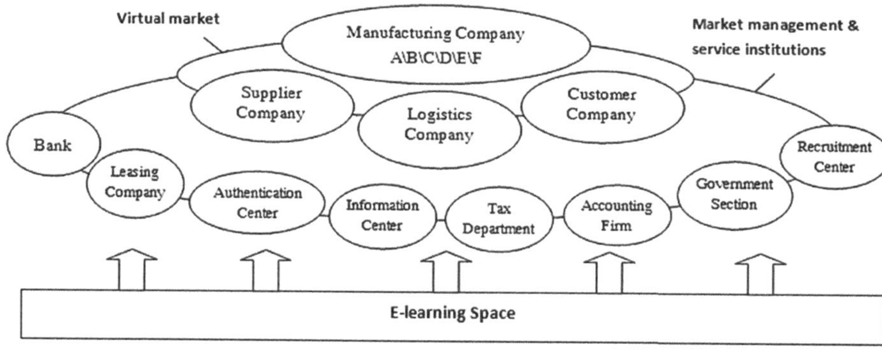

Fig. 1. Design of Virtual Company Program supported by E-learning space

Level 2. The members of Level 1 played different roles in management of virtual manufacturing companies or related virtual economic organizations according to their respective professional backgrounds, by which company's internal institutional framework was established.

Level 3. Every 8 virtual manufacturing companies in Level 2 formed a virtual local market. Every 2 virtual local markets formed a virtual regional market. Every 2 virtual markets formed a virtual country market. Other virtual economic organizations or institutions made up the external service system and market environment.

820 students participated in the Virtual Company program and formed 68 manufacturing companies. Within 6 weeks, these virtual companies will have a virtual operation for three years.

3.2 E-learning Space Design

Without technical support, such large-scale learning activities would not have been carried out. Technology has become a key element of curriculum design. Therefore, we design the E-learning space to support this learning activity based on the mobile LMS system, which includes three supporting functions of resources, collaboration and evaluation (Fig. 2).

Resource Support. In the learning space, we provide a wealth of learning resources and auxiliary resources. Students can access by computers or mobile phones anytime and anywhere, including 8 online professional courses, 3 online case databases (enterprise case database, market case database, and macro-economic case database), 2 activity support resource databases (guidance resource database and auxiliary resource database), and 2 reference resource databases (enterprise law resource database and enterprise management network resource database).

Collaboration Support. We set up online discussion boards for each group, and opened 3 online thematic forums (Business Development Strategy Forum, business management forum, and company culture forum). Besides, we have set up many position communities, including company president, chief financial officer, accounting

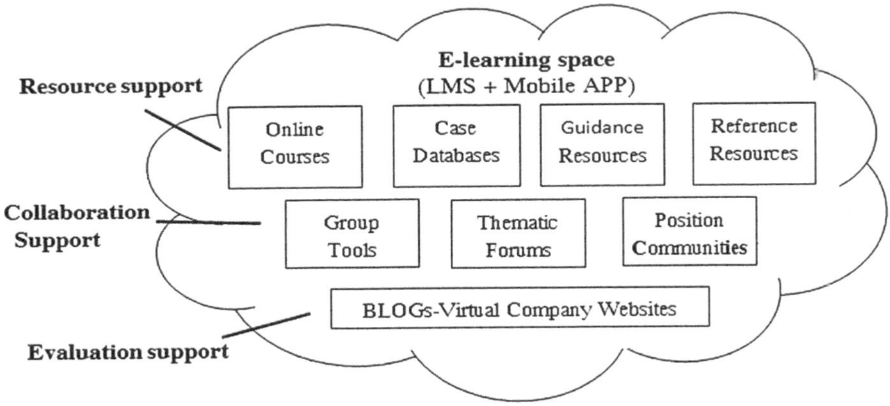

Fig. 2. E-learning space (base on a LMS + Mobile APP)

supervisor, marketing director, sales director, production director, HR Director, purchasing supervisor, Information Supervisor and other different positions. With the help of the collaboration tools, students share the experiences of success and learn from the lessons of failure of others.

Evaluation Support. We require each virtual company to establish its own BLOG, and to publish a group learning log in BLOG and show the outcome of the stage of learning. These BLOGs are not only windows to display the image of the companies, but also platforms for extracurricular interaction.

3.3 Research Methods

In this study, the Five-point Likert Scale was used as a research tool to assess learners' experiences of role-playing collaborative learning in Virtual Company Program. The scale consists of three parts: collaborative willingness, process perception, and output perception (Table 1). Among them, the perception of collaboration process is based on the collaborative learning model of Zhu, including "interaction depth", "information sharing", "collaborative thinking" and "collaborative construction" [8]. With reference to the model, 11 problems are extracted for the analysis of collaborative process perception. Besides, for learning willingness, we evaluate from three aspects: "interest", "effort" and "participation". For learning products, we evaluate four aspects from "quality of the task", "performance of knowledge learning", "performance of professional skills learning" and "performance of collaborative skills learning". Finally, the learner's learning experiences questionnaire contains 18 objective items (in addition to personal information questions).

The collaborative learning experience questionnaire was issued in the last week of the program (anonymous survey). 132 students from 10 randomly selected virtual companies participated in the survey. The reliability analysis showed that the Cronbach α coefficient of the questionnaire was 0.896, indicating that internal consistency of the data was good.

Table 1. Scale of learners' experiences of collaborative learning in Virtual Company Program

Collaborative learning willingness		I am interested in the learning activities
		I am willing to work hard to finish the tasks
		I am willing to take part in the learning activities
Perception of collaboration process	Interaction depth	I can fully express my thoughts
		I can get fast feedback
		It can inspire my reflection and self-evaluation
	Information sharing	I can get different opinions from my peers
		I can get information and resources shared by my peers
	Collaborative thinking	I can respond to my peers quickly
		I can ask my peers questions
		I can turn to my peers for help
		I can provide answers, suggestions, and solutions to my peers
	Collaborative construction	My team has a reasonable division of labor, and can work together to solve the problem
		Peer interaction is smooth, and can help solve problems
Perception of learning output		The quality of the virtual business task is high
		The performance of knowledge learning is high
		The performance of professional skills learning is high
		The performance of collaborative skills learning is high

Semi-structured interview was used to understand the help and challenges of E-learning space for learners. We used TAM as a reference model for interview questions, like "Do you think the online learning platform and resources help you in the program? Can you tell me more about it?" and "What problems of using the online platform and the resource process do you have in the program? Can you tell me more about it?" 10 students from different groups participated in the interview. Through the coding analysis of the interview data, we identified the help or challenge of E-learning space.

4 Results

4.1 Learners' Willingness to Collaborate

In terms of willingness to collaborate, students have shown a very positive attitude, with a mean of more than 4.6 (Table 2). Most of the students were interested in learning activities (mean = 4.697), and more students were willing to work hard to finish their tasks (mean = 4.871), and were willing to participate in learning activities (mean = 4.795). Based on the higher motivation level of the learners, it provided an important guarantee for us to focus on the process of collaborative learning activities and the experience of output.

Table 2. Results of Learners' willingness to collaborate

		N	Mean	Std. deviation
Collaborative learning willingness	Q1	132	4.697	0.461
	Q2	132	4.871	0.336
	Q3	132	4.795	0.405

4.2 Learners' Perception of Collaborative Process

In general, the students' perception of collaborative process was positive, and the average score of each score is above 4.1. However, specific to individual problems, the results showed that learners' attitudes towards collaborative processes were complex (Table 3). In the depth of interaction, majority of students believed that can fully express their ideas (mean = 4.129), and can get fast feedback (mean = 4.273). However, the score of "It can inspire my reflection and self-evaluation" was relatively low (mean = 3.894), indicating interaction depth needs to be improved. In the information sharing, most students believed that they can get different views and opinions from peers (mean = 4.689), and get more information and resources shared by peers (mean = 4.788). However, the performance was not so good in respect of turning to peers for help (mean = 3.553) and providing answers, suggestions and solutions to their peers, (mean = 3.621). We believed that this was related to the long-term learning culture. In the collaborative construction, most of the students agreed that the division of labor was reasonable and can solve the problem (mean = 4.326), but the recognition of efficiency of the interaction was low (mean = 3.992), indicating that there were still some difficulties in the interaction process.

Table 3. Results of Learners' perception of collaborative process

			N	Mean	Std. deviation
Perception of collaboration process	Interaction depth	Q4	132	4.129	0.500
		Q5	132	4.273	0.447
		Q6	132	3.894	0.414
	Information sharing	Q7	132	4.689	0.511
		Q8	132	4.788	0.410
	Collaborative thinking	Q9	132	3.985	0.447
		Q10	132	4.008	0.400
		Q11	132	3.553	0.691
		Q12	132	3.621	0.694
	Collaborative construction	Q13	132	4.326	0.470
		Q14	132	3.992	0.546

4.3 Learners' Perception of Learning Outcome

Most of the students were satisfied with the outcome of role-playing collaborative learning (Table 4). They thought that the quality of the virtual business was high (mean = 4.152) and this program helped knowledge learning (mean = 4.098), professional skills learning (mean = 4.205) and collaborative skills learning (mean = 4.356), among which their collaborative skills have been greatly improved.

Table 4. Results of Learners' perception of learning outcome

		N	Mean	Std. deviation
Collaborative learning willingness	Q15	132	4.152	0.470
	Q16	132	4.098	0.426
	Q17	132	4.205	0.441
	Q18	132	4.356	0.526

4.4 Learners' Perception of E-learning Space

The analysis of interview records showed that 10 participants interviewed agreed that resources and tools provided by E-learning space did help them. Resource support [RS], collaborative support [CS], and evaluation support [ES] were all mentioned, among which resource support was the most prominent (9 mentioned). They don't seem to have many difficulties in technology. Most of the interviewees have relatively rich experience in using LMS, and only 2 of them said they didn't use much before. In the context of collaboration Support, they put forward suggestions for collaborative tools. It showed that they were more inclined to use WeChat or QQ than to use a discussion board or community in LMS. There were also students who pointed out that there would be misunderstandings in non face-to-face communication due to the differences in knowledge background. In terms of evaluation support, the interviewees pointed out that the interactive records left by the E-learning space did not fully respond to their real interaction. Also there were students who thought that "when I look back at the group space page, I really enjoy the harvest of these weeks."

5 Discussion

The study found that the learners obtained a better collaborative learning experience in the Virtual Company Program supported by E-learning space.

First of all, the design of role-playing collaborative learning activities has been recognized by the learners, which can fully stimulate their interest in learning and enable them to generate internal learning motivation [11, 12]. Based on the strong willingness to participate, they are willing to play hard, although there were certain difficulties in the process of collaborative learning. Although differences in background brought communication problems [13], while appealing and collaborative habit were not yet formed [14, 15], the learners showed voluntary cooperation, willing to share and contribution.

Secondly, E-learning space plays an important role for better experience. The information and resources provided the key to the performance support of role playing cooperative learning activities [16]. However, learners are more likely to use familiar communication tools than those integrated with tools in space. Although this situation does not affect the experience, it affects the process records to a certain extent. Even so, E-learning space supports activity evaluation very well by the display function of staged results and final results, and plays an important role in generating positive experience of learning output.

Based on the above research results and practical experience, we propose the following strategies to improve the learners' role-playing collaborative learning experiences supported by E-learning space:

5.1 Promoting the Deep Interaction of Different Roles

The collaborative construction process and effect of different roles in the group are crucial to the whole learning experience. Due to the differences in knowledge background and learning goals, or the influence of cultural habits, the depth of interaction in the group should be fully paid attention to in the process of learning organization. Teachers should intervene moderately and provide interdisciplinary issues and tasks.

5.2 Promoting the Collaboration of the Same Role Among Groups

We should pay full attention to and support the collaboration in the same role among different groups. Because of the limited time in the process, we cannot provide more time and physical space for the interaction of the same role among groups. Using E-learning space can provide collaborative environment for different roles among groups (such as community and forum). In the study, we made an attempt, which was widely accepted by learners.

5.3 Promoting the Perception of Generation in Collaborative Process

In the process of learning, learners' understanding of collaboration still stays at the level of information acquisition and sharing, and the knowledge generation by collaborative interaction is not yet realized. We think it can be improved in two ways: (1) It is necessary to optimize the collaborative tools in the E-learning space, and make use of visual tools and semantic analysis software to make the knowledge generation explicit. (2) Teachers should provide guidance, improve the evaluation system, point out the observation points of the evaluation, and make the learners pay full attention to knowledge in content of interaction.

6 Conclusion

In this study, we have designed a Virtual Company Program supported by E-learning space, using the strategy of role-playing collaborative learning. In the program, students from different majors were assigned to different jobs in various virtual enterprises and virtual government management institutions, and simulated real operation in a complex and dynamic virtual market environment according to business processes and rules. In order to better understand how collaborative learning activities are carried out in the program, we focuses on the students' collaborative learning experiences in this program, and investigates learners' perception of collaborative process, learning output, and supports of E-learning space. It found that most students gained a good learning experience in activity, during which E-learning space played an important role in resource support, collaboration support and evaluation support. But they also met some troubles due to their different knowledge backgrounds, unconsciousness of seeking help and failure to use collaborative tools. Accordingly, we suggest that teachers should provide interdisciplinary tasks to promote further interaction of different roles in a group, provide collaborative environment to promote the collaboration of the same role among groups, and carry out appropriate intervention to promote the perception of generation in collaborative process.

Acknowledgments. This work was supported by the grant from Higher Education Reform Program of Guangdong in 2015 (No. 302).

References

1. Stewart, C., Edwards, H.: Online collaboration: using roleplay to develop skills in resolving conflict. Int. Educ. Stud. **5**(6), 1–10 (2012)
2. Westera, W., Sloep, P.B., Gerrissen, J.F.: The design of the virtual company: synergism of learning and working in a networked environment. Innov. Educ. Train. Int. **37**(1), 23–33 (2000)
3. Qiu, T., Xie, Y., Ni, M., Wu, W.: Development of a Model for Flipped Classroom Supported by PLS: A Case Study. Educational Innovation Through Technology, pp. 241–246. IEEE (2016)
4. Bi, J.J., Yang, X.M.: Constructing personal learning space in the view of connectivism. Chin. Educ. Technol. **8**, 48–54 (2014)
5. Hu, Y., Huang, R.: Learning experience in smart learning environment: definition, elements and scale. E-educ. Res. **12**, 67–73 (2016)
6. Karaman, M.K., Özen, S.O.: A survey of students' experiences on collaborative virtual learning activities based on five-stage model. J. Educ. Technol. Soc. **19**(3), 247–259 (2016)
7. Miao, J., Luo, S., Wang, Q.: Exploring collaborative learning experience in a teacher professional development MOOC. Open Educ. Res. **23**(6), 80–86 (2017)
8. Zhu, Z., Wang, Y., Luo, H.: Synergistic learning for knowledge age: theoretical model, enabling technology and analytical framework. In: Leung, H., Li, F., Lau, R., Li, Q. (eds.) ICWL 2007. LNCS, vol. 4823, pp. 207–217. Springer, Heidelberg (2008). https://doi.org/10.1007/978-3-540-78139-4_19
9. Wang, Y., Zhu, Z.: Multi-fields learning effect in synergistic learning technology system. Mod. Educ. Technol. **19**(12), 35–41 (2009)
10. Rauniar, R., Rawski, G., Yang, J., Johnson, B.: Technology acceptance model (TAM) and social media usage: an empirical study on facebook. J. Enterp. Inf. Manag. **27**(1), 6–30 (2014)
11. Wang, S.: Collaboration factors and quality of learning experience on interactive mobile assisted social E-learning. Turk. Online J. Educ. Technol. **13**(2), 24–34 (2014)

12. Capdeferro, N., Romero, M.: Are online learners frustrated with collaborative learning experiences? Int. Rev. Res. Open Distance Learn. **13**(13), 26–44 (2012)
13. Zhang, X., Zhong, L., Li, M.: Uncovering the interactive learning experience and its effect on learning outcomes in online learning environments. Tsinghua J. Educ. **38**(2), 117–124 (2017)
14. Pinheiro, M.M., Simões, D.: Constructing knowledge: an experience of active and collaborative learning in ICT classrooms. Procedia Soc. Behav. Sci. **64**(64), 392–401 (2012)
15. Aleksic-Maslac, K., Magzan, M., Juric, V.: Social phenomenon of community on online learning: digital interaction and collaborative learning experience. World Scientific and Engineering Academy and Society (2009)
16. Liu, X., Liu, S., Lee, S.H., Magjuka, R.J.: Cultural differences in online learning: international student perceptions. J. Educ. Technol. Soc. **13**(3), 177–188 (2010)

Seamless Co-reading System for Collaborative Group Learning

Chih-Tsan Chang[1,2](✉), Cheng-Yu Tsai[3], Yuen-Ju Li[1], Hung-Hsu Tsai[4], and Pao-Ta Yu[1]

[1] Department of Computer Science and Information Engineering, National Chung Cheng University, Chiayi, Taiwan
{cct99p, csipty}@cs.ccu.edu.tw

[2] Department of Digital Design, MingDao University, Changhua, Taiwan

[3] Department of Research Development, Xengda Technology Co., Ltd., New Taipei, Taiwan

[4] Department of Information Management, National Formosa University, Huwei, Yun-Lin, Taiwan

Abstract. To promote the performance of cooperative learning, this study proposes an online multi-user real-time co-reading system. Through this platform, it assists the teacher and students to increase the coordinative degree of learning activities such that the flipped learning can be seamlessly performed inside or outside the classroom. The multi-user real-time co-reading system is based on the skill of WebSocket to let learners simultaneously watch streaming videos on YouTube almost without delay. This can provide the teacher to guide the student watching the learning video and then get back the feedback from whole class or cooperative groups. According to the feedback, the teacher is able to understand immediately the students' learning condition so that the teacher can adjust the learning material to improve students' learning effect and interest. When students have a learning problem, they can discuss or share the ideas with other members in the chatroom. In addition, the greatest feature of the system is the grouping mechanism different from Skype and JoinNet. The teacher can rearrange cooperative groups based on students' learning condition by their learning feedback from system to give an ideal grouping such that most of students can take higher advantage during their flipped learning.

Keywords: Cooperative learning · Flipped learning · WebSocket YouTube player API

1 Introduction

Most of commercial online synchronous system can let students and teachers to communicate and discuss with each other such as Skpye, JoinNet and Adobe Connect. Some studies demonstrate that students can improve social skills and social consciousness when receiving synchronous learning online [1]. One of the interesting findings was that distance and location made no difference to the learning strategies employed during synchronous discussion [2]. This motivates us to use this mechanism inside classroom to progress the group co-learning. However, as each student watching

S. K. S. Cheung et al. (Eds.): ICBL 2018, LNCS 10949, pp. 287–297, 2018.
https://doi.org/10.1007/978-3-319-94505-7_23

the co-learning media on his/her display device such as notebook, smart phone and tablet, we found that the playing time on each device is not exact the same, called this problem as synchronous problem. Therefore, we find that the skill of WebSocket can improve this problem in contrast to the traditional skill.

Cooperative learning has become one of the approaches of learning. Through collaboration and discussion, every member can understand the learning content to achieve learning goals. The advantage of cooperative learning is students can improve abilities of thinking, personal learning motivation, and interpersonal relationship as well as peer relationship (Slavin 1985) [3]. In this paper, our proposed system not only can solve the synchronous problem, but also can give the activities of group learning more correlatively due to the digital communication without any delay.

Nowadays, for instance, Google Classroom is a blended learning platform offering simple function, such as sharing ideas in chatroom, assigning homework, and grading homework, respectively. Skype and JoinNet offer an interactive sharing platform but a weak chatroom. Although Adobe Connect can provide the near-synchronous function of cooperative learning, it cannot give students a reasonable interactive environment to feed back their learning interest and difficulty. Therefore, we believe that our proposed system is an affordable solution to achieve the requirement of seamless learning activities for group co-learning especially inside the flipped classroom.

2 Literature Review

2.1 Push Technology

Polling is a periodical request from client site to server site via Hypertext Transfer Protocol [4]. As server site receives a request, it will immediately respond to client site. Figure 1 shows the illustration of polling. Although this method can solve the problem of real-time updating, it is still not a good way due to the problem of resource consuming while the server does not have the newest data and it still needs periodically to check the service process in case of the client request.

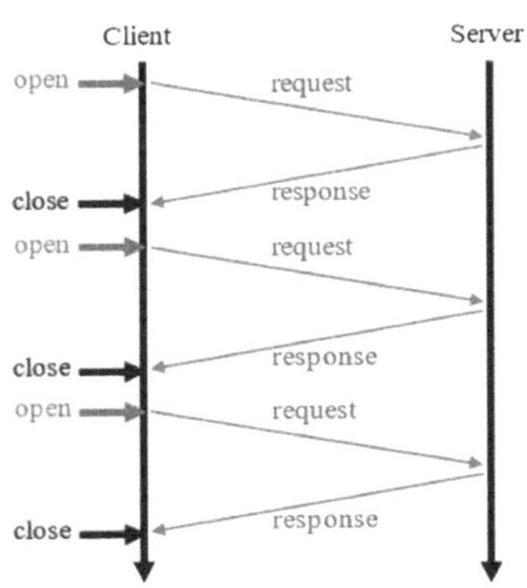

Fig. 1. The illustration of polling.

2.2 WebSocket

WebSocket, standardized by the IETF as RFC 6455 in 2011, is a single TCP connection, which provides full-duplex communication channels. It is easier to exchange the data between the client and the server via WebSocket because it allows the server actively to send data to the client [6]. By using WebSocket API, the client and the server only need a handshake to maintain connection with each other until the connection is closed. Comparing with Hypertext Transfer Protocol, WebSocket launches a request from not only the client but also the server. Figure 2 shows the illustration of WebSocket.

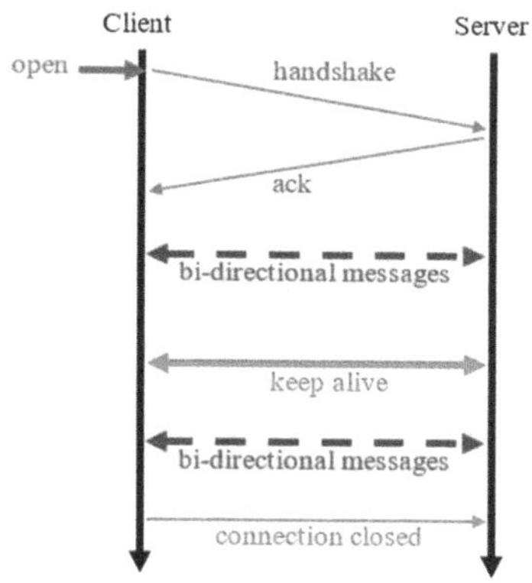

Fig. 2. The illustration of WebSocket

To build up a WebSocket connection, the client needs to send a handshake request to the server [6]. Once the server receives a request from the client, it promptly returns a handshake response, as shown in the example below [7]. The processing of operation will be described in detail as follows [8, 9].

2.3 YouTube IFrame Player API

YouTube IFrame Player API lets us embed YouTube video player easily on our website and can use JavaScript to control the player [10].

Using the API's JavaScript functions, we can queue videos for playback; play, pause or stop those videos; adjust the player volume; or retrieve information about the video being played. Furthermore, we can also add event listeners that will execute in response to certain player events, such as a player state change or a video playback quality change [10].

2.4 Flipped Learning

Flipped classroom is a form of blended learning in which students learn content online by watching video lectures usually at home and do homework in class with teachers and students discussing and solving questions. The teacher interacting with students is more personalized with guiding instead of lecturing [11–13].

Flipped learning strongly excludes to read videos inside lessons that is a self-learning model. It emphasizes about how to best use in-class time with students that is a student-centered model. Actually, flipped learning helps teachers move away from direct instruction as their primary teaching approach toward a more student-centered approach [14, 15].

2.5 Collaborative Reading and Cooperative Learning

Collaborative reading or co-reading is ubiquitous including in classrooms, book clubs, and in less coordinated ways through mass media [16]. In this paper, we emphasize co-reading activities inside a flipped classroom especially with cooperative learning.

There are many theories on cooperative learning. Slavins (1985) described that it was a systematic and structural educational strategy. Teachers divided students in different groups according to different abilities, genders, and races. It could apply to different disciplines and different-aged students [17, 18]. According to Jonhson and Jonhson (1987), students not only had to discuss face-to-face but also had to help and share personal ideas with each other in cooperative learning [19, 20]. Nattiv (1994) regarded cooperative learning as a teaching approach in which students worked together and had a common goal within groups. In additional to this, every student must be responsible for his or her own learning. They also needed to be dependent on each other in all kinds of aspects. Students were usually heterogeneous in groups [21].

The following is the summary of cooperative learning [22].

- Cooperative learning is a systematic and structural educational strategy.
- There are more than two learners in a group.
- Have a common learning goal.
- Students can exchange their own ideas to promote their learning cognitive, social and affective development and inspire their learning motivation in groups.
- Group students according to student's abilities.

There are many methods and theories of cooperative learning since 1970. The commonest cooperative learning methods are Student's Team Achievement Division (STAD), Teams-Games-Tournament (TGT), Jigsaw II, and Learning Together (LT), etc. The following is only to describe the Student's Team Achievement Division which we use in study.

3 System Architecture

An e-Learning platform created by WebSocket and YouTube player is established to meet the purpose of real-time co-reading. The platform will be introduced in three parts, design requirement, system architecture and system design, respectively.

3.1 Design Requirement

We combine the cooperative learning with the e-Learning teaching platform, using WebSocket and YouTube player to create a friendly environment for teachers and students. During the teaching process, the teacher guides students to watch teaching films together and students do team activities in groups. Each member is assigned to a team according to the abilities of the student so that the evaluation will be fair. Figure 3 shows the system architecture including advanced preparations of the session and kinds of session activities.

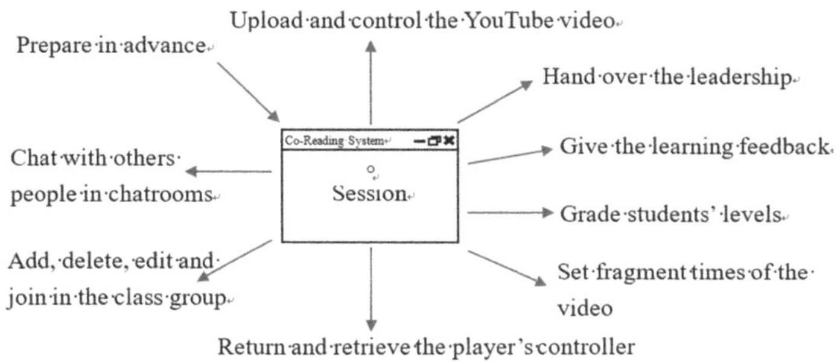

Fig. 3. System architecture

3.2 The Teaching Design of STAD

In order to combine our system with STAD, this section just simply describes the teaching design of STAD as below and Fig. 4 shows the teaching situation of STAD in our system.

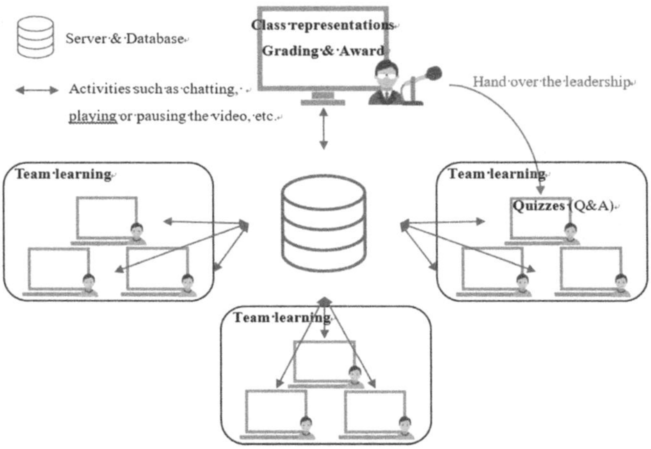

Fig. 4. The concept graph of the co-reading system and STAD

Preparatory Stage

- Instructional Planning
- Heterogeneous grouping
- Prepare teaching materials

Activity Stage

1. The teacher teaches students.
2. Students discuss with their teammates.
3. The teacher asks students to answer questions.
4. The teacher gives a score according to the student's learning performance.
5. The teacher appraises the students' learning condition.

3.3 Structure of Learning Feedback Mechanism

In the teaching process, students may give feedback to the teaching content. The feedback will be shown immediately on teacher's screen. Moreover, the teaching content is analyzed according to three aspects: difficulty, richness and understanding.

- Difficulty: The difficulty levels are divided into very easy, easy, normal, hard, and very hard.
- Richness: The richness levels are divided into very rich, rich, normal, bored, and very bored.
- Understanding: The understanding levels are divided into mastery, a general understanding, normal, a little understanding, and non-understanding.

4 Application of the System

The teacher can create a positive learning environment for students through making proper plans contributing to establish specific cooperative learning technique and laying the foundation for effective teamwork. Based on teaching belief of the teacher, the arrangement of groups can engage teams in learning interactively [22].

4.1 Heterogeneous Grouping

According to students' abilities, the teacher assigns for a group of two to six members. The case of application is based on heterogeneous groups of three members. Moreover, there are nine graduate students and a teacher conducting the learning activities to implement the teaching situation.

4.2 The Preparation of Teaching Materials

The teacher can upload the teaching contents to the YouTube platform and prepare some questions of the curriculum in advance. The case of the application uses Deep Learning as an example of course materials.

4.3 Activity Stage

First, the teacher notifies students of the learning goal and the standard of successful learning in the curriculum to make sure that students understand their goal.

During the process of teaching, the teacher will explain the content as the video is playing. The film will pause at the anchor point so that students can give feedback immediately. When the teaching comes to a section, the teacher can also respect the student's individual leaning feedback immediately in the curriculum. Students' first learning feedback report will be produced to exam students' learning condition. Figure 5 shows the concept graph of class representations and Figs. 6, 7, 8 and 9 show the actual case of class presentations, respectively.

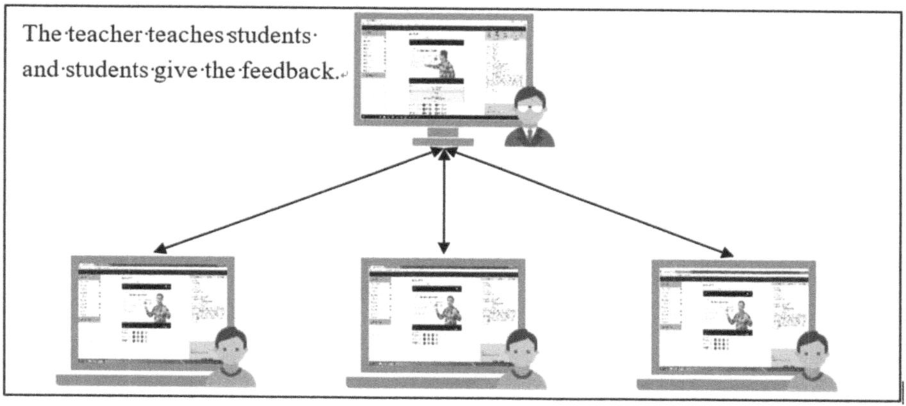

Fig. 5. Class presentations

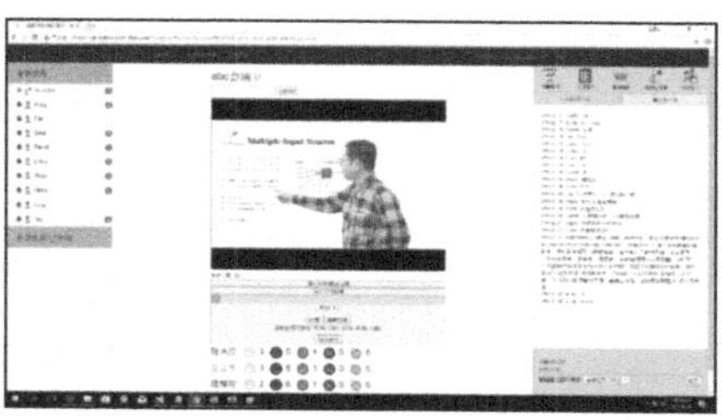

Fig. 6. The teacher's screen of class presentations

Fig. 7. The student's screen of class presentations

4.4 Discuss with Teammates

During the discussion, the teacher can rearrange the team members heterogeneously so that the students with better learning condition can work with the students with worse learning condition, and thus, make each team has the same learning condition. Then, the teacher will hand over the controller and assign questions to the students for

Fig. 8. The case 1 of class presentations

Fig. 9. The case 2 of class representations

discussion as shown in Fig. 10. Students can discuss about the film they just watched as shown in Fig. 11 and the teacher can make the second learning feedback reports according to the discussion.

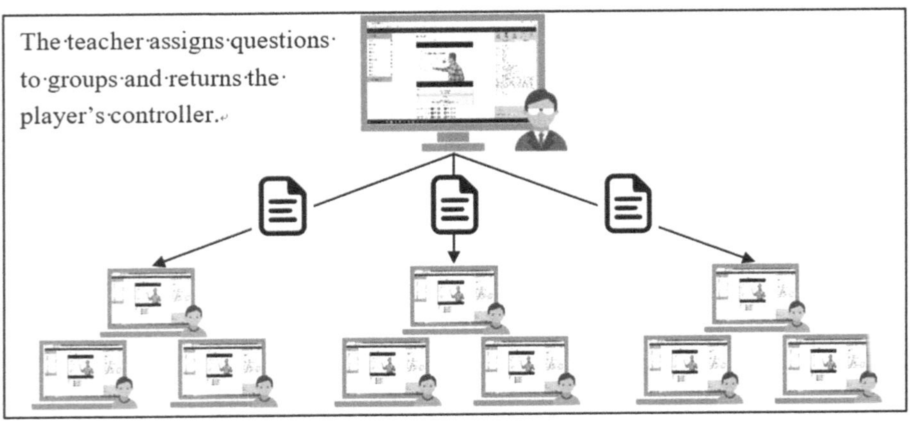

Fig. 10. Assign questions to groups

4.5 Question and Answer

During this section, the teacher can hand over the leadership to a student and let the student response the question as shown in Fig. 12. Afterward the teacher evaluates if students' learning is effective with the first two reports, and replies. For example, the teacher may judge from the learning feedback reports and consider that a certain student is familiar with the teaching content. However, when the teacher asks the student questions, he or she cannot answer at all. Then the teacher can figure out if there is any sign of deception in the students' learning condition.

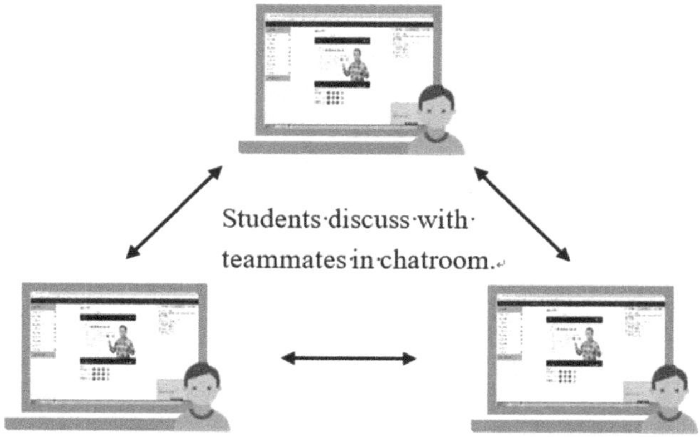

Fig. 11. Discuss with teammates

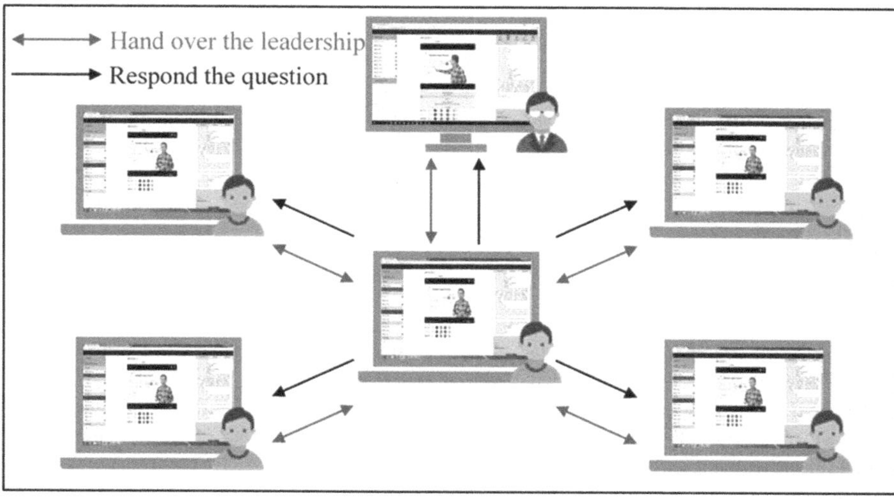

Fig. 12. Respond the question to everyone

5 Conclusions

Compared to Skype, JoinNet and Adobe Connect as shown in Table 1, our system focuses on the cooperative learning (STAD) in the session in the study. Through sharing learning videos, students can discuss and share ideas to engage in cooperative learning. The system also provides the function of handing over the rights of presenter just as Skype, JoinNet and Adobe Connect, and students can give personal opinions to the learning material. The teacher creates the session before he or she joins in the session to upload the teaching video and to set some configurations of the session. Afterwards, students can preview the video in advance after they join in.

Table 1. Different features between each system

Feature	Skype	JoinNet	Adobe connect	My system
Communication protocol	Peer-to-peer	Peer-to-peer	RTMP	WebSocket
Operation of the system	Need installing	Need installing	Web page	Web page
Operation of the meeting	Every members can create a meeting	Start a meeting with the messenger	Every members can create a meeting	Start a meeting by the teacher
Ways of sharing	Screen sharing	Screen sharing	Screen sharing	Video sharing
Hand over the leadership	Yes	Yes	Yes	Yes
Providing voiced messages	Yes	Yes	Yes	No
Providing cooperative learning	No	No	Yes	Yes

Acknowledgements. This work has been supported by the Ministry of Science and Technology of Taiwan under Grants MOST 106-2511-S-194 -001-MY3 and MOST 105-2511-S-194 -002 -MY3.

References

1. Oztok, M., Zingaro, D., Brett, C., Hewitt, J.: Exploring asynchronous and synchronous tool use in online courses. Comput. Educ. **60**(1), 87–94 (2013)
2. Park, Y.J., Bonk, C.J.: Synchronous learning experiences: distance and residential learners' perspectives in a blended graduate course. J. Interact. Online Learn. **6**(3), 245–264 (2007)
3. Li, M.P., Lam, B.H.: Cooperative Learning. The Active Classroom. The Hong Kong Institute of Education, p. 10 (2013)
4. WebSocket Communication Protocol Introduction: Comparison of Polling, Long-Polling and Streaming Principles of Operation. http://www.websocket.org/quantum.html
5. Introduction to Operation of Server-Sent Events. https://www.w3.org/TR/eventsource
6. Wang, V., Salim, F., Moskovits, P.: The Definitive Guide to HTML5 WebSocket vol. 1. Apress, New York (2013)
7. Fette, I.: The WebSocket Protocol (2011)
8. Official Website of WebSocket. http://www.websocket.org/quantum.html
9. YouTube Player API Reference for IFrame Embeds. https://developers.google.com/youtube/iframe_api_reference
10. Downie, N.: Chart.js (2013). http://www.chartjs.org/
11. Tsai, C.-Y., Chang, C.-T., Hsu, J.-M., Tsai, H.-H., Dai, Z.-C., Yu, P.-T.: Toward a highly interactive model of flipped learning. In: Cheung, S.K.S., Kwok, L., Yang, H., Fong, J., Kwan, R. (eds.) ICHL 2015. LNCS, vol. 9167, pp. 173–186. Springer, Cham (2015). https://doi.org/10.1007/978-3-319-20621-9_14

12. Barseghian, T.: Three trends that define the future of teaching and learning. In: KQED, 30 p. (2011). Accessed Apr 2013
13. Tucker, B.: The flipped classroom. Educ. Next **12**(1), 82–83 (2012)
14. Ma, K., Sun, R.: Introducing websocket-based real-time monitoring system for remote intelligent buildings. Int. J. Distrib. Sens. Netw. **9**(12) (2013). Article ID 867693
15. Brusino, J.: The next generation of SCORM: a Q&A with Aaron Silvers (2012). Accessed 3 Nov 2013
16. Marshall, C.C.: Reading and Writing the Electronic Book. Synthesis Lectures on Information Concepts, Retrieval, and Services. Morgan & Claypool Publishers (2009)
17. Adler, A., Gujar, A., Harrison, B. L., O'hara, K., Sellen, A.: A diary study of work-related reading: design implications for digital reading devices. In: Proceedings of the SIGCHI Conference on Human factors in Computing Systems, pp. 241–248. ACM Press/Addison-Wesley Publishing Co., January 1998
18. Slavin, R.E.: Cooperative learning: applying contact theory in desegregated schools. J. Soc. Issues 43–62 (1985)
19. Johnson, D.W., Johnson, R.T., Smith, K.A.: Active Learning: Cooperation in the College Classroom, 2nd edn. Interaction Book Company, Edina (1998)
20. Johnson, D.W., Johnson, R.T.: Learning Together and Alone: Cooperative, Competitive, and Individualistic Learning. Prentice-Hall, Englewood Cliffs (1987)
21. Nattiv, A.: Helping behaviors and math achievement gain of students using cooperative learning. Elem. Sch. J. **94**(3), 285–297 (1994)
22. Chang, C.T., Tsai, C.Y., Peng, S.E., Tsai, H.H., Yu, P.T.: On the design of multi-user streaming feedback system for application of cooperative learning. In: International Computer Symposium (ICS), pp. 656–659. IEEE, December 2016

Improved Flexibility of Learning Processes

Personalized Word Learning for ESL Students via Integration of Implicit and Explicit Profiles

Fu Lee Wang[1], Di Zou[2], and Haoran Xie[3](✉)

[1] School of Science and Technology, The Open University of Hong Kong, Kowloon, Hong Kong SAR, China
[2] Department of English Language Education, The Education University of Hong Kong, New Territories, Hong Kong SAR, China
[3] Department of Mathematics and Information Technology, The Education University of Hong Kong, New Territories, Hong Kong SAR, China
hrxie2@gmail.com

Abstract. Word learning is the one of most fundamental steps for English as Second Language (ESL) students. However, it is a challenge to understand each individual student to provide them with personalized learning experience, since it is difficult to identify various variables like learning style, language proficiency, knowledge background for each learner in an e-learning system. To address this issue, we propose an integrated framework to depict the individual vocabulary proficiency by using the implicit and explicit profiles. The explicit user profiling gives the control of users to specify and modify their vocabulary proficiency so that the users will have a sense of ownership of their personalized data, whereas the implicit user profiling is a non-intrusive method which can record and update the proficiency of learners without explicit manually input from users. In this paper, we attempt to integrate these two kinds of profiles to build a powerful learner profile for personalized vocabulary learning. Furthermore, the preliminary empirical results validate the effectiveness of the integrated framework.

Keywords: Vocabulary acquisition · ESL · Student profiles
Learning analytics · Personalized learning

1 Introduction

The importance of word learning in the development of language has been widely accepted in the educational and linguistic field [5]. In recent years, vocabulary e-learning systems and applications [1,3,13] have become a vital method for ESL learners to learn new words with the development of information technologies. However, it is a challenge to understand each individual student to provide them with personalized learning experience, since it is difficult to identify various variables like learning style, language proficiency, knowledge background for each

S. K. S. Cheung et al. (Eds.): ICBL 2018, LNCS 10949, pp. 301–310, 2018.
https://doi.org/10.1007/978-3-319-94505-7_24

learner in an e-learning system. To cater the needs from different learners, it is critical to understand the above individual factors related to vocabulary learning.

The profiling model is a popular technique for facilitating personalization in various domain-specific applications like web search [9], social media [12], e-learning [14], e-commerce [11] and so on. In the domain of vocabulary learning, a few studies adopted the profiling techniques [13,17,19] for facilitating personalized word learning. There are mainly two kinds of profiling techniques, which are explicit user profiling and implicit user profiling. The explicit user profiling gives the control of users to specify and modify their vocabulary proficiency so that the users will have a sense of ownership of their personalized data, whereas the implicit user profiling is a non-intrusive method which can record and update the proficiency of learners without explicit manually input from users. In our study about the explicit profiling techniques [19], users feel that they have a very good control on their profiles but too much manual efforts is required. In contrast, learners feel that the implicit profiling method is convenient with a bit violation of their privacy in the study about the implicit profiling techniques [13].

To address the challenge of understanding vocabulary proficiency for ESL learners, we propose an integrated framework to depict the individual vocabulary proficiency by leveraging the implicit and explicit profiles. Specifically, the main contributions of this paper are listed as follows.

- We propose an integrated framework which attempts to consolidate the implicit and explicit profiling techniques to build a powerful profile for personalized vocabulary learning;
- We present a updating mechanism to adjust the values which reflect the vocabulary proficiency of each learner in the system by taking the important factors like time or correctness of the answer.
- A preliminary study is conducted by involving real ESL learners in different setting of user profiles, and the empirical results validate the effectiveness of the integrated framework.

The remaining sections of this article will be structured as follows. In Sect. 2, a review about the vocabulary learning system is conducted to understand the holistic view in the field of educational technology. In Sect. 3, we introduce the integrated framework which attempts to consolidate the implicit and explicit profiling techniques and discuss a updating mechanism to adjust the values which reflect the vocabulary proficiency of each learner in the system. In Sect. 4, the experimental procedures, results, and participants are reported and discussed. Section 5 summarizes the findings and potential research topics for our future studies.

2 Related Work

The research studies about the vocabulary learning system become increasingly popular with the rapid development of the information technologies. Chen and Chung [1] presented a personalized mobile English vocabulary learning system based on Item Response Theory and learning memory cycle, which recommends appropriate English vocabulary for learning according to individual learner vocabulary ability and memory cycle. Chen and Li [2] proposed a personalised context-aware ubiquitous learning system or learning English vocabulary based on learner location as detected by wireless positioning techniques, learning time, individual English vocabulary abilities and leisure time, enabling learners to adapt their learning content to effectively support English vocabulary learning in a school environment. Loucky [7] proposed a distance vocabulary learning system by pre-arranging the target vocabulary into bilingual categories under simpler or common semantic field keywords. Huang et al. [3] developed a ubiquitous English vocabulary learning system to assist students in experiencing a systematic vocabulary learning process in which ubiquitous technology is used to develop the system, and video clips are used as the material. Zou et al. [17] adopt the involvement load hypothesis (ILH) [4] to build ILH-based learning profiles for personalized learning task generation. This method was further improved by using the social media data of learners to identify their preferred topics in [13]. More recently, we study the impact of the different word knowledge scales for the word learning [18] and how to use the explicit learner profiles for facilitating the learning task recommendations [19].

3 Methodology

In this section, we firstly introduce the implicit and explicit profiling techniques respectively. Next, we discuss a updating mechanism to adjust the values which reflect the vocabulary proficiency of each learner in the system and how to suggest the learning vocabulary to the learners.

3.1 Explicit Learner Profiling

The processes of the explicit user profiling have been discussed and elaborated in our earlier study [19]. Therefore, in this section, we briefly go through the key notations and definitions for explicit learner profiling processes. The key concept in the explicit profiling is to depict a learn's vocabulary knowledge, which can be formally denoted as a vector of words and the corresponding knowledge levels of these words.

Definition 1. *A* ***learner profile****, denoted by L_i, is a vector of the value pairs:*

$$L_i = (w_1 : \varepsilon_1^i; w_2 : \varepsilon_2^i; ...; w_n : \varepsilon_n^i), \tag{1}$$

where w_a is a words in the system, n is the size of the whole vocabulary in the system, ε_a^i is the knowledge levels of learner i to word w_a, and note that ε_a^i is normalized in the range of $[0, 1]$ to interpret the degree of vocabulary knowledge [19].

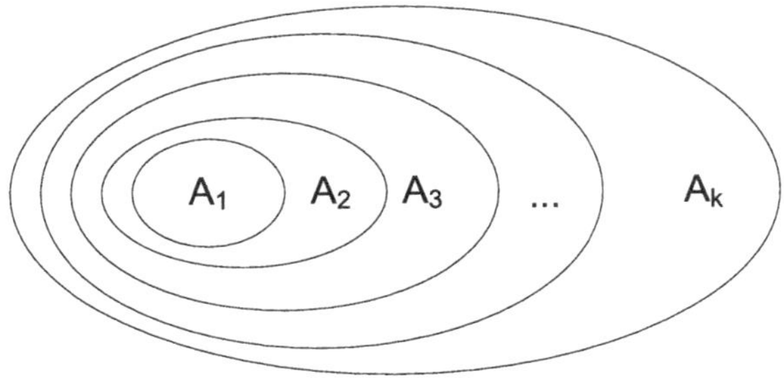

Fig. 1. The nested model for the vocabulary [19]

The whole vocabulary set in the system is categorized to a nested structure by adopting the vocabulary level test [6]. As shown in Fig. 1, the nested structure, formally named vocabulary nest, is defined as follows.

Definition 2. *A* ***vocabulary nest*** *for vocabulary V is denoted as P:*

$$P = \{A_1, A_2, ..., A_k, (A_1 \subset A_2 ... \subset A_k = V)\}, \tag{2}$$

where k is the total levels in a vocabulary nest, and the level of word called ***word rank*** *$r(w_a)$ is defined as the level of minimal vocabulary set to contain the w_a [19].*

The learner can then declare his/her knowledge levels m for the whole vocabulary set to avoid the additional input for each word. The formal definition is given as follows.

Definition 3. *Giving the user-declared knowledge level m, the knowledge level of ε_a^i is obtained by the* ***explicit acquisition function*** *below:*

$$\varepsilon_a^i = \begin{cases} 1 - \alpha^{m - r(w_a) + 1}, & r(w_a) \leq m \\ 0, & r(w_a) > m \end{cases} \tag{3}$$

where α is a factor to give different weights for words in different levels according to the user-declared knowledge level m [19].

3.2 Implicit Learner Profiling

Furthermore, the implicit acquisition method involves acquiring the knowledge level of words from external sources, e.g. a vocabulary test result, examination record. Given a test or examination result, it may have different levels of definition with the system. Therefore, we propose a solution which treats the record (including test/examination) as "a bag of words", and then maps it with the corresponding vocabulary set in the system. In this way, the closest level of difficulty for the vocabulary set is linked to the record directly. Given a record

$d = \{w_1, w_2, ..., w_d\}$ and record corpus D, we adopt the term-frequency and inverse document frequency (TF-IDF) [8] to calculate the word relevance to the document as:

$$rel(w_j) = \frac{f(w_j, d)}{max\{f(w, d) : w \in d\}} \times log \frac{|D|}{|d \in D : w_j \in d|} \tag{4}$$

where the first part is the normalized term frequency for word (term) w_j, the second one is the inverse document frequency which indicates the uniqueness of word w_j to this document d. Then, we rank the top-s relevant words $\{w'_1, w'_2, ..., w'_s\}$ of the document d and find the corresponding level of difficulty by a vote function:

$$vote(A_n) = \sum_{i=1}^{s} 1 - |sign(n - r(w'_i))| \tag{5}$$

where the $sign$ function is to indicate whether the word rank $r(w'_i)$ is equal to n or not. To be clear, the above part in sum can be transformed to the following piecewise function:

$$1 - |sign(n - r(w'_i))| = \begin{cases} 1, & r(w'_i) \neq n \\ 0, & r(w'_i) = n \end{cases} \tag{6}$$

To be specific, if more important words of this record d belong to a vocabulary set (or difficulty level) A_n, then we assume that n is the difficulty level of this document d. Similarly, we regard **rank (or difficulty level)** of a record as the maximal value of vote function.

Definition 4. *Given a record d, the* ***rank (or difficulty level)*** *denoted by* $r'(d)$, *is the maximal value of vote result:*

$$r'(d) = argmax_{(i)} vote(A_i) \tag{7}$$

By obtaining the difficulty level of this document, we therefore are able to find out the mastery level ε_a^i by the following **implicit acquisition function** below.

Definition 5. *Given learner i, word* w_a, *his/her record* d_i *and the grade of record* g_{d_i}, *the mastery level of* ε_a^i *is obtained by the implicit acquisition function as:*

$$\varepsilon_a^i = \begin{cases} g_{d_i} - \beta^{r'(d_i) - r(w_a) + 1}, & r(w_a) \leq r'(d_i) \\ 0, & r(w_a) > r'(d_i) \end{cases} \tag{8}$$

where $r(w_a)$ *denotes the rank of* w_a, $r'(d_i)$ *is the rank of the record* d_i,β *is similar to* α, *which is the damping factor to give different degrees of mastery according to the difficulty levels.*

For the learners who have multiple records, we can treat these multiple record as "a single one" and the learner profile is obtained accordingly. If a learner profile can be obtained in both explicit and implicit methods, then we can adopt the profile fusion method (e.g. linear combination) to handle this case.

3.3 Updating Mechanism

With the learner using the system for vocabulary learning, the knowledge levels of each words in the vocabulary will be changed accordingly. Therefore, a mechanism to update the knowledge levels in the learner profile is necessary. We propose two kinds of updating methods including time-decayed and feedback-driven update in this mechanism.

Time-Decayed Update. The learner may lose some information about recent acquired words if they do not review them, especially for second language (L2) learners. This observation is intuitive and obvious in the process of vocabulary acquisition. Therefore, we employ the time-decayed update by following the Ebbinghaus forgetting curve [10] in learner profile manager as:

$$\varepsilon_i^a|t = e^{-t/\varepsilon_a^i} \tag{9}$$

where $\varepsilon_i^a|t$ is the degree mastery of w_a by learner i without t units of time to review it, $varepsilon_a^i$ is current degree of mastery level. Note that this update operation is only for words that are retained recently, but not those which have been learnt before, e.g the review frequencies are greater than a certain threshold within a reasonable period. Besides, the update operation only works when a certain threshold of time is reached, otherwise it is too resource-consuming.

Feedback-Driven Update. After finishing a certain word-learning tasks, the mastery level of words should be updated accordingly. The feedback-driven update relies on whether the target word are retained or not.

$$\varepsilon_a^i = \begin{cases} 1, & 1-\gamma \le \varepsilon_a^i \le 1, t(w_a^i) = 1 \\ \varepsilon_a^i + \gamma, & 0 \le \varepsilon_a^i \le 1-\gamma, t(w_a^i) = 1 \\ \varepsilon_a^i - \gamma, & \gamma \le \varepsilon_a^i \le 1, t(w_a^i) = 0 \\ 0, & 0 \le \varepsilon_a^i \le \gamma, t(w_a^i) = 0 \end{cases} \tag{10}$$

where γ is the penalty/reward factor to the words in the task ($\gamma \in [0,1]$), $t(w_a)$ is the result whether the word is retained or not ('1' denotes that the word has been retained in the task, otherwise, '0' is given).

3.4 Word Learning Process

The last step of this model is how to suggest a personalized sequence of vocabulary learning tasks according to the information in the learner profile. We use the concept of **word coverage** from our earlier study [13]. This concept word coverage can be used to identify the learning tasks containing unfamiliar words to the learner.

Definition 6. *The* ***word coverage*** *is a measurement function* θ *to estimate unfamiliarity of all target words in a task* t *of learner* i.

$$\theta(t, i) = \sum_{\forall w_a \in t} \varepsilon_a^i \qquad (11)$$

where w_a *is a target vocabulary for learning in the task* t, *and* ε_a^i *denotes the knowledge level of the learner [19].*

4 Experiments

We have invited 32 ESL students to participate in our experiment. These participants have the language proficient with around IELTS Band 5.0, and we randomly divided them into two groups with equal group members. The setting of these two groups are detailed as follows.

- **Control Group.** The control group only adopts the explicit method introduced in the Sect. 3.1 to obtain their knowledge levels for all vocabulary in the system. The setting of control group is almost the same to our earlier study about the explicit profiling method [19].
- **Experimental Group.** The experimental uses the integrated method to consolidate explicit and implicit profiles. For simplicity in this preliminary study, we set the weights of two profiles as equal to 0.5, and adopt the linear combination method (weighted average).

The overall process of the experiments is consisted of three stages. First of all, a pre-test containing 20 target words is conducted to all participants to ensure they have least knowledge at the beginning of the experiment. The second stage is the learning processes, the learning tasks we adopted in the system follow the design, content and assessment criteria in [15,16]. In each cycle of the task learning, two tasks with the maximal unfamiliarity in the system are suggested, and the participant will select one of them. The tasks are set to be very short, which can be completed within 10 mins. The participants will learn about 10 learning tasks within two days. The final stage is a post-test to examine the knowledge of participants about these 20 target words.

The pre-test and post-test results are shown in Fig. 2. We can observe that both group have little knowledge about the target words in the first step (3.3 and 3.2 respectively). We have conduct the significant test among two groups for the pre-test and found that $t > 0.1$ (i.e., there is no significant differences). While the average score of control group in the post-test is 9.4, whereas the experimental group obtained the mean of 10.2 in the post-test. The significant test is also conducted and we find that $t < 0.05$ indicating there is significant differences among two groups. In other words, the fusion of the explicit and implicit profiles can reflect the vocabulary proficiency in a more accurate way.

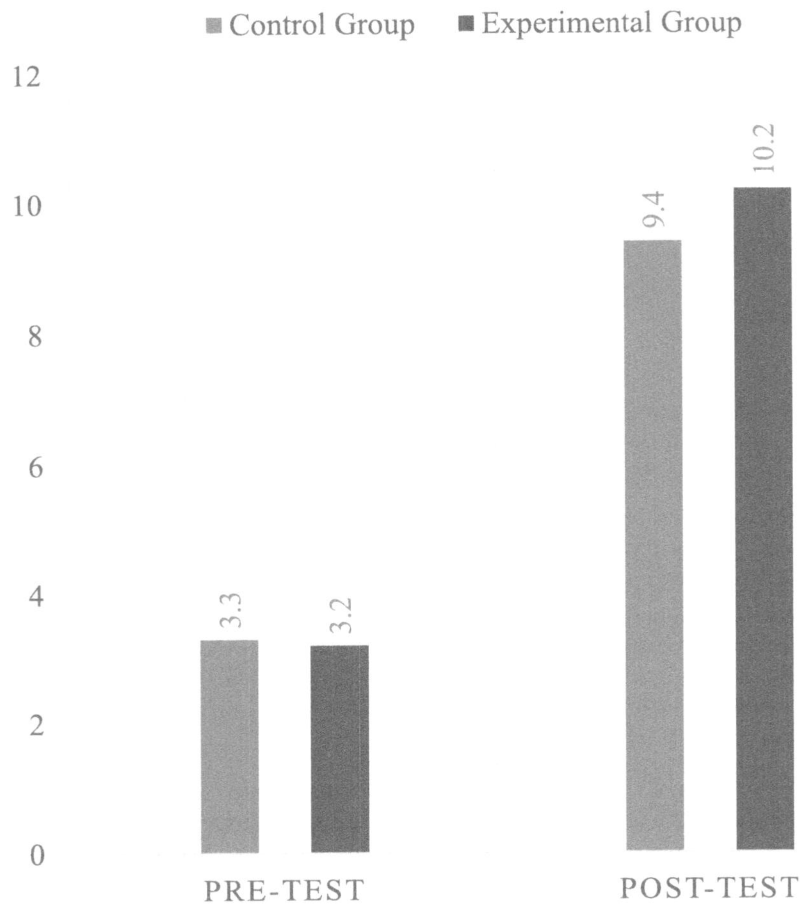

Fig. 2. The pre-test and post-test results in control and experimental group

5 Conclusion

In this article, we propose an integrated framework to consolidate the explicit and implicit profiles to facilitate personalized word learning. Furthermore, we present the updating mechanism during the learning process. In addition, a preliminary experiment is conducted, the results of which validate the effectiveness of the proposed integrated framework. For our future research studies, we plan to investigate the impact of the different weights for implicit and explicit user profiles. Another direction is to invite more participants in the experiments.

Acknowledgement. The work described in this paper was fully supported by the Start-Up Research Grant (RG 54/2017-2018R) of The Education University of Hong Kong and the Innovation and Technology Fund (Project No. GHP/022/17GD) from the Innovation and Technology Commission of the Government of the Hong Kong Special Administrative Region.

References

1. Chen, C.-M., Chung, C.-J.: Personalized mobile English vocabulary learning system based on item response theory and learning memory cycle. Comput. Educ. **51**(2), 624–645 (2008)
2. Chen, C.-M., Li, Y.-L.: Personalised context-aware ubiquitous learning system for supporting effective English vocabulary learning. Interact. Learn. Environ. **18**(4), 341–364 (2010)
3. Huang, Y.-M., Huang, Y.-M., Huang, S.-H., Lin, Y.-T.: A ubiquitous English vocabulary learning system: evidence of active/passive attitudes vs. usefulness/ease-of-use. Comput. Educ. **58**(1), 273–282 (2012)
4. Hulstijn, J.H., Laufer, B.: Some empirical evidence for the involvement load hypothesis in vocabulary acquisition. Lang. Learn. **51**(3), 539–558 (2001)
5. Landau, B., Smith, L.B., Jones, S.S.: The importance of shape in early lexical learning. Cogn. Dev. **3**(3), 299–321 (1988)
6. Laufer, B., Nation, P.: A vocabulary-size test of controlled productive ability. Lang. Test. **16**(1), 33–51 (1999)
7. Loucky, J.P.: Designing distance learning tasks to help maximize vocabulary development. Int. J. Virtual Pers. Learn. Environ. (IJVPLE) **3**(2), 35–58 (2012)
8. Jones, K.S.: A statistical interpretation of term specificity and its application in retrieval. J. Doc. **28**(1), 11–21 (1972)
9. Sugiyama, K., Hatano, K., Yoshikawa, M.: Adaptive web search based on user profile constructed without any effort from users. In: Proceedings of the 13th International Conference on World Wide Web, pp. 675–684. ACM (2004)
10. Wixted, J.T., Ebbesen, E.B.: Genuine power curves in forgetting: a quantitative analysis of individual subject forgetting functions. Mem. Cogn. **25**(5), 731–739 (1997)
11. Wu, D., Im, I., Tremaine, M., Instone, K., Turoff, M.: A framework for classifying personalization scheme used on e-commerce websites. In: 2003 Proceedings of the 36th Annual Hawaii International Conference on System Sciences, 12 p. IEEE (2003)
12. Xie, H., Li, Q., Mao, X., Li, X., Cai, Y., Rao, Y.: Community-aware user profile enrichment in folksonomy. Neural Netw. **58**, 111–121 (2014)
13. Xie, H., Zou, D., Lau, R.Y.K., Wang, F.L., Wong, T.-L.: Generating incidental word-learning tasks via topic-based and load-based profiles. IEEE Multimedia **23**(1), 60–70 (2016)
14. Xie, H., Zou, D., Wang, F.L., Wong, T.-L., Rao, Y.: Discover learning path for group users: a profile-based approach. Neurocomputing **254**, 59–70 (2017)
15. Zou, D.: Comparing dictionary-induced vocabulary learning and inferencing in the context of reading. Lexikos **26**(1), 372–390 (2016)
16. Zou, D.: Vocabulary acquisition through cloze exercises, sentence-writing and composition-writing: extending the evaluation component of the involvement load hypothesis. Lang. Teach. Res. **21**(1), 54–75 (2017)

17. Zou, D., Xie, H., Li, Q., Wang, F.L., Chen, W.: The load-based learner profile for incidental word learning task generation. In: Popescu, E., Lau, R.W.H., Pata, K., Leung, H., Laanpere, M. (eds.) ICWL 2014. LNCS, vol. 8613, pp. 190–200. Springer, Cham (2014). https://doi.org/10.1007/978-3-319-09635-3_21
18. Zou, D., Xie, H., Rao, Y., Wong, T.-L., Wang, F.L., Wu, Q.: A comparative study on various vocabulary knowledge scales for predicting vocabulary pre-knowledge. Int. J. Distance Educ. Technol. (IJDET) **15**(1), 69–81 (2017)
19. Zou, D., Xie, H., Wong, T.-L., Wang, F.L., Kwan, R., Chan, W.H.: An explicit learner profiling model for personalized word learning recommendation. In: Huang, T.-C., Lau, R., Huang, Y.-M., Spaniol, M., Yuen, C.-H. (eds.) SETE 2017. LNCS, vol. 10676, pp. 495–499. Springer, Cham (2017). https://doi.org/10.1007/978-3-319-71084-6_58

The Application Model of Wearable Devices in Physical Education

Rong Miao[1(✉)], Qian Dong[1(✉)], Wen Yong Weng[2], and Xi Yuan Yu[3]

[1] Department of Educational Technology, Graduate School of Education, Peking University, Beijing, China
{miao, st16625m}@gse.pku.edu.cn

[2] Zhejiang Nbugs Technology Limited Company, Zhejiang, China

[3] Zhaoqing NO.1 Experimental Middle School, Guangdong, China

Abstract. The rapid development of wearable technology has led to the expectation that people will apply technology to physical education. But for an independent device, there is a problem that needs to be solved, that is, how to apply it to the PE class. In this research, we design a model using wearable devices to collect data and give feedback in time, and to help teachers grasp students' exercise load timely, so as to ensure students' training safety and promote scientific and effective evaluation. Using this model, the experiment was carried out in the primary school of Zhaoqing City, Guangdong Province to verify the rationality of the design.

Keywords: Wearable devices · Physical education · Model

1 Background

1.1 Research Significance

As a compulsory course, physical education has played an important role in developing students' participation in physical exercise, improving their physical quality, enhancing their physical health and promoting their all-round development. In December 2017, the notice of Ministry of education on the management standard of compulsory education school clearly pointed out that every school should ensure that students exercise time at least 1 h a day, and they should have enough physical education lessons [1].

However, the security problems in physical activities have become one of the main factors that restrict the policy of physical education in primary and secondary schools in China [2]. So how can we guarantee the scientific and rational training of physical education course? How to evaluate whether the student's exercise load reach the standard on the premise of safety of students?

In recent years, wearable devices have been used more and more in education because of its unique advantages of convenience to carry and interaction. In this paper, we introduce wearable devices into physical education.

S. K. S. Cheung et al. (Eds.): ICBL 2018, LNCS 10949, pp. 311–322, 2018.
https://doi.org/10.1007/978-3-319-94505-7_25

1.2 Development of Wearable Devices

In the 1960s, Professor Alex Pentland, director of the Human Dynamics Laboratory at Massachusetts Institute of Technology started a project named wearable computing. In 2012, the emergence of Google Glass has created the first year of using wearable devices.

In Media Lab of Massachusetts Institute of Technology, wearable computing is defined as a combination of multimedia and computer technology and highlight infinitely to input or output instruments in body indistinctly, such as jewelry, glasses or clothes, and it can connect personal LAN function, detect the specific situation or become a private intelligence assistant, and then become user information processing tools in action [3]. In the Horizon Report, wearable technology refers to smart devices, which can be worn by users and take the form of an accessory such as jewelry or eyewear. Smart textiles also allow items of clothing. Wearable format enables the convenient integration of tools into user's everyday life, allowing seamless tracking of personal data such as sleep, movement, location, and social media interactions [4]. For the classification of wearable devices, there is no clear classification at present. Feng Shun tian thinks, according to the physical form, it can be divided into glasses, watches, hand rings, gloves, necklaces, pendant, head hoop, etc. According to its application type, it can be divided into health, safety, game and so on [5].

Through the above definition, wearable devices can be understood as a convenient user - to - day device combined with multimedia, radio, sensor and other technologies. These devices are portable, wearable, user focused, intelligent interactive and highly integrated [6]. They can be used as an information and communication tool seamlessly in learning, living and working environments, and distract users' attention less.

In recent years, with the development of mobile Internet and hardware technology, the function of wearable devices changes. It becomes more convenient, easier to interact and better in real-time performance. Besides, they have been used wider in many fields, such as medical, fire protection, military, disabled aid, entertainment, design etc [7, 8]. Wearable devices also lead to expectation that people will apply them into teaching and learning with their unique advantages.

1.3 Research on the Application of Wearable Devices in Education

With the emergence of products such as Google Glass, Muse and Fitbits, Amazon built a wearable technology store in 2014. Educators begin to rethink the impact of wearable devices on education [9]. The education field has opened the test, development and application of wearable technology, such as recording students' learning behavior, enhancing students' interactive experience and so on.

For example, Victor R. Lee, Joel Drake, Kylie Williamson have applied wearable devices to PE class, they collect data from physical activities, analyze students' physical movement, heart rate, quantify rest time, and compare the steps of tall and short students [10]. Elena et al. [11] have introduced IoT (Internet of Things) technology and wearable technology into task-based child language learning course to help students focus on interaction and track students' interaction behavior.

In order to solve the problem of increasing number of obese and overweight children in post-industrial society, Lindberg et al. [12] have developed a sports game called Running Othello 2 (RO2), which uses wearable devices to record students' movements and heart rate. They evaluate the application of RO2 sports games in PE class of grade three students in South Korea. It shows that students playing RO2 game have better learning effect, higher participation and an increase heart rate.

Song and Xu [13] carried on the analysis to the application of wearable devices in PE class based on SWOT model. They believe that wearable devices in PE class in primary and middle schools can help students construct a motion database for a long time, and it is conducive to teachers' scientific guidance. But the price of devices is high and the function cannot fully meet the daily PE class.

Borthwick et al. [9] believe that as for the application of wearable devices in education, there coexist challenges and problems. On the one hand, it is conducive to the promotion of students' participation, carry out a full range of design, know more needs of students and help establish students' records. On the other hand, wearable devices may have privacy and security problems, like excessive exposure of personal information, data storage and use, etc. In addition, using wearable devices may lead to reform of teaching environment, and the teachers' strategies at school.

2 Application Model of Wearable Devices in Physical Education

2.1 Exercise Load

Exercises load is an important factor to achieve instructional objectives of physical education. It is a quantitative description of the internal and external physical activity of body at a given time. The basic factors that describe the exercise load include content of motion, intensity of motion, quantity of movement and density of motion. The exercise intensity includes the average heart rate during the stage of basic part, the average heart rate, maximum heart rate and heart rate index in PE class [14]. Different types of PE classes have different requirements for exercise load [15]. For example, the new teaching class is generally a medium load, while class for the development of physical quality of students is generally high load. A PE class is usually divided into 3 parts, that is, preparation part, basic part and end part in turn [16].

According to the "primary and middle school students physical exercise load health standards" (WS/T 101-1998) [17], the way to test exercise load is to test each student in a PE class or sports activities at the basic part of 10 s heart rate, and then convert the number into a minute heart rate. If the average heart rate during the basic part is between 120–200 times per min, the exercise load is verified to be appropriate. According to PE monitoring and evaluation of technical specifications (Trial) [18] for primary and middle school in Dongcheng District, Beijing, sport intensity index includes average heart rate, average heart rate during the basic part, maximum heart rate, heart rate index. What's more, it is supplemented by heart rate curve, students and teachers jointly evaluate the scale of the exercise load in PE class.

In this paper, we combine measurement data, students' subjective feelings and teachers' observation to judge the exercise load in PE class. It can collect data from 3 sides. This paper adopts this way to verify reasonableness of the application model.

2.2 Application Model of Wearable Devices

We put forward the WST model as Fig. 1 to help teachers understand students' exercise load timely, adjust training activities, and make early warning for students' physical exercise load that may occur in PE class.

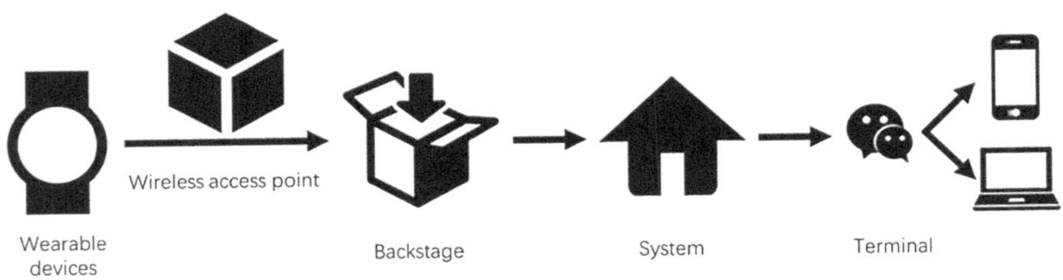

Fig. 1. The WST model of wearable devices applied to physical education

Before PE class, students' basic information data, such as height, weight and grade, are collected into the backstage and connected to the corresponding wearable devices. The wearable devices used in this article is called "love buckle health" (product model: CoCoQCB2). The wearable wristbands are mainly applied to buckle students' health data. By collecting students in real time heart rate data with bracelet, and then through 433M or Bluetooth wireless transmission technology, the devices transmit the data to the server, the server generates the data processing of large data analysis results and suggestions, which would be sent to user terminals.

During students' exercise process, wearable devices collect students' movement data. Then the collected data will be transmitted to the backstage through wireless access point. Next, the backstage analyzes the collected data and imports results into the system. After the certain processing, the system sends the data to user terminals.

During the PE class, teachers can view students exercise data, such as the maximum heart rate, heart rate, heart rate index, etc. through computer, mobile devices. Besides, the data can also be derived through the terminal after class for further analysis.

In WST mode, data collected by wearable devices is processed and analyzed by the system platform, and it is presented on the website, mobile devices and other terminal devices. For PE teachers, it's possible to know students' sports data timely, understand students' exercise load, and realize students' safety more accurately.

3 Experimental Verification Design

3.1 Participants

The participants of this study were 59 fifth-grade students in an elementary school in Zhaoqing City, Guangdong Province. In the experiment, students were randomly divided into two groups, which were labeled as class A (30) and class B (29). In class A and B, 10 students were chosen to wear wearable devices as samples.

The selection of samples follows the following three principles: first, choose among healthy students. According to the definition of health standard WS/T 101-1998 for physical exercise in primary and middle schools, healthy students refer to students who can take physical education according to the syllabus of physical education and exercise regularly. Second, select the students according to their sports performance. The number of level A, B and C in sports achievement in class A is 17, 10 and 3 respectively. While in class B is 22, 5 and 2 respectively. Third, the proportion of boys and girls is appropriate. The number of male, female in class A were 17 and 13 respectively, while class B was 18 and 11 respectively.

3.2 Measurement Tool

In this paper, we design the application mode in PE class, which aims to build a bridge between teachers and students through wearable devices. In addition, through the comparison of teacher observation, traditional pulse measurement and student's subjective feelings expression and the student motion data collected by wearable devices, the three kinds data cross comparison is formed (Fig. 2).

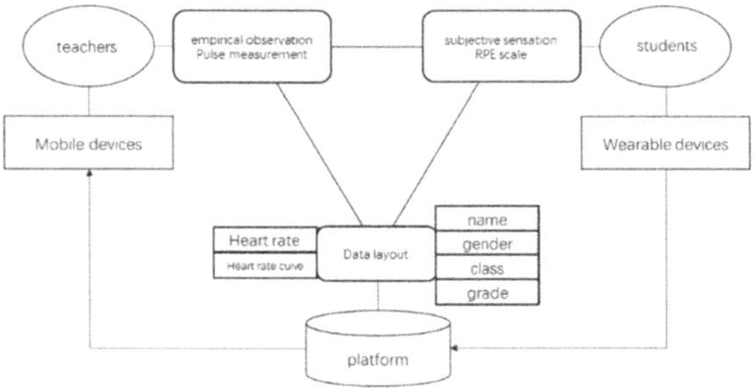

Fig. 2. Research tools design

3.2.1 Heart Rate Measurement

A stopwatch and wearable devices are used to measure the pulse and heart rate.

Traditional pulse measurement refers to the "health standards for physical exercise of primary and middle school students" (WS/T 101-1998) [20]. The wearable device's measurement of heart rate is to get students' heart rate data through a sensor. According to technical specifications for monitoring and evaluation of exercise load in primary and secondary schools in Dongcheng District, Beijing [18], the specific measurement data and standards are as follows.

Average Heart Rate: the average heart rate refers to average heart rate in the whole PE class, and it is appropriate in 130–170 times/min in exercise period. Average heart rate $= \frac{\frac{x_1 + x_n}{2} + x_2 + x_3 + \cdots + x_{n-1}}{n-1}$. x_n means the nth real time heart rate for 3 min.

Maximum Heart Rate: the maximum heart rate refers to the maximum heart rate of students in the whole PE class, generally not more than 200 times/min.

Heart Rate Index: the heart rate index refers to the ratio of the average heart rate to the quiet heart rate. The calculation formula is the heart rate index = average heart rate/quiet heart rate. The quiet heart rate value is when students keep quiet from 5 to 10 min. The suitable heart rate index value is 1.6–1.8 for exercise load.

Heart Rate Curve: the system platform can generate a student's heart rate curve of the whole class and 10 min after class. The diagram takes time as a horizontal coordinate, and the heart rate is a longitudinal coordinate. According to the change of the curve, it is easy to evaluate whether the sports load is suitable. It is qualified that the peak of the heart rate curve appears in the middle part of the basic part in class [19].

3.2.2 RPE Scale

After class, students fill in the RPE scale proposed by Brog [20]. RPE scale is a widely used subjective evaluation of exercise load scale. Scale from 0 to 9 indicates in a sense that there are 10 levels of subjective motion.

3.3 Procedure

The experiment was carried out for three days. Day 1 is the pre-experiment for the aim of testing whether the hand ring and the platform could be used normally. Day 2 and Day 3 are for the formal experiment. The specific process is as follows:

(1) Before class, Students in Class A and Class B wear bracelets 5–10 min to measure the students' quiet heart rate.
(2) On the formal teaching stage, all students complete a 45 min course in accordance with the requirements of the PE teacher. The observation of teachers in class, the use of traditional methods to measure students' pulse will be the reference.
(3) After class, students continue to wear wearable devices (bracelet) for about 10 min and fill in the RPE scale.

4 Data Analysis

Data analysis includes two parts: Part 1 is the analysis of data collected by wearable devices and exercise load reference value. Part 2 is comparison analysis of the data collected by wearable devices (bracelet) and students' pulse data collected by traditional way of measurement. The pulse data is collected from a boy and a girl.

4.1 Wearable Devices Data and Exercise Load

Table 1 is the heart rate data of class A students in the first day and the second day (Fig. 3).

Table 1. Students' heart rate data of Class A

Class A	Day 1				Day 2			
Number times/min	Min heart rate	Average heart rate	Max heart rate	Heart rate index	Min heart rate	Average heart rate	Max heart rate	Heart rate index
Min	**47**	76	94	0.88	**43**	84	116	0.95
Average	**53**	**88**	**134**	**1.112**	**61**	**90**	**140**	**1.099**
Max	64	99	**171**	1.44	75	103	**171**	1.34

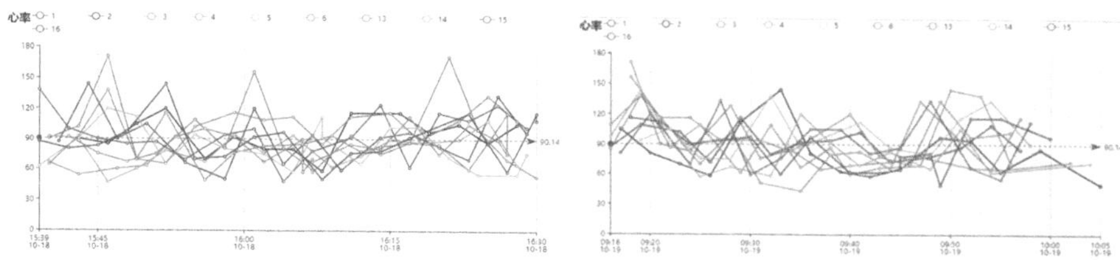

Fig. 3. Heart rate curve of Class A_Day 1 and Day 2

The heart rate data of these two days are similar. Below are the heart rate curve of Day 1 and day 2 in class A.

Table 2 shows the heart rate data of Day 1 and day 2 in class B (Fig. 4).

Table 2. Students' heart rate data of Class B

Class B	Day 1				Day 2			
Number times/min	Min heart rate	Average heart rate	Max heart rate	Heart rate index	Min heart rate	Average heart rate	Max heart rate	Heart rate index
Min	**48**	75	92	0.82	**46**	74	102	0.94
Average	**56**	**86**	**132**	**0.999**	**59**	**88**	**130**	**1.13**
Max	62	95	**171**	1.12	67	107	**163**	1.39

The heart rate data of these two days are also similar. Below are the heart rate curve of Day 1 and day 2 in class B.

From above data, student's heart rate doesn't show consistency, and it seems relatively messy. The reason may be students' movement is by group, and each physical activity interval is about 1 min. For example, students take less than 1 min to

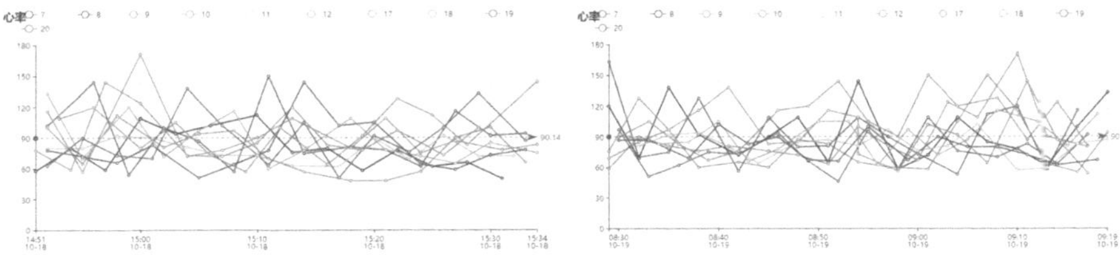

Fig. 4. Heart rate curve of Class B_Day 1 and Day 2

complete running, while the data is collected by 3 min, namely the bracelet probably cannot collect the maximum heart rate of student's movement because of slightly longer time interval, so as to result in heart rate deviation.

Comparing the heart rate index of Class A and B, it is found that the heart rate index measured by wearable devices is much lower than that of exercise standard 1.6–1.8. Through interviewing teachers, they think that the minimum heart rate of students may be 180 times per minute during activity, that is, the data collected by wearable devices is also lower than the teacher's empirical judgement.

In order to explore possible reasons, we compare the students' RPE scale. In the pre-experiment, 55% of the students think that the basic part of the class is a little stronger. On Day 1, the students' data are partially missing. On Day 2, 45% students believe that the strength of the basic part of PE class is suitable, a little strong or strong.

Comparing data collected by wearable devices, teachers' experience, students' RPE scale and exercise standard, both teachers and students think exercise load is appropriate, it should be suitable for standard movement, that is, the heart rate index should be between 1.6–1.8, and the heart rate data collected by wearable devices may be lower.

4.2 Wearable Devices Data and Pulse Measured by Traditional Way

In order to further test whether the hypothesis is right, we compare data collected by wearable devices with pulse measured by traditional way (Table 3). It is important to note that, in general, the heart rate is equal to pulse value. The PE teacher select two students (1 male, 1 female) in class B, to measure students' pulse in real time through the traditional way. The following are the heart rate and traditional pulse data at different minute between 9:00–10:00 (Fig. 5).

We find that for male student, the average heart rate is 129 times/min, quiet heart rate was 78 times/min, heart rate index is 1.67 measured by traditional way. While it shows that the average heart rate is 91 times/min, quiet heart rate is 86 times/min, heart rate index is 1.06 in the bracelet. For female student, the average heart rate is 136 times/min, quiet heart rate is 84 times per minute, heart rate index is 1.62. While it shows that the average heart rate is 103 times/min, quiet heart rate is 77 times/min, heart rate index is 1.34 in the bracelet. By comparing the data, it is found that the heart rate of the bracelet is lower than that of the traditional pulse value. The calculated heart rate index is consistent with teachers' experience and student's subjective feeling. It shows that students' exercise intensity is suitable.

Table 3. Data collected by wearable devices and pulse measured by traditional way

male			
Min	stage	Heart rate	Traditional pulse
15	Before ware-up		78
16		87	
19		109	
20	jogging		108
22	Before shuttle run		114
23		102	
26		72	
29		116	
30	After shuttle run		180
32		80	
34	Practice explanation		102
35	Shuttle run	92	138
38		94	
39			126
41	Practice explanation	102	
42	Crouching start runing		108
44		73	
45	Crouching start runing		210
47			152
48		78	
49	practice		120
51		87	
53	relax		120
54		109	
57		85	

female		
min	Heart rate	Traditional pulse
15		84
18	156	
20		138
21	116	
22		156
24	116	
27	94	
30		144
31	94	
34	83	126
35		120
37	102	
39		116
40	120	
42		144
43	78	
45		174
46	70	
47		174
49	133	126
52	97	
53		132

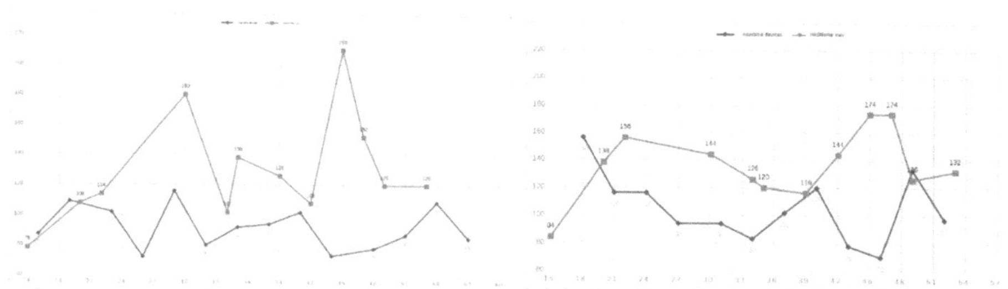

Fig. 5. Comparison of data collected by wearable devices and pulse measured by traditional way of a male student and a female student

By comparing the heart rate data with pulse data, we find that the data of wearable devices is not accurate, it is necessary to improve the accuracy of measured data.

5 Conclusion and Discussion

This study explores the application model of wearable devices in PE class through the quasi experiment. Through analyzing data, we discuss rationality of the application model of wearable devices in PE class and how to improve the function in this model.

5.1 Rationality of the Model

The WST model put independent wearable devices used in PE class, we can collect students' data by wearable devices in time through wireless access point, and then transmit it to the system to be further analyzed, and the final terminal equipment shows the result so that teachers can use mobile phone, tablet and other mobile devices viewing students' data in class. If the student heart rate exceeds 200 per minute, the bracelet can timely vibration alarm, which can prompt students and teachers to ensure that students' training within their personal exercise load.

The WST model can record students' exercise data in the whole process of exercise. On one hand, teachers can get their students' movement data, and make early warning and prompt. On the other hand, the data can be used in educational evaluation and design to assistant teachers to carry out more accurate and scientific activities so as to facilitate students' individualized training. In addition, Using WST model in a long term contributes to the formation of students' personality profiles, promote educational evaluation from empiricism to data, from the group evaluation to individual evaluation, from summarized evaluation to formative evaluation, therefore, it can effectively promote the improvement of PE class.

5.2 Function Improvement of WST Model

In this study, we compare data collected by wearable devices, teacher empirical observation, traditional pulse data and students' subjective feelings to verify the feasibility and rationality of wearable devices applied in PE class.

From the data analysis of bracelet, compared with standard reference, it demonstrates that the minimum heart rate, average heart rate, maximum heart rate and heart rate index indicates students' exercise intensity are relatively low.

From the analysis of RPE scale of students, we find that students' feeling in different stages and heart rate curve in class are consistent with the bracelet data, but there exists a contradiction that the bracelet data is low while the subjective feeling is high.

According to the observation and analysis of the teachers, the data of wearable devices is preliminarily lower. Using traditional way to measure student's pulse and comparing with bracelet heart rate data, it shows that the heart rate data of bracelet is tendency with those of traditional pulse measurement data, but the bracelet data is lower on the whole.

Besides, as we see in the figs, there are a few abnormal points, namely, the bracelet data and traditional pulse data present opposite trend. According to recorded activities, the reason may be activity time intervals between the bracelet and traditional pulse measurement. For example, the bracelet measures data every 3 min, it collects the student's heart rate for third, sixth minutes, but traditional way may measure the fourth, fifth minute data. Shuttle run process is fast, however, training interval is basically less than a minute. It's possible that bracelet collects motion data while traditional pulse measures resting data, which leads to abnormal motion trend.

Based on this, the function of wearable devices applied in the WST model in PE class needs to be improved, and the algorithm needs to be optimized. For example, the time interval between data acquisition is recommended in 1 min and the bracelet needs to continuously improve data accuracy. On the basis of ensuring the stability of data acquisition, the time interval of data measurement and transmission can be shortened.

Furthermore, this research only uses the heart rate as the main index to judge the exercise load of students, other indicators, such as step number, trajectory may also be used in class. At the same time, for different types and age groups, wearable devices can help us test and analyze whether there are differences in reference standards of exercise load. The application of wearable devices to be used in other courses is also the direction of the future study.

References

1. Ministry of Education, People's Republic of China: Notifications of the Ministry of education on the issuance of the standards for the management of compulsory education schools [EB/OL]. http://www.moe.gov.cn/srcsite/A06/s3321/201712/t20171211_321026.html. Accessed 05 Dec 2017
2. Sun, C.: Study on exercise safety problems and countermeasures in primary and secondary schools. Sports Expo **13**, 63 (2011)
3. Wikipedia: Interaction paradigm [EB/OL]. http://zh.wikipedia.org/wiki/Interaction_paradigm. Accessed 02 Apr 2014
4. Adams Becker, S., Freeman, A., Giesinger Hall, C., Cummins, M., Yuhnke, B.: NMC/CoSN Horizon Report: 2016K-12 Edition. The New Media Consortium, Austin (2016)
5. Feng, S.: Development status and trend of wearable devices. Inf. Commun. Technol. **3**, 52–57 (2014)
6. Liu, H., Jun, S., X, Wu: The enlightenment of wearable technology to the construction of intelligent teaching environment. China Educ. Technol. **10**, 57–61 (2016)
7. Yu, N., Chen, D., Xia, H.: New development of wearable computing technology and its applications. Digit. Commun. **39**(4), 13–20 (2012)
8. Johnson, L., Adams, S., Becker, M., Cummings, V., Estrada, A., Freeman, H., DeGette, L., Zhang, T., Yin, B., Yin, L., Bai, X.: New media alliance horizon report (2013 Higher Education Edition) Part I. J. Beijing Radio Televis. Univ. (S1), 5–29+80 (2013)
9. Borthwick, A.C., Anderson, C.L., Finsness, E.S., et al.: Special article personal wearable technologies in education: value or villain? J. Digit. Learn. Teach. Educ. **31**(3), 85–92 (2015)
10. Lee, V.R., Drake, J., Williamson, K.: Let's get physical: K-12 students using wearable devices to obtain and learn about data from physical activities. Techtrends **59**(4), 46–53 (2015)
11. Elena, D.L.G., Camacho, V., Orozco-Barbosa, L., et al.: Introducing IoT and wearable technologies into task-based language learning for young children. IEEE Trans. Learn. Technol. **PP**(99), 366–378 (2016)
12. Lindberg, R., Seo, J., Laine, T.H.: Enhancing physical education with exergames and wearable technology. IEEE Trans. Learn. Technol. **9**(4), 328–341 (2016)
13. Song, Z., Xu, X.: The application of wearable devices in physical education—analysis based on SWOT model. Mod. Sports Sci. Technol. **6**(34), 111–112 (2016)
14. Wang, G., Hu, J.: Analysis on exercise workload and physiology workload. J. Chengdu Sport Univ. (4), 96 (1996)

15. Mao, Z., Lai, T.: How to treat the exercise load in physical education. School Sports China **11**, 28–31 (2006)
16. Huang, J., Qin, Y., An, C., et al.: A survey on exercise load of some primary and middle school students in Dongcheng District, Beijing. Chin. J. School Health **29**(5), 448–449 (2008)
17. Ministry of Health of the PRC: Health standard of physical exercise load for primary and middle school students WS/T 101-1998. Standards Press of China, Beijing (1998)
18. Exercise load monitoring project group in Dongcheng District: Technical specifications for monitoring and evaluation of exercise load in primary and secondary schools in Dongcheng District (Trial) [EB/OL]. https://wenku.baidu.com/view/c939dae4336c1eb91a375df5.html. Accessed 29 Sept 2015
19. Yi, S., Ma, J.: Instruction of physical education and extracurricular sports activities for children and adolescents, pp. 17–20. Medical Publishing House of Peking University, Beijing (2013)
20. Borg, G.A.: Psychophysical bases of perceived exertion. Med. Sci. Sports Exerc. **14**(5), 377 (1982)

Develop the Interactive Feedback Portfolio System with iBeacon Technology Applied in Flipped Classroom Learning Activities

Hung-Hsu Tsai[1(✉)], Xin-Yu Hou[1], You-Ming Yong[1], Kuo-Ching Chiou[2], and Pao-Ta Yu[3]

[1] Department of Information Management, National Formosa University, Yunlin, Taiwan
thh@nfu.edu.tw, {40441125,40241146}@gm.nfu.edu.tw
[2] Department of Finance, Chaoyang University of Technology, Taichung, Taiwan
kcchiou@cyut.edu.tw
[3] Department of Computer Science and Information Engineering, National Chung Cheng University, Chiayi, Taiwan
csipty@cs.ccu.edu.tw

Abstract. The paper proposes an interactive feedback portfolio (IFEP) system with iBeacon technology which is used in classroom to support the flipped classroom learning activities. The use of the IFEP system aims at promoting high interaction in classroom learning, which consists of APPs students used and web-interface functions teachers utilized. Students enable the APP in their smart phones and then the APP scan iBeacon devices. The detection statuses of iBeacon devices in classrooms can be automatically recorded in the cloud space. As a result, students' presence in classroom can be obtained automatically. Teachers can use another function the IFEP system offers to promote the interaction in classroom via displaying questions on the front screen in classroom. Meanwhile, it pushes (multicasts) these questions to students' smart phones via web-socket technology. Subsequently, students employ APP to feedback their responses to these questions. During collecting students' responses, the system also exhibits the temporary results of students' responses on screen and displays count-down time signal. This way can inspire students' interaction and interest to join the quiz-like activities. Teachers can quickly get the results of responses for students' answers. These results including students' presence in classroom and correction rates students' responses can be readily analyzed for their correlations on learning performance in the future. Moreover, teachers can quickly obtain students' learning achievements in classroom and then teachers may adjust their instructional strategies.

Keywords: Interactive feedback portfolio · Flipped classroom
Web socket · iBeacon · Blend learning

S. K. S. Cheung et al. (Eds.): ICBL 2018, LNCS 10949, pp. 323–332, 2018.
https://doi.org/10.1007/978-3-319-94505-7_26

1 Introduction

In the classroom, how to gain students' engagement and immediate feedback is a critical research for blended learning [1]. Especially, within higher education, it is an emerging event to develop the appropriate or easy-operation tools for instructors and students. Nowadays, Kahoot, which is an eLearning tool, was developed to support the kind of classroom learning. Its easy operations can support the learning activities of higher education classrooms. Therefore, one of merits of using Kahoot is that instructors and students can save training time for classroom learning. A feature of designing Kahoot is to add instructional-game fashion. Articles indicate that involving instructional games in the design of learning environments can effectively reach educational goals [2]. The benefits of using Kahoot in classrooms in higher education for teachers and students are to quickly get real-time feedbacks students sent on quizzes, and to enjoyably participate in the kind of highly interactive activity in classroom, respectively. Moreover, the results of surveys on quizzes according to students' feedbacks mentioned above can be used in tailoring teachers' instructional designs or appropriate disciplines.

Another eLearning tool, ZUVIO, for getting immediate feedbacks students offer is an online interactive platform while teaching and learning [3]. Its purpose is to promote instructional quality and students' participation. Teachers start to carry out quizzes in classroom. Subsequently, students utilize various digital devices such as smartphones, tablets, or computers, to immediately provide their answers to questions in quizzes [4].

However, several limits of using Kahoot in classroom learning are given as follows. First, it offers no students identifications to have a difficulty to trace their learning achievements when performing personal learning. Second, it is inappropriate to support the class with many students in classroom due to a limit for students, in the rear region of the classroom, who almost unclearly watch the content on the front screen. Third, students need to type data such as URLs of web servers and pin numbers on their smartphones before starting to answer questions. Moreover, it just shows the final results of students' answer for when time slot of replying each question is expired. Unfortunately, there is no the function of dynamically displaying temporary real-time results of answers students reply during answering each question. As a result, its design lacks the competition-like learning strategy while answering question. Furthermore, students cannot query their answers they ever replied, and also assessments results of answers students offer. Finally, it ignores to keep accumulative results of students' answers for each question in its cloud space. Consequently, it cannot provide appropriate cloud services via computing these accumulative results of students' answers.

Regarding to ZUVIO, there are limits of using it in classroom learning, which are provided as follows. First, it cannot make sure students' presence in classroom. Second, it cannot show questions in the front screen in classroom. Therefore, its design lacks instructional games and competition-like learning strategies. Note that some limits for ZUVIO are skipped here due to the same as using Kahoot. Table 1 presents comparison results of these two tools in terms of several factors including student identification, detection of student presence in classroom, typing data before answering questions, dynamically displaying real-time results, questions display, accumulative results of students' answers for each question, and getting assessment results.

Table 1. Comparison results of these three tools in terms of several factors while involving them in classroom learning.

Limits	Kahoot	Zuvio	IFEP
Student identification	Anonymous	Require students' identification while using APPs	Require students' identification while using APPs
Students' presence in classroom	Yes	No	Yes. Students' APP scan iBeacon devices set up at classroom
Integrating instructional games in the system design	Yes	No	Yes
Providing competition-like learning while answering question	Yes	No	Yes
Typing some data for answering question	Require to type URL and pin number before answering questions	No. It uses APPs to answer questions	No. APPs scan iBeacon devices set up at classroom, and then trigger off a corresponding link saved in iBeacon cloud space
Dynamically displaying temporary real-time results during answering each question	No. After answering each question, the system shows results of students' answers	No. A question sheet is sent to students' APP. The results of students' answers for the question sheet are displayed when finishing answering questions	Yes
Questions displayed in the front screen in classroom	Yes. A disadvantage of its design is that students in the rear area of the classroom have a difficulty to see questions	No	Yes. Questions are not only are displayed in the front screen but also are pushed on students' smartphones
Accumulative results of students' answers for each question are restored in cloud space of the system	No. A need to have accumulative results for each question via computing assessment results for each question on each time	No	Yes
Students can query their assessments results of students' answers and answers they ever replied	No	Yes	Yes
System's cloud space also has a copy of the assessment results for each question sheet and questions in the sheet	No	Yes	Yes

According to the comparisons shown in Table 1, this motivates us to develop the IFEP system with iBeacon technology to improve these tools. The features of the IFEP system are briefly summarized here, which can be found in Table 1. The main features of the design of the IFEP system aim at supporting learning activities of flipped classroom in order to achieve higher interaction teachers and students in classroom. These key functions include automatic detection of student presence in classroom, integrations of both instructional games and competition-like learning strategies, and cloud services for computing accumulative assessment results of students' answers.

In Sect. 2, some related literatures for backgrounds are reviewed. In Sect. 3, the IFEP system is briefly described. In Sect. 4, an instructional design according to the use of the IFEP system to support flipped classroom for learning a course in higher education. Finally, conclusions are drawn in Sect. 5.

2 Backgrounds

2.1 WebSocket

Websocket is a communication protocol over TCP, which is specified in the specification of HTML5. In the traditional HTTP protocol, clients have to connect the web server first, and then web server send web files to clients' web browsers. Moreover, client users require to renew web pages manually, and then the new contents of the web page are sent to clients' web browsers to renew the web page.

Once websocket connections or sessions are set up between client and server, data transformation by two-way communication. When new contents of web pages are updated, the sever can actively push new contents to clients' web browsers. Therefore, a main benefit of using websocket technology is that clients do not need renew web pages manually by a polling way. The purpose of this websocket technology is to offer a mechanism for browser-based applications that need two-way communication with servers that does not depend on opening multiple HTTP connections (e.g., using XMLHttpRequest or <iframe>s and long polling) [5–7].

2.2 A Review of iBeacon

iBeacon is a title of a technology standard, which proposed by Apple company. It offers Mobile Apps (running on both iOS and Android devices) to query beacons in the physical world by listening for signals and react corresponding actions. Obviously, iBeacon technology allows Mobile Apps to get their position on a micro-local scale, and send hyper-contextual content to users based on location. Bluetooth Low Energy is the underlying communication technology for iBeacon.

2.3 Bluetooth Low Energy (BLE)

BLE is a wireless data protocol that connects devices together over a short distance. BLE beacons are an attractive solution for a plethora of Internet of Things (IoT) applications due to lesser power they require than conventional Bluetooth [8]. It is a vital component of billions of products on the IoT market currently [9].

2.4 Flipped Classroom

Flipped classroom (FC) is a learning strategy for blended learning. The goal of flipped classroom learning focuses on having more time in classroom to achieve high interaction between instructors and students. Teachers assign readings before class and students studies readings outside class time. Accordingly, teachers save lecture time in classroom for describing readings because students finished readings before class [10]. Most students agreed the FC over lectures, and their learning can be improved [10]. Each student preferred coming to class with a basic understanding of the learning units. Therefore, students can fully enjoy and engage in class discussion.

2.5 Tom Malone's Theory of Intrinsically Motivating Instruction

Malone proposed three categories, challenge, fantasy, and curiosity, for the essential characteristics of good computer games and enjoyable situations [11].Therefore, these three categories can be referred while developing instructional games for educations. First, for challenge, Malone discovered that most games offer various goals in order to games having challenges for players. Second, for Fantasy, the fantasy involved in a game means intimate materials are learned. The players are capable of utilizing analogies between their existing knowledge about the fantasy world and the unfamiliar things they are learning. Third, for curiosity, according to cognitive structures, there are three of the characteristics of well-formed scientific theories: completeness, consistency, and parsimony. Accordingly, how to engage students' curiosity is to present only sufficient information to make their existing knowledge seem incomplete, inconsistent, or parsimonious. The students are then inspired to learn more so that better cognitive structures can be formed.

3 Descriptions of the IFEP System

3.1 Experimental Environment for the IFEP System

Figure 1 shows an example of the experimental environment while using the IFEP system to support classroom learning. First, once students enable the APP of the IFEP system and then enter the classroom with iBeacon devices, the APP scans available iBeacon devices. The APP automatically uploads iBeacon information such as detection time, distance between the smartphone and the iBeacon, and UUID to the cloud server if it detects available iBeacon devices successfully. Meanwhile, students' identifications are also sent to the cloud server. Then, instructor starts to post questions for a quiz on the front screen in classroom. The IFEP system also pushes the questions to students' smartphones. Subsequently, a timer on the screen begins to count down during replying students' answers to questions. Here the IFEP system can display the temporary real-time histogram of students' answers before timer expired. Figure 2 illustrates an example of displaying temporary real-time histogram of students' answers. There are four items (or answers), A, B, C, and D, to be chosen by students. The numbers of item selection exhibit at y axis in Fig. 2. Then, students can watch continuous changes of the temporary real-time histograms on screen simultaneously.

In the paper, to multicast results to students in classroom for synchronization can be realized by websocket technology. Here displaying a timer to count down the answer time slot is conducted by websocket technology. Figure 2 shows a timer on upper right of screen of smartphone. This circumstance can be regarded as the implementation for competition-like learning strategy. Students touch big color buttons on screen of smartphones to send their answers to the cloud server. The situation can be regarded as applying the instruction-game strategy in the design of the IFEP system. Students can query the assessment results of their answers in the cloud server.

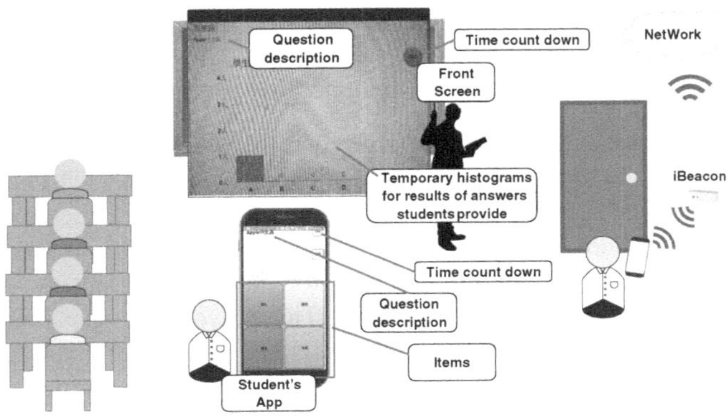

Fig. 1. The experimental environment while using the IFEP system.

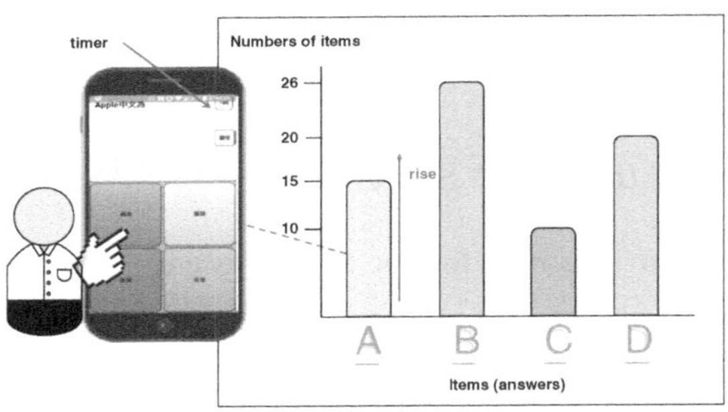

Fig. 2. The histogram of students' answers.

Recently, flipped classroom strategy can be applied for promoting the interaction of classroom or blended learning. Therefore, the IFEP system offers the function of automatically calculating students' presence in classroom via scanning iBeacon devices set up in classroom in advance or before class time. The IFEP system provides teachers with the records of students' presence in classroom. It saves time for teachers who have a need to perform the roll-call procedure in classroom. Accordingly, teachers have more time to proceed other learning activities. Moreover, Malone proposed three categories, challenge, fantasy, and curiosity, for the essential characteristics of good computer games and enjoyable situations [11]. Here these three categories are applied in the design of the IFEP system for performing quizzes in classroom.

- For the challenge, students will wait for displaying unknown questions on front screen and their smartphone.
- For fantasy, the temporary real-time histograms of students' answers can be displayed on the front screen. A timer not only is exhibited in the screen but also is pushed on students' smartphones.
- For curiosity, the APP shows color buttons for touching as inputs and different sounds for the correct or incorrect result for students' responses. Additionally, the IFEP system provides sounds while continuously displaying temporary real-time histogram of students' answers on screen.

Therefore, the design mentioned above has an attempt to attract students' interests to enjoy quizzes activities so as to increase more interaction in classroom learning to support flipped-classroom learning.

3.2 Experimental Environment for the IFEP System

Figure 3 exhibits the architecture of the IFEP system. There are three components for administrator, instructor, and student sites. Administrator can access data to cloud server or maintain cloud server via Response Web Design (RWD). Instructor site access data to cloud server via RWD. The system offers the APP for students. The chief functions the system offers for these three components can be summarized as follows.

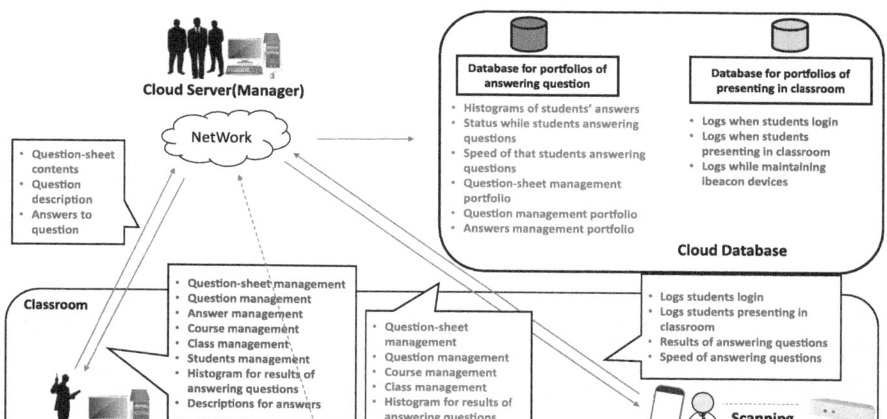

Fig. 3. The architecture of the IFEP system.

- Administrator: Managing cloud databases for portfolios answering question and students' presence in classroom. Maintaining websocket and iBeacon sessions.
- Instructor: Maintaining data for courses, classes, students, question sheets, questions in question sheet, answers to questions, more descriptions to answers, and evaluation results for students' answers.

- Students: Scanning iBeacon devices. Access to question sheets, questions, packets for a timer, answers students ever did, assessment results for students' answers. Uploading data for iBeacon devices and answers to questions.

The benefits of using the IFEP system in classroom learning includes less roll-call time, quick getting students' learning status for learning units, more interesting in enjoying in classroom activities to increase interaction, and easy development of cloud services for analyzing portfolios in cloud database.

4 Instructional Design Supported by the IFEP System

In the paper, an instructional design is proposed for applying flipped classroom in class room learning in higher education, which can be supported by the IFEP system. Figure 4 illustrates the learning procedure of the instructional design. Here the course for experimental instruction is data structure. Up to now, the system just is exploited in the support of teaching the course while applying flipped classroom. There are twenty participants who join in the experimental instruction for the learning procedure. Therefore, only some examples for the use of the IFEP system in the learning procedure can be presented here. The instructional scenario is to suppose instructor already assigns readings or learning units to students as homework before class. Students have to study these learning units outside class time before class. Instructor utilize quizzes for these learning units to perform high interaction within class time for reviewing learning materials (Fig. 5).

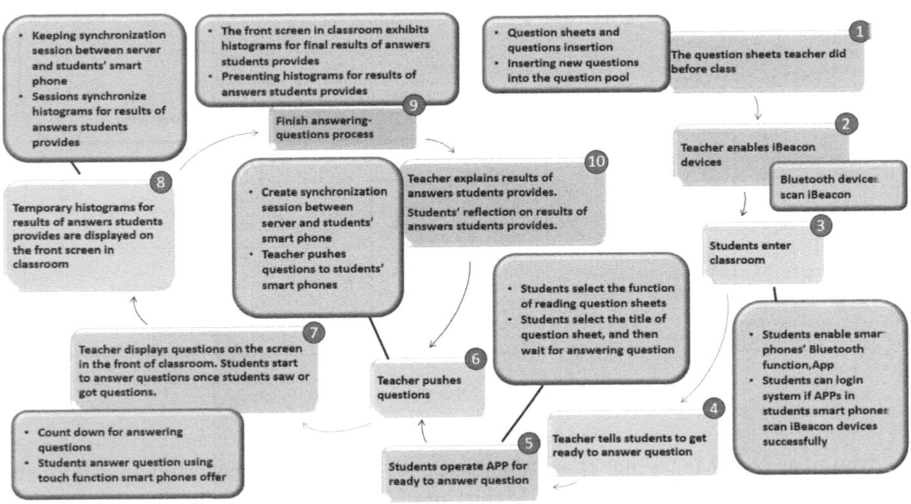

Fig. 4. The learning procedure of applying flipped classroom in classroom learning in higher education, which can be supported by the IFEP system for blended learning.

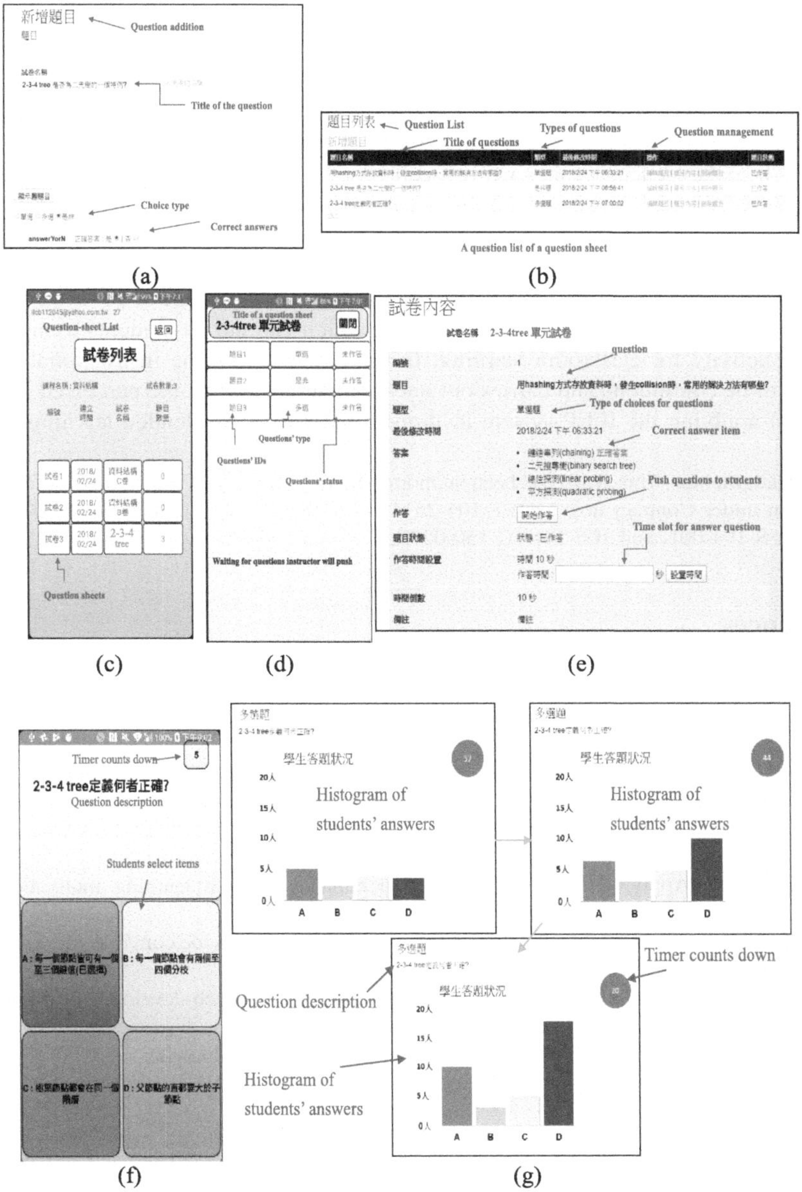

Fig. 5. (a) and (b) show question managements; (c) and (d) display the screen shots of students' APP while waiting for questions instructor will push within a short time; (e) illustrates question-sheet managements including triggering to push questions; (f) shows the screen shots of students' APP while answering questions; (g) illustrates the front screen in classroom, which displays continuous changes of histograms of temporary students' answers and a counting-down timer.

5 Conclusions

The IFEP system with iBeacon technology has proposed in the paper, which can be used in blended learning to support the flipped classroom learning activities. The use of the IFEP system promotes high interaction in classroom learning for conducting quizzes. It makes teachers can save roll-call time because students' presence in classroom can be obtained automatically by detecting iBeacon devices. Therefore, teachers have more time to promote interactions in classroom. The designs of the IFEP system mainly follow the guideline categories of developing instructional games and competition-like learning strategy. As a result, the operations the IFEP system offers are like to play game and to do competitions, which can attract students to engage in the quiz activity for classroom learning. In the future study, the instructional experiments will be continuous and carries out questionnaires to prove the perceived learning effects of applying the IFEP system in flipped classroom for blended learning.

Acknowledgments. This work has been supported by the Ministry of Science and Technology of Taiwan under Contract nos. MOST 105-2511-S-150-003-MY2, 105-2511-S-194-002-MY3, 105-2511-S-194-001, and 106-2813-C-150-027-U.

References

1. Plump, C.M., LaRosa, J.: Using Kahoot! In the classroom to create engagement and active learning: a game-based technology solution for eLearning novices. Manag. Teach. Rev. **2**(2), 151–158 (2017)
2. Cagiltay, N.E., Ozcelik, E., Ozcelik, N.S.: The effect of competition on learning in games. Comput. Educ. **87**, 35–41 (2015)
3. Lo, G., Lin, D., Tang, W.H.: ZUVIO (2015). http://aca.tmu.edu.tw/files/achive/1413_458220f3.pdf
4. Wang, B.T.: Applying PBL and ZUVIO to enhance English learning motivation. Int. J. Cyber Soc. Educ. **9**(1), 1–16 (2016)
5. Mishra, S.: Introduction to WebSockets (2018). https://linode.com/docs/development/introduction-to-websockets/
6. Wang, G.T.: WebSocket (2014). https://blog.gtwang.org/web-development/websocket-protocol/
7. Fette, I., Melnikov, A.: The WebSocket Protocol. Internet Engineering Task Force (2011)
8. Spachos, P.: Computer Communications (2017). https://doi.org/10.1016/j.comcom.2017 12.007
9. Introduction: Bluetooth Low Energy (2018). http://www.ti.com/lit/ml/swrp220/swrp220.pdf
10. Lewis, C.E., Chen, D.C., Relan, A.: Implementation of a flipped classroom approach to promote active learning in the third year surgery clerkship. Am. J. Surg. **215**, 298–303 (2017)
11. Malone, T.W.: What makes things fun to learn? Heuristics for designing instructional computer games. In: The 3rd ACM SIGSMALL Symposium and the First SIGPC Symposium on Small Systems, Palo Alto, California, United States. ACM Press (1980)

Promoting English Pronunciation via Mobile Devices-Based Automatic Speech Evaluation (ASE) Technology

Xiaobin Liu[1], Chunxiao Zhu[1], Jianli Jiao[2], and Manfei Xu[1(✉)]

[1] School of Foreign Studies, South China Normal University, Guangzhou, China
{liuxiaobin, xumanfei}@m.scnu.edu.cn
[2] School of Information Technology in Education, South China Normal University, Guangzhou, China

Abstract. Traditional English teaching in China pays insufficient attention to phonetics teaching and usually leads to learners' poor pronunciation. With the rapid development of the Automatic Speech Evaluation (ASE) technology, many applications are designed to help learners improve their pronunciation. However, no formal conclusion has been made on the effectiveness of ASE-based "imitating-speaking" with immediate feedbacks in English phonetics learning. This study analyzes the validity of the ASE-based "imitating-speaking" by using *Fluent English* as the tool of the two-month experiment. 64 learners in China are chosen as the subjects and they are divided into an experimental group and a control one. The result turns out that ASE-based "imitating-speaking" helps to improve learners' pronunciation and intonation. Moreover, on the basis of the result of the experiment, the study sums up some relative teaching and learning strategies that are employed in this phonetics learning method.

Keywords: Automatic Speech Evaluation · Phonetics teaching
Imitating-speaking · Immediate feedback · MALL

1 Introduction

Language is the key tool of communication and the correctness of pronunciation and intonation is directly related to the validity of communication. A good pronunciation is the key to mastery of a new language, and that to master any language, one only needs to master 50%–90% of its grammar and 1% of its vocabulary while he must master 100% of its knowledge on pronunciation (Gimson 1980). Therefore, phonetics teaching, which is the basis, plays an essential role in English teaching process. Meanwhile, English teaching in junior middle school in China is right the elementary stage of English teaching, indicating that English phonetics teaching in junior middle school forms the basis of the whole English teaching system.

However, there are still many limitations in present phonetics teaching in middle schools. Pronunciation teaching in China is always based on several kinds of practice in the textbook such as syllables, sentences and intonation, and the phonetics teaching procedure in a class is usually carried out in a pattern that the teacher reads as

S. K. S. Cheung et al. (Eds.): ICBL 2018, LNCS 10949, pp. 333–343, 2018.
https://doi.org/10.1007/978-3-319-94505-7_27

demonstration, the students read after that and then the teacher checks and gives feedbacks (Li et al. 2017). In this pattern, there are obvious limitations in time and space for learners. Another factor is due to large-scale of English class with usually more than 50 students. Without specific feedbacks from the teacher based on individual student's problems, it is hard for students to improve Pronunciation by themselves.

Fortunately, with the development of technology, Automatic Speech Assessment Technology has been developed quickly, which leads to the development of many intelligent imitating-speaking applications for English learning based on this kind of technology (Teng et al. 2016). With these applications, after learners read after the sentences by imitation, they can get immediate feedbacks on their pronunciation and intonation, and a score will be given by the applications as well. Therefore, applying these applications to phonetics teaching is hopefully to promote learning validity. However, the problem lies only in the effectiveness of promoting learners' pronunciation and intonation. This is also the aim of present study.

2 Literature Review

Learning English phonetics by imitating and speaking is a learning method that has gained great attention for a long time. Stern (1970) pointed out that the most fundamental and effective way in English phonetics teaching is imitation, which can not only be seen as the basis of making proper responses, but also the first step to reinforce habits of pronouncing. However, traditional "imitating-speaking" phonetics learning mode can only help learners to vaguely perceive some conspicuous characteristics like high pitch and stress acoustically, but cannot help learners accurately master the frequently changing intonation of the target language. In "imitating-speaking" led by their English teacher, the teacher plays the role as a pronunciation model most of the time. While students are practicing by imitating tapes, they need instructions and feedbacks which are always not available.

Fortunately, as the modern information technologies develop rapidly, the modernization of education has also been greatly developed. Many technologies have been applied to the development of learning software or applications, such as Automatic Speech Recognition and Automatic Speech Evaluation (ASE) which can help to give automatic feedbacks to learners. As a result, in addition to teaching knowledge to students in a traditional way, many English teachers also instruct students to learn English after class on the internet.

What's more, during the past decade, technologies of developing mobile devices and mobile internet are being improved at a high speed, and many scholars are trying to apply mobile technologies to English teaching. Mobile Assisted Language Learning (MALL) becomes one of the hottest issues in education. Mobile devices like smartphones and tablet PCs (pads) make MALL possible (Duman and Gedik 2014).

As a result, technology-aided phonetics teaching is drawing more and more attention from scholars and much research has been done on it. For example, some researchers have made researches on speech visualization-based phonetics teaching. Zhou and Zhang (2006) carries out a research on the fluency of English speaking aided by Cool Edit. Xie (2007) uses Speech Analyzer to study sound recognition in English phonetics teaching and sensitiveness on the difference between English and Chinese. Zhuang and Bu (2011) researches on the effect of using *Praat* on improving correctness of college students' pronunciation. Liu et al. (2013) carries out a study on speech visualization-based "imitating-speaking" phonetics teaching and proved its effectiveness on improving learners' pronunciation. Researches have also been made on effectiveness of some other technology-aided phonetics teaching. Xu (2010) proves the effectiveness of ASR-based online software on phoneme teaching. In addition, Sha (2005) points out that the automatic speech recognition and assessment technologies mainly focus on segmental features instead of supra-segmental features, which implies that there are not only advantages but also limitations in teaching phonetics in MALL. Sun and Yang (2012) makes a research into the guiding standards of phonetics teaching in MALL from the aspect of feedback, affirming the value of intelligent timely feedbacks for "imitating-speaking" learning pattern, and also providing suggestions for the design of scientific feedbacks of these kinds of applications.

To conclude, traditional phonetics teaching by "imitating-speaking" are proved to be an effective way in phonetics teaching, and technology-aided phonetics teaching is also hopefully effective. Considering the limitations of traditional "imitating-speaking" learning mode and the advantages of present ASE-based mobile learning applications, it's important to find out whether or not this learning method can help to improve students' pronunciation and intonation positively.

3 The Present Study

The study aims at examining the effect of using ASE in English phonetics teaching by analyzing students' performance on pronunciation, and tries to reveal the value of applying such kind of technology to English phonetics teaching. Based on the aim of the study, the following research questions are designed:

(1) Will the ASE-based "imitating-speaking" phonetics learning mode help to improve students' accuracy of pronunciation and intonation?
(2) If yes, what strategies are employed in it?

At the very beginning of this research, it involves 36 students from Class 1, Grade 7 as the experimental group and 46 students from Class 6, Grade 7 as the control group in a junior middle school of Guangzhou, China. After an analysis on their past performance in speaking English and their performance on the pre-test, only 32 students from each class are chosen for the experiment. When the experiment is being carried out, they have been in Grade 7 for just less than one month.

The reason why we choose these two classes for the experiment is mainly that they are in the charge of the same English teacher and Class 6 is also a parallel class in the grade. Moreover, since their English teacher is the head-teacher of Class 1, Class 1 is chosen as the experimental group for controlling convenience. And the reason why we only choose 32 out of all the students in each class for the experiment is that only those students are active in the experiment with mobile devices available at home.

This study applies the learning app *Fluent English* in teaching English phonetics and examines whether this app can help to improve students' pronunciation and intonation in speaking English, by comparing their performance on pretest before using the app with their performance on post-test after practicing with the app for about two months. All the recording and data from the pre-test, post-test and intervention process are studied and analyzed by adopting quantitative approaches and qualitative approaches.

In this experiment, the following instruments are used.

(1) The smartphone app *Fluent English*. The intelligent "imitating-speaking" learning mode is perfectly designed in this app. It is based on the ASE Technology, in which students can listen to a great number of dialogues, read after the dialogues, and then some feedbacks on students' pronunciation and a score will be given. While learners are using it for learning, it can show how learners' performances are by changing different parts of the reading materials into different colors (Green represents good pronunciation, black represents not-bad pronunciation and red represents wrong pronunciation). What's more, a score is given by the app, which takes both pronunciation and intonation into consideration and shows learners' total performance. Learners can correct their mistakes with the immediate feedback they get from the app. The whole practicing process is designed in the form of finishing tasks of training and passing rounds. If a learner still fails to reac right although he/she has listened to and imitated the original recordings for many times, he/she can ask for help by posing questions to other learners on the app, and make discussion on the questions.
(2) A pre-test and a post-test. These two tests are designed in the form of speaking practice to know their performance on speaking before and after the training The tests consist of some dialogues and a passage for students to read.

All the scores of every test are marked by the students' English teacher and all the data collected are analyzed by using statistics software SPSS 19.0 and MS Excel.

4 Results and Discussion

4.1 Analysis on Pre-test

Before the experiment, it is necessary to know about students' actual level in phonetics and figure out whether the experimental group and control group chosen are of parallel level. Therefore, the two groups are engaged in the same pre-test. We design a phonetics test to ascertain the phonetics proficiency of the subjects. The focus of the test is mainly pronunciation and intonation. All the scores are given according to the standards of the speaking part of the Middle School Entrance Examination by students' English teacher. With the help of SPSS, we analyze these two samples by using the Independent-Sample T-Test with the following result obtained.

As the data in Table 1 show, $t = -0.078 < 1$, and Sig (2-tailed) = 0.938 > 0.05; in Table 2, $t = 0.174 < 1$, and Sig (2-tailed) = 0.862 > 0.05; in Table 3, $t = 0.044 < 1$, and Sig (2-tailed) = 0.965 > 0.05. All of these data show that before the experiment, the English-speaking ability (reading aloud) of the experimental and control groups have no significant difference concerning their pronunciation and intonation, which indicates that they are at the same initial level.

Table 1. The result of the T-test for pre-test focusing on pronunciation

Group	N	Mean	Std. deviation	*t*	Sig. (2-tailed)
Experimental	32	7.2031	0.79168	-	0.938
Control	32	7.2188	0.80259	0.078	

$*p < 0.05$

Table 2. The result of the T-test for pre-test focusing on intonation

Group	N	Mean	Std. deviation	*t*	Sig. (2-tailed)
Experimental	32	7.1094	0.83988	0.174	0.862
Control	32	7.0781	0.56951		

$*p < 0.05$

Table 3. The result of the T-test for the total scores of pre-test

Group	N	Mean	Std. deviation	*t*	Sig. (2-tailed)
Experimental	32	14.3125	1.52268	0.044	0.965
Control	32	14.2969	1.30049		

$*p < 0.05$

4.2 Analysis on Post-test

In the post-test, we make detailed comparisons between the recordings of the experimental group and control group based on three aspects: pronunciation, intonation and total effect, and the three scores focusing on each aspect are given to each recording. The scores are given by the English teacher of the subjects. We make comparisons between the means of the two groups independently on pronunciation, intonation and total effect in independent samples T-test to find out whether there is significance in the difference. The followings are the analysis of the results of the three aspects.

(1) Pronunciation: as can be seen in Table 4, experimental group's mean score is 0.98 points higher than the control group, and the Sig (2-tailed) is 0.00 (<0.05), indicating the difference between the two groups on pronunciation is significant, which proves that the "imitating-speaking" learning mode based on ASE technology is good for improving learner's pronunciation.

Table 4. The result of the T-test for post-test focusing on pronunciation

Group	N	Mean	Std. deviation	*t*	Sig. (2-tailed)
Experimental	32	8.7031	0.65819	6.625	0.000
Control	32	7.7188	0.52267		

$*p < 0.05$

(2) Intonation: as Table 5 shows, the experimental group's mean score is 0.80 points higher than the control group and the Sig (2-tailed) is 0.00 (<0.05), indicating the difference between the two groups on intonation is significant, which proves that the "imitating-speaking" learning mode based on the automatic speech assessment technology is good for improving learner's intonation.

Table 5. The result of the T-test for post-test focusing on intonation

Group	N	Mean	Std. deviation	t	Sig. (2-tailed)
Experimental	32	8.1250	0.72956	4.382	0.000
Control	32	7.3281	0.72523		

*$p < 0.05$

(3) Total effect: According to Table 6, experimental group's mean score is 1.78 points higher than the control group when their standard deviations alter little. The Sig (2-tailed) is 0.00 (<0.05), indicating the difference between the two groups on intonation is significant, which suggests that the "imitating-speaking" learning mode based on the automatic speech assessment technology can help to improve learners speaking ability concerning their pronunciation and intonation.

Table 6. The Result of the T-test for the total scores of Post-test

Group	N	Mean	Std. deviation	t	Sig. (2-tailed)
Experimental	32	16.8281	0.92987	7.671	0.000
Control	32	15.0469	0.92770		

*$p < 0.05$

According to the above data analysis, the answer to the first question of the study is clear: ASE-based "imitating-speaking" can help to improve learners' pronunciation and intonation.

4.3 Discussion

4.3.1 Benefits

According to the experiment and what have been analyzed above, the distinct results of the experimental group and control group suggests that apps like *Fluent English* designed with the "imitating-speaking" phonetics learning mode based on the automatic speech assessment technology can be a useful tool to improve students' performance on pronunciation and intonation.

It can be seen from the research that there are many benefits in learning phonetics using the intelligent "imitating-speaking" mode such as using *Fluent English*. Some definite benefits will be listed taking *Fluent English* as an example. First of all, the app provides varieties of listening materials of different levels for learners. Learners can independently choose practicing materials according to their interests and their learning levels. The pronunciation and intonation of the listening materials in the app are accurate and normative, avoiding the situation that students are misled by inaccurate pronunciation and intonation. Second, visual immediate feedbacks are available while learners are using the app, helping students to correct their mistakes and improve their pronunciation at once. What's more, there is no need for students to worry about embarrassment caused by immediate feedbacks like in traditional classrooms, thus increasing learners' confidence and willingness in speaking. Third, learners can communicate with other learners on the app and be better awarded of others' progress by listening to others' practicing recordings, which makes learners more eager to make progress themselves. In addition, most learners agree that learning phonetics in this way is very interesting. Forth, the teacher can share learning materials to students in case that some students are not active and initiative in the learning, and monitor students' learning situation. Last but not least, learners can learn whenever and wherever they want to learn, leaving behind the problem in traditional learning that students can only learn and get feedbacks in school

4.3.2 Discussion on Strategies

In *Fluent English*, the following learning strategies are mainly employed: *repetition, reinforcement, visualization, resourcing, small-pacing, task-taking and self-encouragement.*

Figure 1 will help to show the strategies mentioned above which will be analyzed as follow.

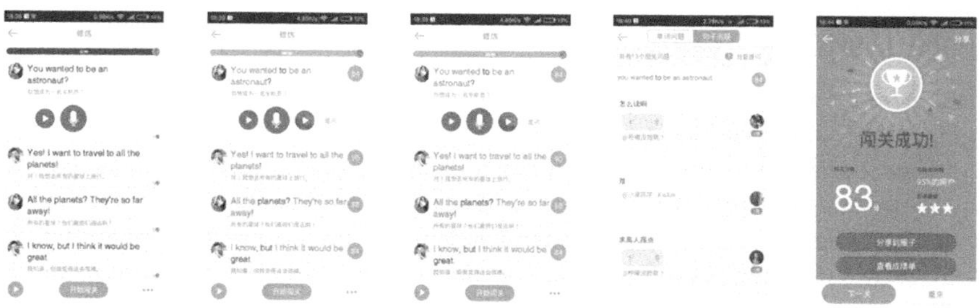

Fig. 1. Screenshots of the smartphone app *Fluent English*

Repetition and reinforcement: in the app, the user has endless chances to listen to original recordings and to record his/her own recordings. Before getting a satisfying score, he/she must listen and read over and over again until mastering the pronunciation and intonation to a certain degree. During this process, good pronunciation will also be reinforced for many times. This strategy implies that English teachers should attach importance to repetition of imitating and reading in daily phonetics teaching, and that feedbacks should be timely and specific. For example, during teaching English phonetics symbols, frequent repetition of reading symbols taught newly should be emphasized. For symbols taught days even months ago, scientific plans for repetition should be organized by the teacher for reinforcement. In other words, symbols newly taught need continuos reinforcement while symbols taught previously need interval reinforcement. The same rule should also be applied to teaching other phonetics elements. What's more, mistakes should be pointed out each time.

Visualization: after each imitating, immediate visual feedbacks will be given to users, with which they can easily know how their performance is and what should be focused on in next imitating (see Fig. 4.2). This strategy suggests that feedbacks can be visually simply comprehensible. For example, in daily phonetics teaching, if a student makes good pronunciation, the teacher can show admiration by nodding or smiling at him/her. If a student makes bad or wrong pronunciation, the teacher can frown a little to inform him/her there is imperfectness in their pronunciation. Visual feedbacks like nodding, smiling or frowning are good visual feedbacks in phonetics teaching as they can be easily understood.

Resourcing: while practicing, if the user finds it difficult to read some words right or get a satisfying score although he/she has imitated the original recording for many times, he/she can ask other users online by posing a question (see Fig. 4.3 & 4.4). Discussion also can be made on the question between the user and other users. The process of asking for help is the process of using resource strategy. In daily phonetics teaching, teachers also need to cultivate students' awareness of using resource strategy and remind students to ask for help when they have questions. Online dictionaries, teachers and classmates are all resource of help. To train students' ability of using resourcing strategy for help in phonetics teaching, when a student comes to the teacher for help, the teacher can even sometimes deliberately refuse to answer and ask the student to solve the problem by himself/herself, reminding him/her of some other ways of getting help.

Small-pacing: different users have different proficiency in phonetics learning, so users' learning pace will be different from each other. Users can design their own learning schedule according to their own situation and reach their goals steps by steps. One user may only practice a course for only once and manages to pass the round, while another user may practice a course for more than five times before passing the round. This strategy shows that it is good for English teachers to help students evaluate themselves correctly and to make learning plans which are divided into many small plans with small goals according to students' own level. For example, for students who are very poor in pronunciation, the teacher should pay more attention to guide them. These students may feel hard to catch up with daily teaching, needing individual extra help from the teacher. Goals set for their learning should be simpler and reachable. Before making a great progress, a series of small goals will be made for it. The teacher should assist these students to make leaning plans one by one and help also should be offered to realize the goals.

Task-taking: as can be seen in Fig. 4.5, practicing is taking tasks. The practicing is designed in the form of finishing tasks of training and passing rounds. This strategy implies that English teachers should take advantage of giving different definite interesting tasks to students in order to keep students' learning motivation. Task-based competition is also helpful in phonetics teaching. For example, group work can be used in phonetics teaching. Tasks like reading dialogue can be given to all the groups.

Each member of each group should take a role and some groups will be invited to perform in front of the whole class. In order to make a better performance, members of a group have to help each other with pronouncing problems. In this task-taking process, students may feel more interested and competitive.

Self-encouraging: the system gives the learners who finish daily task a certain number of stars which can be used like money on the app to buy learning resources provided on the online store of the app. The level of the user in the app will also be higher if he/she gets more stars. These will cause users' motivation to practice more and can be regarded as the employment of self-encouraging. This strategy shows that English teachers can establish a system of praise in daily phonetics teaching to encourage students to practice more and make more progress. For example, in class of low grades, teachers can give the whole class a series of extra practicing tasks like reading dialogues or passages with good pronunciation and intonation to the teacher, and make the rule that students are free to choose to do the tasks or not. Each time a student finishes reading a task with satisfying pronunciation, he/she can get a prize such as a star stick from the teacher. A certain number of stars can be exchanged for a better prize. In this process, students who are active in learning may be greatly encouraged and keep improving to get more admiration. But the form of praise should be scientific, considering students' regulation of physical and mental development. Too much or insufficient prizes are both unacceptable.

5 Conclusion and Research Implications

It is shown in the above study that the use of *Fluent English* does make English phonetics teaching more interesting and effective, and brings positive acceleration for students' English speaking. Answers for the questions put forward before the experiment are very clear: ASE-based "imitating-speaking" can help to improve students' accuracy of pronunciation and intonation, and the strategies employed in the app are mainly repetition, reinforcement, visualization, resourcing, small-pacing, task-taking and self-encouragement. Although there are still a few limitations of apps like *Fluent English* in phonetics learning, it plays an essential and significant role in improving students' pronunciation and intonation and rising students' awareness of speaking well.

This learning mode can not only help to improve students' pronunciation and intonation, but also can help to solve some present problems of phonetics teaching. Students can get immediate specific feedbacks while speaking instead of only general feedbacks from the English teacher which may not be very helpful for some students. What's more, puzzlements caused by some teachers who are not good enough in phonetics themselves can be solved to a certain extent. By using ASE-based "imitating-speaking" phonetics learning mode, the effectiveness of phonetics teaching will be greatly increased, offering more freedom for both students and teachers. Besides, mobile phones or pads are becoming more and more common, making the application of this learning mode more possible. Most importantly, with technology being developed rapidly, more and more phonetics learning apps applying this learning mode will be developed, offering more interesting learning materials and experience for learners.

Nevertheless, although Mobile learning is becoming more and more popular, apps with "imitating-speaking" learning mode based on ASE technology has not been widely used for teaching English phonetics. Even some teachers have never heard of it before or have no idea of taking advantages of them in their daily teaching. The current situation may result from some limitations of applying these kinds of learning apps to phonetics teaching. For one thing, it requires the support of mobile devices and wireless internet. Although mobile devices and wireless internet are becoming more common in normal families, still some students have no access to them. Besides, some parents are not willing to let their children use mobile devices everyday out of worries that their children may use the devices to do things that are not related with study. For other thing, such teaching requires teachers to do extra work after school which occupies teachers' private time.

To conclude, the application of the ASE-based "imitating-speaking" to phonetics teaching in junior middle school can give students more opportunities to speak English with feedbacks. It also offers adequate listening resources to them, solving the problem of students who generally have no idea of where to find appropriate listening and speaking materials. In spite of some limitations of using this learning mode presently, it still can be a good helper in training students' pronunciation and intonation if conditions permit. Its future is also promising as technology and economics develop fast.

Acknowledgment. This paper is the result of the following funds: South China Normal University scientific research foundation for fostering junior teachers in social science (13SK04); Guangdong Higher Education Teaching Reform Project 2015 No. 204; Guangdong "13th Five-Year" Plan Co-funded Project of Philosophy & Social Science (GD16XWW25). The research is also supported by Beijing Competency Edu-Tech Institute. The corresponding author of the paper is Manfei Xu.

References

Duman, G.O., Gedik, N.: Research trends in mobile assisted language learning from 2000 to 2012. ReCALL **02**, 197–216 (2014)

Gimson, A.C.: An Introduction to the Pronunciation of English. Arnold, London (1980)

Stern, H.H.: Perspectives on Second Language Teaching. Ontario Institute for Studies in Education, Toronto (1970)

Li, M., Han, M., Chen, Z., Mo, Y., Chen, X., Liu, X.: Improving English pronunciation via automatic speech recognition technology (Technical report). In: 2017 International Symposium on Educational Technology (2017)

Liu, X., Lin, W., Zhang, W., Hong, X.: An experimental study on speech visualization in English recitation. e-Educ. Res. **04**, 81–86 (2013)

Sha, G.: Computer-assisted instruction and testing of pronunciation: a critical view. Com-Assi. Fore. Lang. Educ. **04**, 67–71 (2005)

Sun, Z., Yang, L.: Feedbacks in the computer-assisted foreign language pronunciation instruction: problems and considerations. Eng. Teach. **11**, 49–52 (2012)

Teng, H., Liu, X., Wang, L.: The research of english pronunciation evaluation system based on the speech recognition technology. J. Yancheng Ins. Tech. (Nat. Sci. Ed.) **03**, 17–22 (2016)

Xie, P.: Application of speech analyzer to English pronunciation teaching. Com-Assi. Fore. Lang. Educ. **06**, 26–29 (2007)

Xu, W.: A study on effectiveness of an ASR-based online software on Chinese college students' phoneme learning. MA Thesis, Hunan University (2010)

Zhou, A., Zhang, C.: Measuring English oral fluency with cool edit pro. Com-Assi. Fore. Lang. Educ. **04**, 67–70 (2006)

Zhuang, M., Bu, Y.: A study on visualization in pronunciation teaching. e-Educ. Res. **02**, 02–98 (2011)

Open Educational Resources

Design Guidelines for Mobile MOOC Learning—An Empirical Study

Jiyou Jia(✉) and Bilan Zhang

Department of Educational Technology, School of Education, Peking University, Yiheyuanlu 5, Beijing 100871, China
{jjy, zhangbilan}@pku.edu.cn

Abstract. With the popularity and convenience of smart phones and Internet, more and more users participate in MOOC (Massive Open Online Courses) via mobile phones or tablet computers. Thus how to design MOOC for mobile learning deserves theoretical study and practical exploration. Based on the review of related literature and the assessment of the APPs provided by six mostly used MOOC platforms, we proposed six guidelines for the mobile MOOC design, i.e. clear navigation, simple layout, linear display, harmonious coloring, smooth video, and full interaction. To verify the rationality of those guidelines, we designed a corresponding survey to investigate the learners' perception and attitude toward the six guidelines implemented in one MOOC in China. The analysis of the survey result demonstrates that the MOOC learners believed those guidelines are valuable in mobile MOOC design and helpful for MOOC learning.

Keywords: MOOC · Mobile learning · Instructional design
Design guidelines

1 Introduction

The Statistical Report on Internet Development in China published in August 2017 by China Internet Network Information Center (abbreviated as CNNIC) shows that up to July 2017, the Internet users in China count 751 Million. Among them 724 Million (96.3%) use smart phones to access Internet. 144 Million are learners of different online resources. Since 2013, MOOC (Massive Open Online Course) has been paid great attention to by Chinese educational authorities, researchers and practitioners. Up to January 2018, more than 3200 MOOCs from more than 460 higher education institutes have been designed and put on usage in more than 10 MOOC platforms, and more than 55 Million learners have accessed those courses.

With the popularity and convenience of smart phones and Internet, more and more users participate in MOOC (Massive Open Online Courses) via mobile clients like smart phones or tablet computers. How to design MOOC for mobile learning to meet the great demand deserves theoretical research and practical exploration. This study will study the related work, examine the common MOOCs' mobile application (APPs),

S. K. S. Cheung et al. (Eds.): ICBL 2018, LNCS 10949, pp. 347–356, 2018.
https://doi.org/10.1007/978-3-319-94505-7_28

propose the design guidelines for mobile MOOC, and survey the MOOC learners about their attitude and feeling about those guidelines.

2 Related Work

In January 2016, we searched the papers in Chinese journals (http://cnki.net) published from 2012 to 2015 with the key words "mobile" and "MOOC", and find 14 related papers. They can be classified into four categories: theory, technology, course design and effect evaluation.

Among those 14 papers, two papers (14.3%) discussed the theoretical foundation of applying smart phones in MOOC instruction (Wang 2015; Yu and Zhou 2014). Five papers (35.7%) addresses technological aspects of mobile MOOC, for example, the design of APPs for MOOC (Chen 2015), System requirement analysis (Zhuc et al. 2014), mobile learning system based on MOOC concept (He et al. 2015), design rationales for mobile MOOC (Feng 2014).

Six papers (42.9%) address mobile MOOC design issues. Lan etc. proposed the concept of Super MOOC (SMOOC) to describe the mobile learning of MOOC with smart phones (Lan et al. 2015). Wang et al. suggested the fragmented learning model for basic university courses featured with smart phones as client machines and enormous MOOC resources (Wang et al. 2015). Wang introduced MOOC resources and flipped classroom concept into the instructional design of an undergraduate course "computer literacy" (Wang 2015). Hu designed a MOOC "Android Programing" and suggested to use smart phones to learn this course (Hu 2015). Zeng (2015) and Li (2014) also suggested the instruction of MOOC with the help of mobile devices.

Only one paper (7.1%) proposed the evaluation indexes of mobile MOOC design, with three first-order indexes and nine second-order indexes, and suggested that mobile MOOC should pay special attention to the design of interface, interaction and video resource (Hu 2015).

Besides Chinese literature we have also searched international researches. Renz et al. (2014) analyzed the demand and supply of mobile MOOC, the APPs supporting MOOC, and the benefit of mobile MOOC illustrated by case studies. Sharples et al. (2015) analyzed some case of mobile MOOCs.

The above literature review shows that the mobile learning of MOOC with smart phones have drawn great attention from researchers and practitioners. Though the demand and supply, theory, technology, course design and so on have been discussed, there have not been sounding design guidelines which can guide the design of mobile MOOCs and whose effect has been assessed. This study will attempt to fill in this gap.

3 The APP Features of Common MOOC Platforms

Because the application (APP) installed in smart phones and tablet computers is the main approach of the users to access MOOCs, this study examined the APPs of common MOOC platforms.

On third March 2016, we tested the APPS of six typical and popular MOOC platforms in China, i.e. XuetangX, NetEase Open Course, Chinese University MOOC, Coursera, edX, and Udacity. The used test client was a smart phone Huawei TAG-AL00. Its screen resolution is 1280 × 720 pixels, its operating system is Android 5.1, and the network is WIFI. The test result is shown in Table 1.

From Table 1 we can see both common and specific features in different MOOC platforms.

Regarding the download statistics, NetEase Open Course, Chinese University MOOC and Coursera reached millions of downloads, followed by XuetangX and Udacity, and edX had the least downloads.

Regarding the functionality, in the homepage three functions are all included: My course, course search.

Regarding the course number, Coursera had most course collections, followed by XuetangX, Chinese University MOOC, edX, and Udacity had the least courses. NetEase Open Course's video resource was the richest.

4 Pilot Experience Survey of Common MOOC APPs

Based on the evaluating index for mobile MOOC proposed by Hu (2015), we designed the evaluation rubric for mobile APPs for MOOCs. It had 3 first-level indexes and 11 second-level items. The first level indexes include course feature, user experience and system feature.

Three student volunteers were enrolled to use this rubric to evaluate the APPs of six MOOC platforms. Every student used his or her own smart phone to test the APPs. The phones' spec is listed in Table 2.

Three volunteers were required to fill in a survey to express their experience of using the Apps to learn the MOOC. Each of the 11 items was measured by the volunteers with the 5-points Likert scale, with 5 as the excellent experience, 4 as very good, 3 as ordinary, 2 as bad and 1 as the worst experience.

The three indexes and 11 items, score means of each item for the six MOOCs given by the volunteers are listed in Table 3. The survey result demonstrates both common and specific features of the APPs of different MOOC platforms felt by the respondents.

Regarding course features, most courses in Coursera and edX were provided by the world-class elite universities, with high-quality and enormous resources; many courses in XuetangX were provided by the professors from Tsinghua-University, one of the top universities in China, and some were provided by overseas universities. Most courses of Chinese University MOOC came from leading universities in China with high-quality. The video courses in NetEase Open Course had various providers and thus uneven qualities. The courses in Udacity had the least quantity and the simplest classification, i.e. computer programming course, many of which supplied guidance on hands-on programming experiment.

Regarding user experience, Chinese University MOOC and Coursera had the most participation tools, while edX had the least tools. Except Udacity and edX, the interface of other MOOC APPs was clear and simple. The interaction function of NetEase Open

Table 1. APP features of common MOOC platforms in China

Platform	XuetangX	Chinese University MOOC	NetEase Open Course	edX	Coursera	Udacity
Country	China			USA		
Website	www.xuetangx.com	www. icourse163.org	www.open.163.com	www.edx.org	www.coursera.org	www. udacity.com
Version	V2.5.0	V1.3.0	V4.0.1	V1.0.09	V2.1.5.1	V1.9.0
Language	Chinese	Chinese	Chinese	Multi language	Multi language	English
Size	20.88 M	18.64 M	6.59 M	9.39 M	15.13 M	5.66 M
Download	60 K	450 K	4070 K	3311	220 K	50 K
Video play and control	Almost smooth	Almost smooth	Smooth	Slow	Smooth	Slow and pause
Homepage	My course, course search, course category, course recommendation and self-service	My learning, course search, course category	My course, course search, course category, watch record	My course, my video, find course, settings, feedback submission	My course, course search, refresh, completed course, current course, upcoming courses	My course, course category
Course content	Course announcement, details, sharing, video, catalog	Announcement, courseware, examination, discussion forum	Video, introduction, catalog, recommendation, forum, favorite, sharing, error feedback	Video, syllabus	Course catalog, video, discussion, assignment, download	Video introduction,
Course number	1027 courses within 21 categories	841 courses within 6 categories	A large number of videos	546 courses within 31 categories	1813 courses within 38 categories	128 courses

Note: the download number is given by “360 phone assistants” statistics.

Table 2. Phone spec of three volunteers

Volunteer	Phone type	Operating system	Screen resolution
A	Apple iphone6	iOS 9	1334 × 750
B	Huawei Glory 6	Android 4.4	1920 × 1080
C	Red Mi 1S	Android4.4.4	1280 × 720

Table 3. The score means of each item from 3 volunteers

Evaluation indexes	XuetangX	Chinese University MOOC	NetEase Open Course		edX	Coursera	Udacity
Course feature	Quality	3.7	4.0	5.0	1.7	4.0	3.7
	Quantity	3.7	3.3	5.0	2.3	3.7	2.7
	Participation tools	2.3	3.7	3.0	1.3	3.7	2.0
User experience	Interface	3.0	4.7	4.3	1.3	3.0	2.3
	Interaction	3.3	4.3	5.0	2.3	4.0	2.7
	Personalization	4.7	3.7	4.7	1.7	3.3	2.0
System features	Compatibility	4.7	5.0	4.7	1.0	3.0	2.3
	Responsiveness	3.7	4.0	4.3	1.7	3.7	2.7
	Supportability	4.3	4.3	5.0	1.7	3.3	2.7
	Use easiness	3.3	5.0	4.7	1.3	3.7	2.3
	Like to use	2.3	4.0	4.7	1.3	2.3	1.3
Overall score		3.6	4.2	4.6	1.6	3.4	2.4

Course, Coursera 和 Chinese University MOOC was better. Except Udacity, all the other APPs supported personalized user setting.

Regarding the compatibility, responsiveness and supportiveness, the three APPS from Chinese providers, i.e. NetEase Open Course, Chinese University MOOC 和 XuetangX, were all advantaged over the three APPS from foreign providers, i.e. Coursera, Udacity and edX. After installation the three Chinese APPs could be perfectly adapted to the phone OS and screen, run without any error, play videos fluently without any pause and caching. The system's feedback to users' question was fast and guaranteed. The APPs was updated timely. The three foreign APPs needed more time of caching by video playing and often paused by playing videos. Except edX and Udacity the other four APPs were easy to be used.

Overall, NetEase Open Course had the highest score, followed by XuetangX, Chinese University MOOC, Coursera, Udacity, and the edX had the lowest score.

The majority of courses in Udacity were about computer programming and needed practice with personal computer which could not be implemented in phones. So the videos in Udacity were just general introduction.

The videos from edX were difficult to be watched mainly because many videos were stored in YouTube and could not be visited by Chinese users.

5 Design Guidelines Supporting Mobile MOOC

Based on the above investigation of existing MOOC platforms and the user experience about using the APPs of those platforms, we propose six guidelines guiding the design of mobile MOOC. They are clear navigation, simple layout, linear display, harmonious coloring, smooth video, and full interaction.

Guideline One: clear navigation. Because smart phones have a smaller screen, and the MOOC has many learning resources and activities, a clear navigation is helpful for the user to find the needed content and function easily and quickly, and to be concentrated on the content and function, rather than on searching. Moreover, a clear navigation is also useful for the platform administrators to manage the modules more efficiently. For the clear navigation, three functions should be included in the homepage: course search, course classification, and my courses. Upcoming courses can also be added to the homepage to announce in advance some upcoming courses.

Guideline two: simple layout. Only necessary elements should be displayed in the layout so that the learner can be focused on the learning content or activity displayed in the small screen.

Guideline three: linear display. All the learning resources and activities including videos, assignment, reading materials etc. should be organized with the order of teaching weeks or content chapters, and linearly displayed in the screen. Through this way the learner can browse all the contents quickly.

Guideline four: smooth video. Lecture video is the most important form of the learning content in MOOCs, and watching video should provide the learner the feeling like listening to the teachers in the classroom. So the smooth video can lead to good user experience, and interrupted video will result in bad user experience. The forwards and backwards function should also be included in the video player so that the learner can watch the video with his or her own pace. Subtitles with different languages should also be selectable for the videos spoken in a foreign language.

Guideline five: harmonious colors. For the mobile screen, interface colors should be arranged reasonably from the point view of aesthetic foundation, and highlight the key content and functions by using eye-catching colors or a higher contrast color layout, for example with black background and white texts.

Guideline six: full interaction. Online forum should be included in the MOOC APPs so that the learner can post and reply to others' post at any time via text input or even through voice speech. This kind of online communication and discussion can not only push the learners to think in more depth and more width, but also provide them with the chance to exchange their emotion and feeling.

6 The Attitude Survey Toward Design Guidelines from Learners of a MOOC

Because the design guidelines were proposed just based on the test result of APPs from six MOOC platforms done by just three volunteers, their reliability and validity need to be confirmed by a larger number of MOOC learners. Therefore we introduced these guidelines to one lecturer Mr. Yang who held one MOOC in "Chinese University MOOC" platform in July 2016, and asked him to consider those guidelines for the design and implementation of his MOOC, "Micro Lecture design and creation".

The website of this MOOC is the following:

http://www.icourse163.org/course/icourse-1001555013?tid=1001628022#/info

This MOOC lasted 5 weeks, and could be accessed either via web browser or mobile APP, which was tested by us in Sects. 3 and 4. There were four components in the APP just as discovered in the pilot test in Sect. 3: announcement, courseware, examination and discussion forum.

By the end of the MOOC, i.e. in August 2016, we designed an anonymous web-based survey to investigate the learners' attitude toward the design guidelines of MOOC. The survey is comprised of three parts: the first part is the learners' demographic data, the second part is the learners' attitude toward the degree that the MOOC followed the design guidelines, and the third part is the learners' feeling about the MOOC APPs they used. All the eight items in the second part and seven items in the third part were measured by the volunteers with the 5-points Likert scale, with 1 as the strongly agree, 2 as agree, 3 as neutral, 4 as not agree and 5 as strongly not agree.

We received 504 valid answers from the MOOC learners. Now we introduce the descriptive statistics of the answers.

In the first part, the learners' demographic data included their gender, age, and MOOC experience. Males counted 203 (40.3%), while females counted 301 (59.7%). The average age was 36.7.

The average number of MOOCs the learners had taken part in was 2.8. It can be inferred that most learners had learned two or three MOOCs and their survey answers were representative. Among 504 learners, 189 used smart phones and 157 used tablet computers for the MOOC learning. The learners using mobile clients counted 346 (68.7%). The other 158 learners (31.3%) used desktop or notebook computers to learn MOOC. Mobile learners counted more than two-thirds of MOOC population and were the majority of MOOC learners.

For the second and third part of the survey containing 15 5-points Likert answer items, reliability and validity test were done with SPSS. For the reliability test, Cronbach's Alpha was 0.969 so that the survey answers' reliability was very good. For the structural validity, the KMO (Kaiser-Meyer-Olkin) value was 0.960, and the significance of Bartlett Ball test was 0.000. So the structural validity of the survey answers was also very good.

The first five items in the second part corresponded to the first five design guidelines for mobile MOOC. The last three items were full lecturer-learner interaction, full learner-learner interaction and full human-computer interaction, and they were the concrete form of the sixth guideline "full interaction". The means and standard deviations of the learners' answers to the eight items are listed in Table 4.

All the means of the learners' answers to the eight items were not greater than 2 which represented the agreeable level. It can be inferred that most learners of this MOOC agreed that the design of this MOOC obey the six guidelines of mobile MOOC proposed by us.

Table 4. The means and standard deviations of the learners' answers to the items in second part

	Clear navigation	Simple layout	Linear display	Smooth video	Harmonious color	Lecturer-learner interaction	Learner-learner interaction	Human-computer interaction
Mean	1.8	1.8	1.8	1.8	1.7	2.0	2.0	2.0
Std. dev.	.78	.76	.75	.81	.75	.88	.87	.84

The third part is comprised of seven items corresponding to MOOC APPs' usability, easy use, stability, compatibility, responsiveness and personalization. The mean and standard deviation of the learner's answers to each item are listed in Table 5.

Table 5. The means and standard deviations of the learners' answers to the items in third part

	Preference to use	Easiness to use	Stableness	Responsiveness	Personalization	Easiness to change functions	Compatibility
Mean	2.0	1.8	1.8	1.9	1.9	1.9	1.9
Std. dev.	1.00	.80	.80	.82	.82	.82	.82

All the means of the learners' answers to the seven items were less than 2 which represented the agreeable level. Therefore most learners of this MOOC agreed that the this MOOC was easy to use, stable, responsive, compatible, and supported personalization.

Table 6. T-test of answer differences from two groups to the questions in the second part

	Group	Mean	Std. dev.	t	Sig. (two sides)
Clear navigation	1	1.7	.677	9.588	.000
	2	2.1	.878		
Simple layout	1	1.7	.676	3.621	.000
	2	2.0	.861		
Linear display	1	1.6	.651	9.589	.000
	2	2.2	.849		
Smooth video	1	1.6	.710	7.757	.000
	2	2.1	.895		
Harmonious color	1	1.6	.652	3.985	.000
	2	2.0	.862		
Lecturer-learner interaction	1	1.9	.859	2.441	.001
	2	2.2	.907		
Learner-learner interaction	1	1.9	.849	.712	.000
	2	2.2	.871		
Human-computer interaction	1	1.9	.783	6.867	.000
	2	2.2	.896		

Table 7. T-test of answer differences from two groups to the questions in the third part

	Group	Mean	Std. dev.	t	Sig. (two sides)
Preference to use	1	1.7	.870	6.769	.000
	2	2.6	.994		
Easiness to change functions	1	1.7	.721	14.682	.000
	2	2.2	.896		
Easiness to use	1	1.7	.696	14.674	.000
	2	2.2	.902		
Stability	1	1.6	.692	15.858	.000
	2	2.2	.902		
Responsiveness	1	1.7	.724	11.801	.000
	2	2.2	.901		
Compatibility	1	1.7	.735	11.053	.000
	2	2.2	.904		
Personalization	1	1.7	.743	7.385	.000
	2	2.2	.895		

In order to find the difference between the learners using mobile clients and those using traditional computers, we divided the learners into two groups, Group 1 with mobile clients (N = 346, 68.7%) and Group 2 with PC or tablet computers (N = 158, 31.3%). We used independent sample T-test to analyze the difference of the two groups' answers to the items in second part and third part. The analysis result shows that the mobile client group's answer means to all items are less than that of non-mobile group at statistically significant level ($p < 0.05$), as shown in Tables 6 and 7. This result implies that the MOOC learners using smartphone and other mobile equipment recognized the six design guidelines more highly than the MOOC learners using personal computers and other traditional equipment, thus perceived more easiness and usefulness from the mobile MOOC learning.

7 Conclusion and Discussion

Based on the review of related literature and the assessment of the APPs provided by six mostly used MOOC platforms, we proposed six guidelines for the mobile MOOC design, i.e. clear navigation, simple layout, linear display, harmonious coloring, smooth video, and full interaction. To verify the rationality of those guidelines, we designed a corresponding survey to investigate the learners' perception and attitude toward the six guidelines implemented in one MOOC in China. The analysis of the survey result demonstrates that the MOOC learners believed those guidelines are valuable in mobile MOOC design and helpful for MOOC learning.

While more and more learners in China and all over the world are participating in MOOCs through smart phones, tablet computers and other mobile clients, MOOC platform designer and administrators, and MOOC lecturers should consider how to orient the MOOC design to the mobile learners. The six design guidelines suggested by this paper could serve a reference for those in charge of MOOC platform and MOOCs.

One limitation of this research is the lack of practical implementation of those guidelines by the authors. Because the authors were neither the designer of the MOOC platform and its APP, nor the MOOC instructors themselves, they could not implement the design guidelines in MOOC APP and MOOC instruction. The authors, just as a third-party, independently evaluated the learners' perception and attitude toward one MOOC in China, whose lecturer was asked to follow those six guidelines. In the future the authors will try to get the chance to use open source MOOC platform such as EdX from MIT to design APP for MOOC, implement the guidelines in one MOOC, and evaluate its effect on learning outcome through empirical study.

Acknowledgement. This research is supported by the project, "Research of instructional design principles for MOOCs based on learning analytics" (No. 2016ZD101), from Online Education Research Center, Ministry of Education (QuanTong Education Fund), China. The authors thank also all the volunteers, lecturers and learners who have participated in the project and in the investigated MOOC.

References

Yu, M., Zhou, J.: The application prospects of mobile MOOCs in higher education. Guangzhou Educ. **15**, 238–239 (2014)
Chen, X.: Android MOOC app design. China Comput. Commun. **4**, 29–30 (2015)
Zhuo, J., Chen, H., Wei, J.: The need analysis of mobile MOOC system. In: Proceedings of the Ninth Management Science Annual Conference (2014)
He, Y., Yan, Z., Chen, W.: The mobile learning platform design based on MOOC. Netw. Secur. Technol. Appl. **2**, 7–8 (2015)
Feng, M.: MOOCS based on mobile learning platform. Sci. Technol. Vis. **18**, 45–46 (2014)
Lan, X., Yang, L., Wang, H., He, G., Guo, Q.: The exploration of MOOC to SMOOC. Shaanxi RTVU J. **17**(1), 5–8 (2015)
Wang, B., Tao, B., Miao, F., Du, X.: Research of fragmented intelligent mobile learning model. J. Jiangsu Open Univ. **26**(4), 51–54 (2015)
Wang, L.: The design of the undergraduate course "Computer Literacy" based on edX. J. Inn. Mong. Norm. Univ. (Educ. Sci.) **28**(1), 96–97 (2015)
Zeng, M.: Micro-courses of mobile MOOC: an effective way to solve the problems of the in-service personnel's training. China Audio Vis. Educ. **3**, 30–34 (2015)
Hu, X.: Mobile MOOC design for vocational education courses. Asia Pac. Educ. **2**(20), 114 (2015)
Li, Y.: The exploration of mobile learning based on MOOCs. Hebei Sci. Technol. Forum **27**(4), 36–38 (2014)
Renz, J., Staubitz, T., Meinel, C.: MOOC to go. international association for the development of the information society. Paper presented at the international conference on mobile learning, 10th, Madrid, Spain, 28 February–2 March 2014
Sharples, M., Kloos, C.D., Dimitriadis, Y., Garlatti, S., Specht, M.: Mobile and accessible learning for MOOCs. J. Interact. Med. Educ. **2015**(1) (2015). https://doi.org/10.5334/jime.ai. Article ID 4

Perceived Usefulness of Open Educational Resources Between Full-Time and Distance-Learning Students

Simon K. S. Cheung(✉)

The Open University of Hong Kong,
Good Shepherd Street, Homantin, Kowloon, Hong Kong
kscheung@ouhk.edu.hk

Abstract. Open educational resources or OER have been recognized as a major source of learning materials for university students. This paper investigates the students' perception on the usefulness of OER with a focus on comparing the perceived usefulness between full-time and distance-learning students, based on a survey carried out at the Open University of Hong Kong in the academic year 2017–18. It is found that both full-time and distance-learning students generally consider OER useful for learning purposes, especially for using the resources to supplement the existing course materials and to get more resources for doing assignments and projects. On different types of OER, open courseware, course materials and e-books are mostly perceived as very useful or useful by both full-time and distance-learning students, while more distance-learning students than full-time students also consider open online courses, tutorials, and open online learning tools and platforms very useful or useful. For both full-time and distance learning students, accuracy and comprehensiveness are key concerns of using OER for learning purposes.

Keywords: Open Educational Resources · Open courseware
Massive Open Online Courses · Open access textbooks · Distance learning
Student perception

1 Introduction

The public internet and world-wide-web came into existence in the 1990s. After two decades, a vast volume of online resources have been openly available to the public through the internet. Examples are the online news, online magazines, online e-books, online games, images, audio and video clips, etc. Out of these online resources, some are educational resources such as online e-books, online courses and online learning tools, openly available for teaching and learning purposes. They are generally called open educational resources or OER. According to the Organization for Economic Cooperation and Development, OER is formally defined as the "digitized materials offered freely and openly for educators, students, and self-learners to use and re-use for teaching, learning and research" [1]. OER have been recognized as a major source of materials for teaching and learning at all levels, from primary and secondary education

S. K. S. Cheung et al. (Eds.): ICBL 2018, LNCS 10949, pp. 357–367, 2018.
https://doi.org/10.1007/978-3-319-94505-7_29

to higher education. They are used in both the traditional classroom-based learning, and distance-learning and online learning.

Like many online resources in the internet, OER contents are continuously growing at a compound rate. There are indeed a number of driving forces behind. First, the internet offers a very convenient means for openly sharing OER to the general public. Second, the broad penetration of information and communication technologies makes the access to the internet very convenient and well affordable. Third, the prevalence of digital culture enables the wide acceptance of using electronic form of learning materials to complement to traditional learning [2, 3]. Fourth, the development of standard open licensing options, such as the Creative Commons [4], simplifies the handling of copyrights for using, reusing, revising and sharing OER [5]. Fifth, official policies on the adoption of OER have been established at both the government and institution levels [6].

Although OER for primary and secondary education have become well available, the majority of the available OER basically aims for higher education. For the vast volume of OER in the Internet, Cheung, et al. attempted to categorize OER for higher education as open courseware, open online courses, open e-books, and open-source learning software and tools [7]. Open courseware refer to the self-contained course materials which are organized for a course of study, usually through self-study, such as OpenCourseWare [8], OpenLearn [9] and iTunes U [10]. Open online courses refer to the online courses openly and freely accessible through the Internet. They differ from open courseware because of allowing online interactions between the teachers and students. Massive open online courses or MOOCs, such as EdX [11], Coursera [12] and FutureLearn [13], are examples. Open e-books cover textbooks and reference books that are accessible online and downloadable for offline usage. Examples are OpenStar CNX [14], College Open Textbooks Collaborative [15] and Project Gutenberg [16]. Open-source learning tools include online dictionaries, encyclopedia, and learning platforms, such as Wikipedia [17], Wiktionary [18], and G-Suite for Education [19].

Following the author's previous study on the distance-learning students' perception on the usefulness of OER in last year [20], this paper continues to investigate the same topic, but with updated figures and a special focus on comparing the perceived usefulness between full-time and distance-learning students. It is based on a survey carried out at the Open University of Hong Kong, which offers undergraduate and postgraduate programmes, in both full-time and distance-learning modes. The survey was conducted in the beginning of the academic year 2017–18 to two separate sets of undergraduate students, full-time students and distance-learning students, through online questionnaires. The students were asked on the frequency of accessing OER and the general perception on the usefulness of different categories of OER, as well as the concerns on the shortcoming of OER. Based on the survey results, the students' general perception is analyzed, and the perceived usefulness is compared between full-time and distance-learning students. The results devise some findings on how OER can be effectively used by full-time and distance-learning undergraduate students for learning purposes.

The rest of this paper is organized as follows. Section 2 is an overview of OER for teaching and learning. Section 3 reports the above-mentioned survey in details. Section 4 summarizes the key findings from the survey results. Section 5 concludes this paper with some discussion.

2 Overview of OER for Teaching and Learning

This section provides an overview of OER, based on the categorization of OER for higher education by Cheung et al. [7]. For teaching and learning in higher education, OER can be categorized as open courseware, open online courses, open e-books, and open-source learning software and tools, as follows.

Open courseware are completed sets of self-contained course materials or learning materials in electronic format. The contents are coherently organized for a course of study. Open courseware are usually offered by higher education institutions and open learning institutions by openly sharing some of their existing courseware or learning materials. Therefore, they are primarily designed for the offering institutions. OCW, OpenLearn and iTunes U are some representative examples [8–10]. OCW provides learning materials of 2,400 courses, mainly from the Massachusetts Institute of Technology [8]. Similar to OCW, the Open University in the United Kingdom offers open and free learning materials of almost 1,000 courses on its OpenLearn platform [9]. The iTunes U was launched by Apple for universities to deliver open and free university-level learning materials, which are mainly lectures, tutorials and demonstratives in audio and video formats [10].

Open online courses are by nature online courses, but freely and openly available for the general public through the internet. They include massive open online courses or MOOC, offered by many world-class universities. Not only offering the necessary course materials, open online courses also allow some online interaction between the teachers and students. Enrollment is required, and the courses are basically instructor-led online courses in a virtual classroom setting. A number of well-known MOOC, such as EdX, Coursea and FutureLearn [11–13]. Launched in 2012 by the Harvard University and the Massachusetts Institute of Technology, EdX becomes MOOC platform offering over 1,000 open online courses of over 90 renowned universities around the world [11]. Similar to the EdX, Coursera is another MOOC platform offering over 2,000 open online courses from 149 higher education institutions [12]. FutureLearn is a MOOC platform launched by a group of higher education institutions in the United Kingdom [13]. Hundreds of open online courses are offered by the institutions together with other partners.

Open e-books are by nature e-books, covering textbooks, reference books, and other books relevant to the study. They are openly and freely accessible online, and downloadable for offline reading through some e-book readers. Open e-books provide textual and graphical contents as the traditional printed books, as well as the digital contents such as multimedia and interactive elements [21, 22]. Openstar CNX, College Open Textbooks Collaborative and Project Gutenberg are some representative examples [14–16]. Initiated by the Rice University, Openstar CNX offers open e-textbooks at the post-secondary level in Mathematics, Science, Social Sciences and Humanities [14]. The College Open Textbooks Collaborative is a consortium of 29 educational organizations to offering hundreds of open textbooks, which are being used by over 2,000 colleges [15]. Project Gutenberg is another well-established platform offering open e-books which can be read online, or downloaded in various formats, including e-Pub and Kindle [16]. Most of the open e-books were previously published e-books by bona fide publishers and proof-read by volunteers.

The last category refers to the open-source learning software and tools, which are different from open courseware, open online courses or open e-books. They are online tools or open-source software that support teaching and learning, such as online dictionaries and other online learning tools, as well as open platforms for individual learning and collaborative learning. Wikipedia, Wiktionary, and G-Suite for Education are some representative examples [17–19]. Wikipedia is a well-known multilingual, web-based and free-content encyclopedia platform for openly editable contents, contributed collaboratively by anonymous volunteers [17]. Similar to the Wikipedia, Wiktionary is an open online dictionary which collects over 5 million English words, 3 million French words, and 1 million words in other languages [18]. Offered by Google, G-Suite is a bundle of open and free applications as well as online cloud storage for learning purposes [19].

3 Survey on the Perception of the Usefulness of OER

This section reports a survey on the perception of the usefulness of OER for learning purposes. The survey was separately conducted to the full-time and distance-learning undergraduate students at the Open University of Hong Kong in the beginning of the academic year 2017–18.

Founded in 1989, the Open University of Hong Kong is a well-established public university in Hong Kong that offers undergraduate and postgraduate programmes, in both full-time and distance-learning modes [23]. In December 2017, an e-mail was sent to two randomly selected sets of students from all undergraduate programmes, one being the full-time students and the other being the distance-learning students, inviting them to complete an online questionnaires. The online questionnaire consists of 3 parts. In the first part, the students were asked on the frequency of accessing OER, and the general perception on the usefulness of OER for different learning purposes. The second part focus on the perception on the usefulness of each category of OER for different learning purposes, while the third part focus on the concerns about the shortcomings of OER.

For the survey, a total of 356 and 293 valid responses were received from the full-time and part-time students respectively. The survey results are reported, separately for full-time and distance-learning students, as follows.

3.1 General Perception on the Usefulness of OER

Table 1 shows the frequency of accessing OER for learning purposes. For full-time students, 83% of the responses often or very often access OER while 23% sometimes access OER, and only 4% seldom access OER. For distance-learning students, 72% of the responses often or very often access OER while 19% sometimes access OER and 10% seldom access OER. In general, the majority of full-time and distance-learning students often or very often access OER. The percentage of full-time students often or very often access OER is higher than that of distance-learning students.

Table 1. Frequency of accessing OER for learning purposes.

Frequency	% of responses (full-time)	% of responses (distance-learning)
Very often (every day)	31%	26%
Often (more than once per week, but not every day)	52%	46%
Sometimes (once per week)	13%	19%
Seldom (less than once per week)	4%	10%
Never	0%	0%

Table 2 shows the full-time students' overall perception on the usefulness of OER, where the majority (over 70%) generally consider OER very useful or useful for being used to supplement the existing course materials and do assignments or projects. About half generally consider OER very useful or useful for being used to prepare tests or examinations. Table 3 shows the figures on the distance-learning students. The majority (over 70%) generally consider OER very useful or useful, not only for being used to supplement the existing course materials and do assignments or projects but also to acquire more knowledge as learning reference.

Table 2. Full-time students' overall perception on the usefulness of OER.

Learning purposes	Very useful	Useful	Neutral	Less useful	Not useful
To supplement the existing course materials	40%	34%	19%	4%	2%
To acquire more knowledge as learning reference	35%	31%	22%	7%	5%
To get resources for doing assignments or projects	43%	31%	17%	6%	2%
To get resources for preparing tests or examination	29%	26%	26%	11%	7%

Table 3. Distance-learning students' usefulness of OER for learning purposes.

Learning purposes	Very useful	Useful	Neutral	Less useful	Not useful
To supplement the existing course materials	42%	34%	19%	3%	2%
To acquire more knowledge as learning reference	40%	34%	19%	4%	2%
To get resources for doing assignments or projects	44%	33%	17%	4%	2%
To get resources for preparing tests or examination	38%	24%	23%	10%	5%

3.2 Usefulness of OER in Learning Activities

In the following, the students' perception on the usefulness of the four categories of OER, namely, open courseware, open online courses, open e-books, and open-source learning software and tools, are reported.

On open courseware, Table 4 shows the full-time students' perception while Table 5 shows the distance-learning students' perception. They the commonality that the majority (over 70%) generally consider open courseware very useful or useful for learning purposes. These open courseware cover the openly shared complete sets of course materials, openly shared lecture notes or class notes, openly shared video clips of lectures or classes, and other supplementary course or learning materials.

Table 4. Full-time students' perception on the usefulness of open courseware.

Types of open courseware	Very useful	Useful	Neutral	Less useful	Not useful
Openly shared complete sets of course materials	52%	25%	18%	3%	1%
Openly shared lecture notes or class notes	52%	27%	17%	2%	3%
Openly shared video clips of lectures or classes	48%	24%	21%	3%	3%
Other supplementary course or learning materials	43%	31%	19%	5%	3%

Table 5. Distance-learning students' perception on the usefulness of open courseware.

Types of open courseware	Very useful	Useful	Neutral	Less useful	Not useful
Openly shared complete sets of course materials	48%	26%	20%	5%	1%
Openly shared lecture notes or class notes	51%	26%	17%	4%	2%
Openly shared video clips of lectures or classes	52%	25%	17%	5%	1%
Other supplementary course or learning materials	46%	30%	19%	4%	2%

On open online courses, Table 6 shows the full-time students' perception while Table 7 shows the distance-learning students' perception. It is shown in Table 6 that about half (38% to 59%) of full-time students generally consider open online courses very useful or useful. However, for distance-learning students, as shown in Table 7, more than half (50% to 72%) generally consider open online courses very useful or useful, in particular, the massive open online courses (self-contained full courses) and open online tutorials on specific topics.

Table 6. Full-time students' perception on the usefulness of open online courses.

Types of open online courses	Very useful	Useful	Neutral	Less useful	Not useful
Massive open online courses (self-contained full courses)	32%	27%	28%	9%	5%
Open online tutorials on specific topics	28%	30%	31%	8%	3%
Small-scale mobile learning courses or apps	18%	21%	40%	12%	9%
Open online interactive help desks or discussion forums	17%	21%	32%	19%	12%

Table 7. Distance-learning students' perception on the usefulness of open online courses.

Types of open online courses	Very useful	Useful	Neutral	Less useful	Not useful
Massive open online courses (self-contained full courses)	46%	26%	22%	5%	1%
Open online tutorials on specific topics	36%	32%	23%	6%	2%
Small-scale mobile learning courses or apps	22%	28%	35%	10%	5%
Open online interactive help desks or discussion forums	28%	28%	29%	11%	4%

On open e-books, Table 8 shows the full-time students' perception while Table 9 shows the distance-learning students' perception. They have the commonality that the majority (over 70%) generally consider different types of open e-books (including self-contained textbooks and self-contained reference books) very useful or useful for learning purposes, except open e-journals, e-journals or e-magazines.

Table 8. Full-time students' perception on the usefulness of open e-books.

Types of open e-books	Very useful	Useful	Neutral	Less useful	Not useful
Open access e-books (self-contained textbooks)	56%	23%	14%	5%	2%
Open access e-books (self-contained reference books)	52%	24%	16%	6%	2%
Open access e-journal, e-periodicals or e-magazines	36%	20%	24%	13%	4%
Open access reports or other open access documentations	43%	26%	20%	9%	3%

On open-source learning software or tools, Table 10 shows the full-time students' perception while Table 11 shows the distance-learning students' perception. They have the commonality that the majority (69% to 82%) consider open online dictionaries or encyclopedia very useful or useful, and more than half (60% to 66%) consider other software or tools very useful or useful. Besides, the majority (73%) of distance-learning students but about half (57%) of full-time students also consider online learning platform very useful or useful.

Table 9. Distance-learning students' perception on the usefulness of open e-books.

Types of open e-books	Very useful	Useful	Neutral	Less useful	Not useful
Open access e-books (self-contained textbooks)	60%	23%	12%	3%	2%
Open access e-books (self-contained reference books)	54%	27%	14%	3%	2%
Open access e-journal, e-periodicals or e-magazines	42%	23%	22%	9%	4%
Open access reports or other open access documentations	45%	27%	19%	7%	2%

Table 10. Full-time students' perception on the usefulness of open learning tools.

Types of open learning tools	Very useful	Useful	Neutral	Less useful	Not useful
Open online dictionaries or encyclopedia	43%	26%	23%	5%	3%
Online anti-plagiarism checker and grammar checker	37%	28%	22%	8%	6%
Other open learning software (mind map, slide builder, etc.)	28%	32%	24%	11%	4%
Online learning platform for self or collaborative learning	27%	30%	30%	10%	3%

Table 11. Distance-learning students' perception on the usefulness of open tools.

Types of open learning tools	Very useful	Useful	Neutral	Less useful	Not useful
Open online dictionaries or encyclopedia	53%	29%	14%	3%	2%
Online anti-plagiarism checker and grammar checker	40%	26%	25%	5%	4%
Other open learning software (mind map, slide builder, etc.)	34%	27%	30%	4%	5%
Online learning platform for self or collaborative learning	39%	34%	18%	7%	3%

3.3 Shortcomings or Concerns of OER

Whilst OER offer many advantages such as providing the general public the freedom to use, reuse, revise and share educational materials, students have concerns on their shortcomings. From the students' perspectives, the quality, readability, completeness and relevancy of the contents are of some known concerns on the shortcomings in using OER, for example, whether the contents are accurate, comprehensive, well organized, and updated [24, 25].

Tables 12 and 13 show the full-time and distance-learning students' concerns on the shortcomings in using OER respectively. While they generally have these concerns, more students have concerns on the accuracy and comprehensiveness than others, as reflected in the percentages – 61% of full-time students and 57% of distance-learning students strongly agree or agree that the contents may not be accurate; 56% of full-time students and 51% of distance-learning students strongly agree or agree that the contents may not be comprehensive.

Table 12. Full-time students' concerns on the shortcomings in using OER.

Shortcomings of OER	Strongly agree	Agree	Neutral	Disagree	Strongly disagree
Contents may not be accurate	24%	37%	25%	11%	3%
Contents may not be up-to-date	17%	29%	33%	15%	7%
Contents may not be comprehensive	19%	37%	28%	11%	4%
Contents may not be well organized	17%	30%	35%	12%	5%

Table 13. Distance-learning students' concerns on the shortcomings in using OER.

Shortcomings of OER	Strongly agree	Agree	Neutral	Disagree	Strongly disagree
Contents may not be accurate	26%	31%	28%	10%	5%
Contents may not be up-to-date	16%	30%	33%	14%	6%
Contents may not be comprehensive	24%	27%	32%	13%	4%
Contents may not be well organized	21%	26%	33%	14%	5%

4 Findings from the Survey Results

The survey results and the findings are summarized below.

- OER are very often or often used by the majority of students (both full-time and distance-learning students) for learning purposes.
- Full-time students generally consider OER very useful or useful for being used to supplement the existing course materials supplementing the course and do assignments or projects. Distance-learning students have the same perception, but also consider OER very useful or useful for being used to acquire more knowledge as learning reference.
- Both full-time and distance-learning generally consider open courseware (the course materials, lecture notes, and video clips of lecture or classes, etc.) very useful or useful for learning purposes.
- In terms of percentage, more distance-learning students than full-time students consider open online courses (in particular, massive open online courses and online tutorials on specific topics) very useful or useful for learning purposes.

- On the open e-books, both full-time and distance-learning students generally consider self-contained textbooks and reference books (but not e-journals or e-magazines) very useful or useful for learning purposes.
- Open online dictionaries and encyclopedia are generally considered to be very useful or useful by both full-time and distance-learning students. Besides, in terms of percentage, more distance-learning students than full-time students consider online learning platform (for self and collaborative learning) very useful or useful for learning purposes.
- Both full-time students and distance-learning students have more concerns on the accuracy and comprehensiveness of the contents in using OER for learning purposes.

5 Conclusion

OER have been widely adopted, especially in higher education. Vast amount of OER contents are available in the internet, and the contents are continuously growing at a compound rate. It is of no doubt that OER benefits both teaching and learning. This paper reports a survey recently carried out at the Open University of Hong Kong on the students' perceived usefulness of using different categories of OER for learning purposes. The results are analyzed with a focus on comparing the students' perception between full-time and distance-learning students.

It is found that OER are generally considered useful by both full-time and distance-learning students, especially as to supplement the existing course materials and do assignments or projects. In particular, open courseware and course materials, e-books, and online dictionaries or encyclopedia are well adopted for learning purposes. It is also found that more distance-learning students than full-time students consider open online courses and open collaborative learning platform useful for learning purposes. This probably reflects that distance-learning students lack some lecture-type learning experience and collaborative learning experience, on which OER can be effectively used as supplements. Finally, the accuracy and comprehensiveness of OER contents are still the students' key concerns. These findings would serve a practical reference in the adoption of OER for teaching and learning.

References

1. OECD: Giving Knowledge for Free: The Emergence of Open Education Resources. Centre for Educational Research and Innovation, Organization for Economic Cooperation and Development (2007)
2. Cheung, K.S., Lam, J., Im, T., Szeto, R.: Exploring a pedagogy-driven approach to e-course development. In: Proceedings of the IEEE International Workshop on Education Technology and Training, pp. 22–25. IEEE (2008)
3. Lam, J., Cheung, K.S., Yau, J., Seto, W., Im, T.: Students' needs of e-courses as complement to traditional learning: a Japanese studies e-course case. In: Proceedings of the International Symposium on IT in Medicine and Education, pp. 876–880. IEEE (2008)
4. Creative Commons: Website of Creative Commons (2018). http://creativecommons.org

5. Yuen, K.S., Chow, L., Cheung, S.K.S., Li, K.C., Tsang, E.Y.M.: Overcoming copyright hurdles in the development of learning materials in the digital era. In: Li, K.C., Wang, F.L., Yuen, K.S., Cheung, S.K.S., Kwan, R. (eds.) ICT 2012. CCIS, vol. 302, pp. 190–200. Springer, Heidelberg (2012). https://doi.org/10.1007/978-3-642-31398-1_17
6. Hoosen, S.: Survey on Governments' Open Educational Resources Policies. World OER Congress, Commonwealth of Learning and UNESCO (2012)
7. Cheung, S.K.S., Li, K.C., Yuen, K.S.: An overview of open education resources for higher education. In: Lam, J., Li, K.C., Cheung, S.K.S., Wang, F.L. (eds.) ICT 2013. CCIS, vol. 407, pp. 26–34. Springer, Heidelberg (2013). https://doi.org/10.1007/978-3-642-45272-7_3
8. MIT: Website of MIT OpenCourseWare (2018). http://ocw.mit.edu
9. OpenLearn: Website of OpenLearn (2018). http://www.open.edu/openlearn
10. Apple: Website of iTunes U (2018). http://www.apple.com/itunes-u
11. EdX: Website of EdX (2018). http://www.edx.org
12. Coursera: Website of Coursera (2018). http://www.coursera.org
13. FurtureLearn: Website of FutureLearn (2018). http://www.futurelearn.com
14. CNX: Website of OpenStar CNX (2018). http://www.cnx.org
15. COTC: Website of College Open Textbooks Collaborative (2018). http://www.collegeopentextbooks.org
16. Gutenberg: Website of Project Gutenberg (2018). http://gutenberg.org
17. Wikipedia: Website of Wikipedia (2018). http://www.wikipedia.org
18. Wiktionary: Website of Wiktionary (2018). http://www.wiktionary.org
19. Google: Website of Google for Education (2018). http://www.google.com/edu
20. Cheung, S.K.S.: Distance-learning students' perception on the usefulness of open educational resources. In: Cheung, S.K.S., Kwok, L-f, Ma, W.W.K., Lee, L.-K., Yang, H. (eds.) ICBL 2017. LNCS, vol. 10309, pp. 389–399. Springer, Cham (2017). https://doi.org/10.1007/978-3-319-59360-9_34
21. Tsang, E.Y.M., Yuen, K.S., Li, K.C., Cheung, S.K.S.: Designing open textbooks for effective teaching and learning. In: Lam, J., Li, K.C., Cheung, S.K.S., Wang, F.L. (eds.) ICT 2013. CCIS, vol. 407, pp. 43–55. Springer, Heidelberg (2013). https://doi.org/10.1007/978-3-642-45272-7_5
22. Cheung, S.K.S., Yuen, K.S., Li, K.C., Tsang, E.Y.M., Wong, A.: Open access textbooks: opportunities and challenges. In: Li, K.C., Wang, F.L., Yuen, K.S., Cheung, S.K.S., Kwan, R. (eds.) ICT 2012. CCIS, vol. 302, pp. 201–210. Springer, Heidelberg (2012). https://doi.org/10.1007/978-3-642-31398-1_18
23. OUHK: Website of Open University of Hong Kong (2018). http://www.ouhk.edu.hk
24. Educause: 7 Things You Should Know About Open Educational Resources. Educause Learning Initiative, June 2010
25. Camilleri, A.F., Ehlers, U.D. Pawlowski, J.: State of the Art Review of Quality Issues Related to Open Educational Resources, JCR Scientific and Policy Reports, Joint Research Centre, European Commission (2014)

Students' Evaluation of SkELL: The 'Sketch Engine for Language Learning'

Yoko Hirata(✉) and Yoshihiro Hirata

Hokkai-Gakuen University, Sapporo, Japan
hira@eli.hokkai-s-u.ac.jp, hirata@hgu.jp

Abstract. The recent development of authentic language data called corpora has made it possible for linguists to create more reliable dictionaries and do linguistic research. The resources are valuable in that they help students learn various lexical and grammatical patterns such as collocations. However, corpora are not used as mainstream teaching materials at schools. It is assumed that for those who haven't had sufficient online language learning experiences, such as Japanese students, it could be difficult to appreciate the efficacy of these resources. Unfortunately, little research has been conducted regarding how students view the utilization and efficacy of these online language resources. This study aims to assess the utility of the corpus driven web-interface, SkELL (Sketch Engine for Language Learning) through students' own evaluations of the tool, as part of an English course at their Japanese university. The major benefit observed by the students was the freedom to access a very large amount of raw English language data, which they can use to investigate various lexical and grammatical combinations related to their studies without additional cost. While the learning curve for SkELL is not as steep as traditional corpus tools, detailed guidance from instructors remains necessary to ensure students are able to take full advantage of the platform.

Keywords: SkELL · Online resources · Language learning · Japanese

1 Introduction, Research and Aim

With the development of various online language learning resources readily available to students, the introduction of authentic language data into mainstream language classroom is steadily becoming an inevitable innovation. While the benefits of these technologies have widely been discussed, their actual utility remains limited due to the various challenges associated with learning how to operate these technologies in classroom settings. One such tool for looking up authentic language data in English is a *concordancer*. The British National Corpus (BNC) and the Corpus of Contemporary American English (COCA) are two catalogues of authentic English that are accessible online, where a keyword search returns a series of *concordance lines*. This layout makes it easy for users to compare many instances of a keyword's use across many contexts. Concordancers have a long history of being used as reference tools to help students correct their lexical and grammatical mistakes in writing courses [1–3]. They also help students learn different complicated rules without providing them with

S. K. S. Cheung et al. (Eds.): ICBL 2018, LNCS 10949, pp. 368–377, 2018.
https://doi.org/10.1007/978-3-319-94505-7_30

detailed explanations of words and grammar [4]. In addition, this assists students in enhancing their autonomous and independent learning [5, 6], which results in encouraging them to get actively involved in their language learning [7]. Unfortunately, one of the problems associated with using online corpora is their usability and narrow functionality. For example, these two concordancers provide incomplete sentences and no ability to search the wider context of an individual search result. This, and other such limitations, lead to difficulties producing effective teaching materials or methods from concordancers, requiring instructors to employ innovative strategies to make full use of them, or to make them accessible to their students. Recent studies have suggested that online educational materials have played important roles in developing their lifelong language skills [8]. Therefore, more research should be conducted on the effectiveness of user-friendly corpora for various groups of students, including strategies for choosing a corpus indexer which matches their needs and preferences. Giving students' an active role in evaluating corpora tools may be one such way to achieve this goal.

Research Background and SkELL

SkELL (Sketch Engine for Language Learning) [9] is a relatively new web-based tool largely containing English (https://skell.sketchengine.co.uk/run.cgi/skell). The tool provides a search engine which returns example sentences containing the search term, as well as collocations and related terms. The corpus indexed is the entire catalogue of articles from the English *Wikipedia* website [10]. Since this is a reference tool it is believed to be effective for both instructors teaching and students learning English [10].

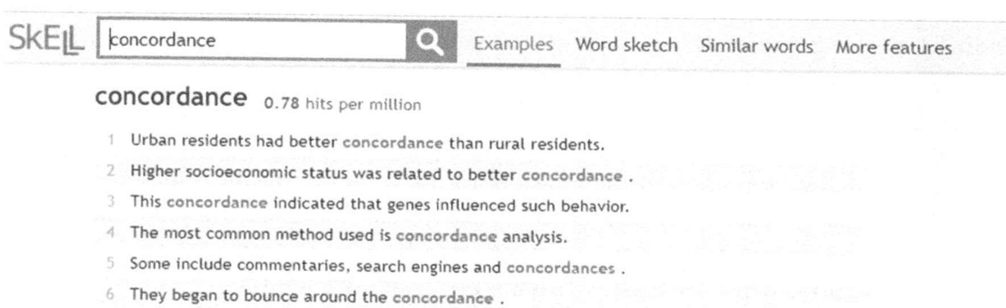

It has clearly been acknowledged that the evaluation of resources plays an important role in the successful language learning [11] and they need to be carefully examined to meet the instructor's need to accomplish their teaching purposes [12]. Although online language learning resources such as SkELL often require students to work on them individually comprehensive investigation into how students evaluate and explore them is indispensable for their smooth implementation in the classroom. However, there are few studies on the effectiveness of student-based evaluations of SkELL. In addition, little has been written on examining students' views on utilizing the reference tool for their language study. In order to maximize the quality of students' English language learning experiences, in-depth analysis of novice users' responses to SkELL is of crucial importance.

Aim of the Study

The aim of this study was to demonstrate how novice SkELL users perceived the utilization of SkELL from an English study perspective. The present study was also aimed at determining how students see the benefits and problems of the tool to improve their English language skills. The study sought to answer the following questions:

1. How can students review and evaluate SkELL?
2. What are the benefits and problems of SkELL from the students' perspectives?
3. How can language instructors encourage students to utilize SkELL effectively?

The results will assist instructors in considering how to integrate online language resources into their language courses in order to meet the specific students' learning needs and goals.

2 Experimental Study

2.1 Participants

The students of this study (n = 26) were lower intermediate Japanese undergraduate students of English in an English course. They were full-time female students between the age of eighteen and twenty-two. The course was offered by the Faculty of Humanities and it was a semester-long blended course providing both a traditional face-to-face and online environment. The course was offered once a week for ninety minutes in a computer lab. The aim of this course was to improve their four skills (reading, speaking, listening and writing) focusing specifically on reading skills.

Although students were used to the traditional language learning approach taken in a large lecture-type classroom where the teacher tended to adopt predominately textbook-based teacher-directed instruction [13], the majority of them had general experience in using computers in the classroom. In addition, all the students had been using the Internet and mobiles in their everyday lives. However, they had no experience in online independent language learning in or beyond the conventional classroom in secondary school where English curricula are exam-oriented.

In Japan, English examination typically involves multiple-choice questions and the Grammar-Translation model, which requires students to translate English to Japanese and vice versa [14]. Students are also accustomed to rote-memorization of words, phrases and grammatical points are taught in isolation without clear contexts, which is the most efficient approach to achieving success in their exams. This marriage between teaching methodology and examinations generally makes English assessment in Japan straight-forward and predictable for both teachers and students, but it is widely considered to be ineffective for developing communication ability [15].

While the course in this study was considered to be a *reading course*, and not one focused on improving communication directly, students were still encouraged to work together and discuss their learning as they worked with SkELL. However, the primary goal in working with SkELL was to supplement their attempts to read and interpret their textbooks using the online resource to create paraphrases or new sentences with target words and phrases. Of the 26 students, only four had experience using online dictionaries, and none had experience using SkELL before they took this course.

2.2 SkELL Project

At the beginning of the course the introductory information on SkELL together with online English monolingual dictionaries were given to the students. The instructor explained the importance of consulting authentic English resources in the classroom. In addition, the instructor strongly encouraged students to consult these reference tools whenever they had trouble with unknown words and phrases. Students were also required to create dialogues and texts using SkELL and present it to the class. The focus in this course was on looking at collocations and the context where the target words and phrases were used, and to summarize and paraphrase the key words and expressions acquired from their textbooks with the help of SkELL. The instructor monitored students' utilization of these tools during class. At the end of the course students were required as an examination to write several short texts including the required five key words and phrases which had been covered in the course. The aim of this written test was to examine whether or not they were able to use the key words and phrases they had learned productively.

2.3 Data Collection

After the project, in order to obtain qualitative and quantitative data, a 20-item questionnaire, including both closed and open questions, was distributed to the students in order to collect their opinions of SkELL evaluation, including the advantages and disadvantages of the tool. The questions sought information about features and the effectiveness in developing their English skills. The rating scale used in the questionnaire was a 10-point Likert Scale with 1 representing "strongly disagree" and 10 representing "strongly agree". In order for students to fully understand the questions, the questionnaires were written in Japanese. For the purpose of attaining a mean response for each question, the responses were totaled and averaged. Standard deviation was then obtained for the purpose of examining statistically meaningful differences between students' responses. The data is presented in this paper as mean $\pm$ SD.

3 Highlights of the Findings

3.1 Closed Questions

The data collected from the students is presented below. As shown in Table 1, the majority of students appreciated the large number of example sentences presented by SkELL (7.0 ± 1.8), and generally felt the tool contributed positively to their English studies (6.9 ± 1.6). Students generally felt the tool was useful for acquiring collocations (6.7 ± 1.9), although there was more variation in whether this improved their overall ability to use these expressions (5.9 ± 2.1).

Table 1. Averages of the students' use of SkELL.

	Mean (SD)
1. SkELL's large volume of example sentences is useful for your English study	7.0 (1.8)
2. Unlike the limited number of example sentences in the dictionary, SkELL helps you learn how words and phrases are used	5.9 (2.1)
3. Using SkELL in the classroom helped you study English successfully	6.9 (1.6)
4. The instructor should strongly encourage you to use SkELL even at home	6.3 (1.6)
5. SkELL helps you learn various collocations	6.7 (1.9)
6. The number of example sentences provided by SkELL is appropriate for your English study	6.8 (1.5)

(N = 26)

The results presented in Table 2 show students had mixed opinions on the usefulness of SkELL in their English studies. They scored SkELL marginally higher than online dictionaries in terms of its usability and efficiency when they study English, however its features did not contribute strongly to their attitudes towards their overall English language studies. But in both cases opinions are not strong, as indicated by respective means and standard deviations of (6.5 ± 1.9) (5.5 ± 1.8).

Table 2. SkELL's students' reading strategies for using the Web.

	Mean (SD)
7. SkELL is superior to dictionaries in that it makes you look at words and/or phrases instead of a single word	6.5 (1.9)
8. SkELL is useful when you prepare for TOEIC exams	6.5 (1.6)
9. SkELL enhances your motivation to study English	5.5 (1.8)
10. SkELL attracts and interests you, so studying with it is fun and entertaining	4.8 (1.8)

(N = 26)

Table 3 shows the students' preferred components of SkELL. The results indicate that students valued the appropriate length of the example sentences provided by SkELL (7.4 ± 1.7). However, calculations from the data set reveals only approximately 27% of students were confident they had learnt how the target words and phrases were to be used in context. Furthermore, approximately half of the students in this project thought using SkELL alone as a reference tool was not sufficient to improve their language skills.

Students were divided on whether or not they thought using SkELL in secondary school was appropriate (6.6 ± 2.4), with the wide deviation resulting from students either strongly agreeing or disagreeing with the notion, with few who were undecided. In terms of language skills gained by using this tool, while improvements were felt in

Table 3. Students' preferred components of SkELL

	Mean (SD)
11. The length of each example sentence in SkELL is appropriate	7.4 (1.7)
12. You need longer example sentences in SkELL	3.7 (1.8)
13. Using both SkELL and dictionaries is indispensable for your English study	7.2 (1.9)
14. You can learn how the target words and phrases are used in context	6.6 (1.7)
15. SkELL should be used in secondary schools	6.6 (2.4)
16. The layout of the website and interface is easy to follow	6.3 (1.4)
17. SkELL assists you in improving your reading skills	7.2 (1.6)
18. SkELL assists you in improving your speaking skills	6.4 (1.5)

(N = 26)

both areas, students generally felt it improved their reading skills more than their speaking skills (7.2 ± 1.6 and 6.4 ± 1.5 respectively).

3.2 Open Questions

While not all students responded here, the comments of those who did shed further light on the benefits and drawbacks experienced while using SkELL in this project.

Benefits

The major benefit of SkELL students pointed out is the number of example sentences provided by this tool. Two thirds of the students commented favorably on this topic; a sampling of their comments is as follows:

> *"Having a lot of raw example sentences helped me learn how to use the target words quite easily and gave me their prediction as to how they are combined with other words."*

> *"Due to its large number of example sentences SkELL gave me a different perspective from dictionaries on how English should be learned."*

> *"SkELL assisted me in learning various lexical and grammatical combinations because of its large number of examples."*

Five students mentioned the advantage of learning how the target words and phrases are used in different contexts.

> *"SkELL is a great tool to show certain words and their accompanying words in certain contexts. It is a good resource of learning how to use words in context."*

Four students commented on the convenience and usability of SkELL.

> *"Due to the appropriate size of colored key words or phrases on the screen, it is easy for me to read sentences on SkELL."*

> *"Sentences provided by SkELL are relatively short, making it easier for me to read them."*

> *"Reading English sentences without their Japanese translations is good for me to learn English."*

> *"SkELL is easier and more convenient than any other language resource websites to look at many usages accompanied with the target words."*

Drawbacks

Again, not all students responded, written comments of those who did shed further light on the major problem students emphasized was the difficulty experienced in understanding the meaning of sentences. Just over half of the students stated that reading example sentences was cumbersome because they needed to consult dictionaries for the meanings of unknown words. One of the students stated as follows:

> *"It took me a long time to come to understand the meaning of the sentences including the target key words and the co-occurring words because I had to look up many words in my dictionary very frequently."*

There were other students who had problems with shortness of sentences and the resultant lack of context as follows:

> *"Each sentence is too short for me to learn how the target words and phrases are used. I wanted to read the sentences in their original sources."*

> *"Due to shortness of example sentences, those with pronouns made it extremely difficult for me to imagine the context in which the target expressions are used."*

In addition, there were also students who were less impressed by the usability of the interface, including a few who struggled with the large numbers of sentences, in contrast to the majority of their classmates:

"Since there are different ways of using SkELL it'll take time for me to get accustomed to it."

"I was overwhelmed with the large number of sentences and therefore was not able to find what I wanted."

"SkELL required me to type correct spelling to get search results."

Three students also wanted SkELL to provide them with Japanese translations of the example sentences.

4 Discussion

The project in this study was introduced on an experimental basis and therefore no well-organized learner training was offered. However, the findings and the comments provided by the students indicate that the majority valued SkELL. The primary utility praised was the number of sentences provided per search. These presented various word combinations which students never encountered in their everyday situations, nor in their textbooks. The questionnaire results regarding the efficacy of the sentences presented by SkELL suggested that many students benefitted from the advantages of being able to examine collocations in many sentences, as well as identify co-occurring words and phrases. For the majority of students this helped them to understand how the target words and expressions are used in context.

On the other hand, a small majority of students expressed their difficulty dealing with the many unknown words included in the sentences their searches returned. In addition, some students were confused by sentences including pronouns because the isolated sentences did not provide the relevant antecedents. This habit of looking at for these antecedents is highly problematic, and indicative of students having been required to reliably identify these nouns as part of their assessment in secondary-school. However, a pronoun can be provided without giving it any clear antecedent and be used to refer to an entire preceding phrase or clause instead of one clear noun antecedent. Therefore, having students practice imaging what these pronouns might be referring to is one way to overcome this drawback of SkELL, and help students begin to analyse difficult sentences with many unknown words more inductively.

While most students saw the large number of example sentences as a benefit, a smaller number experienced the opposite, and found the large number overwhelming. However, even these students were persistent in their desire to utilize SkELL, presumably because they appreciated the opportunity to learn about the various ways in which the words could be used - something that was unavailable to them during secondary school. In fact, if the relationship between students' views on SkELL and their backgrounds in English education could be examined, it is highly likely that we would find that students whose secondary schools relied more prominently on the traditional education methods discussed earlier, would produce students who struggle more with the sentences in SkELL. Since traditional methods rely on word-by-word textual analysis, these students are used to stopping as soon as they encounter an unknown word, instead of trying to work with their existing knowledge to make guesses or inferences about the overall meaning, and moving on.

5 Conclusion

This study examined how Japanese university students of English made use of and evaluated SkELL as part of their course of study. In this pilot study, the number of students who used the tool was too small to draw any concrete conclusions. However, the findings of this study provide new and important insights into how instructors might encourage students to fully utilize this or similar tools in their classrooms. The results reveal that SkELL has good potential to broaden students' English language learning experiences through various authentic language examples. In addition, tools like SkELL provide ample opportunities to develop more authentic materials and classroom activities. For example, students can contextualize the sentences by creating their own original stories and dialogues, or they can practice target expressions by rewriting or expanding the sentences with other words they're learning. Other ideas include encouraging students to find useful combinations of words and phrases for using in various conversational settings. Further in-depth research based on a larger scale study will be conducted to gain a more comprehensive understanding of how SkELL could effectively be implemented in language classes. Apart from an increased sample size, this larger study should include both male and female students, with demographic data provided for responses to both open and closed questions, as well as include actual learning outcomes. This will help instructors draw more reasonable conclusions regarding the further possibilities for effective utilization of authentic language data in the classroom.

References

1. Cargill, M., Adams, R.: Learning discipline-specific research English for a world stage: a self-access concordancing tool? In: Higher Education in a Changing World: Proceedings HERDSA, pp. 56–92. Higher Education Research and Development Society of Australasia Inc., Sydney (2005)
2. Chambers, A., O'Sullivan, I.: Corpus consultation and advanced learners' writing skills in French. ReCALL **16**(1), 158–172 (2004)
3. Frankenberg-Garcia, A.: Learners' use of corpus examples. Int. J. Lexicogr. **25**(3), 273–296 (2012)
4. Hunston, S.: Corpora in Applied Linguistics. Cambridge University Press, Cambridge (2002)

5. Boulton, A., Carter-Thomas, S., Rowley-Jolivet, E.: Issues in corpus-informed research and learning in ESP. In: Boulton, A., Carter-Thomas, S., Rowley-Jolivet, E. (eds.) Corpus-Informed Research and Learning in ESP. Issues and Applications. J. Benjamins, Amsterdam (2012)
6. Gitsaki, C.: Course design to promote student autonomy and lifelong learning skills: a Japanese example? In: Anderson, H., Hobbs, M., Jones-Parry, J., Logan, S., Lotovale, S. (eds.) Supporting Independent Learning in the 21st Century, Proceedings of the Second Conference of the Independent Learning Association, pp. 9–12. Independent Learning Association Oceania, Auckland (2005)
7. Chambers, A.: What is data-driven learning? In: O'Keeffe, A., McCarthy, M. (eds.) The Routledge Handbook of Corpus Linguistics, pp. 345–358. Routledge, New York (2010)
8. Walraven, A., Brand-Gruwel, S., Boshuizen, H.P.A.: How students evaluate information and sources when searching the World Wide Web for information. Comput. Educ. **25**(1), 234–246 (2009)
9. SkELL (Sketch Engine for Language Learning): Lexical Computing Ltd. (2014–2018). http://skell.sketchengine.co.uk/run.cgi/skell
10. Baisa, V., Suchomel, V.: SkELL: web interface for English language learning. In: Horák, A., Rychlý, P. (eds.) Proceedings of Recent Advances in Slavonic Natural Language Processing, RASLAN, pp. 63–70 (2014)
11. Johnson, K.: An Introduction to Foreign Language Learning and Teaching. Longman, Harlow (2008)
12. Ellis, R.: The empirical evaluation of language teaching materials. ELT J. **51**(1), 36–42 (1997)
13. Cooker, L., Torpey, M.: From the classroom to the self-access centre: a chronicle of learner-centred curriculum development. Lang. Teach. **28**(6), 11–16 (2004)
14. Humphries, S., Burns, A.: 'In reality it's almost impossible': CLT-oriented curriculum change. ELT J. **69**(3), 239–248 (2015)
15. Aspinall, R.W.: International Education Policy in Japan in an Age of Globalization and Risk. Global Oriental, Leiden (2013)

Performance Evaluation of ICT-Based Teaching and Learning in Higher Education

Yunxiang Zheng[1], Haozhen Li[1], and Tianxiang Zheng[2(✉)]

[1] School of Educational Information Technology, South China Normal University, Guangzhou, Guangdong, China
zyx@scnu.edu.cn, 21020602@qq.com
[2] Shenzhen Tourism College of Jinan University, Shenzhen, Guangdong, China
zsuzd@163.com

Abstract. ICT (Information and Communication Technology) is crucial to enhancing the quality of higher education by improving students' learning effectiveness and enriching their learning experiences. People are now concerned about the quality, efficiency, effectiveness, and return on investment (ROI) of how ICT is applied in higher education. Performance evaluation is an effective way to solve this problem, with the exceptional advantage of promoting sustainable development. In this paper, a 4-Dimension Performance Evaluation Model and corresponding course-related Performance Evaluation Indicator System in Massive Open Online Course (MOOC) case are proposed to evaluate how ICT is applied in higher education. Our case study with three MOOCs shows that our model and indicator system are helpful in measuring the current status of ICT in higher education while providing suggestions and directions to help the course become more "mature" and lead it to a new stage.

Keywords: ICT in education
ICT-based teaching and learning in higher education
Performance evaluation · Massive open online course

1 Introduction

Adaptive Learning Technology, Augmented Reality and Virtual Reality, Affective Computing, and Robotics are all new technologies that have a promising future in higher education in the coming years [1, 2]. It seems that ICT is developing much faster than ever before; they will definitely transform the education system's structure and revolutionize educational models in the near future. Actually, ICT has been widely and deeply integrated into higher education; one well-known example is MOOC. Undoubtedly, ICT is crucial to enhancing the quality of higher education by improving students' learning effectiveness and enriching student learning experiences. Therefore, many countries have invested enormous manpower, material resources and financial resources into different levels of colleges and universities. Until now, the infrastructure has been well constructed, with all kinds of resources and educational applications running on it.

S. K. S. Cheung et al. (Eds.): ICBL 2018, LNCS 10949, pp. 378–390, 2018.
https://doi.org/10.1007/978-3-319-94505-7_31

We raise two questions here: Does ICT performance meet people's expectations, and how should we evaluate the return on investment (ROI) in higher education? Administrators, teachers, students, parents, and researchers all hold different opinions. There is a tremendous discrepancy in measuring the input and output of ICT in education. Moreover, not enough concern has been placed on the performance of how ICT is applied in teaching and learning at different levels. In other words, we should try to evaluate the performance of ICT in the institute (university), for the courses, and for the teachers and students. To this end, this paper proposes a 4-Dimension Performance Evaluation Model (4DPEM) and corresponding course-related Performance Evaluation Indicator System (c-PEIS) to capture these ideas for evaluating how ICT is applied in higher education and leading it to a new stage.

2 Related Work

Begun in 1990, the Campus Computing Project (CCP) was the largest continuing study of the role of computing, information technology, and e-Learning in American higher education. The project's national studies drew on qualitative and quantitative data to help inform faculty, campus officials, policy-makers, and others interested in a wide array of information technology planning and policy issues that affect colleges and universities in the United States [3]. The CCP was considered the earliest research in this field. In 2001, the CEO Forum on Education and Technology in America produced the School Technology and Readiness (STaR) evaluation system [4]. In 2005, the World Bank performed research in some developing countries to evaluate the application of ICT in education; they focused on ten aspects that could be categorized into four themes [5]. International Telecommunication Union (ITU), United Nations Conference on Trade and Development (UNCTAD), the United Nations Educational, Scientific and Cultural Organization (UNESCO), and dozens of international organizations formed a partnership for measuring ICT for development and began to design and release "core ICT indictors" [6]. In 2006, British Educational Communications and Technology Agency (BECTA) released the Self-Review Framework (SRF) to evaluate ICT development and application level of a school [7]. In 2008, "ICT in Schools" was published by the Department of Education and Science [8]. In 2001, the Chinese Ministry of Industry and Information Technology proposed a scheme for national informatization index. Many provinces and cities released corresponding indicators of their administrative regions according to practical needs.

In recent years, performance evaluation of how ICT is applied in education has become a popular issue, ranging from research frameworks and analysis patterns to evaluation models and evaluation indicators. The enGauge framework used six aspects to assess the effectiveness of ICT in education [4]. Nicol and Coen proposed an INSIGHT model to evaluate ICT in higher education from a cost-benefit point of view [9]. Laurillard proposed a benefits-oriented cost model for technology-enhanced learning [10]. Rajev proposed a performance evaluation of ICT infrastructure in an academic environment [11]. Man conducted a trial of constructing an evaluation model for a university's use of ICT tools [12]. Lu created a method for calculating weight in performance evaluation for ICT [13]. Ma proposed a maturity model that was process-oriented [14]. There are many other studies that this paper does not mention, and together they make important contributions to the development of evaluating ICT in higher education both theoretically and practically.

3 Principles of Performance Evaluation in Higher Education

Performance originates from the company; it is considered as behavioral tendency and achievement in accordance with the overall goals and value pursuit of an organization [15]. Performance is composed of two aspects: behavior and value. It is a comprehensive reflection of processes and results. When applied to education, performance becomes unstable since the result of education is extremely difficult to calculate and evaluate. The following are some principles of constructing performance evaluation models and indicator systems in higher education:

(1) Performance evaluation should be comprehensive, revealing the core value of ICT in higher education. There are four functions for higher education: talent cultivation (teaching and learning), scientific research, education management, and societal service and cultural inheritance. Performance evaluation of ICT in higher education should cover these functions. In addition, there are three apparently different aspects when evaluating ICT in higher education: university (institute), course and teacher. As a result, performance evaluation should cover these aspects and treat them specifically. Note that the element "student" is included in the "course" aspect as its direct beneficiary (output).
(2) Performance evaluation should be performance-oriented, paying attention to performance enhancement and improvement. In a previous article [16], we proposed a performance evaluation meta-model from general and systematic angles to guide and evaluate the long-term effects of ICT in education. The performance-improving trail is about the continual improvement and sustainable development of performance. Our model should be derived from this meta-model to meet this principle.
(3) The model and performance evaluation system should be practical and easy to use. Specifically, the indexes should be specific and collectable from complex aspects of ICT-based teaching and learning, as they play important roles in evaluation and decision-making. In general, Divide-and-Conquer is an ideal way to solve a complex problem. Therefore, dimension reduction and subordinate relations between indicators can be flexibly used.

4 Performance Evaluation Model and Indicator System for ICT-Based Teaching and Learning in Higher Education

4.1 Performance Evaluation Model (PEM)

This paper evaluates performance evaluation by concentrating on the four functions of higher education and using the Capability Maturity Model (CMM) originally proposed in the field of Computer Science [17] to capture the progress or path that the performance undergoes. First, there are four functions of higher education and three aspects of evaluating ICT in higher education, as stated above. Second, performance evaluation normally emphasizes input (investment), process (teaching process in this paper) and output (achievement). Though management (organization or top-level design/planning) can be included in "input", this paper treats it separately as it represents high-level support and remains macroscopically stable. Lastly, we have to take into account the performance-improving trail required in CMM. Accordingly, a 4-Dimension Performance Evaluation Model (4DPEM) is proposed and depicted as Fig. 1, where the X-axis is the performance dimension, the Y-axis is the function dimension, and the Z-axis is the aspect dimension. The missing dimension is the performance-improving trail (dimension T for short), showing how the performance changes over time (just such as the newest 4D printing technology [18]). As this paper discusses performance evaluation and strengthens the importance of performance enhancement, the missing dimension T is always included by default in the following discussion, unless otherwise stated.

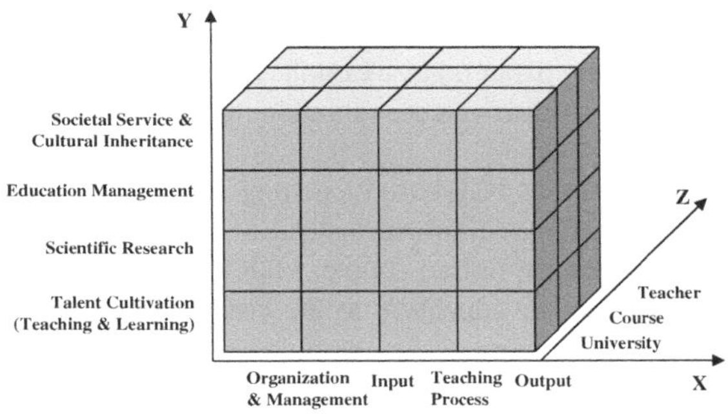

Fig. 1. 4-dimension performance evaluation model (Dimension T is omitted)

Figure 1 is only a skeleton of what our PEM looks like, while in practice each element (indicator) in each dimension should be divided into several parts to reveal its components and structure. For instance, for the X-axis: (1) the Organization & Management indicator can be decomposed into Policy & Documentation, Organizational Structure, Incentive Mechanisms and Inspection Mechanisms, (2) the Input indicator can be decomposed into Early Input (Early Investment) and Follow-up Input (Follow-up Investment), (3) the Teaching Process indicator can be decomposed into Use of Digital Resources, Use of Flexible Teaching Methods, and others, and (4) the Output indicator can be decomposed into Enhancing Students' Learning Ability, Change in Learning Attitude, Social Acceptance, and others. Details can be found in Sect. 4.2.

In addition, it is extremely difficult to put everything in Fig. 1 together when constructing a practical indicator system, as too many items and relations must be considered and decomposed. Dimension reduction seems to be an ideal solution to this problem, i.e., fix one dimension (e.g., Dimension Y) and discuss the other two (e.g., Dimensions X and Z), or fix two dimensions (e.g., Dimensions Y and Z) and discuss the remaining dimension (e.g., Dimension X). Theoretically, there are several combinations. For example 1, we can talk about a university's overall performance within its four functions, which fixes Z and discusses X and Y. For example 2, we can talk about a teacher's performance in scientific research, which fixes Y and Z and discusses X. For example 3, we can talk about a course's performance in talent cultivation, which fixes Y and Z and discusses X. It should be noted that the missing dimension T is also included without explicitly being stated.

4.2 Performance Evaluation Indicator System (PEIS)

From Sect. 4.1, we know that 4DPEM is too general to use in practice, as it leaves too many details undefined. In fact, we need something more specific and operable. As a result, we usually build different targeted indicator systems for different needs. That is, we'll have case-by-case solutions for different scenarios. For instance, we can build a corresponding indicator system for example 1 (a university's overall performance within its four functions) and build another indicator system for example 2 (a teacher's performance in scientific research). These indicator systems are all derived from our 4DPEM and share the same framework, building process and evaluation procedures. Due to space limitations, this paper takes example 3, discussed in Sect. 4.1, as the case to build and illustrate the performance evaluation indicator system in the following sections.

Because this study discusses ICT-based teaching and learning in higher education, "course" here means an ICT-based course instead of a traditional face-to-face course. A popular and prevalent form of online course, MOOC represents a current and future trend in applying ICT in higher education at the course level. Therefore, the MOOC model was selected in the following as the example of dimension Z to build our course-related Performance Evaluation Indicator System (c-PEIS). There are four steps as shown below.

First, as Dimension Y and Z are fixed, we should decompose the four performance indicators of Dimension X into subindicators according to the MOOC's characteristics and functionality in talent cultivation. There is no consensus about the precise characteristics that define open online courses, but there is little disagreement for a MOOC to be described as open enrollment, free, and mass participation. These characteristics imply that the teaching and learning process, interactive discussion among learners, and learning supportive services should all be considered in the candidate lists for performance evaluation subindicators. In addition, indexes of the existing evaluation standard for open online courses show that attention should be paid to the resources offered by the course, including basic and extended resources, instructional design, and course delivery. To create a relatively complete indicator system, this paper analyzes several typical open online course evaluation systems (such as Li [19], Rosewell [20], Lowenthal [21] and Klobas [22]), sorts out most frequently cited items, and then matches and categorizes each with the four indicators mentioned above to generate an initial version of c-PEIS. Then, five experts who have many years of experience in ICT-based teaching were invited to complete a survey to offer their suggestions and comments (Delphi method). 5-point Likert scale was used to measure and collect data.

Table 1. Performance evaluation indicator system for MOOCs

Indicator	KPA (subindicator)	KP
Organization & management	Policy & documentation (OM1)	With supportive policies and adequate documentation to keep the course going/running
		Continually updated in response to international and national statutes
	Organizational structure (OM2)	Having a team that is well-structured with clear divisions
	Sustainable funding and environmental improvement (OM3)	Provide a guaranteed mechanism for sustainable special funding
		Provide a guaranteed mechanism for sustainable resource and environmental improvement
		Learning support service
	Incentive mechanisms and inspection mechanisms (OM4)	Motivation among teachers, developers and assistants
		Establish transparent inspection/assess mechanisms
Input	Early input: rich resources (I1)	Percentage of resources with copyright
		Sufficient resources to meet basic needs
		Enough extended resources
	Early input: clear and focused content (I2)	Content represents the forefront of that field
		The design and implementation of the course are clearly focused
		Content is targeted
	Early input: well-organized content (I3)	The structure conforms to learners' physical and mental development
		Support diverse learning styles
	Follow-up input: humanized support services (I4)	Different supportive services, e.g., email reminders, reply notifications, etc.
		Available user manual and instructions
	Follow-up input: support for meaning construction (I5)	Appropriate learning situations
		Online collaborative learning activities
		Provide tools for inquiry-based learning
	Follow-up input: upgrading and optimizing resources (I6)	Resource redevelopment through updating and reproduction by teachers and students
		Updating and renewing resources regularly
Teaching process	Use of digital resources and media (TP1)	Use learning resources frequently
		Use IT to improve the teaching process to enhance quality and efficiency
	Use of flexible teaching methods (TP2)	Use appropriate teaching methods to link the classroom and the real world
		Learning activity spurs student autonomy
		Help students build the connection between old and new knowledge

(*continued*)

Table 1. (*continued*)

Indicator	KPA (subindicator)	KP
	Use of diversified evaluation (TP3)	Diagnostic evaluation, formative evaluation and summative evaluation are properly used
		Diversified evaluation content, focusing on students' emotional experiences, inquiry abilities and collaboration
		Diversified evaluators, including teacher evaluation and peer- and self-evaluation
	Deep interaction (TP4)	Deep interaction between teacher and students to help solve problems
		Deep interaction among students to alleviate loneliness
		Encourage students to participate in online discussion through different ways
	Scope of sharing (TP5)	Expand course coverage to benefit more
		Share resources in different ways through social networks
	Continuous optimization (TP6)	Continuously stimulate students' intrinsic motivation
		Help students change learning styles
		The course shows distinct disciplinary characteristics and innovation
Output	Achievement of predicted goals (O1)	Predicted goals (content knowledge, skills, etc.) are achieved
	Enhancing students' learning abilities (O2)	Students are able to retrieve, analyze, process, assess and disseminate information
		Students can solve practical problems with their knowledge
		Students can have collaborative group discussions and share viewpoints using technology
		Students can enjoy self-regulated learning using technology
	Change in learning attitude (O3)	Students increase their understanding of learning and innovation
		Students are interested in different learning styles
		Students are satisfied with the learning result
	Development of personality and characteristics (O4)	The course helps forge students' personality and characteristics through personalized learning
	Social acceptance (O5)	The course credit is approved in colleges
		The course is approved by outside companies

After two rounds of surveys, we had the final version. Details can be found in the first two columns of Table 1, where subindicators are transferred to key process areas (KPAs) in accordance with CMM.

Second, dimension T should also be refined according to the meta-model [16] to capture the MOOC's lifecycle and continuous performance enhancement. Judging by the features of open online courses, there should be five explicit stages in its lifecycle, i.e., Initial, Basic, Applied, Innovative and Optimizing. (1) Initial means the course manager (or developer, similarly hereinafter) has no standard processes or means for course construction (making resources, course delivery, evaluation rubric, etc.). The manager does not have a general idea of predicting learning outcomes or upgrading the course with any accuracy. (2) Basic means the course manager has basic course construction skills and controls, with plenty of standardized resources or platforms to support online teaching and learning. (3) Applied means the course crew has pulled together a standard set of process, skills and controls for the entire course, and concentration is shifted to the application of information technology and its integration with teaching and learning to improve quality or change learning styles. (4) Innovative means the course crew has plenty of experience on how to expand the coverage of the course, how to direct innovative reforms for upgrading and how to share their successful experiences. (5) Optimizing means the course crew has accomplished all of the above and now begins to seek optimization in course performance so that the course can be continually updated.

Third, according to CMM, each maturity level is composed of key process areas (KPAs). Each KPA identifies a cluster of related activities that, when performed collectively, achieve a set of goals considered important for that maturity level. Moreover, each KPA is described in terms of key practices (KPs) that, when implemented, help to satisfy that KPA. KP describes things that contribute most to the effective implementation of the "attached" KPA. In this paper, each subindicator is transferred to a KPA, strengthening their contribution to the performance of ICT-based teaching and learning. In addition, key practices are proposed and associated with each KPA according to the core value of that KPA and the key practice's contribution, which are also described in Table 1.

Finally, all of the KPAs are categorized into different maturity levels, showing how to precisely upgrade a course from Initial to Optimizing, as shown in Table 2. The relations between the five maturity levels and the KPAs build a model called the Performance Maturity Model. It can be seen from this model that if all the associated KPAs belonging to a certain maturity level are satisfied, the course is considered to have reached that maturity level. Note that the requirements for a higher level include those of a lower level. For instance, if a course is evaluated and considered level 4, it should satisfy all the KPAs within levels 2, 3 and 4 (there is no KPA in level 1). Tables 1 and 2 together show exactly what c-PEIS looks like.

Table 2. Performance maturity model for MOOCs

Level	Organization and management	Input	Teaching process	Output
1st Initial	N/A			
2nd Basic	Policy & documentation (OM1) Organizational structure (OM2)	Rich resources (I1)	Use of digital resources and media (TP1)	Achievement of predicted goals (O1)
3rd Applied		Clear and focused content (I2) Well-organized content (I3) Humanized support services (I4)	Use of flexible teaching method (TP2) Use of diversified evaluation (TP3)	Enhancing students' learning ability (O2)
4th Innovative	Sustainable funding and environmental improvement (OM3)	Support for meaning construction (I5)	Deep interaction (TP4) Scope of sharing (TP5)	Change in learning attitude (O3)
5th Optimizing	Incentive mechanisms and inspection mechanisms (OM4)	Upgrading and optimizing resources (I6)	Continuous optimization (TP6)	Development of personality and characteristics (O4) Social acceptance (O5)

5 Case Study

The Chinese *iCourse163* platform is the largest and maybe the most popular MOOC platform in China, with more than 1000 courses running as of 2018. In this case study, we randomly selected three courses: Traditional Chinese Medicine and Diagnosis (C1), Multimedia Technology and Application (C2), and Curriculum Design and Evaluation in Elementary School (C3). They are from the fields of Medical Science, Computer Technology and Education and have completely different backgrounds, characteristics and structures; this is to reduce the potential impact or inaccuracy that may be caused by selecting all samples from the same field.

5.1 Methodology

We used the survey method to collect data. We conducted the survey on each course separately; the respondents were managers, teachers and college students in these courses in the fall of 2016, with 85 in C1, 33 in C2 and 34 in C3. The response rate for complete and valid surveys was 100%.

For instrumentation, we adopted benchmarks or scales in [20–22] and got three questionnaires for different participants. For managers, items related to key practices of organization and management (refer to Table 1) constituted most of the survey. For teachers, items related to key practices in course design and development, application and sharing, and teaching effects constituted most of the survey. For students, items related to key practices in application and sharing and learning effects dominated the survey. All the questionnaires began with a demographics section. The survey received preassessment from two experts, and feedback was collected and used to adjust the wording for several items to improve the readability of the survey. After permission was granted to conduct the research, we collected data from managers, teachers and students who had participated in the courses. The survey required 5 to 10 min to complete. All responses were entered into Microsoft Excel for analysis.

When implementing 4DPEM and c-PEIS, one of the most important steps is to determine one-by-one whether a KPA is satisfied. If all the associated KPAs belonging to a certain maturity level are satisfied, the course is considered to reach that maturity level. While each KPA is described in terms of some KPs that help to satisfy the KPA, measuring each KP becomes straightforward in our next step. In our survey, 5-point Likert scale was used to measure each KP, ranging from (1) "totally disagree", to (5) "totally agree". Then, we calculated the average for each KPA by summing the scores of all associated KPs and dividing it by the number of KPs. Only when the average was greater than 4 (out of 5) did we consider the KPA satisfied (3 means "uncertain" in our scale, while 4 means "partly agree").

5.2 Results and Analysis

Due to space limitations, we simply discuss the results of the Teaching Process and Output indicators, which are illustrated in Figs. 2 and 3.

From a performance perspective, it can be seen from Fig. 2 that TP1, TP3 and TP5 of these courses are fully satisfied, which means the courses paid enough attention to the use of digital resources and to the use of diversified evaluation methods to assess students' learning, and they tried their best to share the contents and learning experiences with other learners. Especially for TP5, where all the courses performed well, we conducted further investigation (interviews with the managers) and found that their school leaders continuously supported them and efforts were made to explore inter-school collaboration, which contributes to a large scope of course-sharing (TP5). However, due to insufficient functionality of the platform and lack of teacher awareness of the importance of online interaction among students (and teachers), none of these courses managed to perform well in KPA TP4 (deep interaction among students and teachers), weakening the effect of meaning construction and peer-sharing. On the other hand, from Fig. 3, we know that all these courses also performed well in KPAs O1 and O5, which means the predicted goals were achieved with desirable social acceptance. Further analysis revealed that students' mastery of knowledge and openness to the public both contributed to these two KPAs. However, none of these courses passed O3 and O4, which means students had no sign of changing their learning attitude, even with advanced ICT learning tools, and their development of personality or characteristics are currently ignored. In fact, personalized output can be expected with the aid of ICT and new digital environment.

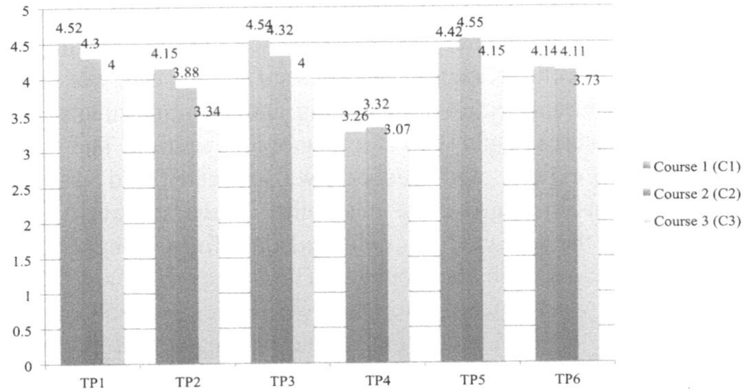

Fig. 2. Teaching process scores for the three courses

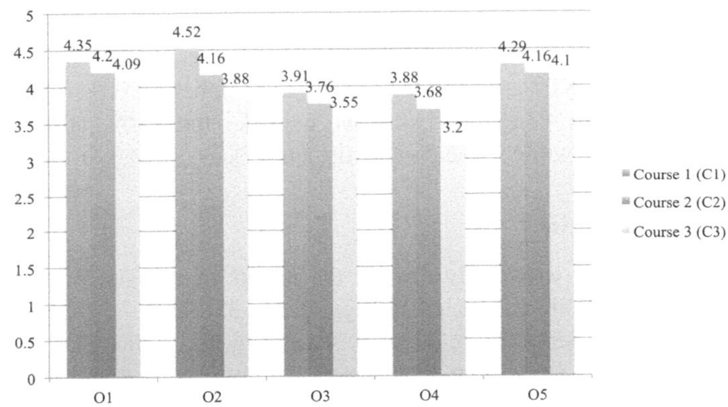

Fig. 3. Output scores for the three courses

From a course perspective, C1 performed comparatively best in both KPAs among these three, whereas C3 was the worst. The reason is that due to insufficient funding, there were only two teachers (including the one in charge) who participated in C3, while there were more than five in C1, resulting in a much greater workload for teachers in C3 than those in C1. Therefore, they were not able to try or use different teaching methods or diversified evaluation instruments, nor did they give enough optimization to continuously update the course. Under these circumstances, it was difficult to promote students' change in learning attitude, let alone their personal development. Consequently, C3 fell behind in these KPAs compared with C1 or C2.

Data analysis and follow-up surveys of the other performance indicators are similar and omitted here. According to Table 2 and the data we've collected and calculated for each course, we draw our final conclusion as follows: Course 1 is now at Level 3 with strengths in areas OM3, TP1, TP3, and O2 and weaknesses in areas I5 and TP4. Suggestions made for this course include providing students with more learning tools to support inquiry-based learning and encouraging students to explore, discover and solve problems collaboratively. Similarly, Course 2 and Course 3 are both at Level 2. Course 2 is hindered mainly by KPA TP2, while Course 3 is hindered by I4, TP2 and O2. By pointing out their strengths and weaknesses, we succeeded in directing the courses to make improvement in specific area(s), which in return will enhance teaching quality and lead them to upgrade to a higher level.

6 Conclusion

ICT is developing faster than ever before; it will definitely transform the education system's structure and revolutionize educational model in the near future. To recognize the actual situation of ICT in higher education, leverage the investment and its return, and increase the quality of teaching and learning and improve sustainable development, performance evaluation should be involved; this helps transform one-off static evaluation into dynamic performance enhancement.

To this end, this paper proposes a 4-Dimension Performance Evaluation Model (4DPEM); this model evaluates the performance of ICT in an institute (a certain university), for the courses, and for the teachers and the students, while emphasizing the functions of higher education as well. It is a general model and serves as a lead for any subsequent (derived) model or indicator system. That is the first contribution of this paper. To verify 4DPEM and get a more specific and practical indicator system within certain fields, a course-related Performance Evaluation Indicator System (c-PEIS) in a MOOC case is constructed as an example to evaluate the MOOC's application in higher education. Based on our meta-model, c-PEIS intrinsically supports the continued improvement and sustainable development of performance. This is the second contribution of this paper. Our case study of three courses on the Chinese *iCourse163* platform shows that 4DPEM and PEIS are helpful for measuring the current status of ICT in higher education while providing suggestions and directions to help the course become more "mature".

Note that 4DPEM and PEIS are far from perfect and need to be updated continually. We hope they have positive referential value for research in this field.

Acknowledgements. This work was supported by the Natural Science Foundation of Guangdong Province under grant 2014A030313427.

References

1. The New Media Consortium: Horizon Report (2017 Higher Education Edition). http://cdn.nmc.org/media/2017-nmc-horizon-report-he-EN.pdf
2. The New Media Consortium: Horizon Report (2016 Higher Education Edition). http://cdn.nmc.org/media/2016-nmc-horizon-report-he-EN.pdf
3. The 2007 National Survey of Information Technology in US Higher Education. http://www.immagic.com/eLibrary/ARCHIVES/GENERAL/CCP_US/C071029G.pdf
4. The CEO Forum School Technology and Readiness Report. http://www.ceoforum.org
5. Trucano, M.: Knowledge maps: ICTs in education. infoDev/World Bank, Washington, DC (2005)

6. International Telecommunication Union: Partnership on measuring ICT for development—core ICT indicators, Geneva (2010)
7. Zuo, X.M.: Literature review of ICT in schools by BECTA. Distance Educ. China **11**, 11–16 (2011). (in Chinese)
8. Department of Education and Science: ICT in schools. Evaluation Support and Research Unit, Marlborough (2008)
9. Nicol, D., Coen, M.: A model for evaluating the institutional costs and benefits of ICT initiatives in teaching and learning in higher education. Res. Learn. Technol. **11**(2) 46–60 (2003)
10. Laurillard, D.: Modelling benefits-oriented costs for technology enhanced learning. High. Educ. **54**(1), 21–39 (2007)
11. Rajev, M.K.G.: A performance evaluation of ICT infrastructure in the academic environment. Asian J. Res. Soc. Sci. Humanit. **7**(4), 320–333 (2017)
12. Man, K.: An evaluation model on ICT tools performance in university's industrial activities: with special concerns on university's organizational characteristics and the academic staff's motivations. In: Abstracts of Annual Conference of Japan Society for Management Information, pp. 123–126 (2013)
13. Lu, C., Li, L.L., Wu, D.: Application of combination weighting method to weight calculation in performance evaluation of ICT. In: 2015 IEEE 15th International Conference on Advanced Learning Technologies (ICALT), pp. 258–259 (2015)
14. Ma, N., Yu, S.Q.: The process assessment and capability maturity model for educational informationization of schools. J. Distance Educ. **1**, 13–17 (2010)
15. Stolovich, H.D., Keeps, E.J.: Handbook of Human Performance Technology, 2nd edn. Jossey-Bass Pfeiffer, San Francisco (1999)
16. Zheng, Y., Xie, Y.: Metamodel for evaluating the performance of ICT in education. In: Cheung, S.K.S., Kwok, L.-F., Shang, J., Wang, A., Kwan, R. (eds.) ICBL 2016. LNCS, vol. 9757, pp. 207–218. Springer, Cham (2016). https://doi.org/10.1007/978-3-319-41165-1_19
17. Software Engineering Institute. The Capability Maturity Model–Guidelines for Improving the Software Process. Addison-Wesley Publishing Company, New York (1995)
18. Skylar, T.: 4D printing: multi-material shape change. Archit. Des. **84**(1), 116–121 (2014)
19. Li, Q., Liu, N.: Towards a MOOC quality assurance framework. Open Educ. Res. **21**(5), 66–73 (2015). (in Chinese)
20. Rosewell, J., Darco, J.: The OpenupEd quality label: benchmarks for MOOCs. Int. J. Innov. Qual. Learn. **2**(3), 88–100 (2014)
21. Lowenthal, P.R., Hodges, C.B.: In search of quality: using quality matters to analyze the quality of massive open online courses. Int. Rev. Res. Open Distance Learn. **16**(5), 83–101 (2015)
22. Klobas, J.E.: Measuring the success of scalable open online courses. Perform. Meas. Metrics **15**(3), 145–162 (2014)

Pedagogical and Psychological Issues

A Case Study to Promote Computational Thinking: The Lab Rotation Approach

Jin Cai[1,2], Harrison Hao Yang[2,3(✉)], Di Gong[2], Jason MacLeod[2], and Yao Jin[1]

[1] Hubei University of Education, Wuhan 430205, China
[2] Central China Normal University, Wuhan 430079, China
[3] State University of New York at Oswego, Oswego, NY 13126, USA
harrison.yang@oswego.edu

Abstract. This paper presents the rationale, design, development, implementation and evaluation of a case study utilizing the lab rotation model of blended learning for teaching computational thinking in Chinese higher education. The principles of computational thinking were integrated into an entry level course that is required among all college students, entitled *Fundamentals of College Computing*. A mixed method research approach was utilized to examine students learning outcomes and perception of the instructional process among 114 first year college students. The results showed that the teaching approach was successful at improving students' computational thinking, particularly on the method and ability dimensions. Recommendations for promoting college students' computational thinking, as well as teaching strategies for implementing this type of a unique lab rotational approach in China are discussed.

Keywords: Mixed method research · Teaching strategies · Blended learning
Computational thinking · Fundamentals of computing

1 Introduction

Computational thinking describes an attitude and skills that are highly demanded [1] and suggested to be fundamental for everyone in the 21st century [2]. Computational thinking more specifically represents a thought process for identifying problems and solutions, which integrates one's knowledge and skills with information and communication technology (ICT) to effectively apply tools and carry out solutions [1, 2]. Over the past decade, computational thinking has begun emerging in a variety of educational standards, including the International Society for Technology in Education, and the Next Generation Science Standards. However, the development of such educational standards is in the early stages and often target the primary and secondary levels of education [3]. Thus, few guidelines exist for teaching computational thinking at the post-secondary level.

In China, the fundamental knowledge and skills of computing have been a college-level instructional requirement for nearly 20 years, and the curriculum has experienced several major reforms in an effort to stay current with the evolution of technology and societal demands [4]. Of the many reforms, the most prominent change to curriculum is

S. K. S. Cheung et al. (Eds.): ICBL 2018, LNCS 10949, pp. 393–403, 2018.
https://doi.org/10.1007/978-3-319-94505-7_32

requiring the integration of computational thinking, beyond basic knowledge and skills for using ICT. While this policy shift represents a positive and proactive effort toward supporting students' academic and professional success, it also presents new challenges for students. Research suggests computational thinking requires time to develop, and that students' may not enjoy the related learning activities because they are not always capable of recognizing the value and application of the skills being transferred [5]. Additionally, computational thinking is difficult, and requires active participation in the learning process which is unlike the traditional teacher-centered learning approaches common in Chinese educational systems [6]. Therefore, it is not surprising that instructors have been documented as facing related challenges of maintaining students' engagement in class [7]. Instructors also face difficulties maintaining up-to-date educational resources amidst rapidly changing technological evolution. More significantly, there is a general lack of research available to assist with the issues of how to teach, assess, and ensure the transfer of individuals' capabilities toward real-life scenarios [3]. These related studies suggest that despite computational thinking being recognized as critically important, a variety of issues are preventing computational thinking from being taught most effectively in Chinese higher education.

This study utilizes a mixed method research approach to examine the blended delivery of a computational thinking course taught via the integration of lecture-based instruction and a cloud classroom. The results document a successful educational approach for teaching computational thinking that contributes knowledge toward the research gap surrounding this critical topic.

2 Conceptual Framework

2.1 Computational Thinking

The basic premise of computational thinking is not new. For example, during the 1960's, there was an argument to establish programming and computing requirements for college students of all disciplines [8]. The following decades increasingly explored a variety of interpretations and definitions of computational thinking [9–11]. However, it was not until Jeannette Wing's influential article [1], that definitional issues began to settle. Wing's most prominent definition of computational thinking is "the thought processes involved in formulating problems and their solutions so that the solutions are represented in a form that can be effectively carried out by an information-processing agent" [2]. The College Board and the National Science Foundation proposed computational thinking to further be described by the following seven big ideas [12]:

(1) Computing is a creative activity
(2) Pattern recognition focuses information and detail towards problem solving
(3) Data and information facilitate knowledge creation
(4) Algorithms are tools for developing and communicating problem solutions
(5) Programming is a process that requires the production of artifacts
(6) Interconnection of digital devices and networks enable computational approaches
(7) Computing enables innovation in other fields of research, education, business, etc.

Based upon such definitional developments, discussion of computational thinking has begun shifting toward the practical aspects of how to teach and assess computational thinking. Some progress has been made; however, large gaps still exist that require empirical exploration and that no clear instructional process for teaching computational thinking has been identified [3, 13, 14]. To date, most research approaching the issue of instructional processes has focus on unique and specific educational applications, such as within discipline-specific courses for computer science [12], interactive media design [15], and robotics [16]. Therefore, the identification of empirically validated multidisciplinary instructional processes for teaching computational thinking of a relevant issues of critical importance.

2.2 The Lab Rotation Model of Blended Learning

The lab rotation model of blended learning is an instruction approach where students rotate on a pre-determined schedule among different locations on a brick-and-mortar campus [17]. For example, between a traditional face-to-face classroom and a computer lab that is utilizing some type of online instruction. The lab rotation approach is different from other rotational models of blended learning, such as the flipped classroom or the station rotation models, in two ways [18]. First, the lab rotation model hosts all classes on a brick-and-mortar campus, which differentiates from the flipped classroom model. Second, the lab rotation model in not contained to only one classroom space, which differentiates from the station rotation model. According to one of our previous studies, the lab rotation model can be able to (1) improve students' learning autonomy, (2) provide students with optional learning materials as often as possible, and (3) provide timely help and guidance for the students [19]. In this study, the lab rotation model is utilized to deliver traditional lecture-based instruction in a multimedia classroom, and computer-based instruction through a cloud classroom in a computer laboratory.

2.3 Traditional Lecture-Based Instruction

Traditional lecture-based instruction describes the basis of a teacher-centered instructional practice which is common among China, as well as many other countries located within the Asia-Pacific [6]. Traditional lecture-based instruction typically entails the verbal delivery of information from an instructor to students with the assistance of a visual display (e.g., chalkboard, dry-erase whiteboard, projection screen) and students' individual learning resources (e.g., text books, notebooks, paper and digital learning resources). Additionally, this educational practice typically utilizes a drill and practice approach for teaching, whereby, interaction is primarily teacher-to-student with only minimal student-to-student communications. In this study, the face-to-face multimedia classroom was utilized two times per week to delivery lecture-based instruction.

2.4 The Cloud Classroom

The cloud classroom typically refers to a ubiquitous virtual space for students to participate in formally assigned tasks and learning activities [20]. That is to say, cloud classrooms are accessible from any Internet-connected digital device, such as smart phones, tablets, and computers. Additionally, cloud classrooms provide instructors the abilities to disseminate communications and learning resources, such as reading materials, assignment instructions, worksheets, video lectures, and grades. In some cases, cloud classrooms also host student-to-student communications and collaboration. In general, the implementation of cloud classrooms has been increasing due to instructors' and students' demands for increased flexibility, as well as educational institutions' interest in attracting more diverse scholarly populations [21]. In this study, a cloud classroom was utilized to deliver two class periods per week of individualized computer-based learning activities in a computer lab. During this time, the instructor supervised the learning environment and was available to troubleshoot issues and provide one-to-one support.

3 Methodology

3.1 Research Objectives

The research objectives of this study were to design, develop, implement, and evaluate a course for broadly teaching computational thinking to first year college students in Chinese higher education.

3.2 Participants and Setting

The participants of this study were 158 first year college students at the Hubei University of Education. The Hubei University of Education is a teacher training instruction of higher education in China that possesses a high percentage of students originating from rural and underdeveloped regions. In China, these types of student demographics typically possess less computer experience, as well as less exposure to the appropriate techniques for using computers in professional settings when compared to their peers originating from more developed urban areas. Therefore, the Hubei University of Education is required to teach ICT skills and computational thinking to all freshmen in order to develop the basic knowledge and skills required for successful computer utilization in academic and professional settings.

The participants were derived from an even distribution of four degree programs, including business English, financial management, medical logistics, and ideological and political studies. Incomplete questionnaire responses were omitted from analysis. Among the original sample of 158 students, the valid response rate for the pre-test (n = 145) and post-test (n = 131) was 92% and 83%, respectively. Student identification codes allowed further refinement of the responses. The final sample (n = 114) included all the students that completed both a valid pre- and post- test. The female-to-male ratio was approximately 5:1, which was a representative gender ratio of the institution's demographic composition and very common among other teaching training institutions in China.

The participants were taught via the lab rotation blended learning approach which utilized a face-to-face multimedia classroom two times per week. In addition, a cloud classroom was used to host two individualized computer-based learning activities in a computer lab two times per week. In total, this paper presents a case study for a full academic semester, which was the equivalent of a 14-week duration of time.

3.3 Course Background: *Fundamentals of College Computing*

The *Fundamentals of College Computing* is a basic computing course that was widely established as a university requirement during the mid-1990's. The learning objective of this course cover the basic computer knowledge and skills, including the usage of Windows operating systems, Microsoft Office products (e.g., Word, Excel, PowerPoint), computer networking, and multimedia applications. At Hubei University of Education, this course is required for first year college student that are not majoring in computer science. Over the past decade, more than 3,000 college students have attended this course on an annual basis. Currently, The *Fundamentals of College Computing* course is delivered in 56 class periods, including 28 class periods of lecture-based instruction (two 45-min classes per week) and 28 class periods of laboratory practice (two 45-min classes per week) where students are required to use computers to complete their given tasks guides by the cloud classroom under the instructors' supervision.

Despite being a required course, the specific course objective and curriculum vary across universities. In the past, the *Fundamentals of College Computing* only taught basic concepts of computer and software utilization; however, most practitioners now commonly agree that the course should be focusing on the development student computational thinking [22, 23]. Nevertheless, a variety of issues remain, including the structure of curriculum, maintenance of learning content, stimulation of student engagement, and transfer of knowledge as measured by students' achievement [7]. In 2017, the pass rate for student enrolled in this course at the Hubei University of Education was only an average of 22% [24]. Such a low success rate clearly illustrates the issue that many college students are lacking basic computing knowledge, skills, and computational thinking capacities. However, with such low rates of success, educators and institutions must also reflect upon their instructional processes and explore new ways of promoting the transfer of knowledge within this crucial discipline.

3.4 Course Design and Development

In order to develop the course, a thorough review of extant research and available open online resources was conducted. Based upon this review, the course original course objectives and learning resource for the *Fundamentals of College Computing* course were expanded to integrate an existing open online course entitled *University Computing*, which was developed at the Beijing Institute of Technology to teach the major concepts of computational thinking. Table 1 provides an overview of original in comparison to the re-designed course established to develop college students' higher-order capacities of computational thinking.

The *iCourse* learning platform (www.icourse163.org) was utilized to host the cloud classroom in this study. *iCourse* is a sharing platform for higher education curriculum resources, which was initially developed through the Chinese Ministry of Education

Table 1. Overview of the re-design *Fundamentals of College Computing* course

	Pre-existing course	Re-designed course	
Course objective	Promoting basic ICT knowledge and skills	Promote higher-order computational thinking through the application of basic ICT knowledge and skills	
Instructional model	Face-to-face	Lab rotation model of blended learning	
Instructional delivery	Multimedia classroom	Multimedia classroom	Computer lab
Pedagogy	Teacher-centered/Lecture-based	Teacher-centered/Lecture-based	Student-centered/Computer-based
Learning objectives	• Introduction to computer operating systems • Introduction to Microsoft Office applications • Introduction to multimedia application • Introduction to computer networking	• Introduction to computer operating systems • Introduction to Microsoft Office applications • Introduction to multimedia application • Introduction to computer networking	• Computer theory and hardware architecture • Computer software platforms • The digitalization of information • Algorithms and programming • Databases & data processing • Multimedia data processing • Computer network platform • Computer-based problem solving
Assessment	Examination of basic ICT knowledge and skills	Examination of basic ICT knowledge and skills	Examination of computational thinking

and Ministry of Finance during the 12th Five-Year Plan. The *iCourse* platform provided independent instruction to students within a cloud classroom that allowed for student-centered learning which required the application of knowledge and skills introduced in the lecture-based instruction that was host in the multimedia classroom. The *iCourse* platform primarily consisted of video lectures, discussion forums, unit assignments, and quizzes. Additionally, the *iCourse* platform was utilized to disseminate announcements and grades, as well as track students' progress and participation. Beyond the *iCourse* platform, there were also several assignments given within the computer lab that required group work cooperation with a presentation required to showcase the final product deliverable.

3.5 Instrumentation

The Computational Thinking Questionnaire [25] was used to measure college student computational thinking. The instrument consisted 24 items and three dimensions, including consciousness (7 items), method (9 items), and ability (8 items). Each item was measured on a 5-point Likert scale ranging from (1) "not at all" to (5) "very much". The original reported dimensional reliabilities were as follows: consciousness (alpha = 0.65), method (alpha = 0.75), and ability (alpha = 0.72). In this study, the pre- and post- test alphas for the consciousness dimension were 0.69 and 0.76, respectively. The pre- and post- test alphas for the method dimension were 0.80 and 0.87, respectively. The pre- and post- test alphas for the ability dimension were 0.83 and 0.87, respectively.

3.6 Data Collection and Analysis Procedure

The *Fundamentals of College Computing* course was implemented during the fall 2017 semester. After receiving administrative permission to conduct the study, the quantitative data was collected with the Computational Thinking Questionnaire via web-based format at the end of the third week (pre-test) and at the end of the fourteenth week (post-test). Students' participation was optional. Identification codes were used to verify that students' completed valid responses for both the pre- and post- tests, which provided confirmation that the data analysis was based upon the same group of participants. The valid questionnaire data was imported into SPSS 22. Cronbach's alpha was used to examine the reliability of the students' responses. A series of *t*-tests were conducted to compare students pre- and post- test results, which provided a quantitative examination of the influence this instructional approach provided for developing college students' computational thinking.

Qualitative data was also collected at the end of the fourteenth week in order to triangulate the quantitative findings, as well as extrapolate a deeper understanding of students' perception of the instructional approach. The qualitative data consisted the transcripts of ten independent semi-structured student interviews.

4 Results

4.1 Overview of Students' Computational Thinking

A series of t-tests were used to compare the level of college students' computational thinking reported on the pre- and post- tests of the Computational Thinking Questionnaire. As shown in Table 2, students' post-test results were observed to be statistically higher than the pre-test results for the overall level of computational thinking, as well as the method and ability dimensions of computational thinking.

4.2 Qualitative Evaluation of the Instructional Approach

Two further examine the students' experiences, ten students were randomly selected to participate in semi-structured interviews. The verbatim transcripts of students'

Table 2. Paired *t*-test analysis of the computational thinking questionnaire

	Pre-test		Post-test		*t*
	M	*SD*	*M*	*SD*	
Computational thinking	3.34	0.45	3.49	0.48	4.21*
Consciousness	3.55	0.48	3.61	0.49	1.51
Method	3.35	0.50	3.51	0.52	3.55*
Ability	3.14	0.56	3.37	0.57	4.75*

$^*p < 0.01$

interviews were thematically analyzed to describe their perceptions of the learning contents and their perceptions of the instructional approach in this context which focused on the development of computational thinking. Three representative themes emerged from the qualitative data, including (1) an overall interest in both the course contents and instructional approach, (2) disinterest because the instructional approach, and (3) disinterest because the course contents. Table 3 illustrates these theme with representative student interview quotes.

Table 3. Thematic analysis of student interview responses

Theme	Representative student quotes
Interested in the course content and instructional approach	"I am not bad at the basic application of these skills. Not only did I participate in this course, but I also participated in other open online courses that I am interested in"
Disinterested because the instructional approach	"I prefer the face-to-face lessons in. I have little interest in the SPOC course. I don't have enough time to watch these video lectures out of class, and I can't control myself well in self-study"
Disinterested because the course content	"I don't want to learn because I do think both the SPOC and the application of MS Office are very difficult for me"

5 Discussion and Conclusion

This study presents the rationale, design, development, implementation, and evaluation of a case study utilizing the lab rotation model of instruction to teach computational thinking in Chinese higher education. The findings indicate that such an approach can be used to broadly meet educational policy requirements in China [4, 22, 23], as well as the urgent societal demands for computational thinking in educational and professional environments [1, 2]. However, further examination of the quantitative findings showed that this preliminary case study was only successful in cultivating the method and ability dimensions of computational thinking. These findings support previous research suggesting that college students' may not immediately recognize the value of the skills there are learning or be aware of the educational progress they are making [5].

Future research is needed to refine the learning contents and instructional pedagogy used in this instructional approach to ensure that a comprehensive spectrum of computational thinking components can be developed, including the consciousness dimension.

The findings of this case study provide a benchmark for broadly teaching computational thinking among a wide variety of degree programs in Chinese higher education, which is a different approach from most previous documentation that discusses specialized subject contexts and learning activities [12, 15, 16]. Additionally, the present study provides empirical data to begin clarifying the well-documented research gap surrounding the more fundamental issue of how to teach computational thinking [3, 13, 14].

Qualitative data from student interviews provided a deeper perspective to understand and interpret the quantitative data. Thematic analysis showed that students were generally satisfied with the instructional approach and learning contents included in the *Fundamentals of College Computing* course. However, some individual differences were identified where students expressed disinterest in either the instructional approach or learning contents. Students that were disinterested with the instructional approach were primarily unsatisfied as a result of the demand for work outside of class when their learning objectives were not completed within the computer lab. These findings have provided valuable feedback that can assist re-design of the course schedule to maintain operable workloads that do not over-burden and disengage individuals that fall behind. In contrast, students that expressed disinterest in the learning content were typically unhappy with the high proportion of contents that were theoretical in nature. This theme of observations provided insights for additional course re-design suggesting more constructivist and collaborative learning activities may be valuable to captivate the interests of a larger percentage of participants.

The findings and implications of this study should be considered with respect to a few research limitations, particularly the participants and the instrumentation. This study focused on the development of computational thinking among first year college students primarily derived from rural and underdeveloped places of origin in China. Future research should include a control group for the pre-test/post-test experimental comparison, as this study only had and investigated the experimental group. Furthermore, future research should explore other levels of education and socio-cultural demographics. Additionally, this study was based upon a three-dimensional conceptualization of computational thinking, which was the selected as the best available tool during the time of the study. Future research should continue to refine abilities to measure more specific conceptualizations of computational thinking.

To conclude, this study describes the rationale for developing college students' computational thinking, and benchmarks an instructional approach utilizing the lab rotation model of blended learning to teach a broad audience of individuals. Preliminary evaluation of the instructional approach showed some successful results at cultivation college students' computational thinking. Future research is encouraged to utilizing this approach in similar socio-cultural contexts to address this critical issue, as well as contribute new evidence to refine the theoretical and practical implications of this case.

Acknowledgements. This work was supported by the Fundamental Research Funds for the Central Universities of Central China Normal University (CCNU14Z02006).

References

1. Wing, J.M.: Computational thinking. Commun. ACM **49**(3), 33–35 (2006)
2. Wing, J.M.: Research notebook: computational thinking: what and why? The Link Magazine, pp. 1–6 (2010)
3. Kalelioglu, F., Gulbahar, Y., Kukul, V.: A framework for computational thinking based on a systematic research review. Baltic J. Modern Comput. **4**(3), 583–596 (2016)
4. Sun, S.X.: The exploration and practice of the reform of basic computer courses in regional universities. Chin. Univ. Teach. **4**, 59–62 (2014). (in Chinese)
5. Miller, L.D., Soh, L.-K., Chiriacescu, V., et al.: Improving learning of computational thinking using creative thinking exercises in CS-1 computer science courses. In: 43rd Frontiers in Education Conference Proceedings, California, pp. 1426–1432. IEEE (2013)
6. Hill, P.: Asia-Pacific secondary education system review series no. 1: examination systems, pp. 1–42. UNESCO, Thailand (2010)
7. Yang, W.Z., Liu, M.K.: Computational thinking oriented multiple blended teaching and its application: take the course of fundamentals of college computer as an example. Audio-Vis. Educ. China **4**, 129–136 (2017). (in Chinese)
8. Newell, A., Peris, A.J., Simon, H.A.: Computer science. Science **157**(3795), 1373–1374 (1967)
9. Knuth, D.: Computer science and its relation to mathematics. Am. Math. Mon. **81**(4), 323–343 (1974)
10. Denning, P.J., Comer, D.E., Gries, D., et al.: Computing as a discipline. Commun. ACM **32** (1), 9–23 (1989)
11. Wulf, W.A.: Are we scientists or engineers? ACM Comput. Surv. **27**(1), 55–57 (1995)
12. CS Principles. http://www.csprinciples.org/home/about-the-project. Accessed 25 Feb 2018
13. Feng, B.Q.: Discussing the practical operation of cultivating computational thinking ability. Chin. Univ. Teach. **9**, 9–12 (2012). (in Chinese)
14. Grover, S., Pea, R.: Computational thinking in K-12: a review of the state of the field. Educ. Res. **42**(1), 38–43 (2013)
15. Brennan, K., Resnick, M.: New frameworks for studying and assessing the development of computational thinking. In: 2012 AERA Annual Meeting Proceedings, AERA, Vancouver, pp. 1–25 (2012)
16. Atmatzidou, S., Demetriadis, S.: Advancing students' computational thinking skills through educational robotics: a study on age and gender relevant differences. Rob. Auton. Syst. **75B**, 661–670 (2016)
17. Staker, H., Horn, M.B.: Classifying K-12 blended learning. Innosight Institute, Boston (2012)
18. Christensen, C.M., Horn, M.B., Staker, H.: Is K-12 blended learning disruptive? An introduction of the theory of hybrids. Clayton Christensen Institute for Disruptive Innovation, California (2013)
19. Cai, J., Zhu, S., Tian, Y.M., Yang, H.H.: Learning from practice: improving blended learning strategies in an educational technology course. Int. J. Innov. Learn. **21**(4), 467–480 (2017)

20. MacLeod, J., Yang, H.H., Zhu, S., et al.: Technological factors and student-to-student connected classroom climate in cloud classrooms. J. Educ. Comput. Res. (2017). https://doi.org/10.1007/s40299-017-0341-6
21. Malikowski, S.R., Thompson, M.E., Theis, J.G.: A model for research into course bridging technology and learning theory. J. Educ. Comput. Res. **26**(2), 149–173 (2007)
22. Zhan, D.C., Nie, L.S., Xu, X.F.: Fundamentals of college computer: a course of basic education of computational thinking for all college students. Chin. Univ. Teach. **4**, 15–20 (2011). (in Chinese)
23. Alliance of Nine Chinese Universities: The Statement of Development Strategy of Computer Fundamental Education of nine universities alliance. Chin. Univ. Teach. **9**, 4 (2010). (in Chinese)
24. Hubei University of Education. A notice of the final examination of 2017–2018, 30 March 2018. http://jwc.hue.edu.cn/98/18/c1328a38936/page.htm. Accessed 2 Apr 2018
25. Wang, J.: Research and practice on the current situation and development of college students' computational thinking. Master's thesis, Chongqing Normal University (2015). (in Chinese)

Parental and Teacher Influence on Secondary Students' Information Literacy

Sha Zhu[1], Di Wu[2(✉)], Liqin Yu[2], Harrison Hao Yang[2,3], Jason MacLeod[2], and Huan Li[2]

[1] Wuhan Huada National E-learning Technologies Co., Ltd., Wuhan 430079, China
[2] Central China Normal University, Wuhan 430079, China
dr.wudi@gmail.com
[3] State University of New York at Oswego, Oswego 13126, USA

Abstract. This study investigated secondary students' level of information literacy in China, as well as examined parents' and teachers' influence toward students' information literacy. The survey method was employed on a sample of 3172 students, 2035 parents, and 851 teachers to examine personal beliefs, attitudes, and technology usage. Students' information literacy was assessed via a web-based examination and the main findings were as follows: (1) a large percentage of students' overall level of information literacy was average or low; (2) teachers' Internet self-efficacy positively predicted students' information literacy, while teachers' in-class ICT usage negatively predicted students' information literacy; (3) parents' Internet attitudes positively influenced students' information literacy. Based on the findings, suggestions for improving students' information literacy were discussed.

Keywords: Information literacy · Secondary students · Influential factors China

1 Introduction

The emergence of technological innovation characterized by big data, cloud computing, and intelligent manufacturing technologies has swept the world, bringing about the transformation to an information society [1, 2]. In the information society, data is at the core of quickly changing economies, and people are expected to be capable of efficient and effective personal, academic, and professional engagement in activities such as selecting, utilizing, applying, managing, and exchanging information [3]. Accordingly, demand for improving information literacy is becoming an important strategy for economic and social development [4]. Therefore, in many developed countries the promotion of information literacy has become a pedagogical issue, and a set of information literacy standards has been established to guide the cultivation of information literacy in formalized educational context [5–12]. The development of secondary students' information literacy, in particular, has been regarded as critical for preparing individuals for future success, as well as for strengthening the productivity of economies [13, 14].

S. K. S. Cheung et al. (Eds.): ICBL 2018, LNCS 10949, pp. 404–415, 2018.
https://doi.org/10.1007/978-3-319-94505-7_33

In response to such modern demands, the Chinese government has emphasized the significance of developing secondary students' information literacy in national strategic plans since the beginning of the 21st century. For example, the *National Medium and Long-Term Education Reform and Development Plan (2010–2020)* stated that, "students are encouraged to use information technology to study and learn independently, to enhance their ability to analyze and solve problems, as well as to accelerate access to the wide applications of these tools" [15]. In January 2017, the State Council promulgated the *Thirteenth Five-Year Plan for the Development of National Education*, and information literacy was regarded as one of the three major capabilities for cultivating students' innovative and entrepreneurial ability [16]. Additionally, according to a government report, the provincial finance investment toward information and communication technology (ICT) in education reached more than four billion Yuan in 2016 [17].

Significant progress has been made; however, despite many efforts and investments, challenges remain facing the development of students' information literacy in China. Previous research suggests students possess only average levels of information literacy, and a "digital gap" exists among individuals' ability levels between rural and urban areas [18]. Due to such information literacy deficits, it is not surprising that research has illustrated many irrational and inappropriate behaviors emerging among students while engaging in online social activities, such as cyberbullying [19, 20], sensitive information self-disclosures [21, 22], and mediated acts of piracy or plagiarism [23].

These related studies highlight that understanding the factors which cultivate and undermine the development of students' information literacy is an issue of critical importance in China. Therefore, this study investigates the level of secondary students' information literacy and examines parental and teacher influential toward information literacy development. The results can provide evidence to support the development of policy for more effectively cultivation of students' information literacy.

2 Conceptual Framework

2.1 Information Literacy

Zurkowski [24] first proposed the phrase "information literacy", and since that time, the definition and conceptualization of information literacy has continuously evolved. Initially, information literacy referred to an ability to utilize information technology to find information for solving problems [25]. In the 1990s, the conceptualization of information literacy was transformed to reflect a set of specific skills, including retrieving, utilizing, organizing, managing, comprehending, analyzing, and evaluating information [26, 27]. In the present, the definition of information literacy has emerged to go beyond basic skills and also entail a set of qualities, including information awareness, information knowledge, and information ethics. To describe the current conceptualization, UNESCO stated that information literacy is "the prerequisite for effective participation in the information society and the basic human rights of lifelong learning" [28].

Based on a thorough review of extant research, the present study is based upon a conceptualization of information literacy with four dimensions: (1) Awareness and Cognition, (2) Scientific Knowledge, (3) Application and Innovation, and (4) Ethics and Law. Awareness and Cognition refers to one's information sensitivity, such as how one understands and interprets information [29, 30]. Scientific Knowledge refers to one's mastery of information theories, methods, and principles of information technology tools. [31, 32]. Application and Innovation refers to one's set of abilities used for information acquisition, identification, storage and management, processing, distribution and communication, and innovative applications [26, 33, 34]. Ethics and Law refers to one's moral principles and understanding of the rules governing information activities [35].

2.2 Related Works

Parent-Level Factors Influencing Information Literacy. Among developed countries with long-established information literacy research, parents' ICT attitudes, Internet self-efficacy, and Internet attitudes may be considered as influential factors toward students' information literacy. For instance, research has shown that students who own computers in the home have a higher level of information literacy [36], and that parents' attitudes towards ICT can influence their children's information literacy [37]. Additionally, research suggests that parents' Internet self-efficacy is positively related to their children's information literacy [38]. Previous study also indicated that parents' internet attitude is significantly correlated with children's level of information literacy [39]. However, few research has examined parental influence toward secondary students' information literacy in China.

Teacher-Level Factors Influencing Information Literacy. It has been widely acknowledged in developed countries that teachers' ICT attitudes, in-class ICT usage, and Internet self-efficacy can be influential factors of students' information literacy. For example, research suggests that teachers' ICT attitudes can indirectly affect students' information literacy by influencing their ICT attitudes [40], and that the appropriate usage of ICT in teaching activities has a positive association with the level of students' information literacy [39]. Research has also claimed that collaborative teaching approach and inquiry-based learning with ICT positively influences the level of students' information literacy [41]. Additionally, teachers' Internet self-efficacy has shown positive impact on the level of students' information literacy in digital information processing and communication [39]. However, few research has specifically focused toward teachers' influence of secondary students' information literacy in China.

3 The Present Study

3.1 Research Question

In order to promote the level of secondary students' information literacy in China, it is necessary to benchmark the status quo of students' information literacy and analyze key influential factors that can be used to make improvements. With respect to the factors influencing students' information literacy, the investigations of personal factors, such as students beliefs, attitudes, and experience has been well documented [42–44]. However, external factors such as parental and teacher influence has received comparatively little attention in China. This is particularly true from a joint perspective, simultaneously considering both parent and teacher influences among one sample, which is more characteristically representative to the natural context of student life. Therefore, the present study was designed to examine how, and to what extent, both parents and teacher display influence toward secondary students' information literacy in China. The following research questions were proposed to guide this study:

Q1: What are secondary students' overall levels of information literacy?
Q2: What are the parental influences that can predict students' information literacy?
Q3: What are the teacher influences that can predict students' information literacy?

3.2 Research Model

Based upon the proposed rationale, conceptual framework, review of extant research, a research model was proposed to describe key parental and teacher influences of secondary students' information literacy in China. As shown in Fig. 1, students' information literacy was the dependent variable, with parent and teacher influences being independent variables.

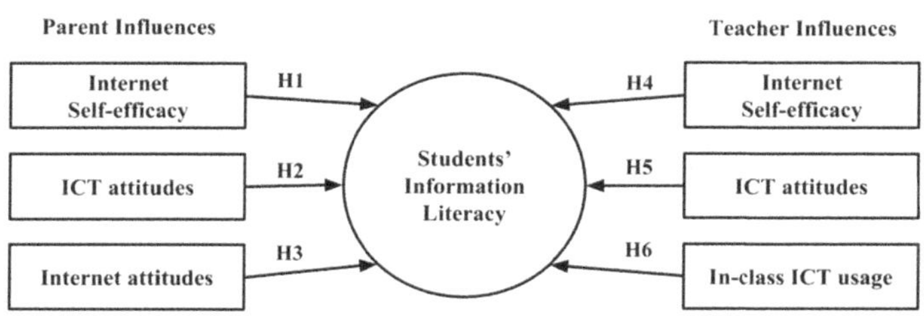

Fig. 1. The proposed research model.

Additionally, the following hypothesized relationships were proposed:

H1: The level of parents' Internet self-efficacy is positively related to the degree of students' information literacy.
H2: The level of parents' ICT attitudes is positively related to the degree of students' information literacy.
H3: The level of parents' Internet attitudes is positively related to the degree of students' information literacy.
H4: The level of teachers' Internet self-efficacy is positively related to the degree of students' information literacy.
H5: The level of teachers' ICT attitudes is positively related to the degree of students' information literacy.

H6: The level of teachers' in-class ICT usage is positively related to the degree of students' information literacy.

4 Methodology

4.1 Participants

The participants consisted of 3172 students, 2035 parents, and 851 teachers. Liu Zhou City, which is located in the Guangxi Zhuang Autonomous Region of China, was the targeted sampling location of this study. Considering the academic stress of students focusing on entrance examinations for transition to senior secondary and higher education, ninth grade and twelfth grade students were not included in this study. Therefore, the participant consisted of only seventh, eighth, tenth, and eleventh grade students, as well as their corresponding parents and teachers. A description of the sample is provided in Table 1.

Table 1. Demographic composition of the sample.

Grade	Students (n = 3172)		Parents (n = 2035)		Teachers (n = 851)	
	Female	Male	Female	Male	Female	Male
Seventh	316	322	370	232	124	47
Eighth	421	393	369	200	122	55
Tenth	529	424	282	233	156	98
Eleventh	472	295	196	153	162	87
Total	1738	1434	1217	818	564	287

4.2 Instrumentation

The present study adopted three different instruments to specifically address the secondary students, parents, and teachers, respectively.

Secondary students' information literacy was measure with a web-based Student Information Literacy Test, which was designed by the research group experts. The test consisted of 91 multiple choice questions assessing the four dimensions of information literacy: Awareness and Cognition (12 items); Scientific Knowledge (20 items); Application and Innovation (44 items); Ethics and Law (15 items). The total possible test score was 100, and the grading weights of the four information literacy dimensions were 15%, 30%, 40%, and 15%, respectively. The recommended threshold that determines a passing score on the Information Literacy Test was 60 out of 100.

The Parental Information Literacy Questionnaire was adopted from previous studies [39, 45, 46] to measure parental influence. The questionnaire consisted of 31 items measuring parents' Internet self-efficacy (11 items), ICT attitudes (5 items), and Internet attitudes (15 items). Items were measured on a 5-point Likert scale. The Cronbach's alpha values obtained in this study were as follows: overall (alpha = 0.93),

Internet self-efficacy (alpha = 0.92), ICT attitudes (alpha = 0.87), Internet attitudes (alpha = 0.85).

The Teacher Information Literacy Questionnaire was adopted from previous studies [39, 45, 47] to measure teaching influence. The questionnaire consisted of 23 items measuring teachers' Internet self-efficacy (11 items), ICT attitudes (5 items), and in-class ICT usage (7 items). Items were measured on a 5-point Likert scale. The Cronbach's alpha values obtained in this study were as follows: overall (alpha = 0.91), Internet self-efficacy (alpha = 0.94), ICT attitudes (alpha = 0.84), in-class ICT usage (alpha = 0.89).

4.3 Data Collection and Analysis Procedures

This study was conducted in December 2017. The sampling of the participants was conducted using a 3-stage cluster sampling method. Cluster sampling involves random selection of naturally occurring groups when it is impossible or impractical to sample the whole population. In the first stage, seven municipal and county areas were randomly selected from the ten total municipal and county areas of Liu Zhou City. In the second stage, one junior secondary and one senior secondary school were randomly selected within each of the seven selected city areas. In the third stage, the students of two classes in each grade (seventh, eighth, tenth, eleventh) were randomly selected to be participants. In addition, all teachers of each grade-level were selected as participants, respectively. Parents of the student sample were also contacted for participation. In most cases, students' parents participated; however, participation was optional and anonymous, so a minority of parents did not participate due to certain personal reasons, such as limited time or unwillingness to be involved in this study, etc.

Descriptive analysis was employed to investigate secondary students' information literacy, and regression analyses were used to explore parental and teacher influences of secondary students' information literacy.

5 Results

5.1 Overview of Secondary Students' Information Literacy

To answer research question one, the level of students' information literacy was explored. An overview of the students' mean scores and standard deviations for information literacy and its four dimensions are provided in Table 2. According to Table 2, secondary students' overall mean information literacy score was approximately 64 out of 100, which implies that an estimated 95% of student scores ranged between 35 to 93. As would be expected, student scores increased as grade-level progressed. These finding suggest that a large percentage of secondary student may actually possess only average or low levels of information literacy in this sampling region.

Table 2. Descriptive data for students' information literacy.

7th grade		8th grade		10th grade		11th grade		All grades	
M	*SD*	*M*	*SD*	*M*	*SD*	*M*	*SD*	*M*	*SD*
52.19	11.71	56.87	12.90	69.91	11.38	73.94	9.21	63.97	14.32

5.2 Parent Influences Toward Students' Information Literacy

To answer research question two, regression analysis was used to explore the relationship between students' information literacy and the parent influences. As shown in Table 3, parents' Internet self-efficacy and ICT attitudes did not significant predictors of students' information literacy, which rejected H1 and H2.

Table 3. Regression analysis of parent influences.

Independent variable	Dependent variable	*B*	*SE*	*β*	*t*
ICT attitudes	Information literacy	.07	.12	.02	.63
	Awareness and cognition	−.00	.01	−.00	−.16
	Scientific knowledge	.04	.05	.02	.78
	Application and innovation	.06	.05	.03	1.08
	Ethics and law	−.02	.03	−.02	−.67
Internet self-efficacy	Information literacy	−.00	.06	−.00	−.06
	Awareness and cognition	.01	.01	.05	1.47
	Scientific knowledge	−.02	.03	−.02	−.61
	Application and innovation	−.01	.03	−.01	−.18
	Ethics and law	.01	.01	.01	.40
Internet attitudes	Information literacy	.16	.07	.08	2.47*
	Awareness and cognition	.03	.01	.11	3.24*
	Scientific knowledge	.04	.03	.04	1.30
	Application and innovation	.08	.03	.09	2.77*
	Ethics and law	.02	.02	.05	1.33

*$p < 0.05$

Parents' Internet attitudes ($t = 2.47$, $p < 0.05$) was found to positively predict students' information literacy, which confirmed H3. Further analysis showed that parents' attitudes toward using the Internet significantly predicted two dimensions of information literacy: Awareness and Cognition ($t = 3.24$, $p < 0.05$); Application and Innovation ($t = 2.77$, $p < 0.05$).

5.3 Teacher Influences Toward Students' Information Literacy

To answer research question three, regression analysis was employed to examine the relationship between students' information literacy and the teacher influences. As shown in Table 4, teachers' Internet self-efficacy ($t = 9.15$, $p < 0.05$) was found to positively predict students' information literacy, which confirmed H4. Further analysis showed that teachers' Internet self-efficacy significantly predicted all dimensions of information literacy: Awareness and Cognition ($t = 2.82$, $p < 0.05$); Scientific Knowledge ($t = 9.25$, $p < 0.05$); Application and Innovation ($t = 8.55$, $p < 0.05$); Ethics and Law ($t = 4.91$, $p < 0.05$).

Table 4. Regression analysis of teacher influences.

Independent variable	Dependent variable	B	SE	β	t
ICT attitudes	Information literacy	−.42	.55	−.03	−.77
	Awareness and cognition	−.10	.07	−.06	-1.43
	Scientific knowledge	.03	.22	.01	.16
	Application and innovation	−.29	.25	−.04	−1.16
	Ethics and law	−.07	.14	−.02	−.52
In-class ICT usage	Information literacy	−2.19	.22	−.41	−9.84*
	Awareness and cognition	−.03	.03	−.05	−1.19
	Scientific knowledge	−.94	.09	−.44	−10.41*
	Application and innovation	−.90	.10	−.38	−8.98*
	Ethics and law	−.33	.06	−.26	−5.84*
Internet self-efficacy	Information literacy	1.81	.20	.25	9.15*
	Awareness and cognition	.07	.03	.08	2.82*
	Scientific knowledge	.74	.08	.26	9.25*
	Application and innovation	.76	.089	.24	8.55*
	Ethics and law	.24	.05	.14	4.91*

*$p < 0.05$

Teachers' ICT attitudes did not significantly predict students' information literacy, which rejected H5. Teachers' in-class ICT usage was shown to negatively predict students' information literacy, which rejected H6. Further analysis showed that teachers' in-class ICT usage significantly predicted three dimensions of information literacy: Scientific Knowledge ($t = -10.41$, $p < 0.05$); Application and Innovation ($t = -8.98$, $p < 0.05$); Ethics and Law ($t = -5.84$, $p < 0.05$).

6 Discussion and Conclusion

This study investigated the overall level of secondary students' information literacy in China, as well as simultaneously examined key parental and teacher influences of students' information literacy. The results showed that the Chinese secondary students possess only average and in some cases low levels of information literacy among seventh, eighth, tenth, and eleventh grade individuals. The findings are consistent with previous studies conducted among Chinese adolescents, which indicated despite high rates of technology utilization, individuals may not be competent and effective with their information technology utilization [18, 48]. Accordingly, this study draws attention to the issue of how to better cultivate information literacy among secondary students in China. Particularly, in ways that emphasize information sensitivity, knowledge of information principles, skills for applying information, and an appropriate moral disposition for participating with information activities.

Examination of parental influence showed that parents' Internet attitudes had a positive impact on students' information literacy. This finding supported previous research in developed countries [39] and implies that parents awareness and understanding of the Internet is critical to their child's information literacy development. Thus, increasing the effectiveness of cultivating secondary students' information literacy is not only the responsibilities of teachers' and students' alone. Parents must also take an active role in the process, for example, through the participation in self-paced technology training to learn basic technical skills, improve their awareness, and reduce personal computer anxieties that may stimulate such negative attitudes [49, 50].

Examination of teacher influences indicated that teachers' Internet self-efficacy can positively predict students' information literacy. These findings aligned previous studies indicating that teachers with higher confidence in using the Internet can more positively effect students' information literacy [39, 51]. Teachers' in-class ICT usage was found to be a negative predictor of students' information literacy. This finding was somewhat surprising; however, the results might be partially explained by the inappropriate usage of information technology in teaching among the Chinese teachers [52]. Previous research has revealed that inappropriate or improperly selected information technology tools can have negative effects on students [53]. Thus, it is suggested that more training programs, mentorship tracks, and research be focused toward the issue of developing more appropriate ICT integration among teachers in China. Through these types of experiences, teachers can develop a comprehensive understanding of the benefits and limitations of using ICT in teaching, which can enable more appropriate usage of in-class ICT.

In conclusion, the development of information literacy among secondary students in China is a critical and multifaceted issue. This study aligns some previous research from developed countries suggesting that parental and teacher influences are critical to the development of students' information literacy. Furthermore, this study highlights an even more significant implication that teachers' in-class ICT utilization may actually be undermining students' information literacy development. All future practical approaches to developing information literacy should consider parents' and teachers' influences, in addition to the traditional focus on students' themselves.

Acknowledgments. The work was supported by the National Key Technology Research and Development Program (No. 2014BAH22F01).

References

1. Castells, M.: The Rise of the Network Society: The Information Age: Economy, Society and Culture, vol. 1. Wiley Blackwell, Oxford (2010)
2. Webster, F.: Theories of the Information Society. Routledge, London (2014)

3. van Laar, E., van Deursen, A.J., van Dijk, J.A., de Haan, J.: The relation between 21st-century skills and digital skills: a systematic literature review. Comput. Hum. Behav. **72**, 577–588 (2017)
4. UNESCO: Towards Media And Information Literacy Indicators. http://www.unesco.org/fileadmin/MULTIMEDIA/HQ/CI/CI/pdf/unesco_mil_indicators_background_document_2011_final_en.pdf
5. American Association of School Librarians & Association for Educational Communications: Information Power: building partnerships for learning. American Library Association (1998)
6. Association of College & Research Libraries: Information Literacy Competency Standards for Higher Education. http://www.ala.org/acrl/sites/ala.org.acrl/files/content/standards/standards.pdf
7. Association of College & Research Libraries: Framework for Information Literacy for Higher Education. http://www.ala.org/arcl/standards/ils_recomm.pdf
8. Australian and New Zealand Institute for Information Literacy: Australian and New Zealand Information Literacy Framework. http://www.caul.edu.au/content/upload/files/info-literacy/InfoLiteracyFramework.pdf
9. Council of Australian University Librarians: Information literacy standard. http://www.caul.edu.au/content/upload/files/caul-doc/InfoLitStandards2001.doc
10. International Association for the Evaluation of Educational Achievement: Preparing for Life in a Digital Age: The IEA International Computer and Information Literacy Study International Report. http://www.iea.nl/fileadmin/user_upload/Publications/Electronic_versions/ICILS_2013_International_Report.pdf
11. Society of College, National and University Libraries: Information skills in higher education: A SCONUL position paper. https://www.sconul.ac.uk/sites/default/files/documents/Seven_pillars2.pdf
12. Society of College, National and University Libraries: The SCONUL Seven Pillars of Information Literacy: Core Model For Higher Education. https://www.sconul.ac.uk/sites/default/files/documents/coremodel.pdf
13. Cha, S.E., Jun, S.J., Kwon, D.Y., Kim, H.S., Kim, S.B., Kim, J.M., Kim, Y.A., Han, S.G., Seo, S.S., Jun, W.C., Kim, H.C.: Measuring achievement of ICT competency for students in Korea. Comput. Educ. **56**(4), 990–1002 (2011)
14. Pourkarimi, J., Nazarzadeh Zare, M.: The assessment of ICT literacy of Iranian teachers through the ISST model. Int. J. Inf. Learn. Technol. **33**(4), 236–247 (2016)
15. The Central People's Government of the People's Republic of China: National Medium and Long-term Plan for Education Reform and Development. http://www.moe.edu.cn/srcsite/A01/s7048/201007/t20100729_171904.html
16. State Council: Notice on Issuing the "Thirteenth Five-Year Plan for the Development of National Education. http://www.gov.cn/zhengce/content/2017-01/19/content_5161341.htm
17. Du, Z.Y.: Deepen the application, integration and innovation; Promote ICT in education comprehensively and deeply. http://www.ict.edu.cn/laws/jianghua/duzhanyuan/n20170508_42983.shtml
18. Li, Y., Ranieri, M.: Are 'digital natives' really digitally competent?—a study on Chinese teenagers. Br. J. Edu. Technol. **41**(6), 1029–1042 (2010)
19. Mishna, F., Schwan, K.J., Birze, A., Van Wert, M., Lacome-Duncan, A., McInroy, L., Attar-Schwartz, S.: Gendered and sexualized bullying and cyber bullying: spotlighting girls and making boys invisible. Youth Soc. (2018). https://doi.org/10.1177/0044118X18757150
20. Kokkinos, C.M., Antoniadou, N., Asdre, A., Voulgaridou, K.: Parenting and Internet behavior predictors of cyber-bullying and cyber-victimization among preadolescents. Deviant Behav. **37**(4), 439–455 (2016)

21. Chen, B., Bryer, T.: Investigating instructional strategies for using social media in formal and informal learning. Int. Rev. Res. Open Distrib. Learn. **13**(1), 87–104 (2012)
22. Chen, W., Xie, X.C., Ping, F., Wang, M.Z.: Personality differences in online and offline self-disclosure preference among adolescents: a person-oriented approach. Pers. Individ. Differ. **105**, 175–178 (2017)
23. Hallam, C., Zanella, G.: Online self-disclosure: The privacy paradox explained as a temporally discounted balance between concerns and rewards. Comput. Hum. Behav. **68**, 217–227 (2017)
24. Zurkowski, P.G.: The Information Service Environment: Relationships and Priorities. Related Paper No. 5. National Commission on Libraries and Information Science, Washington, DC (1974)
25. Rawitsch, D.G.: Minnesota's statewide push for computer literacy. Instr. Innov. **27**(2), 34–35 (1982)
26. Bruce, C.S., Candy, P.C.: Developing information literate graduates: prompts for good practice. In: Information Literacy in Practice, pp. 245–253 (1995)
27. Bruce, C.S.: Seven Faces of Information Literacy. AUSLIB Press, Adelaide (1997)
28. UNESCO: Alexandria Proclamation on Information Literacy and Lifelong Learning. http://www.unesco.org/new/en/communication-and-information/resources/news-and-in-focus-articles/all-news/news/alexandria_proclamation_on_information_literacy_and_lifelong/
29. SCONUL: Information Skills in Higher Education: A SCONUL Position Paper. http://www.sconul.ac.uk/groups/information_literacy/papers/Seven_pillars.html
30. Doyle, C.S.: Outcome Measures for Information Literacy within the National Education Goals of 1990. Final Report to National Forum on Information Literacy. Summary of Findings, U.S. Department of Education (1992)
31. Martin, A.: Literacies for the digital age: preview of Part 1. In: Martin, A., Madigan, D. (eds.) Digital Literacies for Learning, pp. 3–26. Facet Publishing, London (2006)
32. Information Literacy Standards for Student Learning. http://umanitoba.ca/libraries/units/education/media/InformationLiteracyStandards_final.pdf
33. Mutch, A.: Seven faces of information literacy. Int. J. Inf. Manag. **18**(6), 465–466 (1998)
34. Big6 Skills Overview. http://big6.com/pages/about/big6-skills-overview.php
35. Information Literacy Competency Standards for Higher Education, http://www.ala.org/ala/acrl/acrlstandards/informationliteracycompetency.htm
36. Baek, S.G., Kim, D.I., Kim, M.R., Kim, H.S., Yu, Y.L., Park, S.H., Kim, S.W., Kim, M.R.: The development of standardized ICT literacy assessment for secondary school student. Asian J. Educ. **10**(1), 175–198 (2009)
37. Vélez, A.P., Olivencia, J.J.L., Zuazua, I.I.: The role of adults in children digital literacy. Procedia-Soc. Behav. Sci. **237**, 887–892 (2017)
38. Kong, S.C., Li, K.M.: Collaboration between school and parents to foster information literacy: learning in the information society. Comput. Educ. **52**(2), 275–282 (2009)
39. Aesaert, K., Van Nijlen, D., Vanderlinde, R., Tondeur, J., Devlieger, I., van Braak, J.: The contribution of pupil, classroom and school level characteristics to primary school pupils' ICT competences. Comput. Educ. **87**(C), 55–69 (2015)
40. Meelissen, M.R., Drent, M.: Gender differences in computer attitudes: does the school matter? Comput. Hum. Behav. **24**(3), 969–985 (2008)
41. Lai, Y.-L., Guo, S.-J., Tsai, C.-H.: Using collaborative teaching and inquiry-based learning to help elementary school students develop information literacy and information technology skills. In: Kurbanoğlu, S., Špiranec, S., Grassian, E., Mizrachi, D., Catts, R. (eds.) ECIL 2014. CCIS, vol. 492, pp. 436–445. Springer, Cham (2014). https://doi.org/10.1007/978-3-319-14136-7_46

42. Scherer, R., Rohatgi, A., Hatlevik, O.E.: Students' profiles of ICT use: identification, determinants, and relations to achievement in a computer and information literacy test. Comput. Hum. Behav. **70**, 486–499 (2017)
43. Senkbeil, M., Ihme, J.M.: Motivational factors predicting ICT literacy: first evidence on the structure of an ICT motivation inventory. Comput. Educ. **108**, 145–158 (2017)
44. Fraillon, J., Ainley, J., Schulz, W., Friedman, T., Gebhardt, E.: Preparing for life in a digital age: the IEA international computer and information literacy study international report. Technical report, International Association for the Evaluation of Educational Achievement (2014)
45. Liang, J.C., Wu, S.H., Tsai, C.C.: Nurses' internet self-efficacy and attitudes toward web-based continuing learning. Nurse Educ. Today **31**(8), 768–773 (2011)
46. Luan, W.S., Fung, N.S., Nawawi, M., Hong, T.S.: Experienced and inexperienced internet users among pre-service teachers: their use and attitudes toward the internet. J. Educ. Technol. Soc. **8**(1), 90–103 (2005)
47. Vanderlinde, R., Braak, J.V.: The e-capacity of primary schools: development of a conceptual model and scale construction from a school improvement perspective. Comput. Educ. **55**(2), 541–553 (2010)
48. Šorgo, A., Bartol, T., Dolničar, D., Boh Podgornik, B.: Attributes of digital natives as predictors of information literacy in higher education. Br. J. Edu. Technol. **48**(3), 749–767 (2017)
49. Lee, C.L., Huang, M.K.: The influence of computer literacy and computer anxiety on computer self-efficacy: the moderating effect of gender. Cyber Psychol. Behav. Soc. Netw. **17**(3), 172–180 (2014)
50. Gupta, S.: Reducing computer anxiety in self-paced technology training. In: Proceedings of the 50th Hawaii International Conference on System Sciences, pp. 154–163. University of Hawaii at Manoa (2017)
51. Gerick, J., Eickelmann, B., Bos, W.: School-level predictors for the use of ICT in schools and students' CIL in international comparison. Large-Scale Assess. Educ. **5**(1), 5 (2017)
52. He, X., Wray, D.: Digital literacies in a Chinese secondary school. In: Marcus-Quinn, A., Hourigan, T. (eds.) Handbook on Digital Learning for K-12 Schools, pp. 233–249. Springer, Cham (2017). https://doi.org/10.1007/978-3-319-33808-8_14
53. Wajszczyk, R.: A study of the impact of technology in early education. http://www.diva-portal.org/smash/get/diva2:737018/FULLTEXT01.pdf

Development of Computer Competence Courses in Seniors – Shift from Learning Space with Computer-Based Activities to Virtual Platform - Case Study

Miloslava Černá(✉) and Libuše Svobodová

Faculty of Informatics and Management, University of Hradec Kralove, Rokitanskeho 62, Hradec Kralove, Czech Republic
{miloslava.cerna, libuse.svobodova}@uhk.cz

Abstract. This paper deals with the issue of computer literacy development in elderly people in the local intergeneration project. The project is at the crossroads: continue conducting courses in the traditional way or updating the content of courses and learning environment to reflect the changes in technologies and society. Researchers have been involved into the project for the second year and are currently participating in the preparatory phase of suggesting solutions. The aim of the paper is to describe learning environment of current courses, define its weaknesses and justify its unavoidable update. Potential ways to the solution on virtual platform will be proposed for further consideration and implementation at the meeting of directors of involved primary schools with the municipality authority of the city of Hradec Králové. Data stem from the primary and secondary sources. Results are important for authors of the updated courses, as they are considering shift from computer-based learning environment to web-based environment with the study materials online. Schools that organize courses for seniors do not use LMS or any other tools for sharing of materials; they use printed materials. The paper brings a set of potential solutions on updating organization of courses like Clasroom in G+ , or on-line communities.

Keywords: Blended learning · Computer literacy · Elderly people Learning environment · Study

1 Introduction

Society and its future is strongly influenced by two distinctive unstoppable factors, by the ageing society and by the development of information technologies. Information technologies have entered and started to influence lives of the whole of society in both professional and private spheres. Computer literacy is a competence that represents an inseparable part of everyday lives, e.g., people have to cope with electronic payment, ordering services or making appointments with the doctors via the Internet. Currently our society is experiencing a shift to electronic medical prescriptions, which causes, in many elderly people (and not only elderly people) concern, distrust or even fear. People have to adapt to changes and development, it isn't possible to stop the time.

S. K. S. Cheung et al. (Eds.): ICBL 2018, LNCS 10949, pp. 416–425, 2018.
https://doi.org/10.1007/978-3-319-94505-7_34

The elderly people issue has been part of the Faculty research interest for four years. The authors have participated in the research and published their findings; see [1, 2]. Also other colleagues from the Faculty of Informatics and Management are involved in the senior social phenomenon; they run their projects and publish their findings in reputable forums [3–5].

2 Methodology and Goal

2.1 Goal of the Paper

This paper deals with the issue of computer literacy development in elderly people in the concrete local long-term project. Municipality and selected primary schools in the city of Hradec Králové have organized the computer courses for seniors since 2001. Organizers are currently considering changes in courses content as well as their form.

The aim of the paper is to identify the learning environment and its unavoidable update. Potential ways to the solution on virtual platform will be proposed for further consideration and implementation at the meeting of directors of involved primary schools with the municipality authority.

As for applied methodology, primary and secondary sources were used. The paper is based on qualitative research; main tools were *interviews* with project stakeholders (deputy-mayor who is in charge of education, primary school directors and teachers of engaged schools), discussions with pupils and senior attendees of the courses and *observation* of activities, learning atmosphere in individual classes.

Natixis Global Retirement Index (NGRI) opens the issue of elderly people in the Literature review chapter. It forms a kind of technical starting platform enabling the measurement of the retirement climate across nations in the developed world. Then definitions to key terms like computer literacy, blended and hybrid learning are provided. The core part of the paper is the Proposal of potential solutions where adoption of a robust learning management system on the virtual platform is suggested or trendy way of establishing communities in social networks.

3 Literature Review

Literature review draws on professional and scientific literature, websites of selected studies and surveys, statistical offices and other professional sources. It encompasses following areas: definitions to key expressions relevant to the scope of the paper like elderly people, retirement index, computer literacy, blended and hybrid learning.

Old age isn't a definite biological stage, there is no United Nations standard numerical criterion; there is no fixed threshold when people are considered old. Elderly people definition was taken from the statement of the World Health where the chronological age of 65 years is accepted as 'elderly' or older person [6].

3.1 Natixis Global Retirement Index

Retirement is a pressing social and economic issue. According to the report on the 2016 Natixis Global Retirement Index, which was released by Natixis Global Asset Management Old, retirement models got unsustainable; lifespans are expanding, government budgets are shrinking and *policy makers and employers continue to shift the responsibility of retirement funding to the individual* [7]. The Multidimensional Natixis Global Retirement Index GRI has been applied for five years as a complex tool for measuring the retirement climate across nations in the developed world. The index incorporates 18 performance indicators of retiree wellbeing across four broad categories – thematic sub-indices: Finances, Health, Material Wellbeing and Quality of Life [8]. As for the rating of the Czech Republic via the GRI, the data are much more optimistic in *comparison with the general rather sceptical perception of retirement in our country. Compared to 43 countries, the Czech Republic ranked at a relatively decent 16th place*. Overall, Czech seniors are doing better than their peers in Israel, France, Japan or South Korea [9].

Definition of the GRI from the report follows: "The Global Retirement Index assesses factors that drive retirement security across 43 mainly developed economies where retirement is a pressing social and economic issue. The index includes International Monetary Fund (IMF) advanced economies, members of the Organization for Economic Co-operation and Development (OECD), and the BRIC countries (Brazil, Russia, India and China). The researchers calculated a mean score in each category and combined the category scores for a final overall ranking of the 43 nations studied".

The country achieves a balanced set of results across all sub-indices and registers its strongest performance in Material Wellbeing, it reaches sixth position. The country performs well in the Finance sub-index. Its public finances are healthier due to less public debt and a lower tax burden. And its banking sector has a lower proportion of non-performing loans. Quality of Life (23rd) sub-index has improved which is connected higher usage of renewable electricity drive improvement in the environmental factors indicator. As for the Health sub-index the Czech Republic declined to the 27th position. The country sees a fall in its life expectancy score. Life expectancy in women is 81.7 years and in men 75.9 years [8].

3.2 Computer Literacy

Being computer literate becomes a necessity in current society. The IT Education Site defines Computer literate skill as follows: *Computer literate is a term used to describe individuals who have the knowledge and skills to use a computer and other related technology. This term is usually used to describe the most basic knowledge and skills needed to operate software products such as an operating system, a software application, or an automated Web design tool* [10].

According to [11] computer literacy represents basic, *nontechnical knowledge about computers and how to use them. Computer literacy means familiarity and experience with computers, software, and computer systems*. Cambridge dictionary [12] speaks about *the ability to use computers effectively*.

3.3 Definitions of 'Blended Learning' and 'Hybrid Learning'

Definitions of 'blended learning' and 'hybrid learning' vary or these expressions are interchangeable. The academic papers bring slightly different definitions from promoted products on the market. Company Panopto explains blended and hybrid learning expression on their websites presenting their product Video Platform for businesses and universities. "Blended learning is a form of education that takes place both online and in a brick-and-mortar location. Both of these modalities are integrated into a cohesive learning experience for the student. In blended learning scenarios, *"face time" between students and teachers is not replaced by online course delivery*. Rather, the online component of the learning experience usually consists of exercises or additional content that complement the in-class lesson. Often, the term hybrid learning is used almost interchangeably with blended learning. However, there is a subtle distinction. In hybrid learning, a significant portion of the course takes place online. In contrast with blended learning, *a hybrid learning scenario replaces much of the student-teacher "face time" in a brick-and-mortar location with online interaction*" [13].

aNewSpring company presents on their website a learning enhancement platform. They also try to explain both discussed expressions. They state that blended and hybrid learning both are very effective because of the synergy that is created between different ways of studying. *Blended learning utilizes the best online tools to support a teacher-led classroom*, learners are also encouraged to explore and follow their own paths with computer-based modules. A teacher can bring those lessons to life and give them meaning. *Hybrid learning focuses less on the technology* and more on the most effective way to deliver a course to learners, which is different for every company [14].

In academic sphere, the definitions also vary [15] and get outdated. O'Neill et al. [16] defines "Elearning" as instruction delivered electronically via the Internet, Intranets, or CD-ROM or DVD. CD-ROMs or DVD aren't used in the process of education any more or very little. Smart and Cappel [17] stated that they used terms "elearning," "online learning," and "web-based learning" interchangeably in their study on Students' perception of online learning like many other writers. Hybrid and blended learning terms are often used interchangeably, e.g. Kostolanyova et al. [18] "All institutions provided either fully distance education, or the *hybrid (blended) courses* to support the full-time and part-times study programmes" or even joined into one term, e.g. Tashiro et al. [19] describe a taxonomy for *hybrid-blended learning courses* which they developed. Li [20] states in their study that hybrid learning is not only a combination of face-to-face classes with online learning… "it is a mixture of receiving knowledge and discovery learning, a mixture of autonomous learning and collaborative learning, a mixture of process study and evaluation, a mixture of applying media and learning tools".

For the purposes of our research, we applied a modified Hybrid learning term which stems from aNewSpring definition [14]. *Hybrid learning focuses less on the technology and more on the most appropriate way to deliver a course to mixed ability learners with various demands and preferences.*

4 Description of the Courses, Development and Future

Computer literacy courses for elderly people have been regularly organized for 17 years by the municipality of Hradec Kralove and selected primary schools. The awareness of this event got established among the city population due to systematic promotion on the websites of the city and participating primary schools, in reports in local printed media and leaflets at the general practitioners. In the analysed year schools offered 217 places, 162 elderly people were enrolled and 132 successfully completed the course, 111 pupils participated as seniors' assistants.

Pupils from the lower secondary schools teach elderly people how to work with the computer in a ten-week course one hour weekly. There is a primary school teacher in each class, playing mainly administrative and supervising role. Based on the observation in the running classes, teachers' involvement into the process of education varies. Some teachers explain study material in the frontal way, using their computer and a data projector and pupils sit by seniors' site at the computer and work with seniors individually. Some teachers only write the programme of the lesson on the whiteboard, they are there to give advice or solve technical problem. The way of teaching/learning is mostly computer-based.

There is shift from teaching/learning entirely fundamental computer skills to wider horizons especially to work with photography, which was reflected in the design of future courses. *Based on the technological and sociological changes a demand for the development of mobile skills have rapidly increased in the elderly people.* A new course on utilization of smart phones is in the phase of pilot testing. Currently syllabus and study materials are being worked out and finalized. Syllabus consists of four areas: (1) basic setting of the system: work with icons, data usage, and connection to WIFI, (2) applications calendar, alarm clock, contacts, sms, camera, SD cards, (3) Internet, (4) applications: Play Store - Download Maps, Rescue, Weather ….

Likewise new courses are desirable; a new learning space is desirable, too. Course study material is provided to the participants only in printed form, it has been updated four times but always as a textbook. Learning environment for Senior courses consisted of computer classroom, data projector, whiteboard with markers, printed study material, teacher supervising the course and pupils as study assistants of the attendees. Participants of the courses didn't save any files or minutes from the individual lessons onto neither the disc nor virtual learning space or social media. They always started from zero. After discussions with the course organizers at schools, it was stated that it is advisable and desirable to find a space, where participants could save their notes, share ideas and find study material. The issue of selection of the convenient space for running courses was then discussed at the meetings of schools directors and the authority from the municipality education department at the end of the year 2017. The authors of the paper were asked to prepare a draft solution.

5 Proposal of Potential Solutions

We were asked by the municipality deputy-mayor in the field of education to prepare a workshop targeted at the directors of involved primary schools and teachers who have been participating in the project. At the end of March, we are going to present and discuss potential solutions at the regular meeting of directors. It is a sensitive issue, the project has a long tradition and not everyone is willing to make changes when the 'project works'. It is desirable to raise stakeholders' interest and to make suggestions as if they were theirs. Advancement of learning environment is of key importance, innovative use of social media will be offered for consideration. As a motto we have selected "We don't stop playing because we grow old; we grow old because we stop playing". George Bernard Shaw.

Solutions depend on two key factors: the possibilities and equipment of schools and knowledge and needs of seniors.

It might be motivating to move from computer-based learning with textbook support to electronic materials and web-based learning for both seniors and their young lecturers. Pupils are familiar with social media and Moodle Management system. A considerable amount of seniors also use social networks.

There are two main ways which might be adopted, firstly learning management system on the virtual platform and secondly communities in social networks. Both solutions differ significantly and have their pros and contras.

- It is desirable to consider the appropriateness of *Moodle*. The other possibility is deeper cooperation with the University of Hradec Králové, which can offer more sophisticated *Blackboard* learning management system.
- The other possibility is to consider *communities* on social networks in G+ or Facebook or learning space *G Suite for Education in Google+*.

Work in virtual platform is a standard activity at schools, both teachers and students are familiar with it. Faculty of Informatics and Management has been involved in the design and implementation of e-courses for more than two decades and developed an international reputation in this field. University academic researchers and educationist can help the project designers with creation of templates that conform to didactic rules. The key limitation is if there is a responsible person who will administrate the courses in each school as it means another financial burden for the directors. If the courses are located at university environment, the administration is of no problem.

Philosophy of learning space is completely different in communities in social networks. Positive is that the space is much more colourful, the drawback is that the activities in them form a kind of mosaic without systematic support. It is a challenge for the teachers to prepare classes and follow the progress. For example, community Seniors for Computing [21] contains links to free education courses, including age category 55+ like course organized by Goodwill Community Foundation LearnFree (GCFLearnFree.org) [22]. Beside others they offer courses on Hardware: Computers, Technology, Smartphones & Tablets, Technology Buying Guide, Internet & Apps: Email, Internet, Social Media, Google Apps, SharePoint Resources, Photos & Design, Online Safety, Internet, Social Media, Google Apps (now G Suite), Microsoft

Resources, Photos & Design, QuickBooks, Online Safety and courses on Life Skills: like, Personal Finance and learning languages (Fig. 1).

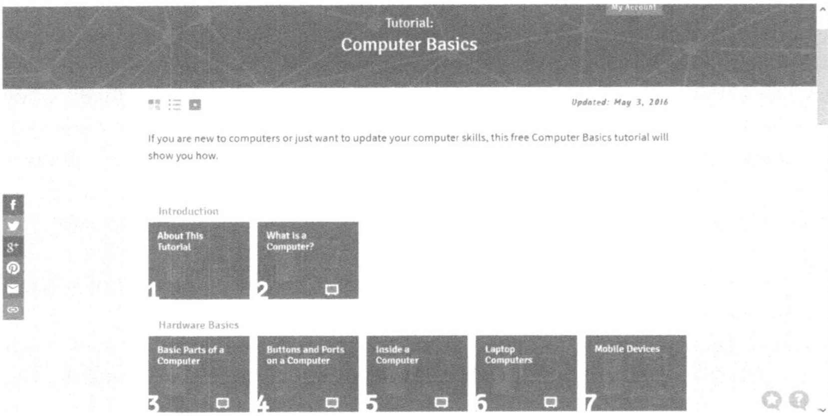

Fig. 1. Tutorial – computer basics [23]

Another inspiring on-line community is 'Seniors Internet Help' - Baby Boomers Online [24]. This community was created to offer help to seniors in the Internet environment (Fig. 2).

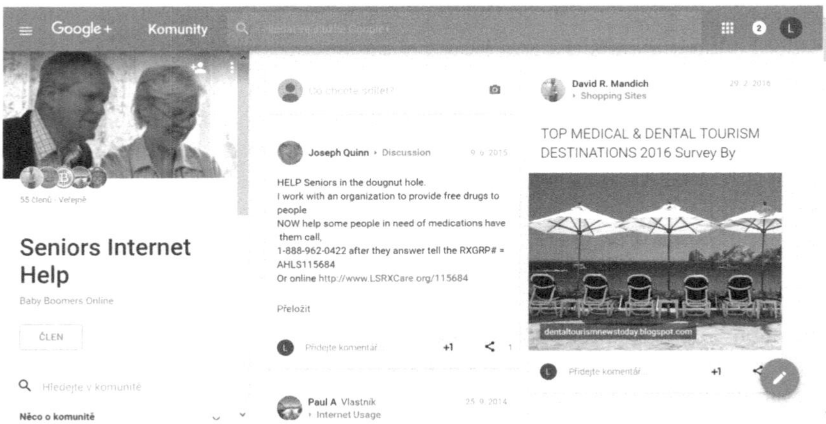

Fig. 2. Seniors internet help [24]

Next proposal, which is offered for further consideration, is a sophisticated G Suite and its part G Suite for Education. Everyone knows G Suite which is a suite of online applications (mail, calendar, shared disk, documents, video calls), the great positive is that people can work on it from any device [25]. Other positives relate to the fact that G

Suite for Education tools are free, ad-free, reliable, secure and have a long tradition of beneficial outcomes (Fig. 3).

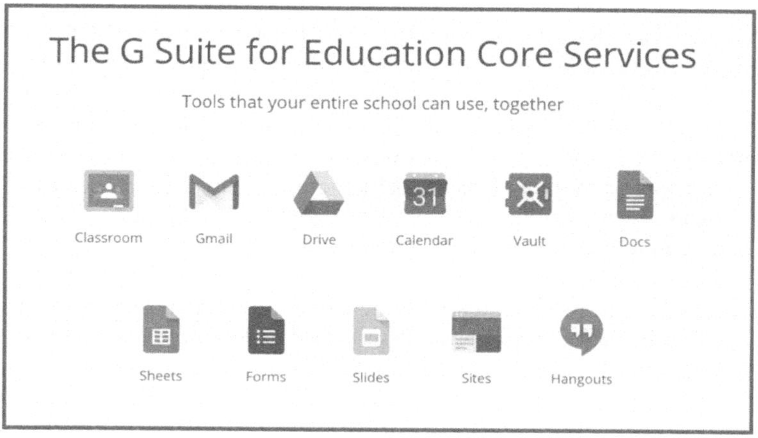

Fig. 3. The G suite for education core services [25]

If the G Suite for Education is found rather complicated we would like to point to the tool Clasroom which was launched just three years ago. We find it as the smart solution as is easy to create and administer. The main menu consists of three main sections: Stream, Students and About the course. Students are given code and then they can add comments and supply contributions. When participants manage this part, they can approach the vertical menu with more sophisticated tools: Course Folder on the disc, Classroom Office, Google Calendars, see more [26].

6 Conclusion and Discussion

Changes are a sensitive issue. Changes are a challenge and disturb stagnation. The project has a long tradition and not everyone is willing to make changes when the 'project works'. That is why suggestions on changes in the content and form of the project have to be formulated carefully with deep respect to work which has been done up to now. The goal of the paper was reached. The learning space has been described together with limitations of current state as well as with the attempts to widen and update the topics of courses to reflect the demand for the development of mobile skills and exploration of other communication channels like Skype in elderly people. Researchers consider advancement of learning environment of key importance. They focus on innovative use of social media and consider the appropriateness of robust learning management systems like Moodle or Blackboard. It is important to keep in mind that the elderly people as course attendees aren't the only participants, there are also pupils their assistants who should feel comfortable in the environment. As for social networks, pupils are familiar with them but as for learning management systems not everyone will be able to use this environment instantly. Further measures will have to be taken not to place just another burden on supervising teachers in classes.

The article does not aim to provide one niche solution. The aim is to prepare ideas, resources and explanations justifying the need of updating learning environment from computer based learning process with episodic blended learning activities to hybrid learning environment in the spirit of the stated definition on hybrid learning. Hybrid learning focuses less on the technology and more on the most appropriate way to deliver a course to mixed ability learners with various demands and preferences [14].

Potential solutions and recommendations will be discussed at the workshop organized by Municipality. Authors believe that the atmosphere will be open to new ideas and that people conducting the courses will bring their solutions as well and will participate in testing and finding the optimum way.

Acknowledgement. The paper is supported by the project SPEV 2018 at the Faculty of Informatics and Management of the University of Hradec Kralove, Czech Republic. In addition, the authors thank Anna Borkovcova for her help with the project.

References

1. Svobodova, L., Cerna, M.: Benefits and pitfalls in utilization of the internet by elderly people. In: Kar, A.K., Ilavarasan, P.V., Gupta, M.P., Dwivedi, Y.K., Mäntymäki, M., Janssen, M., Simintiras, A., Al-Sharhan, S. (eds.) I3E 2017. LNCS, vol. 10595, pp. 135–146. Springer, Cham (2017). https://doi.org/10.1007/978-3-319-68557-1_13
2. Hedvicakova, M., Svobodova, L.: Internet use by elderly people in the czech republic. In: Kar, A.K., Ilavarasan, P.V., Gupta, M.P., Dwivedi, Y.K., Mäntymäki, M., Janssen, M., Simintiras, A., Al-Sharhan, S. (eds.) I3E 2017. LNCS, vol. 10595, pp. 514–524. Springer, Cham (2017). https://doi.org/10.1007/978-3-319-68557-1_45
3. Klímová, B., Marešová, P.: Computer-based training programs for older people with mild cognitive impairment and/or dementia. Front. Hum. Neurosci. **11**, 262 (2017)
4. Šimonová, I., Klímová, B., Poulová, P., Pražák, P.: The use of ICT devices by older people with a special focus on their type and respondents' age: a Czech case study. Educ. Gerontol. **43**(12), 641–649 (2017)
5. Poulova, P., Simonova, I.: Blended learning as means of support within the elderly people education. In: Cheung, S.K.S., Kwok, L.-F., Ma, W.W.K., Lee, L.-K., Yang, H. (eds.) ICBL 2017. LNCS, vol. 10309, pp. 3–14. Springer, Cham (2017). https://doi.org/10.1007/978-3-319-59360-9_1
6. World Health Organization: Proposed working definition of an older person. http://www.who.int/healthinfo/survey/ageingdefnolder/en/. Accessed 15 Feb 2018
7. Study: Retirement security not just the responsibility of individuals. https://www2.im.natixis.com/global/1250227335641/Global+Retirement+Index+2016. Accessed 15 Feb 2018
8. Global Retirement Index. https://www.im.natixis.com/us/resources/2017-global-retirement-index. Accessed 15 Feb 2018
9. Retirement - pension/who lives better life - senior people in the Czech Republic or in other countries. http://moneymag.cz/duchody-penze/9286-kdo-se-ma-lepe-duchodci-v-cesku-nebo-v-jinych-zemich. Accessed 15 Feb 2018
10. Computer literate. https://www.techopedia.com/definition/23303/computer-literate. Accessed 15 Feb 2018

11. Computer literacy. http://www.dictionary.com/browse/computer-literacy. Accessed 15 Feb 2018
12. Computer literacy. https://dictionary.cambridge.org/us/dictionary/english/computer-literacy. Accessed 15 Feb 2018
13. Blended Learning, Hybrid Learning, The Flipped Classroom… What's the Difference? https://www.panopto.com/blog/blended-learning-hybrid-learning-flipped-classroom-whats-difference/. Accessed 15 Feb 2018
14. Blended and hybrid learning. https://www.anewspring.com/blended-and-hybrid-learning/. Accessed 15 Feb 2018
15. Westover, J.H., Westover, J.P.: Engaging Hybrid and Blended Learning in Higher Education. Common Ground Publishing LLC (2014)
16. O'Neill, K., Singh, G., O'Donoghue, J.: Implementing elearning programmes for higher education: a review of the literature. J. Inf. Technol. Educ. **3**, 313–323 (2004)
17. Smart, K.L., Cappel, J.J.: Students' perceptions of online learning: a comparative study. J. Inf. Technol. Educ. **5**, 201–219 (2006)
18. Kostolanyova, K., Jurickova, R., Simonova, I., Poulova, P.: Flexible hybrid learning: comparative study. In: Cheung, S.K.S., Kwok, L.-F., Yang, H., Fong, J., Kwan, R. (eds.) ICHL 2015. LNCS, vol. 9167, pp. 70–81. Springer, Cham (2015). https://doi.org/10.1007/978-3-319-20621-9_6
19. Tashiro, J., Hung, P.C.K., Martin, M.V., Tashiro, R.R.: What really works in hybrid learning: a cognitive perspective. In: Cheung, S.K.S., Kwok, L.-F., Yang, H., Fong, J., Kwan, R. (eds.) ICHL 2015. LNCS, vol. 9167, pp. 15–35. Springer, Cham (2015). https://doi.org/10.1007/978-3-319-20621-9_2
20. Li, K.: Applying grounded theory method in building a hybrid learning activities model. In: Cheung, S.K.S., Kwok, L.-F., Yang, H., Fong, J., Kwan, R. (eds.) ICHL 2015. LNCS, vol. 9167, pp. 82–93. Springer, Cham (2015). https://doi.org/10.1007/978-3-319-20621-9_7
21. Community. https://plus.google.com/u/1/collection/4Kr0MBV. Accessed 15 Feb 2018
22. GCF Learn Free, Who we are. https://www.gcflearnfree.org/info/aboutus/who-we-are. Accessed 15 Feb 2018
23. GCF Learn Free, Computer basics. https://www.gcflearnfree.org/computerbasics/. Accessed 15 Feb 2018
24. Internet help. https://plus.google.com/u/1/s/Seniors%20Internet%20help/top. Accessed 15 Feb 2018
25. G Suite for Education. http://shakeuplearning.com/blog/g-suite-education-need-know/. Accessed 15 Feb 2018
26. Shake up learning, The Teacher's Guide to Google Classroom. http://shakeuplearning.com/the-teachers-guide-to-google-classroom/. Accessed 15 Feb 2018

Enriching Learning Experience - Older Adults and Their Use of the Internet

Blanka Klímova[1], Petra Poulova[1](✉), Pavel Prazak[1], and Ivana Simonova[2]

[1] Faculty of Informatics and Management, University of Hradec Kralove, Rokitanskeho 62, Hradec Kralove, Czech Republic
{blanka.klimova, petra.poulova, pavel.prazak}@uhk.cz
[2] Faculty of Education, Jan Evangelista Purkyně University, Ceské mladeze 8, Usti nad Labem, Czech Republic
ivana.simonova@ujep.cz

Abstract. Ageing is becoming a big social issue nowadays. For example, in 2000 the percentage of older individuals aged 65+ years reached 12.4% worldwide. In 2030, this number should rise to 19% and in 2050 to 22%. Therefore there is a need to prolong an active life of older people, especially by implementing nonpharmacological approaches. And current technological devices and services can assist them in this process. Therefore, the purpose of this study is to explore the use of the Internet among older people in the Czech Republic with respect to their age. The key methods exploited in this study include a questionnaire survey, statistical processing of data collection, as well as evaluation of both empirical and theoretical findings on the research issue. The results indicate that the age is a decisive factor in the use of the Internet by seniors. In fact, the use of the Internet falls with the declining age with the breakthrough age 75+ years. Generally, older people use the Internet for communication purposes with the help of e-mail, the most frequent ICT tool for this generation group. The results also suggest that older people should be trained in the use of the Internet since the training may help them overcome both psychological and social barriers, which represent the constraints in their use of the Internet. Particularly the last presidential election in the Czech Republic has shown the need for education, as the seniors were the most vulnerable group in the area of spreading Fake-news.

Keywords: Age · Blended learning · Elderly · Internet · Survey

1 Introduction

Currently, there is a growing rise of older population groups worldwide. In 2000 the percentage of older individuals aged 65+ years reached 12.4%. In 2030, this number should rise to 19% and in 2050 to 22% [1]. In Europe this population group aged 65+ represent 18% of the 503 million Europeans, which should almost double by 2060 [2]. This trend of aging population causes additional problems such as increased costs on the treatment and care about this elderly people [3, 4]. Therefore there is ongoing effort to extend the active life of this group of people in order to enable them to stay

S. K. S. Cheung et al. (Eds.): ICBL 2018, LNCS 10949, pp. 426–437, 2018.
https://doi.org/10.1007/978-3-319-94505-7_35

economically and socially independent. And current technological devices and services can assist them in this process.

Recent research studies [5–8] have also proved that older generation of people, aged 58–77, are nowadays much more digitally aware than they used to be ten years ago. Currently, more and more people use the Internet. For example, in the USA 64% of older individuals aged 65+ years exploit the Internet [9], in the Great Britain the number of people aged 65+ years has reached 74% [10], and in the Netherlands it is even more – 78% of older people use it [11]. This is caused not only by acquiring more experience through different kinds of community and nationwide projects aimed at older people [12, 13], but also their desire to communicate with their family, e.g. grandchildren, or to find the information they need.

Generally, there are three main preconditions which support the rising use of ICT by older people. These include:

- an increase in the number of older people worldwide;
- ICT as a tool for providing older people with the promise of greater independence;
- the generation of "baby boomers" approaching retirement being relatively comfortable using ICT; they will bring many technology-related skills into their retirement years [14, 15].

Older adults do not form a heterogeneous demographic group since according to the declining age, they have different needs, which place the older people into three different groups: 55–64 years old, 65–74 years old, 75 and more years old [15, 16].

The purpose of this study is to explore the use of the Internet among older people in the Czech Republic with respect to their age.

2 Materials and Methods

The research methodology is introduced in four subchapters comprising (1) the research question and the main research objective, (2) research sample, (3) hypotheses and (4) the tool for testing the hypotheses.

2.1 Research Question and Objective

The current life is characterized by two main features: (1) living in the i-society, where ICT devices have penetrated all spheres of life, and (2) the growing amount of senior population, which requires to support the development of important skills (competences) necessary for living in the i-society which might be new for them in some aspects.

Therefore, the answer to the question how seniors exploit the ICT devices and the Internet in common life is highly topical. Coherently, the research questions focus on two areas:

1. Do seniors exploit the Internet?
2. Is the Internet exploitation impacted by respondents' age?

Reflecting the above mentioned, the main research objective is to discover whether seniors use the Internet and whether the Internet exploitation depends on user's age.

2.2 Research Sample

Totally, 432 respondents participated in the research. They all were residents of Hradec Kralove district and both seniors with active and passive approach to the ICT competence development were represented in the sample. All respondents were physically and mentally healthy and were structured in three groups:

- the so-called 'passive' seniors, i.e., those who do not want to pay attention to acquiring any knowledge of the latest ICT and their exploitation, were represented by respondents living in senior houses (group 1, DD, n = 108);
- the so-called 'active seniors' interested in their further education, particularly in the ICT field and who attended ICT courses held by the Hradec Kralove municipality (group 2, HK, n = 159);
- the so-called 'active seniors' interested in their further education in general who attended courses of the University of the Third Age (group 3, U3V, n = 164).

As the 'passive' seniors are represented by one group of the institutionalized respondents and other 'passive' seniors have not been included in the sample, the authors are aware of the fact that the research sample is of a selective type, not representing the whole population but representing its characteristics in several features only, i.e. in the male/female structure. Consequently, the results cannot be generalized, but they can serve as an introductory study for further deeper research activities.

The respondents' age ranged between 55 years (born in 1961) and 94 years (in 2016, when the research was conducted (born in 1922), as the age of 55 is the starting seniors' age in the Czech Republic [17]. The sample consisted of 317 female (F, 73%) and 11 male respondents (M, 17%) – this distribution follows the structure of the Czech senior population [18]. There were 15 respondents 85+ years old – 12 females and 3 males. Most of the respondents (257; F 188; M 69) were born in the period of 1942-51, i.e., they were 65–74 years old; the oldest ones were 87+ years old.

For the purpose of this research, respondents were structured into three age groups (55–64-year old: 82 respondents; 65–74-year old: 257; 75+-year old: 93), which is a rather common approach, cf. [19, 20].

2.3 Hypotheses

Totally, five hypotheses were tested, three of them relating to the Internet exploitation by the seniors and other two to the impact of respondents' age on the Internet exploitation.

Ad (1) Do Seniors Exploit the Internet?

$H1_1$: Respondents in group 2 (HK, participants of ICT courses) exploit the Internet more compared to respondents in group 1 (DD, living in senior houses).

$H2_1$: Respondents in group 3 (U3V, participants of U3V courses) exploit the Internet more compared to respondents in group 1 (DD, living in senior houses).
$H3_1$: Respondents in group 2 (HK, participants of ICT courses) exploit the Internet more compared to respondents in group 3 (U3V, participants of U3V courses).

Ad (2) Is the Internet Exploitation Impacted by Respondents' Age?

$H4_1$: The proportion of Internet users in 55–64 age group is higher compared to 65–74 age group.
$H5_1$: The proportion of Internet users in 65–74 age group is higher compared to 75+ age group.

2.4 Research Tool

The questionnaire was distributed by the researchers in the senior houses, ICT courses and U3V courses. In the lounge of the senior houses, or after one of the course lessons respondents were provided with basic information on the purpose of the research and they filled in the questionnaire in the printed form.

The questionnaire took approximately 15 min and comprised 10 items covering

- personal data (Q1: gender, age, level of education),
- three yes/no questions (Q2: Did you use ICT in your profession?; Q7: Do you exploit the Internet?; Q9: Do you exploit the Internet in your mobile/smart phone?),
- five multiple-choice questions with one or more answers from 6–12 distractors (Q3: What ICT devices do you own?; Q4: What ICT devices do you use?; Q6: How did/do you acquire the ICT skills/competences?; Q8: What Internet services do you exploit?),
- one open-answer question (Q10: Can you imagine your life without electronic devices? Why?).

One year before the research started, the questionnaire had been piloted in the group of 22 respondents – participants of ICT courses and adjusted to its present final form.

The collected data were processed by the 'R' software version 2.5.1 [21].

3 Research Results

The presentation of the research results is structured into two parts which follow the research questions:

1. Do seniors exploit the Internet?
2. Is the Internet exploitation impacted by the respondents' age?

The process of testing hypotheses included the following steps:

- Collected data were displayed in the contingency table,
- Chi-Square Test of independence was conducted,
- Proportion and Confidence Interval were calculated and p-value computed.

3.1 Do Seniors Exploit the Internet?

The data in this field were collected from one item of the questionnaire. They are summarized in the contingency table below (Table 1), in total and in groups 1–3.

Table 1. Internet exploitation in groups of seniors.

			Group of seniors			Total
			DD	HK	U3V	
Using Internet	No	Count	60	14	27	101
		% within Group	55.0%	8.8%	16.5%	23.4%
	Yes	Count	49	145	137	331
		% within Group	45.0%	91.2%	83.5%	76.6%
Total		Count	109	159	164	432
		% within Group	100.0%	100.0%	100.0%	100.0%

The results show that the Internet is widely used by the 'active' respondents in group 2 (HK, participants of ICT courses; 91.2%), followed by group 3 (U3V, participants of U3V courses; 83.5%), whereas more than half of the 'passive' respondents (DD, respondents living in senior houses; 55%) do not exploit the Internet.

Applying the Pearson chí-square test of independence on the 0.05 significance level, the correlations between the single groups in the Internet exploitation were discovered. The results are displayed in Table 2.

Table 2. Results of Chi-Square Tests for independence of the use of the Internet and group of seniors.

	Value	df	p-value
Pearson Chi-Square	84.249	2	$<2.2e{-16}$
N of valid cases	432		

In order to receive detailed results in single groups, the proportions between them were compared. The calculations of proportion and confidence interval were based on the data in Table 1 and displayed in Table 3.

Table 3. Proportion of the Internet exploitation in single groups.

Group of seniors	Proportion	95% confidence interval
DD	$p_{DD} = 0.45$	(0.355, 0.548)
HK	$p_{HK} = 0.912$	(0.854, 0.949)
U3V	$p_{U3V} = 0.835$	(0.768, 0.887)

Further on, hypotheses H1, H2, H3 stating that:

$H1_1$: The proportion of respondents in group 2 (HK, participants of ICT courses) is higher compared to the proportion in group 1 (DD, living in senior houses).
$H2_1$: The proportion of respondents in group 3 (U3V, participants of U3V courses) is higher compared to the proportion in group 1 (DD, living in senior houses).
$H3_1$: The proportion of respondents in group 2 (HK, participants of ICT courses) is higher compared to the proportion in group 3 (U3V, participants of U3V courses).

Were tested according to Table 4.

Table 4. Hypotheses H1, H2, H3 on the proportion of the Internet exploitation in the single groups

	Null hypothesis	Alternative hypothesis
H1	$p_{HK} = p_{DD}$	$p_{HK} > p_{DD}$
H2	$p_{U3V} = p_{DD}$	$p_{U3V} > p_{DD}$
H3	$p_{HK} = p_{U3V}$	$p_{HK} > p_{U3V}$

The z-test was applied for considering the difference of two population proportions; the results are displayed in Table 5. In the table, instead of z-statistics, which shows an approximate normal distribution, the chí-square distribution of 1 degree of freedom is displayed, which is valid if the null hypothesis is verified.

Table 5. Results of testing hypotheses H1, H2, H3 for the difference between two population proportions

Test	X-squared	df	p-value
H1	66.9	1	<2.2e−16
H2	43.1	1	2.556e−11
H3	3.61	1	0.02873

The results show that on the 0.05 significance level, hypotheses H1, H2 and H3 were verified; on the 0.01 significance level, hypotheses H1 and H2 were verified, whereas hypothesis H3 could not be statistically proved.

These results mean that on the 0.05 significance level there exist statistically significant differences between the groups of the respondents living in senior houses (group 1, DD), attending ICT course (group 2 ICT) and U3V courses (group 3, U3V) in the Internet exploitation as follows: respondents in group 2 (HK, participants of ICT courses) exploit the Internet more compared to the respondents in group 1 (DD, living in senior houses); respondents in group 3 (U3V, participants of U3V courses) exploit the Internet more compared to group 1 (DD, living in senior houses); respondents in group 2 (HK, participants of ICT courses) exploit the Internet more compared to the respondents in group 3 (U3V, participants of U3V courses).

On the 0.01 significance level, statistically significant differences were detected between group 2 (HK, participants of ICT courses) whose respondents exploit the Internet more compared to the respondents in group 1 (DD, living in senior houses) and group 3 (U3V, participants of U3V courses) who exploit the Internet more compared to the respondents in group 1 (DD, living in senior houses). Statistically significant differences between group 2 (HK, participants of ICT courses) and group 3 (U3V, participants of U3V courses) could not be proved.

3.2 Is the Internet Exploitation Impacted by the Respondents' Age?

Reflecting on the date of birth, all seniors were categorized in three age groups: 55–64 year-old (born 1952–1961), 65–74 year-old (born 1942–1951) and 75+ year-old (born 1922–1941). The structure is displayed in the Table 6.

Table 6. The Internet exploitation according to the respondents' age in the single groups of seniors.

			Age groups			Total
			55–64	65–74	75+	
Exploiting the Internet	No	Count	10	47	44	101
		% within age group	12.3%	18.2%	47.3%	23.4%
	Yes	Count	71	211	49	331
		% within age group	87.7%	81.8%	52.7%	76.6%
Total		Count	81	258	93	432
		% within age group	100.0%	100.0%	100.0%	100.0%

The data show a continuous increase in the Internet exploitation in relation to the respondents' age. Whereas the Internet was used by more than half (52.7%%) of the oldest respondents (aged 75+, born 1922–41), which is rather high rate, the proportion surpassed 80% of the users in the respondents aged 74–65 (81.8%; born 1942–51) and those aged 64–55 (87.7%; born 1952–61).

The tendency of increasing proportion of the Internet users in 'younger' age groups was tested by hypotheses H 4 and H5 stating that:

$H4_1$: The proportion of Internet users in 55–64 age group is higher compared to 55–74 age group.
$H5_1$: The proportion of Internet users in 65–74 age group is higher compared to 75+ age group.

Hypotheses were verified according to Table 7.

The z-test was applied for considering two population proportions; the results are displayed in Table 8. In the table, instead of z-statistics, which shows approximate normal distribution, the chí-square distribution of 1 degree of freedom is displayed, which is valid if the null hypothesis is verified.

Table 7. The Internet exploitation according to the respondents' age in the single groups of seniors.

Null hypothesis	Alternative hypothesis
$p_{55-64} = p_{65-74}$	$p_{55-64} > p_{65-74}$
$p_{65-74} = p_{75+}$	$p_{65-74} > p_{75+}$

Table 8. Results of testing hypotheses 4–5 for the difference between two population proportions.

Test	X-squared	Df	p-value
H4	1.13	1	0.144
H5	28.6	1	4.368e−08

The results show that on the 0.05 significance level, hypothesis H4 was falsified and H5 was verified.

These results mean that on the 0.05 significance level the statistically significant difference was not discovered between groups of the 55–64 year-old respondents (born 1952–61) and 65–74 year-old ones (born 1951–42). The statistically significant difference was detected between the respondents 65–74 year-old (born 1942–1951) and 75+ year-old (born 1922–1941).

In addition to the main hypotheses, the authors examined the frequency of the use of the Internet by these older individuals. The findings revealed that more than half of the respondents (53%) exploited the Internet on a daily basis and another 22% of the respondents used it at least once a weak (Fig. 1).

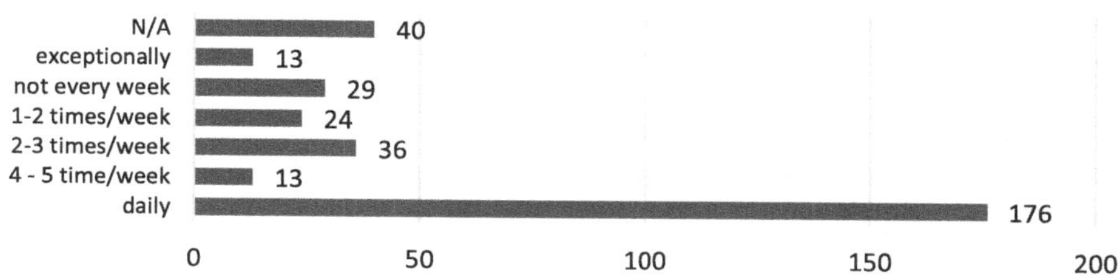

Fig. 1. Frequency of the use of the internet by the respondents.

Furthermore, the authors also dealt with the issue of the Internet activities seniors are engaged in. 72% of the respondents use the Internet for communication and the main tool for it is e-mail. Surprisingly, the second most used service on the Internet was electronic banking (e-banking – 40% of the respondents), closely followed by Skype, photo sharing – 38%). One third of the respondents also reported that they did shopping via the Internet (33% of the respondents) (Fig. 2).

The survey showed that almost none of these seniors nowadays cannot imagine life without the Internet. As they pointed out, it was part and parcel of their present life.

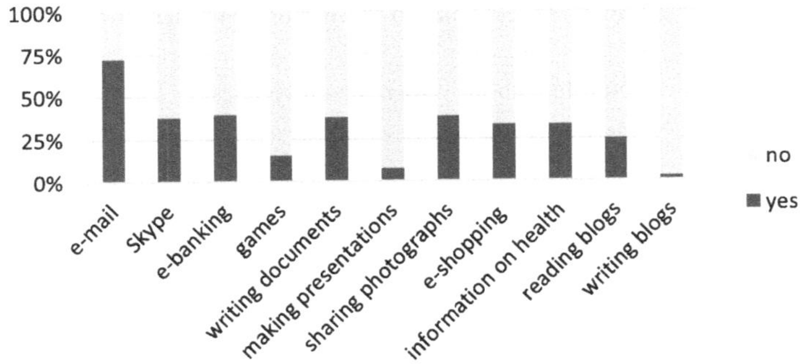

Fig. 2. The internet activities the respondents were engaged in.

4 Discussion

The results reveal that more and more older adults exploit the Internet nowadays and more than half of them exploit it on a daily basis. This is especially true for the age groups (55 years up to 74 years). The breakthrough age in the decrease in the use of the Internet among these people is then 75 years, which is quite common in the developed countries and it is connected with the overall deterioration of cognitive functions at this age [22]. This finding has been also confirmed by van Boekel et al. [11] who report that people reaching the age 74+ years spend the least time on the Internet. The same was discovered by Smith [23], de Veer et al. [24], or Zickuhr and Madden [25]. Nevertheless, even in this age group (75+ years) the situation is improving since the number has almost doubled in five years cf. [11, 23].

The findings suggest that those attending specialized ICT courses had more experience in their use and thus, were more confident and frequent users than those in senior houses and the attends of the University of the Third Age. This fact was also indicated by Choi and DiNitto [26], who claim that older people need to be trained in the Internet use for various purposes since the Internet plays the significant role in their social capital, as well as in removing their psychological barriers. Zheng et al. [27] suggest that older individuals, especially those who feel lonely, should be a target.

Generally, older people use the Internet for communication purposes with the help of e-mail, the most frequent ICT tool for this generation group cf. [28–30]. Nevertheless, the findings of this study indicate that the second most common reason for the use of the Internet is the Internet banking, followed by Skype communication and photo sharing cf. [19, 31]. Similar results were achieved by Choi and DiNitto [26], who report that their older Internet users were engaged in diverse types of Internet activities; almost 86% of the users sent emails/text messages, 51% shopped, paid bills, and/or did banking, and 45% conducted health-related tasks on the Internet. The most recent study by van Boekel et al. [11] distinguished four main clusters of the older Internet users. These include minimizers, aged 74 years, who exploit the Internet the least; maximizers, below 70 years, who use the Internet for all activities; practical users, aged 71 years on average, who exploit the Internet for searching for information, comparing products or the Internet banking; and social users, mainly women, aged 71 years, who use the Internet for social and leisure activities. Most recently, more and more older people have used the Internet for searching for healthcare information [32, 33]. However, older people use only selected eHealth services which include, for example, obtaining information on their health, receiving reminders for scheduled visits, medication instructions, or consulting a doctor at a distance. Furthermore, they use Internet for searching health information about the right nutrition, exercise or weight issues, diseases such as cancer, heart disease, or arthritis, high cholesterol, and health providers [34].

Research also shows that the use of the Internet by older population groups may have a positive effect on enhancement of their cognitive functions, e.g., [35, 36], and thus, help in aging diseases such dementia. Almeida et al. [35], for example, claim that the risk of incident of dementia was about 30% to 40% lower among older computer users than non-users. This has been confirmed by Tun and Lachman [37] who state that the exploitation of computers is linked with improved cognitive competences in adulthood and old age.

The limitations of this study consist in a selective sample of the respondents located in one of the regions of the Czech Republic only and a lack of investigation of other factors such as educational or social status of the respondents.

5 Conclusions

Overall, the findings of this study indicate that the age (and respondents' previous experience in the Internet exploitation, e.g. at work) is a decisive factor in the use of the Internet by seniors. In fact, the use of the Internet falls with the declining age, however, the breakthrough age seems to be 75+ years. The results also suggest that older people should be trained in the use of the Internet since the training may help them overcome both psychological and social barriers, which represent the constraints in their use of the Internet.

The last presidential election in the Czech Republic has clearly demonstrated the need for education not only in the technical aspects of the Internet use but also ethical. As a rule, seniors, without a critical approach, trust the information they receive from emails from known and unknown people and are the most vulnerable group in the area of spreading the so-called Fake-news. Because this training should be focused on the Internet users, blended courses seem to be the most effective approach.

Furthermore, seniors could be divided into three basic age groups according to their special needs, which should be considered when designing new technological devises or services for these aging population groups, which could help them to enhance cognitive functions.

Acknowledgments. The paper is supported by the project SPEV (2018) at the Faculty of Informatics and Management of the University of Hradec Kralove, Czech Republic.

References

1. Transgenerational Design Matters (2009). http://transgenerational.org/aging/demographics.htm. Accessed 10 Mar 2017
2. Patterson, I.: Growing Older. Tourism and Leisure Behaviour of Older Adults. Cabi, Cambridge (2006)
3. Maresova, P., Klimova, B., Kuca, K.: Alzheimer's disease: cost cuts call for novel drugs development and national strategy. Ceska Slov. Farm. **64**, 25–30 (2015)
4. Maresova, P., Mohelska, H., Valis, M., Kuca, K.: Alzheimer disease and its treatment costs, case study in the Czech. Neuropsychiatr. Dis. Treat. **11**, 2349–2354 (2015)
5. Hanson, V.L.: Age and web access: the next generation. In: Proceedings of the 2010 W4A – Technical, Madrid, pp. 7–15 (2009)
6. Hernandez-Encuentra, E., Pousada, M., Gomez-Zuniga, B.: ICT and older people: beyond usability. Educ. Gerontol. **35**, 226–245 (2009)
7. Sayago, S., Blat, J.: Telling the story of older people e-mailing: an ethnographical study. Int. J. Hum. Comput. Stud. **68**, 105–120 (2010)
8. Heart, T., Kalderon, E.: Older adults: are they ready to adopt health-related ICT? Int. J. Med. Inf. **82**, e209–e231 (2013)
9. Pew Research Center: Internet/Broadband fact sheet (2017). http://www.pewinternet.org/fact-sheet/internet-broadband/. Accessed 23 May 2017
10. Office for National Statistics: Internet users in the UK: 2016 (2016). https://www.ons.gov.uk/businessindustryandtrade/itandinternetindustry/bulletins/internetusers/. Accessed 20 May 2017
11. van Boekel, L.C., Peek, S.T., Luijkx, K.G.: Diversity in older adults' use of the Internet: identifying subgroups through latent class analysis. J. Med. Internet Res. **19**(5), e180 (2017)
12. Bishop, J.: Increasing participation in online communities: a framework for human computer interaction. Comput. Hum. Behav. **23**, 1881–1893 (2009)
13. Godfrey, M., Johnson, O.: Digital circles of support: meeting the information needs of older people. Comput. Hum. Behav. **25**, 633–642 (2009)
14. Virginia Assistive Technology System: Assistive technology and Aging. A handbook for Virginians who are aging and their caregivers (2011). http://www.vda.virginia.gov/pdfdocs/Assistive%20Technology%20&%20Aging%20-%20All.pdf. Accessed 19 May 2017
15. Klimova, B.: Use of the Internet as a prevention tool against cognitive decline in normal aging. Clin. Interv. Aging **11**, 1231–1237 (2016)
16. Klimova, B.: Senior tourism and information and communication technologies. In: Park, J.J., Chen, S.-C., Raymond Choo, K.-K. (eds.) MUE/FutureTech -2017. LNEE, vol. 448, pp. 440–445. Springer, Singapore (2017). https://doi.org/10.1007/978-981-10-5041-1_71
17. Czech Statistical Office: Seniors (2017). https://www.czso.cz/csu/czso/seniori. Accessed 16 May 2017
18. Czech Statistical Office: Population by one-year age and sex (2017). https://vdb.czso.cz. Accessed 16 May 2017
19. Benáčová, H., Valenta, M.: Moznosti informaticke vyuky senioru v ČR a EU. [Possibilities of computer science teaching of older people in the Czech Republic and EU.] Systémová Integrace **4**, 77–86 (2009)
20. Slavik, L.: Senior tourism. Diploma thesis, Praha, UK (2012)
21. The R Project for Statistical Computing (2017). https://www.r-project.org/. Accessed 20 May 2017

22. Klimova, B., Simonova, I., Poulova, P., Truhlarova, Z., Kuca, K.: Older people and their attitude to the use of information and communication technologies – a review study with special focus on the Czech Republic (Older people and their attitude to ICT). Educ. Gerontol. **42**(5), 361–369 (2016)
23. Smith, A.: Older adults and technology use (2014). http://www.pewinternet.org/2014/04/03/older-adults-and-technology-use/. Accessed 9 June 2017
24. de Veer, A.J.E., et al.: Determinants of the intention to use e-Health by community dwelling older people. BMC Health Serv. Res. **15**(103), 1–9 (2015)
25. Zickuhr, K., Madden, M.: Older adults and internet use (2012). http://www.pewinternet.org/files/old-media/Files/Reports/2012/PIP_Older_adults_and_internet_use.pdf. Accessed 9 May 2017
26. Choi, N.G., DiNitto, D.M.: Internet use among older adults: association with health needs, psychological capital, and social capital. J. Med. Internet Res. **15**(5), e97 (2013)
27. Zheng, R.Z., Hill, R.D., Gardner, M.K.: Engaging older adults with modern technology: internet use and information access needs. Information Science Reference, USA (2013)
28. Gell, N.M., Rosenberg, D.E., Demiris, G., LaCroix, A.Z., Patel, K.V.: Patterns of technology use among older adults with and without disabilities. Gerontologist **55**(3), 412–421 (2015)
29. Sayago, S., Sloan, D., Blat, J.: Everyday use of computer-mediated communication tools and its evolution over time: an ethnographical study with older people. Interact. Comput. **23**, 543–554 (2011)
30. Prior, S., Arnott, J., Dickinson, A.: Interface metaphor design and instant messaging for older adults. In: Proceedings of CHI 2008 Extended Abstract on Human Factors in Computing Systems, Florence, pp. 3747–3752 (2008)
31. Brush, A.B., Inkpen, K.M., Tee, K.: SPARCS: exploring sharing suggestions to enhance family connectedness. In: Proceedings of the 2008 ACM Conference on Computer Supported Cooperative Work, San Diego, pp. 629–638 (2008)
32. Bujnowska-Fedak, M.M.: Trends in the use of the Internet for health purposes in Poland. BMC **15**, 194 (2015)
33. Bujnowska-Fedak, M.M., Pirogowicz, I.: Support for e-health services among elderly primary care patients. Telemed. J. E-Health **20**(8), 696–704 (2014)
34. Kaiser Family Foundation: E-health and the elderly: how seniors use the Internet for health information. Key findings from a national survey of older Americans (2013). https://kaiserfamilyfoundation.files.wordpress.com/2013/01/e-health-and-the-elderly-how-seniors-use-the-internet-for-health-information-key-findings-from-a-national-survey-of-older-americans-survey-report.pdf. Accessed 9 Oct 2017
35. Almeida, O.P., Yeap, B.B., Alfonso, H., Hankey, G.J., Flicker, L., Norman, P.E.: Older men who use computers have lower risk of dementia. PLoS ONE **7**(8), e44239 (2012)
36. Dodge, H.H., Zhu, J., Mattek, N.C., et al.: Web-enabled conversational interactions as a method to improve cognitive functions: results of a 6-week randomized controlled trial. Alzheimer's Dement.: Transl. Res. Clin. Interv. **1**(1), 1–12 (2015)
37. Tun, P.A., Lachman, M.E.: The association between computer use and cognition across adulthood: use it so you won't lose it? Psychol. Aging **25**, 560–568 (2010)

Author Index

The manufacturer's authorised representative in the EU is Springer Nature Customer Service Centre GmbH, Europaplatz 3, 69115 Heidelberg, Germany. If you have any concerns regarding our products, please contact ProductSafety@springernature.com

Printed and bound by CPI Group (UK) Ltd, Croydon, CR0 4YY
22/09/2026
02220983-0007